EDUCATIONAL EVALUATION

Alternative Approaches and Practical Guidelines

Blaine R. Worthen

Utah State University

and

James R. Sanders

Western Michigan University

Longman

London

370.78
W932e

Educational Evaluation

Copyright © 1987 by Longman Inc.

Longman Inc.
95 Church Street
White Plains, N.Y. 10601

Associated companies:
Longman Group Ltd., London
Longman Cheshire Pty., Melbourne
Longman Paul Pty., Auckland
Copp Clark Pitman, Toronto
Pitman Publishing Inc., New York

Credits appear on page viii.

Senior Editor: Naomi Silverman
Production Editor: Helen B. Ambrosio
Text Design: Angela Foote
Cover Design: Stephan Zander
Production Supervisor: Eduardo Castillo
Compositor: Graphicraft Typesetters Ltd.
Printer and Binder: The Alpine Press, Inc.

Library of Congress Cataloging in Publication Data

Worthen, Blaine R.
　Educational evaluation.
　Bibliography: p.
　Includes index.
　1. Education—Evaluation.　2. Education—United States
—Evaluation.　I. Sanders, James R.　II. Title.
LB1028.W656　1988　　370'.7'8　　86-21409
ISBN 0-582-28551-8 (pbk.)
ISBN 0-8013-0128-9

　　89 90 9 8 7 6 5 4 3

Contents

Credits _____

p. 55 (Table 4.1) reprinted with permission of The Free Press, a Division of Macmillan, Inc. from ENCYCLOPEDIA OF EDUCATIONAL RESEARCH, Fifth Edition, Harold E. Mitzel, Editor in Chief. Copyright © 1982 by American Research Association.

pp. 56-57 (Table 4.2) from THE PROFESSION AND PRACTICE OF PROGRAM EVALUATION, by S. Anderson and S. Ball. San Francisco: Jossey-Bass, Inc., 1978.

p. 67 (Figure 5.1) from EVALUATION AT THE LOCAL LEVEL, by Robert L. Hammond. Tucson, AZ: Project EPIC, undated.

p. 80 (Table 6.1) from SYSTEMATIC EVALUATION, by D.L. Stufflebeam and Shinkfield. Boston: Kluwer-Nijhoff, Inc., 1985.

p. 83 (Figure 6.1) from SYSTEMATIC EVALUATION, by D.L. Stufflebeam and Shinkfield. Boston: Kluwer-Nijhoff, Inc., 1985.

pp. 91-92 "Checklist for Reviewing and Selecting Materials" developed by the Center for Instructional Development and Services, Florida State University, Tallahassee, FL.

p. 93 "Instructional Materials Review Form" developed by the Center for Instructional Development and Services, Florida State University, Tallahassee, FL.

p. 131 (Figure 10.1) from "The Countenance of Educational Evaluation," by R. E. Stake, in TEACHERS COLLEGE RECORD 68, 1967.

p. 136 (Figure 10.2) from "Program Evaluation, Particularly Responsive Evaluation," by Robert E. Stake. Occasional Paper No. 5, Western Michigan University Evaluation Center, Kalamazoo, MI.

pp. 136-137 from "Program Evaluation, Particularly Responsive Evaluation," by Robert E. Stake. Occasional Paper No. 5, Western Michigan University Evaluation Center, Kalamazoo, MI.

pp. 163-164 material reprinted with permission of the Association for Supervision and Curriculum Development from APPLIED STRATEGIES FOR CURRICULUM EVALUATION, edited by Ronald S. Brandt. Copyright © 1981 by the Association for Supervision and Curriculum Development. All rights reserved.

pp. 195-196 material reprinted from IMPROVING AND ASSESSING PERFORMANCE: EVALUATION IN HIGHER EDUCATION. Berkeley, CA: Center for Research and Development in Higher Education, 1975.

p. 255 (Figure 16.3) from PROGRAM EVALUATION AND REVIEW TECHNIQUES: APPLICATION IN EDUCATION, by Desmond Cook. Washington, DC: United States Office of Education Cooperative Research Monograph No. 17.

p. 302 List of definitions reprinted from "Alternatives for Achievement Testing," by J. R. Sanders and S. L. Murray in EDUCATIONAL TECHNOLOGY 16:3, 1976.

p. 303 material reprinted from "Alternatives for Achievement Testing," by J. R. Sanders and S. L. Murray in EDUCATIONAL TECHNOLOGY 16:3, 1976.

pp. 304-305 (Table 18.1) from "Alternatives for Achievement Testing," by J. R. Sanders and S. L. Murray in EDUCATIONAL TECHNOLOGY 16:3, 1976.

p. 315 (Figure 18.1) from "Formative Evaluation: Selecting Techniques and Procedures," by James R. Sanders and Donald J. Cunningham. In EVALUATING EDUCATIONAL PROGRAMS AND PRODUCTS, edited by Gary Borich. Englewood Cliffs, NJ: Educational Technology Publications, 1974.

pp. 372-375 Summary of Standards reprinted from "Summary of the Joint Committee on Standards for Educational Evaluation," in STANDARDS FOR EVALUATION OF EDUCATIONAL PROGRAMS, PROJECTS AND MATERIALS. New York: McGraw-Hill, 1981.

p. 377 (Figure 21.1) from "The Project to Develop Standards for Educational Evaluation: Its Past and Future," by J.M. Ridings and D.L. Stufflebeam. Reprinted with permission from STUDIES IN EDUCATIONAL EVALUATION 1, 1981.

p. 379 (Figure 21.2) from PROGRAM EVALUATION SOURCEBOOK, by R.O. Brinkerhoff, D.M. Brethower, T. Hluckyj and J.R. Nowakowski. Boston: Kluwer-Nijhoff, Inc., 1983.

pp. 383-396 Sample interviews reprinted from "Characteristics of Good Evaluation Studies," by Blaine R. Worthen in JOURNAL OF RESEARCH AND DEVELOPMENT IN EDUCATION 10:3, 1977.

Preface

More than a dozen years ago, our textbook *Educational Evaluation: Theory and Practice* was first published. We were gratified by the reception to that book; the field was young, we had pulled together much of the best of the early literature in it, and our synthesis of that literature remained useful for over a decade.

Gradually, as the field of evaluation matured, our book became dated. New evaluation approaches, procedures, and techniques not included in our text were developed and began to show promise. Also, our experience during the years since we drafted our first manuscript had substantially altered—and, we feel, matured—our thinking about educational evaluation.

At first we considered revising our earlier text. Eventually, it became apparent that a new book, not a revision, would be necessary. We have drawn into it some portions of our former text that our colleagues have suggested to us are most useful and that we judge to be current. Although content drawn from our earlier book represents only 15 percent of this volume, we judge the best of the original Worthen–Sanders text to be included here.

This book differs from its predecessor in several significant ways:

1. It is an integrated textbook, not an edited book of readings (though we have liberally quoted and excerpted what we consider to be the real nuggets from the evaluation literature and incorporated that content with our own).

2. Our coverage of evaluation approaches and models is not only more recent but also much broader, ranging across the entire spectrum of evaluation approaches that have been shown to be useful in educational evaluation. "Adversary evaluation," "responsive evaluation," and numerous other approaches that were too underdeveloped for inclusion earlier are treated at some length here.

3. More than half of this volume is devoted to practical guidelines for planning, conducting, and using evaluations; checklists and step-by-step procedural guides are proposed to assist the inexperienced evaluator learn more quickly how to do many essential evaluation activities.

4. We have incorporated within each chapter *learner aids,* such as orienting questions at the beginning, and applied exercises and lists of further suggested readings at the end of the chapters.

5. We have applied the content of each of the chapters in our "Practical Guidelines" section to a common case study of a fictional evaluation of a school curriculum to show how our suggestions might be carried out in "real life."

6. We have referenced and cited liberally the expanding literature in educational evaluation and allied areas, so that this book will serve both as a useful reference source for the professor of evaluation and a text for the student of evaluation.

In any text, there will be limitations. Space has not permitted us to treat several topics in the depth we desired. Faced with choices of whether to include content that would titillate the theoretician or that which would instruct the practitioner of evaluation, we have chosen the latter.

Sometimes we may rightly be accused of having stated the obvious; our only defense for doing so is the fact that the obvious seems to have escaped many who conduct evaluation studies and even a few who write about doing such studies.

We may also be chastised for traditionalism because we have not included every new proposal dealing with evaluation studies. Yet we refuse to accept as conceptual or methodological breakthroughs all the profound pronouncements or provocative proposals made by luminaries in evaluation. If worthy, new ideas will gradually be proven in the cauldrons of practice; that will be the time for inclusion in a text such as this.

We may also be criticized for dealing with much that is simple. Yet in a book aimed largely at beginners, in a field still relatively young, it would seem a disservice to leapfrog the practicalities to grapple with conceptual and methodological uncertainties and complexities. We leave such matters for the advanced graduate seminar, the occasional paper, or publications designed primarily for circulation among the theorists of evaluation. Our text is designed to be unashamedly practical (though not necessarily *easy*) in addressing the realities of the day-to-day planning and conduct of educational evaluations.

PURPOSE AND AUDIENCE

This book can be used in a variety of ways. It is designed primarily as a basic text for graduate courses in evaluation or related administration, curriculum, or teacher education courses where efforts are made to teach practitioners to assess the effectiveness of their educational endeavors. More ideally suited to a semester-length course or a two-quarter sequence, it can be readily adapted to a one-quarter course by judiciously selecting content to be covered and that to be omitted—the balance will be available to the student who wishes to pursue further reading. Selective picking and choosing of content will also allow portions of this book to be used in providing in-service seminars and workshops on educational evaluation.

This book should also serve well as a reference for practicing evaluators, professors, graduate and advanced undergraduate students, and other educators who desire a comprehensive overview of educational evaluation and references to additional sources of information.

In general, this book is intended to (1) familiarize readers with the variety of alternative approaches proposed for planning and conducting evaluation; and (2) provide practical guidelines helpful with almost any general evaluation approach.

Within this general framework, the more specific goals of this book are these:

1. To help users develop an awareness of and sensitivity to critical concepts and issues in educational evaluation.

2. To help users develop a clear perspective about the role of evaluation in education.

3. To help educators become enlightened users of evaluation in their professional work.

4. To prepare evaluators to conduct useful, feasible, proper, and technically sound evaluation studies.

Although this book will contribute substantially to the development and preparation of professional evaluators, additional education and experience will be necessary to develop further the competencies required in conducting high-quality evaluation studies.

It may be helpful to say a word about the intentions and limitations of this book. First, although tests are used frequently to collect educational evaluation data, this is not a book about testing per se. Second, although many of the evaluation concepts and guidelines discussed here for evaluating educational curriculum in general, or specific programs, products, processes, or practices in particular, also apply to evaluation of educational personnel, this text is not intended as a full treatment of teacher evaluation, university faculty evaluation, or evaluation of any other educational personnel. Third, although the authors have conducted evaluations in a variety of social contexts other than education (for example, youth corrections, health science programs, family planning services, pet welfare programs, and mental health services), a majority of our experience is in conducting evaluations in educational settings such as public and private schools, universities and colleges, and educational units within military, business, industrial, or professional settings. Therefore, whereas the guidelines presented here generalize to many noneducation settings, the primary focus is on educational evaluation. Similarly, although we have conducted a number of evaluations in other countries, the majority of our experience is with educational systems in the United States, and we draw naturally for many of our examples from that which we know best. At the same time, the general concepts, principles, and guidelines offered in this text will generalize across most geographic boundaries and settings and transcend most differences in social and disciplinary context. In short, this book should prove as useful in evaluating a pet welfare program in Kent County, England, or a mental health clinic in Ottawa as it is in evaluating a vocational education curriculum in the San Francisco public schools.

TEACHING AND LEARNING AIDS

To assist instructors and readers in using this book, we include the following teaching and learning aids:

1. Each chapter (hereafter) includes questions that readers should be able to answer at its conclusion.

2. Each chapter contains application exercises readers can use in testing their ability to apply its content.

3. Each chapter includes a list of additional suggested readings.

4. Chapters that provide practical guidelines for planning, conducting, and using evaluation studies include a running case study, unfolded chapter by chapter to illustrate how the guidelines would be applied to a real-life evaluation.

ORGANIZATION

This volume consists of 21 chapters organized into four major parts.

Part One: Basic evaluation roles, concepts, definitions, and distinctions, and consideration of the history of educational evaluation.

Part Two: Six alternative views of how educational evaluations should be conducted, a discussion of philosophical and methodological underpinnings of each, and a comparative analysis of the characteristics and contributions of these alternatives.

Part Three: Practical guidelines for planning and conducting evaluation studies, including
  • Considerations on when to evaluate
  • The origins and context of an evaluation
  • Ways to identify and select evaluative questions and criteria
  • Planning evaluation studies
  • Developing evaluation management plans

Part Four: Practical guidelines for using and evaluating evaluations, including
  • Dealing with political and interpersonal aspects of evaluation
  • Collecting, analyzing, and interpreting evaluation information
  • Reporting and using evaluation findings
  • Evaluating and improving evaluation studies

READER'S GUIDE

To make this book more immediately useful for the multiple audiences it is intended to serve, the following chapter coverage is suggested as one effective way to direct various readers to those chapters and pages they (or their instructors) may wish to cover.

In-service Workshop/Seminar Instructors and/or Participants

If this text were made available sufficiently far in advance of a workshop or seminar, participants could read broadly from any or all sections of the book, as desirable. In addition, extended reading assignments could also be given for participants to complete following a workshop. If, however, reading time is confined to the typical one to two days alloted to a workshop or seminar, then coverage will of necessity be more limited. In such cases, specific chapters could serve as foundations for topical evaluation workshops such as the examples listed below.

1. An Overview of Evaluation and Its Role in Improving Education (Chapters 1 and 3)
2. History of Evaluation Thought in American Education (Chapter 2)
3. Philosophical Foundations of Evaluation in Education (Chapter 4)
4. Alternative Approaches to Evaluation in Education (Chapters 5 through 11, or any *one* chapter could be the basis for a workshop devoted solely to a *particular* evaluation approach, such as "Expertise-Oriented Evaluation Approaches"—Chapter 8)

5. Identifying Questions to be Answered by Educational Evaluations (Chapter 14)
6. Practical Guidelines for Planning Evaluations (Chapters 12 through 16)
7. Data Collection Techniques for Educational Evaluation (Chapter 18)
8. Data Analysis Techniques for Educational Evaluation (Chapter 19)
9. Criteria and Procedures for Evaluating Evaluations (Chapter 21)

Students and/or Professors in One-Quarter-Length University Courses

There are obviously different emphases one might choose in selecting the chapters of this text for any one-quarter class. The proportion of the book that can be covered within one academic quarter will also be influenced greatly by variables such as preferred teaching style and educational level of the students. We propose three possible ways to use this text in quarter-length courses that differ in focus, as suggested by the alternate course titles and content coverage listed below.

1. "An Overview of Educational Evaluation"—A broad "survey" course including some coverage of both evaluation theory and practice. This alternate, which would use about 55 percent of this book's content, would be especially appropriate where students are unlikely to take further formal coursework in evaluation:

Chapter 1, all	Chapter 12, pp. 165–172, 181–185
Chapter 3, pp. 21–24, 34–39	Chapter 13, pp. 186–191, 200–209
Chapter 4, pp. 43–45, 59–61	Chapter 14, pp. 210–212, 220–222, 225–227
Chapter 5, pp. 62–65, 72–75	
Chapter 6, pp. 77–82, 83–85	Chapter 15, all
Chapter 7, pp. 87–90, 96–97	Chapter 17, pp. 281–290, 292–296
Chapter 8, pp. 98–106, 108–111	Chapter 18, pp. 298–300, 323–326
Chapter 9, pp. 113–120, 121–126	Chapter 19, pp. 328–329, 336–339
Chapter 10, pp. 127–130, 134–140, 141–142	Chapter 20, pp. 341–343, 347–348, 360–361, 366–368
Chapter 11, pp. 144–146, 150–158	Chapter 21, pp. 369–376, 396–400

2. "Alternative Approaches to Evaluation"—A course focusing on the conceptual foundations of educational evaluation, with particular emphasis on the diverse approaches that have been proposed for use in evaluation and the uses, strengths, and limitations of each approach: Chapters 1 through 11 and 21 (about 45 percent of the text content).
3. "Practical Guidelines for Planning, Conducting, and Using Educational Evaluations"—A practicum focusing on guidelines, steps, and procedures for all aspects involved in planning and carrying out educational evaluation: Chapters 12 through 21 (about 60 percent of the text content).

Students and/or Professors in Semester-Length Courses or Two-Quarter Sequences

This book is designed for use in its entirety in a semester-length course focusing on both the theory and practice of educational evaluation, such as: "Educational Evaluation: Alternative Approaches and Practical Guidelines," Chapters 1 through 21 (100 percent of the text content).

Obviously, instructors of semester-length courses could also choose to delete chapters or sections of the book to give greater emphasis to other chapters, in ways parallel to the alternatives suggested above for quarter-length courses.

We do not presume to suggest to the evaluation practitioner or advanced students which sections might be most pertinent to their needs. We presume individuals already somewhat familiar with or expert in evaluation will need no guidance to make the best possible use of the contents of this volume.

SUGGESTIONS FOR IMPROVEMENT

We hope that this text will meet your needs, whether you are the instructor, student, or a practicing evaluator for whom this book might serve as a reference or handbook. Whatever your role, we have a request to make. We want very much to receive your comments or suggestions on how to improve future editions of this book. It is our intent to continue to update and modify future editions to make this work as helpful as possible to those who use it; your help will be gratefully received.

We express our appreciation to:
- our many colleagues whose urging and helpful suggestions have prompted us to write this book, most especially Egon Guba, Robert Ingle, Wayne Welch, Carol Tittle, Jim Fortune, Richard Jaeger, Larry Braskamp, Daniel Antonoplos, Gilbert Austin, Nick Eastmond, Adrian Van Mondfrans, and Cecil Clark;
- Barry Fraser and Karen Houghton, for their very helpful curriculum evaluation bibliography; although we aspire to be thorough students of the evaluation literature, their compilation has been most helpful;
- Michael Scriven, for his very useful evaluation thesaurus;
- Mary B. McClelland, who co-authored some application exercises that were adapted for this book;
- The Association for Supervision and Curriculum Development and other copyright holders for permitting us to reprint here portions of our earlier writing to which they hold the rights, and to our many colleagues who have allowed us to reprint excerpts or graphics that exceeded normal quotation privileges;
- Joyce Brinck, for her outstanding and tireless production of this manuscript and her dedication to the completion of myriad tasks associated with it;
- Vicki Spandel for her superb editorial assistance, which went far beyond technical editing to improve substantially the content and presentation;
- Joan Shaw, Karen Ranson, Carmen Bullock, Cathryn Peterson, Becky Valcarce and Marcia Summers for their uncomplaining and excellent technical assistance with the manuscript and associated tasks; and
- our wives, Barbara and Susan, and our families, without whose support and sacrifice this book could not have been written.

Blaine R. Worthen
James R. Sanders

Part One
Introduction

In this initial section of our text, we attempt to accomplish three things.

First, we discuss in Chapter 1 the varying roles evaluation studies can play in education and related fields, current societal expectations of evaluation, and factors that influence how well evaluation can fulfill such expectations.

Second, we discuss in Chapter 2 the historical evolution of evaluation as a growing force in educational improvement.

Third, we define evaluation more specifically in Chapter 3 and try to help the reader distinguish clearly between evaluation and closely related—but different—activities such as research and measurement. We also introduce the reader to two basic distinctions important to educational evaluation.

Our intent in this section is to provide the reader with information essential to understanding not only the content of the sections of our book that follow, but also the broad wealth of material that exists in the literature on evaluation in education and related fields.

Chapter 1
The Role of Evaluation in Improving Education

Orienting Questions

1. What is the difference between formal and informal evaluation?
2. What is the *goal* of evaluation? What *roles* can evaluation play in education?
3. What is an evaluation object? What are some examples of important evaluation objects in education?

In most advanced nations, education is increasingly viewed as a primary means for solving social problems. Indeed, in some cases, the future welfare of nations has been placed squarely on the shoulders of the schools and universities. In the United States, for example, the National Commission on Excellence in Education was created to investigate "the widespread public perception that something is seriously remiss in our educational system," and the "support of all who care about our future" was elicited to aid the commission's work (National Commission on Excellence in Education, 1983, p. 1). The first essential message in the commission's public report, entitled *A Nation At Risk: The Imperative for Educational Reform*, is that the United States' once unchallenged lead in commerce, industry, science, and technological innovation is being overtaken by competitors throughout the world. The commission's panel of distinguished leaders warned that "the educational foundations of our society are presently being eroded by a rising tide of mediocrity that threatens our very future as a nation and a people" (National Commission on Excellence in Education, 1983, p. 5). This report has sparked a national debate on education that echoes similar (if less dramatic) dialogues in countries everywhere.

Admittedly, critics of existing educational systems often overstate their case, focusing so much on the inadequacies of schools that they breed pessimism about the possibility of genuine educational improvement. But even if such pessimism is unjustified, one cannot discount the critics' concerns, for they serve to highlight one key deficit in most educational systems: the lack of effective evaluation. Without careful, systematic inquiry into the effectiveness of either current school practices or new programs, many changes occurring in education become little more than random adoption of faddish innovations. Probably the greatest contributors to this inadequate evaluation are (1) the lack of dependable information about the performance of educational products, practices, and programs; and (2) the absence of established systems for producing such information.

Though it is just one step toward educational improvement, evaluation holds greater promise than any other approach in providing educators with information they need to help improve educational practices. Recognition of this fact has encouraged many educational and governmental leaders to support evaluation, and most educated publics agree that school programs should be evaluated. Parents want information about the curricula and teaching methods used to instruct their children. Other citizen groups want to know what results are being achieved through schools' expenditures of public funds. Because evaluation can help provide this information, lawmakers often use evaluation mandates as a means of legislating school improvement, and school and university officials accept evaluation as a necessary condition for obtaining funds for many educational programs. Many teachers and administrators scan evaluation reports to catch a clue about how well they are doing. In short, evaluation has gained widespread acceptance in education and related fields

INFORMAL VERSUS FORMAL EVALUATION

Evaluation is not a new concept. One dictionary definition of evaluation is, "To determine the worth of: to appraise" (*Webster's New World Dictionary*, 1960, p. 26). Given such broad focus for the term, it can be argued that evaluation has been with us always and that everyone is, in his or her own way, an evaluator. When the English adopted and improved upon the Welsh longbow, it was because the English yeomen saw its advantages over their own crossbows. The longbow could send an arrow through the stoutest armor and was capable of launching three arrows while the crossbow was sending one. In short, the English evaluated the longbow's value for their purposes, deciding that its use would strengthen them in their struggles with the French. So they abandoned the crossbow and perfected the longbow, and the English armies proved invincible during most of the Hundred Years' War. By contrast, French archers experimented briefly with the longbow, then went back to the crossbow—and continued to lose battles. Such are the perils of poor evaluation. Unfortunately, the faulty judgment that led the French to persist in using an inferior weapon represents an informal evaluation pattern that has been repeated throughout history.

Consider the fifth-grade teacher who decides to continue using outdated, phonetically inaccurate, and culturally insensitive reading books in her class rather than the highly regarded, up-to-date, linguistically correct, and culturally sensitive reading curriculum adopted by the school district. Her decision is most probably based upon a highly informal appraisal of the value of the two alternative books to her instructional program. Or, consider the administrators who establish a graduate program to train professional personnel and then, without collecting any data about the program, vote to terminate it before the first graduating class has taken jobs. They too are engaged in evaluation of a sort.

Evaluation then is a basic form of human behavior. Sometimes it is thorough, structured, and formal. More often it is impressionistic and private. Informal evaluation occurs whenever one chooses from among available alternatives—and sometimes informality is the only practical approach. (In choosing an entrée from a dinner menu, only the most compulsive individual would conduct exit interviews with restaurant patrons to gather data in support of his dinner choice.) This informal type of evaluation, choices based on highly subjective *perceptions* of which alternative is best, is not of concern in this book. Our focus is the more formal and systematic approach to evaluation, where choices are based on *systematic* efforts to define criteria and obtain *accurate* information about alternatives (thus enabling the real value of the alternatives to be determined).

EVALUATION'S ROLES AND GOALS

Formal evaluation studies have played many roles in education, including the following:

1. To provide a basis for decision making and policy formation
2. To assess student achievement
3. To evaluate curricula
4. To accredit schools
5. To monitor expenditure of public funds
6. To improve educational materials and programs.

Scriven (1973) notes that evaluation plays many roles in education, even though it has a single goal: to determine the worth or merit of whatever is being evaluated. He made the important distinction that the *goal* of evaluation is to provide answers to significant evaluative questions that are posed, whereas evaluation *roles* refer to the ways in which those answers are used. The goal usually relates to value questions, requires judgments of worth or merit, and is conceptually distinct from roles. Scriven made the distinction this way:

In terms of goals, we may say that evaluation attempts to answer certain *types of question* about certain *entities*. The entities are the various educational instruments (processes, personnel, procedures, programs, etc.). The types of question include questions of the form: *How well* does this instrument perform (with respect to such-and-such criteria)? Does it perform *better* than this other instrument; *What* merits, or drawbacks does this instrument have (i.e., what variables from the group in which we are interested are significantly affected by its application)? Is the use of this instrument *worth* what it's costing?

...the *roles* which evaluation has in a particular educational context may be enormously various; it may form part of a teacher training activity, of the process of curriculum development, of a field experiment connected with the improvement of learning theory, of an investigation preliminary to a decision about purchase or rejection of materials; it may be a data-gathering activity for supporting a request for tax increases or research support, or a preliminary to the reward or punishment of people as in an executive training program, a prison, or a classroom. Failure to make this rather obvious distinction between the roles and goals of evaluation is one of the factors that has led to the dilution of what is called evaluation to the point where it can no longer answer the questions which are its principal goal, questions about real merit or worth. (Scriven, 1973, pp. 61–62)

We shall discuss evaluation's goal further in later chapters. Here we deal more with the roles evaluation plays.

Many authors have attempted to categorize the purposes for which evaluations are conducted. For example, Brophy, Grotelueschen, and Gooler (1974) outlined three major reasons for conducting evaluations:

1. Planning procedures, programs, and/or products
2. Improving existing procedures, programs, and/or products
3. Justifying (or not justifying) existing or planned procedures, programs, and/or products.

Most educators agree that evaluation can serve either a *formative* purpose (such as helping to improve a mathematics curriculum) or a *summative* purpose (such as deciding whether that curriculum should be continued).[1] Anderson and Ball (1978) further describe the capabilities of evaluation, as applied to formal programs, in terms of six major purposes (which are not necessarily mutually exclusive):

1. To contribute to decisions about program installation
2. To contribute to decisions about program continuation, expansion, or certification
3. To contribute to decisions about program modifications
4. To obtain evidence to rally support for a program
5. To obtain evidence to rally opposition to a program
6. To contribute to the understanding of basic psychological, social, and other processes.[2]

It is not our purpose to provide an exhaustive list of all the purposes educational evaluation can serve. There are many. And the list continues to grow as more educators gain experience in using evaluation for their benefit. Support for continued use and improvement of evaluation generally rests on one of the following arguments:

1. There is a need to plan and carry out school improvements in a systematic way that includes (a) identifying needs, (b) selecting the best strategies from among known alternatives, (c) monitoring changes as they occur, and (d) measuring the impact of these changes. Only through this process can educators minimize the chance of misdirected or inconsequential changes and justify expenditures associated with beneficial changes (Stufflebeam & Shinkfield, 1985). Hammond (1973) also made a similar logical argument by stressing the use of systematic evaluation to avoid faddism, overreaction to political pressure, pendulum swinging, reliance on persuasive claims of advocates and salesmen, and resistance to information sharing (that is, a reluctance or simple lack of effort to let staff and the public know what is happening in the school). Alkin, Daillak, and White (1979) documented the use of evaluation to direct decision making about new programs.

2. There is a need for cost-benefit analysis of programs and practices that

require large amounts of money (Madaus, Airasian, & Kellaghan, 1980). A push for accountability in public education (Lessinger & Tyler, 1971; Browder, Atkins, & Kaya, 1973; Webster, 1977) is consistent with this line of reasoning.

3. There is a need to test a number of popular theories (myths?) about the effects of education on student development. Professional experience currently dictates most teaching and school management practices. Yet it seems quite appropriate to ask that experience-based educational decisions be justified and supported. As Cronbach and others (1980, p. 38) noted, "The need for systematic and often subtle information to supplant or confirm casual observations is what generates the call for evaluation."

4. Educators have a professional responsibility to appraise the quality of their school programs, and they constantly seek ways of improving that quality (Spencer, 1964; Cronbach and others, 1980).

5. There is a need to reduce uncertainty about educational practices when experience is limited (Patton and others, 1978; Kennedy, Apling, & Neumann, 1980).

6. There is a need to satisfy external agencies' demands for reports, to legitimize decisions, or to improve public relations through credible, data-based decision making (King, Thompson, & Pechman, 1982).

Evaluation as Political Activity

An example of widely diverse roles evaluation may play is found in the urging of Cronbach and his colleagues (1980, p. 152) that an evaluator go beyond his or her traditional technical, scientific roles to play "...an active role in political events, preferably as a multipartisan who serves the general interest." Thoughtful evaluators have come to realize that evaluation is not just a technical procedure involving instrument development, data collection, and data analysis—it is also a political activity. Information is power, and those who possess information unavailable to others have an advantage. Moreover, whenever the special interests of different individuals or groups are being considered in an evaluation, as they are most of the time, there is opportunity for one point of view to dominate. Attempts to influence the outcomes of an evaluation, or to avoid evaluation altogether, are yet another way in which political influence interplays with evaluation. Brickell (1978), Cronbach and others (1980), House (1973, 1980), and the Joint Committee on Standards for Educational Evaluation (1981) have all examined ways in which evaluation and politics interrelate. This topic will be discussed in further detail in Chapter 17.

THE OBJECTS OF FORMAL EVALUATION STUDIES

Formal evaluation studies have been conducted to answer questions about a wide variety of educational entities, which we shall refer to here as *evaluation objects*. The evaluation object is whatever is being evaluated. Important evaluation objects in education include the following:

- Student development and performance
- Educator qualifications and performance
- Curriculum design and processes
- School organizational structure
- Textbooks and other curriculum materials and products
- Funded or unfunded projects
- Any aspect of school operations (school transportation, food services, health services)
- School budgets, business and finance
- Facilities, media and libraries, equipment
- Educational policies
- School–community relations
- Parent involvement in schools
- School climate
- Ideas, plans, and objectives.

Each of these objects may be analyzed by looking at its component parts, their interactions, and their performance within particular contexts. Objects change over time and within different contexts. The object that is described in one setting or in one time frame may be very different from that same object described elsewhere or at a different time. Descriptions of a program presented in a plan or public relations document, for example, may or may not correspond to reality. Evaluators have found that firsthand experience with the object of the evaluation is the best way to gain valid knowledge about it.[3]

Whatever the evaluation object, the process requires reflection and sensitivity to the values of others if the evaluation is to be adequate. Questions like "What makes a good teacher?" or "What makes a good high school curriculum?" do not have easy answers. The answers are dependent on the students who are being served by the school, on available resources, on conceptions of what schools are for (see Goodlad, 1979, for a provocative discussion of this question), on the research literature that reports relationships between teaching variables or curriculum variables and student development, on accreditation requirements, and certainly on the values of the constituents of the school. But while simple answers do not exist, the benefits to students and eventually to society of addressing these important questions cannot be underestimated.

Potential and Limitations of Educational Evaluation

The usefulness of educational evaluation has led some persons to look to it as a panacea for all the ills of education. But evaluation alone cannot solve all of education's problems. One of the biggest mistakes of evaluators in the 1970s was to promise results that could not possibly be attained. Stake (1982, p. 58) noted this when he said, "Evaluator promises often leap beyond what the proposer has previously accomplished, and also beyond the attainment of anyone in the field." Even ardent supporters of evaluation are forced to admit that many evaluation studies fail to lead to significant improvements in school programs. Why? Partly it's a question of grave inadequacies in the conceptualization and conduct of many educational evaluations. It's also a question of understanding too little about other factors that affect the use of evaluation information, even from studies that are well conceptualized and well conducted. In addition, we may have been limited by our unfortunate tendency to view evaluation as a series of discrete studies, rather than a continuing system of self-renewal.

A few poorly planned, badly executed, or inappropriately ignored evaluations should not surprise us; such failings occur in every field of human endeavor. The real problem is one of frequency and significance. So many key evaluations have been disappointing or have made such little impact that even some evaluation advocates have expressed reservations about evaluation living up to its high potential. Indeed, unless evaluation practices improve significantly in the years ahead, its potential for improving education may never be realized. That need not happen. This book is intended to help educational evaluators, and those who use their results to improve the practice and utility of evaluation in the field of education.

A parallel problem exists when those served by evaluation naively assume that its magic wand need only be waved over an educational enterprise to correct all its malfunctions and inadequacies. As House, Mathison, Pearsol, and Preskill (1982, p. 27) put it, "The expectations of what evaluation can accomplish are often beyond common-sense limits."[4] Though evaluation can be enormously useful, it is generally counterproductive for evaluators or those who depend on their work to propose evaluation as the ultimate solution to every problem or, indeed, as any sort of solution, because evaluation in and of itself won't effect a solution—though it might suggest one. Evaluation serves to identify strengths and weaknesses, highlight the good, and expose the faulty, but not to *correct* problems, for that is the separate step of using evaluation findings.

Evaluation has a role to play in enlightening its consumers, and it may be used for many purposes in education. But it is only one of many influences on educational policies, practices, and decisions. Both its limitations and its benefits must be acknowledged. The remainder of this book is devoted to enhancing an understanding of how evaluation may reach its full potential as a force for improving education.

APPLICATION EXERCISES

1. Discuss the potential and limitations of educational evaluation. Identify some things evaluation cannot do for educators.
2. Within your own institution (if you are a university student, you might choose your university), identify several evaluation objects that you believe would be appropriate for study. For each, identify: (1) the *role* the evaluation study would play, and (2) the *goal* of the evaluation.

SUGGESTED READINGS

NOWAKOWSKI, J., BUNDA, M. A., WORKING, R., BERNACKI, G., & HARRINGTON, P. (1985). *A Handbook of Educational Variables.* Boston: Kluwer-Nijhoff.

SCRIVEN, M. (1973). The methodology of evaluation. In B. R. WORTHEN & J. R. SANDERS, *Educational Evaluation: Theory and Practice*, Belmont, CA: Wadsworth.

Chapter 2
The History of Evaluation in Education

Orienting Questions

1. Prior to 1920, what use was made of evaluation in the field of education? Which American educators of that period used evaluation? How did they use it?
2. Who were the major contributors to the development of educational evaluation between 1920 and 1965? What did each of these individuals contribute?
3. What major political events occurred in the late 1950s and early 1960s that greatly accelerated the growth of evaluation thought?
4. How would you characterize the growth of educational evaluation from 1965 to the present? What are some significant developments that have occurred in the field of evaluation during this period?

Formal evaluation (at least of educational and social programs) has only begun to mature as a conscious, purposeful activity, with major developments occurring over the past 20 years. As noted by some analysts:

> Evaluation, as an established field, is now in its late adolescent years. The bubbling, exciting, fast-developing childhood years of the late 1960s and early 1970s gave way in the mid to late 1970s to the less self-assured, serious, introspective early adolescent years. Now, in the early 1980s, evaluation is making the transition from late adolescence to adulthood. (Conner, Altman, & Jackson, 1984, p. 13)

Yet we should not overlook the forms of evaluation that have served education prior to this recent growth spurt.

THE HISTORY AND INFLUENCE OF EVALUATION IN EDUCATION

Assuming that decisions have always been a part of education, we can safely claim that evaluation has always had a role to play. Informal evaluation, or the way in which people form impressions or perceptions about which educational alternatives are best, is as much a part of education as teaching itself. Yet even formal evaluation, or the use of accurate information and criteria to assign values and justify value judgments, has a much longer and more distinguished history than is generally recognized.

Educational Evaluation: Early History to A.D. 1920

The practice of evaluating individual performance was evident as early as 2000 B.C., when Chinese officials conducted civil service examinations to measure proficiency of public officials. Greek teachers, such as Socrates, used verbally mediated evaluation as part of the learning process. But formal evaluations of educational and social programs were almost nonexistent until the mid-nineteenth century.

Travers (1983) has established that prior to the mid-1800s there was little that could be construed as formal evaluation in American education.[5] Prior to 1837, political and religious beliefs dictated most educational choices. Communities were happy to attract and hold teachers, regardless of their competence, and if a teacher did prove incompetent in those days, formal evaluation was relatively pointless anyway—the school just closed for lack of students.

Americans Henry Barnard and Horace Mann—and later, William Torrey Harris—apparently introduced the practice of collecting data on which to base educational decisions. Their work began in the state education departments of Massachusetts and Connecticut and was continued in the United States Education Bureau with a process for collecting information to assist and support decision making. Thus were sown the seeds of educational evaluation in the United States.

During the period 1838 to 1850, Horace Mann submitted 12 annual reports to the Board of Education of the Commonwealth of Massachusetts. As Travers (1983) reported in detail, these reports identified all current educational concerns, with empirical support. Many of the concerns reported in those annual reports are still relevant today:

- Geographic distribution of schools
- Adequacy of outside supervision
- Financial support for poor students who want to attend school
- Low interest in education among community members
- School finance
- Teacher competency
- Selection or construction of appropriate curriculum materials
- Adequacy of school libraries in rural areas
- Consolidation of small schools
- Teacher training
- Discipline
- Economic benefits in free public education.

In 1845, the Boston School Committee undertook what became known as the

Boston Survey, the first use of printed tests for widescale assessment of student achievement. A sample of Boston students were tested in definitions, geography, grammar, civil history, natural philosophy, astronomy, writing, and arithmetic. Interestingly, the committee was shocked by the low level of performance in 1845 and again in 1846, and discontinued the testing in 1847 because no use was made of the results (Travers, 1983). This precursor to modern-day debate over the value of school testing was the first attempt at objectively measuring student achievement to assess the quality of a large school system.

Later, during the period of 1895–1905, Joseph Rice organized a similar assessment program carried out in a number of large school systems throughout the United States. Because Rice had a reputation as an educational critic, he feared his criticisms might be dismissed as the grumblings of one disgruntled observer. Hence, he set out to document his claims that schooltime was inefficiently used. In his tests of spelling, for example, he found negligible differences in students' performance from one school to another, regardless of the amount of time spent on spelling instruction. He used these data to support his proposals for restructuring spelling instruction. His tests of arithmetic, on the other hand, revealed large differences among schools; consequently, Rice proposed the setting up of standardized examinations (Travers, 1983).

One more interesting contribution by Rice to the field of school evaluation might be noted. In 1915, he published a book entitled *The People's Government: Efficient, Bossless, Graftless.* In it he proposed a system for resolving controversial policy issues; namely, to bring together all relevant facts and present them to a qualified panel of judges. This process, proposed as a means of eliminating graft and waste in government, was an early and little known form of what later emerged as the advocate-adversary or judicial approach to evaluation.

In the early 1900s, Edward Lee Thorndike, called the father of the educational testing movement, helped persuade educators that measuring human change was worthwhile. Measurement technology for determining human abilities flourished in the United States during the first two decades of the present century, and testing emerged as the primary means of evaluating schools. By World War I, somewhere between 18 (Travers, 1983) and 40 (Madaus, Airasian, & Kellaghan, 1980) large school systems had bureaus of school research working on large-scale assessments of student achievement. It was reported that these surveys were used "for a variety of purposes: to diagnose specific system weaknesses, to standardize curricular practice, to evaluate experiments, and to assess the overall performance of a system as well as to make decisions about individuals" (Madaus, Airasian, & Kellaghan, 1980, p. 6).

The testing movement was in full swing by 1918, with individual and group tests being developed for use in many educational and psychological decisions. The Army Alpha (for literates) and Beta (for illiterates) tests, developed and used during World War I, lent credibility to the notion that good decisions about individuals could be made only when objective test information was available. Though the early school system surveys had relied mainly on criterion-referenced tests to gather group information in school subject areas, the 1920s saw the emergence of norm-referenced tests developed for use in measuring individual performance levels.

One other event of interest occurred right before World War I. This was the commissioned evaluation of the Gary, Indiana, public school system by Abraham Flexner, beginning in 1915. The Gary plan was an innovative means of meeting the educational needs of the Gary community. This evaluation was apparently requested by the school superintendent, William Wirt, who was convinced that his schools were the best in the country and who wanted an outside group of individuals to conduct a study of the school system that would prove him right. The evaluation study was completed in 1918, at considerable cost. The conclusions stated that the Gary students were academically inferior to comparison students, but some commentators (for example, Travers, 1983) believe the study was highly biased against the Gary plan. Results aside, this evaluation is the first evidence that we have found of a school board hiring an outside, independent team of evaluators to study and report on a controversial educational program. The political and technical problems inherent in this evaluation study still plague educational evaluations today. Perhaps if the concepts of meta-evaluation and standards for evaluation had been developed back in 1915, the Gary school system might have benefited rather than suffered. After reading an account of the Gary evaluation, one cannot avoid appreciating the way in which educational evaluation has developed during the twentieth century.

Educational Evaluation: 1920–1965

The testing movement continued to flourish during the 1920s and 1930s, with the New York Board of Regents examination appearing in 1927 and the Iowa tests in 1929. By the mid-1930s, over one-half of the United States had some form of statewide testing. The development of standardized achievement tests for use in large-scale testing programs was a natural outgrowth of this trend. In addition, teacher-made achievement tests burgeoned, forming a basis for most school grading systems. Personality and interest profiles were also developed during this period. The military and private industry began using these new tools to evaluate recruits or applicants for personnel selection and classification. During this period, measurement and evaluation were regarded as nearly synonymous, and the term "evaluation" was most often used to mean the assigning of grades or summarizing of student performance on tests. The concept of evaluation, as we know it today, was still evolving.

The 1920s also saw the emergence of the empirically minded school superintendent, embodied in Carleton Washburne of Winnetka, Illinois. Washburne was described as one who "understood the value of facts and figures and [knew] that they had to be collected by experts if they were to be credible" (Travers, 1983, p. 517).[6]

During the 1930s, as part of the progressive education movement, school districts experimented with curricula based on the writings of John Dewey. As such curricula were developed and tried, they were evaluated, albeit informally. Critics of progressive high school curricula were unimpressed with these evaluations, however, and maintained that students educated in progressive high school curricula would fare poorly in higher education programs when compared to students educated in conventional Carnegie-unit curricula. This controversy led to the landmark Eight Year Study, which included a formal plan of evaluation that remains popular today. Ralph Tyler, employed in 1932 as director of the evaluation staff of the study, conceptualized the objectives-based approach to educational evaluation and developed instruments and procedures to measure a wide range of educational outcomes. In reporting their work on the Eight Year Study, Smith and Tyler (1942) provided an evaluation manual that was to dominate thinking in educational evaluation for the next quarter century. Even today, evaluators who employ objectives as the basis for determining whether a curriculum or program is a success (that is, if the objectives are achieved, the curriculum is judged to be successful) are still often referred to as Tylerian evaluators. Later work by Bloom and others (1956), Taba (1962), Krathwohl, Bloom, and Masia (1964), Metfessel and Michael (1967), Bloom, Hastings, and Madaus (1971), and many others followed in the footsteps formed in the 1930s by Ralph Tyler. The United States National Assessment of Educational Progress (NAEP) was also conceptualized by Tyler in the 1960s, following the approach used in the Eight Year Study. Many current statewide testing programs in the United States are also based on the NAEP design.

The 1930s also witnessed a growing influence among national and regional school accreditation agencies in the United States. Although they had been on the scene since the late 1800s and early 1900s, these agencies did not reach their pinnacle of power until the 1930s, for there were charters, standards, and memberships to be developed. Accreditation replaced the system of school inspections, based on a Western European school evaluation approach, that were common in many states in the 1890s (Glass, 1969). Using *Evaluative Criteria,* published by the National Study of School Evaluation, teams of outside educators were sent to review self-study reports of member institutions and to make their own observations. Recommendations from the team determined member institutions' status.

Unlike the Eight Year Study that concentrated on the outcomes of schooling, the accreditation movement concentrated on the resources and processes used in schools. For example, accrediting agencies developed guidelines and criteria to monitor the adequacy of facilities, qualifications of staff, and appropriateness of program design, rather than assessing the educational status of graduates. Accreditation has been a highly influential part of American evaluation since the late 1800s. With the establishment of formal accrediting agencies for schools and colleges came the institutionalization of at least a quasi-evaluation process in American education.

The 1940s and early 1950s generally saw a period of consolidation and application of earlier evaluation developments. School personnel devoted their energies to testing and test development, accreditation, school surveys, and the formation or selection of acceptable objectives for education. The 1950s and early 1960s also saw considerable technical development, building on the Tylerian base. For example, taxonomies of possible educational objectives were published, beginning with the influential *Taxonomy of Educational Objectives: Handbook I: Cognitive Domain* (Bloom and others, 1956). "Bloom's taxonomy," as it came to be popularly called, defined in explicit detail a hierarchy of thinking skills applicable to various content areas. This document continues to be a standard tool both in testing and in curriculum development, design, and evaluation. A sequel companion volume, entitled *Taxonomy of Educational Objectives: Handbook II: Affective Domain* (Krathwohl and others, 1964) has become popularly known as "Krathwohl's taxonomy." It provided, in the same detail as Bloom's taxonomy, an organized structure for evaluating and teaching feelings, emotions, and values. As reference tools for the evaluator, these taxonomies have proven indispensable.

Prior to 1965, the most dramatic change in educational evaluation resulted from the Soviet Union's launch of Sputnik I in 1957. American reaction was nearly immediate. With passage of the National Defense Education Act of 1958, millions of dollars were poured into development of new educational programs. Major new curriculum development projects, especially in mathematics and science (biology, chemistry, and physics), were initiated across the country. Subsequently, funds were made available to evaluate these curriculum development efforts.

The relatively few evaluation studies that resulted revealed the conceptual and methodological impoverishment of evaluation in that era. In many cases, the designs were inadequate, the data invalid, the analyses inaccurate, and the reports irrelevant to the important evaluation questions that should have been posed. Most of the studies depended on idiosyncratic combinations and applications of concepts and techniques from experimental design, psychometrics, curriculum development and, to a lesser extent, survey research. Theoretical work related to educational evaluation per se was almost nonexistent. Few scholars had yet turned their attention to developing evaluation plans applicable to education. Thus, educational evaluators were left to glean what they could from other fields. That their gleanings were meager was noted by Cronbach (1963) in a seminal article criticizing evaluations of the past as largely unhelpful and calling for new directions. Cronbach believed educational evaluation should help developers improve their products during early stages, not just appraise their effectiveness once they were in the marketplace. Although Cronbach's recommendations had little immediate impact, they did stimulate sufficient dialogue among evaluation specialists to launch a greatly expanded conception of evaluation, as will be discussed later.

About the time of Cronbach's pronouncements, civil rights and concern for the disadvantaged began to gain increasing attention at the federal level. The Civil Rights Act of 1964 led to the Coleman Study in 1965–1966 that focused on equality of opportunity for minority children. Even more important to educational evaluation, however, was the passage of the Elementary and Secondary Education Act (ESEA) of 1965, which authorized several educational research, development, and dissemination activities. But the largest single component of the bill was Title I (later Chapter I) educational programs for disadvantaged youth, destined to be the most costly federal education program in American history.

As Congress began its deliberations on the proposed ESEA, it became apparent that if passed, this bill would result in tens of thousands of federal grants to local education agencies, intermediate and state agencies, and universities. Concerns began to be expressed, especially on the Senate floor, that there was absolutely no assurance that the large amounts of money authorized for education would be spent as intended. ESEA was by far the most comprehensive and ambitious education bill ever envisioned, and it was noted that education did not have an impressive record of providing evidence that federal monies thus expended resulted in any real educational improvements. Indeed, there were some in Congress who felt federal funds allocated to education prior to ESEA had sunk like stones into the morass of educational programs with scarcely an observable ripple to mark their passage.

Robert F. Kennedy was among those senators who forcefully insisted ESEA carry a proviso requiring educators to be accountable for the federal monies they received. They were to file an evaluation report for each grant showing what effects had resulted from the expenditure of the federal funds. Although only partially successful (the final version of the bill required evaluation reports under only two of its Titles—I and III), these efforts led to the first major federal mandate for educational evaluation. Translated into operational terms, this meant that thousands of educators were for the first time *required* to spend their time evaluating their own efforts. Project evaluations mandated by state and federal governments have since become standard practice, with evaluation emerging as a political tool to control the expenditure of public funds.

Educational Evaluation: 1965–Present

In 1965, American educators were unprepared to respond effectively to the new evaluation mandate. Few had any expertise in evaluation. As a result, many school districts released their best teachers from classroom duties and pressed them into service as Title I or Title III evaluators. Their only qualifications for the job were experience and training as teachers—hardly relevant credentials for the position at hand. Even those who possessed technical expertise were ill-prepared for the new demands of the federal mandate; their training in experimental research design, measurement, and statistics—while relevant—did not prepare them adequately to conduct evaluation. Nevertheless, some help is better than none, and these technical experts were widely employed. Using the resources known to them, they borrowed heavily from the behavioral, social, and educational sciences to conduct educational evaluation with, as we shall see, dubious results.

That many of the resulting "evaluations" would be inadequate was inevitable. Egon Guba was one who, after an analysis of the evaluation plans contained in a sample of Title III project proposals, concluded that

> It is very dubious whether the results of these evaluations will be of much use to anyone.... None of these product evaluations will give the Federal Government the data it needs to review the general Title III program and to decide how the program might be reshaped to be more effective. (Guba, 1967, p. 312)

Lack of trained personnel was not the only reason for the poor response to the ESEA evaluation mandate. In translating the legislation into operational terms, the United States Office of Education (USOE) had failed to provide adequate guidelines for the local evaluator. In the absence of such guidelines, evaluation designs for each project had to be created *de novo* by inexperienced personnel.

It seems likely that this failure to provide useful guidelines resulted more from lack of knowledge about what a good evaluation should include than from lack of effort on the part of USOE personnel. The expertise and methodology needed was either not available or else it was not adequate to address new evaluation needs. Few scholars had concerned themselves with generalizable evaluation plans for use by local evaluators. Theoretical work in evaluation was almost nonexistent.

The resulting vacuum was quickly filled, however, during the period of 1967–1973, as academics developed new approaches, strategies, and methods for evaluators to use in these federal projects. Beginning in 1967, some observers began circulating their notions about how one should conduct educational evaluations. Their efforts produced several new evaluation "models" touted by the authors as responsive to the needs of Title I and Title III evaluators, and relevant to the ongoing curriculum development efforts sparked by Sputnik. New evaluation approaches were also proposed by educationists in England, Australia, Israel, Sweden, and other countries.

Collectively, these new conceptualizations of evaluation greatly broadened earlier views. As these frameworks for planning evaluation studies were refined, evaluators began increasingly to rely on them for guidance. Although these models couldn't begin to solve all the evaluation problems of local evaluators, they did help them circumvent several of the more treacherous pitfalls common to earlier evaluation studies. Problems caused by mindless application of objectives-based (Tylerian) evaluation methods to every evaluation were revealed. The need to evaluate unintended outcomes of a curriculum was recognized. Values and standards were emphasized, and the importance of making judgments about merit and worth was made clear. These new and controversial ideas spawned dialogue and debate that fed a developing evaluation vocabulary and literature. The result has been a plethora of evaluation articles and books in the past two decades, containing at least 40 formalized or semiformalized evaluation "models" proposed for use in education. (Fortunately, these models can be organized into several more generalizable evaluation approaches, as shown later in Part Two.)

During this period, when the ESEA gave such profound impetus to educational evaluation, other developing trends increased the emphasis on evaluative processes. The growth of teacher militancy, union demands, and calls for civil rights reforms in education all required refined capabilities in evaluation. The increasing public outcry for educational accountability caused educators to rethink education's responsibilities and outcomes and ways of documenting them. Concerns over educational achievement led to student testing at federal and state levels. The National Assessment of Educational Progress, begun in 1964 under the direction of Ralph Tyler, continues today with an annual assessment of performance based on a national sample of students. It was not long until state departments of education began designing state assessment systems, and state legislatures began requiring school reports on student achievement in subjects like reading and mathematics. Most states today conduct some type of statewide testing program.

During the late 1960s and early 1970s, professional associations began encouraging their members to grant evaluation more serious attention. For example, the American Educational Research Association initiated a monograph series in curriculum evaluation. The Association for Supervision and Curriculum Development (ASCD) published evaluation monographs that encouraged curriculum developers to employ better evaluation techniques in assessing the worth of their products. More important, the 1970s gave rise to new professional associations for evaluators. Although Division H in the American Educational Research Association had been created as a professional home for school-based evaluators, no association had yet been created to serve the evaluation specialist exclusively. In 1975, Phi Delta Kappa International provided seed money to establish the Evaluation Network, an interdisciplinary professional association of evaluators. The Evaluation Network quickly grew to several thousand members and sponsored a quarterly publication, *Evaluation News*. The Evaluation Research Society, conceived by Marcia Guttentag and established in 1976, also developed as a multidisciplinary professional association for evaluators. This society also sponsored several publications. Beginning in 1986, a merger of these two associations resulted in a new, broader based American Evaluation Association.

The United States government has made concerted efforts to support and improve evaluation of the nation's educational system. In 1967, the federal government created the Center for the Study of Evaluation, a federally supported research and development center at the University of California, Los Angeles. In 1972, the government created the National Institute of Education (NIE). The NIE focused one of its research programs on evaluation in education, supporting field research that added to our knowledge of evaluation methodology, and also funded research to adapt methods and techniques from other disciplines for use in educational evaluation. During this same period (1968 to 1977), the budget for the Office of Planning, Budgeting, and Evaluation in the United States Office of Education was reported to have grown 1,650 percent (McLaughlin, 1980). One of the most enduring evaluation efforts supported by this federal agency was the operation of a series of Technical Assistance Centers for Title I/Chapter I Evaluation. Initiated in 1976, this nationwide network of centers has gradually expanded its perspective from mandated Title I evaluation and reporting to a broad range of evaluation-related assistance services addressing nearly all aspects of Chapter (Title) I programs.

The professional literature in evaluation has grown exponentially during the past 20 years, with the appearance of (1) numerous manuals, anthologies, and textbooks on selected evaluation issues; (2) journals such as *Evaluation, Evaluation and Program Planning, Evaluation News, Educational Evaluation and Policy Analysis, Evaluation Quarterly, New Directions for Program Evaluation*, and *Evaluation Review*; and (3) annual compilations of evaluation literature published in the *Evaluation Studies Review Annuals*. Talmage (1982) reports that the evaluation literature began to burgeon rapidly around 1974.

A Joint Committee on Standards for Educational Evaluation, created in the

United States in 1975, now includes representatives from most major professional educational associations in the nation.[7] In 1981, this Joint Committee developed the *Standards for Evaluations of Educational Programs, Projects, and Materials,* the first organized statement of principles for sound educational evaluation. A parallel effort by the Evaluation Research Society in 1982 resulted in a second set of standards, proposed to guide program evaluation practices in the diverse fields represented by the Society's membership.

The past decade in educational evaluation may be called one of "professionalization," as the shared knowledge and experience of a great many evaluators in education grew and matured. As was noted earlier in this chapter, ". . . evaluation is making the transition from late adolescence to adulthood." Yet, it must continue to grow and adapt to changing conditions and demands. For example, economic austerity and political conservatism in many nations during the early 1980s have led to retrenchment and reduction in many social and educational programs, especially those sponsored by national governments. The resulting decrease in demand for evaluation of large-scale, federally supported educational programs has led some commentators to make gloomy predictions about the future of evaluation in education and related areas. Some insightful analysts, however, have forecasted that evaluation of educational programs will continue, although the locus and focus will shift increasingly to local education agencies as evaluation's role in improving educational programs becomes institutionalized.

APPLICATION EXERCISES

1. Investigate parallels between the growth of evaluation thought in education and the growth of thought in other educational functions such as curriculum development, testing, and school administration.
2. List several reasons why evaluation in American education probably would not have developed as it did if the federal government had not been involved in educational reform.

SUGGESTED READINGS

Madaus, G., Airasian, P., & Kellaghan, T. (1980). *School effectiveness.* New York: McGraw-Hill.

Madaus, G., Stufflebeam, D., & Scriven, M. (1983). Program evaluation: A historical overview. In G. Madaus, M. Scriven, & D. Stufflebeam (Eds.), *Evaluation models: Viewpoints on educational and human services evaluation.* Boston: Kluwer-Nijhoff.

Talmage, H. (1982). Evaluation of programs. In H. E. Mitzel (Ed.), *Encyclopedia of educational research* (5th ed.). New York: The Free Press.

Travers, R. (1983). *How research has changed American schools.* Kalamazoo, MI: Mythos Press.

Chapter 3
The Concept of Evaluation:
An Overview

Orienting Questions

1. If a person said she was doing an evaluation, what mental images would you have of her work?
2. What are some alternative ways that evaluation has been defined? Which definition do the authors prefer, and why?
3. What are some similarities and differences between educational research and evaluation?
4. When a person measures educational outcomes, has she evaluated the program that produces those outcomes?
5. What are the major differences between *formative* and *summative* evaluations?
6. What difference does it make whether a formative or summative evaluation is conducted by internal or external evaluators?

In the previous chapter on the history of evaluation, the perceptive reader will have noticed that the term *evaluation* was used broadly to encompass many diverse activities, ranging from testing student achievement to conducting accreditation site visits. Also, several evaluation terms and concepts were used without definition, except those that were implicit in context. Although such a general level of discourse was appropriate for that chapter, it is necessary now to become more specific about basic concepts and distinctions in order to provide common concepts and vocabulary for later chapters.

Like many disciplines, educational evaluation has developed its own jargon. For example, "evaluand" is often used to refer to whatever is being evaluated, unless it is a person, who is then an "evaluee" (Scriven, 1981). Moreover, the same terms are often used by different writers to refer to very different concepts or activities; even the term *evaluation* has been used to refer to so many disparate phenomena that the result is a confusing tangle of semantic underbrush through which the student of evaluation is forced to struggle.

The purpose of this chapter is to define evaluation more precisely, differentiate it from other related but different activities, and examine two basic distinctions important to educational evaluation. The remainder of this chapter is divided into five major sections: (1) definition of evaluation and several other related activities; (2) a discussion of evaluation as a form of disciplined inquiry; (3) a discussion of similarities in and differences between educational research and evaluation; (4) an effort to expand the definition of evaluation; and (5) an examination of two basic distinctions in evaluation.

DEFINITION OF EVALUATION AND RELATED ACTIVITIES

There is no widely agreed-upon definition of educational evaluation. Some educators equate evaluation with measurement. Others define evaluation as the assessment of the extent to which specific objectives have been attained. For some, evaluation is synonymous with and encompasses nothing more than professional judgment. Some view evaluation as primarily scientific inquiry, whereas others argue that it is essentially a political activity. There are those who define evaluation as the act of collecting and providing information to enable decision-makers to function more intelligently. And so on.

In Chapter 4, we will discuss at greater length alternative views of evaluation and how these differing conceptions lead to widely varied types of evaluation studies. Our purpose here is only to sort out evaluation from among other educational activities and functions with which it often becomes confused.

Simple Verbal Definitions

Simple verbal definitions[8] of research, evaluation, and measurement are never fully satisfactory. Research, evaluation, and measurement are complicated endeavors; they are ultimately no more than hypothetical constructs that allow us to speak with consistency about certain approaches to the production of information or knowledge. The meaning of the words can be seen by examining the ways scholars use the terms *research, evaluation*, and *measurement* both in their writing and conversation.

This is not to argue that no attempt should be made to differentiate these activities on an abstract, verbal level. Indeed, confusion among the terms accounts for much wasted motion in educational scholarship and complicates the already difficult jobs of conducting evaluations or teaching others how to conduct evaluations.

Despite the shortcomings of simple verbal definitions, they can serve as a point of departure, providing necessary precursors for later discussions.

Evaluation is the determination of a thing's value.[9] In education, it is the formal determination of the quality, effectiveness, or value of a program, product, project, process, objective, or curriculum. Evaluation uses inquiry and judgment methods, including: (1) determining standards for judging quality and deciding whether those standards should be relative or absolute; (2) collecting relevant information; and (3) applying the standards to determine quality. Evaluation can apply to either current or proposed enterprises.

Research is systematic inquiry aimed at obtaining generalizable knowledge by testing claims about the relationships among variables, or by describing generalizable phenomena.[10] The resulting knowledge, which may generate theoretical models, functional relationships, or descriptions, may be obtained by empirical or other systematic methods and may or may not have immediate application.

Measurement (which is usually conceived of more broadly than mere testing) is the quantitative description of behavior, things, or events (mainly how much of a quality, or characteristic, an individual thing or event possesses). Measurement is simply a process for collecting the data on which research generalizations or evaluative judgments will be made. It is a key tool in evaluation and research; engaging in measurement is not, in and of itself, either research or evaluation.

Research is clearly an enormously complex undertaking that goes far beyond simple evaluative findings (for example, Program A is better than Program B on a particular criterion) by trying to ascertain the causes for those findings. The complexity of unraveling causes makes research a luxury few school districts can afford. Research has many of the trappings of evaluation and shares with it many common activities, but it lacks evaluation's explicit judgments of quality.

Evaluation research, a term much used in the social sciences and sometimes in education as well, is, in our opinion, something of a misnomer, and its use seems to obscure more than clarify. Rather than try to define it here, we shall explain in a subsequent section why we avoid using this term in our treatment of educational evaluation.

Why Definition Is Important

Some readers may think that entirely too much fuss is being made over defining "evaluation." Meanings of words are critical, however, because words influence action.

Evaluation is complex. It is not a simple matter of stating behavioral objectives, building a test, or analyzing data, though it may include these activities. A thorough evaluation contains elements of a dozen or more distinct activities, the precise combination influenced by time, money, expertise, the good will of school practitioners, and many other factors. But equally important (and more readily influenced) is the image the evaluator holds of evaluation work: its responsibilities, duties, uniqueness, and similarities to related endeavors.

We frequently meet persons responsible for evaluation whose sincere efforts are negated by the particular semantic problem addressed in this chapter. By happenstance, habit, or methodological bias, they may label the trial and investigation of a new curriculum "research" or "experiment" instead of "evaluation." The inquiry they conduct will be different because they have chosen to call it a "research project" or an "experiment" rather than an "evaluation." Their choice influences the literature they read (it will deal with research or experimental design), the consultants they call in (only acknowledged experts in designing and analyzing experiments), the way they report the results (always in the best tradition of the *American Educational Research Journal* or the *Journal of Experimental Psychology*), and the criteria used to judge how well the study was done (emphasizing objectivity, internal and external validity, and other standards used to judge research practices). These are not necessarily the paths to relevant data gathering or rational decision making about curricula. By way of analogy, established canons of practice exist that underlie sound medical research procedures, but those are not the most relevant procedures that the surgeon must employ when performing a tonsillectomy.

Important as it is to define evaluation, therefore, a final, authoritative definition is illusive, if not impossible, because of the lack of consensus about this phenomenon and just what it comprises. Talmage (1982) has made this point well, noting that, "Three purposes appear most frequently in definitions of evaluation: (1) to render judgments on the worth of a program; (2) to assist decision-makers responsible for deciding policy; and (3) to serve a political function" (Talmage, 1982, p. 594). Talmage also notes that, while these purposes are not mutually exclusive, they receive different emphases in different evaluation studies, thus negating the possibility of any single, correct definition of evaluation.

In general, we have no quarrel with Talmage's analysis, but we would note one point of departure. For us, the first purpose she lists for evaluation—to render judgments of the value of a program—is not just a purpose for evaluation but *is* evaluation. Conversely, the other purposes do not describe what evaluation is but rather what it is *used for*. We choose, therefore, to define evaluation as the act of rendering judgments to determine value—worth and merit—without questioning or diminishing the important roles evaluation plays in decision-making and political activities. We agree with those who note that the important issues in education usually focus on decisions to be made, not judging value for the sake of judging value. But while this ties our definition of evaluation closely to the decision-making context in which evaluation is typically used, it does not narrow the definition of evaluation to serve only decision making.

To understand our view of evaluation better, it is necessary to consider a broader issue, namely, the role of disciplined inquiry in reshaping and revitalizing educational programs and practices.

EVALUATION AS DISCIPLINED INQUIRY

Both educational leaders and the public rightly expect the scientific method to play an important role in educational improvement. Cronbach and Suppes phrased this expectation well in their discussion of disciplined inquiry for education:

> There has been agreement, both within and without the ranks of educators, that systematic investigation has much to offer. Indeed, there is agreement that *massive, lasting changes in education cannot safely be made except on the basis of deep objective inquiry.* (Cronbach & Suppes, 1969, p. 12)

Such systematic investigation, termed by Cronbach and Suppes as "disciplined inquiry," can take many forms (for example, a laboratory experiment or a mail survey); however, there is a quality that is common to each. As Cronbach and Suppes put it,

> Disciplined inquiry has a quality that distinguishes it from other sources of opinion and belief. The disciplined inquiry is conducted and reported in such a way that the argument can be painstakingly examined. The report does not depend for its appeal on the eloquence of the writer or on any surface plausibility. The argument is not justified by anecdotes or casually assembled fragments of evidence. Scholars in each field have developed traditional questions that serve as touchstones to separate sound argument from incomplete or questionable argument. Among other things, the mathematician asks about axioms, the historian about the authenticity of documents, the experimental scientist about verifiability of observations. Whatever the character of a study, if it is disciplined the investigator has anticipated the traditional questions that are pertinent. He institutes controls at each step of information collection and reasoning to avoid the sources of error to which these questions refer. If the errors cannot be eliminated, he takes them into account by discussing the margin for error in his conclusions. Thus the report of a disciplined inquiry has a texture that displays the raw materials entering the argument and the logical processes by which they were compressed and rearranged to make the conclusion credible. . . .
>
> Disciplined inquiry does not necessarily follow well-established, formal procedures. Some of the most excellent inquiry is free-ranging and speculative in its initial stages, trying what might seem to be bizarre combinations of ideas and procedures, or restlessly casting about for ideas. . . . But. . . fundamental to disciplined inquiry is its central attitude, which places a premium on objectivity and evidential test. (Cronbach & Suppes, 1969, pp. 15–16, 18)

Inquiry, thus defined, encompasses several common activities in education, among them educational evaluation. Of course, systematic inquiry is not the only hallmark of evaluation. As Cronbach has also noted, evaluation is both a political and scientific activity:

> Evaluation does, of course, draw on scientific tradition. It has to be judged in part by scientific ideals, and it surely should use all the techniques and principles from relevant science that it can. But science is only part of the story, and, I would say, a subordinate part. If evaluation is not primarily a scientific activity, what is it? It is first and foremost a political activity, a function performed within a social system. (Cronbach, 1977, p. 1)

Although, as noted earlier, one might better view political activity as a major *use* of evaluation, rather than a description of what evaluation is, Cronbach's point should not be lost. Evaluation is not only a scientific activity, as we shall discuss in some detail later in this text. Yet, evaluation *is* based on certain ideals and knowledge, and it differs from many forms of social or educational service in its insistence upon systematic, disciplined inquiry in the broad sense in which this concept was originally defined by Cronbach and Suppes.

Research is obviously an additional example of disciplined inquiry. As noted earlier, both educational research and evaluation have a great deal in common; both depend very heavily on empirical inquiry methods and techniques. If one were to watch tests being administered to students, or observe recording time-on-task data in classrooms, it would often be difficult to know whether the ongoing activity was research or evaluation. When one considers the purpose for which the activity is conducted, research and evaluation have less in common, because the objective of the inquiry is quite different for these activities (as will be shown later in this chapter).

Despite differences in purpose, educational evaluation and research are frequently mistaken for one another. This may not seem particularly serious to the casual observer, but such confusion can have serious consequences indeed for the *researcher* or *evaluator*. The best efforts of an investigator whose responsibility is evaluation but whose conceptual perspective is research usually prove inadequate as either research or evaluation. Because it is especially crucial for the evaluator to distinguish research from evaluation, we will attempt to sharpen the distinction in the next chapter.

SIMILARITIES AND DIFFERENCES IN EDUCATIONAL EVALUATION AND RESEARCH

Thus far we have only attempted to differentiate between broad conceptions of research and evaluation. Distinguishing between such activities is at best extremely difficult and is made more so by the fact that each can be subdivided into several distinct activities. Many researchers have proposed their favored schemes for classifying research (Borg & Gall, 1983; Kerlinger, 1975). Similarly, several evaluators have attempted to classify varying types of evaluation (Worthen & Sanders, 1973; Stufflebeam & Webster, 1980; Brinkerhoff, Brethower, Hluchyj, & Nowakowski, 1983; Worthen, 1984). Although important differences exist among these various types of research and evaluation, there is an ingredient common to all: production of knowledge, however general or specific, not previously available. With this commonality in mind, we will now turn our attention to the more important differences among various types of research.

The distinction between basic and applied research seems well entrenched in educational parlance. Although these constructs might more properly be thought of as the ends of a continuum rather than as a dichotomy, they are useful for differentiating between broad classes of activities.[11] The distinction between the two also helps in subsequent consideration of how research relates to evaluation. Definitions of basic and applied research provided nearly three decades ago by the National Science Foundation still serve to make the distinction:

> *Basic research* is directed toward increase of knowledge; it is research where the primary aim of the investigator is a fuller understanding of the subject under study rather than a practical application thereof. *Applied research* is directed toward practical applications of knowledge. (National Science Foundation, 1960, p. 5)

When successful, applied research results in plans or directives for development; basic research does not. In applied research, the knowledge produced must have almost immediate utility, whereas no such constraint is imposed on basic research. Basic research is intended to enhance understanding, and practical utility of the knowledge is not an issue.

Two variants of applied research are "institutional research" and "operations research," activities aimed at supplying institutions or social systems with relevant data. To the extent that the conclusions resulting from inquiries of this type are generalizable, at least across time, these activities may appropriately be labeled *research*. However, where the object is nongeneralizable information on performance of a program or process, the label *evaluation* might be more appropriate.

Action research, a concept that became popular and then all but disappeared during the 1950s, was also seen as a type of applied research. Proposed as a way to integrate studies into practical educational settings, the idea of action research was that researchable problems or issues are best identified in the classroom or school—where the action is. Immediate research work could be used to generate empirically supported answers that would then be applied. Although the concept of action research had much appeal, it proved to be unworkable for several reasons: Educators could not be released for enough time to carry out needed research, insufficient numbers of educators were trained in research methods, the cost of doing the research did not justify the benefits that were derived, and the problems that were able to be studied in a short period of time were trivial. The important problems required time, personnel, and funds that were unavailable to educational agencies (Hodgkinson, 1957; Clifford, 1973).

Evaluation has sometimes been considered a form of applied research that focuses only on one social program, one curriculum, or one classroom lesson. This view ignores an obvious difference between the two: the level of generality in the knowledge produced. Applied research (as opposed to basic research) is aimed at producing generalizable knowledge relevant to providing a solution to a *general* problem. Evaluation focuses on collecting *specific* information relevant to a particular problem, program, or product.

This brings us again to the term *evaluation research*.

Evaluation Research Defined and Discarded

The term *evaluation research* was popularized in the early 1970s, beginning with Caro's 1971 book, *Readings in Evaluation Research*. Used chiefly among social scientists, the term was adopted by the Evaluation Research Society and has become the model terminology used to describe evaluation in that association and in many evaluation publications by social scientists.

Those who find meaning in the terms *evaluation research* or *evaluative research* (which we shall hereafter treat as synonymous) are quick to separate evaluation research from evaluation. For example, Rossi states that

> evaluation research is not equivalent to evaluation. To the extent that an evaluation is based on empirical evidence collected in ways that are susceptible to replication and treated with due regard to issues of internal, external, and construct validity, then the evaluation in question is evaluation research. The disciplines that have concerned themselves with the methodological problems of empirical research on social systems have been the social sciences (from which I would not exclude parts of education). Whether or not a given individual or organization engaging in evaluation research regards her/himself or itself as doing social science, he/she/it is nevertheless doing so. The

evaluation research in question may be conducted very well or very poorly, but it is social science research.

  This is not to deny the possible validity of a connoisseurial approach to evaluation, in which expert judgments based on eccentric (but insightful) observations play major roles. Indeed, such evaluations may be worth more per resources expended. But they are not social science nor are they evaluation research. (Rossi, 1982a, p. 61)

Rossi views evaluation research, therefore, as the application of social science research methods to evaluation issues. Talmage seems both to support and broaden this perspective when, in attempting to differentiate *evaluation research* from *research* and *experimental research*, she says:

  Evaluation research studies usually lack replicability because the system, program, or phenomenon being studied is dynamic; that is, it is in operation, changeable, and taking place in a naturalistic or field setting. Whereas the canons of scientific rigor are applied to evaluation research as far as possible, it is necessary to augment the study with descriptions of contextual variables, and to utilize the methodologies and perspectives of various disciplines in order best to understand the processes and functioning of the system, program, or phenomenon under study.

  Evaluation of educational programs is one area of evaluation under the rubric of evaluation research; it . . . applies the full range of evaluation research activities from initial design and planning through program implementation and institutionalization. (Talmage, 1982, pp. 594–595)

We have no particular argument with Rossi or Talmage on matters of substance, but we do disagree on interpretation. We agree that research is not equivalent to evaluation, regardless of its modifying adjectives, for, as argued earlier, research and evaluation differ in purpose even when they use the same methods and techniques. But we disagree that an activity should be termed evaluation *research* simply because it uses the experimental paradigm so favored among those social scientists who have shaped the form and direction of most social programs. Experimental research methods or a connoisseurial approach can both be used to evaluate—in other words, judge the worth or merit of—a social or educational program. It is not the tool that determines whether an activity is research or evaluation, but the purpose for which it is employed. It is not the use of social science methods that determines whether evaluation or research is being done, but the purpose for which the activity is being conducted. The neurosurgeon and the pathologist both use a scalpel, but to very different ends. Research and evaluation are no more synonymous, just because they may employ common approaches, tools, and techniques, than performing surgery is synonymous with doing an autopsy. Similarly, the form of inquiry we term *evaluation* may use research methodology (social science or otherwise) without being considered *research*, just as it may rely on cross-examination of expert witnesses to obtain data without being viewed as the practice of law.

  Put simply, we see little to be gained by use of the term *evaluation research*. And much clarity may be lost. To set what we hope will be a trend, there will be no further discussion or use of "evaluation research" in this book.

Characteristics of Inquiry that Distinguish Evaluation from Research

It should be apparent from our previous discussion that some types of evaluation and research[12] resemble one another in certain ways. However, common characteristics shared by research and evaluation should not be allowed to obscure their fundamental differences. Contrasting the "purest" and most distinct forms of each activity admittedly results in oversimplifications, but should clarify some major points that may have been obscured in the previous discussion.[13]

Before focusing on key differences between research and evaluation, we should reiterate an earlier caution from Stake and Denny (1969), which is still timely:

> The distinction between research and evaluation can be overstated as well as understated. The principal difference is the degree to which the findings are generalizable beyond their application to a given product, program, or locale. Almost always the steps taken by the researcher to attain generalizability tend to make his inquiries artificial or irrelevant in the eyes of the practitioner. The evaluator sacrifices the opportunity to manipulate and control but gains relevance to the immediate situation. Researcher and evaluator work within the same inquiry paradigm but play different management roles and appeal to different audiences (Stake & Denny, 1969, p. 374)

It is not our intent to overstate the distinction between research and evaluation. Yet, at a time when each is frequently mistaken for the other, to the detriment of both, we see a need for emphasizing differences more than similarities. What follows are 12 characteristics of inquiry that distinguish between "pure" forms of research and evaluation.

Motivation of the Inquirer. Research and evaluation are generally undertaken for different reasons. Research satisfies curiosity by advancing knowledge; evaluation contributes to the solution of practical problems through judging the value of whatever is evaluated. The researcher is intrigued; the evaluator (or, at least, her client) is concerned.

The researcher may believe that her work has great long-range implications for problem solving, but that is not her primary motivation. If she is very nimble, she won't get bogged down in the seeming paradox that *policy* decisions supporting basic inquiry for its practical payoffs do *not* imply that researchers should focus on practical solutions.

Objective of the Inquiry. Research seeks *conclusions*; evaluation leads to *decisions*. Cronbach and Suppes (1969) distinguished between *decision-oriented* and *conclusion-oriented inquiry* this way:

> In a decision-oriented study the investigator is asked to provide information wanted by a decision-maker: a school administrator, a government policymaker, the manager of a project to develop a new biology textbook, or the like. The decision-oriented study is a commissioned study. The decision-maker believes that he needs information to guide his actions and he poses the question to the investigator. The conclusion-oriented study, on the other hand, takes its direction from the investigator's commitments and hunches. The educational decision-maker can, at most, arouse the investigator's interest in a problem. The latter formulates his own question, usually a general one rather than a question

about a particular institution. The aim is to conceptualize and understand the chosen
phenomenon; a particular finding is only a means to that end. Therefore, he concentrates
on persons and settings that he expects to be enlightening. (Cronbach & Suppes, 1969,
pp. 20–21)

Conclusion-oriented inquiry is here referred to as research; decision-oriented
inquiry typifies evaluation as well as any three words can.

Laws vs. Descriptions.   Briefly stated, research involves *nomothetic* (law-
giving) activities, and evaluation involves *idiographic* (descriptive of the particular)
activities. Research is the quest for laws—that is, statements of relationships
among two or more variables. Evaluation seeks to describe a particular thing and
its unique context with respect to one or more scales of value.

Role of Explanation.   Considerable confusion exists about the extent to
which evaluators should explain ("understand") the phenomena they evaluate. We
do not view explanations as the primary purpose of evaluation. A fully proper and
useful evaluation can be conducted without explaining *what caused* the product or
program being evaluated to be good or bad or *how* it produces its effects. It is
fortunate that this is so, for educational evaluation is so needed and credible
explanations of educational phenomena are so rare. Of course, it would be
wonderful if an evaluation of an outstanding training program managed also to
explain what it was that made the program work so well, just so that good fortune
did not lead to similar expectations for all educational evaluations.

Autonomy of the Inquiry.   Science is an independent and autonomous enterprise. At the beginning of his classic, *The Conduct of Inquiry*, Kaplan (1964) wrote:

> It is one of the themes of this book that the various sciences, taken together, are not
> colonies subject to the governance of logic, methodology, philosophy of science, or any
> other discipline whatever, but are, and of right ought to be, free and independent.
> Following John Dewey, I shall refer to this declaration of scientific independence as the
> principle of *autonomy of inquiry*. It is the principle that the pursuit of truth is accountable
> to nothing and to no one not a part of that pursuit itself. (Kaplan, 1964, p. 3)

Not surprisingly, autonomy of inquiry proves an important characteristic for
typifying research and evaluation. As was seen incidentally in the quote from
Cronbach and Suppes, evaluation is undertaken at the behest of a client, but the
researcher sets her own task. As will be seen later, the autonomy that the
researcher and the evaluator enjoy to differing degrees has implications for how
they should be trained and how their respective inquiries are pursued.

Properties of the Phenomena Assessed.   Educational evaluation attempts to
assess the *value* of a thing, whereas educational research attempts to generate
scientific *knowledge*. Except that knowledge is highly valued and thus worthwhile,
this distinction serves fairly well to discriminate research and evaluation. The
distinction can be given added meaning if *value* is taken as synonymous with *social
utility* (which is presumed to increase with improved health, happiness, and life
expectancy,[14] and if *scientific knowledge* is identified with two of its properties: (1)
empirical verifiability, and (2) logical consistency.

Evaluation seeks to assess social utility directly. Research may yield indirect evidence of social utility, insofar as empirical verifiability of general phenomena and logical consistency may eventually be socially useful. Valuing is the *sine qua non* of evaluation. A touchstone for discriminating between an evaluator and a researcher is to ask whether the inquiry she is conducting would be regarded as a failure if it produced no data on the usefulness of the thing being studied. A researcher answering strictly as a researcher will probably say no.

Generalizability of the Phenomena Studied. Perhaps the highest correlate of the research-evaluation distinction is the generalizability of the phenomena being studied. Three aspects of generalizability can be identified: (1) generalizability across time (Will the phenomenon—perhaps a textbook or a self-concept—be of interest 50 years hence?); (2) generalizability across geography (Is the phenomenon of any interest to people in the next town, the next province, across the ocean?); and (3) applicability to a number of specific instances (Are there many specific examples of the phenomenon being studied or is this the only one?). These three qualities of the object of an educational inquiry can be used to classify different inquiry types, as in Figure 3.1.

Three types of inquiry are represented in Figure 3.1: (1) program evaluation—the evaluation of a complex of people, materials, and organization which make up a particular educational program; (2) product evaluation—the evaluation of a medium of schooling such as a book, a film, or a recorded tape; and (3) educational research.

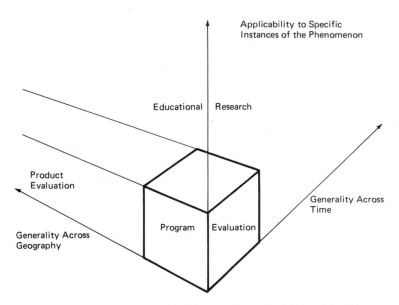

FIGURE 3.1 Three Inquiry Types Classified by the Generalizability of the Phenomenon Investigated*

*The property represented by each axis is absent where the three axes meet and increase as one moves out along each axis.

Program evaluation is depicted in Figure 3.1 as concerned with a phenomenon (an educational program) that has limited generalizability across time and geography. For example, the innovative "ecology curriculum" (including instructional materials, staff, students, and other courses in the school) in the Middletown Public Schools will probably not survive the decade, is of little interest to the schools in Norfolk that have a different set of environmental problems and instructional resources, and has little relationship to other curricula with other objectives. Product evaluation is concerned with assessing the worth of something like a new ecology textbook or an overhead projector that can be widely disseminated geographically, but that similarly may not be of interest 10 years hence, and that produces little or no reliable knowledge about education in general. Educational research focuses on concepts supposed to be relatively permanent, applicable to schooling nearly everywhere, and relevant to numerous teaching and learning contexts.

Criteria for Judging the Activity. Two important criteria for judging the adequacy of research are internal validity (To what extent are the results of the study unequivocal and not confounded with extraneous or systematic error variance?) and external validity (To what extent can the results be generalized to other units—for example, subjects or classrooms—with characteristics similar to those used in the study?).

If one were forced to choose the most important criteria from among the several criteria that might be used for judging the adequacy of evaluation, the five most vital would probably be *accuracy* (the extent to which the information obtained is an accurate reflection—a one-to-one correspondence—with reality), *credibility* (the extent to which the information is believable to clients who need it), *utility* (the extent to which the results are actually used), *feasibility* (the extent to which the evaluation is realistic, prudent, diplomatic, and frugal), and *propriety* (the extent to which the evaluation is done legally and ethically, protecting the rights of those involved.

Identifiable Clients. Research is often conducted with only the most nebulous idea of who may use the results. Conversely, evaluation is generally conducted for a well-defined audience or client group. Evaluators can identify such clients as policymakers, program managers, or concerned publics. Research results, on the other hand, are laid out for general perusal by anyone who finds them interesting or useful.

Relevance of Time. Research sets its own time schedule—barring economic constraints. Evaluation, by contrast, is time-bound; both start-up and duration must adhere to strict schedules if the results are to be useful.

Disciplinary Base. Making educational research multidisciplinary may be a good suggestion for the research community as a whole, but it is doubtful that the individual researcher is well advised to attack her particular area of interest simultaneously from several different disciplinary perspectives. Few persons can fruitfully work in the cracks between disciplines; most will find it challenge enough to deal with the problems of one discipline at a time.

That the educational researcher can afford to pursue inquiry within one paradigm and the evaluator cannot is one of many consequences of the autonomy of inquiry. When one is free to define her own problems for solution (as the researcher is), she seldom asks a question that takes her outside of the discipline in which she was educated. Psychologists pose questions that can be solved by the methods of their own disciplines, as do sociologists, economists, and other scientists. The seeds of the answer to a research question are planted along with the question. The curriculum evaluator enjoys less freedom in defining the questions she must answer. Hence, she may find it necessary to employ a wider range of inquiry perspectives and techniques in order to find her answers.[15]

Preparation. The distinction just discussed, relating to disciplinary bases, has different implications for the education of researchers than for the education of evaluators. Research aimed at producing understanding of such phenomena as school learning, the social organization of schools, and human growth and development can best be accomplished from the perspectives afforded by the relevant social sciences. Consequently, the best preparation for many educational researchers is likely to be a thorough mastery of a relatively traditional social science discipline, coupled with application of the tools of that discipline to educational problems. Given the ambitiousness of preparing a researcher thoroughly in the methods and techniques of her chosen discipline, there is little point in arguing that any one researcher should receive training in more than one discipline. A graduate program that attempts to indoctrinate the same student in social psychology, physiological psychology, and microeconomic theory is likely to produce a researcher so superficially prepared in several areas that she can contribute in none.

By contrast, to the extent that the preparation of evaluators touches on the traditional disciplines at all, it is best that several disciplines be sampled. Only through an interdisciplinary education can the evaluator become sensitive to the wide range of phenomena to which she must attend if she is to properly assess the worth of an educational program. That superficial exposure does not qualify her to conduct in-depth research is simply irrelevant.

The preparation of educational researchers need not be as broad in techniques of inquiry as that for evaluators. Most sociologists' work is none the worse for their ignorance of confounding relations in fractional factorial designs, and who would argue that an experimental psychologist suffers from ignorance of scalogram analysis? The education of researchers must be more concerned with substantive matters (such as Keynesian economics, Skinnerian operant conditioning, or the cognitive dissonance theory) than with methods and techniques. The evaluator, conversely, must be broadly familiar with a wide variety of methods and techniques because one evaluation might require her to use psychometrics, another sociometrics, a third econometrics, and so on.

In preparing both researchers and evaluators, some provisions must be made for the acquisition of practical experience. Doubtless there is no better practical experience for the research trainee than apprenticeship to a competent, practicing researcher. Worthen and Roaden (1975) found that apprenticeship to one researcher over an extended period of time was positively correlated with subsequent research productivity. A protracted apprenticeship to a single evaluator would be inappro-priate, however, because breadth of experience in a variety of settings is essential. Evaluation is unashamedly practical. Whereas the researcher can afford to ignore—indeed, *must* ignore—the countless practical constraints of contemporary schools in constructing her elegant idealizations, evaluation that ignores practicalities is just bad evaluation.

TWO BASIC DISTINCTIONS IN EVALUATION

Prominent evaluation theorists differ widely in their views of what evaluation is and how it should be carried out. We will discuss these differences in some detail in Part Two. Despite these varying perspectives, however, some common concepts and distinctions exist about which there seems to be relatively little debate.[16] These notions, though elemental, have proven powerful in shaping people's thinking about evaluation. In this section, we will discuss two basic distinctions in evaluation and how they apply to educational evaluation studies.

Formative and Summative Evaluation

Scriven (1967) first distinguished between the *formative* and *summative* roles of evaluation. Since then, the terms have become almost universally accepted in the field. Although in practice distinctions between these two types of evaluation may blur somewhat, it seems useful to summarize the major differences noted by Scriven, even at the risk of some oversimplification.

Formative evaluation is conducted during the operation of a program to provide program directors evaluative information useful in improving the program.[17] For example, during the development of a curriculum package, formative evaluation would involve content inspection by experts, pilot tests with small numbers of children, field tests with larger numbers of children and teachers in several schools, and so forth. Each step would result in immediate feedback to the developers, who would then use the information to make necessary revisions.

Summative evaluation is conducted at the end of a program to provide potential consumers with judgments about that program's worth or merit. For example, after the curriculum package is completely developed, a summative evaluation might be conducted to determine how effective the package is with a national sample of typical schools, teachers, and students at the level for which it was developed. The findings of the summative evaluation would then be made avail-able to consumers.

Note that the audiences and uses for these two evaluation roles are very dif-ferent. In formative evaluation, the audience is program personnel—in our example, those responsible for developing the curriculum. Summative evaluation audiences include potential consumers (students, teachers, and other professionals), funding sources (taxpayers or funding agency), and supervisors and other officials, as well as program personnel. Formative evaluation leads to (or should lead to) decisions about program development (including modification, revision, and the like). Summative evaluation leads to decisions concerning program continuation, termination, expansion, adoption, and so on.

It should be apparent that both formative and summative evaluation are essential because decisions are needed during the developmental stages of a program to improve and strengthen it, and again, when it has stabilized, to judge its final worth or determine its future. Unfortunately, far too many educators conduct only summative evaluation. This is unfortunate because the development process, without formative evaluation, is incomplete and inefficient. Consider the foolishness of developing a new aircraft design and submitting it to a "summative" test flight without first testing it in the "formative" wind tunnel. Educational test flights can be expensive too, especially when we haven't a clue about the probability of success.

Failure to use formative evaluation is myopic, for formative data collected early can help rechannel time, money, and all types of human and material resources into more productive directions. Evaluation conducted only when a project nears completion may simply come too late to be of much help.

Of course, the relative emphasis on formative and summative evaluation changes throughout the life of an educational program, as suggested in Figure 3.2, although this generalized concept obviously may not precisely fit any particular curriculum innovation.

Baker (1978) noted that two important factors which influence the usefulness of formative evaluation are *control* and *timing*. If suggestions for improvement are to be implemented, then it is important that the formative study collect data on variables over which program administrators have some control. Also, information that reaches administrators too late for use in improving the program is patently useless.

As will be noted later, many of the evaluation techniques and approaches described later in this book can be used as readily for formative as summative evaluation; the timing of their use and the purpose for which they are employed determines whether they play a summative or formative role.[18]

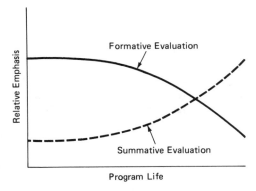

FIGURE 3.2 Relationship Between Formative and Summative Evaluation Across Life of a Curriculum Innovation

An effort to distinguish between formative and summative evaluation on several dimensions appears in Figure 3.3.[19]

Distinguishing Formative and Summative Evaluation in Practice. As with most conceptual distinctions, formative and summative evaluation are often not as easy to distinguish in practice as they seem in these pages. For example, if a program continues beyond a summative evaluation study, the results of that study may be used for both summative and, later, formative evaluation purposes. This may be one factor that led Stake (1969b) to suggest that formative and summative evaluation may be less distinguished by when they are conducted than by what "insiders" and "outsiders" want to know about educational programs.

> In evaluation circles, the terms *formative* and *summative* are heard more and more frequently. These terms have a dramatic effect, distinguishing between what is done *during development* and what is done *when development is finished*. For the purpose of choosing an evaluation strategy, I find this a trivial distinction. For most educational programs—correspondence courses or Montessori programs—development never ends. For a learner, there is a beginning and an end, but for the teacher, the programs are ongoing, ever evolving. What is important is that there are differences between what the "program people" want to know about their program and what "outsiders" want to know. We can make a non-trivial distinction between formative evaluation for the program developer who is planning ahead and trying to choose the best ingredients, and summative evaluation for anyone who is looking at the program, past or present, and who is trying to find out what it is and what it does. (Stake, 1969b, p. 40)

We accept the general wisdom of this caution and admit that sorting ongoing evaluations into formative and summative categories, as such, is unproductive. We

	Formative Evaluation	Summative Evaluation
Purpose	To improve program	To certify program utility
Audience	Program administrators and staff	Potential consumer or funding agency
Who Should Do It	Internal evaluator	External evaluator
Major Characteristic	Timely	Convincing
Measures	Often informal	Valid/reliable
Frequency of Data Collection	Frequent	Limited
Sample Size	Often small	Usually large
Questions Asked	What is working? What needs to be improved? How can it be improved?	What results occur? With whom? Under what condition? With what training? At what cost?
Design Constraints	What information is needed? When?	What claims do you wish to make?

FIGURE 3.3   Differences Between Formative and Summative Evaluation

maintain, however, that the distinction between formative and summative evaluation is relevant to a more important distinction between the purposes and audiences for these two evaluation roles.

Internal and External Evaluation

The adjectives *internal* and *external* distinguish between evaluations conducted by program employees and those conducted by outsiders. An experimental year-round education program in the San Francisco public schools might be evaluated by a member of the school district staff (internal) or by a site-visit team appointed by the California State Board of Education (external). There are obvious advantages and disadvantages connected with both of these roles.

The internal evaluator is almost certain to know more about the program than any outsider, but she may also be so close to the program that she is unable to be completely objective. Seldom is there as much reason to question the objectivity of the external evaluator (unless she is found to have a particular ax to grind) and this dispassionate perspective is perhaps her greatest asset. Conversely, it is difficult for an external evaluator to ever learn as much about the program as the insider knows. Note that when we say *as much*, we refer only to quantity, not quality. One often finds an internal evaluator who is full of unimportant details about the program but overlooks several critical variables. If these bits of key information are picked up by the external evaluator, as is sometimes the case, she may end up knowing much less *overall* about the project but knowing much more of importance. On the other hand, the internal evaluator is much more likely to be familiar with important contextual information (for example, the serious illness of the director's husband, which is adversely affecting the director's work) that would temper evaluation recommendations.

Anderson and Ball (1978) have noted that knowing who funds an evaluation and to whom the evaluator reports largely determines the evaluator's financial and administrative dependence. They argue that independent relationships (that is, external evaluation) generally enhance the credibility of the study, a point with which we agree.

Others, however, question whether external evaluation really results in more credible evaluations. Cronbach and his colleagues (1980) are frankly unsympathetic to the view that the quality of evaluation is enhanced through the use of external reviewers. They take the position that credibility of evaluation studies lies in profession-wide arrangements that ensure the evaluator's freedom to be honest, not in the inherent objectivity of external review. And Campbell (1984) lists insistence on external evaluation as a major error that social science methodologists made in presenting their views of applied social science to government in the 1960s. He calls for cross-validation of studies akin to that conducted in the physical sciences as a better way to obtain objectivity than by depending on the "dogma" of external evaluation.

Evaluators who have survived years of service as "in-house" evaluators or evaluation contractors would likely find these views somewhat quaint and far removed from the political cauldrons in which they have seen (if not felt personally) employment locus and control of perquisites wreak havoc. Control of salary and perquisites can have a very real influence on objectivity and even truth, as Scriven (1976a) has noted in his examination of methods for bias control. Pronouncements to the contrary may have the ring of academic correctness but ignore the political practicalities. Similarly, these scholars' expressed lack of concern over evaluators who are too sympathetic to the program they are evaluating will be viewed as innocent by many veteran evaluators who have all too often seen colleagues' pro-program sympathies lead to unconscionable defenses of the status quo. The call for cross-validation of studies is compelling, using the referent of the physical sciences. But it loses its relevance and potency in the much less replicable realms of educational and social inquiry. It would be nice if educational evaluation studies could be cross-validated as readily as reading meters in the physical sciences. Alas, such is not the case. We continue to believe, despite the arguments of esteemed colleagues to the contrary, that the locus of the evaluator can have a profound effect on the results of an evaluation study. We will expand this point in the next section.

Possible Role Combinations

The dimensions of formative and summative evaluation can be combined with the dimensions of internal and external evaluation to form the two-by-two matrix shown in Figure 3.4.

The most common roles in evaluation might be indicated by cells 1 and 4 in the matrix. Formative evaluation is typically conducted by an internal evaluator, and there are clear merits in such an approach. Her knowledge of the program is of great value here, and possible lack of objectivity is not nearly the problem it would be in a summative evaluation. Summative evaluations are typically (and probably best) conducted by external evaluators. It is difficult, for example, to know how much credibility to accord a Ford Motor Company evaluation that concludes that a particular Ford automobile is far better than its competitors in the same price range. The credibility accorded to an internal summative evaluation (cell 3) of an educational program is likely to be no better. Summative evaluation is generally

	Internal	*External*
Formative	1 Internal Formative	2 External Formative
Summative	3 Internal Summative	4 External Summative

FIGURE 3.4   Combination of Evaluation Roles

best conducted by an external evaluator or agency. In some instances, however, there is simply no possibility of obtaining such external help because of financial constraints or absence of competent personnel willing to do the job. In these cases, the summative evaluation is weakened by the lack of outside perspective, but it might be possible to retain a semblance of objectivity and credibility by choosing the internal summative evaluator from among those who are some distance removed from the actual development of the program or product being evaluated.

The difficulty in conducting objective, credible, internal summative evaluations may be one reason for the report by Franks and Fortune (1984) that few local school districts in the United States are administering any type of summative evaluations to programs funded under Chapter 2 legislation. The view that relaxation of the federal evaluation mandate may be the real cause of this phenomenon is more cynical. Whatever the cause, it should be reiterated that both formative and summative studies of educational programs are needed for long-range improvement of our educational systems.

A very important role—that of the external formative evaluator shown in cell 2—is almost completely neglected in educational evaluations. As implied earlier, the internal evaluator may share many of the perspectives and blind spots of other program staff and, consequently, neglect to even entertain negative questions about the program. The external evaluator, who does not have lengthy familiarity with the program or its context, is much less likely to be influenced by *a priori* perceptions of its basic worth. This is not synonymous with saying that she is predisposed toward judging the program as ineffective. Her orientation should be neither positive nor negative. It should be neutral, uninfluenced by close associations with either the program or its competitors. In essence, the external formative evaluator introduces a cold, hard look of reality into the evaluation relatively early—in a sense, a preview of what a summative evaluator might say. This fresh outside perspective is important and can preclude the disaster that frequently occurs when program staff self-consciously select criteria and variables they believe will prove their program successful, only to have an outside agency (a school board or site-visit team) later recommend terminating the program because their summative evaluation—which focused on other variables or criteria—suggested the program was ineffective. Wisdom would dictate the use of an outside evaluator as part of every formative evaluation. Scriven (1972), although accepting the utility of internal formative evaluation, also argued for this view, saying "it now seems to me that a producer or staff evaluator who wants good *formative* evaluation has got to use some external evaluators to get it" (Scriven, 1972, p. 2).

APPLICATION EXERCISES

1. List the types of evaluation studies that have been conducted in an educational institution of your acquaintance, noting whether the evaluator was internal or external to that institution. Determine whether each study was formative or

summative and whether the study would have been strengthened by having it conducted by someone with the *opposite* (internal/external) relationship to the institution.

2. Select one evaluation study and one research study with which you are familiar. Analyze both to see if they differ on the 12 dimensions identified in this chapter as useful in distinguishing between research and evaluation activities.

SUGGESTED READINGS

CRONBACH, L. J., & SUPPES, P. (1969). *Research for tomorrow's schools: Disciplined inquiry for education.* New York: Macmillan.

SCRIVEN, M. (1973). The methodology of evaluation. In B. R. WORTHEN & J. R. SANDERS, *Educational evaluation: Theory and practice.* Belmont, CA: Wadsworth.

STUFFLEBEAM, D. L., & WEBSTER, W. J. (1980). An analysis of alternative approaches to evaluation. *Educational Evaluation and Policy Analysis, 2*(3), 5–19.

WORTHEN, B. R., & SANDERS, J. R. (1973). *Educational evaluation: Theory and practice.* Belmont, CA: Wadsworth.

Part Two

Alternative Approaches to Educational Evaluation

In Part One we referred to varying roles evaluation studies can play in education and related fields. Readers were introduced to some distinctions related to the concept of evaluation. We hinted at differences that exist among some major schools of evaluation thought. But we have not yet exposed the reader to the range and variety of alternative, often conflicting, conceptions of what evaluation is and how it should be carried out. Doing so is the purpose of this section.

In Part Two we introduce the reader to the wealth of thought and writing that has taken place in evaluation in recent years. In Chapter 4 we address the diversity of evaluation approaches proposed and examine the factors that have contributed to such differing views. Prior efforts to classify the many evaluation approaches into fewer categories are also discussed, along with presentation of the categories that we use throughout the remainder of this section.

In Chapters 5 through 10 we summarize six general approaches to evaluation, one per chapter. These general approaches include those we see as most prevalent in the literature and most popular in use. Within each chapter, we summarize previous thinking and writing pertaining to that approach, discuss how that approach has been used in education, and examine its strengths and weaknesses. Space does not permit exhaustive coverage of any particular evaluation model or conception; the chapters are necessarily too brief to provide the detail about any particular author's view of evaluation that would have been possible had we been willing to limit coverage to the thoughts of only a few evaluation theorists. We have preferred to cover a broader array of evaluation approaches at less depth, providing in each chapter references to which interested individuals may turn for a more in-depth discussion of any particular evaluation model.

We have attempted to include both the "old" and "new" approaches proposed for use in conducting educational evaluation studies. We will likely be criticized by some who do not find their preferred approach featured in our treatment of alternatives, and others may be distressed that we have included approaches they think we should have omitted. Some will accuse us of "traditionalism" because we have not dealt with several new variants that we consider esoteric (for example, poetry or watercolor painting as metaphors for evaluation). No one book can cover all that has been proposed as evaluation techniques or approaches, even if that were its entire content. Our intent has been to avoid bandwagon enthusiasm, however, and introduce approaches that have proven demonstrably useful in at least a few actual evaluation studies, not those that have been merely written about, however provocatively.

In Chapter 11 the characteristics and contributions of the six general alternative approaches we have described are compared, along with cautions concerning discipleship to any one approach and a plea for thoughtful, eclectic use of alternatives, especially where such an approach would strengthen evaluations more than would adherence to a single view.

Chapter 4
Alternative Views of Evaluation

Orienting Questions

1. Why are there so many different approaches to evaluation?
2. How would objectivists and subjectivists differ in their approach to evaluation?
3. Why is evaluation theory, as reflected in different approaches to evaluation, important to learn?
4. What are the different assumptions and arguments that have led some to champion quantitative evaluation methods and others to favor qualitative evaluation methods?
5. What practical issues contribute to the diversity of evaluation approaches?

Like many other young, emerging fields, evaluation is troubled by definitional and ideological disputes. Those who write about evaluation differ widely in their views of what evaluation is and how one should go about doing it. Those who conduct evaluation studies in education and related settings bring to the task diverse conceptions of how evaluations should be structured and carried out. The various prescriptions that have been given for evaluation models are implemented with varying degrees of fidelity, and some evaluations are designed without conscious reference to any existing conceptual framework, thereby resulting, if successful, in yet another evaluation approach. During the past two decades, over 50 different evaluation models have been developed and circulated. Scriven summarized the situation well in saying that

> The proliferation of evaluation models is a sign of the ferment of the field and the seriousness of the methodological problems which evaluation encounters. In this sense, it is a hopeful sign. But it makes a balanced overview very hard to achieve; one might as well try to describe the "typical animal" or the "ideal animal" in a zoo. (Scriven, 1984, p. 49)

Extending the animal metaphor in a somewhat different direction, trying to understand educational evaluation by reading the various commentaries and prescriptions of evaluation's theoreticians is rather like trying to learn what an elephant is like by piecing together reports of several blind people, each of whom happens to grasp a different portion of the elephant's anatomy. The evaluation literature is badly fragmented and is often aimed more at fellow evaluation theorists than at practitioners. Busy practitioners can hardly be faulted for not expending the time necessary to interpret and consolidate these disparate bits of knowledge.

We shall not solve the problem totally in this book. But this chapter and those that follow (Chapters 5 through 11) should clarify the varied alternatives useful in conducting evaluation. Perhaps by the end we will know enough about the elephant to recognize it when we see it.

DIVERSE CONCEPTIONS OF EDUCATIONAL EVALUATION

We have mentioned that at least three different views of educational evaluation have coexisted for the past 50 years. With the ascendency of the measurement movement, evaluation came to be defined as roughly synonymous with educational measurement. This orientation is evident today in the writing of such measurement specialists as Hopkins and Stanley (1981) and Sax (1980). Concurrently, formalization of school and university accreditation procedures led to the view that evaluation is synonymous with professional judgment. This view has persisted in many current evaluation practices where judgments are based on opinions of experts, whether or not the data and criteria used in reaching those judgments are clear. A third conception of evaluation emerged during Tyler's work on the Eight Year Study of the 1930s. In his work, evaluation came to be viewed as the process of comparing performance data with clearly specified objectives. This view is reflected in the next chapter.

Since 1965, new approaches have emerged as prominent methodologists and educationists turned their attention to evaluation methods. Many evaluation "models" emerged, ranging from comprehensive prescriptions to checklists of suggestions. In the absence of a good empirical base for determining the best way to evaluate educational programs, these models have greatly influenced present practices. Some authors opt for a systems approach, viewing evaluation as a process of identifying and collecting information to assist decision-makers. Others focus on the importance of naturalistic inquiry, or urge that value pluralism be recognized, accommodated, and preserved and that those individuals involved with the entity being evaluated play the prime role in determining what direction the evaluation study takes. Some writers propose that evaluations be structured in keeping with legal or forensic paradigms so that planned opposition—both pro and con—is built in. And this barely dents the list of current alternatives.

As Guba and Lincoln (1981) noted, the idea that evaluation should determine the worth of an educational program is one of the few things these diverse approaches have in common. Talmage (1982) concurs, stating that three purposes that appear most frequently in alternative evaluation proposals are "(1) to render judgment on the worth of a program; (2) to assist decision makers; and (3) to serve a political function" (Talmage, 1982, p. 594).

On the other hand, the differing concepts and emphases in these variant evaluation approaches greatly influence the practice of evaluation. As noted previously, "the various models are built on differing—often conflicting—conceptions and definitions of evaluation, with the result that practitioners are led in very different directions, depending upon which model they follow" (Worthen, 1972b, p. 3). Let us consider an example.

If one viewed evaluation as essentially synonymous with professional judgment, the worth of the curriculum would be assessed by experts (as judged by the evaluation client) observing the curriculum in action, examining the curriculum materials, or in some other way gleaning sufficient information to record their considered judgments.

If evaluation is equated with measurement, the curriculum might well be judged on the basis of students' scores on standardized tests.

If evaluation is viewed as a comparison between performance indicators and objectives, behaviorally stated objectives would be established for the curriculum, and relevant student behaviors would be measured against this yardstick, using either standardized or evaluator-constructed instruments. (Note that in this process there is no assessment of the worth of the objectives themselves.)

Using a decision-oriented approach, the evaluator, working closely with the decision-maker, would collect sufficient information about the relative advantages and disadvantages of each decision alternative to judge which was best. However, although the decision-maker would judge the worth of each alternative, evaluation per se would be a shared role.

If one accepted the authors' earlier definition of evaluation (see Chapter 3), the curriculum evaluator would first identify the curriculum goals and then, using input from appropriate reference groups, determine whether the goals were good for the students, parents, and community served. He would then collect evaluative information relevant to those goals as well as to identifiable side effects resulting from the curriculum. When the data were analyzed and interpreted, the evaluator would judge the worth of the curriculum and (usually) make a recommendation to the individual or group responsible for final decisions.

Obviously, the way in which one views evaluation has direct impact on the type of evaluation activities conducted.

ORIGINS OF ALTERNATIVE VIEWS OF EVALUATION

One might wonder why there are so many views of evaluation. But remember, there is no less disagreement about which learning theory is best, which research paradigm is preferable, or which school-management theory is most useful. It is no more reasonable to expect agreement on one approach to educational evaluation than it is to expect agreement on one way to teach or to run a school. Evaluation scholars come from varied backgrounds and have different world views of education and inquiry. As needs for rethinking evaluation have appeared, writers—academics, for the most part—have been amazingly productive and creative in proposing responses to those needs. Often several theorists have worked concurrently and independently to address similar needs but have approached them in very different ways. Thus, the emerging views of evaluation have been widely divergent, sometimes based on conflicting assumptions, and often focused on differing goals or purposes. Evaluation literature will undoubtedly continue to reflect new views as other theorists share their insights.

Before presenting alternative evaluation approaches, we need to consider briefly the factors that led to differing views, including evaluators' diverse philosophical ideologies, cognitive styles, methodological preferences, values, and practical perspectives.

PHILOSOPHICAL AND IDEOLOGICAL DIFFERENCES

There is no univocal philosophy of evaluation, any more than there is a single, universally accepted philosophy of science. And perhaps that lack has not hurt us too much, for, as House (1983b) has noted, we have been doing without one for a long time. The lack of a guiding philosophy has not preempted extensive discourse and debate concerning philosophical assumptions about epistemology and value. Indeed, different approaches to establishing truth or merit are largely responsible for the diversity of views about educational evaluation.

Objectivist and Subjectivist Epistemology

House (1980, 1983a, 1983b) has written extensively and thoughtfully about different philosophies of knowing or establishing truth (epistemology) and how they affect the approach to evaluation one would choose. He has grouped evaluation approaches into two categories: *objectivism* and *subjectivism*.

Objectivism requires that evaluation information be "scientifically objective": that is, that it use data collection and analysis techniques that yield results reproducible and verifiable by other reasonable and competent persons using the same techniques. In this sense, the evaluation procedures are "externalized," existing outside of the evaluator in clearly explicated form that is replicable by others and that will produce similar results from one evaluation to the next. Objectivism is derived largely from the social science tradition of empiricism.

Subjectivism bases its validity claims on "an appeal to experience rather than to scientific method. Knowledge is conceived as being largely tacit rather than explicit" (House, 1980, p. 252). The validity of a subjectivist evaluation depends on the relevance of the evaluator's background and qualifications and the keenness of his perceptions. In this sense, the evaluation procedures are "internalized," existing largely within the evaluator in ways that are not explicitly understood or reproducible by others.

Objectivism has held sway in the social sciences and in educational inquiry for decades. There are, however, many criticisms of objectivist epistemology, as there are of logical positivism in educational science. Campbell (1984) states that, "Twenty years ago logical positivism dominated the philosophy of science. . . . Today the tide has completely turned among the theorists of science in philosophy, sociology, and elsewhere. Logical positivism is almost universally rejected" (Campbell, 1984, p. 27). Scriven (1984) argues that any lingering positivist bias in evaluation should be eliminated. And Guba and Lincoln (1981) have challenged the "infallibility" of the hypothetico-deductive inquiry paradigm because of its limitations in dealing with complex, interactive phenomena in dynamic, septic educational settings. Although less sweeping and conclusive in his critique, House (1980) portrays objectivism as inattentive to its own credibility, presuming validity because of its methodology and, therefore, credible only to those who value such a methodology. He also notes that objectivism conceals hidden values and biases of which its adherents are unaware, because even the choice of data-collection techniques and instruments is not value-neutral, an assumption seemingly taken for granted by objectivist evaluators.

To counter the objectivist hold upon the methodologies of evaluation in education and related areas, criticisms of objectivism have been extreme. Yet subjectivism has been no less soundly criticized, especially by those who see its procedures as "unscientific" and, therefore, of dubious worth. Critics (for example, Boruch & Cordray, 1980) point out that subjectivist evaluation often leads to varying, sometimes contradictory, conclusions that defy reconciliation because that which led to the conclusions is largely obscured within the nonreplicable procedures of the evaluator. Similarly, as House puts it,

> Critics of the phenomenologist epistemology note that there is often confusion over whose common sense perceptions are to be taken as the basis for understanding. Furthermore, if one takes everyday understanding as the foundation of inquiry, does one not merely reconstruct whatever ideologies, biases, and false beliefs already exist? How can one distinguish causal determinants and regularities, the strength of the positivist epistemology, from perceived beliefs? How can one evaluate conflicting interpretations? Phenomenology provides no way of doing so. (House, 1980, p. 254)

And so the dialogue continues. The objectivists depend upon replicable facts as their touchstone of truth, whereas subjectivists depend upon accumulated experience as their way to understanding. Although both epistemologies carry within them "tests" that must be met if their application is to be viewed as trustworthy, they lead to very different evaluation designs and methods, giving rise to much of today's diversity in evaluation approaches.

Utilitarian Versus Intuitionist-Pluralist Evaluation

House (1976, 1983a) has also made a distinction closely related to that of objectivism and subjectivism, namely utilitarian versus intuitionist-pluralist evaluation. Although this is a distinction concerning principles for assigning values, not epistemology, utilitarian and intuitionist-pluralist evaluation approaches parallel the objectivist and subjectivist epistemologies outlined above.

Utilitarian Evaluation.   Utilitarian approaches determine value by assessing the *overall* impact of an educational program on those affected. These approaches have tended to follow objectivist epistemology. In his treatise on "justice in evaluation," House (1976) suggests that utilitarian evaluation accepts the value premise that the greatest good is that which will benefit the greatest number of individuals. Thus, "properly speaking, utilitarianism refers to the idea of maximizing happiness in society" (House, 1983a, p. 49). There is a single, explicitly defined ethical principle operative. As a result, the evaluator will focus on total group gains by using average test scores or some other common index of "good" to identify the "greatest good for the greatest number." The best educational programs are those that produce the greatest gains on the criterion or criteria selected to determine worth. Statewide assessment programs and large-scale comparative evaluations are utilitarian in nature. Most utilitarian-evaluation approaches lend themselves to use by governments or others who mandate and/or sponsor evaluation studies for which managers and public program administrators are the major audiences.

Intuitionist-Pluralist Evaluation.   At the opposite end of the continuum are intuitionist-pluralist approaches to evaluation, which are based on the idea that value depends upon the impact of the program on *each* individual. These approaches have tended to follow subjectivist epistemology. Here the value position is that the greatest good requires the attention to each individual's benefit. Thus,

> The ethical principles are not single in number nor explicitly defined as in utilitarian ethics. There are several principles derived from intuition and experience, but no set rules for weighting them. This captures another meaning of ethical subjectivism—that the ultimate criterion of what is good and right are individual feelings or apprehensions. (House, 1983a, p. 50)

This approach leads to a focus on the distribution of gains by individuals and subgroups (for example, ethnic groupings). There can be no common index of "good," but rather a plurality of criteria and judges, and the evaluator is no longer an impartial "averager" but a portrayer of different values and needs. Data may be test scores, but intuitionist-pluralist evaluators often prefer data from personal interviews and testimonials of program participants. Weighing and balancing the many judgments and criteria inherent in this approach is largely intuitive, and there are no algorithms to help reduce complex evaluative information to any unequivocal recommendation. The perceived merit or worth of an educational program depends largely on the values and perspectives of whoever is judging, and each individual or constituent group is a legitimate judge. "Likewise, the subjective utility of something is based on personal judgment and personal desires. Each person is the best judge of events for himself" (House, 1983a, p. 56). Within limits of feasibility, most intuitionist-pluralist evaluations try to involve as "judges" all individuals and groups who are affected by the program being evaluated, rather than leaving decisions and judgments to governmental sponsors and high-level administrators—as is typically the case with utilitarian evaluation.

The Impact of Philosophical Differences

Evaluators have tended to line up along the several continua described above, or worse, have become polarized in "either-or" dichotomies. Talmage sees this debate over epistemology as a major cause of rifts that permeate the field of evaluation. Speaking of such philosophical differences, Talmage said, "Program evaluation has been greatly affected by this schism: what is considered 'acceptable' evaluation research often depends upon the position taken regarding one or another of these continua" (Talmage, 1982, p. 596). Yet, although differences in philosophy have led to alternative views of evaluation, the philosophical differences are not incompatible. Multiple approaches to describing objects of study, drawn from both objectivist and subjectivist traditions, have been used in the same evaluations to achieve important goals (see, for example, Stake & Easely, 1978; Sanders & Sonnad, 1982).

In choosing a philosophical orientation, evaluators need to consider (1) the credibility of results reported to evaluation clients, (2) the need for exploration when studying unknown phenomena, (3) the importance of understanding or explaining findings, (4) the need to be sensitive to emerging or hidden issues during the evaluation, and, of course, (5) the importance of thoroughly addressing questions posed by the client (that is, meeting the client's expectations) when planning an evaluation. We recognize the right of any evaluator to subscribe totally to the assumptions and premises of one particular ideology. Yet few evaluators who succeed in a wide range of evaluation settings can afford to consider philosophical ideologies as "either-or" decisions. The purist view that looks noble in print yields to practical pressures demanding that the evaluator use appropriate methods based on an epistemology that is right *for that evaluation*, or even multiple methods based on alternative epistemologies within the same evaluation.[20] It is important to know, however, the assumptions and limitations of methods that are drawn from different world views about evaluation.

METHODOLOGICAL BACKGROUNDS AND PREFERENCES

Different philosophical assumptions about knowledge and value give rise naturally to different evaluation methods. Indeed, evaluation philosophy and methodology are so closely intertwined that we might well have discussed both together in the previous section. But we believe it useful to examine separately two methodological issues that have influenced greatly the conduct of evaluation studies: (1) quantitative versus qualitative inquiry, and (2) the difficulty encountered by evaluators in working across disciplinary and methodological boundaries.

Quantitative and Qualitative Evaluation

Much has been said in recent years about quantitative and qualitative evaluation, as evaluators have struggled to sort out the relative utility of these two distinct approaches. To understand this distinction more fully, we must refer to the history of its evolution. Because so many people serving in evaluation roles during the late 1950s and 1960s were educational and psychological researchers, it is not surprising that the experimental tradition quickly became the most generally accepted evaluation approach. The work of Campbell and Stanley (1963, 1966) gave enormous impetus to the predominance of experimental or quasi-experimental approaches. Although some evaluators cautioned that correct use of the experimental model in largely uncontrollable classroom settings might not be feasible, the elegance and precision of the experimental method led most educational evaluators to view it as the ideal.

Not all program evaluators were enamored with the use of traditional quantitative methods for program evaluations, however, and their dissatisfaction led to a search for alternatives. Qualitative and naturalistic methods, largely shunned by most educational evaluators during the 1960s as unacceptably "soft," gained wider acceptance in the 1970s and thereafter as proposals for their application to program evaluations were made by Parlett and Hamilton (1976), Stake (1978, 1980), Eisner (1976, 1979b), Guba and Lincoln (1981), and others.

The rise in popularity of qualitative inquiry methods in education has been noted by social and behavioral scientists concerned with the study of education (see Bogdan & Biklen, 1982; Cook & Reichardt, 1979; Rist, 1980). Bogdan and Biklen speak on the spectacular increase in acceptability of qualitative techniques in educational research:

> A field once dominated by measurement, operationalized definitions, variables, and empirical fact has had to make room for a research approach gaining in popularity, one that emphasizes inductive analysis, description, and the study of people's perceptions . . . dependence on qualitative methods for studying various educational issues is growing . . . qualitative research in education has, or will soon, come of age. (Bogdan & Biklen, 1982, p. xiii)

These same trends are no less true for educational evaluation; if anything, qualitative techniques have gained favor more quickly there.

Before proceeding further, we should delineate more clearly the differences between qualitative and quantitative methods. We find descriptions by Schofield and Anderson (1984) most useful for this purpose.[21] In their view, *qualitative* inquiry generally

> (a) is conducted in natural settings, such as schools or neighborhoods; (b) utilizes the researcher as the chief "instrument" in both data-gathering and analysis, . . . (c) emphasizes "thick description," that is, obtaining "real," "rich," "deep," data which illuminate everyday patterns of action and meaning from the perspective of those being studied . . . , (d) tends to focus on social processes rather than primarily or exclusively on outcomes, (e) employs multiple data-gathering methods, especially participant-

observation and interviews, and (f) uses an inductive approach to data analysis, extracting its concepts from the mass of particular detail which constitutes the data base....

By contrast, these authors state that *quantitative* inquiry generally

focuses on the testing of specific hypotheses that are smaller parts of some larger theoretical perspective. This approach follows the traditional natural science model more closely than qualitative research, emphasizing experimental design and statistical methods of analysis. Quantitative research emphasizes standardization, precision, objectivity, and reliability of measurement as well as replicability and generalizability of findings. Thus, quantitative research is characterized not only by a focus on producing numbers but on generating numbers which are suitable for statistical tests. (Schofield & Anderson, 1984, pp. 8–9)

Although subtle differences exist, other terms used to describe very similar methodological distinctions should be noted here. Guba and Lincoln (1981) contrast the *naturalistic* and *scientific* paradigms. The dichotomy of *subjective* versus *objective* methodology is similar to that of qualitative and quantitative methods as defined above. We should note that all of the dichotomies are largely artificial and should more accurately be thought of as different ends of a continuum (Goetz & LeCompte, 1981), although we will continue to use them dichotomously for simplicity, at least for now.

During the 1960s, sharp disagreements developed between proponents of the newer qualitative approaches and adherents to the more broadly accepted quantitative methods. And the 1970s were marked by debates as the two schools of thought struggled for ascendancy (see, for example, the Page and Stake, 1979, debate). Although some who favor qualitative methods are concerned that the sudden popularity and apparent simplicity of this approach have attracted innocents who employ qualitative inquiry without understanding of its complexity or the competence it demands of its user (Schofield & Anderson, 1984), most advocates are delighted by its increasing acceptance and are quick to attack weaknesses in quantitative inquiry.

Those who favor quantitative methods are, for the most part, distressed by the shift toward qualitative inquiry (notwithstanding the fact that quantitative work is still the dominant approach to educational inquiry, as even casual reading of the most influential journals in education and related areas will reveal). Critics of qualitative evaluation often complain about the subjectivity of many qualitative methods and techniques, expressing concern that evaluation has abandoned objectivity in favor of inexpertly managed subjectivity.

In short, the last two decades have been marked by acrimony between these seemingly irreconcilable methodological persuasions.

Recently, however, the dialogue has begun to move beyond this debate, with analysts increasingly discussing the benefits of integrating both methods within an educational evaluation study (for example, Cook & Reichardt, 1979; Worthen, 1981; and the especially useful summary by Madey, 1982). Stone's (1984) comment about educational research seems to extend to evaluation as well:

Today in educational research, . . . the trend is methodological pluralism and eclecticism. Many formerly-devout quantitative researchers are now trying their hands at qualitative inquiry. The vigorous quantitative/qualitative debate, if not dead, is somehow buried. (Stone, 1984, p. 1)

Yet even here there is not agreement, and scholars hold very disparate views of how far the integration of the qualitative and quantitative paradigms can be carried. Some, like J. K. Smith (1983), see such fundamental differences that they believe there is little hope of meaningful integration. Others, like Guba and Lincoln (1981), acknowledge that complementarity might be *possible* on some dimensions, yet they opt for one paradigm and seem pessimistic about healing the schism:

Can one assume both singular reality and multiple realities at the same time? How can one believe in insularity between the investigator and the object of his investigation while also allowing for their mutual interaction? How can one work simultaneously toward the development of nomothetic and idiographic science? (Guba & Lincoln, 1981, p. 77)

There is a growing chorus, however, of those who are optimistic about the fruitfulness of a complementary approach. For example, Howe (1985) has argued persuasively that adherence to rigid epistemological distinctions between qualitative and quantitative methods is, in itself, nothing more than a dogma held over from logical positivism.

Perhaps Schofield and Anderson (1984) state this position best when they say that

recent years have seen a number of important statements which argue against the traditional view that qualitative and quantitative work are based on fundamentally different paradigms and are thus competing and irreconcilable ways of approaching research. . . . Scholars of this persuasion, many of whom have been deeply involved with evaluation research in the field of education, argue that the distinction between qualitative and quantitative research is a matter of degree rather than of a basic difference which creates an unbridgeable chasm between the two camps. . . .

Reichardt and Cook (1979) argue that method-type is not irrevocably linked to paradigm-type and that the qualitative and quantitative paradigms are neither as rigid nor as incompatible as is commonly assumed. For example, they argue that all research has important subjective elements and that the characterization of quantitative research as objective and of qualitative research as subjective overdraws the distinction between the approaches in numerous ways. . . .

If qualitative and quantitative methods are not rooted in opposite and irreconcilable paradigms but rather are both more or less subjective, more or less valid and the like, there is no reason why they can not be utilized simultaneously. In fact, a number of scholars have recently argued not only that quantitative and qualitative approaches *can* be utilized jointly but that they *should* be so utilized. . . . The basic argument behind this position is that these two research strategies tend to have complementary strengths. . . .

Qualitative research . . . is weak where experimental and other quantitative designs are often strong and strong where such designs are frequently weak. Specifically, qualitative research is not generally able to specify causal connections with the degree of certainty or precision that many quantitative strategies can. However, it is ideally suited to suggesting ideas about social processes, to exploring the context in which the phenomena under investigation occur, and to capturing with both vividness and subtlety the perceptions of the individuals being studied. (Schofield & Anderson, 1984, pp. 12–13, 16–17)

We view quantitative and qualitative methods as compatible, complementary approaches in evaluation of educational programs. We have little interest in extending what we believe to be the relatively meaningless arguments that favor quantitative methods over qualitative, or vice versa. We view both forms of inquiry as appropriate, depending on the purpose and questions for which the study is conducted. Our bias for an ecumenical resolution of this issue permeates and influences this book in ways we hope will prove useful. We echo Stone's conclusion, if only hopefully, that the quantitative/qualitative debate, if not dead, is somehow buried. But if not, we would suggest that the energy of educational scholars and practitioners still being expended in such debate be more productively channeled into conceptualizing and testing procedures for effective integration of quantitative and qualitative methodologies, an area in which there is still very little guidance.

Disciplinary Boundaries and Evaluation Methodology

It is ironic that in a field with such a rich array of alternative evaluation approaches, there still exists a tendency to fall prey to the "law of the instrument" fallacy,[22] rather than adapting or inventing evaluation methods to meet our needs. Our grasp of evaluation still seems partial and parochial, as may be expected in a young field. But it is unfortunate that we seem to carry with us into a new field the methodological allegiances we developed through earlier studies. Too often we fail to encourage methodological flexibility, unthinkingly adopting a single-minded perspective that can answer only questions stemming from that perspective. Today's typical evaluation studies depend largely on methodology adapted from agronomy, some fields in psychology, and to a limited extent, sociology.[23] Those who interpret this statement as critical of these fields have missed the point, for they are esteemed disciplines, with methodologies well suited to pursue research questions within their respective spheres of inquiry. Rather, the point is that evaluation is not a discipline but merely a social process or activity aimed at determining the value of certain materials, programs, or efforts. As such, it necessarily cuts across disciplines, and evaluators are thus denied the luxury of remaining within any single inquiry paradigm.

It has been argued previously (see Chapter 3) that evaluation, unlike research, cannot fix the boundaries of its own inquiry, that evaluation questions are set by clients' needs and might be framed so as to require the tools of several disciplines to answer them. It was asserted that evaluators would need to have the flexibility to use econometrics to collect one type of data, psychometrics for another, sociometrics for a third, and so forth. Yet evaluators often go about the business of evaluation using their preferred methods and drawing little if at all on the alternative paradigms that may be more relevant to the evaluation problems at hand. It is not an easy thing to shuck off the conceptual shackles forged by experience. It is harder yet to expect that busy evaluators will interrupt an evaluation study to set off on an intellectual expedition into the terra incognita of another discipline to discover new methods and techniques perhaps more relevant to the problem at hand than they currently possess. And advising evaluators to be methodologically interdisciplinary sounds somewhat hollow in the absence of graduate programs designed specifically to assist evaluators-to-be in learning how they might do so.

Several writers have recognized the implications of evaluators' methodological preferences. For example, Talmage (1982) divides evaluators into four groups according to methodology: experimentalists, eclectics, describers, and benefit-cost analysts. Table 4.1 summarizes how, in her view, these four methodological positions relate to differences on several other dimensions; an excellent discussion of these differences appears in her original work.

Anderson and Ball (1978) also address how evaluators' predispositions and preferences on both philosophical and methodological dimensions led to differing designs, data collection and analysis methods, and interpretive techniques. Table 4.2 summarizes briefly their views, which are discussed in more detail in their original work.

More examples of alternative methodological preferences and their effect on evaluation studies could be given, but these should suffice. The increasing variety of methodological perspectives gaining legitimacy in educational evaluation is not only increasing the variety of ways evaluations are designed and conducted, but also is adding richness of perspective to a field still too young to opt for any single, ideal evaluation paradigm.

DIFFERENT METAPHORS OF EVALUATION

The importance of metaphors in evaluation has become increasingly clear during the past decade.[24] Worthen (1978) described the rationale that led the Northwest Regional Educational Laboratory to launch a federally supported research effort to identify metaphors from other disciplines that might lead to useful new evaluation methodologies in the field of education:

> If I may use a metaphor, we have proposed...a planned expedition into other fields to find and capture those methods and techniques that might have relevance for educational evaluation and...domesticate them so they will become tractable for our use. Again, limited resources will allow us to explore only so far, so we need to identify early those areas which appear most likely to contain good methodological candidates for domestication. (Worthen, 1978, p. 3)

Continued and enhanced greatly under the leadership of N. L. Smith (1981b, 1981c), and with conceptual contributions by Guba (1978b), this research effort has examined the possibility of using a variety of metaphors, such as investigative journalism, photography, storytelling, philosophical analysis, and literary criticism, to mention only a few. Although several of these metaphors have proven of limited use for educational evaluation, others have yielded many useful new methods and techniques for evaluators in educational settings.

TABLE 4.1

Four Methodological Approaches in Program Evaluation

	Experimentalists	Eclectics	Describers	Benefit-Cost Analyzers
	Cook and Campbell (1979) Riecken and Boruch (1974) Rivlin and Timpane (1975)	Bryk (1978) Cronbach and others (1980) R. S. Weiss and Rein (1972)	Parlett and Hamilton (1977) Patton (1980) Stake (1975)	Haller (1975) Levin (1975) Thompson (1980)
Philosophical base	Positivist	Modified positivist to pragmatic	Phenomenological	Logical/Analytic
Disciplinary base	Psychology	Psychology; sociology; political science	Sociology; anthropology	Economics; accounting
Focus of methodology	Identify causal links	Augment search for causal links with process and contextual data	Describe program holistically and from perspective of the participants	Judge worth of program in terms of costs and benefits
Methodology	Experimental and quasi-experimental designs	Quasi-experimental designs; case studies; descriptions	Ethnography; case studies, participant observation; triangulation	Benefit-cost analysis
Variables	Predetermined as input-output	Predetermined plus emerging	Emerging in course of evaluation	Predetermined
Control or comparison group	Yes	Where possible	Not necessary	Yes
Participants' role in carrying out evaluation	None	None to interactive	Varies (may react to field notes)	None
Evaluator's role	Independent of program	Cooperative	Interactive	Independent of program
Political pressures (internal-external)	Controlled in design; or ignored	Accommodated	Describe	Ignore
Focus of evaluation report	Render "go/no go" decision	Interpret and recommend for program improvement	Present holistic portrayal of program in process	Render judgment

Source: Talmage, 1982, p. 600, Harold E. Mitzel, Editor in Chief

55

TABLE 4.2
Predispositions and Preferences of Evaluators (Including Examples of
Design, Measurement, Analysis, and Interpretation Preferences
Associated with the Principal Dimensions)

	Phenomenological	*Behavioristic*
Design	Clinical or case study	Experimental or quasi-experimental design
Measurement	Subjective measurement methods, content analyses, self-reports	Objective measurement methods, tests, systematic observations
Analysis	Descriptive statistics and nonparametric techniques	Inferential statistics
Interpretation	Judgmental, value-laden	Nonjudgmental

	Absolutist	*Comparative*
Design	One-group design	Experimental or quasi-experimental design with comparison group(s)
Analysis	Within-group analysis	Between-group analysis
Interpretation	Standard-referenced	Comparison-group referenced

	Independent	*Dependent*
Measurement	Goal-free measures	Measures tailored to program goals
Interpretation	Nonclient-oriented	Goal-referenced, client-oriented

	Pragmatic	*Theoretical*
Design	Widely varying	Experimental or quasi-experimental design (hypothesis testing)
Measurement	Ad hoc measures, records	Established measures, construct validity emphasized
Analysis	Widely varying	Inferential statistics
Interpretation	Program-specific conclusions, little generalization (ideographic)	Hypothesis confirmation, generalization (nomothetic)

	Narrow Scope	*Broad Scope*
Measurement	Few and specific measures	Many and global measures
Analysis	Univariate contrasts	Multivariate analyses
Interpretation	Oriented toward component functioning	Oriented toward system functioning

	High Intensive	*Low Intensive*
Design	Repeated measurement occasions (longitudinal)	Infrequent measurement occasions (perhaps cross-sectional)
Measurement	Multitrait; multimethod (triangulation)	Survey tests

TABLE 4.2 CONTINUED

	High Intensive	Low intensive
Analysis	Multivariate analyses, including factor analyses	Univariate analyses, descriptive statistics
Interpretation	Generalization	Description

	Process	Product
Design	Repeated measurement occasions	Experimental or quasi-experimental design, infrequent measurement occasions
Measurement	Observations, logs, interviews	Tests
Analysis	Descriptive statistics	Inferential statistics
Interpretation	Recommendations for program improvement	Recommendations for program continuation, expansion, "accreditation"

Source: Anderson and Ball, 1978, pp. 122–123

One need not consciously seek metaphors in the way the Northwest Regional Educational Laboratory study did. Metaphors underlie and influence much of our thinking. Indeed, one reason for differing evaluation approaches is the different evaluation metaphors held by writers and practitioners. House (1983b) has demonstrated that much of our everyday thinking is metaphorical in nature and extends that point to argue that evaluation thought is also largely metaphorical. Further, he suggests that conflicts between existing evaluation schemes stem from differences in the underlying metaphors held by proponents of those schemes. For example, metaphoric conceptions of social programs equate those programs with industrial production (leading to metaphors based on machines, assembly lines, or pipelines) or with sports contests or games (leading to metaphors of targets and goals).

The influence of such metaphors on evaluation is obvious. For example, one who perceives evaluation as retrospective backtracking of a program to discover the causes of its outcomes is likely to use an approach that resembles forensic pathology, whereas one who holds a connoisseurial metaphor of evaluation will use an approach more akin to literary criticism. Yes, different metaphors account for much of the variation in evaluation approaches.

RESPONDING TO DIFFERENT NEEDS IN EDUCATION

In proposing new evaluation approaches, evaluation theorists have not only been influenced by their different methodological and metaphorical preferences or their different ways of looking at knowledge and how it is achieved. They have also been responding to different needs that they perceived, needs such as school administrators wanting better information for decision making, educators wanting a more systematic way to review school curricula, school personnel struggling for of that which is evaluated (for example, knowledge of mathematics in evaluating a mathematics education program)—some evaluators (for example, Eisner, 1975, 1979a) see such expertise as the *sine qua non* of evaluation. Indeed, without such expertise, their evaluation approach would be futile. Other evaluators (for a better way to articulate the purposes of schooling, federal and state legislators monitoring resource allocation, and local stakeholders hoping to define issues in rational rather than emotional terms.

Various approaches were developed to address each need. In the aggregate, these different approaches help us comprehend the wide range of needs for evaluation in education. We must learn to identify what is useful in each approach when faced with a specific evaluation need, to use it wisely, and not to be distracted by irrelevant evaluation approaches constructed to deal with a different need.

PRACTICAL CONSIDERATIONS

We have traced how epistemological issues, methodological preferences, metaphoric views of evaluation, and different needs all contribute to the diversity of alternative evaluation approaches. Several practical issues also contribute to this diversity.

First, evaluators disagree about whether the intent of evaluation is to render a value judgment. Some (Edwards, Guttentag, & Snapper, 1975; Patton, 1978; and Weiss, 1977) are concerned only with the usefulness of the evaluation to the decision-maker and believe that he, not the evaluator, should render the value judgment. Others (for example, Scriven, 1973; Wolf, 1979; and Worthen & Sanders, 1973) believe the evaluator's report to the decision-maker is complete only if it contains a value judgment. Such differences in views have obvious practical implications.

Second, evaluators differ in their general view of the political roles of evaluation. MacDonald (1976) provides a political classification (described in greater detail in Chapter 10) to illustrate how political orientation affects the style of evaluation conducted: bureaucratic, autocratic, or democratic. Although MacDonald prefers the democratic, he provides a useful analysis of how these different political-orientation issues result in very different approaches.

Third, evaluators are influenced by their prior experience. Although most recent conceptual work in educational evaluation has come from academics in higher education, some of it emanates from practitioners in local and state education agencies. Many of the authors who have shaped our thinking about evaluation have been educational psychologists, specialists in educational and psychological tests and measurements, guidance counselors, school administrators, curriculum specialists, or philosophers. Each theorist has drawn from certain strengths, from experience with certain types of problems and processes in education, and from a way of looking at things that grew out of his or her professional education and career. In the aggregate, the different approaches represent nearly every way imaginable of looking at education; individually, however, they represent limited perspectives.

Fourth, evaluators differ in their views about who should conduct the evaluation and the nature of the expertise that the evaluator must possess. Although this topic is too complex to be treated adequately in this chapter, an illustration might help. Considering one dimension of expertise—substantive knowledge about the content example, Worthen & Sanders, 1984) not only question the need for the evaluator to possess such expertise but also suggest that there may sometimes be advantages in selecting evaluators who are not specialists in the content of that which they evaluate. Such differences in perspective lead to different approaches to evaluation.

Finally, evaluators differ even in their perception of whether it is desirable to have a wide variety of approaches to educational evaluation. Antonoplos (1977) and Gephart (1977) have lamented the proliferation of evaluation models and urged that an effort be made to synthesize existing models. Palumbo and Nachmias (1984) are less sanguine about the possibility of developing an ideal evaluation paradigm, but they propose that making the effort is worthwhile. Conversely, Raizen and Rossi (1981) have argued that the goal of attaining uniformity in evaluation methods and measures, proposed by some as a way to increase quality of information, cannot be attained at the present time without prematurely inhibiting needed development in the field of evaluation. Worthen (1977b) had earlier made a similar point in arguing that efforts to synthesize existing evaluation models would be dysfunctional, an argument that will be expanded later in Chapter 11. Regardless of which view you subscribe to, it is clear that either the inability to generate an idealistic evaluation model (after all, none has been forthcoming since the call for synthesis nearly a decade ago) or resistance to trading the diversity of models for a unified view accounts, at least in part, for the continued variety of approaches that confronts the evaluation practitioner.

THEMES AMONG THE VARIATIONS

Despite the diversity in evaluation approaches, commonalities do exist. Many individuals have attempted to bring order out of the chaos reflected in evaluation literature by developing classification schemes, or taxonomies. Each such effort selected one or more dimensions deemed useful in classifying evaluation approaches. But because evaluation is multifaceted and because it can be conducted at different phases of a program's development, the same evaluation model can be classified in diverse ways, depending on emphasis. Consider the following examples.

Those who have published classification schema include Worthen and Sanders (1973), Popham (1975), Ross and Cronbach (1976), Stake (1975b), Curriculum Development Centre (1977), Stufflebeam and Webster (1980), Guba and Lincoln (1981), House (1983a), Madaus, Scriven, and Stufflebeam (1983), and Worthen (1984). All have influenced our thinking about the categorization of evaluation approaches, but we have drawn especially on our own work and that of House in developing the schema proposed below.

A CLASSIFICATION SCHEMA FOR EVALUATION APPROACHES

We have chosen to classify many different approaches to evaluation into the six categories described below.

1. *Objectives-oriented approaches,* where the focus is on specifying goals and objectives and determining the extent to which they have been attained.
2. *Management-oriented approaches,* where the central concern is on identifying and meeting the informational needs of managerial decision-makers.
3. *Consumer-oriented approaches,* where the central issue is developing evaluative information on educational "products," broadly defined, for use by educational consumers in choosing among competing curricula, instructional products, and the like.
4. *Expertise-oriented approaches,* which depend primarily on the direct application of professional expertise to judge the quality of educational endeavors.
5. *Adversary-oriented approaches,* where planned opposition in points of view of different evaluators (pro and con) is the central focus of the evaluation.
6. *Naturalistic and participant-oriented approaches,* where naturalistic inquiry and involvement of participants (stakeholders in that which is evaluated) are central in determining the values, criteria, needs, and data for the evaluation.

These six categories seem to us to distribute (though not equally) along House's (1983a) dimension of utilitarian to intuitionist-pluralist evaluation, as shown in Figure 4.1 below.

Placement of individual evaluation approaches within these six categories is to some degree arbitrary. Several approaches are multifaceted and include characteristics that would allow them to be placed in more than one category; for convenience we have decided to place such approaches in one category and only reference in other chapters, where appropriate, their other features. Our classification is based on what we see as the driving force behind doing the evaluation—the major questions to be addressed and/or the major organizer(s) that underlie each approach (for example, objectives, or management decisions). Within each category, the approaches vary by level of formality and structure, some being relatively well developed philosophically and procedurally, others less developed. It should be noted that these frameworks deal with conceptual approaches to evaluation, not techniques; discussion of the many techniques that might be used in educational evaluations is reserved for Part Three of this book.

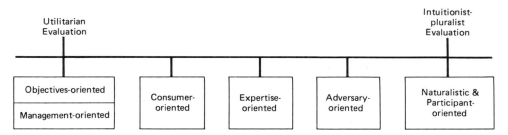

FIGURE 4.1 Distribution of Six Evaluation Approaches on the Dimension of Utilitarian to Intuitionist-Pluralist Evaluation

APPLICATION EXERCISE

1. Think about how you would approach evaluation. Describe the steps you think you would follow. Then, analyze your approach according to your philosophical and methodological preferences. Explain how your background and what you would be evaluating could have affected your approach. Describe other things that might have affected your approach to evaluation.

2. Identify an educational program you would like to see evaluated. List some qualitative evaluation methods that could be used. Now list some quantitative methods that you see as appropriate. Discuss whether it would be appropriate to combine both methods within the same study, including reasons for your conclusion.

SUGGESTED READINGS

GUBA, E. G., & LINCOLN, Y. S. (1981). *Effective evaluation*. San Francisco: Jossey-Bass.

HOUSE, E. R. (1980). *Evaluating with validity*. Beverly Hills, CA: Sage.

HOUSE, E. R. (1983a). Assumptions underlying evaluation models. In G. F. MADAUS, M. SCRIVEN, & D. L. STUFFLEBEAM (Eds.), *Evaluation models*. Boston: Kluwer-Nijhoff.

HOUSE, E. R. (Ed.). (1983b). *Philosophy of evaluation*. New Directions for Program Evaluation, No. 19. San Francisco: Jossey-Bass.

Chapter 5
Objectives–Oriented
Evaluation Approaches

Orienting Questions

1. What aspects of Tyler's approach to evaluation have permeated all later objectives–oriented evaluation approaches?
2. What unique contributions were made by the proposals of Hammond, Provus, and Metfessel and Michael?
3. In what forms has the objectives–oriented evaluation approach been used in education?
4. What are some major strengths and limitations of objectives-oriented evaluation approaches?
5. What is "goal-free evaluation"? Does it have a useful role to play in educational evaluation?

T he distinguishing feature of an objectives–oriented evaluation approach is that the purposes of some educational activity are specified, and then evaluation focuses on the extent to which those purposes are achieved. In education the activity could be as short as a one-day classroom lesson or as complex as the whole schooling enterprise. The information gained from an objectives–oriented evaluation could be used to reformulate the purposes of the activity, the activity itself, or the assessment procedures and devices used to determine the achievement of purposes.

DEVELOPERS OF THE OBJECTIVES-ORIENTED EVALUATION APPROACH AND THEIR CONTRIBUTIONS

Many people have contributed to the evolution and refinement of the objectives-oriented approach to evaluation since its inception in the 1930s, but the individual credited with conceptualizing and popularizing it in education is R. W. Tyler (1942, 1950), for whom this approach has been named.

The Tylerian Evaluation Approach

Tyler's approach to evaluation was developed and used during the Eight Year Study of the late 1930s (Smith & Tyler, 1942). Travers (1983) did note, however, that an earlier work, Waples and Tyler's *Research Methods and Teacher Problems* (1930), set the stage for Tyler's later achievements in evaluation.

Tyler conceived of evaluation as the process of determining the extent to which the educational objectives of a school program or curriculum are actually being attained. His approach to evaluation followed these steps:

1. Establish broad goals or objectives.
2. Classify the goals or objectives.
3. Define objectives in behavioral terms.
4. Find situations in which achievement of objectives can be shown.
5. Develop or select measurement techniques.
6. Collect performance data.
7. Compare performance data with behaviorally stated objectives.

Discrepancies between performance and objectives would lead to modifications intended to correct the deficiency, and the evaluation cycle would be repeated.

Tyler's rationale was logical, scientifically acceptable, readily adoptable by educational evaluators (most of whose methodological upbringing was very compatible with the pretest-posttest measurement of student behaviors stressed by Tyler), and had great influence on subsequent evaluation theorists.

Goodlad (1979) pointed out that Tyler advocated the use of general goals to establish purposes, rather than prematurely becoming preoccupied with formulating behavioral objectives. Of course, the broad goals for any activity eventually require operational definitions so that appropriate measurement devices and settings can be selected. Tyler's belief was that educators primarily needed to discuss the importance and meaning of general goals of education. Otherwise, in Goodlad's words, the premature specification of behavioral objectives would result in objectives that, "could only be arbitrary, restrictive, and ultimately dysfunctional" (Goodlad, 1979, p. 43).

Tyler described six categories of purpose for American schools (Goodlad, 1979). They were (1) acquisition of information; (2) development of work habits and study skills; (3) development of effective ways of thinking; (4) internalization of social attitudes, interests, appreciations, and sensitivities; (5) maintenance of physical health; and (6) development of a philosophy of life.

Over the years, educators have refined and reformulated the purposes of schooling into various forms. Two recent publications provided statements that reflect the thinking of the past 50 years.

First, the Evaluation Center at Western Michigan University developed a *Handbook of Educational Variables* in cooperation with the Toledo, Ohio, Public Schools (Nowakowski and others, 1985). The *Handbook* divided elementary and secondary student development into these seven categories:

1. Intellectual
2. Emotional

3. Physical and Recreational
4. Aesthetic and Cultural
5. Moral
6. Vocational
7. Social

Each one of these categories was analyzed in detail too extensive to reproduce here. Such a resource exemplifies the extent to which Tyler's approach to evaluation has been refined.

A second resource that specifies the purposes of schooling in the United States is Goodlad's (1979) list of 12 goal areas for schools, which includes the following major categories:

1. Mastery of basic skills or fundamental processes
2. Career education/vocational education
3. Intellectual development
4. Enculturation
5. Interpersonal relations
6. Autonomy
7. Citizenship
8. Creativity and aesthetic perception
9. Self-concept
10. Emotional and physical well-being
11. Moral and ethical character
12. Self-realization

Goodlad stressed that evaluation and improvement of American schools cannot make much headway until these purposes have been discussed, accepted, operationally defined, and monitored. It should be clear that a single standardized test of achievement of basic skills provides insufficient data to evaluate our schools. Yet the use of standardized test results is still the most common form of school evaluation discussed in the popular media today.

Tyler stressed the importance of screening broad goals before accepting them as the basis for evaluating an activity. The screen through which potential goals should be filtered includes value questions derived from three sources: philosophical (the nature of knowledge); social (the nature of society); and pedagogical (the nature of the learner and the learning process). Scriven (1967) reiterated the need to evaluate the purposes of any activity as a part of evaluating the activity and its consequences.

The question of how specifically to evaluate goals and objectives was addressed by Sanders and Cunningham (1973, 1974). Their approach was to consider both logical and empirical methods for goal evaluation. *Logical* methods included:

1. Examining the cogency of the argument or rationale behind each objective. If there are no justifiable reasons for a goal or objective, it cannot have much value. The *need* for accomplishing the goal or objective is a critical consideration.
2. Examining the consequences of accomplishing the goal or objective. By projecting logically the consequences of achieving a goal, both strengths and

weaknesses in competing goals may be revealed. Criteria such as utility and feasibility (cost, acceptability, political palatability, training, or other requirements) of the goal or objective could be used here. A search of educational literature may reveal the results of past attempts to achieve certain goals or objectives.

3. Considering whether higher-order values such as laws, policies, fit with existing practices, moral principles, the ideals of a free society, or the Constitution, to see if a goal or purpose is required by or will conflict with such values.

Empirical methods for evaluating goals or objectives included:

1. Collecting group data to describe judgments about the value of a goal or objective. Surveys are the most common form of gathering information about a group's value position.

2. Arranging for experts, hearings, or panels to review and evaluate potential goals or objectives. Specialists can draw from knowledge or experience that may not be otherwise available. Their informed judgment may be very different from the group value data that surveys would produce.

3. Conducting content studies of archival records, such as speeches, minutes, editorials, or newsletters. Such content analyses may reveal value positions that conflict with, or are in support of, a particular goal or objective.

4. Conducting a pilot study to see if the goal is attainable and in what form it may be attained. If no prior experience is available when evaluating a purpose or goal, it may be advisable to suspend judgment until some experience has been gained. Once a broad goal has been made operational, or activities directed toward attaining the goal have been tried, it may take on a different meaning from that which it had in earlier discussions.

Several evaluation approaches developed in education during the late 1960s and early 1970s used goals or objectives as a central focus in the evaluation procedure. These approaches may be seen, therefore, as further refinements of Tyler's approach. Most noteworthy of these objectives-referenced evaluation approaches were those developed by Metfessel and Michael (1967), Hammond (1973) and Provus (1969, 1971; Yavorsky, 1976). They are noteworthy because they added new insights into how educational programs may be studied within the Tylerian tradition.

Metfessel and Michael's Evaluation Paradigm

An early approach to evaluation suggested by Metfessel and Michael (1967) was heavily influenced by the Tylerian tradition. Eight steps in the evaluation process were proposed as follows:

1. Involve the total school community as facilitators of program evaluation.
2. Formulate cohesive model of goals and specific objectives.
3. Translate specific objectives into a communicable form applicable to facilitating learning in the school environment.

4. Select or construct instruments to furnish measures allowing inferences about program effectiveness.
5. Carry out periodic observations using content-valid tests, scales, and other behavioral measures.
6. Analyze data using appropriate statistical methods.
7. Interpret the data using standards of desired levels of performance over all measures.
8. Develop recommendations for the further implementation, modification, and revision of broad goals and specific objectives.

One of the primary contributions of Metfessel and Michael was in expanding the educational evaluator's vision of alternative instruments that might be used to collect evaluation data. Interested readers will find their lists of alternative instruments for data collection (Metfessel & Michael, 1967; Worthen & Sanders, 1973, pp. 276–279) to be a valuable guide.

Hammond's Evaluation Approach

Hammond[25] was interested not only in determining whether goals or objectives were achieved but also in finding out why some educational innovations failed while others succeeded. To help the evaluator search for factors that influence the success or failure of any educational activity, Hammond developed a three-dimensional cube (Hammond, 1973) for use in describing educational programs and organizing evaluation variables (see Fig. 5.1). Hammond called his cube a "structure for evaluation."

The three dimensions of the cube are:

1. *Instruction*: Characteristics of the educational activity that is being evaluated.
   a. *Organization*: Time, scheduling, course sequences, and organization of the school, including vertical (graded or ungraded) and horizontal (self-contained, cooperative teaching, or departmentalized) organization.
   b. *Content*: Topics to be covered.
   c. *Method*: Teaching activities, types of interaction (for example, teacher-student, media-student), teaching/learning theory.
   d. *Facilities*: Space, equipment, expendable materials.
   e. *Cost*: Funds required for facilities, maintenance, personnel.
2. *Institution*: Characteristics of individuals or groups involved with the educational activity being evaluated.
   a. *Student* (column 1 of the cube): Age, grade level, sex, family background, social class, health, mental health, achievement, ability, interests.
   b. *Teacher, administrator, educational specialist* (columns 2, 3, and 4 of the cube): For each role, one might attend to age, sex, race or religion, health, personality, educational background and work experience, pertinent personal characteristics (work habits).
   c. *Family* (column 5 of the cube): Degree of involvement with the activity being evaluated, general characteristics such as culture or language, family

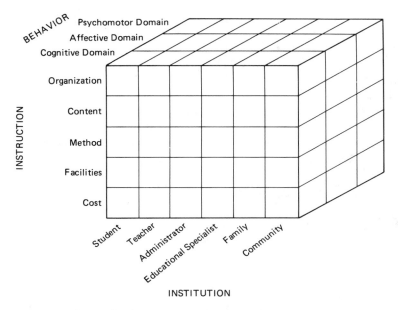

FIGURE 5.1 Structure for Evaluation

Source: Hammond, 1973, p. 158.

size, marital status, income, educational level, affiliations (for example, religion, politics, union).

  d. *Community* (column 6 of the cube): Geographical setting, history, demographics, economic characteristics, social and political characteristics.
3. *Behavioral Objectives*: Objectives of the educational activity being evaluated.
  a. *Cognitive objectives*: Knowledge and intellectual skills.
  b. *Affective objectives*: Interests, attitudes, feelings, and emotions.
  c. *Psychomotor objectives*: Physical skills, coordination.

Hammond's cube is made up of 90 potentially useful cells. Any cell may be examined to determine the types of evaluative questions that might be generated. For example, an evaluator might examine the cell formed by the interaction of *content* (from the Instruction dimension), *teacher* (from the Institution dimension), and *affective objectives* (from the Behavioral Objectives dimension). What questions does this configuration of factors suggest? Here are just a few of many possible examples:

  • How well are teachers using the subject matter of this program in achieving its (or their) affective objectives?
  • How do teachers feel about the content and the program's affective objectives?
  • Is the content of the program sufficient for teachers to accomplish their affective objectives?
  • Are teachers prepared to use this subject matter to accomplish the program's affective objectives?

Hammond's evaluation structure is a valuable heuristic tool the evaluator can use in analyzing the successes and failures of an educational activity in achieving its objectives. If all cells in the cube were equally pertinent to a given evaluation study, the evaluator would have 90 cells to use for generating evaluation questions! Generating and responding to so many questions would be a monumental but extremely helpful task. Often, however, many of the cells prove irrelevant to a given evaluation, and frequently only a few cells apply.

Beyond the introduction of his cube, Hammond's approach to evaluation deviated little from the Tylerian approach, proposing the following steps in evaluating school programs:

1. Defining the program.
2. Defining the descriptive variables (using his "cube").
3. Stating objectives.
4. Assessing performance.
5. Analyzing results.
6. Comparing results with objectives.

Provus's Discrepancy Evaluation Model

Another approach to evaluation in the Tylerian tradition was developed by Provus, who based his approach on his evaluation assignments in the Pittsburgh, Pennsylvania, public schools. Provus viewed evaluation as a continuous information management process designed to serve as "the watchdog of program management" and the "handmaiden of administration in the management of program development through sound decision making" (Provus, 1973, p. 186). Although his was in some ways a management-oriented evaluation approach, the key characteristic of Provus's proposals stemmed from the Tylerian tradition. Provus viewed evaluation as a process of (1) agreeing upon standards (another term used in place of "objectives"[26]), (2) determining whether a discrepancy exists between the performance of some aspect of a program and the standards set for performance, and (3) using information about discrepancies to decide whether to improve, maintain, or terminate the program or some aspect of it. Provus called his approach, not surprisingly, the Discrepancy Evaluation Model.[27]

As a program or educational activity is being developed, Provus conceived of it as going through four developmental stages, to which he added a fifth optional stage:

1. Definition
2. Installation
3. Process (interim products)
4. Product
5. Cost-benefit analysis (optional)

During the *definition*, or design, stage, the focus of work is on defining goals, processes, or activities, and delineating necessary resources and participants to carry out the activities and accomplish the goals. Provus considered educational programs to be dynamic systems involving inputs (antecedents), processes, and outputs (outcomes). Standards or expectations were established for each. These standards were the objectives on which all further evaluation work depends. The evaluator's job at the design stage is to see that a complete set of specifications is produced and that they meet certain criteria: theoretical and structural soundness.

At the *installation* stage, the program design or definition is used as the standard against which to judge program operation. The evaluator performs a series of congruency tests to identify any discrepancies between expected and actual installation of the program or activity. The intent is to make certain that the program has been installed as it had been designed. This is important because studies have found that teachers vary as much in implementing a single program as they do in implementing several different ones. The degree to which program specifications are followed is best determined through firsthand observation. If discrepancies are found at this stage, Provus proposed either changing the program definition, making adjustments in the installation (such as preparing a special in-service workshop), or terminating the activity if it appears that further development would be futile.

During the *process* stage, evaluation is to focus on gathering data on the progress of participants (for example, students) to determine whether their behaviors changed as expected. Provus used the term *enabling objective* to refer to those gains that participants should be making if program goals are to be reached. If certain enabling objectives are not achieved, the activities leading to those objectives are revised or redefined. The validity of the evaluation data would also be questioned. If the evaluator finds that enabling objectives are not being achieved, another option is to terminate the program if it appears that the discrepancy cannot be eliminated.

At the *product* stage, evaluation is to determine whether the *terminal objectives* for the program have been achieved. Provus distinguished between immediate outcomes, or *terminal objectives*, and long-term outcomes, or *ultimate objectives*. He encouraged the evaluator to go beyond the traditional emphasis on end-of-program performance and make follow-up studies a part of evaluation.

Provus also suggested an optional fifth stage that called for *cost-benefit analysis* and comparison of results with similar cost analyses of comparable educational programs. In recent times, with funds for education becoming scarcer, cost-benefit analyses have become an essential part of almost all educational evaluations.

The Discrepancy Evaluation Model was designed to facilitate development of educational programs in a large public school system, and later it was applied to statewide evaluations by a federal bureau. A complex approach that works best in larger systems with adequate staff resources, its central focus is on use of discrepancies to help managers determine the extent to which program development is proceeding toward attainment of stated objectives. It attempts to assure effective program development by preventing the activity from proceeding to the next stage until all identified discrepancies have been removed. Whenever a discrepancy is found, Provus suggested a cooperative problem-solving process for program staff and evaluators. The process involved asking (1) Why is there a discrepancy? (2) What corrective actions are possible? and (3) Which corrective action is best? This process usually required that additional information be gathered and criteria developed to allow rational, justifiable decisions about corrective actions (or terminations). This particular problem-solving activity was a new addition to the traditional objectives-oriented evaluation approach.

The evaluation approaches outlined here have been referred to not only as objectives-oriented evaluation approaches, the term we prefer, but also as "objectives-referenced" evaluations, "objectives-performance congruence" approaches, "performance congruence" models, and other similar terms. In each, assessment of the extent to which objectives have been attained is the central feature.

HOW THE OBJECTIVES-ORIENTED EVALUATION APPROACH HAS BEEN USED

The objectives-oriented approach has dominated the thinking and development of educational evaluation since the 1930s, both here in the United States and elsewhere. Its straightforward procedure of letting objectives achievement determine success or failure and justify improvements, maintenance, or termination of educational activities has proved an attractive prototype.

In the 1950s and early 1960s, curriculum evaluation and curriculum development procedures were based almost entirely on Tyler's conception of evaluation developed during the Eight Year Study. Taba, who worked with Tyler in the Eight Year Study, was one who influenced the field of curriculum development with an objectives-oriented model that included the following steps:

1. Diagnosis of needs
2. Formulation of objectives
3. Selection of content
4. Organization of content
5. Selection of learning experiences
6. Organization of learning experiences
7. Determining the "what" and "how" of evaluation (Taba, 1962, p. 12)

The technology of objectives-oriented evaluation was refined by Mager (1962), who went beyond simple insistence that objectives be prespecified in behavioral terms to insist that objectives must also contain the attainment levels desired by educators and the criteria for judging such attainment. Insistence on the use of behavioral objectives sparked a profession-wide debate that began in the 1960s and still continues. Several educators (Gideonse, 1969; Popham, 1973a, 1973b, 1975) have championed the use of behavioral objectives, whereas others (for example, Atkin, 1968) contend that specification of behavioral objectives is not really helpful to curriculum development or sound curriculum evaluation.

Whether or not one believes behavioral objectives are useful, one cannot help being distressed by the mindlessness that ran rampant through education wherein educators were encouraged to state every intent—however trivial—in behavioral terms. In some schools, the staffs were spending so much time and energy stating everything they wanted to teach in behavioral terms that they hardly had time to teach. Training every teacher to use a recipe for translating every aspiration into a behavioral objective wastes time and resources and distorts what education should be. This is especially true when teachers are used to writing objectives intended more for evaluation than for instruction. It is, after all, the evaluator who is supposedly skilled in the language of operationalization. We think the evaluator should take the following stance in working with program personnel: "Give me an objective in any form, just so I understand what your intent is. As an evaluator, I will translate your objective into behavioral terms and have you review my statement to make certain I have not distorted your intent." That approach makes more sense than trying to train all educators to be evaluators.

The pendulum obviously needed to move from the irresponsible position that educators do not need objectives because, after all, they "know in their hearts they are right." But education moved too far in the opposite extreme when it spawned the religion of behaviorism and the disciples who applied it unintelligently. One can hardly oppose using instructional objectives and assessing their attainment, but the use of dozens or even hundreds of objectives for each area of endeavor, not uncommon a few years ago, amounted to a monopolization of educators' time and skills for a relatively small payoff. Although vestiges of this philosophy are still evident in some schools, the press for behavioral reductionism seems to have diminished. Had the push for behavioral objectives not been contained, disenchanted educators may well have refused to have anything to do with evaluation—an outcome that would have had serious consequences for education.

Though the debate has shifted from a focus on proper statement of objectives to that of how the objectives are to be measured, it still divides the field of evaluation.

Bloom and Krathwohl were influential in refining the objectives-oriented approach to evaluation with their work on the previously discussed taxonomies of educational objectives in both the cognitive (Bloom and others, 1956) and affective domains (Krathwohl and others, 1964). With the development of these taxonomies of objectives, curriculum specialists had powerful tools to aid them in using Tyler's approach. Bloom, Hastings, and Madaus (1971) also prepared a handbook for educators to use in identifying appropriate objectives for instruction in the subject matter taught in school and for developing and using measurement instruments to determine students' levels of performance in each subject. Cronbach (1963), who also worked with Tyler on the Eight Year Study, developed an approach to using objectives and associated measurement techniques for purposes of course and curriculum improvement.

But the blockbuster, in terms of expenditure, has been the objectives-referenced or criterion-referenced testing programs originated in the 1960s and 1970s by federal and state governments. The National Assessment of Educational Progress (NAEP) was originated in the mid-1960s under the leadership of Tyler. This federal program was designed to collect performance data periodically on samples of students and young adults in the essential subjects of American education. Great care was taken to select objectives generally accepted in this country as desirable achievements at the different stages of development measured (ages 9, 13, 17, and adult). Public reports have, since the mid-1960s, described the ability of Americans in these age groups to answer questions in subjects considered important.

Like those of the Eight Year Study, the instruments and objectives of NAEP have been made available to educators, but they have received limited use. Virtually every state has developed its own form of annual statewide testing, and many have generally followed the NAEP approach.

Derivative "objectives-oriented" movements in education, in the form of school accountability (Lessinger, 1970; Lessinger & Tyler, 1971), competency or minimum competency testing (Bunda & Sanders, 1979; Jaeger & Tittle, 1980; Madaus, 1983), objectives- and criterion-referenced collections and exchanges (Instructional Objectives Exchange, 1969; Clearinghouse for Applied Performance Testing, 1974), and federal project monitoring (such as the TIERS System for Title I projects developed by Tallmadge & Wood, 1976) appeared in the late 1960s and continue to be influential. For example, most states in the United States now have a competency testing program used to determine whether children have mastered the minimal objectives established for their respective grade levels. The tradition begun by Tyler over 50 years ago has had remarkable staying power.

STRENGTHS AND LIMITATIONS OF THE OBJECTIVES-ORIENTED EVALUATION APPROACH

Probably the greatest strength and appeal of the objectives-oriented approach to evaluation in education lies in its simplicity. It is easily understood, easy to follow and implement, and produces information that educators generally agree is relevant to their mission. This approach has stimulated so much technological development over the years that the processes of specifying objectives and developing or finding appropriate measurement procedures and instruments have been finely honed. The literature on objectives-oriented evaluation is extensive, filled with creative ideas for applying the approach in classrooms, schools, school districts, and beyond (Cronbach, 1963; Lindvall, 1964; Popham, Eisner, Sullivan, & Tyler, 1969; Metfessel & Michael, 1967; Bloom, Hastings, & Madaus, 1971; Morris & Fitzgibbon, 1978).

The objectives-oriented evaluation approach has caused educators to reflect about their intentions and to clarify formerly ambiguous generalities about educational outcomes (Mager, 1962). Discussions of appropriate educational objectives with the community being served have given objectives-oriented evaluation the appeal of face validity—the program is, after all, merely being held accountable for what its designers said it was going to accomplish, and that is obviously legitimate.

As a result of the attention placed on this approach, tests have improved, and technically sound measurement practices have broadened to include unobtrusive (Webb, Campbell, Schwartz, & Sechrest, 1966) and non-paper-and-pencil evidence (Sanders & Sachse, 1977). These and other advances in the measurement of *outcomes* in education may be tied to the outcome orientation of Tyler. These advances, added to the many instruments, objectives pools, and step-by-step guides that have been placed in the hands of educators by various projects, have greatly expanded the available resources for educational evaluation during the twentieth century.

Useful as this approach to evaluation seems to its many adherents, critics have asserted that it (1) lacks a real evaluative component (facilitating measurement and assessment of objectives rather than resulting in explicit judgments of merit or worth), (2) lacks standards to judge the importance of observed discrepancies between objectives and performance levels, (3) neglects the value of the objectives themselves, (4) ignores important alternatives that should be considered in planning an educational program, (5) neglects transactions that occur within the program or activity being evaluated, (6) neglects the context in which the evaluation takes place, (7) ignores important outcomes other than those covered by the objectives (the unintended outcomes of the activity), (8) omits evidence of program value not reflected in its own objectives, and (9) promotes a linear, inflexible approach to evaluation. Collectively, these criticisms suggest that objectives-oriented evaluation can result in tunnel vision that tends to limit evaluation's effectiveness and potential.

To some extent, the rather elaborate technology developed to support this evaluation approach makes its use appear seductively simple to novice evaluators only partially familiar with its philosophical and practical difficulties. The assumption that education is a technology—a body of techniques leading to prespecified means—has been criticized by Waks (1975), who pointed to potential problems with the philosophical underpinnings of this approach.

A recently passed law in one of our states is a classic example of poor use of the objectives-oriented evaluation approach. The General Assembly mandated that each school district should report once a year both to its local constituency and to the state the extent to which the district had achieved its stated goals and objectives. All a district had to do was to announce some general goals and specific objectives, carry out its program for a year, and at the end of the time report how well it had done on those goals and objectives. Although it is often important to know whether a district is attaining its stated objectives, such is not always the case. It depends largely on whether the goals were worth attaining in the first place. Some goals that are attainable are hardly worth the effort. Some goals are attained because they were set too low or had already been attained, not because the program was effective. The situation is almost analogous to that in which one needs to identify which children in a classroom are in good health and which are suffering from malnutrition, and height is considered a relevant indicator. There would be at least a measure of foolishness in asking each child to make his own tape measure, use it in measuring his height, and then report how well he has attained the height he desired to reach at that point or whether he is too tall or too short for his age.

A related difficulty lies in the frequent challenge of trying to ascertain the goals or objectives of many educational endeavors. Evaluators have found that the objectives listed on paper do not always match those in the minds of program staff. As a result, their activities may conflict with or deviate from publicly stated objectives, sometimes for good reasons. Professional educators will not become slaves to stated objectives if they believe alternative courses of action or goals are desirable. Such individuals tend to argue against strident and unthinking application of an objectives-oriented approach.

A related and perhaps more pervasive problem is the fact that many educators have not articulated objectives for their curricula or programs in any interpretable form. This is not to say they have no idea of where they are going or what they want to accomplish (although that is sometimes unfortunately the case), but rather that they are unaccustomed to thinking or speaking in "behavioral" language familiar to objectives-oriented evaluators. The evaluator may find it necessary to elicit clear statements of intent in an almost Rogerian fashion rather than translate those statements into behavioral terms as deemed necessary (not forgetting to ask those whose intentions they reflect if there have been distortions in the translation). Given the fact that many evaluators, lamentably, are not equipped by disposition or training to assist educators in this way, the objectives-oriented approach to evaluation frequently results in the verdict that a program cannot be evaluated, when the problem lies more with narrow understanding of the approach and/or the insistence that all educators must become experts in behavioral specification before this method can be used.

Who really determines the goals and objectives? Do they include all important outcomes? Have all those affected by the program agreed upon these particular goals or objectives? Who has determined that a particular criterion level is more defensible than alternatives? On what evidence? These and other questions must be addressed if an objectives-oriented approach is to be defensible.

Overemphasizing the testing components of this evaluation approach can prove dangerous. "Teaching for the test" is only human when a teacher's performance is evaluated by how well students do on standardized or statewide assessment tests. Madaus (1983) describes how competency testing invariably turns into *minimum* competency testing when expectations for achievement become bounded by test content. Such narrowing of educational purposes is a negative, albeit unintentional, consequence this approach may have had.

We should not leave our discussion of limitations of objectives-oriented evaluation without noting that Scriven's perception of its limitations led him to develop his now widely known proposals for goal-free evaluation (Scriven, 1972). Although intentionally the opposite of objectives-oriented approaches, it seems logical to discuss this proposal here.

Goal-Free Evaluation

The rationale for goal-free evaluation can be summarized as follows: First, educational goals should not be taken as given; like anything else, they should be evaluated. Further, goals are generally little more than rhetoric and seldom reveal the real objectives of the project or changes in intent. In addition, many important program outcomes do not fall in the category of goals or objectives anyway (for example, establishing a new vocational education center will create additional jobs—a desirable outcome—but never an explicit goal of the center). Scriven believes the most important function of goal-free evaluation, however, is to reduce bias and increase objectivity. In objectives-oriented evaluation, an evaluator is told the goals of the project and is therefore immediately limited in her perceptions—the goals act like blinders, causing her to miss important outcomes not directly related to those goals.

For example, suppose an evaluator is told that the goals of a dropout rehabilitation program are to (1) bring dropouts back into school, (2) train them in productive vocations, and (3) place them in stable jobs. She may spend all her time designing and applying measures to look at such things as how many dropouts have been recruited back into school, how many have been placed and remain placed in paying jobs, and so forth. These are worthwhile goals, and the program may be successful on all these counts. But what about the fact that the crime rate of other (nondropout) children in the high school has tripled since the dropouts were brought back into the school? Indeed, a hidden curriculum seems to have sprung up: stripping cars. This negative side effect is much more likely to be picked up by the goal-free evaluator than by the objectives-oriented evaluator working behind her built-in blinders.

The following are major characteristics of goal-free evaluation:
- The evaluator purposefully avoids becoming aware of the program goals.
- Predetermined goals are not permitted to narrow the focus of the evaluation study.
- Goal-free evaluation focuses on *actual* outcomes rather than intended program outcomes.
- The goal-free evaluator has minimal contact with the program manager and staff.
- Goal-free evaluation increases the likelihood that unanticipated side effects will be noted.

It might be helpful to point out that objectives-oriented and goal-free evaluation are not mutually exclusive. Indeed, they supplement one another. The internal staff evaluator of necessity conducts a goal-directed evaluation. She can hardly hope to avoid knowing the goals of the program, and it would be unwise to ignore them even if she could. Program managers obviously need to know how well the program is meeting its goals, and the internal evaluator uses goal-directed evaluation to provide such administrators with that information. At the same time, it is important to know how others judge the program, not only on the basis of how well it does what it is *supposed* to do but also on the basis of what it *does* in all areas, on *all* its outcomes, intended or not. This is the task for the external goal-free evaluator who knows nothing of the program goals. Thus, goal-directed evaluation and goal-free evaluation can work well together. And while the major share of a program's evaluation resources should not go to goal-free evaluation, it is tragic when all resources go to goal-directed evaluation on a program where the goals do not even begin to include the important educational outcomes.

APPLICATION EXERCISE

1. Mrs. Jackson is a member of the faculty of Greenlawn Middle School in Antioch, Ohio. Although students are still grouped by grades, within each grade a team of teachers cooperates to develop lessons that are interdisciplinary. Individual members of the team have been assigned responsibility for the areas of English, mathematics, science, and social studies. Mrs. Jackson has decided to evaluate her area of responsibility—the seventh-grade English section of the instructional program. Her evaluation tentatively includes:

   a. Administration of a standardized English achievement test in September and June. She plans to compare the means of the pre- and posttest groups with national norms for the tests.

   b. Monthly interviews of a 10 percent sample of her class to assess student reaction to the English portion of the instructional program.

   c. Complete record keeping of students' progress so assessment may be made of their eighth-grade performance.

   d. Observation by an outside observer twice a month, using a scale she has devised to record pupil interaction during class discussions.

   e. Comparison of the performance of Mrs. Jackson's seventh-grade class on the standardized tests with the performance of the seventh grade at Martindale Junior High School, a traditional junior high.

   Using what you have just learned about Tyler's approach to evaluation, how Hammond's cube can be used in evaluation, and how Provus's Discrepancy Evaluation Model works, advise Mrs. Jackson on her evaluation design. What questions should she be addressing? How could she organize her evaluation? How might she change her design to make it better?

SUGGESTED READINGS

BLOOM, B. S., HASTINGS, J. T., & MADAUS, G. F. (1971). *Handbook on formative and summative evaluation of student learning.* New York: McGraw-Hill.

GOODLAD, J. (1979). *What schools are for.* Bloomington, IN: Phi Delta Kappa Educational Foundation.

HAMMOND, R. L. (1973). Evaluation at the local level. In B. R. WORTHEN & J. R. SANDERS, *Educational evaluation: Theory and Practice.* Belmont, CA: Wadsworth.

METFESSEL, N. S., & MICHAEL, W. B. (1967). A paradigm involving multiple criterion measures for the evaluation of the effectiveness of school programs. *Educational and Psychological Measurement, 27,* 931–943. Also in B. R. WORTHEN & J. R. SANDERS (1973), *Educational Evaluation: Theory and Practice.* Belmont, CA: Wadsworth.

NOWAKOWSKI, J., BUNDA, M. A., WORKING, R., BERNACKI, G., & HARRINGTON, P. (1985). *A handbook of educational variables.* Boston: Kluwer-Nijhoff.

POPHAM, W. J. (1975). *Educational evaluation.* Englewood Cliffs, NJ: Prentice-Hall.

PROVUS, M. (1971). *Discrepancy evaluation.* Berkeley, CA: McCutchan.

SMITH, E. R., & TYLER, R. W. (1942). *Appraising and recording student progress.* New York: Harper & Row.

Chapter 6
Management-Oriented
Evaluation Approaches

Orienting Questions

1. Why has the management-oriented approach to evaluation been so popular among school district, state, and federal government leaders?
2. What are the developmental stages of an educational program and how can management-oriented evaluation help in program development?
3. What techniques are most useful for context evaluation? Input? Process? Product?
4. What are some similarities and differences between Stufflebeam's CIPP evaluation model and UCLA's evaluation model?
5. What are some major strengths and limitations of the management-oriented evaluation approach?

The management-oriented evaluation approach in education is meant to serve decision-makers. Its rationale is that evaluative information is an essential part of good decision making, and that the evaluator can best serve education by serving administrators, policymakers, school boards, teachers, and others in education who need good evaluative information. Developers of this method have relied on a systems approach to education in which decisions are made about inputs, processes, and outputs. By highlighting different levels of decisions and decision-makers, this approach clarifies who will use the evaluation results, how they will use them, and what aspect(s) of the system they are making decisions about. The decision-maker is always the audience to whom a management-oriented evaluation is directed, and the decision-maker's concerns, informational needs, and criteria for effectiveness guide the direction of the study.

DEVELOPERS OF THE MANAGEMENT-ORIENTED EVALUATION APPROACH AND THEIR CONTRIBUTIONS

The most important contributions to a management-oriented approach to evaluation in education have been made by Stufflebeam and Alkin. In the mid-1960s, both recognized the shortcomings of available evaluation approaches. Working to expand and systematize thinking about administrative studies and educational decision making, they built upon concepts only hinted at in the earlier work of Bernard, Mann, Harris, and Washburne. During the 1960s and 1970s, they also drew from management theory (for example, Braybrooke & Lindblom, 1963). Both Stufflebeam and Alkin make the decision(s) of program managers the pivotal organizer for the evaluation. Program objectives are not the main concern. In the models proposed by both theorists, the evaluator, working closely with administrator(s), identifies the decisions the administrator must make and then collects sufficient information about the relative advantages and disadvantages of each decision alternative to allow a fair judgment based on specified criteria. The success of the evaluation rests on the quality of teamwork between evaluators and decision-makers.

The CIPP Evaluation Model

Stufflebeam (1969, 1971, 1983; Stufflebeam & Shinkfield, 1985) has been an influential proponent of a decision-oriented evaluation approach structured to help administrators make good decisions. He views evaluation as "the process of delineating, obtaining, and providing useful information for judging decision alternatives" (Stufflebeam, 1973a, p. 129). He developed an evaluation framework to serve managers and administrators facing four different kinds of educational decisions:

1. *Context evaluation*, to serve *planning decisions*. Determining what needs are to be addressed in an educational program helps in defining objectives for the program.

2. *Input evaluation*, to serve *structuring decisions*. Determining what resources are available, what alternative strategies for the program should be considered, and what plan seems to have the best potential for meeting needs facilitates design of program procedures.

3. *Process evaluation*, to serve *implementing decisions*. How well is the plan being implemented? What barriers threaten its success? What revisions are needed? Once these questions are answered, procedures can be monitored, controlled, and refined.

4. *Product evaluation*, to serve *recycling decisions*. What results were obtained? How well were needs reduced? What should be done with the program after it has run its course? These questions are important in judging program attainments.

The first letter of each type of evaluation—context, input, process, and product—have been used to form the acronym "CIPP," by which Stufflebeam's evaluation model is best known. Table 6.1 summarizes the main features of the four types of evaluation, as proposed by Stufflebeam and Shinkfield (1985, pp. 170–171).

As a logical structure for designing each type of evaluation, Stufflebeam proposed that evaluators follow these steps:

A. *Focusing the Evaluation*
   1. Identify the major level(s) of decision making to be served; for example, local, state, or national.
   2. For each level of decision making, project the decision situations to be served and describe each one in terms of its locus, focus, criticality, timing, and composition of alternatives.
   3. Define criteria for each decision situation by specifying variables for measurement and standards for use in the judgment of alternatives.
   4. Define policies within which the evaluator must operate.
B. *Collection of Information*
   1. Specify the source of the information to be collected.
   2. Specify the instruments and methods for collecting the needed information.
   3. Specify the sampling procedure to be employed.
   4. Specify the conditions and schedule for information collection.
C. *Organization of Information*
   1. Provide a format for the information that is to be collected.
   2. Designate a means for performing the analysis.
D. *Analysis of Information*
   1. Select the analytical procedures to be employed.
   2. Designate a means for performing the analysis.
E. *Reporting of Information*
   1. Define the audiences for the evaluation reports.
   2. Specify means for providing information to the audiences.
   3. Specify the format for evaluation reports and/or reporting sessions.
   4. Schedule the reporting of information.
F. *Administration of the Evaluation*
   1. Summarize the evaluation schedule.
   2. Define staff and resource requirements and plans for meeting these requirements.
   3. Specify means for meeting policy requirements for conduct of the evaluation.
   4. Evaluate the potential of the evaluation design for providing information that is valid, reliable, credible, timely, and pervasive.
   5. Specify and schedule means for periodic updating of the evaluation design.
   6. Provide a budget for the total evaluation program.
      (Stufflebeam, 1973b, p. 144)

TABLE 6.1

Four Types of Evaluation

	Context Evaluation	Input Evaluation	Process Evaluation	Product Evaluation
Objective	To define the institutional context, to identify the target population and assess their needs, to identify opportunities for addressing the needs, to diagnose *problems* underlying the *needs*, and to judge whether proposed objectives are sufficiently responsive to the assessed needs.	To identify and assess *system capabilities*, alternative program *strategies*, procedural *designs* for implementing the strategies, budgets, and schedules.	To identify or predict in process, *defects* in the procedural design or its implementation, to provide information for the preprogrammed decisions, and to record and judge procedural events and activities.	To collect descriptions and judgments of outcomes and to relate them to objectives and to context, input, and process information, and to interpret their worth and merit.
Method	By using such methods as system analysis, survey, document review, hearings, interviews, diagnostic tests, and the Delphi technique.	By inventorying and analyzing available human and material resources, solution strategies, and procedural designs for relevance, feasibility and economy. And by using such methods as literature search, visits to exemplary programs, advocate teams, and pilot trials.	By monitoring the activity's potential procedural barriers and remaining alert to unanticipated ones, by obtaining specified information for programmed decisions, by describing the actual process, and by continually interacting with, and observing the activities of project staff.	By defining operationally and measuring outcome criteria, by collecting judgments of outcomes from stakeholders, and by performing both qualitative and quantitative analyses.
Relation to decision making in the change process	For deciding upon the *setting* to be served, the *goals* associated with meeting needs or using opportunities, and the *objectives* associated with solving problems; that is, for *planning* needed changes. And to provide a basis for judging outcomes.	For selecting *sources of support*, solution strategies, and procedural *designs*; that is, for *structuring change* activities. And to provide a basis for judging implementation.	For *implementing and refining the program design and procedure*; that is, for effecting *process control.* And to provide a log of the actual process for later use in interpreting outcomes.	For deciding to *continue, terminate, modify,* or *refocus* a change activity. And to present a clear record of effects (intended and unintended, positive and negative).

Source: Stufflebeam and Shinkfield, 1985, pp. 170–171

The UCLA Evaluation Model

While he was director of the Center for the Study of Evaluation at UCLA, Alkin (1969) developed an evaluation framework that paralleled closely some aspects of the CIPP model. Alkin defined evaluation as "the process of ascertaining the decision areas of concern, selecting appropriate information, and collecting and analyzing information in order to report summary data useful to decision-makers in selecting among alternatives" (Alkin, 1969, p. 2). Alkin's model included the following five types of evaluation:

1. *Systems assessment*, to provide information about the state of the system. (Very similar to context evaluation in the CIPP model.)
2. *Program planning*, to assist in the selection of particular programs likely to be effective in meeting specific educational needs. (Very similar to input evaluation.)
3. *Program implementation*, to provide information about whether a program was introduced to the appropriate group in the manner intended.
4. *Program improvement*, to provide information about how a program is functioning, whether interim objectives are being achieved, and whether unanticipated outcomes are appearing. (Similar to process evaluation.)
5. *Program certification*, to provide information about the value of the program and its potential for use elsewhere. (Very similar to product evaluation.)

Both the CIPP and UCLA frameworks for evaluation appear to be linear and sequential, but the developers have stressed that such is not the case. For example, the evaluator would not have to complete an input evaluation or a systems assessment in order to undertake one of the other types of evaluation listed in the framework. Often evaluators may undertake "retrospective" evaluations (such as a context evaluation or a systems assessment) in preparation for a process or program improvement evaluation study, believing this evaluation approach is cumulative, linear, and sequential; however, such steps are not always necessary. A process evaluation can be done without having completed context or input evaluation studies. At other times, the evaluator may cycle into another type of evaluation if some decisions suggest that earlier decisions should be reviewed. Such is the nature of management-oriented evaluation.

More recent work on the CIPP model has produced working guides for types of evaluation included in that framework. For example, Stufflebeam (1977) advanced the procedure for conducting a *context* evaluation with his guidelines for designing a needs assessment for an educational program or activity.

A guide for use in *input* evaluation was developed by Reinhard (1972). The input evaluation approach that she developed is called the *advocate team technique*. It is used when acceptable alternatives for designing a new program are not available or obvious. The technique creates alternative new designs that are then evaluated and selected, adapted, or combined to create the most viable alternative design for a new program. This technique has been used successfully by the federal government (Reinhard, 1972) and by school districts (Sanders, 1982) to generate options and guide the final design of educational programs.

Procedures proposed by Cronbach (1963) provided useful suggestions for the conduct of *process* evaluation.

Techniques discussed in Chapter 18 of this book (most notably goal-free evaluation and comparative experimental designs) provide information useful in conducting *product* evaluations, as do approaches to evaluation discussed later in Chapter 7.

Other Management-Oriented Evaluation Approaches

In Chapter 5, Provus's Discrepancy Evaluation Model was described as an objectives-oriented evaluation model. Some aspects of that model are also directed toward serving the information needs of educational program managers. It is systems-oriented, focusing on input, process, and output at each of five stages of evaluation: program definition, program installation, program process, program products, and cost-benefit analysis. Even cursory scrutiny of these five types of evaluation reveal close parallels to the CIPP and UCLA evaluation models with respect to their sensitivity to the various decisions managers need to make at each stage of program development.

The utilization-focused evaluation approach of Patton (1978) in one respect could also be viewed as a decision-making approach. He stressed that the process of identifying and organizing relevant decision-makers and information-users is the first step in evaluation. In his view, the use of evaluation findings requires that decision-makers determine what information is needed by various people and arrange for that information to be collected and provided to those persons.

The systems analysis approach has also been suggested by some to be an evaluation approach (for example, House, 1980; Rivlin, 1971; Rossi, Freeman, & Wright, 1979) and if we agreed we would place it with others covered in this chapter. However, we do not consider systems studies to be evaluation because of their narrow research focus on establishing causal links between a few preselected variables and on cost analyses. We consider such studies to be good examples of social research rather than evaluation.

HOW THE MANAGEMENT-ORIENTED EVALUATION APPROACH HAS BEEN USED

The CIPP model has been used in school districts and state and federal government agencies. The Dallas, Texas, Independent School District, for example, established an evaluation office organized around the four types of evaluation in the model. All evaluation activities in that district fall into one or more of these categories. The Saginaw, Michigan, public schools also structured their evaluation work by using the CIPP model, as did the Lansing, Michigan, public schools, and evaluations systems in the Cincinnati and Columbus public school systems in Ohio.

The management-oriented approach to evaluation has guided educators through program planning, operation, and review. Program staff have found this approach a useful guide to program improvement.

This evaluation approach has also been used for accountability purposes. It provides a record-keeping framework that facilitates public review of educational needs, objectives, plans, activities, and outcomes. School administrators and school boards have found this approach useful in meeting public demands for information.

Stufflebeam and Shinkfield (1985) described these two uses of the CIPP model as shown in Figure 6.1:

	Decision Making *(Formative Orientation)*	*Accountability* *(Summative Orientation)*
Context	Guidance for choice of objectives and assignment of priorities.	Record of objectives and bases for their choice along with a record of needs, opportunities, and problems.
Input	Guidance for choice of program strategy. Input for specification of procedural design.	Record of chosen strategy and design and reasons for their choice over other alternatives.
Process	Guidance for implementation.	Record of the actual process.
Product	Guidance for termination, continuation, modification, or installation.	Record of attainments and recycling decisions.

FIGURE 6.1   The Relevance of Four Evaluation Types to Decision Making and Accountability

Source: Stufflebeam and Shinkfield, 1985, p. 164.

STRENGTHS AND LIMITATIONS OF THE MANAGEMENT-ORIENTED EVALUATION APPROACH

This approach has proved appealing to many evaluators and program managers, particularly those at home with the rational and orderly systems approach, to which it is clearly related. Perhaps its greatest strength is that it gives focus to the evaluation. Experienced evaluators know how tempting it is simply to cast a wide net, collecting an enormous amount of information, only later to discard much of it because it is not directly relevant to the key issues or questions the evaluation must address. Deciding precisely what information to collect is essential. Focusing on informational needs and pending decisions of managers limits the range of relevant data and brings the evaluation into sharp focus. As House put it (using the term "decision making approach" to describe the CIPP model and related approaches),

> the decision making approach provides a valuable insight into evaluation. It stresses the importance of the utility of information. Evaluation information is meant to be used. Connecting evaluation to decision-making underlines the purpose of evaluation. It is also practically useful to shape an evaluation in reference to actual decision-making considerations. Even if one cannot define precisely the decision alternatives, one can eliminate a number of lines of inquiry as being irrelevant. (House, 1980, p. 232)

The management-oriented approach to evaluation was instrumental in showing evaluators and educators that they need not wait until an activity or program has run its course before evaluating it. In fact, educators can begin evaluating even when ideas for programs are first discussed. Because of lost opportunities and heavy resource investment, evaluation is generally least effective at the end of a developing program. Of course, educators have found that it's never too late to begin evaluating, even if a program has been in place for years. The decisions are simply different.

The management-oriented evaluation approach is probably the preferred choice in the eyes of most school administrators and boards. This is hardly surprising given the emphasis this approach places on information for decision-makers. By attending directly to the informational needs of people who are to use the evaluation, this approach addressed one of the biggest criticisms of evaluation in the 1960s: that it did not provide useful information.

The CIPP model, in particular, is a useful and simple heuristic tool that helps the evaluator generate potentially important questions to be addressed in an evaluation. For each of the four types of evaluation (CIPP), the evaluator can identify a number of questions about an educational undertaking. The model and the questions it generates also make the evaluation easy to explain to lay audiences.

The management-oriented approach to evaluation supports evaluation of every component of an educational program as it operates, grows, or changes. It stresses the timely use of feedback by decision-makers so that education is not left to flounder or proceed unaffected by updated knowledge about needs, resources, new developments in education, the realities of day-to-day operations, or the consequences of providing education in any given way.

A potential weakness of this approach is the evaluator's occasional inability to respond to questions or issues that may be significant—even critical—but that clash with or at least do not match the concerns and questions of the decision-maker who essentially controls the evaluation.

House also issued a warning when he asked,

> Why should the decision-maker, who is usually identified as the program administrator, be given so much preference? Does this not put the evaluator at the service of top management and make the evaluator the "hired gun" of the program establishment? Does this not make the evaluation potentially unfair and even undemocratic? The answer is that these are potential weaknesses of the decision-making approach. (House, 1980, p. 231)

To build on House's point, we might want to consider the policy uses of evaluations by what Cronbach and others (1980) called the *policy-shaping community*. The policy-shaping community includes: (1) public servants, such as responsible officials at the policy and program levels and the actual operating personnel; and (2) the public, consisting not only of constituents, but also influential persons such as commentators, academic social scientists, philosophers, gadflies, and even novelists or dramatists. Few policy studies have been found to have a direct effect on the policy-shaping community, but evaluations can and do influence these audiences over time. Policy, as a reflection of public values, may be seen as a never-ending aspect of education that continues to be molded or revised as issues, reforms, social causes, and social values change or come to the forefront of attention. We need to remember, as Cronbach has noted, that one important role of the evaluator is to illuminate, not to dictate, the decision. Helping clients to understand the complexity of issues, not to give simple answers to narrow questions, is a role of evaluation.

Another limitation is that, if followed in its entirety, the management-oriented approach can result in costly and complex evaluations. If priorities are not carefully set and followed, the many questions to be addressed using a management-oriented approach can all clamor for attention, leading to an evaluation system as large as the program itself and diverting resources from program activities. In planning evaluation procedures, management-oriented evaluators need to consider the resources and time available. If the management-oriented approach requires more time or resources than are available, another approach may have to be considered.

As a case in point, consider the classroom teacher who has to make decisions about next week's lesson plans. Because of his time limitations, and the limited information that is readily available to him, this teacher may be able to use only the CIPP or UCLA models informally, as an armchair aid. As with any approach, the management-oriented evaluator needs to be realistic about what work is possible and not to promise more than can be delivered.

Finally, this evaluation approach assumes that the important decisions can be clearly identified in advance, that clear decision alternatives can be specified, and that the decisions to be served remain reasonably stable while the evaluation is being done. All of these assumptions about the orderliness and predictability of the decision-making process are suspect and frequently unwarranted. Frequent adjustments may be needed in the original evaluation plan if this approach is to work well.

APPLICATION EXERCISE

A public school system successfully demonstrated its need for federal support for an elementary compensatory education program. They received a $500,000 grant to be spent over a period of three years from July 1, 1986 to June 30, 1989. On March 15, 1986, the Superintendent convened a meeting of the Assistant Superintendent of Elementary Instruction and 30 principals of elementary schools eligible to participate in the proposed program. It was their decision that a thorough evaluation of the reading and mathematics programs in these schools should be completed by September 30, 1986 to identify needs. Alternative strategies for solving needs would then be evaluated and a program would be chosen for the elementary compensatory education project. They also decided to establish an evaluation team that would be responsible for:

1. Conducting the evaluation of the reading and mathematics programs of the eligible schools

2. Evaluating alternative programs to meet the needs of the 30 schools
3. Continually monitoring the program, which would be implemented starting in 1986
4. Collecting information to be reported annually (on June 30 for each year of the grant) to the United States Department of Education.

Using what you have just learned about management-oriented evaluation approaches, advise the evaluation team members about how they should proceed (assuming that it is now March 1986). Be as detailed in your planning as you can be.

SUGGESTED READINGS

ALKIN, M. C. (1969). Evaluation theory development. *Evaluation Comment, 2*, 2–7. Also excerpted in B. R. WORTHEN & J. R. SANDERS (1973), *Educational evaluation: Theory and Practice*. Belmont, CA: Wadsworth.

STUFFLEBEAM, D. L. (1983). The CIPP model for program evaluation. In G. F. MADAUS, M. SCRIVEN, & D. L. STUFFLEBEAM (Eds.), *Evaluation models*. Boston: Kluwer-Nijhoff.

STUFFLEBEAM, D. L., FOLEY, W. J., GEPHART, W. J., GUBA, E. G., HAMMOND, R. L., MERRIMAN, H. O., & PROVUS, M. M. (1971). *Educational evaluation and decision making*. Itasca, IL: F. E. PEACOCK.

STUFFLEBEAM, D. L., & SHINKFIELD, A. J. (1985). *Systematic evaluation*. Boston: Kluwer-Nijhoff.

Chapter 7
Consumer-Oriented Evaluation Approaches

Orienting Questions

1. Consumers of educational products often use product evaluations done by others. If someone were doing product evaluations for you, what criteria would you want that person to use?
2. What educational products are found in most schools? How are purchasing decisions made? What criteria seem to be most important in the selection process?
3. What does the consumer-oriented evaluation approach suggest for those involved in curriculum development?
4. How has the consumer-oriented evaluation approach been used in education?
5. What are some major strengths and limitations of the consumer-oriented evaluation approach?

Independent agencies or individuals who have taken responsibility to compile information on educational products, or assist others in doing so, have promoted the consumer-oriented evaluation approach. Educational products include virtually any aspect of education available in the marketplace: curriculum packages, workshops, instructional media, in-service training opportunities, staff evaluation, forms or procedures, new technology, software and equipment, educational materials and supplies, and even services to schools.

Sales of educational products in the United States alone exceeds $500 million annually. As competition has grown in the educational product industry, marketing strategies have become creative, but often they are not calculated to serve the best interests of the consumer or student. For this reason, some educational evaluators have actively urged consumer education, independent reviews of educational products patterned after the Consumers Union approach, and requirements for objective evidence of product effectiveness. Proposed checklists for rating products and product evaluation reports are two typical outgrowths of this approach.

The consumer-oriented approach to evaluation is predominantly a summative evaluation approach. Developers of educational products have come to realize, however, that using the checklists and criteria of the consumer advocate while the product is being created is the best way to prepare for subsequent public scrutiny. Thus, the checklists and criteria proposed by "watchdog" agencies have become tools for formative evaluation of products still being developed.

DEVELOPERS OF THE CONSUMER-ORIENTED EVALUATION APPROACH AND THEIR CONTRIBUTIONS

The importance of consumer-oriented evaluation seems to have been first recognized during the mid- and late 1960s as new curriculum packages and other educational products began to flood the market. Prior to the 1960s, most materials available to educators were textbooks. With the influx of funds earmarked for product development and federal purchases, however, the marketplace swelled.

Scriven's Concerns and Checklists

Scriven (1967) made a major contribution to this approach with his distinction between formative and summative evaluation. The summative role of evaluation, he said, "[enables] administrators to decide whether the entire finished curriculum, refined by use of the evaluation process in its...[formative] role, represents a sufficiently significant advance on the available alternatives to justify the expense of adoption by a school system" (Scriven, 1967, pp. 41–42). Criteria that Scriven suggested for evaluating any product included the following:
- Evidence of achievement of important educational objectives
- Evidence of achievement of important noneducational objectives (for example, social objectives)
- Follow-up results
- Secondary and unintended effects, such as effects on the teacher, the teacher's colleagues, other students, administrators, parents, the school, the taxpayer, and other incidental positive or negative effects
- Range of utility (that is, for whom will it be useful)
- Moral considerations (unjust uses of punishment or controversial content)
- Costs.

Later, Scriven (1974b) published a product checklist that expanded his earlier criteria. This new product checklist was the result of reviews commissioned by the federal government, focusing on educational products developed by federally sponsored research and development centers and regional laboratories. It was used in the examination of over 90 educational products, most of which underwent many revisions during that review. Scriven stressed that the items in this checklist were *necessitata,* not *desiderata.* They included the following:

1. *Need.* Number affected, social significance, absence of substitutes, multiplicative effects, evidence of need.
2. *Market.* Dissemination plan, size, and importance of potential markets.
3. *Performance—True Field Trials.* Evidence of effectiveness of final version, with typical users, with typical aid, in typical settings, within a typical time frame.
4. *Performance—True Consumer.* Tests run with all relevant "consumers," such as students, teachers, principals, school district staff, state and federal officials, Congress, and taxpayers.
5. *Performance—Critical Comparisons.* Comparative data provided on important competitors such as no-treatment groups, existing competitors, projected competitors, created competitors, and hypothesized competitors.
6. *Performance—Long Term.* Evidence of effects at pertinent times is reported, such as a week to a month after use of the product, a month to a year later, a year to a few years later, and over critical career stages.
7. *Performance—Side Effects.* Evidence of independent study or search for unintended outcomes during, immediately following, and over the long-term product use.
8. *Performance—Process.* Evidence of product use provided to verify product descriptions, causal claims, and the morality of product use.
9. *Performance—Causation.* Evidence of product effectiveness provided through randomized experimental study or through defensible quasi-experimental, ex post facto, or correlational studies.
10. *Performance—Statistical Significance.* Statistical evidence of product effectiveness to make use of appropriate analysis techniques, significance levels, and interpretations.
11. *Performance—Educational Significance.* Educational significance is demonstrated through independent judgments, expert judgments, judgments based on item analysis and raw scores of tests, side effects, long-term effects and comparative gains, and educationally sound use.
12. *Cost-effectiveness.* A comprehensive cost analysis, including expert judgment of costs, independent judgment of costs, and comparison to costs for competitors.
13. *Extended Support.* Plans for postmarketing data collection and improvement, in-service training, updating of aids, and study of new uses and user data.

These are stringent standards, to be sure, but defensible and important—although few textbooks or curriculum packages now on the market would satisfy all of them. Perhaps no one educational product will ever be judged successful on all these criteria, but producers' efforts to meet these standards would have a marked effect on improving the efforts of educational developers.

Scriven continues to be the most avid and articulate advocate of the consumer-oriented evaluation approach, although he is not blind to weaknesses in some of its applications, as noted in the following observation:

We should add a word about what may seem to be the most obvious of all models for a consumerist ideologue, namely *Consumer Reports* product evaluations. While these serve as a good enough model to demonstrate failures in most of the alternatives more widely accepted in program evaluation, especially educational program evaluation, it must not be thought that the present author regards them as flawless. I have elsewhere said something about factual and logical errors and separatist bias in *Consumer Reports* ("Product Evaluation" in N. Smith, ed., *New Models of Program Evaluation*, Sage, 1981). Although *Consumer Reports* is not as good as it was and it has now accumulated even more years across which the separatist/managerial crime of refusal to discuss its methodologies and errors in an explicit and nondefensive way has been exacerbated many times, and although there are now other consumer magazines which do considerably better work than *Consumer Reports* in particular fields, *Consumer Reports* is still a very good model for most types of product evaluation. (Scriven, 1984, p. 75)

Other Checklists and Product Analysis Systems

In the mid-1960s, Komoski was a leader in establishing the Educational Products Information Exchange (EPIE) as an independent product review service modeled after the Consumers Union. Through its newsletter (*EPIE Forum*) and published reports,[28] EPIE has provided much needed evaluative information to state departments of education and school districts that subscribe to its service. EPIE checklists and curriculum analysis guides have also been valuable tools for the educational consumer. In addition, EPIE collects and disseminates information being used in school settings.

Likewise, checklists developed by Morrisett and Stevens (1967), Tyler and Klein (1967), and Eash (1970) have been useful aids to educators responsible for compiling information for use in selecting educational products. The Curriculum Materials Analysis System (CMAS) developed by Morrisett and Stevens, for example, includes the following guidelines for product analysis:[29]

1. *Describe the characteristics of the product*: Media, materials, time needed, style, costs, availability, available performance data, subject matter and content, dominant characteristics of curriculum forms.
2. *Analyze its rationale and objectives*: Describe and evaluate rationale, general objectives, specific objectives, behavioral objectives.
3. *Consider antecedent conditions in using this product*: Pupil characteristics, teacher capabilities and requirements, community and school characteristics, existing curriculum and curriculum organization (vertical and horizontal).
4. *Consider its content*: The cognitive structure, skills to be taught, affective content.
5. *Consider the instructional theory and teaching strategies used in this product*: Appropriateness of teaching strategies, forms, modes, or transactions.
6. *Form overall judgments*: Be sure to consider other descriptive data, reported experiences with the product, pilot tryouts, and outside recommendations.

A variety of product evaluation checklists have been developed and used over the past several years by individual evaluators and agencies. Many serve as valuable guides from which one might develop a checklist tailored for one's own situation. The following checklists developed by the Florida Department of Education (1980) and Patterson (undated) provide good examples of concise review forms useful for heuristic purposes.

LEVEL I

Equipment and Storage Considerations

	yes	no	don't know	N/A*
If equipment is needed to use the materials, is the equipment available and accessible?				
Is space available in the classroom to store the materials?				
Is work space available in the classroom so that materials can be used properly?				

Materials-Use Considerations

	yes	no	don't know	N/A*
Are teachers' guides included in the materials?				
If the materials require innovative or unusual strategies, are there indications that the strategies used in the materials can easily be integrated into your present system, without having long-term negative effects on student learning and classroom management?				
Have materials been field-tested in similar situations and found to be successful?				

Cost Considerations

	yes	no	don't know	N/A*
Is there enough money in the budget?				
Will the materials be used often enough to justify the cost?				
Can parts of the materials be purchased separately from the overall package?				
Can you afford to continue using the materials?				
Are materials well made and likely to withstand repeated use?				

*Not applicable

LEVEL II

Content Considerations

	yes	no	don't know	N/A*
Does the content match course objectives?				
Is the content appropriate?				

Functions-of-Instruction Considerations

	yes	no	don't know	N/A*
Are the materials likely to gain and maintain the learner's attention?				
Are the materials likely to inform the learner of the objective?				
Do the materials provide for recall of relevant learning?				

Do the materials present learning content in appropriate ways?

Do the materials provide learning guidance?

Do the materials provide an opportunity to practice?

Is feedback on the performance provided within the materials?

Are there provisions within the materials for assessing the learner's performance?

Do the materials provide for retention and transfer?

Instructional Strategies Considerations

Are materials practical and easy to use?

Stereotyping and Bias Considerations

Do materials avoid stereotypes and bias?

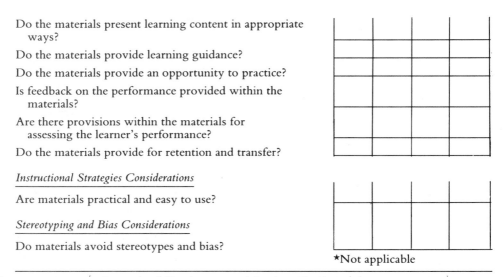

★Not applicable

Source: Center for Instructional Development and Services, Florida State University

HOW THE CONSUMER-ORIENTED EVALUATION APPROACH HAS BEEN USED

As mentioned previously, the consumer-oriented approach to evaluation has been used extensively by government agencies and independent educational consumer advocates such as EPIE to make information available on hundreds of products.

The Joint Dissemination Review Panel (JDRP) in the United States Department of Education has established a classic example of a consumer-oriented evaluation system by setting standards (Tallmadge, 1977) for new educational programs that it will recommend for adoption. Those that pass the JDRP review are approved through the National Dissemination Network for dissemination to school systems throughout the United States.

A role for state departments of education or other educational service agencies, such as intermediate school districts, in using this approach has been discussed by several states in recent years. Rather than evaluating products themselves, and then disseminating their findings to school districts, or merely listing available products, states and service agencies have discussed using standard forms to compile and then disseminate evaluation information about any new product. Guidelines developed for this purpose (Sanders, 1974) address four aspects of a product: its educational processes, content, transportability, and effectiveness. In each case the central concern has been, "What does one need to know about a product before deciding whether to adapt or install it?" Questions posed within each category include the following:

Process Information

1. What is the nature and frequency of interactions among (combinations of) students/teachers/administrators/relevant others? Have these interactions been evaluated?

Instructional Materials Review Form:

Marvin Patterson
Center for Studies in
 Vocational Education
Florida State University

Title(s)_____ _____ Author(s) _____ Publisher _____ Latest Copyright Date _____	☐ Retain for Committee Review ☐ Bibliography Only ☐ Reject (Comments:

Use the following code to rate materials:
+   means yes or good quality   —   means no or poor quality
o   means all right, but not of especially good quality   NA   means not applicable

						Committee Members
						1. Does the content cover a significant portion of the program competencies?
						2. Is the content up-to-date?
						3. Is the reading/math level appropriate for most students?
						4. Are objectives, competencies, or tasks stated in the student materials.
						5. Are tests included in the materials?
						6. Are performance checklists included?
						7. Are hands-on activities included?
						8. How many outside materials are required? + means 0-1 materials o means 2-3 materials — means 4+ materials
						9. Would you use these materials in your training program?
						If the materials to this point appear to be a possible choice for selection, continue with your review. Stop if the materals appear to be too poor for further consideration.
						10. Is a Teacher's Guide included which offers management suggestions for the materials?
						11. Is the material presented in a logical sequence?
						Quality Judgments. Use +, o, — to rate the quality of the products.
						12. Quality of objectives, competencies, and/or tasks
						13. Degree of match between learning activities and objectives.
						14. Quality of test items and degree of match with objectives.
						15. Quality of performance checklists and degree of match with objectives.
						16. Quality of directions for how students are to proceed through the materials.
						17. Quality of drawings, photographs, and/or other visuals.
						18. Overall design of the learning activities for individualized instruction.
						19. Emphasis on safety practices (when needed)
						20. Degree of freedom from bias with respect to sex, race, national origin, age, religion, etc. (see provided guidelines).
						21. Quality of management procedures for teachers (teacher's guides, etc.).
						22. (Optional) List the career-map competencies covered by these materials.

Comments:

Source: Center for Instructional Development and Services, Florida State University

2. Is the teaching strategy to be employed described so that its appropriateness can be determined? Has the strategy been evaluated?
3. Is the instructional schedule required by the program or product described so that its feasibility can be determined? Has the schedule been evaluated?
4. Are the equipment and facilities required by the program or product described so that their feasibility can be determined? Have they been evaluated?
5. Are the budget and human resource requirements of the program or product listed so that their feasibility can be determined? Have the following requirements been included?
   a. Start-up and continuation budget requirements?
   b. Administration/teaching staff/parent or advisory committees/student resource requirements?
   c. In-service?
6. Is evaluation an integral part of the (a) development, and (b) implementation of the program or product?

Content Information

1. Is the existence or lack of basic program or product elements, such as the following, noted?
   a. Clearly stated objectives?
   b. Sufficient directions?
   c. Other materials required?
   d. Prerequisite knowledge/attitudes required?
   e. Fit with disciplinary knowledge base and existing curriculum and sequence of a school?
2. Have these elements been evaluated?
3. Has the content of the program or product been evaluated by recognized content specialists?
4. Is there sufficient information about the program or product rationale and philosophy to permit a decision about whether it is within the realm of school responsibility or consistent with a district's philosophy? (School responsibility has traditionally encompassed such areas as intellectual development, personal development, citizenship, social development, educational and personal adjustment, physical growth and development.)
5. Do the objectives of the program or product have cogent rationales? Are they compatible with the school philosophy and the values of the community?

Transportability Information

Referring to the Bracht and Glass (1968) treatment of external validity, three elements relating to transportability appear critical: (1) geography and setting, (2) people, and (3) time.

1. What information is available regarding classroom/school/community settings in which the program or product has been used effectively, in terms of:

    a. Size/numbers?
    b. Organization?
    c. Political factors?
    d. Legal issues?
    e. Facilities?
    f. Wealth?
    g. Occupational factors?
    h. Geographical indices (for example, rural/urban)?
    i. Cultural factors?
    j. Public/nonpublic factors?
    k. Philosophical issues?

2. What information is available concerning the teachers/students/administrators/relevant others with whom the program or product has been used effectively in relation to the following:
    a. Age/grade?
    b. Experience?
    c. Entrance knowledge?
    d. Expectations/preferences/interests?
    e. Ethnic/cultural makeup?

3. What information is available regarding the time of year in which the program or product has been used effectively?

4. Does the program or product have special requirements in areas such as the following:
    a. Training?
    b. Organization or facilities?
    c. Additional materials or equipment?
    d. Research people/specialists?

Effectiveness Information

1. Has technically sound information about the effects of the program or product on its target audience been obtained using one of more of the following procedures:
    a. Comparison to established base (pre-post)?
    b. Prediction (make success estimates using regression techniques)?
    c. Comparison to local or state norms?
    d. Comparison against objectives or predetermined standards?
    e. Comparison of student and/or teacher behaviors to those for competing programs or products?

2. Is there evidence that the program or product has eliminated a documented need, such as
    a. Cost savings?
    b. Improved morale?
    c. Faster learning rate?

3. Is immediate and follow-up effectiveness information available?

These questions could easily be cast into a checklist formed by using the following response categories:

YES	*NO*	*IMPLIED*	*NOT APPLICABLE*
Information available:			

Although not necessarily a product evaluation enterprise, the *Mental Measurement Yearbooks* (Mitchell, 1985) must be mentioned as a form of consumer-oriented evaluation. These yearbooks contain critical reviews of commercially available tests marketed in the United States and several other English-speaking countries. As educational products, these tests deserve the same scrutiny any product receives, and the *Mental Measurement Yearbooks* have provided a valuable service in this regard to educators.

STRENGTHS AND LIMITATIONS OF THE CONSUMER-ORIENTED EVALUATION APPROACH

Developers of the consumer-oriented approach to evaluation have provided a valuable service to educators in two ways: (1) they have made available evaluations of educational products as a service to educators who may not have the time or information to do the job thoroughly; and (2) they have advanced the knowledge of educators about the criteria most appropriate to use in selecting educational products. The checklists that have evolved from years of consumer-oriented product evaluations are useful and simple evaluation tools.

Consumers have become more aware of the sales ploys of the education industry, thanks to the efforts of consumer-oriented evaluators. Educators are (or should be) less vulnerable to sales tactics than they were 20 years ago. They are (or should be) more discriminating in the way they select products.

The educational product industry has a long way to go, however, in being responsive to educators' needs. Just ask a textbook sales rep for information about the performance or proven effectiveness of his product, and see what kind of information you get. Most of the time it will be either anecdotal testimony or scanty, poorly conceived product evaluation. Very seldom do corporations spend the time or money needed to acquire acceptable information about their products' performance. Educational consumers must insist on such information if the educational product industry is to take product evaluation seriously.

The consumer-oriented approach to evaluation is not without drawbacks (although they seem small compared to its benefits). It can increase the cost of educational products. The time and money invested in product testing will usually be passed on to the consumer. Moreover, the use of stringent standards in product development and purchase may suppress creativity because of the risk involved. There is a place for trial programs in schools before products are fully adopted. By developing long-term plans for change, educators can give untested products a chance without consuming large portions of the budget. Cooperative trial programs with the educational product industry may be in the best interest of all.

Finally, the consumer-oriented approach to evaluation threatens local initiative development because teachers or curriculum specialists may become increasingly dependent on outside products and consumer services. Educators need to place the purchase of outside products in perspective so that they are not overly dependent on the availability of other people's work. We agree with those who contend that we need to be less concerned with developing and purchasing teacher-proof products and more concerned with supporting product-proof teachers—teachers who think for themselves and who take the initiative in addressing student needs.

APPLICATION EXERCISE

Teachers in each academic department of a senior high school are given a choice of curricular programs to use in their classrooms. This policy is designed to take full advantage of the range of capabilities of individual faculty members. All faculty members are required to prepare an evaluation of their program and circulate these reports among the faculty. These evaluations are to be conducted in keeping with the evaluation guidelines established by the curriculum council. The guidelines require:

1. A statement from each teacher at end of year about the goals for his course and an assessment of the extent to which these goals were met using the selected program.
2. Submission of information from each teacher about the comparison of his pupils' performance and the performance of pupils using a different curricular program.
3. An outside assessment of the appropriateness of the selected program for the teacher's stated goals.
4. A comparison of student performance on standardized tests to national norms.
5. A complete list of test items used during the year. Results for each item to be reported.

Using what you have just learned about consumer-oriented evaluation, what changes in the evaluation process would you suggest to the curriculum council? How could faculty reports be structured so that other schools could benefit from their consumer reports?

SUGGESTED READINGS

SCRIVEN, M. (1974b). Standards for the evaluation of educational programs and products. In G. D. BORICH (Ed.), *Evaluating educational programs and products.* Englewood Cliffs, NJ: Educational Technology Publications. Also in W. J. POPHAM (Ed.). (1974). *Evaluation in education.* Berkeley, CA: McCutchan.

TALLMADGE, G. K. (1977). *Ideabook: JDRP.* (ERIC DL 48329). Washington, DC: U.S. Government Printing Office.

Chapter 8
Expertise-Oriented
Evaluation Approaches

Orienting Questions

1. What are the arguments for and against using professional judgment as the means for evaluating educational programs?
2. Under what conditions would accreditation, blue-ribbon panels, or connoisseurship be methods of choice for conducting an evaluation?
3. What criteria would you use to screen experts in order to select the best for an expertise-oriented evaluation?
4. What differences exist between formal and informal professional review systems?
5. What are some major strengths and limitations of the expertise-oriented evaluation approach?

The expertise-oriented approach to evaluation, probably the oldest and most widely used, depends primarily upon professional expertise to judge an educational institution, program, product, or activity. For example, the worth of a curriculum would be assessed by curriculum or subject-matter experts who would observe the curriculum in action, examine its content and underlying learning theory or, in some other way, glean sufficient information to render a considered judgment about its value.

Although subjective professional judgments are involved to some degree in all the evaluation approaches described thus far, this approach is decidedly different because of its direct, open reliance on subjective professional expertise as the primary evaluation strategy. Such expertise may be provided by the evaluator(s) or by someone else, depending on who offers most in the substance or procedures being evaluated.

Several specific evaluation processes are variants of this approach, including doctoral oral examinations, proposal review panels, professional reviews conducted by professional accreditation bodies, reviews of institutions or individuals by state or national licensing agencies, reviews of educators' performance for decisions concerning promotion or tenure, peer reviews of articles submitted to "refereed" professional journals, site visits of educational programs conducted at the behest of the program's sponsor, reviews and recommendations of prestigious "blue-ribbon" panels, and even the critique offered by the ubiquitous expert who exists, at least one to every educational system, and whose *raison d'etre* is to serve in a self-appointed watchdog role.

To impose some order, we choose to organize and discuss these various manifestations of expertise-oriented evaluation within four categories: (1) formal professional review systems; (2) informal professional review systems; (3) ad hoc panel reviews; and (4) ad hoc individual reviews. Differences in these categories are shown in Table 8.1, along the following dimensions:

1. Is there an existing structure for operating the review?
2. Are published standards used as part of the review?
3. Are reviews scheduled at specified intervals?
4. Does the review include opinions of multiple experts?
5. Do results of the review have an impact on the status of whatever is reviewed?

To this we have added a fifth category, namely educational connoisseurship and criticism, to discuss an interesting expertise-oriented approach that does not fit neatly into the other categories or dimensions shown in Table 8.1.

Site visitation, frequently the mode for conducting expertise-oriented evaluations, is not itself an approach to evaluation; rather, it is a method that might be used not only here but also with other evaluation approaches. Site-visit methods and techniques are discussed in Chapter 18, along with other techniques often used by expertise-oriented evaluators.[31]

DEVELOPERS OF THE EXPERTISE-ORIENTED EVALUATION APPROACH AND THEIR CONTRIBUTIONS

It is hard to pinpoint the origins of this approach, for it has been long with us. It was formally used in education in the 1800s, when schools began to standardize college entrance requirements. Informally, it has been in use since the first time an

TABLE 8.1

Some Features of Four Types of Expertise-Oriented Evaluation Approaches

Type of Expertise-Oriented Evaluation Approach	Existing Structure	Published Standards	Specified Schedule	Opinions of Multiple Experts	Status Affected by Results
Formal Review System	Yes	Yes	Yes	Yes	Usually
Informal Review System	Yes	Rarely	Sometimes	Yes	Usually
Ad Hoc Panel Review	No	No	No	Yes	Sometimes
Ad Hoc Individual Review	No	No	No	No	Sometimes

individual to whom expertise was publicly accorded rendered a judgment about the quality of some educational endeavor (and history is mute on when that occurred). Several movements and individuals have given impetus to the various types of expertise-oriented evaluations, as described below.

Formal Professional Review Systems

We would define a formal professional review system as one having (1) structure or organization established to conduct periodic reviews of educational endeavors; (2) published standards (and possibly instruments) for use in such reviews; (3) a prespecified schedule (for example, every five years) on which reviews will be conducted; (4) opinions of several experts combining to reach the overall judgments of value; and (5) an impact on the status of that which is reviewed, depending on the outcome.

   Accreditation.   To many, the most familiar formal professional review system is that of *accreditation*, the process whereby an organization grants approval of educational institutions. Beginning in the late 1800s, national and regional accreditation agencies gradually supplanted in the United States the borrowed Western European system of school inspections, and these became a potent force in education during the 1930s. Education was not alone in institutionalizing accreditation processes to determine and regulate the quality of its institutions. Parallel efforts were underway in other professions, including medicine and law, as concern over quality led to wide scale acceptance of professionals judging the efforts of fellow professionals. Perhaps the most memorable example is Flexner's (1910) examination of medical schools in the United States and Canada in the early 1900s, which led to the closing of numerous schools he cited as inferior. As Floden (1983) has noted, Flexner's study was not accreditation in the strict sense, because medical schools did not participate voluntarily, but it certainly qualified as accreditation in the broader sense: a classic example of private judgment evaluating educational institutions.

   Flexner's approach differed from most contemporary accreditation efforts in two other significant ways. First, Flexner was not a member of the profession whose efforts he presumed to judge. An educator with no pretense of medical expertise, Flexner nonetheless ventured to judge the quality of medical training in two nations. He argued that common sense was perhaps the most relevant form of expertise:

> Time and time again it has been shown that an unfettered lay mind, is...best suited to undertake a general survey.... The expert has his place, to be sure; but if I were asked to suggest the most promising way to study legal education, I should seek a layman, not a professor of law; or for the sound way to investigate teacher training, the last person I should think of employing would be a professor of education. (Flexner, 1960, p. 71)

It should be noted that Flexner's point was only partially supported by his own study. Although he was a layman in terms of medicine, he was an *educator*, and his judgments were directed at medical *education*, not the practice of medicine, so even here appropriate expertise seemed to be applied.

Second, Flexner made no attempt to claim empirical support for the criteria or process he employed because he insisted that the standards he used were the "obvious" indicators of school quality and needed no such support. His methods of collecting information and reaching judgments were simple and straight-forward: "A stroll through the laboratories disclosed the presence or absence of apparatus, museum specimens, library, and students; and a whiff told the inside story regarding the manner in which anatomy was cultivated" (Flexner, 1960, p. 79).

Third, Flexner dispensed with the professional niceties and courteous criticisms that seem to typify even the negative findings yielded by today's accreditation processes. Excerpts of his report of one school included scathing indictments such as "Its so-called equipment is dirty and disorderly beyond description. Its outfit in anatomy consists of a small box of bones and the dried-up, filthy fragments of a single cadaver. A cold and rusty incubator, a single microscope, . . . and no access to the County Hospital. The school is a disgrace to the state whose laws permit its existence" (Flexner, 1910, p. 190).

Although an excellent example of expertise-oriented evaluation (if expertise as an educator, not a physician, is the touchstone), Flexner's approach is much more like that of contemporary educational evaluators who see judgment as the *sine qua non* of evaluation and who see many of the criteria as obvious extensions of common sense (for example, Scriven, 1973). But today's educational accreditation systems seem for the most part to have grown up differently. Whereas Flexner's review used the same process and standards for all medical schools reviewed, there is much more variability in contemporary national and regional accreditation systems in education. Agencies in the United States, such as the North Central Association (NCA) for accrediting secondary schools or the National Council for the Accreditation of Teacher Education (NCATE), have developed dualistic systems that include some minimum standards deemed important for all schools, along with an internal self-study component in which institutions can present their unique mission and goals, defend their reasonableness and importance, and report on how well that self-study approach is accomplishing its goals and what capa-bilities it offers for the foreseeable future. These two facets of accreditation are emphasized to greatly different degrees in various accreditation systems, leading Kirkwood (1982) to criticize accreditation for lacking "similarity of aims, uni-formity of process, or comparability among institutions" (Kirkwood, 1982, p. 9), whereas others complain that the imposition of external standards by accrediting agencies denies institutions the opportunity of developing unique strengths.

Current accreditation systems also depend on the assumption that only members of a profession are qualified to judge the activities of their peers. Not only are accreditation site-visit team members drawn from the profession or occupation whose work they will judge, but also the standards and criteria are developed solely by members of that professional fraternity.[32] For example, "The standards of techniques for accreditation of schools of teacher education have been deter-mined by committees, comprised mainly of practicing teachers and teacher educa-tors" (Floden, 1983, p. 262).

Although accreditation has historically focused on the adequacy of facilities, qualifications of faculty, and perceived appropriateness of the educational design and processes used, rather than to assess the educational status of school graduates, several current accreditation systems aspire to justify their criteria and standards on the basis of empirical links to performance of program graduates (for example, Dickey & Miller, 1972; Study Commission, 1976). In large part such efforts are reactions to critics of accreditation who have typified accreditation as (in private correspondence from an unnamed colleague) "a bunch of anachronistic old fogies who bumble about with meters, measuring lighting and BTUs and counting the ratio of children per toilet, but failing to measure anything which could be conceived by any stretch of the imagination as related to what children are learning." Though obviously far overdrawn, such a caricature strikes a sensitive nerve among people responsible for accreditation systems, and such criticisms may account, at least in part, for a gradual de-emphasis on such quantitative indicators as square footage per student or number of volumes in the library and a move toward more qualitative indices dealing with purposes of schooling.

As accreditation systems have matured, they have taken on commonalities that extend to the accreditation of most primary, secondary, and professional schools, permitting Scriven (1984) to describe the distinctive features of contemporary accreditation as including (1) published standards; (2) a self-study by the institution; (3) a team of external assessors; (4) a site visit; (5) a site-team report on the institution, usually including recommendations; (6) a review of the report by some distinguished panel; and (7) a final report and accreditation decision by the accrediting body. Although not every accrediting system follows this prescription completely,[33] this is an excellent description of most accreditation systems operating in education today.

Although viewed by some (for example, Scriven, 1984) as not truly an evaluative system, others (see Orlans, 1971, 1975) see accreditation as very much evaluative. Regardless of which view one holds, most would agree that accreditation has played an important role in educational change. Publication and application of the *Evaluative Criteria* (National Study of School Evaluation, 1978) has helped shape recent changes in secondary schools in the United States. It is true that accrediting agencies have little real power over agencies who fail to take their recommendations seriously, as Floden states:

> If accreditors instruct an institution to make particular changes, three options are open. First, officials may amass the necessary funds and make the changes. Second, they may decide the changes cannot be made and close their doors. Third, they may decide not to worry about what the accreditors say and make no changes. If an institution exercises either of the first two options, the aims of accreditation have been realized. When the third option is taken, the process of accreditation has failed to achieve its main purpose. (Floden, 1983, p. 268)

Yet in our experience, the third option is only infrequently exercised. Fully accredited status is, if nothing more, a symbol of achievement highly valued by most educational institutions. Although there may be much room for improvement in the accreditation process, it appears to be a formal review process that will be with us for a long time and, if the upsurge of thoughtful analyses of accreditation issues, problems, and potential (for example, Kells & Robertson, 1980) is any indication, there is reason to be optimistic that its impact can be positive.

Other Formal Review Systems. Despite the wide reach of accreditation, there are those who feel it is an incestuous system that often fails to police itself adequately. As House (1980) has stated:

> Public disenchantment with professionally controlled evaluation is reflected in the declining credibility of accrediting agencies. At one time it was sufficient for an institution to be accredited by the proper agency for the public to be assured of its quality —but no longer. Parents are not always convinced that the school program is of high quality when it is accredited by the North Central Association. In addition, political control of accrediting activities is shifting to state governments. (House, 1980, p. 238)

Because of such concerns over accreditation's credibility, coupled with the pervasive feeling that decisions "closer to home" are preferable, many state boards or departments of education are conducting their own reviews of elementary, secondary, and professional schools. Although these typically supplement rather than supplant reviews by private accrediting bodies, and generally use similar review strategies, they seem of greater consequence to institutions and programs reviewed because negative reviews result not only in loss of status but also possible loss of funding or even termination.

Consider, for example, the Utah State Board of Regent's system for reviewing academic departments within the state's tax-supported universities and colleges.[34] The process and the structure for conducting these reviews have been formalized, general standards exist, a review schedule (every seven years) has been established, teams of experts in the academic discipline (also some "outsiders" to avoid bias and promote breadth of perspective) are used, and the results can influence both the future funding for the department and even its continued existence (though that is a rare outcome, indeed).

Newly proposed personnel evaluation procedures in education, such as competency tests for teachers, could eventually become institutionalized evaluative systems of a sort should they survive the political crossfire that makes any teacher-evaluation system an easy target for a demanding but uninformed public.

Informal Professional Review Systems

Many professional review systems have a structure and set of procedural guidelines and use multiple reviewers. Yet some lack the formal review system's published standards or specified review schedule. For example, in the United States, state departments of education were required by federal law, over a period of many years, to establish a system to evaluate all programs and projects funded under a specific funding authorization designed to increase innovation in schools. Compliance varied widely, but those states that conscientiously complied established an evaluation structure in which districts receiving such funds were reviewed by teams of experts on a scheduled basis (for example, annually), with the results used to determine future funding levels and program continuation.[35]

Other examples of informal expertise-oriented review systems include review of professors for determining rank advancement or tenure status. Such reviews generally follow institutionalized structures and procedures, include input from several professional peers,[36] and certainly can influence the status of the individual professor. Sometimes review schedules are set (for instance, some university policies require annual reviews of individuals in any rank lower than professor for five years or more), but usually the timing is dependent on the applicant's petitioning for review whenever he or she feels prepared. Reviewers rarely use prespecified, published standards or criteria. Such standards are developed by each rank and promotion committee (a group of expert peers) within broad guidelines specified by the university and department and possibly by an existing statement of the role the individual is expected to play in contributing to those goals.

 A graduate student's supervisory committee, composed of experts in the student's chosen field, is another example of an informal system for conducting expert-oriented evaluation. Structures exist for regulating such professional reviews of competence, but the committee members determine the standards for judging each student's preparation and competence. Few would question whether results of this review system affect the status and welfare of graduate students.

Some may consider the systems for obtaining peer reviews of manuscripts submitted to professional periodicals to be examples of informal professional review systems. Perhaps. Many journals do use multiple reviewers, chosen for their expertise in the content of the manuscript, and sometimes empaneled to provide continuity to the review board. In our experience, however, the review structure and standards of most professional organs shift with each appointment of a new editor, and reviews occur whenever manuscripts are submitted, rather than on any regular schedule. In some ways, journal reviews may be a better example of the ad hoc professional review process discussed below.

Ad Hoc Panel Reviews

Unlike the ongoing formal and informal review systems discussed above, many professional reviews by expert panels occur only at irregular intervals, when circumstances demand. Generally, these reviews are related to no institutionalized structure for evaluation and use no predetermined standards. Such professional reviews are usually "one-shot" evaluations prompted by a particular, time-bound need for evaluative information. Of course, a particular agency may, over time, commission many ad hoc panel reviews to perform similar functions without their collectively being viewed as an institutionalized review system.

Funding Agency Review Panels. Many funding agencies use peer-review panels to review competitive proposals. Reviewers read and comment on each proposal and meet as a group to discuss and resolve any differences in their various perceptions.[37] Worthen (1982) provided a manual of proposal review guidelines and instruments for use by external review panels, including (1) preparing for the proposal review (selecting reviewers, structuring review panels, preparing and training reviewers in the use of review instruments); (2) conducting the proposal review (individual evaluation procedures, total panel evaluation procedures, methods for eliminating bias); and (3) presenting results of proposal reviews (summarizing review results). Justiz and Moorman (1985) and Shulman (1985) have also discussed particular proposal review procedures that depend upon the professional judgment of panels of experts.

Blue-Ribbon Panels. A prestigious "blue-ribbon panel," such as the National Commission on Excellence in Education, which was discussed in Chapter 1, is an example of an ad hoc review panel. Members of such panels are appointed because of their experience and expertise in the field being studied. Such panels are typically charged with reviewing a particular situation, documenting their observations, and making recommendations for action. Given the visibility of such panels, the acknowledged expertise of panel members is important if the panel's findings are to be credible. On more local scales, where ad hoc review panels are frequently used as an evaluative strategy on almost all types of educational endeavors, expertise of panel members is no less an issue, even though the reviewers may be of local or regional repute rather than national renown.

Although recommendations of ad hoc panels of experts may have major impact, they also may be ignored, for there is often no formalized body charged with the mandate of following up on their advice.

Ad Hoc Individual Reviews

Another form of expertise-oriented evaluation in education resides in the ubiquitous individual professional review of any educational entity by any individual selected for her expertise to judge its value. Employment of a consultant to perform an individual review of some educational program or activity is commonplace. Such expert review is a particularly important process for evaluating educational textbooks, instructional media products, educational tests, and the like. Such instructional materials need not be reviewed on site, but can be sent to the expert, as suggested by Welch and Walberg (1968). A good example is the review of commercially available tests used by the Buros Institute (see Mitchell, 1985).

Educational Connoisseurship and Criticism

The roles of the theater critic, art critic, and literary critic are well-known and, in the eyes of many, useful roles. Critics are not without their faults (as we shall discuss later), but they are good examples of direct and efficient application of expertise to that which is judged. Indeed, few evaluative approaches in education are likely to produce such parsimonious and pithy portrayals as that of one Broadway critic who evaluated one new play with a single-line summary: "The only thing wrong with this play is that it was performed with the curtain up!"

Although not championing one-line indictments, Eisner (1975, 1976, 1979a, 1979b) does propose that educators, like critics of the arts, bring their expertise to bear in evaluating the quality of education. Eisner does not propose a scientific paradigm but rather an artistic one, which he sees as an important qualitative, humanistic, "nonscientific" supplement to more traditional inquiry methods.[38]

Eisner (1975) has written that this approach requires *educational connoisseurship* and *educational criticism*. Connoisseurship is the art of appreciation—not necessarily a liking or preference for that which is observed, but rather an awareness of its qualities and the relationships among them. The educational connoisseur, in Eisner's view, is aware of the complexities in educational settings and possesses refined perceptual capabilities that makes the appreciation of such complexity possible. The connoisseur's perceptual acuity results largely from a knowledge of what to look for (advance organizers, or critical guideposts), gained through a backlog of previous relevant experience.

The analogy of wine tasting is used by Eisner (1975) to show how one must have a great deal of experience[39] to be able to distinguish what is significant about a wine, using a set of techniques to discern qualities such as body, color, bite, bouquet, flavor, aftertaste, and the like, to judge its overall quality. The connoisseur's refined palate and "gustatory memory" of other wines tasted is what enables him or her to distinguish subtle qualities lost on an ordinary drinker of wine and to render judgments, rather than mere preferences. Connoisseurship does not, however, require a public description or judgment of that which is perceived, for the latter moves one into the area of criticism.

"Criticism is the art of disclosing the qualities of events or objects that connoisseurship perceives" (Eisner, 1979a, p. 197), as when the wine connoisseur either returns the wine or leans back with satisfaction to declare it of acceptable, or better, quality. Educational evaluators are cast as educational critics whose connoisseurship enables them to give a public rendering of the quality and significance of that which is evaluated. Criticism is not a negative appraisal, as Eisner presents it, but rather an educational process intended to enable individuals to recognize qualities and characteristics that might otherwise have been unnoticed and unappreciated. Criticism, to be complete, requires description, interpretation, and evaluation of that which is observed. "Critics are people who talk in special ways about what they encounter. In educational settings criticism is the public side of connoisseurship" (Eisner, 1975, p. 13). Educational evaluation, then, becomes educational criticism. The evaluator is the "instrument," and the data-collecting, analyzing, and judging are largely hidden within the evaluator's mind, analogous to the evaluative processes of art criticism or wine tasting. As a consequence, the expertise—training, experience, and credentials—of the evaluator is crucial, for the validity of the evaluation depends on her perception. Yet, different judgments from different critics are tolerable, and even desirable, for the purpose of criticism is to expand perceptions, not to consolidate all judgments into a single definitive statement.

Kelly (1978) has also likened educational evaluation to criticism by using literary criticism as his analogy. Although different in some features from Eisner's approach, it is similar enough to be considered as another example of this expertise-oriented evaluation approach.

HOW THE EXPERTISE-ORIENTED EVALUATION APPROACH HAS BEEN USED

As we noted earlier, this evaluation approach has been broadly used by both national and regional accreditation agencies. Two rather different types of accreditation exist. One is *institutional accreditation*, where the entire institution is accredited, including all of its more specific entities and activities, however complex. In essence, such institutional endorsement means the accrediting body has concluded that the educational institution, in general, meets acceptable standards of quality. The second type is *specialized or program accreditation*, which deals with various subunits in an institution,[40] such as particular academic or professional training programs. As Kirkwood has noted, "institutional accreditation is not equivalent to the specialized accreditation of each of the several programs in an institution" (Kirkwood, 1982, p. 9). Rather, specialized accrediting processes are usually more specific, rigorous, and prescriptive than are those used in institutional accreditation. Most specialized accreditation bodies are national in scope and frequently are the major multipurpose professional associations (for example, the American Psychological Association or the American Medical Association), whereas institutional accreditation is more often regional and conducted by agencies that exist solely or primarily for that purpose (for example, in the United States, the North Central Association or the New England Association).

A good example of how accreditation by private professional agencies and government-sponsored professional reviews are combined comes from Bernhardt's (1984) description of the evaluation processes of state, regional, and national education agencies, which collectively oversee teacher education programs in California:

> Colleges and Universities in California must be accredited or approved by at least three agencies to offer approved programs of teacher education. Private institutions must first have the approval of the State Department of Education's Office of Private Postsecondary Education (OPPE) to offer *degree* programs. Public institutions must be authorized by their respective California State University and University of California systems. Second, institutions must be accredited by the Western Association of Schools and Colleges (WASC). Then, institutions must submit a document that states that the program is in compliance with all CTC guidelines in order to gain the approval of the Commission on Teacher Credentialing (CTC).
>
> In addition to OPPE, WASC, and CTC accreditation, educational institutions often choose to be accredited by the National Council for Accreditation of Teacher Education (NCATE). (Bernhardt, 1984, p. 1)

Yes, formal professional review systems are alive and well, at least in California.

Other uses of expertise-oriented evaluation are discussed by House (1980), who notes the upsurge of university internal-review systems of colleges, departments, and programs. He notes that such professional reviews are not only useful in making internal decisions and reallocating funds in periods of financial austerity but also may deflect suggestions that such programs should be reviewed by higher-education boards.

Uses (and abuses) of peer review by governmental agencies have been discussed by scholars in many disciplines (see Anderson, 1983; Blanpied & Borg, 1979; Gustafson, 1975). Justiz and Moorman (1985) listed several suggestions one panel of experts made for how the United States National Institute of Education might improve its peer-review processes: (1) identify individuals with recognized expertise and impeccable credentials to serve as members of review panels; (2) provide for continuity and stability of review procedures and review groups by staggering memberships on continuing review committees; and (3) separate the scientific and technical review of proposals from general educational and social goals (adopting a two-tier system similar to the successful system used by the United States National Institute of Health). That some of these recommendations seem obvious is itself a commentary on the need for more thoughtful attention on the part of governmental agencies to the use of expert review as an evaluation approach.

Some funding agencies have also used panels of prestigious educators to evaluate the agencies to which research and development awards had been made. For example, the United States Office of Education empaneled review teams to visit and evaluate each member within its federally funded network of regional laboratories and university-based research and development centers, even though the evaluation focused on only some important outcomes (see Stake, 1970).

As for uses of Eisner's educational criticism approach, we are familiar with few applications beyond those studies conducted by his students (Alexander, 1977; McCutcheon, 1978; Vallance, 1978).

STRENGTHS AND LIMITATIONS OF THE EXPERTISE-ORIENTED EVALUATION APPROACH

Collectively, expertise-oriented approaches to evaluation have emphasized the central role of expert judgment and human wisdom in the evaluative process and have focused attention on such important issues as whose standards (and what degree of publicness) should be used in rendering judgments about educational programs. Conversely, critics of this approach suggest that it often permits evaluators to make judgments that reflect little more than personal biases. Others have noted that the *presumed* expertise of the reviewers is a potential weakness.

Beyond these general observations, the various types of expertise-oriented evaluation approaches have their own unique strengths and weaknesses. Formal review systems such as accreditation have several perceived advantages. Kirkwood (1982) lists accreditation's achievements:

(1) in fostering excellence in education through development of criteria and guidelines for assessing institutional effectiveness; (2) in encouraging institutional improvement through continual self-study and evaluation; (3) in assuring the academic community, the general public, the professions, and other agencies that an institution or program has clearly defined and appropriate educational objectives, has established conditions to facilitate their achievement, appears in fact to be achieving them substantially, and is so organized, staffed, and supported that it can be expected to continue doing so; (4) in providing

counsel and assistance to established and developing institutions; and (5) in protecting institutions from encroachments that might jeopardize their educational effectiveness or academic freedom. (Kirkwood, 1982, p. 12)

The thoroughness of accreditation agencies has prevented the sort of oversimplification that can reduce complex educational phenomena to unidimensional studies. Other desirable features claimed for accreditation include the external perspective provided by the use of outside reviewers and relatively modest cost.

Of all these advantages, perhaps the most underrated is the self-study phase of most accreditation processes. Although it is sometimes misused as a public relations ploy, self-study offers potentially great payoffs, frequently yielding far more important discoveries and benefits than does the later accreditation site visit. Together, internal self-study and external review provide some of the advantages of an evaluative system that includes both formative and summative evaluation.

Formalized review systems also have nontrivial drawbacks. We have already commented on public concerns over credibility and increasing public cynicism that professionals may not police their own operations very vigorously. Scriven has called accreditation "an excellent example of what one might with only slight cynicism call a pseudo-evaluative process, set up to give the appearance of self-regulation without having to suffer the inconvenience" (Scriven, 1984, p. 73). The steady proliferation of specialized accrediting agencies suggests that there may indeed be truth to the suspicion that such processes are protectionist, placing professional self-interest before that of the educational institutions or publics they serve. Further, proliferation of review bodies, whether for reasons of professional self-interest or governmental distrust of private accreditation processes, can place unbearable financial burdens on educational institutions. Bernhardt (1984) suggests that the California system, which was described earlier, is too expensive to operate under current budgets, that it is not efficient, and that it is effective only for determining institutional compliance—not educational quality. Perhaps one accreditation visit may be relatively cost-efficient, as noted above, but multiple reviews can boost costs to unacceptable levels.[41] This concern is exacerbated if one credits findings (see Guba & Clark, 1976) that seem to suggest that contemporary accreditation procedures have not demonstrated much effectiveness in changing or eliminating poor-quality institutions.

Scriven (1984) has cited several problems with accreditation: (1) no suggested weightings of a "mishmash" of standards ranging from trivial to important, (2) fixation on goals that may exclude searching for side effects, (3) managerial bias that influences the composition of review teams, and (4) processes that preclude input from the institution's most severe critics.

Informal peer-review systems and ad hoc professional reviews reflect many of the advantages and disadvantages discussed above for accreditation. In addition, they possess unique strengths and limitations. Some pundits have suggested that such expert reviews are usually little more than a few folks entering the school without much information, strolling through the school with hands in pockets, and leaving the school with precious little more information, but with firm conclusions based on their own preconceived biases. Such views are accurate only for *misuses* of expert-oriented evaluations. Worthen (1983) and Worthen and White (1986) have shown, for example, how ad hoc panel on-site reviews can be designed to yield the advantages of cross-validation by multiple observers and interviewers, while still maximizing the time of individual team members to collect and summarize a substantial body of evaluative information in a short time span. Such ad hoc review panels can also be selected to blend expertise in evaluation techniques with knowledge of the program, and to avoid the naive errors that occur when there is no professional evaluator on the review team (Scriven, 1984).

Disadvantages of expert-oriented peer reviews include the public suspicion that review by one's peers is inherently conservative, potentially incestuous, and subject to possible conflict of interest. If evaluators are drawn from the ranks of the discipline or profession to be evaluated, there are decided risks. Socialization within any group tends to blunt the important characteristic of detachment. Assumptions and practices that would be questioned by an outsider may be taken for granted. These and other disadvantages led us (Worthen, 1974b; Worthen & Sanders, 1984) to point to serious problems that can occur if a program is evaluated only by those with expertise in program content.

House has noted that confidentiality can be another problem because professionals are often loathe to expose their views boldly in the necessary public report. This normally results, he says, in "two reports, one an inside confidential report revealing warts and blemishes, the 'real' report, and a public report which has been edited somewhat. This dual reporting seems to be necessary for professional cooperation, but of course it makes the public distrustful" (House, 1980, pp. 240–241).

Obviously, the question of interjudge and interpanel reliability is relevant when using expert-oriented evaluations because so much depends on the professionalism and perception of the individual expert, whether working alone or as a team member. The question of whether a different expert or panel would have made the same judgments and recommendations is a troublesome one for advocates of this approach, for by its very definition, replicability is not a feature of expertise-oriented studies. Moreover, the easy penetration of extraneous bias into expert judgments is a pervasive concern.

Finally, the connoisseurship-criticism approach to educational evaluation shares, generally, the strengths and limitations of the other expertise-oriented evaluation approaches summarized above, in addition to possessing unique strengths and weaknesses. Perhaps its greatest strength lies in translating educated observations into statements about educational quality. Prior training, experience, and "refined perceptual capabilities" play a crucial role in every expertise-oriented approach to evaluation, but they are perhaps best explicated in Eisner's connoisseurship-criticism approach. One cannot study his proposals and still lampoon expertise-oriented evaluation as a mere "hands-in-pocket" stroll through the school.

The connoisseurship-criticism approach also has its critics. House (1980) has cautioned that the analogy of art criticism is not applicable to at least one aspect of educational evaluation:

It is not unusual for an art critic to advance controversial views—the reader can choose to ignore them. In fact, the reader can choose to read only critics with whom she agrees. A public evaluation of an educational program cannot be so easily dismissed, however. Some justification—whether of the critic, the critic's principles, or the criticism—is necessary. The demands for fairness and justice are more rigorous in the evaluation of public programs. (House, 1980, p. 237)

R. Smith (1984) is perhaps the harshest critic of the "educational criticism" approach to evaluation, fearing that "educational criticism will be esteemed more for its quality as literature and as a record of personal response than for its correct estimates of educational value" (R. Smith, 1984, p. 1). He continues by attacking Eisner's conception of educational criticism on philosophical and methodological grounds, and two of Smith's points are germane here. First, he quarrels with Eisner's contention that educational connoisseurs require no special preparation for their role by noting that anyone wishing to be an educational connoisseur-critic must possess the skills of literary criticism, knowledge of the theories of the social sciences, and knowledge of the history and philosophy of education, as well as sensitivity and perceptiveness—no small feat for the person whose primary training may be, for example, in the teaching of mathematics. How many could really qualify as educational connoisseurs is an important question. Second, Smith questions whether the same methodology is useful for judging the wide array of objects Eisner includes as potential objects of criticism. "Do the same nondiscursive techniques serve the criticism of classroom life, textbooks, and school furniture?" (R. Smith, 1984, p. 14). Probably not.

APPLICATION EXERCISE

The Metropolitan Community Action Organization of Los Angeles received federal funds to establish a one-year education program for adults who have been unable to find employment for 18 consecutive months. A program was implemented that had two major components: (1) the teaching of basic skills such as reading, mathematics, and English as a foreign language, and (2) the teaching of specific vocational skills such as typing, shorthand, key punching, and drafting. The program was designed by adult-education specialists from a local university and representatives of the educational task forces of local unions.

Adults were tested as they entered the program by using standardized batteries in reading and mathematics. Entrants scoring below a grade equivalent of 8.0 were assigned to appropriate levels of reading and/or mathematics instruction. Individual instruction was also provided for students who were not comfortable using the English language. Vocational offerings varied and depended on the unions' assessment of potential job openings in the Los Angeles area. Many of the vocational classes were held in the premises of places of business or industry. A few were conducted in the facility provided for the adult education program.

Using what you have learned about expertise-oriented evaluation approaches, indicate how these approaches might be used in the evaluation of this program.

What purposes could they serve? What could they contribute that other approaches might neglect or not address well? What process and criteria would you use to select your experts and to evaluate their performance?

SUGGESTED READINGS

EISNER, E. W. (1979a). *The educational imagination: On the design and evaluation of school programs.* New York: Macmillan.

FLODEN, R. E. (1980). Flexner, accreditation, and evaluation. *Educational Evaluation and Policy Analysis*, 20, 35–46.

KELLS, H. R., & ROBERTSON, M. P. (1980). Post-secondary accreditation: A current bibliography. *North Central Association Quarterly*, 54, 411–426.

KIRKWOOD, R. (1982). Accreditation. In H. E. MITZEL (Ed.), *Encyclopedia of educational research* (Vol. 1, 5th Ed.). New York: Macmillan and The Free Press.

National Study of School Evaluation (1978). *Evaluative criteria.* Arlington, VA: Author.

Chapter 9
Adversary-Oriented Evaluation Approaches

Orienting Questions

1. When and why would one want to use an adversary-oriented approach to evaluation?
2. Is the adversary-oriented approach limited to courtroom formats? What variations of this approach might be used for program evaluation? Can you give an example of a use for each variation?
3. Do adversary-oriented evaluations always have two opposing views?
4. What are the major strengths and limitations of adversary-oriented evaluation approaches?

Most approaches to educational evaluation rest in part on the assumption that the evaluator should be impartial toward that which he evaluates. Evaluators who hold this view exert considerable effort trying to prevent their personal biases from influencing their findings and judgments.

Yet the truly insightful evaluator is aware that the potential for evaluator bias to influence the outcomes of the study can never be excluded, that even the choice of methods to control bias may be biased. Why did the evaluator choose to collect these particular data as opposed to other data that might have been collected? Why were these particular instruments used instead of others that were available? Why were some individuals interviewed but not others? Each such choice permits personal preferences, prejudices, or preconceptions to slip unnoticed (even by the evaluator) into the evaluation in ways that might significantly alter its outcomes. The evaluator cannot divorce himself from the evaluation.

When one considers other aspects of the evaluator's role, such as interpreting information, framing conclusions, and determining value, the possibility that personal values may influence the results is more obvious. Might the accreditation team's evaluation of the nonsexist counseling course have been more favorable if the team had not been all male? Would the school board have been quicker to believe the glowing evaluation of the superintendent's pet science curriculum if they had not recently reviewed the evaluator's application for the associate superintendency? Who will know that the harsh evaluation of a computer-assisted math curriculum stemmed more from the evaluator's aversion to computers than from any of the curriculum's attributes? In short, the notion that any evaluator can be a paragon of impartiality is naive. The best that any evaluation approach can hope for is to control bias sufficiently so that it does not significantly distort or alter results.

Where most evaluation approaches attempt to reduce bias, the *adversary-oriented approach* aspires to balance it, attempting to assure fairness by incorporating both positive and negative views into the evaluation itself. We would consider an evaluation adversary-oriented if both sides of issues or questions were argued, one side by advocates (those in favor) and the other by adversaries (those opposed). Various types of data (ranging from test scores to human testimony) might be selected and used by either side as evidence to support its arguments. Generally some type of hearing would be held so that the opposing views could be presented and debated before whoever would serve as "judge" or "jury" to decide on the relative merits of the opposing cases. There would be no presumption that the proponents and opponents of a curriculum being evaluated would be unbiased in appraising it. On the contrary, we would expect their biases to surface as they mounted their respective defenses of, or attacks on, the curriculum. And by encouraging biases on both sides to surface, we help ensure a balanced method of gathering information regarding the curriculum.

Adversary-oriented evaluation, then, is a rubric encompassing a collection of divergent evaluation practices that might loosely be referred to as *adversarial* in nature. In its broad sense, the term refers to all evaluations in which there is planned opposition in the points of view of different evaluators or evaluation teams—a *planned* effort to generate *opposing* points of view *within* the overall evaluation.[42] One evaluator (or team) serves as the program's advocate, presenting the most positive view of the program possible from the data, while another evaluator (or team) plays an adversarial role, highlighting any extant deficiencies in the program. Incorporation of these opposing views within a single evaluation reflects a conscious effort to assure fairness and balance and illuminate both strengths and weaknesses of the program. As Levine (1982) has put it,

> In essence, the adversarial model operates with the assumption that truth emerges from a hard, but fair fight, in which opposing sides, after agreeing upon the issues in contention, present evidence in support of each side. The fight is refereed by a neutral figure, and all the relevant evidence is weighed by a neutral person or body to arrive at a fair result. (Levine, 1982, p. 270)

Several types of adversarial proceedings have been invoked as models for adversary evaluations in education, including judicial proceedings, congressional and other hearings, and structured debates, each of which we shall consider in this chapter.

DEVELOPERS OF ADVERSARY-ORIENTED EVALUATION APPROACHES AND THEIR CONTRIBUTIONS

Adversary-oriented evaluation approaches can subsume, draw from, and be incorporated within other evaluation approaches. For example, there is considerable dependence on expert-oriented evaluation (discussed in Chapter 8) in many adversary proceedings (for example, the use of expert witnesses in trials and congressional hearings). Adversary evaluation also shares with the evaluation approaches discussed in Chapter 10 dependence on multiple perspectives about what is evaluated. (Indeed, one such approach, transactional evaluation, proposes the use of proponents and opponents of planned changes on evaluation teams charged to study innovations.) We distinguish adversary evaluation, however, by its use of planned, structured opposition as the primary core of the evaluation and by its derivation from metaphors drawn from more venerable adversarial paradigms.

Origins of Adversary-Oriented Evaluation. Rice (1915) proposed an evaluation method intended to eliminate graft and increase governmental efficiency by presenting facts about waste and corruption to a mock "judge and jury." Although only partly aimed at education, Rice's approach is the first proposed use of "adversary evaluation" with which we are familiar. The idea was not further developed, however, for 50 years. Guba (1965) suggested that educational evaluation might use aspects of the legal paradigm. If trials and hearings were useful in judging truth of claims concerning patents and products, and if human testimony were judged acceptable for determining life or death, as in the judicial system, then might not legal proceedings be a useful metaphor for educational evaluation? Might there be merit in evaluation "trials," in taking and cross-examining human testimony, and in using the concept of advocacy to assure that evaluation fairly examined both sides of issues?

At first, Guba's ideas seemed to fall on deaf ears, for that was the era when evaluators were about the business of refining the application of social science research methods (for example, experimental design) to educational evaluation, as well as developing promising new approaches drawn from other relevant paradigms (management-oriented approaches based on decision theory and systems analysis). But gradually a few colleagues began to test the utility of Guba's suggestions.

The first self-conscious effort to follow a particular adversary paradigm was made in 1970 by Owens. Designed to test the usefulness of a modified judicial model, the evaluation focused on a hypothetical curriculum and included pre-trial conferences, cases presented by the "defense" and "prosecution," a hearings officer, a "jury" panel of educators, charges and rebuttals, direct questioning and redirected questions, and summaries by the prosecution and defense. The reports (Owens, 1971, 1973) were intriguing to the community of educational evaluators and led to further conceptual and empirical work on the adversary approach (for example, Kourilsky, 1973; Wolf, 1973, 1975; Levine, 1974; Stake & Gjerde, 1974;

Kourilsky & Baker, 1976; Owens & Hiscox, 1977; Worthen & Owens, 1978; Levine & Rosenberg, 1979; Owens & Owen, 1981; and House, Thurston, & Hand, 1984). Several of these studies involved what might best be termed *advocate-adversary evaluation,* where an advocate evaluator presents the most favorable review possible and an adversary evaluator presents the most critical and damaging case that might be made, but there are no adversarial interactions or rebuttals surrounding the two stated positions.[43]

As these efforts to develop the adversary approach continued, several evaluations occurred that could be judged truly adversarial in nature (for example, Hiscox & Owens, 1975; Wolf, 1975; Stenzel, 1975; Nafziger, Worthen, & Benson, 1977; Levine and others, 1978; Wolf, 1979; Brathwaite & Thompson, 1981; Madaus, 1981; Popham, 1981). These studies have used widely divergent styles, and reactions to them have been mixed (as will be discussed later).

In the balance of this chapter we shall consider three general approaches to adversary evaluation: (1) adaptations of the legal paradigm and other "two view" adversary hearings; (2) adaptations of quasi-legal and other adversary hearings where more than two opposing views are considered; and (3) use of debate and other forensic structures in adversary evaluations.

The Judicial Evaluation Model and Other 'Pro and Con' Adversary Hearings

The "fight theory" underlies most models of litigation for resolving differences among opposing parties. According to Auerbach, Garrison, Hurst, and Mermin, (1961), this theory holds that the facts in a case can best be determined if each side tries as hard as possible, in a keenly partisan spirit, to provide the court with evidence favorable to that side. Although not disagreeing with the advantages of this posture, Frank (1949) has cautioned that disadvantages occur when "the partisanship of the opposing lawyers blocks the uncovering of vital evidence or leads to a presentation of vital testimony in a way that distorts it" (Frank, 1949, p. 81). Efforts to adapt aspects of the legal paradigm for use in educational evaluation have attempted to capitalize on the potentials cited by Auerbach and colleagues while avoiding the pitfall of which Frank warns.

Owens (1973) listed several characteristics of the adversary proceeding that he believed made it more appropriate for educational evaluations than adaptations of more familiar models:

1. The rules established for handling the adversary proceedings are quite flexible.
2. Complex rules of evidence are replaced by a free evaluation of evidence based solely upon whether the evidence is considered by the hearings officer to be relevant.
3. Both parties can be required before the trial to inform the hearings officer of all relevant facts, means of proof, and names of witnesses.
4. A copy of the charges is furnished to the hearings officer and defendant

before the trial and the defendant has the option of admitting in advance to certain charges and challenging others.

5. Witnesses are allowed to testify more freely and to be cross-examined.
6. Experts are often called upon to testify even before the trial.
7. Pretrial conferences of the hearings officer with both parties tend to make the trial less a battle of wits and more of a search for relevant facts.
8. In addition to the two parties involved, other interested groups may be permitted to participate. (Owens, 1973, pp. 296–297)

Owens also indicated that adversary proceedings in education should not be used to replace existing designs for data collection and analysis, but rather to provide an alternative way of interpreting, synthesizing, and reporting evidence.

The work of Wolf (1973, 1975) has been particularly thoughtful in relation to how evaluators might better define evaluation issues, what role personal testimony might play in evaluation, procedures for direct questioning and cross-examination, and rules of admissibility of evidence. Borrowing concepts from both jury trials and administrative hearings, Wolf proposed the *judicial evaluation model*, which included a statement of charges, opposing counselors, witnesses, a judge or hearings officer, and a jury panel. Four stages are proposed:

1. *Issue generation*: identification and development of possible issues to be addressed in the hearing
2. *Issue selection*: elimination of issues not at dispute and selection and further development of those issues to be argued in the hearing
3. *Preparation of arguments*: collection of evidence, synthesis of prior evaluation data to develop arguments for the two opposing cases to be presented
4. *The hearing*: including prehearing discovery sessions to review cases and agree on hearing procedures, and the actual hearing's presentation of cases, evaluation of evidence and arguments, and panel decision.

Wolf (1975, 1979) made clear that his intention was merely to use the law as a metaphor for educational evaluation, not to replicate legal procedures. He was also prompted by critiques of problems in applying the legal paradigm to educational evaluation (for example, Popham & Carlson, 1977; Worthen & Rogers, 1977) to argue that his model was not an adversarial debate or adversary evaluation, as such: "the metaphors of law are just that—metaphors.... Once the concepts are taken too literally, the object of judicial evaluation then becomes *winning*. This is precisely *not* what the JEM [judicial evaluation model] strives for" (Wolf, 1979, p. 22).[44]

Levine and Rosenberg (1979) have provided an insightful examination of numerous issues in adapting legal analogs for use in evaluation (for example, the burden of proof and use of presumptive evidence). They point out that although adversary models such as jury trials, administrative hearings, appellate proceedings, and arbitration hearings all have unique ways of using evidence and argument, they also have important similarities, including (1) an existing controversy between two or more parties; (2) formal case presentation by advocates for each position; (3) facts heard and decision rendered by an impartial arbiter; and (4) decision based solely upon argument heard and evidence presented during the proceeding.

Adversary Hearings with More than Two Opposing Views

Many committee hearings are not adversarial. Some of the review panels discussed in Chapter 8 (such as blue-ribbon panels) may hold public hearings to collect information pertinent to their charge. Appointed commissions charged with the resolution of controversial issues (for example, the National Commission on Excellence in Education described in Chapter 1) frequently hold hearings to obtain evidence and opinions relevant to their mission. House (1980) has cited as one such example the frequent use in England of commissions and councils headed by prominent citizens to provide guidance to government policymakers. Hearings held by most committees and commissions are decidedly not adversarial in structure, however, for no efforts are made to articulate or contrast opposing points of view.

Several other types of committee hearings are structured to identify and explore all the points of view represented in a particular context. Although not "adversarial" in the strict sense of the word, because, as Smith (1985) has noted, they explore a variety of positions, not just pro and con, we prefer to include them here because (1) they reflect multiple viewpoints, which often are in conflict with one another, thus perhaps qualifying as "multiadversarial" in nature; and (2) they frequently use hearing processes, questioning, cross-examination, interaction concerning alternate viewpoints, and summary statements of the various positions, all procedures typical of the two-sided "pro and con" adversary hearing. St. John (undated), in referring to such hearings as the "committee approach" to evaluation, listed as key characteristics the following:

- All of those with a stake in the evaluation—decision-makers, evaluators, program personnel, clients, and other interested persons—are brought together in the same place at the same time for a careful review of the issues at hand.
- A public hearing with testimony, questioning, cross-examination, and summary statements *produces a full exposition of evidence and illuminates differing points of view about that evidence.*
- The committee hearing method consists of public, verbal, face-to-face interactions, and therefore generates a high degree of personal involvement. Consequently, committee hearings are likely to have a strong impact on those involved, as well as on those who observe them.
- Because interaction between different points of view takes place, a process of communication and education occurs, and the evaluation makes its impact as it is happening. (St. John, undated, p. 2; italics added)

St. John also suggested that committee hearings "...may be useful...when the impact of the evaluation and its follow-through depends on the *consensus of multiple perspectives*, and such consensus is unlikely without significant interaction" (p. 3, italics added). Had he said "presentation of multiple perspectives," we would agree fully, for there are obviously instances where consensus among disparate views is not attained, yet issues are resolved through hearing and weighing the evidence supporting those alternate viewpoints enroute to a decision that may or may not be consensual. We see the focus of such "adversary" committee hearings as the presentation and examination of multiple perspectives that illuminate all legitimate views prior to final resolution of the issues.

The most frequently proposed model for this type of adversary evaluation is the congressional or legislative investigative hearing (Stenzel, 1982; Levine and others, 1978). With origins nearly as old as the origins of parliamentary process, congressional hearings seek to gain information or unveil truth. Although chief counsel and possibly minority counsel might be assigned to assist the committee, the viewpoints are seldom dichotomous partisan views but rather reflect a broad spectrum of individual and group positions (witness the well-known example of the Watergate hearings). Ensuring that all these important views are heard sometimes requires special powers (for example, subpoenaing witnesses), which would seem more difficult to enact and possibly less appropriate in educational settings.

Adversary Debates and Other Forensic Structures

Several approaches that qualify as adversary-oriented do not employ hearing processes. For example, Kourilsky (1973) proposed that pro and con arguments be presented to a decision-maker, who would examine the evidence and question the presenters, ultimately arriving at the decision that seemed fair given both positions. Kourilsky and Baker (1976) described an adversary model in which two teams prepared, respectively, affirmative and negative appraisals of that which was evaluated (the preparation stage), met to present the views to one another, cross-examining and critiquing one another's contentions on prespecified criteria (the confrontation stage), and engaged in open-ended discussions until reconciliation of views was attained and translated into written recommendations in a single report. Levine (1974) proposed that a resident adversary or critic might be assigned to a research project to challenge each bit of information collected, searching for other plausible explanations. The Stake and Gjerde (1974) strategy of having two evaluators prepare separate reports summing up opposing positions for and against the program is yet another variant adversarial approach that does not depend on a hearing format.

Donmoyer (undated) proposed a "deliberative" approach to evaluation, which focused on assessing and balancing alternative conceptions of reality and the differing value positions underlying these conceptions. "Because deliberative evaluation is primarily concerned with fostering understanding of alternative conceptions of reality," the evaluator's role is "to foster interaction and facilitate communication *among* representatives of various stakeholder [groups]..." (Donmoyer, undated, pp. 9–10). Donmoyer saw different world views as the cause of underlying disputes, which could be resolved by open presentation of alternative views in some type of educational forum:

Through the process of communication, those who disagree can, in principle, at least, expand their understanding of an issue by viewing that issue from their opponents' perspectives. (Donmoyer, undated, p. 11)

Nafziger and others (1977) described an adversary evaluation design employing a modified debate model for presenting data collected in a comprehensive evaluation to ensure that both sides of controversial issues were illuminated. This model was used in an adversary evaluation of a statewide team-teaching program in Hawaii.

HOW THE ADVERSARY-ORIENTED EVALUATION APPROACH HAS BEEN USED

The Hawaii evaluation conducted by Nafziger and his colleagues is the only example we know that made any effort to follow the debate model, as opposed to other forensic models. The program evaluated was a controversial "team-teaching" program. Two evaluation teams were formed, and once they had agreed on the basic design for the evaluation, they were randomly assigned positions as the program's advocate or adversary. Each team drew from the common data provided for in the original design and, in addition, was free to collect supplemental data. The teams wrote and exchanged reports and then prepared written rebuttals. Finally, the team leaders presented their reports and arguments verbally and rebutted their opponents' arguments in a standard debate format, before influential Hawaiian educational, governmental, and private leaders, who were given opportunities to ask questions of both team leaders.

The written final reports and live debates sparked great interest, including wide viewing of two television airings of an hour-long condensed version of the debate. Further, Hawaiian decision-makers were very favorable toward the adversarial format of the evaluation (Wright & Sachse, 1977). Despite such receptivity, and selection of this evaluation by the American Educational Research Association as the best all-around evaluation study of 1977, some participants in this study later expressed serious misgivings about aspects of this particular adversary approach (Worthen & Rogers, 1980) or about adversary evaluation in general (Popham & Carlson, 1977).

Several adversary-oriented evaluations have incorporated aspects of the legal paradigm. Wolf's judicial evaluation model has been used in (1) the evaluation of Indiana University's undergraduate teacher education programs (Wolf, 1975; Arnstein, 1975); (2) examination of the United States Bureau of Education for the Handicapped's implementation of a law mandating that all handicapped children have available a free and appropriate education (Wolf & Tymitz, 1977); (3) studying policy formulation in a local school district (Wolf, 1978), and (4) a formative evaluation of the effectiveness of "networking" among agencies in Virginia's employment and training program (Braithwaite & Thompson, 1981). A modified version of the judicial evaluation model (which omitted the jury or panel whose purpose in previous applications was to make recommendations or decisions) was used in the highly publicized Clarification Hearings on Minimum Competency Testing sponsored by the United States National Institute of Education (Herndon, 1980; National Institute of Education, 1981; Madaus, 1981; Popham, 1981).

Other adversary hearings employing legal methods include Owens (1971), described earlier in this chapter, and an evaluation of an experience-based career education program for high school students (Hiscox & Owens, 1975; Owens, Haenn, & Fehrenbacher, 1976), which produced a videotaped hearing presided over by a law professor serving as "judge," with professors of evaluation as the defense and prosecution "attorneys." In an evaluation of doctoral candidacy procedures in a university psychology program, a public hearing resembling a jury trial was used (Levine, 1976; Levine and others, 1978).

Aspects of both the legal and debate models were employed in an evaluation of an experimental undergraduate program in liberal arts at the University of Illinois (Stenzel, 1976). A debate consisting of opening arguments, rebuttals, and final summaries of both advocate and adversary positions was presented to a panel of judges, following the appellate court hearing in which such a panel decides issues under contention.

Clyne (1982) summarized the uses of the adversary process in educational evaluation: (1) summative evaluation; (2) formative evaluation; (3) social science debate; (4) policy analysis and debate; (5) school governance and local decision making; and (6) issue resolution and policy formation. Worthen and Rogers (1980) reported that a survey of a group of key educators and policymakers showed most (81 percent) thought adversary evaluation was appropriate for summative evaluation, whereas only 15 percent felt it should be used in formative evaluation. Braithwaite and Thompson (1981) disagreed, stating that their study showed adversary evaluation could also serve well in formative evaluation. In their evaluation of the national Clarification Hearings on Minimum Competency Testing, Estes and Demaline's (1982) surveys showed that most participants or potential users of such evaluations view adversarial approaches as more useful for summative than formative decisions.

STRENGTHS AND LIMITATIONS OF THE ADVERSARY-ORIENTED EVALUATION APPROACH

Some strengths and weaknesses transcend particular adversary approaches and speak to the merits of the adversarial concept itself.[45] For example, most observers would agree that building opposing viewpoints into an evaluation tends to illuminate both the positive and negative aspects of an educational program better than most other evaluation approaches. Adversary approaches also tend to broaden the range of information collected. A strength common to all of the adversary approaches is the interest they create on the part of their intended audiences. Indeed, one of this approach's greatest strengths is that it can satisfy the audience's informational needs in an interesting, informative manner. Nearly everyone loves a contest.

Adversary-oriented evaluation is also sufficiently broad and pluralistic that it can be combined with other approaches. For example, there is nothing to prevent the use of an expertise-oriented evaluation approach by both teams in an adversary-oriented study, any more than it would violate this approach for the advocate to use a participant-oriented approach while the adversary employed a management-oriented approach.

Openness to diverse viewpoints and open participation by stakeholders who might be excluded by most other approaches are other advantages. Further, this diversity increases the educative value of the hearings.

Another general advantage to adversary-oriented evaluation is that it anticipates (and largely blunts) the nearly inevitable criticisms offered by anyone whose position is not supported by the findings. It is difficult to argue that an evaluation is unfair if it examines and presents *both* sides of an issue. Use of adversary evaluation to diffuse political heat may be an unexpected fringe benefit of this approach.[46] Because opposing views are incorporated *into* the evaluation, most of the pros and cons are argued in an open forum, diverting much subsequent criticism of the evaluation itself. In short, there is more openness to examining issues rather than focusing on one particular point of view. This is consistent with findings from social psychology literature in persuasion and communication research (see Paulson, 1964) that suggest that opinions are modified more readily when both positive and negative views are reported.

Another advantage is the substantial, rigorous planning required of most adversary evaluations (no one wants to be humiliated by an opponent gloating over an easy victory). Few evaluation studies are so carefully planned as those with an adversary orientation.

Adversary evaluation also has, in a sense, a built-in "meta-evaluation": an evaluation of the evaluation. The collection, analysis, and interpretation of data used to support any point of view will be painstakingly criticized by those in opposition. All that remains is to do a more general meta-evaluation of the overall study.

The use of direct, holistic human testimony is frequently cited as a strength of adversary-oriented evaluations, as is cross-examination of that testimony.[47] Considerable use can be made of expert witnesses, thus enabling experts to draw inferences that might elude "lay" educators. Testing of hidden biases is another strength of this approach, as is examination of alternative interpretations of evidence.

Certain legal metaphors may be particularly useful. For example, the British judicial system's pretrial "exploration for discovery" provides an opportunity for opposing barristers to disclose to one another their cases and supporting evidence in the interest of finding any common ground. When two adversaries agree on any data, interpretation, or conclusion, it lends great credence to that aspect of the evaluation. The requirement that any evidence presented be understandable also precludes the type of obfuscation and educational "baffle-gab" that permeates many traditional evaluation reports.

To summarize the discussion thus far, we believe an adversary-oriented evaluation approach may be useful when (1) the object of the evaluation affects many people, (2) controversy about the object of the evaluation has created wide interest, (3) decisions are summative, (4) evaluators are external, (5) clear issues are involved, (6) administrators understand the intensity of adversary-oriented evaluations, and (7) resources are available for additional expenses required by adversarial strategies.

Despite their potential for making evaluation findings more interesting and meaningful to educational decision-makers, adversary-oriented approaches to evaluation are not yet sufficiently well developed to serve as a standard or model for future efforts. As yet there is little beyond personal preference to determine whether such evaluations would best be patterned after jury trials, congressional hearings, debates, or other adversarial arrangements. Preoccupation with the respective paraphernalia of these various approaches could cause evaluators to overlook the benefits that might accrue from use of adversary-oriented evaluation, namely, including planned opposition among evaluators. Despite its intriguing possibilities, we are not convinced that the legal paradigm is necessarily the best pattern. Evaluators may forthrightly protest (for example, Wolf, 1975, 1979) that rigid adherence to a legal model is not intended, yet many continue clinging to the more trivial courtroom rituals that seem unnecessary or downright inappropriate in educational evaluation—what Owens (1973) has called "entanglement in legal technicalities." For instance, replicating the theatrical aspects of the courtroom in adversary hearings is distracting and has made a mockery of some educational evaluations. Cloaking the person presiding over an educational hearing in a black robe seems as pretentious and inane as placing powdered wigs on senators presiding over congressional hearings.

Use of the legal paradigm can also result in a seductive slide into what might be termed an "indictment mentality," which can do a disservice both to evaluation efforts and to the programs being evaluated. Adversary-oriented evaluation literature that invokes the legal model tends to use terms such as "statement of charges" (Hiscox & Owens, 1975), "defendant" (Levine & Rosenberg, 1979), "not guilty" (Levine, 1982), "trial by jury" (Wolf, 1975), and the like. That orientation may be appropriate when there is a formal complaint against an educational program, as in the occasional investigation of some education program for malfeasance, misuse of funds, or gross mistreatment of students. But such situations are rare; and formal complaints, plaintiffs, and litigants are conspicuously absent in the typical educational evaluation—and rightly so. Educational evaluation should aspire to improve educational programs, not determine their guilt or innocence. Although evaluators must of necessity render judgments of worth, judging merit is not the same thing as determining guilt.

It is not only the vocabulary of the legal model that is problematic but also its characteristic of serving only when there is a problem to be solved. There is already too much tendency to view evaluation as something done when a program is in trouble, when there is a crisis or failing that requires correction. It would be unfortunate if this tendency were exacerbated and evaluations conducted only when a complaint had been lodged, an accusation leveled, an offending program accused. It is precisely this orientation that we fear may be a side effect of basing evaluations on the legal model, or on any model meant to be applied only in problem solving or crisis situations. It would be far more salutary if educators came to view evaluation as something routinely carried out to help them keep programs operating at maximum effectiveness and efficiency.

Of course, one can use aspects of the legal paradigm, such as cross-examination by adversaries, without requiring full or even partial courtroom procedures (as demonstrated by congressional hearings or interviews conducted jointly by partisan interviewers). Wolf (1975) and Hiscox and Owens (1975) have shown that one can adapt portions of the legal model without adopting it in its entirety.

Another general concern with adversary-oriented evaluation is whether it provides decision-makers with the full range of needed information. Presentation of strong pro or con positions might increase the probability of an extreme decision. In emphasizing polar positions, educators stand to both gain and lose. They may gain a broader spectrum of data and with more diverse interpretations provided to decision-makers; few other evaluation approaches seem likely to push as far in both positive and negative directions. But in broadening that spectrum, they may compromise the very neutrality so essential to rational decision making.[48]

As mentioned earlier, decision-makers may place greater confidence in conclusions and recommendations agreed to by both sides. Although this seems patently sensible, experience with adversary evaluations suggests such agreement is unlikely to be a spontaneous byproduct of the sparring and jousting that often occurs between adversaries. Most adversary approaches have a competitive element; it is expected that one of the adversaries will win and the other lose. When competition is high, cooperation tends to be lower. Mutual agreements are often abandoned in the adversaries' rush to turn every opposing argument to their own advantage. When winning is at stake, seemingly rational opponents question the obvious. And shared conclusions are not easily come by. Most adversary-oriented evaluation approaches could profit from a better mechanism for seeking and reporting areas of agreement.

Popham and Carlson (1977) point to "disparity in proponent prowess" as a deficit of adversary evaluation, claiming it is all too likely that the case will be decided because of a disparity in skill of the competing teams (or individuals), with the audience influenced more by the persuasiveness of the protagonists than by the strength of the evidence that supports their arguments. The potential for a skilled orator without solid supportive data to sway the "jury" by eloquence alone is, unfortunately, a real possibility.

Assignment of adversaries to pro or con positions is also a difficult matter because of the possible biases that they might bring with them. As noted at the beginning of this chapter, one object of adversary-oriented evaluation is not elimination of bias but rather balancing and publicizing of that bias. Of course, biases are unlikely to be eradicated by assignment to a position. Imagine the plight of Ralph Nader if he were assigned to defend a program or product.

It may not be an explicit assumption, but many adversary-oriented evaluations proceed as if there were an unspoken *obligation* to present two *equally convincing* cases, pro and con. Naturally, no one would tolerate an advocate who presented a weaker case than the data warranted; but what about one who erred in the other direction, feeling compelled to keep up with the opposition, even if it meant straining or ignoring the data? Such an orientation might be appropriate in a forensic society wherein the result of the debate seldom had much effect on the proposition being argued, but not in an evaluation where the outcome will influence real programs and real people.

Like the legal paradigm, the debate model also has irrelevancies that should be strained out before it is applied to education. The touchstones of debate are polemics and persuasion, not truth, which is central to the validity of evaluation studies. Debaters surely use facts and cannot normally afford to ignore the evidence at hand. But seldom is the debater forced to adhere as tightly to the plain, unadorned facts as is the conscionable evaluator. Logic can provide a permissive climate for manipulating data until the form is favorable. Probably more sophistry results from debaters' perversions of syllogistic logic than any other form of self-deception. A skilled debater can often build a remarkably strong case on a very flimsy foundation.

Many commentators have pointed out that adversary–oriented evaluations are time-consuming and expensive, requiring extensive preparation and considerable investment of human and fiscal resources (for example, Owens, 1973; Stenzel, 1982; Popham & Carlson, 1977). Braithwaite and Thompson (1981) said the judicial evaluation model's most serious problem is that it is a "heroic model," requiring

> a large number of participants, many of whom are in important roles. We utilized four case presenters, seven panelists, a hearing officer, a panel facilitator, a nonparticipant observer, and two research assistants in addition to ourselves, 13 witnesses, and two speakers who provided contextual statements at the outset of the hearing. (Braithwaite & Thompson, 1981, p. 16)

Levine and others (1978) estimated that over 80 percent of their effort in an evaluation using an adaptation of a jury trial went into preparing the case and managing the process, and less than 20 percent went into the actual hearing. Kourilsky and Baker (1976) noted as a potential snare of adversary evaluation the temptation to report all of the voluminous information collected with this approach. In short, questions have been raised about whether the adversary approach to evaluation is worth its considerable costs.

The real question, however, is not cost, but cost-effectiveness or cost-benefit. On these dimensions it seems apparent that benefit must be argued on grounds that adversary evaluation increases representativeness of the data, fairness of the instruments, communication between evaluators and decision-makers, and identification of all the pros and cons. Whether adversary evaluation really provides additional benefits must remain an open question until someone sees fit to research the issue.

A final concern of critics of adversary-oriented evaluations is that those who serve as judges are fallible arbiters. Popham and Carlson (1977) have worried about the lack of a process for appealing unwise decisions by arbiters, stating that the lack of a "higher court of appeals" in educational evaluation precludes rectifying improper judgments.[49] House (1980) echoes this concern and also lists as a criterion the contention that the "adversary model" may resolve conflicts but has limited potential for getting at the truth of a matter. He quotes Ramsey Clark, former United States Attorney General, as saying, "If there is a worse procedure for arriving at the truth, I don't know what it is."

APPLICATION EXERCISE

The curriculum council for a large school district decided that one of the major weaknesses of the elementary curriculum was its writing program. Junior high teachers reported that students were generally unable to write cohesive, descriptive paragraphs. On the recommendation of the council, six elementary schools were selected to participate in a pilot project to develop an elementary writing program. The nucleus of the developmental staff consisted of the faculty of these schools. This staff included also a specialist in creative writing from the local university and a representative from the curriculum council. The staff worked together for eight weeks in the summer to develop a program that would be used in all six grades. When school opened, they met twice weekly to discuss the way the course was progressing and to act on the recommendations of the evaluation team. The evaluation team had been appointed by the curriculum council and had the following responsibilities: (1) decide what questions should be asked of the program; (2) select the appropriate criteria for success of the program; and (3) gather information about the program and give it to the program staff with recommendations that they either improve, terminate, or maintain the program.

How could adversary-oriented evaluation approaches be used to address the evaluation needs of the council? Provide details about who would be involved, what the procedures would involve, what reports would be generated, and how the results might be used.

SUGGESTED READINGS

KOURILSKY, M. (1973). An adversary model for educational evaluation. *Evaluation Comment,* 4(2), 3–6.

LEVINE, M. (1982). Adversary hearings, In N. L. SMITH (Ed.), *Communication strategies in evaluation.* Beverly Hills, CA: Sage.

OWENS, T. R. (1973). Educational evaluation by adversary proceeding. In E. R. HOUSE (Ed.), *School evaluation: The politics and process.* Berkeley, CA: McCutchan, pp. 295–305.

STENZEL, N. (1982). Committee hearings as an evaluation format. In N. L. SMITH (Ed.), *Field assessments of innovative evaluation methods.* New Directions for Program Evaluation, No. 13. San Francisco: Jossey-Bass.

WOLF, R. L. (1975). Trial by jury: A new evaluation method. *Phi Delta Kappan, 57*(3), 185–187.

Chapter 10
Naturalistic and Participant-Oriented Evaluation Approaches

Orienting Questions

1. What led to the development of naturalistic and participant-oriented evaluation approaches?
2. What are some of the fundamental principles that naturalistic and participant-oriented evaluators follow when they conduct their evaluations?
3. What problems might a naturalistic or participant-oriented evaluator have with a client who wants a detailed evaluation plan in hand before allowing the evaluation to begin? How could the evaluator deal with this requirement?
4. Should naturalistic or participant-oriented evaluations limit their practice to qualitative methods? Why?
5. How has each of the evaluation approaches described in this chapter been used?
6. What are the major strengths and limitations of naturalistic and participant-oriented evaluation approaches?

Beginning in 1967, several evaluation theorists began to react to what they considered to be the dominance of mechanistic and insensitive approaches to evaluation in the field of education. These theorists expressed concerns that evaluators were largely preoccupied with stating and classifying objectives, designing elaborate evaluation systems, developing technically defensible objective instrumentation, and preparing long technical reports, with the result that evaluators were distracted from what was really happening in education. Critics of traditional evaluation approaches noted that many large-scale evaluations were conducted without the evaluators ever once setting foot in the participating classrooms. What began as a trickle of isolated comments grew to a deluge that flooded evaluation literature in education and the social sciences. More and more practitioners began publicly to question whether many evaluators really understood the phenomena that underlie their numbers, figures, charts, and tables. An increasing segment of the educational community argued that the human element, which was reflected in the complexities of everyday reality and the different perspectives of those engaged in education, was missing from most educational evaluations.

Consequently, a new orientation to evaluation was born, one that stressed firsthand experience with educational activities and settings. This general approach, which grew quickly during the 1970s and 1980s, is aimed at observing and identifying all (or as many as possible) of the concerns, issues, and consequences integral to educational enterprise.

In large part a reaction to perceived deficits in other evaluation approaches, this orientation encompasses a wide variety of more specific proposals that might be generally tied together by their acceptance of the intuitionist-pluralist philosophy of evaluation (see Chapter 4). Most of those who contributed to the development and use of this evaluation approach exhibit a preference for naturalistic inquiry methods as described later in this chapter, as opposed to conventional nomothetic science—hence our use of the term *naturalistic*. Moreover, most advocates of this approach see as central the significant involvement in the evaluation of those who are participants in the endeavor being evaluated—hence the descriptor *participant-oriented*.[50]

The evaluator portrays the different values and needs of all individuals and groups served by the program or curriculum, weighing and balancing this plurality of judgments and criteria in a largely intuitive fashion. Thus, what is judged "best" depends heavily on the values and perspectives of whichever groups or individuals are judging. By involving participants in determining the boundaries of the evaluation, evaluators serve an important educative function by creating better informed educators.

DEVELOPERS OF NATURALISTIC AND PARTICIPANT-ORIENTED EVALUATION APPROACHES AND THEIR CONTRIBUTIONS

In an important sense, Stake (1967) was the first evaluation theorist to provide significant impetus to this orientation in the field of education. His paper, "The Countenance of Educational Evaluation," with its focus on portrayal and processing the judgments of participants, was to alter dramatically the thinking of evaluators in the next decade. Along with his later writings (Stake, 1975a, 1975b, 1978, 1980), he provided conceptions and principles that have guided the evolution of this evaluation approach. Stake's early writings evidenced his growing concern over dominance of educational evaluation by parochial, objectivist, mechanistic, and stagnant conceptions and methods. Guba's (1969) discussion of the "failure of educational evaluation" provided further impetus at the time to the search for an alternative to the rationalistic approach to evaluation. Parlett and Hamilton (1976) complained that the predominant "agricultural-botanist" research paradigm was deficient for studying innovative educational programs, and they presented an alternative "illuminative evaluation" approach that followed a social anthropology paradigm. Rippey (1973) decried the insensitivity of existing evaluation approaches to the impact of an evaluation upon the incumbents in roles within the system being evaluated; he proposed "transactional evaluation" as a more appropriate evaluation approach for systems undergoing evaluation and resultant changes. MacDonald (1974, 1976) expressed concern over existing evaluation approaches' misuses of evaluation information for questionable political purposes, opting instead for "democratic evaluation," designed to protect the rights and informational needs of the whole "community" involved. Guba and Lincoln (1981) reviewed the major approaches used in educational evaluation and rejected all except Stake's notion of responsive evaluation, which they incorporated with naturalistic inquiry to create an evaluation approach they proposed as superior to all alternatives for education. Patton (1975, 1978, 1980) added substantially to the literature on participant-oriented evaluation through his reports of his field-evaluation experiences. Numerous others have also suggested naturalistic or participant-oriented evaluation approaches, or methodologies that are compatible with them (for example, Kelly, 1975; MacDonald & Walker, 1977; Kemmis, 1977; Hamilton, 1976; Stenhouse, 1975; Bullock, 1982; Fetterman, 1984; and Simons, 1984, to name only a few).

Diverse as these proposals are for variants of this general evaluation approach, two threads seem to run through all of them. The first, as Wachtman (1978) notes, is

> disenchantment with evaluation techniques which stress a product-outcome point of view, especially at the expense of a fuller, more holistic approach which sees education as a human endeavor and admits to the complexity of the human condition. Each author argues that instead of simplifying the issues of our humanity we should, in fact, attempt to understand ourselves and education in the context of its complexity. (Wachtman, 1978, p. 2)

Second, in most of these writings, value pluralism is recognized, accommodated, and protected, even though the effort to summarize the frequently disparate judgments and preferences of such groups is left to the intuitive sagacity and communication skills of the evaluator.

Those who use the naturalistic and participant-oriented approaches to evaluation typically prepare descriptive accounts—"portrayals," as they have come to be called—of a person, classroom, school, district, project, program, activity, or some other entity around which clear boundaries have been placed. Not only is the entity richly portrayed but it is clearly positioned within the broader context in which it functions.

In addition to commonalities noted above, evaluations that use this approach generally include the following characteristics:

1. *They depend on inductive reasoning.* Understanding an issue or event or process comes from grass-roots observation and discovery. Understanding emerges; it is not the end product of some preordinate inquiry plan projected before the evaluation is conducted.

2. *They use a multiplicity of data.* Understanding comes from the assimilation of data from a number of sources. Subjective and objective, qualitative and quantitative representations of the phenomena being evaluated are used.

3. *They do not follow a standard plan.* The evaluation process evolves as participants gain experience in the activity. Often the important outcome of the evaluation is a rich understanding of one specific entity with all of its idiosyncratic contextual influences, process variations, and life histories. It is important in and of itself for what it tells about the phenomena that occurred.

4. *They record multiple rather than single realities.* People see things and interpret them in different ways. No one knows everything that happens in a school. And no one perspective is accepted as *the* truth. Because only an individual can truly know what he or she has experienced, all perspectives are accepted as correct, and a central task of the evaluator is to capture these realities and portray them without sacrificing education's complexity.

Of the many authors who have proposed naturalistic and participant-oriented evaluation approaches, we have selected for further description here those whom we see as having been most influential in shaping this orientation.

Stake's Countenance Model

Stake's (1967) early analysis of the evaluation process had a major impact on evaluation thinking and laid a simple but powerful conceptual foundation for later developments in evaluation theory. He asserted that the two basic acts of evaluation are *description* and *judgment* (the "two countenances" of evaluation). Thus the two major activities of any formal evaluation study are full description and judgment of that which is being evaluated. To aid the evaluator in organizing data collection and interpretation, Stake created the evaluation framework shown in Figure 10.1.

Using this framework, the evaluator would (1) provide background, justification, and description of the program rationale (including its need); (2) list intended antecedents (inputs, resources, existing conditions), transactions (activities, processes), and outcomes; (3) record observed antecedents, transactions, and outcomes (including observations of unintended features of each); (4) explicitly state the standards (criteria, expectations, performance of comparable programs) for judging program antecedents, transactions, and outcomes; and (5) record judgments made about the antecedent conditions, transactions, and outcomes. The evaluator would analyze information in the description matrix by looking at the congruence between intents and observations, and by looking at dependencies (contingencies) of outcomes on transactions and antecedents, and of transactions on antecedents. Judgments would be made by applying standards to the descriptive data.

The countenance model thus gives evaluators a conceptual framework for thinking through the procedures of a complete evaluation.

Transactional Evaluation

Rippey (1973) used the term *transactional evaluation* to draw attention to the effects of disruptions in an organization on incumbents in the roles in the system under-

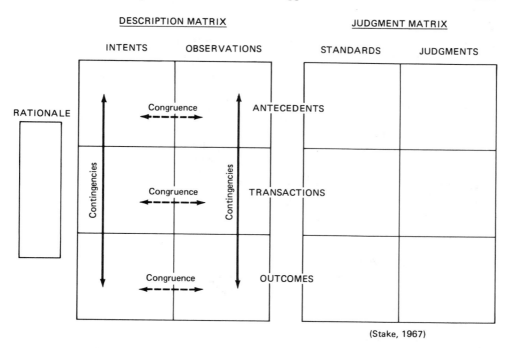

FIGURE 10.1   Stake's Layout of Statements and Data to Be Collected by the Evaluator of an Educational Program

Source: Stake, 1967.

going change. This new approach was "concerned with the system undergoing change rather than with the outcomes of the system's activity" (Rippey, 1973, p. xiii). Transactional evaluation is, therefore, a strategy for managing dysfunctions that occur within an organization in the midst of change (for instance, when a school is introducing a new program or revising an area of the curriculum). Donmoyer encapsulated it well:

> Rippey's transactional orientation emerged from the realization that programs which have been judged extremely successful in one situation can, in a different situation, be sabotaged by program participants whose values and self-interests are threatened. The transactional approach, therefore, changes evaluation's focus from a program's educational outcomes to the disequilibrium in the social system which program change inevitably brings. The approach encourages stakeholders within the social system to participate on evaluation teams and demand alterations in innovative programs which the stakeholders consider desirable. (Donmoyer, undated, p. 10)

By recognizing institutional disruptions brought about by change, transactional evaluation evidences concern with the effects on the "changers"—the staff and administrators. By attempting to alleviate these disruptions, evaluation becomes a strategy for conflict management. Rippey proposed uncovering sources of conflict and then getting proponents and opponents of the innovation involved in developing and carrying out an evaluation plan, with the evaluation specialist providing technical assistance. Such an evaluation approach is needed, Rippey contended, because

> Change, introduced in response to external needs and pressures, will have the following results:
>   1. It will have unexpected consequences as well as those intended.
>   2. It will affect the entire organization, not just the part included in the formal plan.
>   3. It will cause a certain amount of dislocation because of the competition for resources (including the students' time) and the shift of roles and expectations, which may place an individual in a situation incongruent with his needs. (Rippey, 1973, p. 12)

Five phases are proposed for transactional evaluation, as follows:
1. *Initial*—"trouble spots" identified by "neutral" evaluation.
2. *Instrumentation*—data collected in meeting of various interest groups.
3. *Program development*—redefinition to reflect "group consensus" goals and values.
4. *Program monitoring*—groups agree to implement and monitor new program.
5. *Recycling*—process recycled as new conflicts emerge.

Thus, Rippey proposed using continuous evaluation of changes, by both proponents and opponents of the change, to resolve conflicts about the expected and unexpected consequences of educational innovations. The result was to move the human element in educational evaluation more directly into the spotlight. Although some may view transactional evaluation as a management-oriented evaluation approach because of its emphasis on evaluation as conflict management, or as adversary evaluation because of its inclusion of opposing pro and con points of view in planning and conducting the evaluation, we think it belongs here because of its central focus on attending to the interests of the key participants in the educational system under consideration.

Illuminative Evaluation

Parlett and Hamilton (1976) proposed an evaluation approach, which they called *illuminative evaluation*, that would involve intensive study of an educational program as a whole—its rationale and evolution, operations, achievements, and difficulties in the school context or "learning milieu." The purpose of their approach, proposed as especially applicable to small-scale programs, would be to illuminate problems, issues, and significant program features. Based on the social anthropology paradigm, and somewhat on psychiatry and sociology participant observation research, this approach grew from disenchantment with the classical experimental paradigm, which Parlett and Hamilton termed an *agricultural-botany paradigm*, suggesting that it is a more appropriate paradigm for plants than people. Illuminative evaluation is primarily concerned with description and interpretation, not measurement and prediction. No attempt is made to manipulate or control variables, but rather to take the complex educational context, as it exists, and attempt to understand it.

The importance of studying the context of school programs, according to Parlett and Hamilton, is that a variety of factors influence programs in any evaluation, such as constraints (legal, administrative, occupational, architectural, financial); operating assumptions held by faculty (arrangement of subjects, curricula, teaching methods, grading); educators' individual characteristics (teaching style, experience, professional orientation, private goals); and students' perspectives and preoccupations. Also, the introduction of changes within the school context will set off repercussions and unusual effects. The evaluator's task is to provide a comprehensive understanding of the complex reality surrounding the program—to "illuminate" by sharpening discussion, disentangling complexities, isolating the significant from the trivial, and raising the level of sophistication characterizing debates. Although illuminative evaluation concentrates on information gathering, not decision making, it is expected that different groups will look to the evaluator's reports to help make difficult decisions. The illuminative evaluator does not pass judgment, but rather attempts to discover, document, and discuss what the innovation comprises and what it is really like to be a participant in it.

The process of evaluation proposed by Parlett and Hamilton has three basic stages:

1. *Observation*, to explore and become familiar with the day-to-day reality of the setting being studied.
2. *Further inquiry*, to focus the study by inquiring further on selected issues.
3. *Explanation*, to seek to explain observed patterns and cause-effect relationships.

Progressive focusing is recommended for use throughout the evaluation as a technique for refocusing and narrowing the study, thereby allowing more concentrated attention to emerging issues.

Emphasizing classroom process, subjective information, and naturalistic inquiry, the illuminative evaluation approach depends largely on data from observations, interviews, questionnaires and tests, and documents or background sources. "Triangulative" combinations of such data are proposed to provide a more accurate portrayal of reality. The focus of this approach requires that the illuminative evaluator spend substantial periods of time in the field.

Democratic Evaluation

MacDonald (1974, 1976) delineated three tyes of evaluation studies that differed in their selection of roles, goals, audiences, techniques, and issues, as follows:

1. *Bureaucratic evaluation*, where the bureaucratic agency sponsoring the evaluation, not the evaluator, controls the evaluation information and "owns" the evaluation report.
2. *Autocratic evaluation*, where the evaluator retains ownership of the evaluation study and reports findings to the sponsoring agency and in academic journals.
3. *Democratic evaluation*, where the evaluator performs an information service to the whole community—sponsors and participants alike—with neither the evaluator nor sponsoring agency having any special claim on the findings.

Expressing a strong preference for the democratic evaluation approach, MacDonald viewed evaluation as primarily a political activity that had as its only justification the "right to know." He argued, however, that, "People own the facts of their own lives," and he proposed that those being evaluated have the final say—veto power—over the content and release of the evaluation report.

Pluralism of values is recognized in this approach, and the range of audiences served by an evaluation report is a major criterion for judging a study's success. House (1983a) cited this evaluation approach as that which corresponds most closely to the classic liberal, individualistic approach to political pluralism:

> The evaluation model that most closely corresponds to this version of liberal pluralism is MacDonald's democratic evaluation (1974). MacDonald sees the evaluator as a "broker in exchanges of information between groups," representing a range of interests, presenting information accessible to non-specialists, giving informants confidentiality and control over the data, having no concept of information misuse, negotiating with sponsors and participants, and making no recommendations. The evaluator feeds information to audiences and lets the market work things out. Each person makes use of the information as he sees fit with the evaluator removed from interpretation. The evaluator operates on a set of procedural regulations, which control information flow. (House, 1983a, p. 61)

An interesting proposal is that the democratic evaluator should make no recommendations. MacDonald believed that evaluation reports should aspire to be nonrecommendatory "best sellers," which are widely read because of their inherent interest, nontechnical style, and usefulness and appropriateness of their information.

Responsive Evaluation

During the early 1970s, Stake began to expand his earlier (1967) writing more obviously into the realm of naturalistic and participant-oriented evaluation. Although the seeds of this explication lie in his earlier work, Stake's more recent conceptions of "responsive evaluation" (1972, 1975b, 1978, 1980) are implicitly less formal and explicitly more pluralistic than his earlier countenance model.

Responsive evaluation's central focus is in addressing the concerns and issues of a "stakeholder" audience.[51] Stake noted that he was not proposing a new approach to evaluation, for "responsive evaluation is what people do naturally in evaluating things. They observe and react" (Stake, 1972, p. 1).[52] Rather, Stake saw this approach as an attempt to develop a technology to improve and focus this natural behavior of the evaluator. Stake stressed the importance of being *responsive* to realities in the program and to the reactions, concerns, and issues of participants rather than being *preordinate*[53] with evaluation plans, relying on preconceptions and formal plans and objectives of the program. Stake defined responsive evaluation as follows:

> An educational evaluation is *responsive evaluation* if it orients more directly to program activities than to program intents; responds to audience requirements for information;

and if the different value-perspectives present are referred to in reporting the success and failure of the program. (Stake, 1975a, p. 14)

A major reason for proposing responsive evaluation is Stake's perception that the ultimate test of an evaluation's validity is the extent to which it increases the audience's understanding of the entity that was evaluated. Improved communication with stakeholders is a principal goal of responsive evaluation. "The responsive approach tries to respond to the natural ways in which people assimilate information and arrive at understanding" (Stake, 1972, p. 3).

The purpose, framework, and focus of a responsive evaluation emerge from interactions with constituents, and those interactions and observations result in progressive focusing on issues (similar to the progressive focusing in Parlett and Hamilton's "illuminative evaluation" described earlier). Responsive evaluators must interact continuously with members of various stakeholding groups to ascertain what information they desire and the manner in which they prefer to receive such information. Stake described the responsive evaluator's role this way:

> To do a responsive evaluation, the evaluator of course does many things. He makes a plan of observations and negotiations. He arranges for various persons to observe the program. With their help he prepares for brief narratives, portrayals, product displays, graphs, etc. He finds out what is of value to his audience. He gathers expressions of worth from various individuals whose points of view differ. Of course, he checks the quality of his records. He gets program personnel to react to the accuracy of his portrayals. He gets authority figures to react to the importance of various findings. He gets audience members to react to the relevance of his findings. He does much of this informally, iterating, and keeping a record of action and reaction. He chooses media accessible to his audiences to increase the likelihood and fidelity of communication. He might prepare a final written report; he might not—depending on what he and his clients have agreed on. (Stake, 1975b, p. 11)

As one might infer from the above description, responsive evaluators are relatively disinterested in formal objectives or the precision of formalized data collection; they are more likely to be at home working within the naturalistic or ethnographic paradigm, drawing heavily on qualitative techniques. Feedback to the various stakeholders is more likely to include portrayals and testimonials rather than more conventional evaluation data. Such portrayals will frequently feature descriptions of individuals in case studies based on a small sample of those affected by the program or process being evaluated. Reports to audiences will underscore the pluralism within the educational setting. A single set of recommendations is highly improbable; recommendations are more likely to be of the conditional sort where judgments about the "best" program or the "preferred" course of action will vary, depending on who is doing the judging and what criteria they use to ascertain value. Maxwell (1984) has published a rating scale that could be used to assess the quality of responsive evaluations.

Stake (1975b) used the "clock" shown in Figure 10.2 as a mnemonic device to reflect the prominent, recurring events in a responsive evaluation:

FIGURE 10.2   Prominent Events in a Responsive Evaluation

Source: Stake, 1975b, p. 19.

Although the evaluator might best begin the evaluation at twelve o'clock and proceed clockwise, Stake has emphasized that any event can follow any other event, and at any point the evaluator may want to move counterclockwise or cross-clockwise, if events warrant such flexibility. Further, many events may occur simultaneously; many will occur several times during an evaluation. The "clock" serves to remind evaluators that flexibility is an important part of using this naturalistic and participant-oriented approach.

One revealing comparison of responsive and preordinate evaluation approaches was provided by Stake's analysis of what percentage of time evaluators of each persuasion would spend on several evaluation tasks:

	Preordinate (%)	Responsive (%)
Identifying issues, goals	10	10
Preparing instruments	30	15
Observing the program	5	30

Administering tests, etc.	10	—
Gathering judgments	—	15
Learning client needs, etc.	—	5
Processing formal data	25	5
Preparing informal reports	—	10
Preparing formal reports	20	10

(Stake, 1975b, p. 20)

Stake (1978) also advanced acceptance of the naturalistic and participant-oriented approach to evaluation by expanding on its rationale. This approach, he said, has appeal because

1. It helps audiences for the evaluation understand the program if we pay attention to the natural way in which they understand and communicate about things.
2. Knowledge gained from experience (tacit knowledge) facilitates human understanding and extends human experience.
3. Naturalistic generalizations, which are arrived at by recognizing similarities of objects and issues in and out of context, are developed through experience. They serve to expand the way in which people come to view and understand educational programs.
4. By studying single objects, people accumulate experiences that may be used to recognize similarities in other objects. We add to existing experience and human understanding.

We have given more space to responsive evaluation than to other naturalistic and participant-oriented evaluation approaches because we agree, at least in part, with the following assessment of Guba and Lincoln (1981):

> responsive evaluation can be interpreted to include all other models. Evaluation models, as we have used that term, are differentiated on the basis of their organizers. The organizer of the responsive model is audience concerns and issues. If some audience wants to see information relating to the achievement of objectives, that is admissible within the responsive rubric. If another audience wishes to influence or service decisions, assess general effects, or elicit critical judgments, that too can be provided for within the responsive model. The responsive model can accommodate any other organizer, while other models can accommodate only the organizer on which they are based. The resulting flexibility gives the responsive model power beyond that of any of its competitors. (Guba & Lincoln, 1981, p. 38)

One might question whether or not responsive evaluation, so broadly defined, may lose its uniqueness and meaning. Such a broad claim for superiority, mis-understood, could also result in less able evaluators attempting to pass off inferior evaluations, which would be rejected as examples of any other evaluation approach, by labeling them as "responsive" evaluation. That prospect tempts one to narrow the definition of responsive studies to exclude atrocities that do not deserve inclusion under any rubric. But one may as well rail against use of the term "creativity" because of the largely abortive efforts to define and measure that construct as to argue for limiting the broad perspective of responsive evaluation because those incapable of doing quality evaluation work, by any definition, may try to creep under the shelter of the broader conception Guba and Lincoln propose. In the final analysis, each evaluation must be judged by its usefulness, not its label. Used intelligently and competently, responsive evaluation techniques have great potential for enhancing the quality of any evaluation study.

Naturalistic Evaluation

In *The Flame Trees of Thika*, Elspeth Huxley (1982) makes this astute observation:

> The best way to find things out is not to ask questions at all. If you fire off a question, it is like firing off a gun—bang it goes, and everything takes flight and runs for shelter. But if you sit quite still and pretend not to be looking, all the little facts will come and peck round your feet, situations will venture forth from thickets, and intentions will creep out and sun themselves on a stone; and if you are very patient, you will see and understand a great deal more than a man with a gun does.

Huxley's words sum up the spirit of the naturalistic evaluation approach better than could any academic description. Yet it is important to move beyond the prosaic to try, as House has done, to understand the structure of reality underlying this approach. He labeled as "naturalistic" evaluation any evaluation that

> aims at naturalistic generalization (based on the experience of the audience); is directed more at non-technical audiences like teachers or the general public; uses ordinary language and everyday categories of events; and is based more on informal than formal logic. (House, 1983a, p. 57)

Although House and others had written of naturalistic approaches to evaluation, Guba (1978a) provided the first comprehensive discussion of the merits of introducing naturalistic methods into educational evaluation. He differentiated between naturalistic inquiry, rooted in ethnography and phenomenology, and "conventional" inquiry, based on the positivist, experimental paradigm. He not only outlined several reasons for preferring naturalistic inquiry but also analyzed major methodological problems confronting naturalistic inquirers. His monograph contributed greatly toward formulation of naturalistic evaluation methodology.

The most significant work in this area, however, is the later work of Guba and Lincoln (1981), which carefully linked naturalistic inquiry to Stake's responsive evaluation, and then described procedures for implementing this approach. Their more recent work (Lincoln & Guba, 1985) extended their discussion of the naturalistic method of inquiry.

According to Guba and Lincoln, the major role of evaluation is one of responding to an audience's requirements for information in ways that take account of the different value perspectives of its members. By taking a naturalistic approach to evaluation, the evaluator is studying an educational activity *in situ*, or as it occurs naturally, without constraining, manipulating, or controlling it. Naturalistic inquiry casts the evaluator in the role of a learner, and those being studied in the role of informants who "teach" the evaluator. The dominant perspective is that of the informant, because the evaluators learn their perspectives, learn the concepts they use to describe their world, use their definitions of these concepts, learn the "folk theory" explanations, and translate their world so the evaluator and others can understand it.[54]

Guba and Lincoln stress that the criteria used to judge the rigor of scientific inquiry also hold for naturalistic inquiry, but require some reinterpretation. For instance, if one were concerned about the "truth" of an evaluation for particular subjects in a particular context, the naturalistic evaluator would be concerned with *credibility* of findings rather than internal validity. Corroboration of data through cross-checking and triangulation are two methods used by the naturalistic evaluator to establish credibility.

If one were concerned with the *applicability* of an evaluation in other contexts or for other subjects, the naturalistic evaluator would look at the *fit* of the evaluation findings rather than external validity. Applicability is enhanced through the use of working hypotheses that should be tested in other contexts, and through the use of "thick description," which is a "literal description of the entity being evaluated, the circumstances under which it is used, the characteristics of the people involved in it, the nature of the community in which it is located, and the like" (Guba & Lincoln, 1981, p. 119).

If one were concerned with the *consistency* of evaluation findings (that is, whether the same finding would result if the study were repeated), the naturalistic evaluator would consider the study's *auditability* rather than reliability. By having a second team review the documentation and reasoning underlying the evaluation, the evaluator can determine whether agreement on the findings can be reached. Halpern (1983) has developed an extensive model for auditing naturalistic inquiries.

Finally, if one were concerned about the *neutrality* of the evaluation, the naturalistic evaluator would look at the evaluation's *confirmability* rather than its objectivity. Data should be factual and confirmable. The naturalistic evaluator will require that the information generated by the evaluation can be confirmed.

The naturalistic evaluator proceeds by first identifying stakeholders. Their value positions are important, for it is their perspectives that should be reflected in the evaluation. Concerns and issues are elicited from interviews with the stakeholders and from naturalistic observations by the evaluator.

The naturalistic evaluator's data-collection task is defined by certain kinds of information that will be sought:

- Descriptive information about the object of the evaluation and its context
- Information responsive to concerns (documenting them, seeking causes and consequences, and identifying possible actions)
- Information responsive to issues (clarifying them, identifying potential courses of action to resolve them)

- Information about values (clarifying them, finding out about their source and degree of conviction)
- Information about standards to be used in the evaluation (identifying criteria, expectations, and needs).

Through the use of interviews, observations, nonverbal cues, documents, records, and unobtrusive measures, the naturalistic evaluator uses field notes and records as the sources of this information. Descriptions are used not only as data but also as a reporting technique.

Looking Back. The five naturalistic and participant-oriented evaluation approaches we have described above collectively reflect a new orientation in the field of educational evaluation. They are similar in important ways, yet each is unique. As Hamilton, Jenkins, King, MacDonald, and Parlett (1977) noted in reviewing a collection of actual evaluations that follow this general orientation, they display "a family resemblance, not an enclosed orthodoxy guided by a tacit uniformity of practice" (Hamilton and others, 1977, p. 235). Hamilton (1977), however, provided a useful general description of "pluralist evaluation models" that serves to summarize the five we have discussed:

> In practical terms, pluralist evaluation models...can be characterized in the following manner. Compared with the classic models, they tend to be more extensive (not necessarily centered on numerical data), more naturalistic (based on program activity rather than program intent), and more adaptable (not constrained by experimental or preordinate designs). In turn, they are likely to be sensitive to the different values of program participants, to endorse empirical methods which incorporate ethnographic fieldwork, to develop feedback materials which are couched in the natural language of the recipients, and to shift the locus of formal judgment from the evaluator to the participants. (Hamilton, 1977, p. 339)

HOW NATURALISTIC AND PARTICIPANT-ORIENTED EVALUATION APPROACHES HAVE BEEN USED

In one sense, given the breadth of this general evaluation approach, one could almost include as examples any educational evaluation that has used ethnography, case studies, storytelling, qualitative techniques, and the like. We will resist that temptation, recognizing that many studies may use some of the apparatus of participant-oriented or naturalistic evaluation without being good examples of this approach. Rather, we would point to a few examples that reflect conscious efforts to follow this evaluation approach.

Rippey (1973) has described how the concept of transactional evaluation has been used to aid in the process of change in different types of organizations. Likewise, Parlett and Dearden (1977) provide examples of the use of illuminative evaluation in evaluation of higher-education programs.

The arts in education was the focus of an extensive evaluation project using the responsive evaluation approach (Stake, 1975a). In this project, and an earlier one that evaluated a program for talented youth (Stake & Gjerde, 1974), responsive evaluation procedures were used to address issues of immediate interest to evaluation audiences.

Malcolm and Welch (1981) provide an example of a naturalistic case study of a Catholic junior college in Minneapolis, Minnesota. Of particular interest are the authors' personal reactions to such topics as the evaluators' preparations, note-taking in the field, phases in planning for the study, interviewing, data analysis and report writing, and final editing and validation.

The use of descriptive, naturalistic case studies to report on the actual use of a new educational program is well illustrated in reports distributed by the Agency for Instructional Television (Sanders & Sonnad, 1982). Other uses of the naturalistic and participant-oriented approach to evaluation have been reported by Wolcott (1976), Wolf and Tymitz (1977), Patton (1980), Guba and Lincoln (1981), Welch (1981), Spindler (1982), Hébert (1986), and Williams (1986a).

STRENGTHS AND LIMITATIONS OF NATURALISTIC AND PARTICIPANT-ORIENTED EVALUATION APPROACHES

Introduction of evaluations using this approach has prompted more acrimonious debate than almost any development in educational evaluation within the last two decades. Critics of this approach discount it as hopelessly "soft-headed" and argue that few if any educational evaluators are either virtuous or intellectually agile enough to wield masterfully the seductively simple yet slippery and subtle tools that this approach requires. Champions of pluralistic, responsive approaches reply that they can be readily used by any sensitive individual and that they are infinitely richer and more powerful than other approaches and, indeed, can subsume them, because they are flexible and do not preclude the use of other approaches within them, should that be desired by the evaluator's sponsor. Our intent here is not to add to what we see as a largely unproductive, divisive debate, but rather to summarize briefly some of the pros and cons thus far advanced for this approach.

Few would argue against the claim that naturalistic and participant-oriented evaluation has emphasized the human element in evaluation. It directs the attention of the evaluator to the needs of those for whom an evaluation is being done, and it stresses the importance of a broad scope—looking at education from different viewpoints. Those who use this approach view education as a complex human undertaking and attempt to reflect that complexity as accurately as possible so that others may learn from it. The potential for gaining new insights and usable new theories in education from this approach stands among its greatest strengths. Other advantages of this method are its flexibility, attention to contextual variables, and encouragement of multiple data-collection techniques designed to provide a view of less tangible but crucial aspects of human and organizational behavior. In addition, this approach can provide rich and persuasive information that is credible to audiences who see it as reflecting genuine understanding of the inner workings and intricacies of the program.

As with other approaches to evaluation, the strengths of this approach may also prove to be its limitations. Attempts to simplify the evaluation process have proven popular and effective in the past, as evidenced by the 50-year dominance of the objectives-oriented evaluation method. Thus, an approach that stresses complexity rather than simplicity may ultimately prove more popular with theorists than with practitioners, however sound it may be on other grounds.

Critics of this approach have found its subjectivity a serious limitation, even though such arguments could be mounted against every other approach to evaluation (as noted in lengthy discussions of this issue by Guba, 1978a, and Guba & Lincoln, 1981). Because of their reliance on human observation and individual perspective, and their tendency to minimize the importance of instrumentation and group data, advocates of this approach have been criticized for "loose and unsubstantiated" evaluations. Sadler (1981) discusses intuitive data processing as a potential source of bias in naturalistic evaluations. Walker (1974) notes that ethnographic field work can take so much time to complete that the situation often changes or the administrator has to make a decision before the evaluation findings are available. Crittenden (1978) complains that excluding judgment from the evaluator's role makes some participant-oriented approaches nonevaluative. Further, failure to suggest ways of weighing or combining individual standards into overall judgments about the program is viewed as making pluralistic, participant-oriented evaluation difficult for all but the most sensitive and skilled evaluators. Parlett and Hamilton (1976) concede that dependence on open-ended techniques and progressive focusing in this approach make evaluator partiality a potential problem.[55] Although supportive of using naturalistic techniques when the evaluation needs warrant, Williams (1986b) notes that compromises in evaluation standards are usually necessary when conducting naturalistic inquiry.

The cost of using the naturalistic and participant-oriented approach to evaluation has been viewed by some as a serious limitation, especially during times of tight budgets. This approach can be labor-intensive, often requiring full-time presence of the evaluator in the field over an extended period. The time it takes to prepare field notes and reports using this approach is at least as long as it takes for the initial observations. Some commentators (for example, Lewy, 1977) disagree, asserting that responsive-evaluation approaches take less time than other evaluation approaches, but the weight of opinion still suggests that resources (personnel, time, funds) must be considered a nontrivial limitation to wide-scale application of this approach, especially in large educational programs.

The labor intensity of naturalistic and participant-oriented approaches to evaluation limits the number of cases that can be studied intensively. Consequently, it is critical that cases be selected carefully and, even then, that conclusions not be extended beyond what those cases will allow. On the whole, evaluators using this approach are well-advised to be cautious in making interpretations and drawing conclusions. Most results might best be considered contextually anchored facts on which to base—and then test—tentative generalizations.

APPLICATION EXERCISE

As newly appointed director of Co-curricular Activities for the John F. Kennedy High School, you decide to conduct an evaluation of the co-curricular program in the school. The most current information about the program is found in the faculty handbook, published at the opening of each school year. This description reads as follows:

> The John F. Kennedy High School offers a wide range of co-curricular activities for its 2,000 students. Among the various activities are clubs, intramural and varsity sports, band, choir, orchestra, and various service programs such as Red Cross. Clubs are organized by students and assigned a faculty advisor by the Dean of Students. Meetings are scheduled on Monday–Thursday evenings and held in the cafeteria, auditorium, or gymnasium of the school. Varsity sports activities are directed by members of the Physical Education faculty. Intramural sports are organized by home rooms and directed by a faculty member appointed by the Dean of Students. Band, choir, and orchestra are under the direction of members of the music department. Service programs are organized by students who must also find a faculty member who is willing to advise them.

You feel that this description does not provide you with sufficient insight into the program; you decide to conduct an evaluation of the current program before undertaking any modifications or restructuring of the program.

As a naturalistic and a participant-oriented evaluator, how would you proceed to plan and conduct the evaluation?

SUGGESTED READINGS

GUBA, E. G., & LINCOLN, Y. S. (1981). *Effective evaluation.* San Francisco: Jossey-Bass.

LINCOLN, Y. S., & GUBA, E. G. (1985). *Naturalistic inquiry.* Beverly Hills, CA: Sage.

STAKE, R. E. (1967). The countenance of educational evaluation. *Teachers College Record, 68,* 523–540. Also in B. R. WORTHEN & J. R. SANDERS (1973). *Educational evaluation: Theory and practice.* Belmont, CA: Wadsworth.

STAKE, R. E. (1975b). *Program evaluation, particularly responsive evaluation.* (Occasional Paper No. 5). Kalamazoo, MI: Western Michigan University Evaluation Center.

STAKE, R. E. (1978). The case study method in social inquiry. *Educational Researcher, 7,* 5–8.

Chapter 11
Alternative Evaluation Approaches: A Summary and Comparative Analysis

Orienting Questions

1. What are some cautions to keep in mind when considering the alternative evaluation approaches?
2. Did you find one evaluation approach that you feel most comfortable with, or did you find useful ideas coming out of each approach?
3. Would you miss much if you ignored all but one approach, which you then used for all evaluations? What are some dangers of always using the same evaluation approach?
4. What negative metaphors underlie certain evaluation models? Why is that a concern?
5. What has each of the alternative evaluation approaches contributed to the conceptualization of evaluation?
6. What are some of the major contributions that the various evaluation approaches, viewed collectively, make to the practice of educational evaluation?
7. How might the various evaluation approaches be used together in an actual evaluation?

In Chapter 4 we presented a variety of ways to classify evaluation approaches—including our schema, which organizes the proposed approaches into six categories: objectives-oriented, management-oriented, consumer-oriented, expertise-oriented, adversary-oriented, and naturalistic and participant-oriented evaluation. Together these six represent the major current schools of thought about how to approach educational evaluation. And collectively, Chapters 5 through 10 summarize the theoretical and conceptual underpinnings of the primary evaluation models on which today's educational evaluators draw. It is, therefore, appropriate to ask how useful these models are.

The answer is "very useful indeed," as we shall discuss shortly. But first we feel compelled to offer several cautions.

CAUTIONS ABOUT THE ALTERNATIVE EVALUATION APPROACHES

Four cautions about the collective conceptions of evaluation presented in Chapters 5 through 10 are worthy of consideration here.

The Seminal Writings in Evaluation Are neither Models nor Theories

In a young field there is inevitably a good bit of conceptual floundering as notions are developed, circulated, tried out, refined, and challenged by new alternatives. Until a solid knowledge base begins to guide practice, any new field is likely to be guided by the positions, preferences, and polemics of its leaders. Some may argue that this is inappropriate. But the point is that it is also inevitable, for no new field or discipline is born full grown. Yet it is also appropriate to ask how far have the conceptions of leaders led the field, and in what direction.

Given the fact that educational evaluation grew in part out of scientific inquiry, it is not surprising that many evaluators have aspired to do science. As evaluational practitioners turned toward the various evaluation "models" as sources of guidance, many began asking how close educational evaluation was to becoming a science or discipline in its own right. Perhaps political, social, or situational naivete fosters the hope that evaluation will one day grow into a scientific discipline. That day, if attainable, would seem far off. Education itself is not a discipline but rather a professional field that draws its content from several disciplines.

Neurath and others (1955) note that scientific advancement in any field is often directly related to existence of a "univocal language," one in which there is one and only one term for each construct and where each important construct is so named. The semantic undergrowth in the field of evaluation could hardly be termed univocal; some clearing of redundant verbiage is clearly called for.

If one applies standard criteria for scientific models, the various evaluation approaches do not seem to qualify in any but the loosest sense. Even the less rigorous dictionary definitions of "models" seem ill-suited for the current evaluation literature. The most relevant definition is "something eminently worthy of imitation, an exemplar, an ideal," but without clearer operational guidelines and procedures, most evaluation "models" are so vague and general as to elude emulation in any strict sense.

If not models, then what about theories? Here again, our conceptions in evaluation seem not to fit. What we have come to call the theoretical underpinnings of our field lacks important characteristics of most theories. Our evaluation writings are not axiomatic or deductive bodies of knowledge. They do not enable us to develop, manipulate, or interrelate laws and explanations. They do not permit us to predict or explain. They are not tested in the empirical crucible or interrelated with or validated against other relevant bodies of knowledge.[56] In short, they are not theories.

If not models or theories, what are those influential conceptions about evaluation we have used six chapters of this book to present? Quite simply, they are individuals' conceptions about the field of evaluation, their efforts to order the content of a new and partial field into some kind of logical structure. They are sets of categories, lists of things to think about, descriptions of different kinds of evaluation, and exhortations to (perhaps) be heeded. Useful? Very. But theories? Models? No, clearly not.

'Discipleship' to a Particular Evaluation 'Model' Is a Danger

> Into the street the Piper stept,
>   Smiling first a little smile,
> As if he knew what magic slept
>   In his quiet pipe the while;
>
>   (Robert Browning, *The Pied Piper of Hamelin*)

Every evaluation approach described in this book has adherents who believe that a better evaluation will result from that orientation than from alternatives. Fair enough. We have no quarrel with those who follow particular persuasions, just so they do so intelligently, knowing when and where their preferred approach is not applicable, as well as when and how to apply it.

What is troublesome, however, is that every evaluation approach also has some unthinking disciples who are convinced that a particular approach to evaluation is right for every situation.[57] There really are evaluators who are "CIPP-model" loyalists, or unswerving adherents of the discrepancy evaluation model, or those who hold the tenets of responsive evaluation like articles of faith. Many evaluators unthinkingly follow a chosen evaluation approach into battle without first making certain the proposed strategy and tactics fit the terrain and will attain the desired outcomes of the campaign. Insisting that the judicial evaluation model be used for an internal formative evaluation where the issues, not to mention the program, are vague and amorphous is as foolish as mounting a cavalry attack across a swamp.

Ideally, evaluation practitioners will be sufficiently at home with a variety of evaluation approaches to select one appropriate for the situation, rather than distorting the interests and needs of the evaluation's audience(s) to make them fit a preferred approach.

Combining Evaluation Approaches into One Omnibus Evaluation Model Is Unwise, Even if Possible

The proliferation of proposals for how to do educational evaluation has frustrated some writers. Antonoplos laments the "saturation of education with evaluation models" (1977, p. 7) and argues that it (1) inordinately confuses the person who wants an evaluation conducted; (2) causes methodological problems in planning and implementing evaluation studies; (3) fragments and reduces efforts to build evaluation theory; and (4) makes the task of the learner horrendous. He calls for empirical research on the effectiveness of existing models and proposes "synthesizing them in a manner that is parsimonious, that prevents premature closure, and that reduces burdensome verbiage" (Antonoplos, 1977, p. 9).

Gephart (1977) suggests that the diversity of evaluation models is illusory:

> I think it much more logical to assume there is one model than to assume there are multiple models. Circumstances are such that it appears to be some larger number than one because *we do not know enough about the process* to see that they all fit together, let alone to understand *how* they fit together. (Gephart, 1977, pp. 1–2)

Continuing his call for a synthesis of the alternative approaches, Gephart (1978) complains that "the multiple model mess has become dysfunctional!" and argues that the only real difference in the models "is the verbiage used to describe the elements of the 'different' models" (Gephart, 1978, pp. 2–3). Proposing six dimensions for use in synthesizing existing evaluation models, Gephart notes that the evolving nature of educational evaluation requires that any synthesis remain open to change as the field advances.

Were it possible to achieve, a synthesis would unravel evaluation's currently tangled literature, especially if the purpose of the synthesis were limited to identifying similarities in approaches. One might profitably analyze the various evaluation approaches in terms of their concepts and constructs, assumptions and orientations, terminology and (where provided) proposed methodology—and then ask to what extent these approaches really look at different but related evaluation phenomena. Perhaps, with all approaches viewed in aggregate, a more complete portrayal of evaluation would emerge. If a synthesis accomplished nothing more than to bring into the present jungle of terminology some semblance of semantic cultivation, the effort would be useful.

Yet, there are inherent dangers in attempting to synthesize alternatives, especially if the intent is to create the "one model" (of which Gephart speaks) generally applicable in education.

First, the alternative evaluation approaches described in the preceding chapters are based on widely divergent philosophical assumptions. Although some are compatible enough to be fruitfully combined, integrating all would be a philosophical impossibility, for key aspects of some approaches are directly incompatible with central concerns of others.[58] One might "synthesize" diverse ethnic cultures in an unprejudiced societal "melting pot," but there is little hope of creating a similar synthesis of the inhabitants of a zoo. The analogy to educational evaluation is distressingly apt. It would be unfortunate if efforts to synthesize diametrically opposed approaches into one "model" resulted in so much philosophical dilution that the whole was truly less than the sum of its parts.

Second, as mentioned earlier, unthinking discipleship is a tendency among at least some educational evaluators. If a more prestigious synthesized evaluation model were created, it seems likely that disciple-prone evaluators would gather around the new banner in greater numbers than for any previous approach. There would be little advantage in trading provincial bondage to become vassals of a strong centralized monarchy. Intellectual bondage is intellectual bondage no matter where it exists.

A more serious danger lies in the fact that moving toward one omnibus model at this time could bring premature closure to expansion and refinement within the field. Our conceptions are still too untried and our empirical base too weak for us to be very certain of which notions should be preserved and which discarded. How does one go about synthesizing undeveloped, untested hunches and speculative statements? It would seem far preferable to tolerate our contradictory and confusing welter of ideas and make of them what we can than to hammer them into a unified but impoverished conception of evaluation. "The dangers are not in working with models, but in working with too few, and those too much alike, and above all, in belittling any efforts to work with anything else" (Kaplan, 1964, p. 293). Just because we can synthesize does not mean we should. As Kaplan puts it,

> A model is always possible, but it is not always useful in a given state of knowledge.
> What limits its usefulness is not usually an inadequacy in our knowledge of. . .the subject-matter. The requirements of a model then impose a premature closure on our ideas. . .[and] limits our awareness of unexplored possibilities of conceptualization. We tinker with the model when we might be better occupied with the subject-matter itself. . .incorporating it in a model does not automatically give such knowledge scientific status. The maturity of our ideas is usually a matter of slow growth, which cannot be forced. . . . Closure is premature if it lays down the lines for our thinking to follow when we do not know enough to say even whether one direction or another is the more promising. (Kaplan, 1964, p. 279)

A final concern has to do with whether we would really be enriched if the multitude of schemes and suggestions for how to do an evaluation could somehow be streamlined into one or two more sophisticated guidelines. Evaluation contexts are so different that it is difficult to conceive of any one or two models that would be relevant to all. For all their crudity and imperfection, diverse models offer a richness of perspectives—especially if one uses evaluation approaches eclectically (where philosophical compatibility permits), as we shall propose later.

The Choice of Evaluation Approach Is Not Empirically Based

If one accepts our view that it is useful to have a variety of evaluation alternatives, the next logical question is, how will one know which approach is best for a given situation? And that question is devilishly difficult to answer because of one simple fact: There is almost no research to guide one's choice.

Over the years many evaluators have called for a program of research on evaluation (for example, Stufflebeam and others, 1971; Worthen, 1972b, 1977b; Antonoplos, 1977). For the most part, their calls have fallen on deaf ears.[59] The lack of an adequate empirical base is probably the single most important impediment to development of a more adequate evaluation theory and models. In the absence of relevant evidence, about which model works best under which circumstances, adherence to any one model rather than another is largely a statement of philosophy or a profession of faith. As Scriven muses,

> There has been a good deal of work on "evaluation models" which are hybrids between ways of conceptualizing evaluation and reminders as to how to do it. These range from the highly relativistic and value free approaches of many Tyler students and Malcolm Provus' Discrepancy Evaluation, through the touchy-feely school of transactional and responsive evaluation (Rippey and Stake respectively) to the extremely far-reaching and absolutistic approach that I have espoused. Each can, I believe, contribute something of value to most clients, but beyond that I can hardly make a dispassionate judgment. (Scriven, 1976b, pp. 28–29)

Antonoplos is more specific:

> there is little agreement or data to support the efficacy of one definition, model or approach over another and. . .empirical data are needed to determine the extent to which the various models are theoretically and operationally different and the particular goals or purposes for which they are best suited. (Antonoplos, 1977, p. 4)

Years after he first pointed out the need for such research, Stufflebeam was forced to conclude that "there has been very little empirical research on the relative merits of different approaches to evaluation. Clearly, the field of evaluation could profit from systematic examinations of the feasibility, costs, and benefits of competing conceptualizations. . . ." (Stufflebeam, 1981, p. 4).

Until we have solid information about the relative effectiveness of the numerous evaluation approaches, choices among alternatives will remain a matter of the evaluator's preference.

Negative Metaphors Underlying Some Approaches Can Cause Negative Side Effects

In Chapter 4 we discussed how different evaluation metaphors have led to widely diverse evaluation approaches. This leads us to a disquieting fact about these underlying metaphors: namely, that they are predicated upon negative assumptions that fall into one of two categories.

First, several metaphors tacitly assume there is something wrong in the system being evaluated; a patient has died and the cause of death must be discovered (for example, forensic medicine or pathology); a scandal has emerged and the truth must be uncovered (investigative journalism or investigative social research); or allegations have been made and must be investigated (adversary hearings). Such indictment mentality is short-sighted and should be discouraged.

Second, several metaphors are based on assumptions that people will lie, evade questions, or withhold information as a matter of course. For example, in Douglas's (1976) volume on investigative social research, he notes that most social research techniques are based on a cooperative methodology that assumes candor and honesty once one builds rapport with interviewees, informants, etc. Instead, he proposes an alternate confrontive methodology for handling dishonesty and evasion, which he asserts are typical in situations fraught with anxiety and threat.

If we accept Glass's (1975) thesis that evaluation is basically anxiety provoking to those being evaluated, then we could readily conclude that Douglas's methods would be appropriate for collecting data in most educational evaluations. But that would be tantamount to saying that individuals whose programs are being evaluated are prone to be deceitful, dishonest, and evasive, which is an absurd generalization on its face. To champion any evaluation methodology that leads to mutual distrust between evaluators and educational practitioners would not only be wrongheaded but also self-defeating.

Which brings us to a critical question: Can one draw on metaphors such as investigative journalism, investigative social research, congressional hearings, and the like without their serving as Trojan horses to carry insidious assumptions into the precepts and practice of evaluation? We have uneasy visions of educational evaluators marching in the wake of Ralph Nader, evaluating the educational enterprise with no more care than that shown in Nader's assault on the Educational Testing Service and the school testing industry. Or imagine an evaluation analog to Senator Proxmire's "Golden Fleece Awards." Cohen (1978) tells of how irresponsible distortions of his own research by a *National Enquirer* reporter led Proxmire to request the formal report of Cohen's research from the sponsoring National Science Foundation. The spectre of evaluation becoming a degenerate example of tabloid journalism is frightening—and perhaps not so farfetched as we'd like to think. It would be unfortunate to try broadening evaluators' perspectives and succeed only in creating a muckraker mind-set.

One way to avoid some of these problems would be to evoke more positive metaphors, such as the health maintenance approach to medicine. Diagnoses and prescriptions (however unpalatable) are likely to be accepted more gracefully if it is apparent from the outset that the primary objective is not only to uncover and eradicate what is wrong but also to identify and strengthen what is working well.

CONTRIBUTIONS OF THE ALTERNATIVE EVALUATION APPROACHES

If, as argued earlier, the evaluation approaches suggested in the literature are not models or theories, and if there is no empirical basis for deciding which to follow when designing and conducting a particular evaluation, then of what worth are they? Of considerable worth, actually. A novice evaluator may not use Scriven's (1974a) modus operandi method of evaluation, but probably no month passes without that evaluator somehow making conscious use of the concepts of formative or summative evaluation Scriven introduced to our thinking. Individuals may spend years as evaluators and never once use Stufflebeam's (1971) "CIPP model" of evaluation, but most likely they have checked one or more of their evaluation designs against Stufflebeam's (1973b) list of steps in designing evaluations. In similar ways, most of the evaluation approaches summarized in prior chapters influence in important ways the practice of evaluation.

Thinking back to evaluations we have done, our colleagues' work was used in this way in almost every study. As noted earlier,

Although I have developed some preferences of my own in doing evaluations, probably 75 percent of what I do is application of what I have distilled from others' ideas. Doubtlessly, all who have been repeatedly exposed to the evaluation literature have absorbed much "through the pores," as it were, and now reapply it without cognizance of its source. Although few of us may conduct our evaluations in strict adherence to any "model" of evaluation, few of us conduct evaluations which are not enormously influenced by the impact of our colleagues' thinking on our own preferences and actions. (Worthen, 1977b, p. 12)

The alternative conceptions about how evaluation should be conducted—the accompanying sets of categories, lists of things to think about, descriptions of different strategies, and exhortations to heed—influence the practice of educational evaluation in sometimes subtle, sometimes direct, but always significant ways. Some evaluation designs adopt or adapt proposed approaches. Many educational evaluators, however, conduct evaluations without strict adherence (or even intentional attention) to any "model," yet draw unconsciously in their philosophy, plans, and procedures on what they have internalized through exposure to the literature. So the value of the alternative approaches lies in their capacity to help us think, to present and provoke new ideas and techniques, and to serve as mental checklists of things we ought to consider, remember, or worry about. Their heuristic value is very high; their prescriptive value seems much less.

COMPARATIVE ANALYSIS OF CHARACTERISTICS OF ALTERNATIVE EVALUATION APPROACHES

So many new concepts have been presented in Chapters 5 through 10 that the reader might be feeling challenged to assimilate all of it. The matrix in Figure 11.1—a comparative analysis of the characteristics, strengths, and limitations of the six approaches—should help. The aspects of each approach that we have chosen to highlight are as follows:

1. *Proponents*—Individuals who have written about the approach.
2. *Purpose of Evaluation*—The intended use(s) of evaluation proposed by writers advocating each particular approach, or purposes that may be inferred from their writings.
3. *Distinguishing Characteristics*—Key descriptors associated with each approach.
4. *Past Uses of the Approach*—Ways in which each approach has been used in education.
5. *Contributions to the Conceptualization of an Evaluation*—Distinctions, new terms or concepts, logical relationships, and other aids suggested by proponents of each approach that appear to be major or unique contributions.
6. *Criteria for Judging Evaluations*—Explicitly or implicitly defined expectations that may be used to judge the quality of evaluations that follow each approach.
7. *Benefits*—Strengths that may be attributed to each approach and reasons why one might want to use this approach (what it can do *for* you).
8. *Limitations*—Risks associated with use of each approach (what it can do *to* you).

FIGURE 11.1 Comparative Analysis of Alternative Evaluation Approaches

	Objectives-Oriented	Management-Oriented	Consumer-Oriented	Expertise-Oriented	Adversary-Oriented	Naturalistic & Participant-Oriented
1. Some Proponents	Tyler, Provus, Metfessel and Michael, Hammond, Popham, Taba, Bloom, Talmage	Stufflebeam, Alkin, Provus	Scriven, Komoski	Eisner, Accreditation Groups	Wolf, Owens, Levine, Kourilsky	Stake, Patton, Guba and Lincoln, Rippey, MacDonald, Parlett and Hamilton
2. Purpose of Evaluation	Determining the extent to which objectives are achieved	Providing useful information to aid in making decisions	Providing information about educational products to aid decisions about educational purchases or adoptions	Providing professional judgments of quality	Providing a balanced examination of all sides of controversial issues or highlighting both strengths and weaknesses of a program	Understanding and portraying the complexities of an educational activity, responding to an audience's requirements for information
3. Distinguishing Characteristics	Specifying measureable objectives, using objective instruments to gather data, looking for discrepancies between objectives and performance	Serving rational decision making, evaluating at all stages of program development	Using criterion checklists to analyze products, product testing, informing consumers	Basing judgments on individual knowledge and experience, use of consensus standards, team/site visitations	Use of public hearings, use of opposing points of view, decision based on arguments heard during proceedings	Reflecting multiple realities, use of inductive reasoning and discovery, firsthand experience on site

4. *Past Uses*	Curriculum development, monitoring student achievement, needs assessment	Program development, institutional management systems, program planning, accountability	Consumer reports, product development, selection of products for dissemination	Self-study, blue-ribbon panels, accreditation, examination by committee, criticism	Examination of controversial programs or issues, policy hearings	Examination of innovations or change about which little is known, ethnographies of operating programs
5. *Contributions to the Conceptualization of an Evaluation*	Pre-post measurement of performance; clarify goals; use objective tests and measurements that are technically sound	Needs to: identify and evaluate needs and objectives; consider alternative program designs, evaluate them; watch the implementation of a program, look for bugs and explain outcomes; see if needs have been reduced or eliminated; meta-evaluation; guidelines for institutionalizing evaluation	Lists of criteria for evaluating educational products and activities; archival references for completed reviews; formative-summative roles of evaluation bias control	Legitimation of subjective criticism; self-study with outside verification; standards	Use of forensic and judicial forms of public hearing; cross-examination of evidence; thorough presentation of multiple perspectives; focus on, and clarification of issues	Emergent evaluation designs; use of inductive reasoning; recognition of multiple realities; importance of studying context; criteria for judging the rigor of naturalistic inquiry

FIGURE 11.1 CONTINUED

	Objectives-Oriented	Management-Oriented	Consumer-Oriented	Expertise-Oriented	Adversary-Oriented	Naturalistic & Participant-Oriented
6. Criteria for Judging Evaluations	Measurability of objectives; measurement reliability and validity	Utility, feasibility, propriety, and technical soundness	Freedom from bias, technical soundness, defensible criteria used to draw conclusions and make recommendations; evidence of need and effectiveness are required	Use of recognized standards; qualifications of experts	Balance, fairness, publicness, opportunity for cross-examination	Credibility, fit, auditability confirmability
7. Benefits	Ease of use, simplicity, focus on outcomes, high acceptability, forces objectives to be set	Comprehensiveness, sensitivity to information needs of those in a leadership position, systematic approach to evaluation, use of evaluation throughout the process of program development, well operationalized with detailed guidelines for implementation, use of a wide variety of information	Emphasis on consumer information needs, influence on product developers, concern with cost-effectiveness and utility, availability of checklists	Broad coverage, efficiency (ease of implementation, timing), capitalizes on human judgment	Broad coverage, close examination of claims, aim toward closure or resolution, illumination of different sides of issues, impact on audience, use of a wide variety of information	Focus on description and judgment, concern with context, openness to evolve evaluation plan, pluralistic, use of inductive reasoning, use of a wide variety of information, emphasis on understanding

8. *Limitations*	Oversimplification of evaluation and education, outcomes-only orientation, reductionistic, linear, over-emphasis on student testing	Emphasis on organizational efficiency and production model, assumption of orderliness and predictability in decision making, can be expensive to administer and maintain, narrow focus on the concerns of leaders	Cost and lack of sponsorship, may suppress creativity or innovation, not open to debate or cross-examination	Replicability, vulnerability to personal bias, scarcity of supporting documentation to support conclusions, open to conflict of interest, superficial look at context, overuse of intuition, reliance on qualifications of the "experts"	Fallible arbiters or judges, high potential costs and consumption of time, reliance on investigatory and communication skills of presenters, potential irrelevancies or artificial polarization, limited to information that is presented	Nondirective, tendency to be attracted by the bizarre or atypical, potentially high labor intensity and cost, hypothesis generating, potential for failure to reach closure

ECLECTIC USES OF THE ALTERNATIVE EVALUATION APPROACHES

The purpose in the foregoing comparative analysis is to provide key information on the strengths, limitations, and primary uses of each approach. The information in Figure 11.1 is not intended to imply that any one approach is "best"; rather, it is our contention that each approach can be useful. The challenge is to determine which approach (or combination of concepts from different approaches) is most relevant to the task at hand.

Perhaps an experience of one of the authors in attempting to answer a question of a student in a graduate evaluation seminar will help make the point.

> We were conducting a several-week-long examination of various authors' evaluation models and how each might be applied to do an evaluation, when one student asked,... "What model do you usually use?"...I pointed out that I did not believe there was one best model, that each has its strengths, and that I simply used whichever model was most appropriate to the situation at hand.
>
> "How do you know which one is most appropriate?" she queried. I...talked about things like looking at the purpose of the evaluation, the kind of decision needed, limitations of the model, and so on,...and concluded...that a lot of it was in experience and, although a little tough at first, they would all get the hang of it once they had done a few evaluations.
>
> "Maybe it would help," she stated, "if you could give us a few examples of where you've used one of the models and then show us why you picked it."
>
> That seemed like a very useful suggestion,...so I began to sort through my mental files to find the very best examples of where I had used one of the evaluation models. Then I began to sort to find *any* examples of where I had used one of the models. I discarded evaluation after evaluation because I really had not used the model, whatever it was, fully. There were truncated CIPP evaluations (Stufflebeam, 1973a) since I seldom seemed to be called on early enough to do much with context or input evaluations. There were applications of Hammond's cube (Hammond, 1973) for selecting variables, but the rest of the evaluation failed to follow Hammond's ideas. Each was incomplete as an example of use of the models, and I struggled for more pure examples to offer.
>
> Finally, I remembered using Stake's "Countenance" model (1967) in its entirety in evaluating an administrators' training program. That one was memorable because it had been a class project where two students and I took it on...so they could get the experience.... That one brought others to mind and before long I was able to give examples of using several of the models in the way they were intended to be used. The intriguing realization was that every one of those examples came from class projects conducted jointly with students, where I had intentionally adhered to the models to demonstrate their features. I could not recall a single "lone-wolf" evaluation of my own where I had consciously selected any single model to guide the study. Instead, for several years I had been designing each evaluation *de novo*, pulling pieces of the models in as they seemed relevant. Certain features of some models I used frequently, others seldom or never.
>
> That realization seemed worth sharing, although in the process I felt a twinge of disloyalty toward some of my esteemed colleagues and friends for never really using their models in my work.... The class was slightly taken back at first by my heretical

revelation, but they seemed comforted when I pointed out that there were distinct advantages in eclecticism, since one was free to choose the best from diverse sources, systems, or styles (I failed to mention any of the potential philosophical perils of such an approach). Warming to the idea, I argued that one could choose the best features of each model and weave them into a stronger overall approach—really a classic bit of cake-having and cake-eating. . . .

We talked for the remainder of the class about why each evaluation required a somewhat different mix of ingredients, how synthesis and eclecticism were not identical, and why an eclectic approach may be useful. . . . (Worthen, 1977b, pp. 2–5)

The authors of this text are both self-confessed eclectics in our evaluation work, choosing and combining concepts from the evaluation approaches to fit the particular situation, using pieces of various evaluation approaches as they seem appropriate. In very few instances has either of us adhered to any particular "model" of evaluation. Rather, we find we can ensure a better fit by snipping and sewing together bits and pieces off the more traditional ready-made approaches and even weaving a bit of homespun, if necessary, rather than by pulling any existing approach off the shelf. Tailoring works.

Obviously, eclecticism has its limitations (after all, it has been derided as the discipline of undisciplined minds), and one obviously cannot suggest that we develop an "eclectic model" of evaluation, for that would be an obvious non sequitur. And the uninformed could perform egregious errors in the name of eclecticism, such as proposing that a program's objectives be evaluated as a first step in conducting a goal-free evaluation, or laying out a preordinate design for a responsive evaluation. Assuming that one avoids mixing evaluation's philosophically incompatible "oil and water,"[60] the eclectic use of the writings presented in the preceding chapters has far more potential advantages than disadvantages, whether that eclecticism means combining alternative approaches or selectively combining the methods and techniques inherent within those approaches.

Evaluators who have urged that more thoughtful attention be given to eclecticism include Talmage (1982), Cronbach and others (1980), Cronbach (1982), and Conner and others (1984). Yet eclectic use of the evaluator's tools is a lamentably infrequent occurrence in educational evaluation. Much of educational evaluation's potential lies in the scope of strategies it can employ and in the possibility of selectively combining those approaches (Worthen, 1981). Narrow, rigid adherence to single approaches must give way to more mature, sophisticated evaluations that welcome diversity. Admittedly, this will be a challenging task. But that does not lessen its importance.

DRAWING PRACTICAL IMPLICATIONS FROM THE ALTERNATIVE EVALUATION APPROACHES

All the educational evaluation approaches we have presented have something to contribute to the practicing evaluator. They may be used heuristically to generate questions or uncover issues. The literature contains many useful conceptual, methodological, political, communicative, and administrative guidelines. Finally, the approaches offer powerful tools that the evaluator may use or adapt in his work.

Later in this book we will look at practical guidelines for planning and conducting evaluations. Many of these guidelines have been developed as part of a particular approach to evaluation. Fortunately, however, they are generalizable, usable whenever and wherever needed. Just as a skilled carpenter will not use only a hammer to build a fine house, so a skilled evaluator will not depend solely on one approach to plan and conduct a high-quality evaluation.

Let us now turn to practical uses of the tools that evaluation practitioners, theorists, and methodologists have generated.

APPLICATION EXERCISE

Pupils entering the first grade in a particular small town were routinely tested, using the *Metropolitan Reading Readiness Test*. Typically, these students scored at or above the established national norms for the test. On the 1985 and 1986 administrations of the test, however, student performance fell significantly below national norms. In attempts to interpret this sudden drop in students' entry-level scores, school officials compared first grade classes from 1975 to 1985 on the following characteristics:

1. Nature of half-day kindergarten experience
2. Performance on mental ability tests
3. Kindergarten teachers' education and professional experiences
4. Socioeconomic background of students.

Students entering the first grade in 1983 or 1984 had equivalent kindergarten experiences and performed at least as well as their predecessors on mental ability tests. The educational level and professional experience of the kindergarten teachers during the 10-year period was comparable. School officials discovered that the average family income had risen sharply during the 10 years. Further analysis of the data showed that this rise was due largely to an increase in the number of families in which both parents were employed. School officials hypothesized that the mothers' absence from the home adversely affected pupils' readiness levels. On the basis of this information, the school system applied for and received a grant to establish a municipal day-care center for young children of working mothers. It was planned that the center would be staffed by women in the community who had extensive experience in caring for preschool children. Only children of working mothers were to be included in the program.

An evaluation plan was developed, calling for:

1. Identification of a population of preschool children in the town whose mothers did not work and who did not attend the center.
2. Comparison of those children's performance on the *Metropolitan Reading Readiness Test*, at the end of the program's first year, with performance of preschool children who attended the center.

3. A thorough weekly examination of the range of effects of the day-care center on preschool children, using direct observation.
4. A monthly survey of the community's reactions to the day-care center.
5. Determination of the long-range effects of the program by following the day-care center children through the first three grades and comparing their progress with that of children who had not attended the center.

Using each of the six evaluation approaches discussed in Chapters 5 through 10 in this book, decide whether you agree or disagree with the evaluation plan just described. For each approach, describe how that approach might lead you to proceed differently with the evaluation. Do you see any combination of approaches that would be particularly useful in evaluating this program?

SUGGESTED READINGS

GUBA, E. G., & LINCOLN, Y. S. (1981). *Effective evaluation*. San Francisco: Jossey-Bass.

HOUSE, E. R. (1980). *Evaluating with validity*. Beverly Hills, CA: Sage.

MADAUS, G. F., SCRIVEN, M., & STUFFLEBEAM, D. L. (1983). *Evaluation models: Viewpoints on educational and human services evaluation*. Boston: Kluwer-Nijhoff.

STUFFLEBEAM, D. L., & SHINKFIELD, A. J. (1985). *Systematic evaluation*. Boston: Kluwer-Nijhoff.

Part Three
Practical Guidelines for Planning Evaluations

In Part One we discussed basic evaluation roles and concepts and described the history of educational evaluation. In Part Two we examined factors that led to alternative conceptions of evaluation, summarized the key characteristics and strengths and weaknesses of six general evaluation approaches, and argued for thoughtful use of those approaches, including eclectic combining of features of the alternative approaches, when doing so would be advantageous.

Which bings us to the heart of this book—practical guidelines. In this part we begin to provide guidelines that we believe will be helpful to evaluators, regardless of which evaluation approach or combination of approaches they might elect to use. We also focus on guidelines for planning evaluation efforts (and in Part Four focus on guidelines for conducting evaluations). We begin Part Three by examining in Chapter 12 reasons that lead to evaluations being initiated, considerations in deciding when to evaluate ("always" is a common but incorrect answer), and how to determine who should conduct the evaluation. In Chapter 13 we discuss the importance of the evaluator understanding the educational setting and context in which the evaluation will take place, as well as the importance of characterizing accurately that which is to be evaluated. Two crucial steps in evaluation planning—identifying and selecting evaluative questions and criteria, and planning the information collection, analysis, and interpretation—are examined in detail in Chapters 14 and 15. Chapter 16, which ends Part Three, presents guidelines for developing management plans for evaluation studies and consideration of the importance of establishing evaluation agreements and contracts.

The focus of the chapters that follow is decidedly practical. Although we will continue to quote or reference other sources, these chapters are not intended as scholarly reviews of the content covered. Were such reviews to be included, several of these chapters could each fill a textbook. Our intent is only to introduce enough information to give both the evaluator and user of evaluation an awareness of how to proceed and direction to more detailed coverage of many (especially technical) topics in other textbooks. Experience and further study will have to suffice to teach the rest.

INTRODUCTION OF A CASE STUDY

To help readers apply the content of the chapters in this and the following section, we have included a case study, which we will thread through the chapters. At the end of each chapter is a section on "Application to the Case Study," where we will attempt briefly to describe how we would apply some of the content of that chapter to one particular evaluation of a public school curriculum. It is important to point out that not *all* of the content in *any* chapter can be applied to the case study; such an attempt would double the length of this book. We have selected only those few concepts to discuss within the case study that we think will be most helpful in making or clarifying our points. We hope that this case study will help to show how at least some of the guidelines we discuss could be applied to a real evaluation.

Setting the Stage—The Case Study

The case study we will use is one first prepared for use by the Association for Supervision and Curriculum Development (ASCD) in their instructive and entertaining examination of applied strategies for curriculum evaluation (Brandt, 1981). "Knowing that few school districts can afford to hire noted authorities to evaluate their programs, [the ASCD] invited six experts to describe what they might do if they were asked to evaluate the Radnor humanities curriculum" (Brandt, 1981, pp. vii–viii), a real curriculum that existed in the Radnor Middle School in Wayne, Pennsylvania, but which was only described to the six experts in brief written form. The written description of the Radnor humanities curriculum provided to the six evaluators is presented below (in the form of a short report of the humanities curriculum review committee, prefaced by a brief stage-setting introduction by the ASCD editor). Beginning in Chapter 12 of this book, and extending through Chapter 21, one of the six proposals for how the evaluation should be conducted (Worthen, 1981) is presented, by permission of ASCD, and adapted and extended as necessary to fit the needs of this text.

Two introductory comments are appropriate. First, only one of the six approaches to evaluating the Radnor curriculum outlined in the ASCD book could be included here, and that one is a rather eclectic "multiple method" style we have come to favor. The other chapters in the ASCD book illustrate how other individuals would apply their preferred evaluation approaches, such as participant-oriented, expertise-oriented, or decision-oriented evaluation. Collectively, these chapters illustrate how a variety of evaluation approaches might be applied to a single curriculum. We strongly endorse the entire ASCD book as excellent supplemental reading to this text.

Second, we have left the evaluation case study in the informal, singular, first-person form in which it first appeared, and have included in Chapter 12 the introduction that provides a framework for the case study, as it appears there and throughout the next several chapters of this text.

Now for the description of the Radnor curriculum.

THE RADNOR HUMANITIES CURRICULUM

"How have you evaluated this program?" asked the president of the board of education. She seemed determined to maintain an air of objectivity, but the atmosphere was growing tense in the school library where the board was meeting.

The main business of the evening was a report on the middle school's humanities program. Prepared by a committee of 11 educators and six parents, the report was the product of more than 30 committee meetings plus discussions with students, staff, and citizens, and correspondence with other schools. It explained philosophy, listed goals and objectives, described the curriculum in detail, made specific recommendations, and included a rationale for each recommendation. It even listed a number of alternatives that had been considered, but which were rejected as undesirable.

All students in the sixth, seventh, and eighth grades were required to take the humanities course, which was taught two days a week by four teachers, including an artist and a musician, all members of a separate humanities department. The arts—everything from literature, drama, film, music, and dance, to architecture and the visual arts—were used to develop the students' "understanding of all that it means to be human." Looking at a Van Gogh painting of a Flemish mining family at dinner, for instance, students might be asked, "Would you like to be invited to dinner here?" as well as, "What tones and colors did the painter use?" They might listen to Humperdink's opera, *Hansel and Gretel*, or "She's Leaving Home," by the Beatles. Examples were drawn from African and Oriental cultures as well as from European and American.

The program should be continued, the report said, with some modifications, including a new organizational framework based on the concepts and skills being taught, and increased emphasis on writing and other language skills.

Several board members and parents were not satisfied. A woman who was a member of the study committee, but who had not attended most meetings, read a statement expressing concern about the general direction of American education and objected to "values clarification" and "secular humanism" in the program. (The teachers insisted they did not use techniques such as those advocated by Simon, Howe, and Kirschenbaum in *Values Clarification: A Handbook of Practical Strategies for Teachers and Students*, New York: Hart, 1972.)

Others said a humanities course would be more appropriate for older students, who would have the background to appreciate it, but that students in the middle school needed more basic knowledge first. One board member asked what impact the program was having on students and how it could be measured.

Pointing out that the program had been in limbo for more than a year, the principal, assistant superintendent for curriculum, and the superintendent gave strong personal endorsement and asked for an immediate decision. Several parents added their support. But when the meeting ended at 11:00 P.M., the board had postponed acceptance of the committee's report until they could talk privately with the principal about how the program could be scheduled and staffed in light of declining enrollments.

Ten days later, a majority of the board members voted to permit continuation of the humanities course. Still, evaluation remained an issue. In reply to the question about measurement, the principal had said it couldn't be done statistically; the course did not teach children *what* to think and feel, it taught them *to* think and feel. (Brandt, 1981, pp. vi–vii, reprinted by permission)

Evaluation of the Radnor Humanities Curriculum

In the remaining chapters, practical guidelines for various aspects of evaluation will be discussed and then applied, in turn, at the end of each chapter, to the preceding humanities curriculum.

Chapter 12
Clarifying the Evaluation Request and Responsibilities

Orienting Questions

1. Suppose you received a telephone call from a potential client asking if you would do an evaluation. What are some of the first questions you would ask?
2. Are there times you would decline a request for evaluation? If so, under what conditions?
3. Why is the political environment of an evaluation an important early consideration in clarifying the evaluation request?
4. What are some advantages and disadvantages in having an evaluation conducted by an external evaluator?
5. What criteria would you use to select an external evaluator?

In the preceding chapters we discussed evaluation's promise for improving education. As we've seen, educational and legislative leaders in many countries look to evaluation as a key to making their schools better. The potential and promise of evaluation may create the impression that it is *always* appropriate to evaluate and that every facet of every educational endeavor should be evaluated.

Such is not the case. The temptation to evaluate everything may be compelling in an idealistic sense, but it ignores many practical realities.

In this chapter we discuss how the evaluator can better understand the origin of a proposed evaluation and judge whether or not the study would be appropriate.

To clarify the discussion, we need to differentiate here among several groups or individuals who affect or are affected by an evaluation study: sponsors, clients, participants, stakeholders, and audiences.

An evaluation's *sponsor* is the agency or individual who authorizes the evaluation and provides necessary fiscal resources for its conduct. Sponsors may or may not actually select the evaluator or be involved in shaping the study, but they have ultimate authority concerning the evaluation, except when they delegate that authority.

The *client* is the specific agency or individual who requests the evaluation. In many instances, the sponsor and client are synonymous—but not always. For example, in a third-party evaluation of a school district's program for gifted children, the district (client) requests and arranges for the actual study, but the requirement and funding for the evaluation both originate with the state education department (sponsor).

Obviously, the evaluator "participates" in the evaluation study; indeed, he conducts it. But we use the term *participants* to refer to those with whom the evaluator interacts during the planning and conduct of an evaluation, and/or from whom evaluation information is elicited. Participants usually include the client(s) —at least during the planning stages—and those from whom data are collected (for example, students to whom tests or attitude scales are administered).

Stakeholders are those who may be directly affected by evaluation results. School officials, program staff, and parents are common stakeholders. Evaluation sponsors, clients, and participants are usually stakeholders, but some stakeholders do not fall into these groups. For example, it is possible (though probably not wise) to evaluate a school district's program for gifted students without ever interacting with the program teachers. Obviously, those teachers might be affected greatly by the study's outcomes, so they are clearly stakeholders, although they might not be participants.

Audiences include individuals, groups, and agencies who have an interest in the evaluation and receive its results. Sponsors and clients are usually the primary audiences and may occasionally be the only audiences. Generally an evaluation's audiences will also include all stakeholders and participants, although that is not always so. For example, elementary school students might be participants in an evaluation of their school's reading program, being observed, tested, or interviewed; but only in some circumstances would they likely display much interest in the results of that evaluation. More will be said about evaluation audiences in Chapter 13.

UNDERSTANDING THE REASONS FOR INITIATING THE EVALUATION

It is important to understand what prompts an evaluation. Indeed, determining the purpose is probably the most important decision the evaluation sponsor will make in the course of an evaluation. And understanding that purpose is probably the most important insight the evaluator can have. If some problem prompted the decision to evaluate, if some stakeholder has demanded an evaluation, the evaluator should know about it. Presumably, the decision to evaluate stemmed from someone's need to know. Whose need? What do they want to know? Why?

Sometimes the evaluation client can answer such questions directly and clearly. Unfortunately, that is not always the case, and the evaluator's task is made more difficult when the client has no clear picture of what the evaluation should accomplish. It is not uncommon to find that the clients or sponsors are unsophisticated about evaluation procedures and have not thought deeply about possible ramifications or results. As one evaluator noted,

I have found that the purpose of evaluation depends on many factors, and their interrelationships must be uncovered before the study is planned. It is not always obvious, even to the persons who commission the evaluation study, *why* the evaluation is being planned. It is through program observation, reading of proposals and materials, and the probing of intents and expectations from program, administrative, and funding personnel that the purpose of the evaluation is clarified. (Bracht, 1974, p. 1)

Such probing is necessary to clarify purposes and procedures. Where sponsors or clients are already clear about what they hope to obtain, it is no less crucial for the evaluator to understand their motivations. She can often do so by exploring—with whoever is requesting the evaluation—such questions as these:

1. Why is this evaluation being requested? What is its purpose? What questions will it answer?
2. To what use will the evaluation findings be put? By whom? Who else should be informed of the evaluation results?
3. What is to be evaluated? What does it include? Exclude? During what time period? In what settings? For whom is this object intended? Who will participate? What are its goals and objectives? What need is it intended to address? Who is in charge of it? Has it ever been evaluated before?
4. How much time and money are available for the evaluation? Who is available to help with the evaluation? Is certain information needed right away?
5. What is the political climate and context surrounding the evaluation? Will any political factors and forces preclude a meaningful and fair evaluation?

The foregoing questions are only examples, and evaluators might add or subtract others. What is important is that, through careful questioning and listening, the evaluator comes to understand the purpose for the evaluation. Not all purposes are equally valid. Brinkerhoff and his colleagues (1983) suggest that an evaluation purpose is defensible if it meets these criteria:

- *Clear* (understood by important audiences)
- *Accessible* (disseminated to those who have a right to know)
- *Useful* (the information produced will be used)
- *Relevant* (intended to meet an information need that will serve the program)
- *Humane* (can be accomplished without harming those involved or affected)
- *Compatible* (congruent with goals of the sponsor, client, participants, and stakeholders)
- *Worthwhile* (its probable benefit justifies its probable costs).

By listening closely to the client's reasons for initiating the evaluation, the evaluator can determine whether a formative or summative role for the evaluation is intended and can also suggest to the client other reasons for evaluating that may prove even more productive. Thus, the evaluator may reorient the entire evaluation in useful ways even before it begins.

Informational and Noninformational Uses of Evaluation

Educational evaluation is usually intended to enhance our understanding of the educational value of whatever is evaluated. That understanding depends, in turn, on the adequacy of the information collected. But evaluation also has noninformational uses, a fact that Cronbach and his colleagues underscore in arguing that the very incorporation of evaluation into a system makes a difference. They conclude that "the visibility of the evaluation mechanism changes behavior" (Cronbach and others, 1980, p. 159), citing as an analog how drivers' observance of speed limits is affected by police officers' patrolling the highways in plainly marked patrol cars. They also suggest that the existence of evaluation may help convince stakeholders that the system is responsive, not impervious to their feedback.

Such noninformational uses notwithstanding, evaluation studies are used primarily for informational purposes such as: (1) deciding whether to adopt a new program or product; (2) determining whether to continue, modify, expand, or terminate an existing program; (3) examining the extent to which the operation of an educational endeavor is congruent with its design; (4) judging the overall value of an educational program, its relative value and cost compared to competing programs; and (5) helping evaluation sponsors, clients, participants, and stakeholders determine whether identified problems are being solved. Cronbach and colleagues allude to several of these uses in their statement that

> Decision making is proceeding well if participants reach decisions with their eyes open. Something is wrong when they support choices they would reject if they saw the likely consequences clearly. Not knowing what each program will accomplish, a citizen may support an attractive option that has little genuine promise. This is wasteful. Worse, it permits the illusion that, because "something has been done," the problem has been vanquished. Those who settle for a glittering promise lose their momentum and their influence. (Cronbach and others, 1980, p. 155)

Cronbach and colleagues also emphasize another important informational use of evaluation in pointing to the educative function of evaluation, noting that "the evaluator, holding the mirror up to events, is an educator.... The evaluator settles for too little if he simply gives the best answers he can to simple and one-sided questions from his clients. He is neglecting ways in which he could lead the clients to an ultimately more productive understanding" (Cronbach and others, 1980, pp. 160–161).

CONDITIONS UNDER WHICH EVALUATION STUDIES ARE INAPPROPRIATE

The foregoing examples all represent *appropriate* uses of evaluation studies. But evaluations are not always used appropriately. Several circumstances in which evaluations are, at best, of dubious value and, at worst, harmful, are outlined here.

Evaluation Would Produce Trivial Information

Heretical as this may sound to some, sometimes an educational program simply lacks sufficient impact to warrant the expense of formal evaluation. Some educational programs are one-time efforts with no potential for continuation. Some programs are provided at such low cost to so few people that the need for more than informal evaluation is unlikely. Common sense must dictate when a program has enough impact to warrant formal evaluation of its effectiveness.

Evaluation Results Will Not Be Used

Too often the professed "need" for an evaluation is merely an unreasoned assumption that every program must be evaluated. Evaluation is of dubious value unless there is commitment by someone to use the results. There may be some value in a "decision-free Nader's Raiders" type of evaluator capability in the field of education, but given the scarcity of evaluation resources (both financial and human) and the demand for evaluation information to support important decisions, it seems a questionable investment at present.

Sometimes there are important decisions to be made, but it is clear that they will be made for reasons unrelated to evaluative data. A program may, for instance, have sufficient political appeal that administrators are determined to continue it regardless of what any evaluation study shows.[61] In this case, evaluation can play no role except—assuming the data cooperate—to justify program continuation, a whitewash function that prostitutes evaluation's role. Evaluators should avoid meaningless ritualistic evaluations or pro forma exercises, where evaluation only appears to justify decisions actually made for personal or political reasons.

Of course, such dubious (and, one hopes, rare) motives are not always apparent. One of the most frustrating situations the evaluator will confront is to learn, *after* the evaluation has been completed, that the client or sponsor was not really open to conclusions that contradicted preconceived notions. If it becomes clear during the evaluation that conclusions are predetermined, conscionable evaluators will disentangle themselves at the earliest opportunity.

Evaluation Cannot Yield Useful, Valid Information

Sometimes, despite an important pending decision, it appears highly unlikely that an evaluation study will produce any relevant information. For example, consider a decision about whether to continue a dropout prevention program. Here information about the program's effects on dropout rates, graduation percentages, and so forth would be relevant. But what if the program only started one month before the school board must make its decision? The probability of obtaining dependable information (even predictive information) about the program's effectiveness in that length of time is so slight that it would seem wiser to spend one's energies convincing the school board to delay the decision. Similarly, a variety of constraints beyond the evaluator's control (for example, inadequate resources, lack of administrative cooperation or support, limited time in which to collect decent evaluation data, impossible evaluation tasks, and inaccessible data essential to the evaluation) can prevent the evaluator from providing useful information. Well-intentioned but naive clients may request "mission impossible" evaluations that yield only wasted efforts and disappointment. The evaluator needs to recognize when an evaluation is doomed to fail from the beginning. If unreasonable constraints preclude a professionally responsible evaluation, it would be wise not to undertake the evaluation. A bad evaluation is worse than no evaluation at all; poor evaluation data can readily mislead and lull educators into the false security of thinking the misinformation they have really portrays their efforts.

Evaluation Is Premature

Educational programs in a tryout phase nearly always benefit from well-conducted formative evaluation (barring reasons listed hereafter). But one cannot be so quick to conclude that a summative evaluation would be appropriate. Premature summative evaluations are among the most insidious misuses of evaluation, prompting concerns such as those expressed by Campbell:

> Another type of mistake involved *immediate evaluation*, evaluation long before programs were debugged, long before those who were implementing a program believed there was anything worth imitating.
>
> When any one of them, after a year or so of debugging, feels they have something hot, a program worth others borrowing, we will worry about program evaluation in a serious sense. Our slogan would be, "Evaluate only proud programs!" (Think of the contrast with our present ideology, in which Washington planners in Congress and the executive branch design a new program, command immediate nationwide implementation, with no debugging, plus an immediate nationwide evaluation.) (Campbell, 1984, pp. 35–37)

Summative evaluations are also rather futile with nebulous, ill-defined programs, to say nothing of those that have been inadequately implemented or poorly managed. Such difficulties have increased attention on the concept of "evaluability assessment" during recent years (see Wholey, 1979; Jung & Schubert, 1983). Evaluability assessment is simply the process of determining the feasibility of conducting an evaluation study. Although we shall not use the term further in our discussion, this section covers and goes beyond evaluability assessment, as we examine how to determine whether an educational program is capable of being evaluated.

No Qualified Evaluators Are Available

It is obviously pointless to conduct an evaluation if no qualified evaluator is available. We shall say more later about assessing the potential evaluators' qualifications and about determining costs.

Propriety of Evaluation Is Doubtful

Evaluations are undertaken for many reasons—some noble and some not. When the evaluator can discern that the reasons for undertaking the study are honorable and appropriate, the chances of the evaluation being a success are enhanced. But the evaluator must also be able to identify less noble reasons, including those that strain or violate professional principles. It would be unwise to proceed with any evaluation if its propriety is threatened by conflict of interest, jeopardy to participants in the study, or any other factors.

Ethical evaluators refuse to undertake thinly disguised "hatchet jobs," where an evaluation is structured to "get" a particular person or project. Any immoral or illegal uses of information are to be avoided by the evaluator. Confidential information cannot and should not be released in any form that would harm individuals, groups, or institutions. Hence, the evaluator needs to be cautious about promising findings to audiences that have no business receiving certain information. Here the evaluator plays an important role as watchdog over the client's welfare of others.

Evaluation Is Forced, Regardless of Appropriateness

None of the preceding reasons for deciding *not* to evaluate matter much if there is a legal requirement that a particular educational program be evaluated. Unfortunately, funding agencies are not always careful to determine whether an evaluation would be useful or whether—for one of the reasons discussed here—it would be wiser not to evaluate. Given a legal mandate, there is obviously no alternative but to proceed with the evaluation, making the best of a bad situation and doing everything possible to extract some worthwhile information.

DETERMINING WHEN AN EVALUATION IS APPROPRIATE

The various possible circumstances we have discussed here underscore the importance of being clear, cautious, and correct from the very first discussions about an evaluation. Some barriers to the successful completion of an evaluation may be foreseeable at the outset. The evaluator needs to recognize danger signals and, unless modifications are possible, terminate further discussion before too much time and money have been invested. The evaluator shares responsibility for determining the appropriateness of evaluation requests, identifying situations where an evaluation would be inappropriate, and correcting (or avoiding) those situations.

Checklist of Steps for Determining When to Conduct an Evaluation

The following checklist should help the evaluator decide when to initiate an evaluation.

	Check one for each item	
	Yes	No

Step 1. *Is there a legal requirement to evaluate?* (If yes, initiate the evaluation and ignore the rest of this checklist; if no, go to Step 2.)

Step 2. *Does the object of the evaluation have enough impact or importance to warrant formal evaluation?* (If yes, go to Step 3; if no, formal evaluation is unnecessary and you should discontinue further use of this checklist.)

Step 3. *Are there human and fiscal resources available for the evaluation?* (If yes, go to Step 4; if no, you'd best find them before proceeding.)

Step 4. *Is the object of the evaluation ready for evaluation?* (If yes, go to Step 5; if no, evaluation is premature and should be delayed until development and debugging are completed.)

Step 5. *Is the object of the evaluation well enough defined, implemented, and managed to permit a fair evaluation?* (If yes, go to Step 6; if no, delay the evaluation until these defects have been corrected, then go to Step 6.)

Step 6. *Is there an important decision to be made for which evaluation information would be relevant?* (If yes, go to Step 7; if no, evaluation is inappropriate; discontinue further use of this checklist.)

Step 7. *Is it likely that the evaluation will provide dependable information?* (If yes, go to Step 8; if no, discontinue.)

Step 8. *Is the evaluation likely to meet acceptable standards of propriety?* (see Chapter 21) (If yes, go to Step 9; if not, discontinue.)

Step 9. *Will the decision be made exclusively on other bases and uninfluenced by the evaluation data?* (If yes, evaluation is superfluous, discontinue; if no, go to summary.)

SUMMARY:
Based on Steps 1–9 above, *should an evaluation be conducted?*

DETERMINING WHETHER TO USE AN EXTERNAL EVALUATOR

In the previous section we discussed *when* to conduct an evaluation. We now consider *who* will conduct the evaluation. Despite the importance of formative evaluation, we will concentrate on the use of external evaluators for summative evaluation. This is because formative evaluation studies are typically performed by program staff—that is, *internal* evaluators.[62] Summative evaluations are typically conducted by persons or agencies *external* to the program, and the program administrator faces the crucial decision of selecting an evaluator from a pool of relative unknowns and then structuring a good evaluation study. This discussion is aimed at helping the program administrator with this task.

Many ways exist to arrange summative evaluations including the use of internal program staff as evaluators or external evaluators (also called third-party evalua-tors, independent evaluators, evaluation consultants, or evaluation contractors). However, the use of an internal staff member becomes problematic, creating concerns about independence, potential bias, credibility, and conflict of interest (Scriven, 1976a; Anderson & Ball, 1978). In some instances, however, there is simply no possibility of obtaining external help because of limited funds or absence of competent personnel. In these cases, the summative evaluation is weakened by the lack of outside perspective, but it might be possible to boost impartiality and credibility by choosing an internal summative evaluator as far removed as possible from the actual development of the program or product being evaluated (see, for example, Scriven, 1976a). Unfortunately, this compromise is seldom satisfactory, and the remainder of this section focuses on the advantages and disadvantages of using external evaluators, either singly or in combination with internal evaluators.

Advantages of External Evaluations

The advantages of using an external agency or individual[63] to conduct the summa-tive evaluation can be summarized as follows:

1. The external evaluation is more likely to be impartial (that is, capable of replication with comparable results by different but equally competent evaluators) because external evaluators' findings are rarely colored by any vested interest in the program's success or failure.[64]

2. The external evaluation is more likely to be credible (that is, capable of being believed or trusted), especially if the program is controversial and evaluation findings are to be used in settling a dispute.

3. External evaluation enables an agency to draw on evaluation expertise beyond that possessed by agency staff. Many school systems and other educational agencies simply do not find it feasible to hire sufficient numbers of evaluation specialists to conduct the evaluations needed in the system; but they can obtain the necessary expertise through external evaluators. Moreover, external evaluators fit into more flexible staffing arrangements, because there is no need for continuing financial commitment, as is the case with internal evaluators. Thus, the particular skills of several individual external evaluators might be employed at appropriate stages, with each being paid only for the specific services needed.

4. External evaluators bring with them a fresh, outside perspective. Unlike the internal evaluator, they see both the forest and the trees, often detecting un-warranted assumptions that are accepted by insiders.

5. Sometimes persons associated with an educational program are more willing to reveal sensitive information to outsiders (if trust exists) than they are to on-site evaluators, who they fear may inadvertently breach their confidentiality because they are continually on-site and in contact with others involved in the program.

In addition, the use of an external evaluator is often a legal requirement.

Disadvantages of External Evaluations

Although we support the concept of external evaluation, potential disadvantages must be recognized and compensated for. Possible (although not necessary) disadvantages include the following:

1. It is sometimes difficult to ascertain from afar the competence of the external evaluator (a problem dealt with later in this chapter).

2. The external evaluator may, at least at the outset, be unfamiliar with the phenomenon being evaluated and its context, possibly adding to the time required to collect important, relevant facts.

3. Negotiations with an external evaluator may delay start-up of an evaluation, and feedback during the evaluation may be less immediate than with an internal evaluator.

4. Because of the usual communication and travel costs, external evaluations are typically more expensive than internal evaluations, especially if extensive on-site data collection is required. (The temptation to economize should be carefully weighed, however, against potential sacrifice in impartiality, credibility, and technical competence.)

None of these disadvantages is compelling in itself, but they should be considered along with the advantages in deciding whether to obtain external evaluation. In our opinion, unless unusual circumstances make one or more of the disadvantages more salient than usual, the decision should almost always be "yes."

Checklist of Steps for Determining Whether to Use an External Evaluator

The following is proposed as a checklist for deciding whether or not to use an external agency or individual to conduct the evaluation.

	Check one for each item	
	Yes	*No*
Step 1. *Is there a legal requirement that the evaluation be conducted by an external evaluator?* (If yes, initiate the search for an external evaluator; if no, go to Step 2.)		
Step 2. *Are financial resources available to support any use of an external evaluator?* (If yes, proceed to Step 3; if no, discontinue use of this checklist and conduct the evaluation internally.)		
Step 3. *Does the evaluation require specialized knowledge and skills beyond the expertise of internal evaluators who are available to do the evaluation tasks?* (If yes, initiate the search for an external evaluator; if no, go to Step 4.)		

	Check one for each item	
	Yes	*No*

Step 4. *Are credibility, impartiality, and/or outside perspective of concern to the audiences for which the evaluation is conducted?* (If yes, proceed to Step 5; if no, discontinue and question the sanity of the evaluation's audiences.)

Step 5. *Is there an external evaluator possessing the necessary technical competence who is available and willing to do or assist with the evaluation?* (If yes, arrange for his/her assistance; if no, conduct the study internally, but expect a loss of credibility, objectivity, and external perspective.)

SUMMARY:
Based on Steps 1–5 above, *should this evaluation be conducted by an external evaluator?*

Advantages of Combining Internal and External Evaluation

Internal and external evaluation are far too often viewed as mutually exclusive. They need not be. Combining the two approaches can compensate for several of the potential disadvantages listed previously. For example, the external evaluator's unfamiliarity with the program is unlikely to be a serious problem if she works in tandem with an internal evaluator who can quickly provide the necessary contextual information. Travel costs can be greatly reduced by having the internal evaluator collect the bulk of the necessary data, working under the supervision of the external evaluator to assure impartiality and credibility.

External evaluators can "audit" internal evaluation studies to certify that they are methodologically sound and unbiased. Similarly, external evaluators can assist with key tasks where bias might inadvertently occur, such as designing the evaluation, selecting or developing instruments, drawing conclusions from data, and the like. Such partnerships incorporate the advantages of external evaluation without requiring that the entire evaluation be conducted externally. Perhaps even more important, through the resulting teamwork, external evaluation specialists help increase the skills of internal evaluators, thus preparing them to conduct future evaluation activities.

SELECTING AN EXTERNAL EVALUATOR

Selecting an external evaluator is neither simple nor trivial.[65] Once an educational agency has decided to use an external evaluator, it is important to obtain the services of an individual or agency with the necessary competence and sensitivity to do the job well. There is no better way to guarantee a bad evaluation than to turn it over to someone who is inept. Relationships with stakeholders can be irreparably harmed by an insensitive or unresponsive evaluator. Misleading or incorrect information is easy to generate and disseminate but difficult to eradicate. Therefore, great care should be exercised in choosing external evaluators.

No simple algorithm or agreed-upon set of criteria exist for selecting an evaluator,[66] though several writers have offered their suggestions. Before summarizing these suggestions or providing our checklist of proposed steps, it is necessary to consider two areas that are directly relevant to any effort to derive selection criteria for evaluators: (1) competencies necessary for educational evaluators; and (2) evaluator certification.

Competencies Needed by Educational Evaluators

There have been several conceptual and/or empirical efforts to identify the tasks required of educational evaluators and more specific competencies (knowledge, skills, and sensitivities) required to perform those tasks well (for example, Owens, 1968; Worthen & Gagné, 1969; Glass & Worthen, 1970; Anderson, Soptick, Rogers, & Worthen, 1971; Schalock & Sell, 1972; Ricks, 1976; Anderson & Ball, 1978; Owenby & Thomas, 1978). In addition, several attempts have been made to synthesize the common threads from prior conceptual or empirical efforts in hopes of identifying evaluation tasks and competencies commonly considered important (for example, Payne, 1974; Worthen, 1975a; Millman, 1975; Sanders, 1979; Worthen & Sanders, 1984). Even summarizing the evaluation competencies listed via these efforts is beyond the scope of this book, but a few comments seem in order.

First, the overlap among various lists is reassuringly high. We would be concerned if there were substantial disagreement among professional evaluators regarding critical competencies—but such is not the case.

Second, the few areas where the lists of competencies do not overlap result, we believe, from (1) different publication dates (new issues and needs in evaluation are being discovered continually); (2) differences in level of detail; and (3) differences in the evaluation philosophy of the authors (some emphasize technical, others subjective or artistic competencies).

We have included in Appendix 1 a listing of general *areas* of competence we consider important to enable evaluators to conduct high-quality evaluations.

Certification or Licensure of Educational Evaluators

Unfortunately, not all evaluators are equally competent, nor are they all equally scrupulous. Except for a bit of evaluation terminology, some so-called evaluators know little more about evaluation than their clients. Some self-styled evaluators possess only a smattering of the competencies alluded to (and referenced) in the preceding section, and their involvement can jeopardize the quality of an entire evaluation.

Clients often have difficulty determining whether a particular evaluator is genuinely well prepared. After all, how many evaluators could discern clearly the degree of expertise possessed by a self-proclaimed fiscal auditor, as long as the latter used a bit of the language and some of the elementary processes auditors employ? Some educational agencies have commissioned development of conceptual and technical procedures to prevent being "ripped off" by incompetent but crafty charlatans who manage to pass themselves off as evaluators.[67]

It is hardly surprising that many agencies have called for help in assuring the quality of evaluation work in education. Among the most frequent suggestions has been a request for some type of certification or licensing for evaluators working in educational settings (see Worthen, 1972a; Gagné, 1975). Certification or licensure was proposed as a way to assure that individuals had to meet certain minimum qualifications to receive a professional "seal of approval" from professional peers. Although these proposals have not been widely implemented, the state of Louisiana has instituted a program for certifying educational evaluators (Stufflebeam, 1984), which might lead to similar developments in other areas. Where such systems exist, they could prove useful in identifying and selecting competent evaluation help. Meanwhile, in the absence of any widespread certification or licensure for evaluators, *caveat emptor*—let the buyer beware—has become an altogether too familiar motto.

Possible Approaches to Selecting an Evaluator

Thus far we have referenced lists of important competencies and sensitivities desirable in any evaluator. We have pointed out that almost no certification or licensing systems exist to help educators identify qualified evaluators. Important as these considerations are, however, they fall short of collectively providing clear procedural guidelines for use in selecting evaluators, for they are not easy to set in operation.

We learn about most prospective evaluators by word of mouth. Sometimes we seek and obtain résumés for individuals, or "capability statements" prepared by evaluation contracting agencies. But seldom is it easy to obtain direct information on several items of potential importance. One might ascertain a fair bit about an evaluator's expertise in relevant subject matter or evaluation methods by perusing a résumé, but a well-crafted résumé can mask a lack of expertise. Similarly, it is unlikely that you will much learn from résumés or casual conversation concerning the prospective evaluator's ability to maintain ethical standards, deal with qualitative data, or perform a dozen other important evaluation tasks. Only the boldest client will press the evaluator in the manner suggested by one state education agency:

> Be particularly persistent in pressing for explanations when data analysis plans are formulated. Evaluators are inclined to perform analyses to generate results that can be interpreted only by the most highly trained statisticians (which the evaluator may or may not be and which the primary audiences probably are not). To test whether your evaluators will be able to make sense of the results of a proposed analysis, ask for an explanation of several ways the results might turn out and what results would mean in each case. If they cannot do this, tell them to use another analysis—one they can both

understand and explain. If that doesn't work either, replace them or have them hire a consultant who knows how to deal with the more technical aspects of your evaluation. (Illinois State Board of Education, 1982, p. 5)

Not an unreasonable suggestion, but almost as tough as sidling up to the prospective evaluator to ask whether she had done any canonical correlations lately, or whether her interpersonal skills would enable her to interact comfortably with multiple stakeholder groups. Obtaining such information directly is the province of the courageous, if not the impudent.

There are, however, ways to ascertain which prospective evaluators are well qualified to do the work. Five approaches for judging prospective evaluators' qualifications are discussed briefly in the following paragraphs.[68]

1. *Formal academic preparation of the evaluator.*[69] It is always possible for someone to accumulate many credit hours in a field of study without becoming very knowledgeable in that field. Many people go through university degree—even graduate degree—programs without being demonstrably enlightened. It is equally possible for very able people to become competent evaluators without benefit of any formal academic training in evaluation methodology. Yet, in the absence of more valid indicators, it would seem appropriate to consider the field of study in which a person holds a degree, the credit hours accumulated in evaluation, and the presence of specific courses or sequences relevant to developing evaluation competencies per se. It also seems wise to ask whether the academic training was provided by mentors who themselves possessed credentials as evaluators.

2. *Evaluation experience of the evaluator.* There is an old saying in education that it is hard to tell whether a person who has been a teacher for 10 years has had 10 years of teaching experience or one year of teaching experience 10 times. Similarly, some people have carried the title of *evaluator* for years without engaging in any activities that could rightly be termed evaluation. Yet again, in the absence of better measures, the probabilities for success would seem to favor that contractor with prior evaluation experience.[70]

3. *Professional orientation of the evaluator.* Where one is free to influence the choice of external evaluator and evaluation approach, it would seem pointless to choose an evaluator who was predisposed against the approach preferred by the agency's manager and staff. Although dangers exist in selecting evaluators so carefully tailored for the task that one can predict their judgments in advance, it makes little sense, for example, to expect an evaluator whose preferred approach is educational connoisseurship to be at home conducting an empirically based objectives–oriented evaluation.

Lai (1978) suggests interviewing prospective evaluators to discuss their preferred methods and philosophies. Brophy and others suggest the following:

Any process used to determine the merit or worth of a program necessarily involves evaluator judgments. Judgments are reflected in the selection of variables requiring attention, the sources from which data are obtained, the techniques used to gather information, and the messages finally conveyed to an audience. Because so many judgments may be made, the client may wish to inquire into the philosophical and methodological orientation of the evaluator, his motivation for wishing to conduct an evaluation, his knowledge of the problem under study, his experience, his capacity to work with people, and his ability to report information. Such information about the evaluator (similar questions might be raised about the client) provides insight into how a particular evaluator may make judgments. The client is then better prepared to select the appropriate evaluator for the specific program, procedure, or product to be evaluated. (Brophy and others, 1974, p. 8)

4. *Track record of the evaluator.* How well a person performed as an evaluator in prior studies should be the ultimate criterion in determining whether she receives another contract. An obvious limitation of this criterion is that it might prejudice the decision against newcomers fresh from doctoral programs and seeking first jobs, or new agencies staffed by competent—but relatively inexperienced—evaluators. This limitation is more than offset, however, by the advantages this criterion holds for client protection.

Perhaps the best way to judge previous performance is to examine *work samples* in the form of written evaluation reports or other products of the evaluator's previous evaluation activities. This is especially useful if previous evaluations were in any way similar to those desired by the client.

Some cautions are necessary here, however. For one thing, many evaluations are essentially group efforts. The product of a group is not always a reliable basis for judging the work of one member. Even where the report is the result of one person's efforts, the client may lack the necessary technical knowledge to judge the quality of the work. Requesting reviews by other expert evaluators may not be feasible. There are also instances where competent evaluators produce poor reports through no fault of their own but because program personnel with (or for) whom they were working would not cooperate in carrying out the evaluation design. These problems only suggest that any reviews of work products be applied sensibly and in conjunction with other measures.

In many situations it is not possible to obtain samples of previous evaluation work. Few evaluation studies find outlets in professional journals and most are fugitive documents unless supplied by the author. Sometimes distribution of evaluation results is restricted by contract. But whether or not work samples are available, *references from former clients* should be sought.

Client references are not restricted to personnel in the program that was evaluated. The sponsor and secondary audiences (for example, school boards) are equally appropriate sources of information on an evaluator's work. Obviously, though, even this criterion is no protection against the unscrupulous evaluator who lists as a reference a superintendent of schools without mentioning that the superintendent is his father-in-law. (The discussion of ethical standards for evaluators in Chapter 17 is relevant here.)

Numerous individuals and agencies seem to have far greater talent in producing convincing proposals than in delivering what's promised. The use of references or work samples should help to identify serious gaps between what an evaluator purports to be able to do and what she can in fact do.

5. *Personal style and characteristics of the evaluator.* Although intangible and elusive, personal traits are sometimes as important as all the formal training, experience, philosophical orientation, and prior performance combined. Clients cannot always count on a shiftless eye to signify honesty. Yet, some personal characteristics can be identified through interviews with the potential evaluator or those who know her work. If an evaluator is personable during an interview, that bodes well for her ability to interact well with others. If she seems argumentative and unresponsive, it seems pointless to consider her services further, no matter what her technical qualifications or record. If the evaluator talks in gibberish and cannot communicate effectively and clearly in an interview, it is unlikely that her later evaluation reports will be intelligible. Obviously, no evaluator is perfect. However, certain traits—such as sensitivity or eloquence (even under some pressure)—are critical and quite readily discernible.

Checklist of Steps for Selecting an Evaluator

The following is proposed as a checklist of criteria to consider in selecting an evaluator.[71]

	Evaluator appears to be: *(Check one for each item)*		
	Well Qualified	*Cannot Determine Qualifications*	*Not Well Qualified*
1. To what extent does the *formal training* of the potential evaluator qualify him/her to conduct evaluation studies? (Consider items such as major or minor degree specialization; specific courses or course sequences in evaluation methodology; qualifications of persons with whom training was taken, if such qualifications are known; possible need for content specialization.)			
2. To what extent does the *previous evaluation experience* of the potential evaluator qualify him/her to conduct evaluation studies? (Consider items such as length of experience; relevance of experience.)			
	Acceptable Match	*Cannot Determine Match*	*Unacceptable Match*
3. To what extent is the *professional orientation* of the potential evaluator a good match for the evaluation orientation and approach required by the task at hand? (Consider items such as philosophical and methodological orientations.)			

	Well Qualified	Cannot Determine Qualifications	Not Well Qualified
4. To what extent does the *previous performance* of the potential evaluator qualify him/her to conduct evaluation studies? (As judged by work samples or references.)			

	Acceptable	Cannot Determine Acceptability	Unacceptable
5. To what extent are the *personal style and characteristics* of the potential evaluator acceptable? (Consider items such as honesty, character, interpersonal and communication skills, offensive personal mannerisms, etc.)			

	Well Qualified & Acceptable	Cannot Determine Qualifications or Acceptability	Not Well Qualified and/or Unacceptable
Summary Based on questions 1–5 above, *to what extent is the potential evaluator qualified and acceptable, to conduct the evaluation?* If "well qualified and acceptable," or "not well qualified and/or unacceptable," decisions are obvious. If "cannot determine qualifications or acceptability" on basis of initial information, seek additional information and/or assistance from colleagues with expertise in evaluation to make this critical judgment.			

CASE STUDY APPLICATION

At first, I was fooled by ASCD's request that led to this "case study."[72] The task appeared straightforward enough. "Would you," ASCD editor Ron Brandt had asked over the telephone, "be willing to write a chapter for a book on evaluation? We will give you a description of a real school program—sort of a case study—and would like you to explain, in a general way, how you would go about evaluating it." Straightforward. Simplicity itself. So I agreed.

Then the case study arrived from ASCD; it was a description of a humanities curriculum in a middle school in the Radnor Township (Pennsylvania) School District. It contained the report of the Humanities Curriculum Review Committee and a brief overview that provided an introduction (see p. 162). I read the material quickly, worried vaguely that the description was so incomplete that it might not provide much focus for an evaluation, and then dropped the missive into my ASCD file; the deadline was still months away.

Months passed. So did the deadline. A skillfully worded reminder from the editor prodded my conscience, and I retackled the task, beginning by rereading the program description sent by ASCD. I had been right. The writing was lucid, it provided a general outline of the humanities program, gave the general context and some issues surrounding it, and even provided some details about rationale, objectives, schedules, and the like. But it struck me as not nearly enough. Somehow, I have never learned to design an evaluation that is really "on target" without knowing a good bit about not only the program but also the educational and political context in which it is embedded, the personnel who operate it, the population it is intended to serve, availability of resources for the program (not to mention the evaluation), and so on. Without such information, deciding how to aim the evaluation is largely guesswork, and the odds are high that it will miss the mark. How, I wondered, could ASCD expect any evaluator to make a clean hit on such an obscure target?

To put it bluntly, I felt frustrated at the realization that it simply was not feasible to extract from what I had received a clear enough picture of the program and the factors influencing it to permit me to design an evaluation I would feel comfortable defending. Were I like some clairvoyant colleagues who seem not to need much information about a program to launch a full-fledged evaluation, or like the enviably certain and single-minded souls who push and pull every evaluation problem until it can be solved by their preferred evaluation approach, I might have worried less. But somehow I have been afflicted with an abiding conviction that the evaluation approach should be tailored to fit the evaluation problem or need, not the reverse. So I continued to fret about the ambiguity of the request.

Then suddenly the realization hit me. The fuzziness of that target was no accident. By providing purposefully incomplete information about the Radnor humanities curriculum, ASCD was forcing each author to fill in the gaps, and in so doing, to reveal clearly the personal preferences and predilections that make each evaluator's approach unique and render evaluation still more of an art than a science.

Finally, I decided to take the liberty of imagining that the evaluation has already been planned and conducted, thus permitting a description of what has already happened. This shift in tense is important, because it allows exploration of the interactive, iterative nature of evaluation design, which is difficult to see when one looks only at the artificially one-dimensional evaluation plan.

I have chosen to use imaginary journal entries and file artifacts to communicate many of my thoughts about how the evaluation might be conducted. In doing so, I have liberally interpreted the Radnor context; I have made many assumptions about what went on as the evaluation unfolded; I have invented fictional characters[73] and events to suit my purposes; and in the process I have probably unintentionally maligned at least some of the principal actors in the Radnor drama. If so, it is hoped that I have at least done so equitably. My sincere apologies are extended to Principal Janson and others for any violence I may have done to their school system or sensibilities.

My journal entries cover a 12-month period during the design, conduct, and reporting of the evaluation of the humanities program. I have also annotated these entries and artifacts under "author comments" to help underscore important points.

> *Journal Entry: October 11.* Today was the first of three days I've agreed to spend here in Washington, D.C., serving as a member of an advisory panel to read proposals for the USOE. Tonight at dinner, Grayson Millman, another of the panelists, told me he had recently been asked to recommend an evaluation consultant to do an evaluation for a school district in Pennsylvania which he worked with a couple of years ago to set up a standardized testing program. I'm not quite clear on what it's about, except I believe it's some kind of junior-high art program that is drawing fire from some "back to basics" folks, at least that's what he thinks. Not sure I want to get involved, even should they ask me, which is a long shot, since Grayson says they're considering several possible consultants but only have the resources to hire one, especially if it's someone who has to fly in.
>
> Guess I'm a bit reluctant since, from what I can gather, the school is being pressured to have the evaluation done, and I'm a bit wary of being brought into situations where the locals have been forced to set up an evaluation, but want to let you know that they're not going to be forced to like it. Being unwanted and unwelcome is "unfun," and it makes establishing rapport a real upstream swim. Maybe I'm jumping at shadows, though, because of some prior experiences I'm not eager to repeat, like the time a faculty member in a college several of us were evaluating stood up in a public meeting and defined "waste" as "a busload of evaluators going over a cliff—with two empty seats!" Quaint sense of humor, that.
>
> All I really know about this Pennsylvania art program, however, is that the decision to evaluate it has been made. Anyway, I told Grayson I would be willing to talk about it if they should contact me. Gave him a business card to give them. (Glad to pawn these old ones off, since they'll soon be obsolete with that inane nine-digit zip code system coming in. I expect I'll live to see zip codes of 25 digits or so.)

Author Comments. Sometimes the evaluator is identified and selected early enough to help determine whether or not it is appropriate to evaluate a particular educational endeavor. More often, however, the decision has been made before the evaluator is ever contacted. In such cases, the client has presumably made the right choice in deciding to evaluate or else the decision to evaluate has been made at a higher administrative or governing level, in an equally rational way, one would hope. All the evaluator can do is to be sensitive to the possibility that evaluation may be premature or unwarranted for reasons discussed earlier in this chapter. Should that be the case, the professionally responsible evaluator will so advise, urging that the evaluation not go forward until or unless it is appropriate, as was discussed earlier. The fact that it is idealistic to expect all evaluators, whose earnings may be reduced if the evaluation does not continue, to suggest terminating a premature or otherwise inappropriate evaluation underscores how important it is for those who decide when to initiate an evaluation to consider all the factors in the earlier checklist.

October 19. Received an interesting call today from a Mrs. Janson, principal of a middle school in Radnor Township (somewhere near Philadelphia). She asked if I might be willing to consider undertaking an evaluation of the program Grayson Millman told me about. Turns out that it's a somewhat controversial humanities curriculum in her school. Seems board of education members have asked for the evaluation. She made it clear to me that she wasn't asking me to do it, but only if I'd be interested, since they're still deciding who they want. Grayson gave my card to the superintendent, and Mrs. Janson says she has inherited the job to call several evaluators to find out who might be interested and available to do the study.

She didn't seem at all hostile toward having part of her school's curriculum evaluated, so maybe it's not as hot an issue as I'd thought. Besides, she said no one would believe the results of the evaluation unless it were conducted by an outsider. Anyway, I told her I would be interested, tentatively, at least, and sent her the résumé she requested. I hoped she might mention who else she was considering, but she didn't. No reason why she should, since I guess this could be viewed as a "competitive" situation, although I'm not really panting over the opportunity. It's been a while since I've been asked to throw my hat into the ring, but no harm, I guess.

Author Comments. If one is dealing with evaluation "prima donnas" who feel above being compared with other possible consultants or contractors, there may be wisdom in quietly collecting information about the candidates for the job and then calling only the chosen individual. Conversely, if one is dealing with evaluators whose egos are that inflated, it may be wiser to avoid them altogether, on the premise that an exalted self-concept and the sensitivity necessary to do good work seldom coexist.

October 24. Mrs. Janson's secretary called from Radnor today and asked if I had a graduate transcript I could send. I told her no, saying I doubted if it would be helpful even if I had one, since those courses were taken 20 years ago. She asked if I had much coursework or background in the humanities. I told her no, not much. She seemed a bit flustered asking those questions, until I offered to send her copies of a couple of evaluation reports I had done and a few names of folks for whom I had done evaluation work in the past 4–5 years. Suggested she ask Mrs. Janson if that wouldn't suffice, since it seems a lot more relevant and a whole bunch easier to locate. I've no idea where to even look for my transcript. Mother is the only one who ever wanted one until now.

Author Comments. Some wisdom should guide the rigor with which information about evaluators (in the checklist on p. 180) might be pursued. The relevance of formal academic preparation fades with the passage of time and intervening experience becomes more important. Asking for documents or information not only of dubious utility but also not convenient for the evaluator to provide may discourage interest, unless the evaluator is salivating over the opportunity. Of course, if the evaluation is in Tahiti, or the contract is large and lucrative, one can ask for nearly outrageous information and some evaluators will try to provide it. No evaluator should object, however, to being asked for a few work samples or references of clients previously served. If they do object, that should raise a red flag to further discussions.

October 31. Grayson called from Penn State today and said he'd been at Radnor yesterday and heard I was going to be doing the external evaluation. That's news to me—I've not heard a word since I sent the stuff to them last week. Sounds as if they may have made a decision. Gray said he didn't know who else they were considering, but guessed they may not have had many well-qualified persons interested in the job. I had hung up the phone before I realized what he'd said! Reminds me of my old psychometrics prof who was fond of saying one could always look good if compared to a norm group made up of stuffed owls.

APPLICATION EXERCISE

1. Develop a list of questions that you can keep by your telephone in case requests for your evaluation services begin to accelerate. (Word that you have read this book may spread!)
2. Devise an agenda for an initial interview with a client so that you can cover all important early considerations. (What items can't you cover in an interview? How will you find answers to these questions?)

SUGGESTED READINGS

CRONBACH, L. J., and others (1980). *Toward reform of program evaluation.* San Francisco: Jossey-Bass.

GUBA, E. G., & LINCOLN, Y. S. (1981). *Effective evaluation.* San Francisco: Jossey-Bass.

HOUSE, E. R. (Ed.). (1973). *School evaluation: The politics and process.* Berkeley, CA: McCutchan.

STUFFLEBEAM, D. L., and others (1971). *Educational evaluation and decision making.* Itasca, IL: F. E. Peacock.

Chapter 13
Setting Boundaries and Analyzing the Evaluation Context

Orienting Questions

1. How might an evaluator identify intended evaluation audiences?
2. How does one set boundaries around whatever is to be evaluated?
3. What dimensions or characteristics should be included in describing evaluation objects?
4. What resources and capabilities are necessary to an adequate evaluation study?
5. What should the evaluator consider in analyzing the political context in which an evaluation will occur? What impact would political considerations have on conduct of the study?

In the preceding chapter we dealt with deciding whether to conduct an evaluation, deciding whether to use an external evaluator, and judging the qualifications of competing evaluators. In this chapter we turn our attention to four other important considerations: identifying evaluation audiences, setting boundaries on whatever is evaluated, analyzing available resources, and analyzing the political context.

IDENTIFYING INTENDED AUDIENCES FOR AN EVALUATION

Evaluation studies result in some type of report. It is therefore essential that the evaluator know the various audiences for that report, as well as how each might use the evaluation's findings. In this section we discuss the identification and involvement of appropriate evaluation audiences.

Identifying the Multiple Audiences for an Evaluation

An evaluation is adequate only if it collects information from and reports information to all legitimate evaluation audiences. An evaluation of a school program that answers only the questions of the school staff and ignores questions of parents, children, and community groups is simply a bad evaluation. Each legitimate audience must be identified, and the evaluation plan should include their objectives or evaluative questions in determining what data must be collected. Obviously, because some audiences will usually be more important than others, some weighting of their input may be necessary. Correspondingly, the evaluation plan should provide for eliciting appropriate evaluation information from each audience with a direct interest in the program, as well as providing information to each such audience. But how does one identify all the legitimate audiences?

At the outset, the evaluator must realize that the sponsor and client usually represent a primary audience. Yet there are almost always additional important audiences for the evaluation's results, including participants and stakeholders. Indeed, the evaluation's sponsor often supports the study to provide information for other audiences—such as the evaluated program's staff.

Working with the evaluation client and/or sponsor, the evaluator must strike a reasonable balance in deciding whether to define audiences broadly or narrowly. Few evaluations hold sufficient interest to warrant news releases in the *Wall Street Journal* or the *London Times*. But the more frequent mistake is settling on too narrow a range of audiences. Educators and educationists seldom omit themselves from the ranks of contributors or recipients of important evaluation results. Policymakers, managers, and representatives of those working in the educational "trenches" are usually selected to guide evaluations and consume their products. And community members and representatives of other influence groups are increasingly numbered among the evaluation's audiences. But there is still a regrettable tendency to respond to the squeaking wheel, targeting evaluation studies to those who are vociferous, strident, or powerful. What about the retired folks without school-age children, who are uninvolved in the PTA and who are often regarded only when their numbers and approaching school bond issues or other tax increases for educational purposes make it prudent to ignore them no longer? And what of the high school students and their parents? Raizen and Rossi (1982) recommend that the United States Department of Education identify "right-to-know" user audiences and develop strategies to address their needs:

> Perhaps the most neglected audience for evaluation studies consists of program beneficiaries and their representatives. We believe that this neglect is not so much intentional as it is produced by the very real difficulties of defining this set of audiences in a reasonable way. In order to more closely approximate the ideal that all those having a recognized interest in a program should have reasonable access to evaluation results, the Department should consider dissemination of evaluation reports freely to groups and organizations that claim to represent major classes of beneficiaries of education programs.... It is to be expected that such right-to-know groups will be different for different evaluations.... (Raizen & Rossi, 1982, p. 50)

A useful checklist to help evaluators identify important evaluation audiences was developed by Owens (1977) and listed those needing the evaluation findings, distinguishing between those who need the information to make decisions and those who need it simply to be informed. We have developed a similar checklist[74] (see Fig. 13.1).

The greater the number and diversity of audiences to be served, the more

EVALUATION AUDIENCE CHECKLIST

Entity to be Evaluated				(Check all appropriate boxes)	
				To Be Informed	
Individuals, Groups or Agencies Needing the Evaluation's Findings	To Make Policy	To Make Operational Decisions	To Provide Input to Evaluation	To React	For Interest Only
Funding Agencies/Sponsors					
Governing Boards					
Educational Administrators					
Teaching Faculty					
Other Staff Members					
Students					
Parents of Students					
Other Intended Beneficiaries					
Sponsors of Other Beneficiaries (e.g., Institutions)					
Public–Community Members					
Community/Lay Advisory Group					
Supporters					
Opponents					
Other Stakeholders					
Professional Colleagues					
Professional Associations/ Organizations					
Potential Adopters					
Libraries/Dissemination Networks					
Others (list)					

FIGURE 13.1   Checklist of Evaluation Audiences

complex and costly the evaluation. Conversely, for political and practical reasons, the evaluator can ill-afford to ignore certain constituents. Thus, the question of who the audiences are and how they are to be served is a crucial one.

It is doubtful that any one evaluation would have all the audiences listed in Figure 13.1, but it is certain that every entry in that list will be a legitimate audience for many evaluation studies. The checklist is intended only to help evaluators and clients think broadly of the audiences for the evaluation and the purpose that might be served in providing them with the evaluation information. Once that is done, it is important to determine what information each audience needs and will use. Differing interests and needs often require that evaluation reports be tailored for specific audiences, in ways discussed further in Chapter 20.

Once the appropriate evaluation audiences have been identified, the list should be reviewed periodically as the evaluation progresses because audiences can change. It is particularly important to be certain no important audience has been omitted.

Importance of Identifying Evaluation Audiences

The aggregated viewpoints of various evaluation audiences provide focus and direction to the study. Unless evaluators direct the evaluation clearly at their audiences from the outset, results are likely to have little impact.

Discussing who will use evaluation results and how helps clarify what role evaluation will play. In the formative role, insiders use results to improve the program[75] being evaluated, with little threat to its well-being, and good potential for benefiting it. In the summative role, outsiders use results to make decisions about program continuation, termination, or selection, or the apportionment of resources. In this role, evaluation can be threatening to some, representing a means of control; hence, the evaluator should be cautious of *premature* summative evaluation when the program being evaluated has not had a chance to develop fully.

Involvement of Evaluation Audiences in Understanding Reasons for Initiating an Evaluation

As noted in Chapter 12, most evaluators have at some time been misled (perhaps inadvertently) into undertaking an evaluation, only to find at some point that its underlying purpose was quite different from what they had supposed. Such misunderstanding is much more likely if an evaluator talks only to one audience. Dialogue with multiple audiences clarifies the reasons behind an evaluation (except for the rare case where a manipulative individual may intentionally obscure the real purposes—in those cases even contact with multiple audiences would be less useful than truth serum in discerning the real reasons for the evaluation).

The intended users of evaluation results are important stakeholders. They should be asked what information they need and when they need it. Both the medium and message of any reports should be tailored to their way of looking at education, their usual ways of learning, and their information needs. They may also be sources of information during the evaluation, or may assist later in reviewing or interpreting raw data.

DESCRIBING WHAT IS TO BE EVALUATED: SETTING THE BOUNDARIES

Setting boundaries is a fundamental step in gaining a clear sense of what an evaluation is all about. No evaluation is complete without a detailed description of the program being evaluated. Poor or incomplete descriptions can lead to faulty judgments—sometimes about entities that never really existed. For example, the concept of team teaching has fared poorly in several evaluations, resulting in a general impression that team teaching is ineffective. Closer inspection shows that what is often labeled as "team teaching" provides no real opportunities for staff members to plan or work together in direct instruction. Obviously, better descriptions would have precluded these misinterpretations. One can only evaluate adequately that which one can describe accurately.

Because most objects of educational evaluations operate within a larger context, they can be described at several levels of generality. For example, we might describe a particular evaluation as covering (1) computer-mediated language arts instruction in the schools; (2) a particular example of computer-mediated language arts instruction; (3) the WANDAH computer-enhanced writing program; (4) use of the WANDAH writing program to teach gifted grade 10 through grade 12 students in the Middletown High School; or (5) use of the WANDAH writing program in a particular Middletown High School English class.

Evaluators are frequently asked to help evaluate entities as vague as "our school math program." Does that include the districtwide mathematics curriculum for all grade levels, the districtwide math curriculum at a particular grade level, a particular school's total curriculum in math, that school's fourth-grade math program, or the mathematics curriculum in a particular fourth-grade classroom? Should the evaluation focus on the instructional materials, instructional procedures, or both? Answering such questions establishes boundaries that help the evaluation make sense.

The importance of good description increases in proportion to the complexity and scope of what is evaluated. As Carter has noted,

> Indeed, it is surprising how often the first step in a large evaluation contract is to do an extensive description of the program itself. The federal monitors of the program usually know how the program is supposed to work, but they freely admit that they do not know the range of variation involved in its implementation. (Carter, 1982, pp. 40–41)

Factors to Consider in Characterizing the Object of the Evaluation

The evaluator can demarcate the object of the evaluation and the study itself by answering these questions:

- What need does the program exist to serve? Why was it initiated? What are its goals? Whom is it intended to serve?
- What does the program consist of? What are its major components and activities, its basic structure and administrative/managerial design? How does it function?
- What is its setting and context (geographical, demographic, political, level of generality)?
- Who participates in the program (for example, which grades, students, staff, administrators)? Who are other stakeholders?

- What is the program's history? How long is it supposed to continue? When are critical decisions about continuation to be made?
- When and under what conditions is the program to be used? How much time is it intended to take? How frequently is it to be used?
- Are there unique contextual events or circumstances (for example, contract negotiations, teacher strikes, changes in administration) that could affect the program in ways that might distort the evaluation?
- What resources (human, materials, time) are consumed in using the program?
- Has the program been evaluated previously? If so, what outcomes/results were found?

The evaluator should also seek to clarify what is *not* included in the program to be evaluated.

How to Describe the Object of the Evaluation

Answers to questions posed in the preceding section can be obtained in a variety of ways and from a variety of sources. Three basic approaches to collecting descriptive information are: (1) reading documents with information about the object; (2) talking with various individuals familiar with the object; and (3) observing the object in action. Each is discussed briefly here.

Descriptive Documents. Most educational programs are described in proposals to funding agencies, planning documents, reports, minutes of relevant meetings, correspondence, publications, and so on. Taking time to locate and peruse such documents is an important first step in understanding any entity well enough to describe it correctly.

Interviews. Helpful as they are, written documents almost never provide a complete or adequate basis for describing the object of the evaluation. It is almost always necessary to talk at length both with those involved in planning or operating the program and with those who may have observed it in operation. In evaluating a new preservice teacher-education program funded by the Ford Foundation, for instance, the evaluator would be well-advised to learn how the program is (and is supposed to be) operating—not only from the university faculty and administrator(s) responsible for running the program, but also from Ford Foundation sponsors, student trainees in the program, school personnel who supervise the university students in practice teaching, and so on. It is important to interview representatives of all the relevant audiences to determine which issues and concerns are common.

Observations. Much can be learned by observing programs in action. Evaluators may wish to do the observation or, depending on the nature of the program, ask relevant content or process experts to make the observations. Often observations will reveal variations between how the program *is* running and how it is *intended* to run that an evaluator may not discover through interviews or reading.

Dealing with Different Perceptions

Clarifying what is to be evaluated reduces the chances that the evaluator will later be accused of evaluating the wrong thing, of conducting an evaluation that was too narrow in scope, or of failing to take important factors into account.

As a case in point, Cronbach and others relate early steps taken by Coleman and his colleagues in their study of equal educational opportunity in the mid-sixties:

> When the Coleman team set to work, it judged that the survey commissioned by Congress could not be launched without decoding the congressional phrase "inequality of educational opportunity." When the team sought the help of informants from various groups, it discovered that segments of the population did indeed read different meanings into the phrase. There were those who saw racial mixture as the chief concern, others who looked at teacher quality, still others who emphasized the morale and intellectual tone of the school, and finally, there were those who argued that only the end result of pupil progress mattered. (Cronbach and others, 1980, pp. 171–172)

In cases where disagreements over the nature of the object of the evaluation exist, the evaluator is often well-advised to look at each interpretation. By letting various audiences attach whatever meaning they wish to the object and then focusing on results that are relevant to that meaning, the evaluator can address the information needs of multiple audiences. Moreover, the evaluator can educate audiences by helping them look beyond their particular perspectives.

Sometimes it is important for evaluators to obtain formal agreement from the client that a description is accurate. Rarely, unprincipled educators who dislike some less-than-glowing evaluation findings take refuge in the claim that "You haven't understood our program" or "What you've described isn't the program we are running!" We are not speaking here of instances where a careless evaluator has failed to understand or to describe accurately the program, but rather where insecurity or other unadmirable motives lead the program's manager to redefine the program verbally so that evaluation findings seem no longer to apply. Because it is difficult to predict when this educational version of the age-old "shell game" may occur, and nearly as tough to prove which walnut shell hides the real program, it is often advisable to develop documented, mutually agreed-upon descriptions of the evaluation object.

Redescribing the Object as It Changes

It is important to portray the actual character of the object not only as it begins but also as it unfolds (a fact we will expand on in later chapters). A critical point for evaluators to remember is that the object to be evaluated frequently changes during evaluation. This may be due in part to the responsiveness of program managers to feedback that suggests useful refinements and modifications. It is also often the case that an object, such as an individualized tutorial writing program, is not implemented by users in quite the way its designers envisioned. Some adaptations may be justifiable on educational grounds, some may result from naivete or misunderstanding, and some may stem from purposeful resistance on the part of users determined to expunge something objectionable from the original conception. Regardless, the evaluator must describe at the end of the evaluation what was actually evaluated, and that may be quite different from what was originally planned.

Guba and Lincoln (1981) provide an excellent discussion of reasons why changes in the evaluation object (which they call the "evaluand") might occur:

> The evaluator who assumes that an implemented evaluand will be substantially similar to the intended entity is either naive or incompetent. Thus, field observations of the evaluand in use, of the setting as it actually exists, and of the conditions that actually obtain are absolutely essential.
>
> Variations in the entity, setting, and conditions can occur for a variety of reasons. In some cases the reluctance or resistance of the actors in the situation produces unwanted changes. Adaptations to fit the evaluand to the local situation may have to be made. The simple passage of time allows the action of various historical factors to make their contribution to change. Most of all, the continuing activity of the evaluator himself, if it is taken seriously by the actors and if it produces meaningful information, will contribute to a continuously changing set of circumstances. (Guba & Lincoln, 1981, p. 344)

A Sample Description of an Evaluation Object

To help illustrate the key points in this section, we include the outline description of a program evaluated by one of the authors and some of his colleagues in the Northwest Regional Educational Laboratory (NWREL). Although not proposed as necessarily exemplary, this outline should illustrate many of the points discussed previously and help identify useful ways to describe evaluation objects. This description is drawn from an evaluation of nine alternative teacher–education programs initiated by the University of British Columbia. One of the first tasks in the evaluation was to understand each of the nine programs and prepare an accurate description of each program that could be agreed upon by all concerned. What follows is (1) the outline used for all nine descriptions that were completed at the outset of the evaluation,[76] and (2) a summary of how the program descriptions were to be developed.

TASK-ORIENTED TEACHER EDUCATION PROGRAMME (TOTE)
A. *Programme Description*
 1. *Program Title*
 2. *Short Title Used in This Report*
 3. *Date Started*
 4. *Needs*
 5. *Programme Goals*
 6. *Types of Students for Whom the Programme Is Designed*
 7. *Student Outcomes Expected from the Programme*
 8. *Basic Structure and Scheduling Characteristics*
 9. *Content*
 10. *Administrative and Managerial Procedures*

11. *Number and Types of Instructional Personnel*
12. *Approximate Number of Students Enrolled*

The following quotation from the final evaluation report outlines how the actual program descriptions were developed.

A. *Description of Each Alternative Program*

An essential first step in the evaluation was that of making certain that each alternative program was portrayed accurately to NWREL staff conducting the evaluation so that they would not only understand fully that which they evaluated, but also so they could be certain that others from whom judgments about any program were elicited similarly understood that program. To facilitate this understanding, steps were taken for NWREL evaluators to reach agreement with each alternative program director on a description of the program which could be judged accurate by all parties. The following steps were used to produce such descriptions.

1. *Preparation of initial drafts.* Each alternative program proposal was analyzed carefully in an attempt to produce an accurate description of the program on as many of the following dimensions as possible: precise title for the program; the date the program began; the need which led to the development of the program; major goals or objectives which the program is designed to attain; the type of student for which the program is designed; student outcomes expected from the program; the basic structure and scheduling characteristics of the program; content of the program, including the courses or practicum requirements of the program and the associated experiences or activities required of students; administrative and managerial arrangements and procedures for operating the program; the number and type of instructional and support personnel who operate the program; and the number of students who enrolled in the program and attrition rates to date. Sample program descriptions were drafted using the above dimensions and submitted to review by three British Columbia school district superintendents and assistant superintendents to determine if such descriptions would provide sufficient information to enable superintendents to respond intelligently to questions about how well such programs would meet the needs they have for well prepared classroom teachers. The reviews were all favorable and resulted only in minor revisions. Subsequently, program descriptions for all the alternative programs were drafted in the common format suggested and abstracted to be as parsimonious as possible without distorting the description. The regular elementary and secondary teacher education programs were described in similar fashion by the directors of the elementary and secondary divisions of the Faculty.

2. *Review by program supervisors.* The program descriptions were distributed to each alternative program supervisor and to the directors of the elementary and secondary divisions for review by the program supervisor or director and anyone he chose to advise him in developing a completely accurate program description.

3. *Preparation of final program descriptions.* On November 20–22, NWREL evaluators met with each alternative program supervisor and the directors of the regular programs to check each program description for completeness and accuracy. Where the description was found to be incomplete or inaccurate, the program supervisor or director was asked to assist in revising the description to make it accurate. Final drafts were completed jointly by the NWREL evaluators and program supervisors and mutual agreements were reached that the descriptions were accurate for each alternative program and for the regular elementary and secondary programs. Program supervisors were allowed to make additional changes up to the time the descriptions were mailed to all B.C. superintendents in a survey described hereafter . . . . The program descriptions incorporated in the

summaries of each program presented later in this report appear there in the form in which they were actually mailed to B.C. superintendents and to persons preparing to serve as members of the site visit teams. (Worthen, Owens, & Anderson, 1975, pp. 12–14)

ANALYZING THE RESOURCES AND CAPABILITIES THAT CAN BE COMMITTED TO THE EVALUATION

Before discussing the importance of determining the level of resources and energies that should be committed to a particular evaluation study, it may be useful to focus briefly on a pervasive attitude that leads many educators to question the utility of evaluation. We quote here part of an excellent discussion of this attitude and how deeper insight would lead to more intelligent use of evaluation in education.

This attitude manifests itself in the view that evaluation is an "added-on-extra," something to be considered only if there are surplus funds. For example, if I receive a $50,000 grant to produce a programmed text but must spend $5000 on evaluation, then I am left with only $45,000 with which to produce the text. In other words, evaluation decreases the monetary resources of the project without producing any tangible product. Evaluation does not write chapters or teach students.

The trouble with this view is that it confuses price and cost. Quite clearly, the *price* of evaluation services is $5000. But what is the cost? Is it positive or negative? We believe that the evaluation can and should involve no net positive cost to the producer, tax-payer, or consumer. This is the doctrine of Cost Free Evaluation (CFE),...and it should apply to both formative and summative evaluation. As mentioned, evaluation will have a price; it will appear as a line in the budget. But it should not be a programmatic negative; rather it should be designed to have cost-saving and/or effectiveness-increasing consequences for the project.

The most obvious way evaluation can save money is by terminating unsuccessful projects. This represents a savings to the tax-payer or consumer. But evaluation can make more constructive suggestions than termination. For example, formative evaluation should demonstrate ways to improve quality without increasing costs. When evaluation is diagnostic (i.e., identification of the particular features that are producing the observed effects) it is clear that recommendations for improvement will often result. The ultimate consumer of education (e.g., student, teacher, administrator, taxpayer) will benefit since evaluation should serve as a guide to selection between options and, therefore, provide immediate and potential gains in quality and/or savings. Getting the right student into the right program would represent a major increase in educational effectiveness.

Finally, the doctrine of Cost Free Evaluation has some serious consequences for the evaluator. Program evaluators should insist that their work offers a good chance of producing cost savings or quality gains worth the price before contracting for the job. They need to be careful to avoid disruptive evaluation procedures. Other consequences might include: (1) the evaluation report should be treated as a product itself (e.g., getting feedback on early drafts from those assessed); (2) using client facilities with care regarding their cost; (3) trying to make the client more aware of evaluation procedures and less reliant on consultant help (i.e., the evaluator as educator); and (4) returning unused funds even if contractually entitled to them.

In sum then, in at least one respect, evaluation is just like any other commodity— people expect to get what they pay for, they want fair return on their dollars. Further, this is true of students as well as program managers. Once the distinction between evaluation and credentialing is made clear, it becomes possible to use evaluation as a teaching device. That is, once evaluation is seen not solely as a means to certify accomplishment but also as a means to help students succeed, it opens the way for greater use of evaluation. Evaluation should be viewed as an adjunct to teaching-learning strategies. Good teaching cannot take place without good evaluation. As soon as it becomes clear that evaluation helps produce better products (everything from students to textbooks), it will cease being viewed as an "added-on-extra" and come to be an expected service. (Hodgkinson, Hurst, & Levine, 1975, pp. 189–191)

Analyzing Financial Resources Needed for the Evaluation

Even when the client is converted to the doctrine of cost-free evaluation, determining what resources can be devoted to evaluation is difficult. As Cronbach and others have noted, "Deciding on a suitable level of expenditure is...one of the subtlest aspects of evaluation planning" (Cronbach and others, 1980, p. 265).

Ideally, this decision should be made in consultation with the evaluator, whose more intimate knowledge of evaluation costs would be of great help. Unfortunately, there may not be sufficient rapport between evaluator and client to foster such collaborative planning. Indeed, in many situations the client may initially proceed independently to set budgetary limits for the study. Sometimes the evaluator is informed how much money is available for the evaluation. Frequently, however, the amount of money available is not made clear, and, in such cases, the evaluator must choose from among at least three courses of action. First, he could design the least costly evaluation study possible, present the design and cost estimate to the client, determine if such an "economy model" evaluation would provide the information needed by the client, and negotiate from there. Second, he could design the "ideal" study, initially ignoring cost; then, once the design was complete, estimate its cost, present the design and budget to see if it was acceptable and affordable to the client, and negotiate both scope of work and budget downward as necessary. Third, he could press the client to set a level of funding for the study and then design the evaluation to fit this constraint.

When the client is unsure how to budget, the second option (the "ideal" study) seems appropriate, but a fourth option may be even better. An evaluator can propose two or three different levels of evaluation that differ in cost and comprehensiveness—perhaps a "Chevrolet" and a "Cadillac" evaluation, for example—from which the client can select. Clients are often unaware of the possibilities of evaluation design, of what information evaluations might be able to produce, or of the cost of evaluation services. Faced with decisions about trade-offs and budget limitations, the client also needs to know about alternatives and their consequences in order to make a good decision. Budgeting could be the last step in planning an evaluation. On the other hand, if budget limits are known at the beginning, they will affect (and usually enhance) planning decisions that follow.

Ideally, evaluation plans and budgets should remain flexible, if at all possible. Circumstances will change during the study, and new information needs and opportunities will unfold. And if every dollar and every hour of time are committed to an inflexible plan, the results will fail to capitalize on the new insights gained by evaluator and client. Even the most rigid plan and budget should include provisions for how, by mutual agreement, resources might be shifted to accomplish evaluation tasks that take on new priority through changing circumstances.

Analyzing Availability and Capability of Evaluation Personnel

Budget is only one consideration affecting the design of an evaluation study. Personnel is another. Frequently, evaluators can make use of qualified personnel who are on site for reasons other than evaluation. Teachers can collect data. Secretaries can work part-time typing, searching records, or the like, at no cost to the evaluation budget.[77] Graduate students seeking internship experience or working on dissertations or course-related studies can undertake special assignments at minimal cost to the evaluation budget. Volunteers from parent-teacher associations, junior leagues, other community groups, or church groups can often perform nontechnical evaluation tasks. Calls for volunteers from among these various groups often pay off. And involving volunteers not only helps contain costs but also sparks interest in the evaluation among stakeholders.

Whenever people who are not evaluation specialists conduct or assist with evaluation tasks, the evaluator faces unique responsibilities that cannot be neglected: orientation, training, and quality control. Evaluation personnel who lack specialized training or relevant experience require orientation to the nature of the study, its purposes, and the role they will be asked to play. They must understand their responsibilities, not only in completing evaluation tasks in a quality and timely manner but also in representing the evaluation team and its sponsoring organization. Naive and unprepared evaluation staff (volunteers or otherwise) can play havoc with an evaluation if they interact abrasively with others, misrepresent the nature or purpose of the study, betray anonymity or confidentiality, or even dress inappropriately for the setting. Evaluation volunteers or adjuncts must also be trained in the skills required to do the tasks assigned. They must follow strict, detailed guidelines, or errors are likely to occur. Even then, careful supervision and spot-checking are usually required.

Whenever "nonevaluator" personnel are used to expand an evaluation effort at low cost, the risk of bias is present. Personal considerations must not influence the way in which participants (for instance, teachers) or stakeholders (parents, for example) conduct their evaluation tasks. It is easy to allow presuppositions to color one's perceptions. Although few seem likely to be so unprincipled, it is also easy to alter or distort the data to make it fit one's prior conclusions. Thus, to protect the study's validity and credibility it is essential that an evaluator using "local" personnel in the evaluation provide adequate supervision and also audit and authenticate everyone's work by spot-checking and verifying all data collection and analysis. Given conscientious supervision, monitoring and auditing, local staff or volunteers can make a useful "cost-free" contribution to an evaluation.

Of course, using unskilled personnel may not always be as economical as it first appears. It is in the evaluator's best interest to consider carefully the qualifications of available assistants, including their commitment and responsibility, before including them.

Analyzing Other Resources and Constraints for Evaluations

The availability of existing data, including files, records, previous evaluations, documents, or other data-collection efforts to which the evaluation may be attached, is an important consideration. The more information that must be generated *de novo* by the evaluator, the more costly the evaluation.

The availability of needed support materials and services is also important. Existing testing programs, computer services, routine questionnaires, or other information services are all possible resources that could be drawn upon at little or no cost to the evaluation if they already exist for other purposes.

The evaluator should also take into account the relevance of existing evaluation approaches and methods for the specific study being considered. The methodological or technological state of the art necessary to respond successfully to a particular evaluation request may be so underdeveloped or new that a major research and development effort will be required before the evaluation can be launched. Pioneering can require considerably more time, effort, and money than either evaluator or sponsor can afford to spend.

Time must be considered a resource. The evaluator does not wish to miss opportunities for making the evaluation useful because of tardy reports or data collection and analysis. Knowing when to be ready with results is part of good planning. It is ideal to have sufficient time to meet all information needs at a pace that is both comfortable and productive. Limited time can diminish an evaluation's effectiveness as much as limited dollars.

ANALYZING THE POLITICAL CONTEXT FOR THE EVALUATION

Evaluation is inherently a political process. Any activity that involves applying the diverse values of multiple constituents in judging the value of some object has political overtones. Whenever resources are redistributed or priorities are re-defined, political processes are at work. And consider the political nature of decisions regarding whose values are attended to, how they are weighted, what variables are studied, how information is reported and to whom, how clients and other audiences intend to use evaluative information, what kind of support is given to the evaluation and by whom, what potentially embarrassing information is hidden, what possible actions might be taken to subvert the evaluation, and how the evaluator might be co-opted by individuals or groups.

Political processes begin to work with the first inspiration to conduct an evaluation and are pivotal in determining the purpose(s) to be served and the interests and needs to be addressed. Political considerations permeate every facet of evaluation from planning through the reporting and use of evaluation results.

We have reserved our more extensive discussion of political factors in evaluation for Chapter 17. But we cannot leave this chapter without saying a few words about the importance of analyzing the political context in which the evaluation will be conducted while there is still time to recognize and retreat from a political holocaust that could render an evaluation useless.

Upon receiving any new request to undertake an evaluation, the evaluator might consider the following questions:

1. Who would stand to lose/gain most from the evaluation under different scenarios? Have they agreed to cooperate? Do they understand the organizational consequences of an impartial evaluation?
2. Which individuals and groups have power in this setting? Have they agreed to sanction the evaluation? To cooperate?
3. How is the evaluator expected to relate to different individuals or groups? Impartial outsider? Advocate? Future consultant or subcontractor? Confidant? Assistant? What implications does this have for being co-opted?
4. From which stakeholders will cooperation be essential? Have they agreed to provide full cooperation? To allow access to necessary data?
5. Which stakeholders have a vested interest in the outcomes of the evaluation? What steps will be taken to give their perspective a fair hearing without allowing them to preclude alternative views?
6. Who will need to be informed during the evaluation about plans, procedures, progress, and findings?
7. What safeguards should be incorporated into a formal agreement for the evaluation (for example, reporting procedures, editing rights, protection of human subjects, access to data, meta-evaluation, procedures for resolving conflicts)?

Answers to these questions will help the evaluator determine whether it will be feasible and productive to undertake the evaluation study. More will be said in Chapter 17 about political, interpersonal, and ethical considerations that influence educational evaluations.

DETERMINING WHETHER TO PROCEED WITH THE EVALUATION

In Chapter 12 we talked about identifying reasons for the evaluation; such reasons provide the best indicators of whether an evaluation will be meaningful. In this chapter we have discussed the importance of understanding who will use the evaluation information, and how, and we have suggested ways to identify relevant audiences. We have stressed the importance of delimiting what is evaluated, and analyzing fiscal, human, and other resources to determine feasibility. And we have cautioned evaluators to consider whether any political influences might undermine the evaluation effort.

Unfortunately, we can offer no simple algorithm for balancing all these factors in making a final decision about whether to proceed with the evaluation. Thoroughness in considering the factors outlined in this and the preceding chapter, insight, thoughtfulness and common sense are the ingredients essential to a sensible decision about when to agree to do an evaluation. Yet even the most insightful evaluator with considerable experience will sometimes make an unwise decision, which is our cue to return to the case study we left at the end of Chapter 12.

CASE STUDY APPLICATION

November 2. Mrs. Janson, the Radnor principal, called today and told me I'd been picked by the committee to do their evaluation, if I would. I agreed tentatively (having just received the cost estimate for Brad's orthodontics), but told her I couldn't make a final commitment without knowing more about the program, precisely why they want it evaluated, what use they would make of the evaluation findings, the resources available for the evaluation study, and so on. She promised to send some written materials for me to review.

Author Comments. To agree to undertake an evaluation without first knowing a bit about the program to be evaluated strikes me as a potential disservice to both the program and the evaluator. Only an evaluator who is naive, avaricious, or supremely confident that his evaluation skills or approach will solve any evaluation problem would plunge in with so little information. Having once met all three of those criteria, I have more recently repented, and during the last decade have insisted on learning enough about the program, prior to committing to evaluate it, to be certain I could be of some help.

November 8. Spent a few minutes this evening reading through materials I received from Radnor Township School District. They sent a brief report of their Humanities Curriculum Review Committee, which listed committee membership; outlined their activities; gave goals, objectives, and rationale for the curriculum; and included an outline of the proposed content and a schedule for implementation. They also listed other alternatives they had considered and rejected, even explaining why, which is a helpful inclusion. No clue in the materials, however, to some of the more important things I need to know before I decide whether I can be of any real help to them. Spent a while jotting down some questions I want to ask the principal.

Author Comments. Later examination of artifacts in my "Radnor School District Evaluation" file would reveal the following list of questions.

Artifact No. 1

   1. How old is the humanities curriculum in the Radnor School District? The humanities curriculum review committee was launched in 1978, just over a year ago—but what about the curriculum? Is it well established or new? Entrenched or struggling to find root?

   2. Have there been any previous efforts to evaluate the humanities program? If so, by whom, when, what were the findings, and how did they affect the program?

   3. Why does the board want the program evaluated now? What are the political forces at work? If it is controversial, who are the advocates (beyond the obvious)? The opponents? What sparks the controversy?

4. What decision(s) will be made as a result of the evaluation? Will the evaluation really make a difference, or is it merely for show?

5. How broadly did the curriculum committee sample opinions of the public, the students, teachers, administrators, outside specialists? To what extent did those groups really have a chance to give input? Were they well enough informed for their input to be on target? How much do they feel they were really listened to—did their input really shape the outcome?

6. How well is the humanities department at Radnor School integrated with the other departments? Is the relationship congenial, competitive? Any problems here?

7. What are the costs of the humanities program (dollars, time)? Any problems here?

8. What resources are available to conduct the evaluation? How good a job do they really want? (If evaluation budget is inadequate, are there staff members in the school or district who might be assigned to spend time helping collect some of the data, working under my supervision? May not cost much less overall, considering staff time, but should substantially reduce cash outlay for the district, for consultant time, travel, per diem. Use this only in areas where bias isn't too much of a concern or where I can check and correct pretty well for any bias that creeps in.)

9. What access will I have to collect data I need? Are there any problems with the teachers' association or contracts, policies on testing students, and so forth, that would constrain me if I wanted to observe classrooms, interview teachers or test students? What about policies concerning control of the evaluation report(s), review or editorial rights they may insist on, my rights to quote, release, and so on?

10. Are there any other materials that might give me a better feel for the program? What about the unit lesson plans the schedule says should be developed by now?

11. And lest I forget. Rhetoric aside, are they really serious about attaining *all* the goals they have laid out? In a mere two hours per week over three school years? Or are those goals just window dressing to sell the program?

Author Comments. Most of these questions simply seek descriptive information essential to know how (or whether) to conduct the evaluation. Questions 3, 4, 5, 7, 8, and 11 may also suggest a hint of cynicism or suspicion; yet the failure to ask and answer such questions has sent more rookie evaluators baying down wrong trails, en route to unproductive thickets of irrelevant findings, than any other single oversight.

November 9. Called Mrs. Janson, principal of Radnor Middle School. She responded to several of my questions, but as we got into the discussion, it became apparent that she couldn't really answer some of them without presuming to second-guess the board or others. After a bit, she asked, in view of all the questions I was posing, how much information I really thought I would need before I could sit down and outline an evaluation design that would tell them what they needed to know. I pointed out that was precisely the problem. I wasn't yet certain just what it was they needed to know; hence all my questions. I suggested to Mrs. Janson that the most feasible way to proceed would be for me to visit the school for two or three days, talk with her and some other members of the committee (including a parent or two), visit with some board members, observe some humanities classes, review the written units, and see if I couldn't get my questions answered, along with a lot of other questions that will probably occur to me in the process. I suggested that I could then leave with her a rough draft of an evaluation plan that I thought would answer their questions; they could review it and decide if they wanted me to proceed with any or all of it. That way they would know in advance how I intended to carry out the evaluation and what data I proposed to collect, rather than discovering at the end of the evaluation that they didn't really place much stock in the approach I had used or that I had omitted information they viewed as critical. Mrs. Janson immediately saw the wisdom and advantage in my suggestions. She seems delightfully perceptive. Arranged to visit Radnor next week.

Author Comments. In reaching agreements about the conduct of an evaluation, the evaluator should not be the only person to exhibit caution. Evaluation clients should also look carefully at what is proposed before they commit precious resources to the evaluation. Although most evaluators of my acquaintance are well-intentioned, and a majority of those competent, there are yet too many charlatans and hucksters who lack the scruples and/or the skills necessary to do good evaluation work. Atrocities committed by such have gone far to breed skepticism that many educators extend undeservedly to well-qualified, reputable evaluators. Even with well-intentioned, competent evaluators, potential clients can have no assurance *a priori* that their particular approach to evaluating the program will be very helpful.

It is for these reasons that I generally suggest that the evaluator and client interact enough to clarify in some detail what the evaluator is proposing before they "plight their troth." This might require the client to invest a small amount of resources to cover out-of-pocket expenses and a day or two's time for the evaluator (or more than one evaluator) to talk with representatives of the various audiences for the evaluation, probe areas of unclarity, and provide at least a rough plan to which the client can react. In my judgment, that small investment will yield important returns to the client and avoid the later disenchantment that often occurs as an evaluation unfolds in ways never imagined by a client (but perhaps envisioned all along by the evaluator).

The best possible results of such a "preliminary design" stage are sharper, more relevant focusing of the evaluation and clarity of understanding that will undergird a productive working relationship between evaluator and client throughout the study. The worst that can happen is that a small proportion of the resources will be spent to learn that there is a mismatch between what the evaluator can (or is willing to) deliver and what the client needs. That is small cost compared to discovering the mismatch only after the evaluation is well underway, the resources largely expended, and an untidy divorce the only way out of an unsatisfactory relationship.

> *November 14.* Just completed an interesting day and evening in the Radnor School District trying to get a fix on their humanities program. Had informative discussions with Mrs. Janson, Mr. Holton (chairman of the committee), two humanities teachers,

and one parent who served on the committee. All are staunch "loyalists" for the program, but they don't seem closed-minded about it. Not that they are really clamoring for an evaluation—I gather that interest comes mostly from the board—but they seem open to looking at the program and have been candid in responses to my questions. The humanities teachers were the most guarded; not too surprising, I suppose, for it appears they may have a lot at stake. They and Mrs. Janson were all quick to record their skepticism about using tests and statistics to measure something as ethereal as the humanities. The humanities teachers seemed dumbfounded to learn that my Ph.D. is not in some branch of the humanities. One asked how anyone except an expert in humanities could presume to evaluate a humanities curriculum. I countered by pointing out that I write doggerel, publish an occasional short story, and once even tried to sell an oil painting. He wasn't easily impressed. I debated whether to trot out my well-practiced arguments about why evaluators need not be specialists in the content of what they evaluate, but decided the moment was not right for conversion.

I asked each person I talked with what questions they would like an evaluation study to answer and how they would use the findings. I'll do the same tomorrow and then make up a master list.

Also read lesson plans for several of the units. No obvious clues there, except that some units appear to focus more on stuffing students with facts than engaging them in higher-level mental processes that might better help them attain the lofty goals they've set for the curriculum. I'll need to look at some other lesson plans to see if I just pulled a biased sample. Also observed a humanities class in action, much of which focused on varying styles used by artists in the different art periods.

What have I learned so far? Quite a bit, I think, but I'll wait until I complete tomorrow before I try to summarize it.

Author Comments.   Although this journal entry may not really reflect a full day's work for the ambitious evaluator, it reflects some of the types of information the evaluator might try to obtain in informal interviews and perusal of written information and other materials. Whereas the evaluator's thoughtfully prepared questions might be the core of such interviews, often the most useful information comes from probing leads that open during the conversation. Rogerian counseling may yet contribute useful skills to educational evaluation.

The discovery that the evaluator is not a specialist in the content or processes at the heart of the program being evaluated is often a rude shock to the client who is honestly confused as to how such a neophyte in the relevant subject matter could possibly be of help. Having concluded that evaluators need not be content specialists except when certain evaluation approaches (for example, expertise-oriented evaluation) are used, I used to try to convert clients with repeated and lengthy appeals to reason. Experience (and exhaustion) have convinced me of the wisdom of eschewing such appeals in favor of simple promises to obtain judgments of relevant substantive experts as part of the evaluation. Invoking patience is infinitely easier than persuasion and, in this case, seems as productive, because I have never had a client continue to worry this point after the client has seen how relevant content expertise plays a part in the evaluation design.

November 15. Met with three members of the board of education for lunch. Found them all frankly skeptical, in varying degrees, about the value of the middle school's humanities curriculum. One, an engineer, really seemed to have his mind made up. He described the humanities curriculum as a "puff course," and argued there was greater need for more formal reading instruction and work in the sciences at this age level and that the "interdisciplinary frills" could wait until students had mastered the basics. He forecast the outcome of "any honest evaluation" with such certainty that I suspect he may be impervious to any evaluative data that may show the program to have merit.

The other board members seemed less definite, but both called for rigorous, tough evaluation that will "tell it like it is." The board president indicated the program had never been formally evaluated and she felt it was difficult to defend continuation of a program, about which serious questions were being raised, in the absence of objective measurements that show it is working. We talked at length about program costs, what decisions will result from the evaluation, and who will make them. A most useful interview, especially when I got them to list the questions they would like to see addressed by the evaluation. I think board members are leaning but have not yet made up their minds.

Spent the morning reviewing another set of lesson plans. No fact sheets these; on the contrary, they contained much that strikes me as esoteric for the seventh-grader. But I'll await the judgment of humanities experts on that one.

Author Comments. Before beginning any evaluation that relates to continuation or termination of a program, I always try to ferret out whether there is really any need to evaluate—that is, have those who hold the power to make the decision already made up their minds (with little probability they will change them), regardless of the results of the study? That perspective stems from the sad realization that perhaps 75 percent of my first several years as an evaluator was spent generating methodologically impeccable but altogether useless evaluation reports—useless because I wasn't sharp enough to recognize the symptoms of ritualistic evaluation.[78]

Now this doesn't mean that one aborts every evaluation where the decision-makers are found to be tilted toward one view or another. To take that stance would be to eliminate evaluations of most programs governed by human beings. But it does mean that one should check and be convinced there really are decision alternatives that the evaluation can influence. If not, I can muster little defense for the expenditure of time and money to carry out the study.

November 15 (continued). This afternoon I met again with Mrs. Janson, then with a third humanities teacher, and finally with two teachers, one each from the English and social science departments. Now I feel a need to boil down all the rough notes I've taken to try to see what I have learned and what I yet need to learn about the program. That should help me be ready for the special session Mrs. Janson has arranged with the committee tomorrow.

Artifact No. 2

Memo to the File

November 15

Re: Radnor Humanities Program: Summary of Information Learned On-site,
     November 14–15.

1. Radnor Township School District has had a humanities curriculum for 10 to 11 years, but it has evolved and mutated several times. With the exception of the additional structure and more skill emphasis, the current program has not changed greatly in the past three years.

2. The humanities curriculum has never been formally evaluated.

3. During the past year or two, community concerns have risen about the need for more academic content, more basic skills development, etc., and the humanities curriculum has come to be viewed increasingly as a frill by important segments of the community, including some board members.

4. "Values clarification" does not appear to be a real issue, except in the minds of a strident few (including one committee member). The real issue seems to be that of devoting more time to the basic subjects vs. spending it on an interdisciplinary program aimed at using the arts to help students "understand and appreciate all that it means to be human." The differences appear to be honest ones of philosophy and conviction, not those of convenience or self-interest, at least for the most part. Although there is no public outcry evident, the skepticism reflected by the board seems to reflect the trend in the community (as perceived by those involved).

5. The curriculum committee made no systematic effort to obtain input from a broad or representative sampling of parents or others prior to their October report. They did hold public meetings attended by some parents, and parents on the committee reported conversations they had had with other parents, but community input was really quite limited.

6. The humanities department is isolated physically in a separate building from other departments with which it might be expected to be integrated. There does not appear to be much integration across the departments.

7. The fiscal costs of the humanities program really reside in the collective salaries of the four humanities teachers (close to $80 thousand in total). There are no texts or other significant dollar costs. There does appear to be an interest on the part of some board members in the possible savings if the program were eliminated, because the board has expressed interest in making any staff reductions that might be made without reducing the quality of schooling offered to its students.

8. "Opportunity costs" are a key issue for those in the community who favor the "back-to-basics" notion discussed above. Within the school, faculty members in science and social science are particularly concerned about this, for time spent on their subjects was cut back to make room for the required humanities courses.

9. Within the school, faculty members in the science and social science departments are reported to be generally unenthusiastic about the program, those in the reading department about evenly split for and against it, and those in the English department generally favorable. The latter may relate to the fact that some of the humanities teachers apparently have good credentials in English, plus more seniority in the district than the current staff in the English department. If humanities folds, those staff members might be given jobs in the English department, putting jobs of some of the English faculty on the line. Support under those circumstances may be more pragmatic than idealistic.

10. The board really wants to make a "go-no-go" decision and is asking for a summative evaluation to provide them with information to help them decide intelligently. All my instincts tell me that, if there were no evaluation, or if the evaluation were not credible to the board, they would ultimately discontinue the program. But I am equally convinced that an evaluation showing the program to be producing the benefits its sponsors claim for it could yield a positive board decision to allow its continuation.

11. There is apparently about $3,000 available for the evaluation this school year, with any subsequent follow-up funding (if necessary) to be decided by the board. The district is willing to assign some of its staff to assist in collecting data I might specify.

12. District policy will permit me access to whatever data sources I need. The district would not restrict my rights to quote, use, or release the report at my discretion.

13. There are no other written materials at present beyond the unit lesson plans I have reviewed. Other lesson plans are under development.

14. The staff does seem genuine about the program's goals, although some awareness seems to be creeping in that it may be difficult to help students understand "all that it means to be human" in a lifetime, let alone two hours a week for 27 months.

15. The primary audiences for the evaluation seem to be (1) the board; (2) the humanities curriculum study committee; and (3) district and school staff not included on the committee but influenced by the outcomes. Important secondary audiences would include parents and students.

16. There is a sharp difference in the type of data preferred by the various audiences. Mrs. Janson represented the point of view of the humanities department staff and a majority of the committee when she said, "Numbers won't tell the story—this type of program defies quantitative evaluation." Board members called for hard data, however, with one saying, "If you can't quantify it somehow, it probably doesn't exist." Others noted they found testimonials unconvincing and would hope for something more substantial. When informed of those sentiments and asked to react to them in light of her own pessimism about quantitative measurement of student outcomes in humanities, Mrs. Janson said she would love to see some good "numerical" proof that the program was working, for she wasn't sure anything else would convince the board. She acknowledged that testimonials were likely to fall on deaf ears, but she was skeptical that anything else could be produced.

17. Radnor has only one middle school. If one wished to find the most comparable students for a possible control group comparison, the Welsh Valley or Balla Cynwyd Middle Schools in the Lower Merion Township School District, also in the west Philadelphia suburbs, would be the best bets. Or, might there be some way to relax temporarily the requirement that all students in the middle school must go through the humanities curriculum, so that some might spend that time in the more traditional subject matter? That may not be feasible, but I need to probe this more. Without some sort of comparison, I worry that we might pick up student gains (losses) and attribute them to the curriculum, whereas they really stem from maturation, or the "Classes for Youth" series on Channel 7.

Author Comments.   These simulated conclusions are what I believe, reading between the lines, one might find if one spent a couple of days working in the Radnor School context. Although these conclusions may be inaccurate, they represent the types of information that should be gleaned in an initial visit to a program.

In one sense, the evaluation has already begun, and some of these conclusions represent evaluation findings. Yet many are still impressionistic and would need further confirmation before I would lean on them too heavily. For now, their primary utility would be to focus my design and further my data-collection efforts. More important, much of what has been collected constitutes the basic stuff of "program description."

Without using space to comment on each item in my "memo," let me draw attention to two things.

First, specification of audiences for the evaluation findings is an essential, often neglected, part of evaluation design. Let us hope memo items 15 and 16 help make that point, if only on one dimension.

Second, memo item 17 alludes to the possibility of finding an appropriate comparison group. Space does not permit me to create enough of the context to outline in any sensible way what such a design might look like, for it could take many forms, dependent on the conditions, or might prove inappropriate altogether. The specifics of any comparative design are less important here, however, than the fact that I would probably *try* to include a comparative element in any evaluation of a program such as this one, if feasible. Such an approach can get to the heart of the issues of effectiveness and opportunity cost, where most other approaches are weaker or even speculative in this regard. If one chooses, for whatever reason, to evaluate a program without looking at whether it produces the desired outcomes more efficiently or humanely than alternative programs (or no program at all), one never knows just what has been gained by choosing that particular program or lost by rejecting other, possibly better, alternatives.

Now, lest I be accused of falling prey to the "law of the instrument," let me hasten to note that I probably use a comparative evaluation design in fewer than half of the evaluations I conduct. Sometimes they simply are not feasible; sometimes they are irrelevant to the questions posed; sometimes I find it too much of an uphill struggle to disabuse educators of the widely held view that comparative experiments are irrelevant or harmful; and sometimes I'm simply not creative enough to come up with one that makes sense. But none of these facts dissuades me from the feeling that one should look carefully at the power of the comparative element in evaluation. Were this a real-life evaluation, I would work hard to see if a reasonable comparison could be included to get at issues such as relative effectiveness and cost of students spending time in the humanities curriculum versus other alternatives.

November 16. Held a half-day meeting with Mrs. Janson, six other members of the curriculum committee, and the president of the board of education. Spent the first hour checking my perceptions about the program to make sure I was on track, and the next hour was devoted to discussing and resolving issues.

First, we talked at length about the polarization that seemed to be developing over the program and discussed the possibility of using an adversary evaluation approach in at least some parts of the study. That unnerved some of the group who felt there were too many adversaries as it was. I explained that I thought the approach had considerable merit when controversy already existed and opposing positions could be highlighted *within* the study rather than a battle waged around the evaluation. I explained that adversary evaluation attempts to assure fairness through seeking both positive and negative perspectives, that both sides of the issue should be illuminated, and that the range of information collected would tend to be broader. Equally important, critics would be much less likely to discount the evaluation as being biased. After some discussion of costs of collecting parallel information, we decided tentatively that the adversary approach might serve best in three ways: (a) plan to include the opinions of both strong supporters and detractors of the program—lay out the opposing points of view clearly and collect data insofar as possible to test these opposing claims; (b) enlist the aid of two well-selected evaluators, assign one to defend and one to attack the program, then have both review my evaluation design to see if additional data are needed to make their case as strong as possible; and (c) after the data are in, have my two colleagues review them and, as part of the final report, present and debate their cases, pro and con, on the basis of the evidence yielded by the study. Then the board can be the "jury" and reach a verdict. Not really the full "adversary model" of evaluation, I admit, but the group resonated to some of those concepts from it and felt they would be helpful in ensuring fair play, plus being an excellent report technique. . . .

Author Comments.   Some might suggest a more full-blown application of the judicial "model" of evaluation here, complete with opposing counsel, taking of testimony, cross-examination, and other accoutrements of the courtroom, possibly including a gavel and black-robed judge. Although the latter is patently a pathetic parody, careful introduction and cross-examination of testimony can play a valuable role in many evaluations. Before I would commit the time and money necessary to set up a full-blown adversary trial or hearing for an educational program, however, I would ask whether there is a less cumbersome, equally valid way to get at the facts and opinion that witnesses might proffer, while maintaining the essence of what I view important in the adversarial approach. In this case, I think there is.

> *November 16 (continued).* Second, some of the teachers asked whether I really understood the program well enough to evaluate it. Would the program I evaluated really be *their* program, or my misconception of it? I suggested I write a description of the program and send it to Mrs. Janson. She and the humanities teachers could correct any errors in it, so we can reach agreement on just what it is that is being evaluated.

Author Comments.   Why would I have the client review my written description of the program? Because of too many uncomfortable experiences of two types. First, my best efforts (and penetrating insight) notwithstanding, I have occasionally found late in an evaluation that I have not fully understood some basic aspects of the entity I was in the process of evaluating. As a result, I have had to scramble to patch a leaky evaluation design to keep the study afloat.

Even more troublesome are the infrequent instances when I understand the program perfectly well, but when the results are the least bit critical, program directors play an annoying variation of the shell game. Claims are made that the "program" evaluated is not the real program at all, and new descriptions different from those originally provided to the evaluator are offered as proof.

A simple remedy to both these problems is for me to write at the outset my best description of the program and its important elements, then provide that to the clients for their reaction, correction, rewriting—whatever it takes for them to agree and "sign-off" that the product of our joint effort represents an accurate description of their program. That keeps me from making foolish oversights or getting sandbagged by finding that someone has moved the program since the data were collected. Personal preferences aside, I would recommend this step for virtually all evaluations; it seems the epitome of arrogance to think one can evaluate adequately that which one cannot describe accurately.

APPLICATION EXERCISE

Select some educational entity you think should be evaluated. Identify the audiences you think such an evaluation should serve. Describe whatever is to be evaluated (on characteristics specified in this chapter) and analyze the political context for the evaluation and the resources and capabilities necessary to conduct a successful evaluation.

SUGGESTED READINGS

BRINKERHOFF, R. O., BRETHOWER, D. M., HLUCHYJ, T., & NOWAKOWSKI, J. R. (1983). *Program evaluation: A practitioner's guide for trainers and educators*. Boston: Kluwer-Nijhoff.

HODGKINSON, H., HURST, J., & LEVINE, H. (1975). *Improving and assessing performance: Evaluation in higher education*. Berkeley, CA: University of California Center for Research and Development in Higher Education.

OWENS, T. (1977). *Program evaluation skills for busy administrators*. Portland, OR: Northwest Regional Educational Laboratory.

Chapter 14

Identifying and Selecting the Evaluative Questions, Criteria, and Issues

Orienting Questions

1. How do you decide what evaluative questions the evaluation should answer? How can you identify appropriate questions?
2. How can you sort out questions that are important from those that are trivial?
3. What role should the evaluator play in determining what questions will be addressed in the evaluation? What role should the client play?
4. In identifying and selecting evaluative questions, what different concerns and activities are involved in the *divergent* and *convergent* phases?
5. How does one go about identifying questions and concerns of stakeholders?
6. How can needs assessment and snowball sampling be used to identify evaluative questions and criteria?

Evaluations are conducted to answer questions, apply criteria to judge the value of something, or address issues someone has raised. Evaluation questions, criteria, and issues are necessary for good evaluation planning and action. Without them, the evaluation will lack focus, and the evaluator will have considerable difficulty explaining what will be examined, how, and why.

The evaluator's primary responsibility is to gather and interpret information that can help key individuals and groups improve efforts, make enlightened decisions, and provide credible information for public consumption.

The process of identifying and selecting questions, criteria, and issues to be addressed by the evaluation is critical. It requires careful reflection and investigation, for if important questions are overlooked or trivial questions are allowed to consume evaluation resources, the result could be:

- Little or no payoff from the expenditure for the evaluation.
- A myopic evaluation focus that misdirects future efforts.

- Loss of good will or credibility because an audience's important questions or issues are omitted.
- Disenfranchisement of legitimate stakeholders.
- Unjustified conclusions.

Even though evaluation questions and/or issues may be poorly articulated, they are usually attended to in some cursory fashion. Not so with evaluation criteria, which are sometimes never articulated at all. It is always disconcerting to read through an evaluation report and be unable to find anywhere a statement of the criteria or standards used to determine whether a program was a success or failure. Yet without such standards or criteria, measurements and observations cannot be translated into value judgments. For example, is an in-service program for teachers successful if 75 percent of the teachers attend? That all depends on the rationale for the program and the attendance standard that would signal success or failure. What about a 70-percent attendance rate in a high school mathematics class—is that good or bad? Again, it depends on the standard. If it is a college preparatory class with high attendance expectations—say a standard of 95 percent—70 percent is very poor. If it is a remedial mathematics class for dropouts who are returning to school on a part-time basis, the expectation might be considerably lower—say 50 percent—and an attendance rate of 70 percent might be noteworthy. These over-simplified examples should underscore the point that a statement of standards and criteria is essential to every good evaluation.

Cronbach (1982) uses the terms *divergent* and *convergent* to differentiate two phases of identifying and selecting questions for an evaluation. We will adopt these helpful labels in the discussion that follows.

In the *divergent phase*, as comprehensive a "laundry list" of potentially important questions, criteria, and issues as possible is developed. Items come from many sources, and little is excluded, for the evaluator wishes to map out the terrain as thoroughly as possible, considering all possible directions.

In the *convergent phase*, evaluators *select* from the "laundry list" the most critical questions, criteria, and issues to be addressed. As we shall see later in this chapter, the process of setting priorities and making decisions about *the* specific focus for an evaluation is a difficult and complex task.

During the evaluation, new questions, criteria, and issues are likely to emerge. The evaluator must remain flexible, allowing modifications and additions to the evaluation plan when these seem justified.

Now let us consider the divergent—and then the convergent—phase in some detail.

IDENTIFYING APPROPRIATE SOURCES OF QUESTIONS AND CRITERIA: THE DIVERGENT PHASE

Cronbach summarizes the divergent phase of planning an evaluation as follows:

> The first step is opening one's mind to questions to be entertained at least briefly as prospects for investigation. This phase constitutes an evaluative act in itself, requiring collection of data, reasoned analysis, and judgment. Very little of this information and

analysis is quantitative. The data come from informal conversations, casual observations, and review of extant records. Naturalistic and qualitative methods are particularly suited to this work because, attending to the perceptions of participants and interested parties, they enable the evaluator to identify hopes and fears that may not yet have surfaced as policy issues.

* * * * * *

The evaluator should try to see the program through the eyes of the various sectors of the decision-making community, including the professionals who would operate the program if it is adopted and the citizens who are to be served by it. (Cronbach, 1982, pp. 210, 212–213)

If the evaluator is to obtain genuinely diverse viewpoints, she must "throw a broad net" to encompass a wide variety of sources:

1. Questions, concerns, and values of stakeholders.
2. The use of evaluation "models," frameworks, and approaches (such as those in Part Two of this book) as heuristics.
3. Salient issues raised in the education or evaluation literature.
4. Known criteria drawn from relevant research literature.
5. Professional standards, checklists, guidelines, instruments, or criteria developed or used elsewhere.
6. Views and knowledge of expert consultants.
7. The evaluator's own professional judgment.

Each of these sources will be discussed in more detail in the following pages.

Identifying Questions and Concerns of Stakeholders

Perhaps the single most important source of evaluative questions, concerns, and criteria is the project or program's stakeholders—its clients, sponsors, participants, and affected audiences. Yet, as Hodgkinson and his colleagues (1975) point out, many evaluators do not know how to work directly with a client or fear that their objectivity will be compromised by talking to project staff. We cannot overemphasize the importance of garnering the questions, insights, perceptions, hopes, and fears of the evaluation study's stakeholders, for such information should be primary in determining the evaluation's focus.

To obtain such input, the evaluator needs to identify individuals and groups who are influenced or affected by whatever is being evaluated. A tough, but not impossible task, as Weiss observes:

No procedural mechanisms appear capable of identifying, let alone representing, the entire set of potential users of evaluation results or the questions that they will raise. But in the normal course of events, adequate representation of stakeholders seems feasible. (Weiss, 1984, p. 259)

Identifying stakeholders may be easier if one uses a checklist that includes the following: (1) *policymakers* (such as legislators or governing board members); (2) *administrators or managers* (those who direct and administer the educational program or entity evaluated); (3) *practitioners* (those who operate the program); (4) *primary consumers* (those intended to benefit, such as students, or their parents); and (5) *secondary consumers* (such as citizen and community groups who are affected by what happens to primary consumers).

Once stakeholders are identified, they should be interviewed to determine what they would accept as evidence that the object of the evaluation was either being conducted well or was something they would like to see continued. They should be asked to share any concerns about the evaluation object or ideas about how it should be changed. Asking what they would do with the answers to their evaluative questions, why they are concerned about a particular aspect of the evaluation object, or why they would value particular outcomes can help the evaluator judge the thoughtfulness and importance of particular questions and criteria proffered by stakeholders.

There is no single technique for eliciting evaluative questions from stakeholders, but we believe a simple and direct approach works best. For example, we might begin this way: "If I could collect information to answer any evaluation question you might wish to have answered about your program, what question would that be? In other words, what question would best tell you whether or not your program is doing what you want it to do?" Like pickles in a jar, evaluative questions are easier to get out after the first one has been extracted. Some probing—"How do you tell a good program from a bad one? What would you look at?" "Wouldn't you also want to know _____?"—may help clients focus their thinking. The question "What else would you like to know?" generally produces abundant responses. This is no time to be judgmental or to point out that some suggested questions may be currently unanswerable. This is the time for generating all the evaluation questions possible. The time for weighing and selecting the subset of questions to be ultimately pursued is later, in the convergent stage.

Additional specific procedures for guiding evaluator-participant interactions can be found in the writings of advocates of responsive evaluation (for example, Stake, 1975a, 1975b; Parlett & Hamilton, 1976; Guba & Lincoln, 1981). And the concept of stakeholder-based evaluations (Bryk, 1983) provides additional guidance for the evaluator in processing information obtained from others.

By grounding the evaluation plan in the concerns of key people, the evaluator takes steps to assure that the evaluation will be useful and responsive to constituents who may have differing points of view.

For example, consider a leadership training project funded by an external foundation. Interviews with stakeholders of such a program might produce the following questions:

1. (From the project administrator) Are we running on time and within our budget? Are we meeting Foundation expectations for this project? Are there potential trouble spots of which the project administrator should be aware? How can we demonstrate project impact?

2. (From project staff) What materials and procedures have been developed from other projects that we might use? Are there expectations for our work of which we should be aware? How do we measure up to those expectations?

3. (From participants toward whom the project is aimed) What is the project doing to make our programs better? What evidence is there that it is working?

4. (From the Foundation) Is the project doing what it promised? What evidence is there that variables targeted for change have actually changed? How cost-effective is this project? What evidence is there that the school district will continue the project once Foundation funds are terminated?

5. (From the school district administration) What continuing expenses are going to exist once Foundation support terminates? Is this project having district-wide impact? Would this project serve as a model for other change efforts in our district? What permanent changes in our district are resulting from this project?

Using Evaluation Models, Frameworks, and Approaches as Heuristics

In exploring different approaches to evaluation in Part Two of this book, we noted that the specific conceptual frameworks and models developed under each approach play an important role in generating evaluation questions. This is one place in the evaluation process where the conceptual work done by the different evaluation theorists pays considerable dividends.

In reviewing the evaluation literature summarized in Part Two, the evaluator is directed toward certain questions. Sometimes a framework fits poorly and should be set aside, but usually something of value is suggested by each approach, as the following examples illustrate.

The *objectives-oriented approach* guides us to ask whether goals and objectives are available and to what extent they are achieved. Have the goals and objectives been evaluated? Are they defensible? Achievable? Under what conditions or in what settings? What would prevent their achievement? Hammond's "Cube" can be used to generate up to 90 questions. The Discrepancy Evaluation Model raises other questions about standards, program design, program installation, achievement of process, terminal and ultimate goals, and cost-benefit analysis.

The particular *management-oriented approach* developed by Stufflebeam generates questions about the context (need), input (design), process (implementation), and product (outcomes) for a program. Management-oriented approaches also remind us to learn about the decisions that are to be guided by the evaluation: for example, what do decision-makers need to know, and when do they need to know it?

The *naturalistic and participant-oriented approach* reminds us that we should listen to what stakeholders have to say even during informal conversations. The *process* of education is critical and we should try to understand the different ways that people view it, the different meanings placed on it. Portraying education in its full complexity as a means of educating audiences should be of utmost concern. The Countenance Model offers a framework for us to ask questions about rationale, intents, actual events, and standards. We are reminded that full descriptions of the *actual* object of the evaluation and the context in which it operates should be included in our evaluation.

The *consumer-oriented approach* has generated many checklists and sets of criteria that may be of considerable value to us when considering what to study in an evaluation.

The *expertise-oriented approach* has produced standards and critiques of education that reflect the criteria and values used by contemporary experts in education.

The *adversary-oriented approach* reminds us to look for both strengths and weaknesses of the object we are evaluating and to include evaluative questions, concerns, and criteria from both the strongest proponents and opponents of that which is being evaluated.

To the extent that these conceptual frameworks can stimulate questions that might not emerge from other sources, they are important sources for evaluators to consider in the divergent phase of focusing the evaluation.

Using Salient Issues Raised in the Education, Social, or Evaluation Literature

The educational evaluator must keep current on issues in education and evaluation so that the evaluation plan will reflect current social values.

For example, enthusiastic sponsors and participants may not think to question the appropriateness of using public tax dollars to support certain social or ideological programs in the school. Or, the trade-offs between what might be gained and lost by expanding fine arts or humanities offerings and reducing time for math and science may not have been considered. The evaluator has a responsibility to raise such questions.

Commissions and task forces are sometimes formed by national, regional, or local governments to study particular issues of interest to governmental leaders. The Commission on Excellence report, "A Nation at Risk," completed under the Reagan administration, is a good example. Such reports raise provocative questions, and although they frequently make unsubstantiated claims, they usually reflect current social concerns, issues, and beliefs. They may also serve to draw an informed evaluator's attention to issues that should be raised during a particular evaluation. Questions about important current issues may be omitted if the evaluator fails to raise them, with the result that the evaluation may be considered informative but devoid of information on the "real issues facing education today."

Obviously, we are not proposing a faddish "bandwagon" approach to determine what questions will be addressed by an evaluation study, but it would be naive indeed not even to consider the relevance of educational and social issues permeating current professional literature and other media.

Using Knowledge Reported in the Research Literature to Develop Criteria

What do we really know about what works in education? Contrary to what many critics of the educational research community would have us believe, we know a great deal. One has merely to read through the pages of the *Review of Educational Research,* the *Encyclopedia of Educational Research,* the *Phi Delta Kappan,* the *Reviews of Research in Education*, the *Annual Reviews of Psychology,* and *Psychological Bulletin* to find substantiated principles of what works in education.

Admittedly, our knowledge is as yet partial, but it would be patently foolish for designers of a new educational program or textbook to overlook the knowledge that we have gained from research during this century. The compiled research findings related to the object of the evaluation are hard to refute.

Using Professional Standards, Checklists, Guidelines, Instruments, and Criteria Developed or Used Elsewhere

Many efforts at setting standards have been criticized as based on the opinions of experienced educators rather than on research. Critics want to see the relationship between standards and valued educational outcomes substantiated. These standards nonetheless often reflect the value judgments of respected experts. For example, if one were looking at the quality of a particular school, criteria developed by the National Committee for Citizens in Education (1982) about characteristics of outstanding schools could be used. These criteria include the following:
1. High and realistic expectations are held for students.
2. Effective leadership is exerted by a strong principal.
3. Emphasis is placed on instruction.
4. Appropriate discipline is maintained.
5. Regular assessment of progress is conducted.
6. Positive attitudes are expressed often.
7. Respect for students is shown by school personnel.
8. An effective school organization is in place.
9. Parent involvement is encouraged and appreciated.
10. School pride and school spirit can easily be felt.

In a publication entitled "Good Schools: What Makes Them Work," the National School Public Relations Association (1981) cited the following policy statement from the Education Commission of the States regarding components of a good school:
1. Schools place a high value on the uniqueness of the individual. Teachers look for and emphasize strong points.
2. Achievement is the school's focus and instruction time is protected from interruptions and intrusions. Time structures permit a high degree of flexibility and students are given the time they need on tasks. Attention is given to aesthetic, moral, and social development, as well as intellectual growth.
3. Instruction is monitored and evaluated for quality. Activities use the resources of the total community. Students, parents, and community members make decisions about school processes.
4. The school is realistic in its undertakings, recognizing its limitations. The principal is the key person in the school.
5. Balance is achieved between differences or opposing forces. Students with diverse backgrounds are brought together. Organization is provided without

bureaucracy. The focus is on the needs and goals of students. (National School Public Relations Association, 1981, p. 88)

The *Evaluative Criteria* developed by the National Study of Secondary School Evaluation (1973) are widely accepted by educators as a statement of standards educators want schools to attain. Given their use in school accreditation, any school wishing to be accredited by agencies adopting these standards can ill-afford to ignore them.

Although less widely known and used than the *Evaluative Criteria*, the Southern Association's Cooperative Study in Elementary Education (1951) published a set of standards for elementary schools similar to those developed by the National Study of Secondary School Evaluation. Here is a summary of their standards:

1. Knowledge of the children to be taught. Do we know
   - what differences exist among the children in school?
   - what conditions are needed for learning to proceed smoothly and effectively?
2. Scope of the program. Is there a comprehensive program that includes development in
   - mental and physical health and safety (satisfaction, self-confidence, cleanliness, health services, first-crime prevention)?
   - intellectual skills (including basic skills, language arts, arithmetic, science, social studies)?
   - social living (respect, meaning of democracy, moral values)?
   - aesthetic appreciations and expression (environment, creative work, experiences)?
3. Organization for learning. Is there a balanced program of learning experiences that includes
   - balance in target subjects?
   - balance in learning opportunities?
   - time on task?
   - minimum disruptions?
   - resource people and materials, special teachers?
   - grouping of children?
   - provisions for exceptional children?
   - released time for teachers?
4. The teaching-learning process. Does the process include
   - teacher-pupil planning, goal setting?
   - making use of a variety of learning experiences and media?
   - evaluating pupil progress frequently?
5. Resources. Do resources include
   - community resources?
   - a building located on a spacious, conveniently located site which is landscaped and free from undue noise, disagreeable odors, traffic hazards, unsightly surroundings? Does it have adequate playgrounds, garden plots, walks, driveways, parking areas? Does it provide adequate space, facilities?
6. Personnel. Does the personnel configuration include

- sufficient numbers of teachers, balanced by age, sex, training?
- high-quality staff (working with children, parents, other adults, fellow teachers)?
- auxiliary staff?
- sufficient administrative staff (leaders, coordinators, training, working with children, parents, teachers, supervisory skill)?

Evaluators should be aware of efforts to set standards such as the examples above and should use them to generate questions or criteria that are pertinent to a particular evaluation. They are important resources for evaluators to have in their tool kits.

One caution is important. As Tittle has pointed out indirectly in her thoughtful analysis of contextual influences on professional standards, standards set by autonomous professional groups are in and of themselves likely to be more convergent than divergent. Tittle states:

> . . . professional standards codify acceptable practice for a field.
>
> In professions which are autonomous, the standards are set by the members of the profession. Such standards are a product of general consensus within the profession, and often represent the results of much negotiation and compromise. (Tittle, 1984, p. 3)

Thus, compromise and consensus in developing sets of professional standards may rob them of diversity; only using them as one source in conjunction with others justifies their inclusion in a discussion of the divergent phase of evaluation planning. The same would be true for several of the other sources of evaluative questions and criteria discussed below.

Asking Expert Consultants to Specify Questions or Criteria

Evaluators are often asked to evaluate some aspect of education outside their area of expertise. For example, evaluating a school's reading program may require calling on an outside reading specialist to specify questions and criteria that reflect current knowledge and practice. That evaluation specialists must elicit input from content experts is widely recognized.[79] Scriven (1973, 1974a) asks that serious consideration be given to subject-matter experts' opinions of the quality of curriculum materials. Stake (1967) proposes that evaluators seek out, process, and report opinions of "persons of special qualification," presumably including content specialists. Provus (1969) proposes that subject specialists serve with evaluators as part of the same team. Stufflebeam and his colleagues (1971) point out that the evaluator often appropriately plays an "interface role" between content experts and audiences for the evaluation. Hively, Maxwell, Rabehl, Sension, and Lundin (1973) suggest using subject-matter experts as informants and further propose drawing continually on the expertise of social scientists during goal setting. Cronbach and colleagues (1980) and the Joint Committee on Standards for Educational Evaluation (1981) likewise recommend using teams of experts for most evaluations.

In the case of evaluating a school reading program, for example, the consultant could be asked not only to generate a comprehensive list of questions to be addressed but also to identify previous evaluations of reading programs, standards set by professional organizations such as The International Reading Association, and research on the criteria and methods for evaluating reading programs. If there is concern about possible ideological bias, the evaluator might employ more than one independent consultant.

Local college and university departments of education or specialists employed by intermediate school districts or service centers can offer good advice on selecting a consultant.

Using the Evaluator's Professional Judgment

The evaluator should not overlook her own knowledge and experience when generating potential questions, criteria, and issues. Experienced evaluators are accustomed to describing the object of the evaluation in detail and looking at needs, costs, and consequences. Perhaps the evaluator has done a similar evaluation in another setting and knows from experience what questions proved most useful. Professional articles, papers, or presentations describing similar evaluations may also be helpful in identifying evaluative questions or criteria for the present case. Professional colleagues in evaluation and education can suggest additional questions or criteria.

Evaluators are trained, at least in part, to be skeptics, to raise (one hopes) insightful questions that otherwise may never have been considered. This training is never more valuable than during the divergent phase of identifying evaluative questions, criteria, and issues, for some important questions may be omitted unless the evaluator raises them herself.

An experienced and insightful evaluator looking at a new educational project might raise questions like these:

- Are the purposes the project is intended to serve really important? Is there sufficient evidence of need for the project as it is designed? Are other more critical needs going unattended?
- Are the goals, objectives, and project design consistent with documented needs? Are scheduled activities, content, and materials consistent with needs, goals, and objectives?
- Have alternative strategies been considered for accomplishing the project's goals and objectives?
- Based on evaluations of other similar projects, what questions were addressed that should be incorporated into this evaluation?
- Based on experience with other similar projects, what new ideas, potential trouble spots, and expected outcomes can be projected?
- What indicators of project success will be accepted? Can such indicators be determined with instruments or technical "state of the art"?
- What critical elements and events should be examined and observed as the project develops?

- Have the critical events of the project occurred on time and within budget?
- What impact does the project have on ancillary but crucial side effects such as increasing children's humaneness or reducing undesirable stereotypes?

Summarizing Suggestions from Multiple Sources

Somewhere in the divergent process the evaluator will reach a point of diminishing returns, where no new questions are being generated. Assuming each available resource has been tapped, the evaluator should stop and examine what she has obtained: usually, long lists of several dozen potential evaluative questions, along with criteria and issues to be addressed. So that the information can be more readily assimilated and used later, the evaluator will want to organize the evaluative questions into categories. Here certain evaluation frameworks, such as Stufflebeam's CIPP model, Stake's Countenance Model, Provus's Discrepancy Evaluation Model, or Hammond's "Cube" may be useful. The evaluator might adopt labels from one of these frameworks or create a new set of categories tailored to the study. Regardless of the source, having a manageable number of categories is essential in organizing potential questions and communicating them to others. Evaluation issues and criteria should be similarly organized.

It will be obvious to thoughtful evaluators and stakeholders that it is not feasible to address all identified questions, criteria, and issues in any one study. Practical considerations must limit the study to what is manageable. Some questions might be saved for another study; others might be disgarded as inconsequential. Such winnowing is the function of the convergent phase.

SELECTING THE QUESTIONS, CRITERIA, AND ISSUES TO BE ADDRESSED: THE CONVERGENT PHASE

Cronbach introduces well the need for a convergent phase of evaluation planning:

> The preceding section [the divergent phase] spoke as if the ideal were to make the evaluation complete, but that cannot be done. There are at least three reasons for reducing the range of variables treated systematically in an evaluation. First, there will always be a budget limit. Second, as a study becomes increasingly complicated, it becomes harder and harder to manage. The mass of information becomes too great for the evaluator to digest, and much is lost from sight. Third and possibly most important, the attention span of the audience is limited. Very few persons want to know all there is to know about a program. Administrators, legislators, and opinion leaders listen on the run.
>
> The divergent phase identifies what could *possibly* be worth investigating. Here the investigator aims for maximum bandwidth. In the convergent phase, on the contrary, he decides what incompleteness is most acceptable. He reduces bandwidth by culling the list of possibilities. (Cronbach, 1982, p. 225)

No evaluation can answer responsibly all the questions generated during a thorough, divergent planning phase. So the question is not *whether* to winnow these questions into a manageable subset, but rather *who* should do it and *how*.

Who Should Be Involved in the Convergent Phase?

Many evaluators write and behave as if selecting crucial, practical evaluative questions were the sole province of the evaluator. Not so. In fact, under no circumstances should the evaluator assume sole responsibility for selecting the questions and issues to be addressed or the evaluative criteria to be applied. This task requires close interaction with stakeholders. The sponsor of the evaluation, key audiences, and individuals or groups who will be affected by the evaluation should all have a voice.

Indeed, some evaluators are content to leave the final selection of questions to the evaluation sponsor or client. Certainly this lightens the evaluator's task. In our view, however, taking that easy course is a disservice to the client. Lacking the advantage of the evaluator's special training and experience, the client may well wind up posing a number of unanswerable questions for the study.

How Should the Convergent Phase Be Carried Out?

How can the evaluator work with the multiple stakeholders to select the targets for the evaluation? To begin with, the evaluator must determine what criteria should be used to rank the potential evaluative questions. Cronbach and others (1980) propose the following criteria:

> So far we have encouraged the evaluator to scan widely; only in passing did we acknowledge that all lines of inquiry are not equally important. How to cut the list of questions down to size is the obvious next topic.
>
> . . . simultaneous consideration is given to the criteria . . . [of] prior uncertainty, information yield, costs, and leverage (that is, political importance).
>
> These criteria are further explained as follows:
>
> The more a study reduces uncertainty, the greater the information yield and, hence, the more useful the research.
>
> Leverage refers to the probability that the information—*if* believed—will change the course of events. (Cronbach and others, 1980, pp. 261, 265.)

We draw on Cronbach's thinking in proposing the following criteria for determining which proposed evaluation questions should be investigated.

1. *Who would use the information? Who wants to know? Who will be upset if this evaluation question is dropped?* If limitless resources were available, one could argue that (except for invading rights of privacy) anyone who wishes to know has, in a democratic society, the right to information about what is evaluated. Rarely are resources limitless, however, and even if they were, prudence suggests a point of diminishing returns in collecting evaluative information. Therefore, if no important audience will suffer from the evaluator's failure to address a particular question, one might well give it a lower ranking or delete it.

2. *Would an answer to the question reduce present uncertainty or provide information not now readily available?* If not, there seems little point in pursuing it. If the answer already exists, then the question can be addressed easily with little cost to the evaluator or client.

3. *Would the answer to the question yield important information?* Some answers satisfy curiosity—but little more. Where limited resources force choices, the importance of an answer should be an obvious criterion for inclusion.

4. *Is this question merely of passing interest to someone, or does it focus on critical dimensions of continued interest?* Priority should be given to critical questions of continuing importance.

5. *Would the scope or comprehensiveness of the evaluation be seriously limited if this question were dropped?* If so, it should be retained if at all possible.

6. *Would the answer to the question have an impact on the course of events?* If the question could affect policy or operating decisions, there is good reason to address it, if resources permit.[80]

7. *Is it feasible to answer this question given available financial and human resources, time, methods and technology?* Limited resources render many important questions unanswerable. Better to delete them early than to breed frustration by pursuing impossible dreams. Not all questions are equally costly to answer. Perhaps this seems obvious, but it is so commonly ignored that Cronbach's reminder is important:

> The evaluator, working within fixed resources, reduces the initial list of questions to a manageable subset; then he budgets resources unequally over the survivors (holding back some reserves). Not many questions drop entirely out of consciousness. . . . It is sensible to pick up inexpensive information. Recording incidental observations costs almost nothing, while it costs somewhat more to cull data from records produced by normal operations and still more to collect fresh data. (Cronbach, 1982, p. 239)

The seven criteria just noted can be cast into a simple matrix (see Fig. 14.1) to help the evaluator and client narrow the original list of questions into a manageable subset.

Figure 14.1 is proposed only as a general guide and may be adapted or used

	Evaluation Question:						
Would the Evaluation Question. . .	*1*	*2*	*3*	*4*	*5*	*. . .*	*n*
1. Be of interest to key audiences?							
2. Reduce present uncertainty?							
3. Yield important information?							
4. Be of continuing (not fleeting) interest?							
5. Be critical to the study's scope and comprehensiveness?							
6. Have an impact on the course of events?							
7. Be answerable in terms of A. financial and human resources?							
B. time?							
C. available methods and technology?							

FIGURE 14.1   Matrix for Ranking or Selecting Evaluative Questions

flexibly. For example, one might expand the matrix to list as many (*n*) questions as exist on the original list, then simply complete the column entries by answering "yes" or "no" to each question, or alternately assigning some numerical rating. Numerical ratings offer the advantage of helping weight or rank questions. However the matrix is used, the evaluator and client (and representatives of other stakeholder groups, if possible) should work together to complete it. Although the evaluator may have the say on what is feasible, the relative importance of the questions will be determined by the client and other stakeholders. Scanning the completed matrix reveals quickly which questions are not feasible to answer, which are unimportant, and which can and should be pursued.

Of course, this is only one way to narrow down the original list. The evaluator may simply wish to go through the organized "laundry list" and, for each potential question, jot a few words or phrases, keeping in mind the criteria summarized in Figure 14.1. The evaluator might place an asterisk (*) beside each question that appears a sure candidate for selection, then review the overall scope of selected questions and the feasibility of answering all of them in a quality manner. Has the potential utility of the evaluation been compromised in any way so far? Is feasibility still a concern?

At this point, the evaluator should sit down with the sponsor and/or client to review what could have been addressed in the evaluation (the "laundry list"), what seems most reasonable (those with asterisks), and what issues still exist in making selections (feasibility, scope, potential utility, any concerns the sponsor or client may have).

Whether the evaluator prefers to work directly from the original "laundry list" or to use a matrix like that in Figure 14.1, we cannot stress too strongly the importance of conducting this activity—which will focus the entire evaluation study—interactively with the evaluation client. The sponsor or client will likely want to add or subtract selected questions, possibly negotiating an increased or reduced scope for the study or debating rationales for adding or dropping certain questions. The evaluator may find it necessary to defend her own professional judgment or the interests of unrepresented stakeholders. This can be difficult. If the sponsor or client demands too much control over the selection of evaluative questions (for example, requiring inclusion of unanswerable questions or those likely to yield one-sided answers), the evaluator must judge whether her position has been compromised. If it has, it is probably in the best interest of all concerned to terminate the evaluation at this point. Conversely, the evaluator must refrain from insisting on her own preferred questions and overriding legitimate concerns of the sponsor or client.

Usually the evaluator and client can agree on which questions should be addressed. Reaching a congenial consensus (or compromise) goes far toward establishing the sort of rapport that turns an evaluation effort into a "partnership" in which the client is pleased to cooperate. A feeling of "shared ownership" greatly enhances the probability that evaluation findings will be used.

If the evaluator and the client and/or sponsor have done all the winnowing out of evaluative questions, it is important to check the acceptability of the resulting subset with other important stakeholders. To facilitate this, the evaluator might type the list of questions to be addressed with a short explanation indicating why each is important. If the matrix (Fig. 14.1) is used, a copy should be provided. The list of questions and/or matrix should be shared with each important stakeholder in the evaluation. They should be informed that this tentative list of questions is being given to them for two reasons: (1) to keep them informed about the evaluation, and (2) to elicit their reactions, especially if they feel strongly about adding or deleting questions. Sufficient time should be set aside for their review before the final list is produced.

Concerned comments merit a direct response. The evaluator should meet with any who are dissatisfied with the list of questions, and with the sponsor if need be, to discuss and resolve concerns to everyone's satisfaction before continuing. To push for premature closure on legitimate issues surrounding the scope of the evaluation is one of the worst mistakes the evaluator can make. Unresolved conflicts will not go away, and they can be the undoing of an otherwise well-planned evaluation.

One caution: A timeworn but effective ploy used by those who wish to scuttle an unwanted evaluation is to raise unresolvable objections. The astute evaluator should recognize strident insistence on biased or unanswerable questions. She can counter them by giving an advisory committee of stakeholders, including the conflicting parties, the task of hearing and making recommendations on the evaluative questions to be addressed. As we discuss in later chapters, advisory groups composed of stakeholders are a useful and effective part of many successful evaluation studies.

REMAINING FLEXIBLE DURING THE EVALUATION: ALLOWING NEW QUESTIONS, CRITERIA, AND ISSUES TO EMERGE

Many evaluations are flawed by evaluators who relentlessly insist upon answering initially agreed-upon questions, regardless of intervening events, changes in the object of the evaluation, or new discoveries. During the course of an evaluation, many occurrences—for example, changes in scheduling, personnel, and funding; unanticipated problems; evaluation procedures that are found not to work; lines of inquiry that prove to be dead ends; new critical issues that emerge—require new or revised evaluation questions. Because such changes cannot be foreseen, Cronbach and his associates propose that

> Choice of questions and procedures, then, should be tentative. Budgetary plans should not commit every hour and every dollar to...the initial plan. Quite a bit of time and money should be held in reserve. (Cronbach and others, 1980, p. 229)

When changes in the context or object of the evaluation occur, the evaluator must ask whether that change should affect the list of evaluation questions. Does it make some questions moot? Raise new ones? Require revisions? Would changing questions or focus in the middle of the evaluation be fair? The evaluator should discuss any changes and their impact on the evaluation with the sponsor, client, and other stakeholders. Allowing questions and issues to evolve, not committing to an evaluation carved in stone, fulfills Stake's concept of responsive evaluation discussed in Chapter 10.

A word of warning, however. Evaluators must not lose track of questions or issues that—despite possible changes—remain important. Resources should not be diverted from vital investigations just to explore interesting new directions. Flexibility is one thing, indecisiveness another.

Once the evaluative questions (and/or criteria, issues, or objectives) have been agreed upon, the evaluator can complete the evaluation plan. Next steps in the planning process are covered in Chapters 15 and 16.

CASE STUDY APPLICATION

The reader is reminded that on November 14 and 15, the evaluator, during on-site interviews, had asked all those interviewed (the school principal, three humanities teachers, the humanities curriculum committee chairperson, one teacher each from the English and social science departments, one parent, and three members of the school board) what questions they would like the evaluation study to answer. We return to the saga on November 16, midway through a half-day meeting of the evaluator with the principal, six other members of the curriculum committee, and the president of the Board of Education.

November 16 (continued). Having dealt with some other key issues, we spent the bulk of the meeting laying out the skeleton of an evaluation plan, which I suggested we do together. Some of the committee wanted the evaluation to focus on the curriculum goals and objectives, using those as organizers for collecting and reporting the data. But the board president noted that the objectives were only part of the program, and she listed several important questions she felt would be overlooked if we were bound by the objectives. That was tremendous! It usually takes a fair bit of Rogerian counseling to get people to look beyond their written objectives, so I was quick to take the opportunity to tout the advantages of using evaluative questions as key organizers in an evaluation study. To illustrate, I put on the blackboard the questions I had gleaned over the past two days that they and others had said they would like the evaluation to answer. They got involved, started categorizing and collapsing questions, added others, and before we knew it, we had 17 evaluative questions that they all agreed should be dealt with in the study, plus a handful that were left in but viewed as lower in priority.

Before we finalized the list of questions, I proposed they let me review some other professional sources for additional questions we may want to add but might not think of in one short meeting. They agreed, and all but two of the committee members said they could get together again tonight. So we agreed to meet again at 7:00 P.M.

Spent the next several hours back in the office they've let me use, trying to think of additional evaluation questions we should consider asking. Several additional questions occurred as I got thinking about Stake's and Eisner's approaches to evaluating the arts, so now I've inserted some questions on how the various stakeholders view the process of education, as well as what expert humanities "connoisseurs" might say about this program. Also pulled a couple of relevant questions from the Commission on Excellence report. The smartest thing I did, however, was to call Dewey Pitcher, Associate Dean of the College of Humanities back on campus. I know he used to do a lot of accreditation and site-visit work, and wondered if he could tune me in to any sets of written standards for humanities programs that might be floating around in some relevant professional group, or perhaps give me a clue to research in the area of humanities or earlier evaluations of other similar humanities programs that might be useful. He was really helpful, even though he didn't cite any standards, as such, and told me if I wanted a literature review done to update his "already extensive" knowledge, I'd have to hire a research assistant, not expect him to peruse the library shelves for me (I guess you can afford to get crusty when you get to be an associate dean). Anyway, he turned out to be a goldmine, reeling off about two dozen questions he'd want answered about any humanities program. Even though we had already thought of most of them, there were 8 or 10 that were new and struck me as important. Now I feel ready and armed for tonight's meeting.

Author Comments. It is paramount to include representatives of all important audiences in the design of an evaluation study. Without that step, it is your evaluation design; with their involvement, there is an excellent chance they will see it as their design. What better way to have someone understand evaluation and use its results than to get that person involved as a partner in its conduct?

For me, an easy first step is to ask everyone directly or indirectly involved in the program what questions he or she would like to see answered by the evaluation study. Evaluators should feel free to inject their questions (and may need them for "pump-priming" so others get a feel for what is meant by "evaluative questions"), but a major portion of these questions should be drawn from those with a stake in the outcome of the study.

If time permitted, I would examine the relevant research literature personally and peruse the professional writings that describe good (and bad, if I can find them) humanities programs, for in them I would expect to find seeds to still more evaluative questions. I would also see examination of previous evaluations of similar humanities programs to be essential (if they exist and can be found). And I would always ask the expert in the field—someone who "knows the territory." If the expert is knowledgeable, sometimes she can provide a reasonable shortcut to help you identify key issues, concerns, and questions that would not be feasible for you to ferret out on your own.

The examples used in this hypothetical case study may not suffice in a real evaluation, but they should illustrate some of what goes on in the divergent phase of identifying evaluative questions. Now to the convergent phase.

> *November 16 (continued).* Met with the group again tonight and shared with them the additional questions I had generated. I listed several criteria on the blackboard and we used those as yardsticks to determine whether or not to include each question. This is a pleasant group; usually someone has apoplexy over one or more of the questions that threatens some particular sacred cow. Not so this time, except when I asked "What evidence exists that the goals of the curriculum are really important?" That one raised dust for a minute or two, but they accepted it after the shock that anyone would presume to ask it wore off. After a bit they almost seemed to relish the answer, presuming I'd get the answer they would predict.

With the addition of the new questions, some of the earlier ones dimmed by comparison and were quickly dropped. We reordered the rest by priority and agreed on 14 that are crucial, plus four others we'll try to answer if resources permit. The board president had a tough time letting go of one pet question that was just not feasible without a $50,000 study, but finally made it.

Once we got set and agreed on the questions, I suggested we spend our remaining time trying to get the group to help me identify where to begin to look for answers to the questions. (To be continued in Chapter 15).

Author Comments.   The criteria mentioned in the above journal entry are those shown earlier in Figure 14.1, which I always find useful and prefer to use if possible. Jim Sanders feels more at home with his laundry list and asterisks. Both work. The key is to find that approach which you can use to help stakeholders in the evaluation converge on the subset of evaluation questions that are (1) of most importance, and (2) feasible. The importance of narrowing the focus to a reasonable number of important, answerable questions that are satisfactory and interesting to key audiences is so obvious that one might wonder why we trouble to state it. Actually, it really is not so obvious to many evaluation practitioners. We have witnessed numerous instances where evaluators launched their study with long lists of unranked, unselected evaluation questions, only to end up months later frustrated and criticized because they had only produced answers to a few, and those were not the questions the clients cared about most. Indeed, if we had 10 dollars for every case like that we have seen, Jim and I would be basking in the Bahamas rather than penning these pages.

APPLICATION EXERCISE

1. Consider an evaluation that would have meaning for you and your institution or employer. Using what you now know about generating and then selecting questions, criteria, and issues for the evaluation, generate a list of evaluative questions you would want to address.
2. Obtain a copy of a report from a completed evaluation study. Consider the questions that were addressed. Were there any critical oversights? Was the evaluation limited or comprehensive in scope?

SUGGESTED READINGS

BRINKERHOFF, R. O., BRETHOWER, D. M., HLUCHYJ, T., & NOWAKOWSKI, J. (1983). *Program evaluation: A practitioner's guide for trainers and educators.* Boston: Kluwer-Nijhoff.

CRONBACH, L. J. (1982). *Designing evaluations of educational and social programs.* San Francisco: Jossey-Bass.

CRONBACH, L. J., AMBRON, S. R., DORNBUSCH, S. M., HESS, R. D., HORNIK, R. C., PHILLIPS, D. C., WALKER, D. F., & WEINER, S. S. (1980). *Toward reform of program evaluation.* San Francisco, Jossey-Bass.

PATTON, M. Q. (1978). *Utilization-focused evaluation.* Beverly Hills, CA: Sage.

SCRIVEN, M. (1967). The methodology of evaluation. In R. E. Stake (Ed.), *Curriculum evaluation*. American Educational Research Association Monograph Series on Evaluation, No. 1. Chicago: Rand McNally. Also in B. R. WORTHEN & J. R. SANDERS (1973). *Educational evaluation: Theory and practice*. Belmont, CA: Wadsworth.

Chapter 15
Planning the Information Collection, Analysis, and Interpretation

Orienting Questions

1. What are some activities or functions common to all evaluations that must be considered in planning any evaluation study? (*Hint*: One of them is "collection of information.")
2. What circumstances make it necessary and appropriate to change the original evaluation plan?
3. What advantages are there in identifying information needs in advance, insofar as possible?
4. What utility does *sampling* have in educational evaluations?
5. How do the evaluative questions selected for the study relate to the rest of the evaluation plan?

$\mathbf{M}$uch has been said in earlier chapters about the need to "focus" the evaluation study—to understand what is to be evaluated, why the evaluation has been proposed, what the evaluation's sponsor, client, and other stakeholders want to learn, and what criteria they would use to make judgments. But is this evaluation planning? Yes. When the focus of a study has become clear, is the evaluation plan complete? No, for focusing is only one part of developing an evaluation plan.

To explain the relationship between focusing and planning an evaluation, we turn to the earlier work of Stufflebeam (1968, 1973b). He proposes that one first *focus the evaluation* to determine what information is needed. He also proposes four functions common to various kinds of evaluation, namely information *collection, organization, analysis,* and *reporting.* To develop an evaluation design, Stufflebeam maintains one must plan how each of these functions would be carried out. Finally, he proposes that developing a plan for *administering the evaluation* is an integral part of an evaluation design. Stufflebeam's (1973b) resultant structure for developing evaluation designs includes these six activities/functions:

1. *Focusing* the evaluation
2. *Collecting* information
3. *Organizing* information
4. *Analyzing* information
5. *Reporting* information
6. *Administering* the evaluation

In Chapters 12 through 14 we dealt with various aspects of *focusing the evaluation* (Phase 1 above). Understanding the origin and context of a proposed evaluation and identifying and selecting the evaluative questions and criteria most appropriate for the study are all aspects of focusing the evaluation. In this chapter we focus on Phases 2 through 5, *collecting, organizing, analyzing,* and *reporting* information. Before addressing these topics, we wish to remind the reader of three important points.

Flexibility in Conducting Evaluations.   One should not infer that the steps involved in evaluation are sequential and linear. We might have used almost as conveniently here Stake's "clock" (shown as Fig. 10.2, in Chapter 10), which emphasizes that one may move back and forth among evaluation functions, from data analysis to more data collection, to reporting, back to reanalysis, etc. Whatever schematic is used to portray them, all evaluations have in common these facts: (1) they involve data collection, analysis, and interpretation, and (2) the evaluator must plan how these functions will be fulfilled.

The Need for Conceptual Clarity.   In earlier chapters we outlined several different approaches to evaluation and described how each might be used to perform different evaluation roles. Then we provided practical guidelines (especially in Chapters 13 and 14) to help the evaluator focus the evaluation study. It would seem difficult for an evaluator to go through activities such as we have proposed without developing a fairly clear notion of the role the evaluation will play and a general idea of the type of evaluation study that will best suit that role. Such conceptual clarity is essential to any good evaluation plan.

Yet far too often evaluators arrive at this point, after considerable interaction with the evaluation client and other stakeholder groups, still unable to articulate clearly the purposes or procedures of the evaluation. By now, the evaluator should exhibit a clear understanding of the particular evaluation he is proposing. Is he planning a formative or summative evaluation? Is it a comparative evaluation design or a single program evaluation? Is the evaluation to be objectives-oriented, with the design built around the measurement of specific objectives, or goal-free, with the design built around independently generated evaluative questions? Answers to questions such as these should be apparent in any good evaluation plan. If they are not, the evaluator should settle them in his mind (and that of the client) before proceeding further. Without clarity on these points, the focus for the evaluation is fuzzy indeed, and it would be an accident if the remainder of the evaluation were anything but a muddle.

The Need for Flexibility in Evaluation Plans.   Flexibility permits necessary redirection of the evaluation plan in response to the needs of the client that become increasingly clear as the evaluation is focused and refocused during the study. But once the evaluative questions, issues, and criteria are agreed upon, the evaluator should be about the business of completing the (initial) evaluation plan. To waffle at this point is to risk losing opportunities to collect important information. There is a great difference in genuinely *responsive* evaluation, which is continuingly flexible, and *haphazard* evaluation, which attempts to disguise procrastination and lack of forethought as responsiveness.

IDENTIFYING AND JUSTIFYING INFORMATION NEEDS AND VARIABLES

In Chapter 14 we dealt with identifying and selecting those evaluative questions[81] that the evaluation study would answer. Once the evaluative questions are known, the next logical step is to determine what information will enable the evaluator to give intelligent answers to each question. For example, consider the question, "Have the critical program activities occurred on time and within budget?" To answer this question, the evaluator would need to know, among other things, which activities were identified as critical; the program time frames and budget, by activity; when each critical activity began and ended; and the total cost of each critical activity.

The information needs in the preceding example seem very straightforward. But in practice they are often much more complex. For example, consider the question, "What impact does the computer-based WANDAH program have on the writing performance of high school students in the Jefferson High WANDAH writing classes?" To answer the question it would be necessary to first decide what specific variables would define "impact on writing." Writing performance could be viewed either holistically or analytically, or both. Once the needed information and variables for measurement had been specified, it would be necessary to specify the levels of the variable to be measured and to determine how information produced by the various measures would be pooled to answer the question. Holistic measures of students' writing ability might involve judgments made by panels of the overall quality of students' papers, before and after exposure to WANDAH. An analytic approach might include measures of syntactic density, numbers of T-units, percent of "to be" verbs, or average sentence length before and after using WANDAH. Or students' writing performance might be measured according to the extent and effectiveness of revisions from one draft to another. In this armchair example, we can beg the choice, but were we actually conducting the study we would be required to decide which type of information would be best and precisely what variables and measures should be used to provide such information.

The evaluator should obviously involve the client and other stakeholders in deciding what information would best answer each evaluative question. But the evaluator plays an active and pivotal role, as Cronbach and his colleagues have observed:

> The evaluator, then, should be far more than a passive notetaker trying to locate variables to study. From his own knowledge or from his consultation with experts he

should come to understand the problem area and the history of similar programs well enough to suggest likely points of breakdown and possible unfortunate side effects. He can reasonably become devil's advocate, imagining the complaints that opponents might voice about the program. The evaluator can also suggest outcome variables that others have failed to mention, so that his clientele can decide whether data are wanted on these. (Cronbach and others, 1980, p. 170)

Specifying Information Needs in Advance

Not all evaluators believe it is possible for people to identify their information needs in advance. For example, Weiss (1984) says the answer is maybe/maybe not...

> ...although it lists toward maybe not. As cognitive psychologists have demonstrated and as decision theorists have learned to their regret, people do not always know in advance what they will need to know in order to make a decision.... Unless situations are routine and repetitive, the human cognitive apparatus is not always up to the task of foreseeing which information will be critical. Moreover, the assumption that evaluation requests can be defined early in the study relies on a vision of an orderly and predictable environment. It assumes that organizations can schedule their choices and calculate their information needs with confidence that things will go as planned. In fact, neither the political environment nor the organizational milieu is stable. Program decision making is beset by unexpected occurrences from inside and outside the organization. Long experience with the development of management information systems and with managers' inability to specify their needs correctly is instructive here. (Weiss, 1984, p. 259)

Weiss' insights are sound and applicable to our discussion, for predictability is a scarce commodity in most educational systems. Further, educators are not specially trained or accustomed to identifying advance information for decision making. But we think Weiss' analysis is a bit too pessimistic and would view it as more accurate had she said "not *all* people know in advance," or "unpredictable influences prevent people from identifying in advance *all* the information they will need." Changing circumstances almost always renders some initially critical information trivial or irrelevant. Were that fact to preclude early identification of information needs, evaluation studies could only be reactive—to their detriment. Not all information needs can be identified in advance, but surely many can, and should be. Identifying information needs at the outset does not preclude changing them (and the evaluation) as circumstances dictate. But it does offer the advantage of following a plan for collecting information that continues to be viewed as important throughout the evaluation—and in our experience, that is often the great majority of the information identified as important in the first place.

Once the evaluation has been focused (see Chapters 13 and 14), most effective evaluators tend to develop and follow a blueprint that outlines what information they need to collect and what the sources of that information are. At the very least, they know how (as Scriven puts it) to lay snares at critical points in the game trails. Conversely, the novice evaluator goes about randomly turning over stones or beating the brush to see what he can find. No evaluation can depend on a random, scattered "here a little, there a little" approach to data collection. Once the evaluation is focused, an adequate evaluation plan should specify what information must be collected. If the evaluation is objectives-oriented, the plan will specify what information will help determine whether objectives were attained. If the evaluation is built around evaluative questions (of the "What would you need to know to decide whether the program was a success or a failure?" variety), the evaluation plan should specify what information will answer those questions. And in every case, information needs should suggest sources from which that information can be obtained. Failure to attend to these seemingly pedestrian but truly critical steps is one of the greatest single reasons so many evaluations produce little useful information.

Comprehensiveness/Inclusiveness of the Needed Information. No evaluation can hope to collect all relevant data, nor would that be desirable, for there will always be inconsequential data not worth the bother. Collecting too much data is seldom the concern, however. The greater problem is collecting enough data—or more precisely, collecting data on enough important variables to be certain one has included in the evaluation all major and relevant considerations. A good evaluation includes all the main effects, with provisions for remaining alert to unanticipated side effects. A good comparative evaluation doesn't stop with comparing performance of students in an experimental computer-based mathematics program with that of a control group that receives no mathematics instruction. It goes on to identify the critical competitors—other experimental math programs using computers, math programs covering similar content but using only printed materials, and so forth—and compares performance of their students with that of those in the experimental program. In short, the weak evaluation is almost always characterized by a narrow range of variables and omission of several that are important. The wider the range and the greater the number of critical variables included, the better the evaluation generally is.

Identifying Appropriate Sources of Information

Once needed information has been agreed upon, the source(s) of that information must be specified. For example, let us say that to answer the question "Have the critical program activities occurred on time and within budget?" it was agreed that needed information would include program time frames and budget by activity, costs for each activity, and documentation of when each critical activity began and ended. The primary information source for such items would typically be the program administrator. Secondary sources (used as necessary to supplement or cross-check information and perceptions) might be the organization's accountant or budget officer, funding agency officials of the program if externally funded, or program participants (for information on timing and direction of activities).

To answer the question "What impact does the computer-based WANDAH program have on the writing performance of high school students in the Jefferson High WANDAH writing class?" let us assume that it had been decided that information was needed on one holistic measure (teachers' judgments of overall writing quality on one assignment) and one analytic measure (percent of "to be" verbs). The source of information for both would be the students in the WANDAH classes (and students in some non-WANDAH classes, if a comparison group were used). The source is not the teacher or the rater who counts the "to be" verbs; they only judge, score, or transmit information about writing performance, and that information obviously emanates from the students.

Policies that Restrict Information Sources. It is important to identify, early in planning an evaluation, the policies within which the evaluation must operate. For example, teacher contracts may specify that teachers may be contacted for information only if such contact is approved in advance by the local professional education association (or union). Or the evaluator may learn that students can be surveyed or tested only if the data-collection instrument is first approved by a statewide "Educational Data Acquisitions Committee." Certain school files containing student or teacher information may be closed by "rights of privacy" policies or open to the evaluator only within certain circumstances or constraints. Such policies may curtail or restrict access to primary data sources.

Some evaluators try to ascertain if any existing policies will affect their study even before they identify the major evlauative questions their study will address. We prefer not to be constrained by policy considerations quite so early, however. Restrictive or enabling policies will become apparent quickly enough if the evaluator identifies the best possible sources of information needed for the study and then asks the client whether there are any policies restricting use of those sources to gather information.

If reconsideration of the policy is deemed inappropriate, the evaluator will have to obtain information from secondary sources or forego collecting it altogether. Questions that become unanswerable because of policy constraints needn't be tossed out. Retaining them in the evaluation plan can be instructive.

Using Existing Data as an Information Source. Evaluators (and clients) sometimes overlook the fact that not every question must be answered by collecting original data. Evaluators would be wise to see if information relevant to any of the evaluation questions already exists in readily available form. For example, are there extant evaluation reports, status reports, or data collected for other purposes that might provide complete or partial answers to some evaluation questions? If so, there is little reason to duplicate efforts. N. L. Smith (1982b) provides a very useful example of some public data resources that might be consulted in relation to several types of evaluation questions. Thoughtful evaluators should identify parallel information resources that might exist at the local level.

One word of caution. Just because data exist does not mean the data must be used. We have no sympathy for the evaluator who permits evaluation questions to be wrested into nearly unrecognizable form only so they can be answered by available information. Such distortion of an evaluation's intent is not excusable by claims of heightened efficiency.

Commonly Used Information Sources. Within each evaluation study, information sources will be tailored to answer the particular questions posed. Obviously, information sources may, therefore, be as idiosyncratic as the related questions. There are several commonly used information sources, however, including the following:[82]

- Persons for whose benefit the program is intended (for example, students or trainees)
- Persons who carry out the program (teachers or other staff)
- Persons who administer the program (principals or program directors)
- Persons who set program policy (school boards, for example)
- Persons who planned or funded the program (state education agency staff; legislators; federal funding agency officials, and so forth)
- Persons or groups who might be affected by the program evaluation (parents and other stakeholder groups)
- Persons with special expertise in the program's content or methodology (university specialists, for example)
- Program events or activities that can be observed directly
- Contextual evidence concerning the program's effectiveness
- Existing public documents (reports; proposals, etc.)
- Existing files (student performance records)
- Existing data bases (statewide or districtwide test scores)

Client Involvement in Identifying Information Sources. The client's role in identifying information sources is nearly as important as is client involvement in determining what information is needed. The evaluator will often, by dint of experience, be able to identify good sources of information that may not have occurred to the client. Almost as often, the client will be able to identify useful sources of information that may otherwise escape the evaluator's attention. It is simple enough to ask the client, "Do you have any suggestions where we might best obtain such information?" This sort of collaboration not only yields helpful answers but further enhances the shared ownership of the evaluation by the client and evaluator.

Identifying Appropriate Methods and Instruments for Collecting Information

Once the evaluator has specified where or from whom the needed evaluation information will be obtained, the next step is specifying the particular methods and instruments for collecting the needed information. Returning to our earlier examples, information about the timeliness and cost of critical program events might be obtained through personal interviews with the program administrator, budget officer, and program participants or through perusal of program budget and schedule documents. Information about the impact of the WANDAH program on students' writing ability might be collected by the previously mentioned holistic measure (teachers' judgments of overall writing quality on a given assignment) or analytic measure (percent of "to be" verbs in one writing assignment).

There are countless ways to classify data-collection methods and instruments. Although not exhaustive, we have found the following classification scheme[83] useful in prompting neophyte evaluators' thinking about possible methods of data collection.

I. DATA COLLECTED DIRECTLY FROM INDIVIDUALS IDENTIFIED AS SOURCES OF INFORMATION
   A. SELF-REPORTS
      1. Diaries or Anecdotal Accounts
      2. Checklists and Inventories
      3. Rating Scales
      4. Semantic Differentials
      5. Questionnaires
      6. Interviews
      7. Written Responses to Requests for Information (for example, letters)
      8. Sociometric Devices
      9. Projective Techniques
   B. PERSONAL PRODUCTS
      1. Tests
         a. supplied answer (essay, completion, short response, and problem-solving)
         b. selected answer (multiple-choice, true-false, matching, and ranking)
      2. Samples of Work
II. DATA COLLECTED BY AN INDEPENDENT OBSERVER
   A. WRITTEN ACCOUNTS
   B. OBSERVATION FORMS
      1. Observation Schedules
      2. Rating Scales
      3. Checklists and Inventories
III. DATA COLLECTED BY A MECHANICAL DEVICE
   A. AUDIOTAPE
   B. VIDEOTAPE
   C. TIME-LAPSE PHOTOGRAPHS
   D. OTHER DEVICES
      1. Graphic Recordings of Performance Skills
      2. Computer Collation of Student Responses
IV. DATA COLLECTED BY USE OF UNOBTRUSIVE MEASURES
V. DATA COLLECTED FROM EXISTING INFORMATION RESOURCES OR REPOSITORIES
   A. REVIEW OF PUBLIC DOCUMENTS (proposals, reports, course outlines, etc.)
   B. REVIEW OF INSTITUTIONAL OR GROUP FILES (files of student records, fiscal resources, minutes of meetings)
   C. REVIEW OF PERSONAL FILES (correspondence files of individuals reviewed by permission of correspondent)

D. REVIEW OF EXISTING DATA BASES (statewide testing program results)

Numerous other ways of categorizing information-collection techniques have been provided; of these, the listing of multiple measures provided by Metfessel and Michael (1967) and Brinkerhoff and others (1983) are useful examples.

Reviewing the Adequacy of Information-Collection Techniques. Many evaluators choose data-collection techniques or instruments more for their familiarity than for their appropriateness. Evaluators may frequently find familiar techniques applicable, but equally often, new approaches must be sought. Stufflebeam makes a similar observation:

> Only recently have educational evaluators begun to realize that evaluation needs a respectable methodology that is built from the ground up. That is, the techniques of evaluation must be built to serve the information needs of the clients of evaluation. (Stufflebeam, 1981, p. 5)

Once information-collection techniques have been specified for each evaluative question, the evaluator should review them, as a set, to assess their technical soundness, availability, relevance, and usability, asking these questions:

- Will the information to be collected provide a comprehensive picture of what is evaluated?
- Are the information-collection procedures legal and ethical?
- Will the cost of any data-collection procedure be worthwhile, given the amount and kind of information it will provide?
- Can the information be collected without undue disruption to the project?
- Can the procedures be carried out within the time constraints of the evaluation?
- Will the information collected be reliable?
- Does the data-collection plan make use of already existing data?

Role of the Client in Collecting Evaluative Information. In most instances, collecting the evaluation information is the province of the evaluator, not the client, for reasons discussed in earlier chapters (for example, conflict of interest, technical competence). Yet in some circumstances economy might dictate that the evaluator obtain assistance from staff members or others whose time is controlled by the client. Actual data collection must be carried out under the evaluator's supervision, however, to assure accuracy and impartiality. It is the evaluator who must vouchsafe the ultimate quality of the evaluation information—the core of the evaluation. Therefore, despite any salutary effects that "partnership efforts" may have at this stage, we counsel caution in assigning data-collection responsibility to anyone who is not part of the evaluation team.

Determining Appropriate Conditions for Collecting Information

It is not enough to specify only the methods and instruments for collecting information; the evaluator must also assure that the conditions within which those methods and instruments are employed are appropriate. Perhaps the most common concerns are these: (1) Will sampling be used in collecting the information? (2) How will the information actually be collected? and (3) When will the information be collected? A few words about each of these concerns may be helpful.

Specifying Sampling Procedures to Be Employed.   Some innocents have stated that researchers use sampling because they are concerned with generalizing their findings to large populations, whereas evaluators do not use sampling procedures because they are concerned only with describing and judging what exists in the particular case. Such logic misses the key point: Sampling is as useful and efficient for drawing inferences about more circumscribed populations as for large populations.

An example should help. If one were asked to evaluate the effect on student achievement of a particular statewide, ninth-grade curriculum in Texas, it is unlikely that he would propose testing every ninth grader in the Texas public school system. The cost would likely be prohibitive and probably unjustified as well. Careful use of scientific sampling procedures permits the evaluator to select and test a much smaller sample while still generalizing with a high degree of confidence about the likely performance of the entire Texas ninth grade.

In many educational evaluations, it would be feasible to collect certain kinds of data from entire populations. For example, in an evaluation of a countywide vocational educational program, it might be possible (dependent on budget and time) to administer a paper-and-pencil test to each of the 118 students enrolled in the program. If the test were group-administered, it would seem desirable to test the whole population. Conversely, if one wished to collect interview data, it would seldom be practicable to interview all 118 students. Sound sampling procedures would be used to select a feasible number of representative students from whom interview data could be collected, with inferences from those data generalized to the entire student population.

Sampling, then, is a tool to be employed by the evaluator whenever resources or time are limited and wherever sampling would not diminish the confidence that could be placed in the results. We have no quarrel (resources permitting) with the evaluator who compulsively insists on using a particular data-collection technique (for instance, questionnaire survey) with every individual involved, unless such preoccupation uses up resources and forces the omission of other methods (such as observations, interviews, document analysis, tests) that might yield equally or even more important information. We would usually prefer to see sampling employed with multiple data-collection techniques rather than to see all the resources for an evaluation expended to collect data from the entire population using a single instrument.

Specifying How Information Will Be Collected.   Collecting information to answer evaluation questions is normally the job of the evaluator or team members working under his direction. Not infrequently, however, it will be necessary for others to help. In a national field test of an instructional packet designed to teach metric conversion to elementary students, teachers may need to administer tests in their classrooms. Obviously there are drawbacks with such a procedure, but careful instructions about how to administer the test (perhaps coupled with an announced audit process wherein a small fraction of the classrooms will be retested by the evaluator) can result in sufficient consistency to warrant confidence in the data.

For each type of data collection it is therefore necessary to specify *who* will collect the data, as well as *conditions* under which it will be collected. Will students be tested by the teacher in the classroom, in groups, or will they be taken out of class by the evaluator to be tested individually in the principal's office or teacher's lounge? Answers to such questions are important to evaluation planning.

Specifying When the Information Will Be Collected. It seems almost a truism to say that evaluation information collected too late to bear on the relevant course of events is not useful. Timeliness is essential. In determining when information should be collected, the evaluator must consider three criteria:

- When will the information be needed?
- When will the information be available?
- When can the information conveniently be collected?

Knowing when information will be needed establishes the latest allowable date for collecting it because time must be allowed to analyze, interpret, and report results. Availability is also an issue. It is patently absurd to schedule student "posttesting" for early June if the school year ends in late May, yet we have seen evaluators who have discovered this fact too late. It is also inefficient to return repeatedly to a school or classroom to collect data that could have been collected only once, given better planning. If the evaluator specifies the time for each data-collection technique, it is easy to see whether data pertaining to other evaluation questions might be conveniently collected at the same time, using the same technique. It seems obvious, doesn't it? Yet this simple bit of planning is often overlooked.

Determining Appropriate Methods and Techniques for Organizing and Analyzing Information

Evaluators must plan the format in which information will be collected, in addition to designating means for coding, organizing, storing, and retrieving it (Stufflebeam, 1973b). An example might underscore this point. A consultant of our acquaintance was once called by a school district to help analyze "some evaluation data we have collected and would like to analyze in the next week or two." Upon asking to see the data, our friend was led to a room nearly half the size of a normal classroom. There were the data—thousands of students' notebook diaries bound in bundles, by classroom and school, filling the room and stacked floor to ceiling, except for passageways. Our friend's first fear was that the data might topple over on him; his second was that district officials might really believe all that data could be analyzed in such a short time, if at all. After some discussion with our friend, school officials realized that analyzing a random sample of the data—stratified by school, grade level, classroom, student, and time of day—was all that was possible. It also occurred to them that they could have greatly simplified the lives of the students and spared their time (not to mention the forests of the Northwest) if that had been all the data they had collected in the first place.

Specifying How Information Is to Be Analyzed. For each evaluation question, the evaluator should describe the way in which collected information will be analyzed. This requires two steps: (1) identifying the statistical *techniques* to be employed for analyzing both quantitative and qualitative information, and (2) designating some *means* for conducting the analysis. For instance, in the example above, central tendency and dispersion descriptive statistics could be used with quantitative data, or content analysis for qualitative data. The "means" might refer to the evaluator's working on a programmable desk calculator, a graduate assistant employing a minicomputer, or the evaluator using the university mainframe computer system.

Determining Appropriate Ways to Interpret and Report Evaluation Findings

Statistical reports do *not* speak for themselves. Different people looking at the same results may attach very different interpretations to them, depending on their values, past experiences, and personal expectations. For this reason it is useful to share the results of data analyses with the evaluation client and other key audiences to elicit their interpretations of what those results mean. The evaluation plan should allow for the recording of multiple or conflicting interpretations, and all interpretations should take multiple perspectives into consideration.

The evaluation plan should include not only procedures for interpreting the information collected but also criteria for making those interpretations. Workable criteria demand thoughtful selection and explicit description to preclude any misunderstanding when results are interpreted or reported. Value judgments are, after all, the essence of evaluation.

In later chapters we discuss at greater length helpful procedures for interpreting data analysis results, as well as some common misinterpretations of evaluation findings. Here our concern is only with pointing out the importance of carefully planning interpretation procedures.

Specifying the Particulars of Evaluation Reports. For each evaluation question selected, the evaluator should specify when answers and interpretations should be prepared, and for whom. For some questions, frequent periodic reports may be appropriate; for others, a single report. Some reports should be formal technical documents; others may take the form of memoranda, informal discussions, oral presentations, or meetings.

A good way to plan the reporting of evaluation findings is to use a matrix that specifies for each evaluation question (1) the audience, (2) the content to be included, (3) the reporting format, (4) the date of the report, and (5) the context in which the report will be presented.

An example follows:

Evaluation Question	Audience for the Report	Report Content	Report Format	Reporting Schedule	Context for Presenting Report
1. Have the critical program events occurred on time and within budget?	1. Program staff	1. Progress to date; problems needing attention.	1. Memorandum and verbal presentation.	1. Beginning of each month.	1. Presentation at staff meeting, with one-page written summary.
2. What impact does WANDAH have on students' writing ability?	2. School principal, language arts faculty, school board.	2. Findings of student performance on holistic and analytic measures.	2. Written report, with oral briefing, plus executive summary.	2. Preliminary report on March 15; final report on May 1.	2. Briefing and discussion of preliminary report with faculty and principal; written final report to them and executive summary to board, with oral briefing as requested by board.

Once the evaluator has planned reports for each evaluation question, he should review the reports, as a set, to see whether collectively they provide the needed information in a usable form. In Chapter 20 we discuss evaluation reporting at some length. At the planning stage, however, we cannot improve on a very useful set of questions suggested by Brinkerhoff and colleagues:

1. Are report audiences defined? Are they sufficiently comprehensive?
2. Are report formats, content, and schedules appropriate for audience needs?
3. Will the evaluation report balanced information?
4. Will reports be timely and efficient?
5. Is the report plan responsive to rights for knowledge and information with respect to relevant audiences? (Brinkerhoff and others, 1983, p. 48)

Use of Simple Worksheets to Summarize an Evaluation Plan

It may be useful to summarize briefly our discussion of those items that collectively form the outline of an evaluation plan. For each evaluative question (or objective) used to focus the study, it is important to specify the following:

1. *Information required* to answer the question (or determine whether the objective has been attained).
2. *Source(s)* of that information.
3. *Method(s) for collecting* the information.
4. *Information collection arrangements*, including
   a. sampling procedure (if any).
   b. collection procedure (who collects information; under what conditions).
   c. schedule for collection.
5. *Analysis procedures.*
6. *Interpretation procedures* (including criteria).
7. *Reporting procedures*, including
   a. audience(s) for report.
   b. report content.
   c. report format.
   d. schedule for reporting.
   e. context for reporting.

An efficient way of completing these steps is to use a matrix with the first column listing the evaluative questions (or objectives), and subsequent column headings corresponding to each important element of the plan—as shown in the example on the opposite page.

Naturally, there is nothing to say that one must use every column of the matrix for it to prove useful. Nor is there anything magical or immutable about the headings we have provided; they can be modified to suit the evaluator. For example, a more simplified matrix such as that shown in Figure 15.1 has proven useful in many evaluation studies. This more simple version is especially useful with clients, who can more readily assist in completing this "short form," and

Evaluative Question	Information Required	Information Source	Method for Collecting Information
1. What changes in self-concept of Hispanic students occur due to use of the materials?	1. Prepost self-concept data on those Hispanic students using and those not using materials.	1. Hispanic students using materials and Hispanic students not using materials.	1. Quasi-experimental design, using (A) Wooley self-concept test, (B) Observation of student behavior in Nebraska self-concept simulation.

Sampling	Information-Collection Arrangements		Analysis Procedures
	Collection Procedure	Schedule	
1. All Hispanic students in 2 classes using materials, (N = 50); random sample of 2 of 8 classes of Hispanic students in which materials not used (N = 50).	1(A) Wooley self-concept test group-administered by evaluator in both experimental classes and control classes. (B) Teachers structure Nebraska simulation in all classes; trained observers rate students' demonstrated self-concept.	1(A) Pretest in September; posttest in May. (B) Observations in September (pre-), and May (post-).	1(A) Inferential statistics comparative analysis (e.g. ANCOVA). (B) Inferential statistics comparative analysis; and content analysis of observer debriefing on overall perceptions, based on observation.

Interpretation Procedures	Reporting Procedures			
	Audience(s)	Content	Format	Schedule	Presentation Context

Interpretation Procedures	Audience(s)	Content	Format	Schedule	Presentation Context
1(A) Share obtained statistical results, including statistically significant differences, with audiences; ask them to rate practical significance of findings, in terms of specified criteria. (B) Same as above, plus discussion with staff of observer's briefing summary.	1. District administrators, curriculum director, special programs director, school principals, teachers. Secondary audience of parents and Hispanic community leaders.	1. Executive summary; description of evaluation study procedures, data analyses, findings, and recommendations.	1. Written final report, plus oral briefing for district administrators, using evaluative summary.	1. June 1 for written report; June 8 for briefing.	1. Written report in hand of audiences 1 week before briefing, which will summarize and answer questions.

with funding agencies, who have found such matrixes useful in understanding what is proposed by the evaluator. The evaluator can, of course, subsequently add columns and detail as desired, for his own purposes.

A simple device of this type is among the most useful tools an evaluator can employ for summarizing or communicating an evaluation plan to clients and other audiences.

CASE STUDY APPLICATION

November 16 (continued). With the time remaining in our meeting, I proposed we use the evaluation questions we had agreed on to flesh out an evaluation plan. We took a few of the questions and, using a matrix I offered, went through the exercise of identifying information we would need to answer them, listing where and how we would obtain the information, and so on. It was great to see the enthusiasm of several of the group when

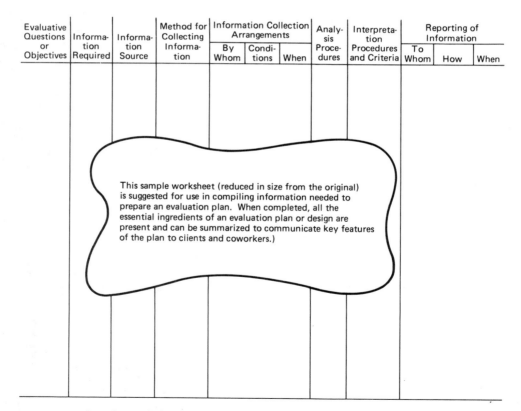

Evaluative Questions or Objectives	Information Required	Information Source	Method for Collecting Information	Information Collection Arrangements			Analysis Procedures	Interpretation Procedures and Criteria	Reporting of Information		
				By Whom	Conditions	When			To Whom	How	When

This sample worksheet (reduced in size from the original) is suggested for use in compiling information needed to prepare an evaluation plan. When completed, all the essential ingredients of an evaluation plan or design are present and can be summarized to communicate key features of the plan to clients and coworkers.)

FIGURE 15.1   Sample Worksheet for Summarizing an Evaluation Plan

they began to realize how simple and straightforward it was. Once they had the hang of it, I suggested they fill out as much of the matrix as they could for the remaining questions and then send it to me. I would try to refine it, flesh out the evaluation plan, and send it back to them for their final approval.

Didn't get the plan finished, but I feel good about what we were able to accomplish. More important, this isn't going to be *my* evaluation plan, it is at least *ours*, if not *theirs*, built on questions they posed, and answered by information from sources they specified.

Author Comments. Using questions (or objectives, if you prefer) as a springboard, I generally use a simple-minded, two-dimensional matrix to communicate to clients, funding agencies, report readers (and myself) how information is to be collected to answer each evaluative question. Jim Sanders and I evolved that matrix in our early joint evaluation work, way back in 1969, and its seeds are contained in less pedestrian and explicit form in early writings of Stufflebeam (1968). Our version may be embarrassingly simple, but it is enormously useful.

December 3. Received the draft of the Radnor group's effort to fill out the matrix for the remaining evaluative questions for their study. They got most of it filled out and had some interesting ideas I may not have thought of. Think I'll save a copy and use in my evaluation seminar to prove my point that much of evaluation planning, *sans* its mystique, is simple logic and should be shared by the client, with the evaluator providing technical help as and where it's needed.

Author Comments. Perusal of my handout for Spring quarter 1980 would reveal the document appearing as Artifact No. 3, of which only a few samples are shown here in the interest of space.[84]

Yes, I do think it useful to have the client not only help identify possible sources of information but also possible ways to collect it. Methodological expertise notwithstanding, the evaluator seldom has the client's intimate feel for the program, such as who is really involved, who knows what, and even how certain groups or individuals might respond to proposed data-collection techniques. Obviously the client should not be left to focus the evaluation alone, but there seems little reason for failing to involve the client as a partner at the design stage.

A few comments about the matrix are in order. First, these sample evaluative questions do not pretend to be complete. Several key questions are obviously omitted: for example, questions about students' learning of concepts presented in the curriculum.

Second, this simulated (but realistic) example of how the matrix might look obviously reflects a first draft in need of considerable refinement. Questions should be raised about whether other sources of information should be included or present sources excluded. Strategies for data collection and instruments are still vague in some instances and need to be checked for cost and feasibility.

Third, even when it is refined, there is no claim that this is the only way a good

Artifact No. 3
Sample Items From the Radnor Township Draft Evaluation Design

Evaluative Questions	Information Required	Source of Information	Strategy/Method of Collecting Information
1. To what extent are the program objectives shared by important groups?	Ratings of importance of objectives.	a. Board of Education b. Hum. Curr. Review Comm. c. Teachers d. Parents e. Other community members	a–b. Individual interviews. c–e. Mailed questionnaire to all teachers, samples of others, using Phi Delta Kappa goal-ranking procedure.
2. To what degree does the curriculum address all the stated objectives?	Coverage of stated objectives in lesson plans and other materials.	a. Humanities faculty b. External humanities experts	a. Faculty analysis of curriculum, match to objectives. b. Review/critique of lesson plans and materials.
4. Is the content of the lesson plans faithful to the humanities?	Substantive adequacy of lessons and other materials.	External humanities experts	Expert review of lesson plans and materials.
5. Are social attitudes in the community such that the curriculum can be successfully implemented here at this time?	Attitudes of community members and influence groups toward the humanities.	a. Community members b. Community influence groups (for example, PTA and service club officers)	Mailed questionnaire survey to sample of community's citizens plus all identified "influence leaders."
9. Do the lesson plans and other curriculum materials use sound?	Knowledge of instructional theory.	Expert in instructional theory	Expert review of lesson plans and materials.
13. Do student attitudes demonstrate that the curriculum is producing the desired results?	Attitudes of students toward the values and concepts taught in the curriculum.	Students	a. Comparative design, using attitude scales, observation, and unobtrusive measures; and. . .? b. Simulated situations, role-playing to get at real student attitudes (for example, attitudes toward elderly, stereotyping of elderly).

246

evaluation could be designed. I would argue, however, that it is a systematic way to produce a good evaluation design, where the evaluator can assure it is technically sound and the client can be sure it is acceptable on other grounds.

Finally, the matrix contains "pieces" of the evaluation that still need to be summarized to yield the real evaluation design. For example, summarizing the columns on methods and arrangements for collecting information will normally identify several questions to be posed to the same source (for instance, teachers), using the same method (such as a mailed questionnaire). Economy of time and effort (and the respondent's patience) will generally result from collecting all the information in a single instrument. Such summarization also quickly reveals inconsistencies and proposals in the draft that are not feasible.

> *December 6.* Completed the evaluation design for the Radnor humanities curriculum today. In the process, I realized we had never explicitly agreed on the standards or criteria the board would use in determining whether or not to continue the program, even though we had discussed them in relationship to the evaluative questions and I had talked individually with some board members about them. So I called Mrs. Reese, the board president, and asked her if she might be able to help me with that. We agreed she should go to her colleagues on the board with the list of evaluative questions and ask them, "What kind of answer to this question would convince you to continue the program? To discontinue it?" Given answers to those questions, we can list some pretty explicit criteria that will help me decide what emphasis to place on the various kinds of data.

Author Comments.   There are many ways one might go about setting criteria for determining whether an entity like this humanities curriculum should be continued or jettisoned. The example offered here is admittedly somewhat tardy if you believe that the only criteria of importance are those held by the formal decision-makers. Yet I find formal decision-makers seldom work in a vacuum and are often influenced by what standards other groups use to judge the program. Once I tended to blurt out, within moments of an introductory handshake with a decision-maker, "Okay, now what criteria do you intend to use to determine whether or not to continue the program?" I am now more patient. Indeed, I like to share the full range of questions various groups hold to be important with the formal decision-makers—in this case the board—and ask them, in essence, whether the answer to that question would influence them either to continue or to scrap the program. Not only can one generate criteria in this way but there is also the possibility of expanding the horizons of those who must make difficult decisions.

> *December 13.* Mrs. Reese called back today after polling the board members on criteria. She reported that she and one other member of the board think all the questions should be used to decide whether to keep the humanities curriculum. But consensus of the board is that the most important criteria relate to three areas: (1) how well students are performing in basic skills (writing and other language skills); (2) whether students are attaining the general and specific goals of the curriculum (critical thinking, appreciation of cultural, ethnic, and social diversity); and (3) whether the patrons of the school wish to see the curriculum continued. With that information, I can complete the evaluation plan and send a copy off to Mrs. Janson tomorrow.

Author Comments.   Mrs. Reese may not have reported formalized criteria, per se, but she has given the stuff of which criteria are made. I have nothing against decision-makers who tell me they intend to continue a program only if "the mean score of students exceeds the 74th percentile on the vocabulary section of the ITBS," just as long as they can defend their rationale and chosen instrument. Conversely, I have a great deal against the arbitrariness that typically underlies such statements. I would much rather have a glimmer of what decision-makers really think important (and some future opportunity to help them reflect more specifically on how they intend to apply the criteria) than to deal with the artificial precision built into too many of today's so-called criteria.

> *December 14.* Completed the Radnor evaluation plan tonight. Was disappointed to find I had to cut out some things I feel are important because there simply isn't enough time and/or money to do them. Alas. Still, I think the plan is a good one, given the constraints we're operating under. I did list in a section on "limitations of this evaluation" those things I deemed important but had to sacrifice due to shortage of resources.

Artifact No. 4.
Outline of the Humanities Program Evaluation

  I. Introduction
     A. History and Description of the Humanities Curriculum
     B. Purposes of the Evaluation
     C. Audiences for Evaluation
     D. Constraints and Policies Within Which the Evaluation Must Operate
 II. Evaluation Plan
     A. Overview
        1. Possible comparative elements
        2. Planned opposition: use of the adversary evaluation approach
        3. Sequencing and interrelationship of components
        4. Evaluative questions to be addressed by the study
        5. Criteria for judging the program
     B. Work Unit 1.0.   Curriculum Analysis
        1. Expert review: humanities specialists
        2. Expert review: instructional design specialist
     C. Work Unit 2.0.   Collection of Extant Data
        1. Existing records
        2. Unobtrusive measures
     D. Work Unit 3.0.   Mailed Questionnaire Surveys
        1. Survey populations/samples
        2. Survey instruments
        3. Follow-up techniques
        4. Nonresponse bias checks
     E. Work Unit 4.0.   Student Measures
        1. Cognitive measures
           a. Basic skills
           b. Humanities content

       2. Affective measures
         a. Attitude scales
         b. Simulated situation: role-playing
    F. Work Unit 5.0. Evaluation Team On-site Visit
       1. Classroom observation
       2. Interviews
         a. Students
         b. Teachers
         c. Parents
         d. Board members
III. Reporting of Results
    A. Preliminary Report: Exit Interview of On-site Team
    B. Final Report and Executive Summary
    C. Review of Draft Reports
    D. Debating the Pros and Cons
IV. Personnel
    A. External Evaluation Team
    B. Radnor Staff (Supervised Participation)
 V. Schedule
    A. Work Flow
    B. Deadlines
VI. Budget

Author Comments. Space prohibits commentary on each of the points in this sketchy outline of the plan, but elaboration may be helpful on a few points that may not be self-evident.

First, for reasons outlined earlier, I would try to get comparative snapshots of the students in the program and other comparable youngsters on variables outlined in work units II–C and II–E. Without more information about the availability of other comparison groups and willingness to allow their use, one could only temporize at this stage, laying out a possible comparative design in II–A and promising, should that not prove feasible, to direct the resources assigned to that effort into more intensive data collection within Radnor on those variables.

Second, within each "work unit" proposed, I would preview *briefly* the type of instrument I would use (listing specific instruments if they are already in existence) and the proposed data analysis.

Third, in work unit 1.0, I would propose sending program goals and lesson plans to the appropriate experts and having them conduct their analyses from afar, unsullied by the rhetoric of the enthusiastic program staff. If resources did not stretch far enough to cover the day or two of consultant time needed here, one could have appropriately selected members of the on-site evaluation team to complete this task.

Fourth, in work unit 2.0, I would envision collection of information on variables such as instances of in-school problems among different ethnic groups, membership in elective dance, drama, or art classes, museum attendance, and the like.

Fifth, in work unit 4.0, I would probably depend on a combination of criterion and norm-referenced measures to get at the basic skills. In addition, I would want to sample students' written products, given the emphasis the curriculum places on that area. In the humanities content, local criterion-referenced measures should be constructed, working cooperatively with the humanities faculty to make certain the items reflect important concepts. In addition, I would want to select a good measure of critical thinking to get at those ambitious program goals.

In the affective area, I would again work closely with teachers to design self-report scales that would assess student attitudes (such as "appreciation" and "sensibility") toward the various content areas. As a supplement, I would structure simulated situations and role-playing opportunities where a smaller sample of students could react directly to stimuli, making choices that reveal relevant attitudes (for instance, stereotypic perceptions of the elderly).

Sixth, I would use an intensive on-site visit of two or three days duration as one of the major sources of data. For all its limitations, there is a great deal to be said for good old-fashioned professional judgment by those who know the territory. So I would be certain to include both humanities experts and evaluation specialists on a team of four or five people. With careful advance scheduling, orientation of the team to the evaluative questions and the interview schedules, splitting the team up to conduct individual interviews, and then coming back to debrief and synthesize findings, a good bit can be accomplished in a reasonably short time (if the team survives the inhumane pace).

Seventh, once the instruments and instructions for their use were completed, I would rely heavily on Radnor district staff to assist with much of the on-site data collection and tabulation, thus greatly amplifying the data that can be collected on a small evaluation budget. The cynic might worry that anxiety over the results could lead to embellishment of these data, but that seems a small risk if one builds-in spot-checks at each step of data collection and coding.

Finally, this evaluation plan proposes what might be called an eclectic, "multiple-source, multiple-method" evaluation, with all the advantages inherent in such an approach. It also incorporates where appropriate the adversary approach, in ways outlined earlier in the journal entry for November 16. But is the plan manageable? Can it be done? That brings us to the next chapter.

APPLICATION EXERCISE

Prepare planning worksheets like the one provided in Figure 15.1 in this chapter. Then list the evaluation questions that you generated for application exercise Number 1 in Chapter 14. Finally, complete the remainder of the worksheets. (Fun, eh?)

SUGGESTED READINGS

BRINKERHOFF, R. O., BRETHOWER, D. M., HLUCHYJ, T., & NOWAKOWSKI, J. R. (1983). *Program evaluation: A practitioner's guide for trainers and educators.* Boston: Kluwer-Nijhoff.

Chapter 16
Developing a Management Plan for the Evaluation

Orienting Questions

1. How can you organize time, responsibilities, and resources so that all evaluation tasks are accomplished in a first-rate and timely manner?
2. How can you estimate the time needed to conduct evaluation activities?
3. What are some advantages of using PERT or Gantt charts?
4. What resources must be considered when developing evaluation budgets?
5. How could a detailed management plan help you? When would such a plan not be desirable?
6. Why would a formal evaluation contract or agreement between evaluator and client be useful? Under what circumstances would such a contract be more important? Less important?

Conducting a thorough and systematic evaluation study is a complex undertaking, from planning (which we have discussed previously in Chapters 12 through 15) through implementing those plans (which we shall discuss in later chapters). To make the effort successful, the evaluator must effectively manage not only the evaluation activities but also the resources allocated to carry them out.

Evaluation management is multifaceted. An evaluation manager must supervise other staff; serve as liaison to evaluation clients, participants, and other evaluation stakeholders; and identify and cope with political influences. Effective management also demands communication and reporting skills. Needed resources must be identified, allocated, and monitored. Periodically, the manager must review all evaluation activities to ensure that schedules are being respected and that all activities meet the high technical standards expected.

An evaluation, whether a team or single-person effort, cannot afford disorganized "planning" or oversights. As the Joint Committee on Standards for Educational Evaluation (1981) reminds us, professional evaluators are responsible for planning cost-effective evaluations. A management plan is needed to structure and control resources—including time, money, and people. Of course, even the best-laid plans must be open to change in response to fluctuating circumstances. But the need for flexibility in no way diminishes the need for a plan. An old Chinese proverb states: "The best leader often appears not to lead at all." Similarly, the best evaluation manager may be rather inconspicuous, but he or she will be in control behind the scenes.

What should a good management plan include? The answer is—everything a conscientious manager needs to be concerned with. The management plan must specify all needed resources and indicate how they should be allocated. It must also include plans for preventing policy restrictions or political influences from undermining the study, and procedures for assuring high-quality procedures and results.

In this chapter we discuss ways to develop and use a good management plan. Specifically, we address six topics: (1) estimating and managing the time needed to conduct evaluation activities; (2) analyzing personnel needs and responsibilities; (3) estimating costs and developing a budget; (4) complying with established policies, protocol, and ethical standards; (5) judging, monitoring, and revising the evaluation plan to assure adherence to high-quality standards; and (6) establishing evaluation agreements and contracts. The reader who wishes additional information about managing evaluation studies is referred to St. Pierre (1983).

ESTIMATING AND MANAGING TIME FOR CONDUCTING EVALUATION ACTIVITIES

The first step in developing a management plan is to prepare a work plan for all tasks that will be involved in the evaluation. This work plan can easily be based on the list of evaluation questions selected for the study. A simple worksheet (much like those used in earlier chapters) can be used to list the questions, along with the tasks that must be performed to answer each question. For each task, the manager must estimate beginning and ending dates, the number of personnel involved and their costs, other resources required, and the total budget. This information may then be entered on a management plan worksheet. A sample worksheet for three hypothetical evaluation questions is shown in Figure 16.1.

Once such a worksheet has been prepared, time frames may be worked out. We will discuss two types of time-related project management approaches: *PERT* systems and *Gantt* charts.[85]

PERT Charts

"PERT" is an acronym for "Program Evaluation and Review Technique" and was developed by the United States Department of Defense as a management tool for complex military projects. Cook (1966) was instrumental in adapting this technique to educational research and evaluation.

Through PERT, complex projects can be blueprinted as a network of *activities* and *events*. Every activity has one event marking its starting point and one marking its ending point. And each activity has a time estimate. Some evaluators, to get best- and worst-case scenarios, use three time estimates: most optimistic, most

FIGURE 16.1   Sample Management Plan Worksheet

Evaluation Question	Tasks	Estimated Task Beginning & Ending Dates	Personnel Involved & Estimated Costs	Other Resources Needed & Costs	Total Task Cost
1. Have the critical events of the program occurred on time and within budget?	1a. List program critical events, time schedule for each, and budget for each.	1a. First month of program.	1a. Evaluator, 5 days at $150 per day = $750.	1a. None.	1a. $750.
	b. Monitor progress and expenditures for critical events.	b. Beginning to end of each month of program.	b. Evaluator, 2 days at $150 per day = $300 per month of program.	b. None.	b. $300 per month.
	c. Prepare and present monthly reports.	c. Last week of each month of program.	c. Evaluator, 2 days at $150 per day = $300 per month of program.	c. 1 day of clerical time = $40 per month of program.	c. $340 per month.
2. Is these sufficient evidence of need for the program as it is designed? Are there other more critical needs that are not being addressed?	2a. Search for assessment of needs.	2a. First day of program or before.	2a. Evaluator, one day at $150 per day = $150.	2a. None.	2a. $150.
	b. If no needs assessment exists, plan and conduct needs assessment.	b. First month of program.	b. Evaluator, 10 days at $150 per day = $1,500.	b. Consultants, 2 for 3 days at $200 = $1,200; research assistant, 10 days at $100 = $1,000.	b. $3,700.
	c. Prepare written report for project administrator.	c. Fourth week of program.	c. Evaluator, 2 days at $150 per day = $300	c. Clerical time, 1 day at $40 = $40	c. $340.
	d. Meet with program administrator.	d. End of fourth week of program.	d. Evaluator and program administrator, 2 hours at $19 per hour = $38.	d. None.	d. $38.

253

FIGURE 16.1 CONTINUED

Evaluation Question	Tasks	Estimated Task Beginning & Ending Dates	Personnel Involved & Estimated Costs	Other Resources Needed & Costs	Total Task Cost
3. Have alternative strategies for accomplishing goals and objectives been considered?	3a. Search for program planning document.	3a. First day of program or before.	3a. Evaluator, one day at $150 per day = $150.	3a. None.	3a. $150.
	b. If no planning document exists, plan and conduct analysis of alternative ways to achieve project objectives.	b. First month of program or before.	b. Program evaluator, 10 days at $150 per day = $1,500.	b. Literature search, $50.	b. $1,550.
	c. Prepare written report for project administrator.	c. Fourth week of program.	c. Evaluator, 2 days at $150 = $300.	c. Clerical time, 1 day at $40 = $40.	c. $340.
	d. Meet with program administrator.	d. End of fourth week of program.	d. Program evaluator and program administrator, 2 hours at $19 per hour = $38.	d. None.	d. $38.

pessimistic, and most realistic. Events are symbolized with a circle, activities with lines, and arrows to indicate direction, as shown in Figure 16.2 Solid lines indicate activities, dotted lines refer only to sequential constraints, showing that one event must be completed before another can begin.

Were PERT being used as proposed by its developers, a time estimate would be added to each solid line in Figure 16.2, and the "critical path" (the longest possible route, in time, between events 1 and 11) would be calculated to highlight those activities where relaxed deadlines are least tolerable.

As useful as PERT is, it can be cumbersome and time–consuming,[86] and may be most useful in large, complex studies where overlooking details may create unresolvable problems.[87] In many instances, a simplified version of PERT, using the same general logic, is sufficient. Seldom have we found a PERT system more detailed than that shown in Figure 16.3 to be necessary or even useful. We do counsel evaluators to make rough time estimates of all activities (solid lines) and to

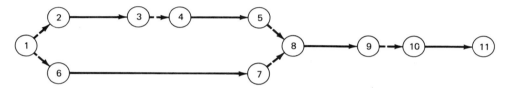

1 = Begin Testing Project
2 = Begin Item Tryout
3 = Complete Item Tryout
4 = Begin Item Revision
5 = Complete Item Revision
6 = Begin Development of Administration and Scoring Procedures
7 = Complete Development of Administration and Scoring Procedures

8 = Begin Student Testing
9 = Complete Student Testing
10 = Begin Test Scoring
11 = Complete Test Scoring

FIGURE 16.2 Partial Example of a PERT Network

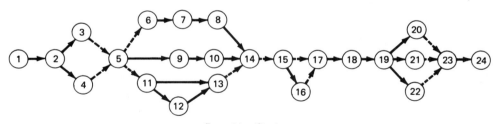

Event Identification

1. Start Project
2. Complete Objectives
3. Complete Data Paradigm
4. Complete Hypotheses
5. Start Item Construction
6. Start Universe Definition
7. Start Sampling
8. Start Sample Selection

9. Start Tryout
10. Start Final Form
11. Start Interviewer Selection
12. Complete Administrative Procedures
13. Complete Schedules
14. Start Field Interview
15. Start Data Coding
16. Complete Follow-up

17. Start Tabulation
18. Start Statistical Tests
19. Complete Tests
20. Complete Interpretation
21. Complete Tables
22. Complete Charts
23. Start Narrative
24. Complete Narrative

FIGURE 16.3 Summary Network for Survey Research Project
Source: Reprinted from Cook, 1966, p. 43.

identify the critical path that suggests where punctuality is most urgent. We should also note that computer programs for PERT and similar management networks show promise of being very helpful (drawing the charts, revising them with updated information) and may eventually permit more sophisticated use of management systems than is possible where noncomputer systems described above are used.

PERT is useful in identifying activities that can occur simultaneously and in delegating staff to those activities. PERT networks also help the evaluator plan time estimates and identify which events must be completed before others can begin. In a complete evaluation, the PERT chart can be used to check progress against the planned schedule, and to revise assignments or activities as necessary to keep from overshooting deadlines. Such planning helps the evaluator avoid overloading staff or overcommitting resources. Balancing work flow and available resources also helps minimize "down times" when some staff members have nothing to do, while others struggle feverishly to keep pace.

Gantt Charts

Gantt charts (Clark, 1952) are simple displays that include proportionate, chronologically scaled time frames for each evaluation task. A Gantt chart lists tasks on the vertical axis and a time scale on the horizontal axis. A horizontal line is drawn for each task to show how long it will take. An evaluator (or anyone) can look at a Gantt chart and tell at a glance when activities will begin and how long each will continue. Gantt charts are easy to prepare, and in addition to their management benefits, they can be effective in communicating evaluation plans. A sample Gantt chart is shown in Figure 16.4.

Advantages of PERT or Gantt Charts

Usually the evaluator will use either a PERT or a Gantt chart, but not both. PERT charts take longer to prepare than Gantt charts and can become very complex if

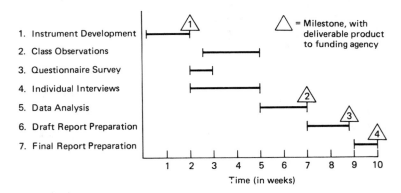

FIGURE 16.4   Example of Showing Milestones on a Gantt Chart

detailed networks exist, but they do force the manager to contemplate personnel assignments for the project in detail. Gantt charts communicate well with non-technical audiences and are simple to prepare. For this reason, Gantt charts often appear in proposals or reports intended for lay audiences, whereas PERT charts are more frequently used internally for detailed evaluation planning.

Both PERT and Gantt charts can help highlight important interim deadlines (or "milestones," as they are often termed by funding agencies) that must be met if the overall evaluation study is to be completed on time. On PERT charts, the critical path automatically highlights such events. On Gantt charts, important milestones can be keyed with symbols (see Fig. 16.4).

Charts reflect, but do not direct, a manager's thinking. A chart is only useful if all steps are accounted for and if time estimates are realistic.

It is essential that sufficient time be allowed for all aspects of the evaluation, from focusing the evaluation study through final reporting. Good evaluation management never places key actors under unrealistic constraints that jeopardize the quality of their performance.

ANALYZING PERSONNEL
NEEDS AND ASSIGNMENTS

The quality of any evaluation depends heavily on the capability and energy of those who carry it out. In some instances, only one individual—the evaluator—may be responsible for everything. Most typically, others—secretarial personnel, assistants, consultants, or evaluation colleagues—will also be involved.

Perhaps the first concern of any evaluation manager is whether qualified individuals are available to carry out the various evaluation tasks. Answering this question demands specifying clearly the roles and responsibilities of each individual. In proposing how to develop an implementation plan for evaluation, Suarez (1981) outlines "personnel role specifications" as the first step: specify who would manage the study, complete the evaluation design, select or develop instruments, collect data, analyze data, write summary reports, and so on.

In analyzing personnel needs and roles, we have found it useful to outline, as specifically as possible, the activities to be accomplished and the time estimates and personnel responsibilities for each. Once role assignments and time estimates are completed, they can be summarized in a sample worksheet (see Fig. 16.5) that suggests personnel needs.

Typically, an evaluation management plan includes *personnel loadings* for each person involved. Personnel loadings are summaries of the work assignments, by phase of the evaluation, in units called *full-time equivalents*, or *FTEs*. An FTE of 0.20, for example, means that a person will spend 20 percent of his or her work time on that particular phase of the evaluation. FTEs can range from 0.0 to 1.00 for any phase. The personnel loadings can be used to check for overloaded or underutilized personnel, and can alert the evaluator of the need to assign more part- or full-time staff to certain tasks.

Figure 16.5 summarizes the project analysis phase of the evaluation in three

Personnel Loadings (FTE) for
Phase 1— Project Analysis (1 month)

	Project Monitoring	Needs Assessment	Design Assessment
Evaluation Staff:			
Project Evaluator	.45	.65	.66
Secretary	.05	.05	.05
Consultants (2)	---	.15 ea.	---
Research Assistant	---	.50	---
Project Staff:			
Project Administrator	---	.01	.01

FIGURE 16.5   Sample Personnel Loadings for an Evaluation Study

parts: project monitoring, needs assessment, and design assignment. The personnel loadings for our management plan of this one-month phase would be as shown in Figure 16.5.

Even a cursory review of Figure 16.5 shows that the project evaluator is overloaded: Her FTEs for the three activities in this phase total well over 100 percent of her work time. Because the research assistant is only committed half-time, perhaps he could take part of the load. Otherwise, more evaluation staff should be hired, or the proposed tasks scaled back.

The secretary is very lightly loaded (if this project is her only responsibility), and it might be possible for her to assume more responsibility for routine tasks that require no technical training.

The project administrator (manager of the program being evaluated, *not* the manager of the evaluation) will probably be pleased to see that the evaluation during this phase consumes little of his time. Conversely, he may be chagrined to learn that an activity he viewed as fairly complicated will require only 2 percent of his time.

Personnel loadings, followed by a reanalysis of personnel needs and assignments, are an important part of good evelution management.

ESTIMATING COSTS OF EVALUATION ACTIVITIES AND DEVELOPING EVALUATION BUDGETS

Evaluation costs money. And it is hard to place a dollar value on the information or insights that evaluation yields. Evaluators are sometimes told that the cost of their services diverts funds that could have been used to strengthen educational services or products. (This ignores the fact that evaluation is usually an important aid to development or management of those very educational services or products.) Evaluators also often compete with one another for evaluation contracts where cost of services is an important consideration. For both these reasons, the pressure to keep down evaluation expenses is strong.

The continuing use of evaluation suggests that many educational policymakers consider it well worth the costs. Some evaluators (for example, Scriven, 1974a) have proposed the possibility of "cost-free" evaluation, suggesting not that evaluation services be offered for nothing, but rather that the benefits of implementing the evaluator's recommendations equal or exceed the expense of a well-conceived, well-conducted study). An evaluation always costs "too much" if the results are useless.

In the discussion that follows, we limit our focus to direct dollar costs, ignoring the nondollar and indirect costs of evaluation, such as opportunity costs,[88] time loss, political, human, and hidden costs—such as the need for research and development to solve unanticipated methodological problems. The reader is referred to the volume by Alkin and Solmon (1983) for a more complete treatment of evaluation costs and benefits.

Resources Needed in Educational Evaluations

Typically, an evaluation budget comprises the following 10 categories:[89]

1. *Evaluation staff salary and benefits.* The amount of time that staff members must spend on evaluation tasks and the level of expertise needed to perform particular evaluation tasks both affect costs.

2. *Consultants.* Staff expertise determines whether outside consultants will be needed. Managers face a difficult management choice: whether to employ adequate evaluation staff on a continuing basis so that they will be available as needed, or keep only a "skeleton staff" of evaluators, using consultants for particular evaluation assignments. Even if the first option is selected, consultants are frequently asked to provide special expertise or independent perspectives.

3. *Travel and per diem (for staff and consultants).* Costs here depend on the amount of field work and the degree of personal interactions required to design and conduct an evaluation.

4. *Communications (postage, telephone calls, etc.).* This category includes both fixed costs (for example, continuing monthly billings for telephone hookups and postage meters) and variable costs (for special communication efforts, such as long-distance calls).

5. *Printing and duplication.* Costs here cover preparation of data-collection instruments, reports, and any other documents.

6. *Data processing.* Costs in this category cover quantitative data analysis: systems design, data coding and checking, data storage and retrieval, computer programming, computer use (time, paper) for manipulating or analyzing data, and computer-based bibliographic searches. The costs for qualitative information analysis are usually covered under staff or consultant personnel.

7. *Printed materials.* This category includes the costs for acquiring data-collection instruments and library materials.

8. *Supplies and equipment.* This category covers the costs of specific supplies as well as equipment that must be purchased or rented.

9. *Subcontracts.* This category includes expenditures for any contracted evaluation-related services such as accounting, legal services, test development, and so forth.

10. *Overhead (facilities, utilities).* The greater the use of external personnel and services, the lower the overhead costs. Typically, however, an institution must bear certain fixed overhead costs (that is, those of maintaining an adequately equipped physical plant) regardless of what arrangements are made for the evaluation.

Developing Evaluation Budgets

Following are brief directions for estimating budgets within each of the 10 cost categories just presented.

    1. *Salaries and benefits.* To calculate salary estimates, multiply the number of days used for each evaluation staff member in the personnel loadings table by his or her daily salary rate, *or* multiply the individual's FTE (from personnel loading table) by the unit FTE rate (daily, monthly, or annual). Calculate fringe benefits for each person by multiplying a percent of salary (for example, 25 percent) by the salary estimate. Most organizations have a set benefit rate for each category of personnel (faculty, staff, etc.).

    2. *Consultants.* Multiply the number of days each consultant will work by the consultant's rate (which must be obtained from each consultant independently). No fringe benefits are calculated for consultants.

    3. *Travel and per diem.* Estimate the total mileage for all automotive travel and multiply by the sponsoring institution's accepted mileage rate or a negotiated rate. Where longer distances require air travel, estimate the round-trip cost of each trip for each person (including consultants) and total all such costs. Be sure to include ground transportation (taxis, rental cars, parking). Necessary per diem costs for lodging and meals should also be calculated for each person (including consultants), and then summed. Per diem often varies greatly by country, region, and city; estimated costs of meals and rooms must be realistic and based on the locale in which the evaluation will be conducted.

    4. *Communications.* Multiply the number of days needed for the evaluation by fixed daily service costs (telephone service, postage meter). Then add an estimate for necessary long-distance telephone, postage (this can be a large item when mail surveys are used), and special services (such as express mailings, large packages, etc.).

    5. *Printing and duplication.* Estimate the printing costs of documents and reports. Also, estimate duplication costs associated with document production and publication, photocopying and library searches.

    6. *Data processing.* For quantitative data analyses, work with the chosen data-processing center to estimate computer time (both central and peripheral processing time) needed for data storage, retrieval, and analysis. Multiply the time required by the rates for central and peripheral computer use. Then estimate the amount of time data-processing specialists (computer programmers and others) will need to plan and implement data processing, and multiply this estimate by the daily or hourly rate of such specialists. Be sure to estimate the costs of coding, key punching, verifying, and entering data (usually by multiplying anticipated hours of staff time by hourly rates). It is always wise to allow some discretionary money for reanalyzing, correcting mistakes, or carrying out additional work suggested by preliminary analysis.

7. *Printed materials.* Estimate the costs of buying instruments, books and reports, and conducting library computer searches.

8. *Supplies and equipment.* Estimate the costs of consumable materials (pencils, paper, typing supplies, audiotapes), as well as the costs of rentals or purchases for typing or recording. Organizations that have an estimated daily cost for evaluation office supplies can simply multiply that daily rate by the estimated number of days needed to complete the evaluation.

9. *Subcontracts.* All subcontracts must be negotiated before the final evaluation budget can be completed. Each subcontractor will submit an independent budget.

10. *Overhead.* Most organizations have fixed percentages of a total budget, or of personnel salaries and benefits, that they charge as operating overhead. This percentage often varies according to how much of an evaluation is done in the office versus "in the field." If no set overhead rate exists, the evaluator must estimate how much of the cost for office space, electricity, heating, furniture, and other operating costs should be appropriately charged to the evaluation.

Once costs in each budget category have been calculated, a total cost for the evaluation can be determined. This first estimate often exceeds the evaluator's or client's expectations. When this happens, review each line item and ask how the work could be completed at less cost. Some effective cost-saving measures include

- Using available volunteers or low-cost workers to reduce staff salaries and benefits (taking care, however, not to compromise quality control)
- Using local specialists for data collection to reduce travel costs
- Asking less-expensive staff to perform nontechnical, routine tasks
- Borrowing (equipment, people, materials, and supplies)
- Seeking "in-kind" contributions from the organization in which the evaluator is employed (often done for good public relations) or the sponsoring agency
- Reducing the scope of the evaluation, perhaps deferring some parts for later
- Using existing instruments, data, or reports
- Using inexpensive data collection when precision can be sacrificed without severe consequences
- Using public media to disseminate results
- Using services when rates are cheapest (for example, nighttime computer runs or evening long-distance telephone calls)
- "Piggybacking" on other studies
- Increasing efficiency through good management (such as our proposed use of PERT in developing a management plan).

How Much Does a Good Evaluation Cost?

A favorite dinner conversation topic among evaluators is speculating what proportion of an educational program's budget should be committed to evaluating that program. Brinkerhoff and others (1983, p. 187) state: "A rule of thumb is that an evaluation budget should be approximately 10 percent of the program or project budget" (these authors are also quick to note that percentages are only rough estimates and may fluctuate widely, with good reason). Stake suggests a lower range of 2 percent to 5 percent as possibly adequate, arguing that "The quality of the study is not likely to be related to its cost. The principal concern is to get able persons working on the study. Sometimes they cost very little, sometimes they are not available at any price" (Stake, 1976, p. 29). If rules of thumb are useful, we tend to think that 10 percent more often results in a better study than does the lower percentages proposed by Stake, but his point cannot be dismissed. We caution against assuming any direct correlation between quality and expenditure. One can neither assume that budgets well above 10 percent are inflated nor that those well below signal inadequate evaluation (even though that may often be the case).

For example, we are familiar with one evaluation that cost over 50 percent of the program's budget. No one thought the price high, for the program was of crucial importance, complex, and challenging to evaluate, and it was slated for adoption (if it were effective) by all the schools within a populous state. At the other extreme (discounting "whitewash" or "lick and promise" evaluations, where a tiny investment signals pro forma fulfillment of a requirement, rather than a sincere effort to collect evaluative information), we are familiar with one award-winning evaluation[90] that cost only a fraction of 1 percent of the budget of the program it evaluated (partly because of use of extant testing programs and other cost-saving mechanisms). Thus, we try not to make assumptions linking percentage of program budget to evaluation quality. The more the percentage sinks below 10 percent, in *most* evaluations, however, the more apprehensive we grow that either (1) the evaluation's sponsor is naive about the costs of doing quality evaluation, or; (2) sincere interest in quality evaluation may be lacking.

Smith and Smith (1985) conducted two interesting studies showing that the various categories within evaluation budgets vary widely in proportion, according to the size of study, methodology, travel distance, and the like. But on the average, they found that approximately 61 percent of the total direct-cost evaluation budget went to personnel; travel consumed 7 to 17 percent; consultants 0 to 6 percent; data processing 0 to 6 percent; materials, supplies, duplication and communication 6 to 10 percent; and "other" 10 to 14 percent; overhead added another 13 to 14 percent to the total direct costs.

COMPLYING WITH ESTABLISHED POLICIES, PROTOCOL, AND ETHICS

The draft management plan should be reviewed carefully for its propriety. It is important not to overlook organizational or ethical practices that are expected of evaluators as professionals. The evaluator must assure that organizational policies and protocol are being followed and that agreements established for the evaluation are respected in generating questions, collecting data, and interpreting or reporting results.

Furthermore, certain ethical and legal considerations must be built into the management plan to assure that the rights of participants are protected. Evaluators must not promise something—such as payments for participation in the evaluation—that they cannot deliver. Further, they need to protect confidentiality or anonymity if that has been promised and avoid invasion of privacy. Data that may be harmful to individuals should not be reported without thoughtful consideration of whether such reporting is necessary.

Legally, the evaluator is governed by public laws regarding access to data and protection of human subjects. If certain potentially harmful data may be subpoenaed later, the evaluator should consider whether it is necessary to collect it in the first place. Protection of Human Subjects committees, established in the United States by the National Research Act of 1974, should have time to review plans and instruments used in the evaluation. Finally, the evaluator and, where relevant, the organization for which she works are fiscally accountable for all income and expenditures. National governments and many states or provinces regulate accounting whenever public funds are expended. In any event, some accounting system is essential. The costs of violating laws governing any aspect of the evaluation can greatly exceed the costs involved in designing appropriate safeguards.

JUDGING, MONITORING, AND REVISING THE EVALUATION PLAN

Quality control is essential in managing any evaluation study. The manager is responsible for seeing that the evaluation design is the best possible, given the circumstances and resources available. Careful attention to each of the following three activities will help.

Evaluating the Evaluation Design. Stufflebeam (1973b, p. 148) notes the importance of considering "the potential of the evaluation design for providing information which is valid, reliable, credible, timely, and pervasive." In Chapter 21 we discuss in detail how one might evaluate an evaluation design. Here we only wish to stress the importance of doing so. Without an effective evaluation design, acquiring good data is only a lucky accident.

Monitoring Adherence to the Evaluation Design. Architects take pains to design buildings that are not only aesthetically pleasing but also structurally sound. The task of the building contractor is to follow the architect's blueprint faithfully, adhering to all essential specifications. The building supervisor ensures that blueprints are not misread and that architectural specifications are followed. In evaluation, as in architecture, blueprints are useful only when they are followed. Every good management plan specifies how evaluation activities will be monitored to be certain the original design is implemented faithfully. Even if the same evaluator develops and implements the design, that does not guarantee that the design won't be constructed merely to impress the client, then scrapped later in favor of a helter-skelter approach.

Revising the Evaluation Design as Needed.   When the sunken living room keeps filling with groundwater it is time to consider altering the original blueprint—either moving the living room up to the next level or perhaps adding a swimming pool. Similarly, unanticipated circumstances may require changes in an evaluation plan. It is futile to follow an obsolete plan. Provisions should be made for periodic examination of the original design and for modification and redirection as necessary. The need for occasional revision does not suggest that designing an evaluation in the first place is wasted effort. On the contrary, it is far simpler to alter a sound blueprint than to build without any blueprint at all—and much less threatening to one's reputation as an architect—or evaluator.

ESTABLISHING EVALUATION AGREEMENTS AND CONTRACTS

Many potential problems that arise during evaluation can be more readily solved if client and evaluator share a firm understanding. Even among administrators and evaluators with the highest possible professional standards and ethics, conflicts can and do arise—usually in the absence of well-documented agreements concerning important procedures. As Guba and Lincoln note:

> Evaluations are done for clients who commission the evaluation, provide for its legitimation, and pay for it. Since he who pays the piper calls the tune, the evaluator must have a firm understanding with the client about what the evaluation is to accomplish, for whom, and by what methods. The evaluator also needs to be protected against certain arbitrary and possibly harmful or unethical actions by the client, just as the client needs to be protected against an unscrupulous evaluator. The means for achieving these understandings and establishing these safeguards is the evaluation contract. (Guba & Lincoln, 1981, pp. 270–271)

Anderson and Ball, quoting Samuel Goldwyn's wry comment that "oral agreements aren't worth the paper they're written on," add the following:

> For major evaluation efforts, a formal, legal contract should be negotiated; not to have one would be foolish for both parties. In smaller evaluation efforts, a formal contract might be unnecessary, but even then a letter of agreement . . . makes excellent sense. In either case, the agreement should spell out not only the financial arrangements but also the main elements and requirements of the planned evaluation. (Anderson & Ball, 1978, p. 155)

It is obviously too late to draft a formal evaluation agreement after the evaluation is underway; such an agreement should be developed prior to launching the evaluation study. A comprehensive discussion of how to establish evaluation agreements and contracts appears elsewhere (Worthen & White, 1986) and will not be reported here, except for the following checklist that summarizes some important items and issues to include in an evaluation agreement and steps that should be taken in negotiating such an agreement.

Checklist for Establishing an Evaluation Agreement

The following checklist is proposed for assessing whether essential issues have been addressed in the evaluation agreement and related negotiations.

	Check one for each item	
	Yes	*No*
1. Are negotiations initiated early enough to permit the evaluator enough entry and lead time to use the evaluation methods and instruments judged appropriate for the study?		
2. Have adequate provisions been made for the development of an evaluation design through one of the following: preparation of design for set fee; preparation of design as the first phase of the contract; or preparation of design under an initial contract, with a separate contract for implementing the design.		
3. Does the evaluation agreement contain a. identification of evaluation client/sponsor?		
b. identification of evaluation contractor?		
c. description of the evaluation object?		
d. statement of the general purpose of the evaluation?		
e. specification of the evaluation's intended audiences?		
f. specification of the authorization for conducting the study?		
4. Are the information needs for the study clearly listed?		
5. Is there a summary of the overall evaluation plan that includes a. the general design and methods of inquiry to be used?		
b. sources of information for the study?		
c. methods and techniques for data collection, analysis, and interpretation?		
d. general reporting strategies to be used?		
6. Does the negotiated Scope of Work include a. the procedures to be employed by the evaluator and a time schedule for their performance?		

   b. adequate descriptions of the products to be expected from the evaluation and deadlines for their delivery?

   c. criteria for judging that the contract has been fulfilled?

7. Does the agreement specify
   a. human resources and key personnel to be involved?

   b. financial resources necessary to do the work?

   c. material resources necessary to do the work?

   d. time necessary to complete the work?

8. Have the negotiations dealt with the respective responsibilities of the client and contractor concerning
   a. the identification of the scope of the inquiry?

   b. access to data and records?

   c. managing or preventing disruptions?

9. Does the agreement deal with
   a. editorial authority? rights of prior review?

   b. misuse or nonuse of findings or reports?

   c. dissemination rights (publication and copyright)?

   d. other uses of evaluation information produced (for example, "piggybacking" of research interests)?

10. Does the negotiated agreement deal with
   a. potential conflicts of interest?

   b. provisions for maintaining informants' confidentiality and anonymity?

   c. professional autonomy of the evaluator?

   d. possible legal issues?

11. Has an adjudication and conflict-resolution procedure been established?

12. Has a basis for payment been established?

13. Have the primary negotiators been identified?

	Check one for each item	
	Yes	*No*
14. Have those who will be affected by the evaluation been invited to participate at a secondary level in the negotiations, at least by representation?		
15. Has a time and resource limit for negotiations been set by mutual agreement?		

SUMMARY
Based on questions 1–15 above, *have negotiations been sufficiently successful to warrant awarding a contract or contracts for accomplishment of the evaluation design and conduct of the evaluation?*

CASE STUDY APPLICATION

December 15. Felt a bit foolish this morning when teaching my graduate evaluation class. I was summarizing the major points I've covered in lectures since the midterm (trying to prep them for the upcoming final), and I was right in the middle of talking about the importance of a management plan when I suddenly realized I hadn't yet developed one for the Radnor study. A few trite phrases like "Practice what you preach" nagged at my concentration until I resolved to set the matter right, tonight.

Which I did. After class, I spent several hours laying out a management plan that included the timelines for various activities, role and task assignments, a budget, and procedures I'll use to make sure we adhere to Radnor's policies and to the standards for conducting evaluations, not to mention the design itself. Sent a copy of the management plan to Mrs. Janson.

Author Comments. Again, in the interest of space and simplicity, the document appearing as Artifact No. 5 is limited to a management plan for the sample items listed in Artifact No. 3 for the case study application in Chapter 15.

December 15 (continued). As I worked out the management plan, I could see that some questions could be asked in one operation. For example, questions 2 and 4 involved external experts in the Humanities and I could have them responding to both evaluation questions for the same consulting fee. Such efficiency!

I considered combining evaluation questions 1 and 5, too, but then thought better of it because they really address two very different issues, and I thought it might confuse the community members to cover both at once. I also wanted to include community influence groups in getting answers to question 5, while not going to the same sources as for question 1. That reasoning led me to plan to conduct separate surveys for questions 1 and 5.

Artifact No. 5: *Summary of the Management Plan*

Evaluation Question	Tasks	Estimated Task Beginning & Ending Dates	Personnel Involved & Estimated Costs	Other Resources Needed & Costs	Total Task Cost
1. To what extent are the program objectives shared by important groups?	1a. Develop & pilot-test questionnaire and cover letter to be used for interviews and mail surveys.	1a. January 1–January 15	1a. Evaluator, 3 days at $150 per day = $450	1a. 3 days of clerical time at $40 per day = $120	1a. $570
	1b. Develop sampling plan.	1b. January 1–January 15	1b. Evaluator, 1 day at $150 per day = $150	1b. 1 day of clerical time at $40 per day = $40	1b. $190
	1c. Develop follow-up and nonresponse bias check procedures.	1c. January 1–January 15	1c. Evaluator, 1 day at $150 per day = $150	1c. None	1c. $150
	1d. Conduct interviews & mail survey with follow-up.	1d. January 20–February 15	1d. Evaluator, 5 days at $150 per day = $750; Research assistant, 5 days at $75 per day = $375	1d. Travel expense = $10; postage = $25; duplication = $50	1d. $1,210
	1e. Analyze data.	1e. February 20–March 1	1e. Research assistant, 5 days at $75 per day = $375	1e. Computer time = $25	1e. $400
	1f. Prepare reports.	1f. March 1–March 15	1f. Evaluator, 5 days at $150 per day = $750	1f. 5 days of clerical time = $200; duplication = $50	1f. $1,000
2. To what degree does the curriculum address all the stated objectives?	2a. Identify humanities faculty who will analyze curriculum and objectives; meet with them to describe the task; collect their reports.	2a. January 15–January 30	2a. Evaluator, 1 day at $150 per day = $150	2a. Humanities faculty, donated time.	2a. $150

Task	Date	Personnel costs	Other costs	Total
2b. Analyze reports from humanities faculty.	2b. January 31–February 5	2b. Evaluator, 1 day at $150 per day = $150	2b. None	2b. $150
2c. Prepare summary report of faculty analyses.	2c. February 5–February 10	2c. Evaluator, 1 day at $150 per day = $150	2c. 1 day of clerical time = $40; duplication = $5	2c. $195
2d. Identify consultants to serve as external humanities experts	2d. January 15–January 20	2d. Evaluator, 1/2 day at $150 per day = $75	2d. None	2d. $75
2e. Call each consultant, describe the task, and enlist their support.	2e. January 20–January 21	2e. Evaluator, 1/2 day at $150 per day = $75	2e. Telephone long distance = $25	2e. $100
2f. Mail out packets of material to external experts	2f. January 20–January 25	2f. Evaluator, 1 day at $150 per day = $150 (includes time to prepare review forms)	2f. 1 day of clerical time = $40; postage = $25	2f. $215
2g. Receive consultant reviews.	2g. February 15	2g. Consultants, 2 at 2 days each at $200 per day = $800	2g. Return postage = $25	2g. $825
2h. Prepare summary report of external reviews.	2h. February 15–February 20	2h. Evaluator, 2 days at $150 per day = $300	2h. 1 day of clerical time = $40; duplication = $5	2h. $345
4. Is the content of the lesson plans faithful to the humanities?				
4a. Identify consultants to serve as external humanities experts (use same people being used for Task 2g, hence Tasks 4a–4e will coincide with Tasks 2d–2h).	4a. January 15–January 20	[Personnel and estimated costs for Tasks 4a–4e coincide with those for Tasks 2d–2h—no new costs]	[Personnel and other costs for Tasks 4a–4e coincide with those for Tasks 2d–2h—no new costs]	No additional costs. Costs of these tasks have been figured into the estimated costs for Tasks 2d–2h.
4b. Call them and enlist their support.	4b. January 20–January 21			

Evaluation Question	Tasks	Estimated Task Beginning & Ending Dates	Personnel Involved & Estimated Costs	Other Resources Needed & Costs	Total Task Cost
	4c. Mail out.	4c. January 20–January 25			
	4d. Receive responses.	4d. February 15			
	4e. Prepare summary report of responses.	4e. February 15–February 20			
5. Are social attitudes in the community such that the curriculum can be successfully implemented here at this time?	5a. Develop and pilot-test questionnaire and cover letter.	5a. March 1–March 15	5a. Evaluator, 3 days at $150 per day = $450	5a. 3 days of clerical time = $120	5a. $570
	5b. Develop sampling plan.	5b. March 1–March 15	5b. Evaluator, 1 day at $150 per day = $150	5b. 1 day of clerical time = $40	5b. $190
	5c. Develop follow-up and nonresponse bias check procedures.	5c. March 1–March 15	5c. Evaluator, 1 day at $150 per day = $150	5c. None	5c. $150
	5d. Conduct survey with follow-ups.	5d. March 20–April 10	5d. Research Assistant, 2 days at $75 per day = $150	5d. Postage = $25; duplication = $50	5d. $225
	5e. Analyze data.	5e. April 15–April 30	5e. Research Assistant, 5 days = $375	5e. Computer time = $25	5e. $400
	5f. Prepare reports	5f. May 1–May 15	5f. Evaluator, 5 days = $750	5f. 5 days of clerical time = $200; duplication = $50	5f. $1,000

Evaluation question	Task	Dates	Personnel costs	Other costs	Total cost
9. Do the lesson plans and other curriculum materials use sound instructional theory?	9a. Identify consultants to serve as experts in instructional theory.	9a. January 15–January 20	9a. Evaluator, no additional cost since it can be done along with Task 2d	9a. None	9a. None
	9b. Call each expert, describe the task, and enlist their support.	9b. January 20–January 21	9b. Evaluator, no additional cost—do along with Task 2e	9b. Telephone, long distance = $10	9b. $10
	9c. Mail out packets of material to external experts.	9c. January 20–January 25	9c. Evaluator, 2 days = $300 (includes 1½ days to prepare review forms)	9c. 1 day of clerical time = $40; postage = $10	9c. $350
	9d. Receive experts' reviews.	9d. February 15	9d. Consultants, 2 at 2 days each at $200 per day = $800	9d. Return postage = $10	9d. $810
	9e. Prepare summary report of external reviews.	9e. February 15–February 20	9e. Evaluator, 1 day = $150	9e. 1 day of clerical time = $40; duplication = $2	9e. $192
13. Do student attitudes demonstrate that the curriculum is producing the desired results?	13a. Design pretest, posttest control group experimental study.	13a. April 15–April 20	13a. Evaluator, 1 day = $150	13a. Clerical support, 1 day = $40	13a. $190
	13b. Enlist cooperation of participating school officials.	13b. April 20–May 1	13b. Evaluator, 1 day = $150	13b. None	13b. $150
	13c. Develop and pilot-test instruments for measuring performance on dependent variables.	13c. May 1–May 30	13c. Evaluator, 12 days = $1,800; Research assistant, 10 days = $750	13c. Clerical support, 4 days = $160; duplication = $50	13c. $2,760
	13d. Randomly assign students to treatments; conduct training for instructors.	13d. August 20–August 21	13d. Evaluator, 3 days = $450; Research assistant, 5 days = $375	13d. Clerical support, 2 days = $80; duplication = $50	13d. $955

Evaluation Question	Tasks	Estimated Task Beginning & Ending Dates	Personnel Involved & Estimated Costs	Other Resources Needed & Costs	Total Task Cost
	13e. Conduct limited case studies of experimental and control classes.	13e. August 25 November 1	13e. 2 case-study researchers, 8 days each at $200 per day = $3,200	13e. Clerical support, 20 days = $800; duplication = $50; cassette tapes = $10; travel = $500	13e. $4,560
	13f. Collect pre- and postdata.	13f. August 25–26; October 30–31	13f. Evaluator, 4 days = $600; Research assistant, 4 days = $300	13f. Duplication = $50; travel = $12	13f. $962
	13g. Analyze data.	13g. November 1– November 10	13g. Evaluator, 2 days = $300; Research assistant, 4 days = $300	13g. Computer time = $30	13g. $630
	13h. Prepare reports.	13h. November 1– November 20	13h. Evaluator, 10 days = $1,500	13h. Clerical support, 10 days = $400; duplication = $25	13h. $1,925

Artifact No. 5 (continued)

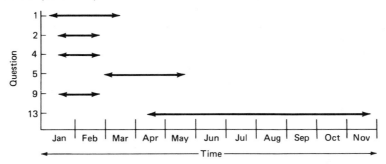

As I worked out my management plan it became obvious that I should line up a part-time research assistant right away. Otherwise the good students would be unavailable when I needed them. I also needed to reserve some secretarial time at points when I would need it. My department head said it would be OK to use our department secretary, as long as we ran the project through the university and paid the reduced "overhead" costs the university would require. The evaluation budget will reimburse my institution for this shared time.

As I developed the management plan, I was again reminded that I have been wise not to resign my full-time job at the university to become an evaluation consultant. The "up" times and "down" times for this project are going to be erratic, as usual; were I depending solely on consulting, I would surely need something to fill in the spaces. Of course, other projects could do that, but it isn't always possible to control events so that all projects are synchronized. A sure course toward a nervous breakdown is to have too many projects out of sync.

December 15 (continued). The Gantt chart for the main evaluation questions listed in the plan revealed the following pattern of project activities. This chart should be a useful tool to communicate the evaluation plan to the folks at Radnor. I didn't break it down by task because the chart got to be too cluttered.

Each evaluative question could be broken down by task for an internal project

Artifact No. 5 (continued):
Personnel Loadings (Days)

	Evaluative Question					
	1	*2*	*4*	*5*	*9*	*13*
Evaluation Staff:						
Evaluator	15	9 · · · · · · · ·→		10	3	33
Research Assistant	10	—	—	7	—	23
Secretary	9	3 · · · · · · · ·→		9	2	37
Humanities						
Consultants (2)	—	2 ea · · · · · ·→		—	—	—
Instructional Theory						
Consultants (2)	—	—	—	—	2 ea	—
Case Study Researchers (2)	—	—	—	—	—	8 ea
Radnor Staff						
Humanities Faculty	—	2 ea	—	—	—	—

management review (so that milestones and progress toward them could be checked on a daily basis), and I'll do that when I get time.[91]

The personnel loadings for the evaluation activities turned out to be much as I expected, fairly typical for midsize evaluation studies.

December 15 (continued). It appears that a part-time research assistant and a part-time secretary will serve the needs of this project nicely. I may want to delegate some of my load to boost up the time of the research assistant on the project while lightening my own. Depends on the reaction to the budget I proposed.

Artifact No. 5 (continued)

Evaluation Staff Salaries	$21,104	
(Evaluator, Research Assistant, Secretary)		
Consultants	4,800	
(Humanities experts—4,		
Instructional Theory Experts—2,		
Case Study Researchers—2)		
Travel	522	
Postage	120	
Telephone	35	
Duplication	437	
Computer	80	
Supplies (tapes)	10	
Total Direct Costs (Questions 1, 2, 4, 5, 9, and 13)		$27,108
Indirect Costs (8% of Direct Costs)		2,169
BUDGET TOTAL FOR SELECTED QUESTIONS		$29,277

December 15 (continued). When I added up this budget, I was utterly amazed—I had no idea it would add up so fast. All the costs are well grounded on detailed planning for this project, but Mrs. Janson may have a stroke. Yet, I realized that I had not even budgeted for some little things like normal office supplies, and my travel budget was low and would only allow me to use fairly local external consultants.

I might try to talk the university into lowering the indirect cost rate, but I suspect chances of that are slim to none; they need to cover things like utilities, facilities, and equipment that I would be using. If I took the project on privately (working out of my basement), then I'd have to buy a typewriter for my secretary! So the budget seems barely adequate, yet to them, it might seem unreasonably high. We'll just need to wait and see how Mrs. Janson reacts.

I also went back over the Radnor evaluation design to see how it stacked up on the 11 general meta–evaluation criteria I've advocated.[92] Using the 11 criteria as a starting point, I rated it (unbiasedly, of course) as follows.

1. *Conceptual Clarity*. Fairly good, given the sections on purposes of the study, the use of adversary and comparative elements, and how the components fit together. Should have been more explicit about the summative nature of the study, however.

2. *Characterization of the Object of the Evaluation*. Excellent, as judged by the humanities department head, who edited my written program description, and then "certified" it as accurate.

3. *Recognition and Representation of Legitimate Audiences*. Good, since I identified what everyone agrees to be the major audiences (and am collecting data from each of them as well). I was not clear in my section on reporting on plans for transmitting the final results to the various audiences, however. Change the gold star to silver.

4. *Sensitivity to Political Problems in the Evaluation.* Good, largely due to: (1) the advantages of the adversary "pro and con" reports; (2) clarity and agreements about the policies within which the evaluation will be conducted; (3) the use of humanities experts to assure that relevant content expertise will be applied; and (4) the comfort the humanities staff has taken in knowing they will see a draft of the final report before it "goes to press."

5. *Specification of Information Needs and Sources.* Excellent. Here is where the matrix (and a compulsive-obsessive personality) pays off.

6. *Comprehensiveness/Inconclusiveness.* Excellent. Drawing evaluative questions from all the groups, plus tossing in some of my own, resulted in an array of variables that I believe represents a very comprehensive set. If something is happening in that humanities program, we will spot it.

7. *Technical Adequacy.* (?) Too early to tell. The recipe looks sound enough, but the real "proof of the pudding" is still in the future. It is easier to describe instruments to be constructed than to construct them so they meet acceptable technical specifications.

8. *Consideration of Costs.* Poor. I really missed the boat here. Having ascertained the dollar cost of the program earlier and having talked a lot about opportunity costs, I didn't make my intentions for handling either of these very explicit in the plan itself. I need to rectify that.

9. *Explicit Standards/Criteria.* Good. They are there, but some may not feel they are explicit enough as stated. I think they communicate.

10. *Judgments and/or Recommendations.* (?) To me, making judgments and recommendations is an integral part of the role I play as an evaluator. But I never say much about that at the design stage—I just do it automatically when it comes time to report.

Maybe that should be clearer in the evaluation plan so the client knows what to expect.

11. *Reports Tailored to Audiences.* Fair. I noted that there would be (1) an omnibus technical evaluation report that self-consciously includes all the details, and (2) a short executive summary of major findings, using nontechnical language and graphs (in place of tabular presentation of data analyses). That was tossed off too quickly, however, with little thought about whether all audiences would find one or the other of those reports appropriate; whether there should be an oral presentation to the board, complete with multicolored overheads; and a one-page summary in case the press wants to run something. I need to think more about this long before we get to the reporting stage.

Author Comments. Evaluations are often designed (mine, at least) under pressure of deadlines. I would like in my lifetime to design an evaluation where I had sufficient time to build the design, carefully cross-checking each part for compliance with criteria that I and others view as touchstones of a good evaluation. I hope that after some years of worrying about them, those standards have become second nature and their consideration instinctive at each stage of the work. Realistically, unless one suffers delusions of grandeur, it seems safer to check one's plan against any of the extant lists of meta-evaluation criteria. They might be as simple as the one used here or as comprehensive as the published evaluation standards that took half a decade or more in their development.[93] At the design stage, I care less about which set of criteria is applied than I do about the fact that time is taken for careful review of the design to see if there are critical flaws or omissions.

Also, it takes at least a measure of arrogance (or naivete) to assume that one can objectively judge the adequacy of one's own evaluation plans. Although I have done so, under pressures of time, I would prefer (and usually manage) to have an evaluation colleague whose expertise I respect review my design for me. Perhaps, had I done so in the present instance, the results would have been different, and blind spots I would carry forward into the conduct of the study could have been eliminated.

> *December 21.* Mrs. Janson called today and indicated the board and committee had given the go-ahead on the plan I submitted, with the only suggested changes coming in the deadline and budget. The board has decided they cannot delay a decision about the humanities curriculum as long as they had originally planned. Instead, they want to make a decision by May 15 so they will have time, should they decide to discontinue the program, to plan for its phase-out and provision of alternative curricular offerings for the students.
>
> That disappoints me, for it will be a real hurry-up job to develop the instruments, supervise the data collection, coordinate the on-site visit, and orchestrate the expert reviews of the materials by that deadline. Fortunately, most of the design can still be implemented and completed within the deadline, although it will be tight. The greatest problem this new deadline causes is the loss of any chance to look at changes in students over time—something I had intended with the cognitive, affective, and unobtrusive measures of student behavior. So I have taken out the pretest-posttest stuff and will depend much more on the site visit. That weakens the evaluation, but one hopes the combination of perspectives left in the study will still be strong enough to yield solid findings. One good thing came from this; they agreed to fold the consultant review into the site visit, using a team including both humanities experts and us evaluators, so that should help.
>
> Anyway, I cut out those activities that couldn't be completed by May, revised the Gantt chart and budget accordingly, ready to send it back to Radnor as an appendix to the evaluation agreement I'll draft tomorrow. It does shave the budget a bit, which is good, but not too much, what with increasing the travel budget some. Mrs. Janson noted that the consultants would have to hitchhike to stay within the original travel budget I'd proposed.

Author Comments.   The best-laid plans of mice and evaluators often go awry. (That is why evaluators need to be not only intellectually flexible but also emotionally resilient.) It is not uncommon for deadlines to be abruptly shifted for reasons far less reasonable than that which I invented as the rationale of the Radnor board. Let me strike another blow for eclectic, multiple-method evaluation designs; they are considerably more robust to changes than are their more single-minded counterparts. If one depends on a single strategy for collecting information and it so happens that changing circumstances disrupt that strategy, there is much less likelihood that the evaluation will succeed.

December 22. Spent a while this morning trying to draft a written evaluation agreement to send to Mrs. Janson. Frankly, I couldn't get my heart into it. The sample contract I was trying to copy was so stuffy that I got to where I wanted to choke every time I hit another "whereas," "wherefore," or "party of the second part."

Maybe I'm a bit cowardly, but I can't get my nerve up to send a stiff, legalistic contract to Radnor and ask those people to sign it. I feel like they'd suspect they'd hired a lawyer, not an evaluator. The last thing I want to do is go into this evaluation with them feeling like I don't trust them. I'm already an outsider, and an evaluator, so that's two strikes against me. I'm not about to waste my third strike by creating the impression with them that there is no basis for good, old-fashioned trust. Maybe I'm suffering from an overdose of Christmas spirit, but I think I'll let a brief letter suffice.

Artifact No. 6

December 22

Mrs. Anne Janson, Principal
Radnor Middle School
13 Ideal Circle
Radnor, PA 19087

Dear Mrs. Janson:

I was pleased to learn from you earlier today that you and your colleagues have generally accepted my evaluation plan, subject to the modifications in activities, schedule, and costs on which we have agreed. I have made the necessary alterations and a revised copy is enclosed.

If you would be comfortable with a fairly informal agreement, I see no need for much formality. Will it suffice to say that I will do the evaluation for the $29,277 outlined in the budget attached to my revised plan? Also, let's agree that I'll follow the plan attached, and we can incorporate it by reference into this letter of agreement.

Anything else we need to agree or modify can be worked out comfortably as necessary, I am sure.

If this is agreeable, please countersign this letter below, retain one copy for your records, and return one to me.

I look forward to working with you.

Sincerely yours,

Author Comments. The evaluation plan provides a good basis for finalizing the agreement between evaluator and client, but there should be some form of written agreement or letter of understanding that incorporates the plan, agrees on reporting deadlines, budget, and the like. I would urge development of such an agreement in virtually any significant evaluation enterprise. Some may see seeds of distrust in such urging. I agree, but the distrust is not of the motives or character of the principal parties; it is merely distrust of their total recall of an understanding made months earlier.

In larger evaluation studies, a more detailed and formal contractual agreement will be necessary.

The above entry represents two "cop-outs." The first is by our mythical evaluator who would rather be comfy than safe, friendly than correct. I used to feel just like him, *until* I'd been "burned" a few times. Now I get tempted to write down and obtain my teenager's signature on agreements to replace gasoline in the family car. Well, almost tempted. We'll have to wait and see how our evaluator fares and whether his casual approach to evaluation contracting comes back to haunt him at a later date.

Meanwhile, the second cop-out is letting my evaluator cop-out, not just to make an instructional point but also to keep the number of pages for this section within bounds. My rationalization is that the reader who really wants to peruse sample evaluation contracts can find several—even one laced liberally with "whereas" and "wherefore"—elsewhere (Worthen & White, 1986).

APPLICATION EXERCISE

1. Use the worksheets that you developed as an application exercise in Chapter 15 to prepare a detailed management plan for your study, including a PERT or Gantt chart, team assignments, and a budget.
2. Develop a draft of a formal agreement between you (as the hypothetical evaluator) and whoever would have to authorize and legitimate (and possibly fund) your study. (Draw on those items specified in this chapter as important in any evaluation contract; see if you agree they are applicable in your situation.)

SUGGESTED READINGS

CLARK, N. (1952). *The Gantt chart*. London: Pitman and Sons.
COOK, D. L. (1966). *Program evaluation and review techniques: Applications in education.* Washington, DC: U.S. Office of Education Cooperative Research Monograph No. 17.
WORTHEN, B. R., & WHITE, K. R. (1986). *Evaluating educational and social programs: Guidelines for proposal reviews, onsite evaluation, evaluation contracts, and technical assistance.* Boston: Kluwer-Nijhoff.

Part Four
Practical Guidelines for Conducting and Using Evaluations

In Part Three we provided guidelines for planning evaluations. In Part Four we focus on guidelines for conducting and using evaluations, beginning in Chapter 17 with suggestions for dealing with political and interpersonal aspects of evaluation. In Chapter 18 we examine several methods and techniques for collecting evaluation information, and in Chapter 19 we provide an overview of selected methods and techniques for analyzing that information. Chapter 20 deals broadly with various aspects of reporting and using evaluation results, and Chapter 21 provides standards and procedures for evaluating evaluation plans, activities, and reports.

None of the chapters in this section purport to treat completely their respective topics. A textbook could be devoted to each chapter (and, indeed, many texts do exist on several of those topics). Each chapter is intended only to introduce the topic and provide practical suggestions for how to use the material in an actual evaluation. References to more extensive discussions of each topic are provided for those who wish more detailed information.

Chapter 17
Dealing with Political, Ethical, and Interpersonal Aspects of Evaluation

Orienting Questions

1. What types of bias can result from the evaluator's *interpersonal, financial,* or *organizational* relationships? How might such biases be minimized or eliminated?
2. What ethical standards should be followed in conducting evaluation studies? Why is each important?
3. To what extent is evaluation a political activity?
4. What types of political pressures cause the most serious problems in evaluation studies? How can the evaluator cope with such pressures?

By now, we hope we have made the point that evaluation is not only —or even primarily—a methodological and technical activity. Important as methodological and technical expertise are to good evaluation, that importance is often overshadowed by the interpersonal, ethical, and political influences that shape the evaluator's work. Many a good evaluation, unimpeachable in all technical details, has failed because of interpersonal insensitivity, ethical compromises, or political naivete. It is pointless to promise to collect sensitive data (principals' ratings of teachers, for instance) without first obtaining permission from the office or individual who controls those data. Agreements must be reached early in any evaluation about such issues as access to data and safeguards against misuse. Program staff must be guaranteed opportunities to correct factual errors without compromising the evaluation itself. These issues exist in almost every evaluation, and the more explicitly they are dealt with, the more likely the evaluation is to succeed.

Evaluators can no longer afford to content themselves with polishing and plying their tools for collecting, analyzing, and reporting data. They must consider how evaluation reports will be received by important stakeholders; whether the results of the evaluation will be suppressed, misused or ignored; how to deal with pressures for immediate data or oversimplified questions; and how to prevent "evaluation anxiety" from disrupting clients or unduly influencing evaluation results. Ignoring such concerns is self-defeating, for human, ethical, and political factors pervade every aspect of an evaluation study. As Guba and Lincoln put it,

> Political and human factors are inevitably present in every evaluation situation and must be dealt with. They cannot be regarded as mere peripheral annoyances that distract the evaluator from his "real" task. The evaluator ought to be able to satisfy himself, at the beginning of each evaluation, that the information likely to result from the evaluation will be worth it in terms of the political imbalance and the human dysfunctionality that it will certainly induce. The evaluator who moves ahead without regard to these issues is not only incompetent but unethical as well. (Guba & Lincoln, 1981, pp. 301–302)

In this chapter we deal with four important topics: (1) communication between evaluator and stakeholders; (2) biases inherent in certain client-evaluator inter-relationships; (3) ethical issues and considerations in evaluation; and (4) political pressures and problems in evaluation.

ESTABLISHING AND MAINTAINING GOOD COMMUNICATIONS AMONG EVALUATORS AND STAKEHOLDERS

The evaluation literature contains numerous pronouncements that good communications are an essential part of both evaluation and the politics that inevitably surround evaluation studies.[94] Yet we continue to find many criticisms of evaluators' communication practices and many examples of poor communication cited in our contemporary literature (the tedious and voluminous technical report offered, for instance, as the sole end product of an evaluation study). Perhaps the message has not sunk in. Perhaps evaluators get too caught up in technical matters and deadlines to attend to communication. Whatever the reason, poor communication can be lethal to an evaluation.

Sometimes the client needs to be reminded that honest evaluation entails risk. Sanctions and cooperation need to be obtained from those in power. Reporting procedures must be clear to everyone at the outset, and clients and evaluators should agree on ways to maintain open communications, assure fairness and impartiality in the evaluation, and resolve any conflicts that might arise during the study.

We offer the following practical recommendations for interpersonal communications in evaluation:[95]

1. *Prepare stakeholders for evaluation.* Develop an "evaluation spirit" by informing participants about the purpose and benefits of the evaluation. Resistance to evaluation comes naturally to most people, and not knowing what to expect can only increase such resistance. Evaluators can minimize defensive attitudes by not insisting on clients' participation where it isn't essential. And though the quality of the evaluation cannot be sacrificed for the sake of goodwill, there is always room for negotiation and compromise.

2. *Foster stakeholder participation.* Increase the involvement of stakeholders by
- Providing a clear opportunity for involvement and allowing time for it.
- Developing awareness of the evaluation (presenting the concept and structure

of the evaluation to stakeholders, clarifying what will be looked at or asked about, and providing reading materials as appropriate).

- Clarifying what the evaluation effort will lead to and what follow-up might occur.
- Capitalizing on various stakeholders' familiarity with the object of the evaluation (recognizing that no one person has the full range of experience with all school-related functions).
- Encouraging constructive criticism (inviting stakeholders to challenge assumptions or weaknesses, encouraging divergent perspectives, encouraging a spirit of fairness and openness, and discouraging dogmatic adherence to outside directives).

3. *Plan adequate time for carrying out all of the evaluation.* Consider forming a committee to plan and schedule all evaluation work. This committee may help decide if the scope of the evaluation must be reduced to allow enough time for all planned activities.

4. *Invite and nurture outside participation.* Remember that parents, school board members, students, taxpayers, and resident experts are all potential stakeholders. Their participation not only strengthens the evaluation but also signals to school staff that this is an important project. A spirit of negotiation and compromise, rather than unilateral action, should be fostered. The evaluator should also recognize and respect the power structure within the school setting. Not listening to important stakeholders generally means damaging—or even losing—the trust, respect, and rapport you have worked hard to gain.

5. *Link long-term goals to immediate actions.* People like to see achievements, so set intermediate goals as stepping stones to long-term goals. Recognize, however, that not all goals will be immediately achievable; that doesn't mean they should be discarded.

6. *Assign responsibilities.* Involving many participants fosters commitment to change and development of new plans.

7. *Put a premium on memos, meetings, and informal "chats."* People need and like to feel informed. The confidence that comes with knowing what's going on helps build an "evaluation spirit" and common understanding about the evaluation.

8. *Recognize and protect the rights of individuals.* To foster courtesy, confidentiality, and human dignity, the Joint Committee proposes the following standard of propriety: "Evaluators should respect human dignity and worth in their interactions with other persons associated with an evaluation" (Joint Committee on Standards for Educational Evaluation, 1981, p. 81).

UNDERSTANDING POTENTIAL BIAS RESULTING FROM THE EVALUATOR'S INTERPERSONAL, FINANCIAL, AND ORGANIZATIONAL RELATIONSHIPS WITH OTHERS

Many people are skeptical about the possibility of human beings rendering completely unbiased judgments (see Lang & Lang, 1953; Mitroff, 1974). Thoughtful analysts (for example, Scriven, 1976a; Anderson & Ball, 1978; Perloff, Padgett,

& Brock, 1980) note—and we agree—that evaluators are no less susceptible to bias than are their counterparts in other walks of life:

> . . . most individuals—evaluators included—pride themselves on their keen intuition and insightful observation of others. Most of us are quite unaware of the shortcomings of those intuitions. It is our contention, therefore, that biases impact powerfully on evaluators' judgments, inferences, and decisions, and in large part because evaluators are unaware of their influence. (Perloff and others, 1980, p. 12)

Perhaps the myth that evaluators are less biased than others is partly attributable to the popular view that evaluation is an "objective" enterprise, involving valid and reliable data and allowing no subjectivity. That optimistic view has been recognized as rather naive, however. Choices are by nature subjective. And evaluators increasingly realize that bias—inadvertent or conscious—can intrude subtly into nearly every choice they make—from selecting an evaluation approach to designing a report. Indeed, the portrait of the completely dispassionate and unbiased evaluator must be hung alongside that of the unicorn and other quaint folklore characters.

A full discussion of sources of bias in educational evaluation transcends the scope of this book. We have discussed some sources of bias, in passing, while examining topics in earlier chapters. Perloff and his colleagues (1980) provide a provocative analysis of how various social and cognitive biases can influence evaluation. We treat here a narrower concern, namely, how the evaluator's relationship to and dependence upon others can seriously bias her judgments. Every evaluation is a complex of interpersonal, financial, and organizational interrelationships between the evaluator and numerous other actors in the evaluation context. We shall discuss briefly each type of interrelationship and its potential for biasing the evaluator's judgments.[96]

Interpersonal Relationships and Bias

It is apparent to even the casual observer that individuals' feelings toward one another can color their judgments, not only about each other but about practically anything with which the other person is perceived to be associated. Hence, we have legal restrictions on testimony about one's spouse, and antinepotism policies that prohibit individuals from being placed in positions where they would need to make decisions about the salary, promotion, or job security of a family member.

Obviously an evaluator must decline an invitation to evaluate a curriculum developed by her sister-in-law. But a less conspicuous source of bias lies in interpersonal relationships that may influence the evaluator in more subtle but equally potent ways. Consider the school district evaluator who is assigned to evaluate a program being piloted by her weekly tennis doubles partner (a fact unknown to the superintendent who made the assignment). Or the external evaluator who finds herself unable to say anything positive about a program directed by an individual whose political and religious views are dramatically opposed to her own. Or the staff member assigned to evaluate products developed by colleagues who share office space, coffee breaks, and membership on the office's bowling team. But relational entanglements need not be so blatant to be problematical. As Anderson and Ball note,

> These relationships . . . influence the morale of the evaluation staff and the program staff. That is, they affect not only such principled and abstract topics as bias and ethics, but also such bread-and-butter issues as the evaluator's mood on Friday afternoon after a week of either repeated friction or relative harmony with program personnel. (Anderson & Ball, 1978, p. 127)

They might have gone on to say that the evaluator's mood will in turn affect such principled concerns as bias and ethics, for the impact of affect on behavior is too well known to require comment here. This does not argue for a cold, aloof evaluator, impervious to human attachments, but for awareness that myriad aspects of interpersonal relationships can color and alter the thinking and judgment of an evaluator, and that these factors must therefore be thoughtfully controlled. Failure to do so will result in the evaluator being co-opted in ways that are likely to bias seriously the outcomes of the study. As Scriven argues,

> The simplest instance of bias in program evaluation is the case of the evaluator who is part of the program staff and loses objectivity because of social and economic bonds to the development staff, compounded by the cumulative effect of repeated acceptance (or rejection) of evaluative suggestions. The resulting situation of quasi-coauthorship (or frustrated coauthorship) naturally destroys the external credibility of the evaluation and often the validity of the evaluative judgments. (Scriven, 1976a, p. 120)

Financial Relationships and Bias

Sir Robert Walpole said that "all men have their price," the implication being that anyone can be bought. And although there are enough examples of incorruptibility and integrity around to prove Walpole's assumptions exaggerated, there are still enough corrupt individuals to give some credence to his cynical view of human nature.

Evaluators hold no claim to moral eminence. There is little reason to believe they are either more or less vulnerable than anyone else to the pressures and influences of financial advantages. We doubt there are many instances of educational evaluators being bribed to sway an evaluation one way or another, but financial pressures are not always so obvious and direct.

For example, consider the unenviable plight of the evaluator who is employed by the very agency whose program she is evaluating. To illustrate how thorny this situation can be, let us describe an actual case.

An evaluator of our acquaintance—we'll call him John—was employed by a United States government-supported research center whose mission was to develop and test exemplary programs and practices for schools. Assigned to direct the center's evaluation unit, John in due time completed an evaluation of a center program designed to improve secondary school students' mathematics performance and attitudes toward math (AMP). The AMP program was expensive

—Congress had invested over one million dollars in its development—and while John found that students liked the program, there wasn't a shred of evidence to suggest that it had any impact at all on students' performance. Troubled by the implications of reporting such information to the funding agency through which Congress had initiated the program, John finally worded his draft report to convey that the *evaluation* was to blame for AMP's failure to produce evidence of success. The summary of his report read as follows (italics ours).[97]

> *Summary.* The results of this study indicate that the Accelerated Mathematics Program (AMP) was somewhat effective in developing positive attitudes toward mathematics, in the sense that students tended to like the AMP materials. The study supplied no evidence, however, from which either long- or short-term student performance changes in mathematics ability can be inferred. *The results do not necessarily indicate that AMP was not effective in promoting change in math performance, but that a variety of shortcomings and limitations of the evaluation design did not allow for the identification and measurement of these changes.*

And how did the funding agency respond to this obvious effort to soften the bad news? Their reaction to the draft report came in a letter, which is reprinted below.

Dear John:

Thank you for the three draft copies of the AMP Impact study. I look forward to the final report.

I hope that our future efforts will be structured so that statements such as those in the "summary" will not have to be made. Instead, I hope that we will be able to say something *positive* in the final report about changes in important performances. I have heard so many good things about AMP that I am disheartened by the lack of evidence that it has short-term performance effectiveness and that I cannot therefore argue for its potential for long-term effectiveness.

The issue here is straightforward. The best argument for funding centers such as yours that I can make internally here in the Department and externally with the Congress is that our products lead to measureable changes for good in American schools. Regardless of the positive "feelings" I get about AMP, it appears we cannot justify all the effort in terms of performance criteria, as per your draft report. That is a drawback. But one which I think we can overcome in future efforts, hopefully in your final report.

> Sincerely,
>
> Lawrence T. Donaldson
> Chief Administrator

The message is blatantly clear. John better find something positive to prove AMP and its cohort programs are worth the investment, or funding could be withdrawn, the program would fold, and John himself would be looking for other employment. It would take a robust soul indeed not to feel some ethical strain in such a situation, especially when his salary comes directly from the threatened program! Fortunately, though John equivocated at first, this story eventually had a happy ending. The final report told the true story, and John was able to assume the role of evaluator (with a clear conscience) on the development staff for another program at the same center.

Even when the evaluator is external to the agency whose programs or products are being evaluated, financial dependence can be a potential source of bias. Consider, for example, an external evaluation consultant or firm dependent on "repeat business"—a dilemma Brickell (1978) outlines entertainingly. The possibility of future evaluation contracts, or consulting, in this case, depends on how well the client likes the most recent evaluation completed by the evaluator. No problem here if the client has a penchant for the truth, even if it might reflect negatively on the program. But what if the client goes rigid at the first hint of criticism? The evaluator who wants future work from such a person must—as Brickell puts it—bite the hand that feeds her while appearing to lick it.

Even if the evaluator is not dependent on repeat business, she may find herself dependent on the client for funds to complete the study in hand. Seldom is an evaluator given all the funds for an evaluation up front. Clients usually wish to see interim products before releasing all the dollars necessary to carry the study to completion. The apparent or unspoken desire of the client to see positive results could very well introduce bias to interim evaluation findings.

In summary, the evaluator's financial relationship with and dependence upon the client must be reviewed carefully to determine whether these factors are likely to bias the study.

Organizational Relationships and Bias

Organizational relationships may be of greater concern to the evaluator than immediate financial gain. The relationship between the evaluator and the program being evaluated can determine not only her present financial welfare but possibly her future employment. Further, an organization may exert great (or total) control over the evaluator's other perquisites—such things as office space, access to secretarial resources, access to and use of facilities and record-keeping systems—even the convenience of available parking space. The way the organization exercises this control to make the evaluator's life easier or more difficult can certainly cause problems with bias.

To make this point, we present eight possible organizational relationships between evaluator and the program being evaluated (see Fig. 17.1).

Generally, the potential for bias is higher when the evaluator is employed by the organization whose program is being evaluated than when the evaluator is employed by an outside agency. In addition, bias is more likely when the "organizationally employed" evaluator reports to the director of the program being evaluated than when she reports to someone outside that program. And as noted earlier, the evaluation consultant who is dependent on repeat business may be more

Evaluator Employed	*To Do One Evaluation or Successive Evaluations*	*Evaluator Reports*
1. Within organization which has responsibility for the program being evaluated	1. Successive evaluations	1. Directly to director of program being evaluated
2. Within organization which has responsibility for the program being evaluated	2. One evaluation	2. Directly to director of program being evaluated
3. Within organization which has responsibility for the program being evaluated	3. Successive evaluations	3. To someone outside the program being evaluated but within the same organization
4. Within organization which has responsibility for the program being evaluated	4. One evaluation	4. To someone outside the program being evaluated but within the same organization
5. By outside agency	5. Successive evaluations	5. As consultant or contractor to director of program being evaluated
6. By outside agency	6. One evaluation	6. As consultant or contractor to director of program being evaluated
7. By outside agency	7. Successive evaluations	7. Directly to outside funding agency which supports the program
8. By outside agency	8. One evaluation	8. Directly to outside funding agency which supports the program

FIGURE 17.1   Organizational Relationships of Evaluator to Client

vulnerable to bias because of a perceived need to please the client. In short, the candor and the objectivity an evaluator demonstrates in conducting an evaluation are likely to decrease in direct proportion to the amount of control the client (the unit or program being evaluated) has over the evaluator's job security, salary and perquisites.

Some authors (for example, Cronbach and others, 1980) are unsympathetic to concerns that the locus of the evaluator's employment may influence the results of the evaluation. Such a stance ignores the very real influence that control of salary and perquisites can have on objectivity and even truth. Any assertion that such mundane matters are unlikely to influence an evaluation's outcome must seem quaint to "in-house" evaluators or evaluation contractors who have survived years of service in political cauldrons in which they have seen (if not felt personally) employment locus and control of perquisites wreak havoc.

Bias and Evaluation Roles.   The discerning reader has probably already noted that our discussion in the preceding sections omits one important consideration—whether the evaluation is formative or summative. In discussing the pros and cons of an evaluator's financial and administrative dependence or independence from the client, Anderson and Ball make this observation:

> Dependent relationships may promote the evaluator's responsivity to particular program needs. This can be worthwhile when the purpose of the evaluation is to improve the program. . . . However, dependence can be counterproductive when the purpose of the evaluation is to provide a credible, global assessment of the program's impact (Scriven, 1967). Skeptics will certainly question positive evaluation results produced by a dependent evaluator. (Anderson & Ball, 1978, p. 129)

It would seem obvious that the external, independent evaluator is to be preferred in summative evaluations, although as we have noted in the prior section, "independence" is defined by a variety of factors often not considered. For example, it strains credibility to argue that an external evaluator is truly independent when she is selected and paid by the client to carry out a summative study (even though independence is more likely here than if the evaluator were internal, and hence under even more direct client control).

Stated differently, co-optation, ego-involvement, and bias are undesirable in any evaluation, but they are doubly so in summative evaluation studies, where any conflict of interest is on a direct collision course with the purpose of such studies.

MAINTAINING ETHICAL STANDARDS: CONSIDERATIONS, ISSUES, AND RESPONSIBILITIES FOR EVALUATORS AND CLIENTS

Sadler (1981) states that evaluation bias can take three different forms: (1) unconscious distortions resulting from the evaluator's idiosyncratic background and experience; (2) biases introduced unwittingly by limitations in the evaluator's information-processing abilities; and (3) ethical compromises or distortions resulting from the evaluator's perception of possible payoffs and penalties. This last category, actions for which the evaluator (or client) is personally culpable, provides the focus for this section.

Drawing on Sadler's notions, as well as on our own work and that of Guba (1975), we might postulate the following forms of "evaluation corruptibility" that result from ethical compromises or distortions:

- Willingness, given conflict of interest or other perceived payoffs or penalties, to twist the truth and produce positive findings
- Intrusion of unsubstantiated opinions because of sloppy, capricious, and unprofessional evaluation practices
- "Shaded" evaluation "findings" resulting from intrusion of the evaluator's personal prejudices or preconceived notions
- Obtaining the cooperation of clients or participants by making promises that cannot be kept
- Failure to honor commitments that could have been honored.

Whether such problems result from the evaluator's incompetence or from more morally reprehensible causes, they still result in seriously compromised or outright discredited evaluations. It may matter greatly, on moral grounds, whether evaluation results are distorted because the evaluator is unconscionably self-serving, or because she is simply ignorant of how to discover and portray reality. But in practical terms the result is the same. Therefore, those who conduct and those who are served by evaluation studies share a responsibility for becoming informed about relevant ethical issues.

Proposed Ethical Standards in Evaluation

Beginning in the mid-1970s, several professional organizations contemplated evaluation's ethical issues. Two major organizations in the United States have published proposed sets of standards for evaluation practice (the Joint Committee on Standards for Educational Evaluation, 1981, and the Evaluation Research Society, 1982). Although dissimilar in level of detail and organization, the two sets overlap heavily in content (Stufflebeam, 1982). Both address the issue of ethical conduct. One of four major areas of concern listed by the Joint Committee, for instance, is that of "propriety," and specific standards in this area include

- Formal obligation
- Conflict of interest
- Full and frank disclosure
- Public's right to know
- Rights of human subjects
- Human interactions
- Balanced reporting
- Fiscal responsibility.

Other authors have also implicitly or explicitly listed ethical standards for evaluators (for example, Anderson & Ball, 1978; Fetterman, 1983; Straton, 1977; Brophy and others, 1974). For the most part, their concerns have been well covered by the Joint Committee on Standards; however, expansion in a few areas indicated by these authors may be helpful here.

Formal obligation goes beyond agreement on technically adequate evaluation procedures and includes such issues as clearly warning clients about the evaluation's limitations and not promising too much.

Conflict of interest cannot always be resolved. But if the evaluator makes her values and biases explicit in as open and honest a way as possible, in the spirit of "let the buyer beware," clients can at least be alert to biases that may unwittingly creep into the work of even the most honest evaluator.

The public's right to know and *full and frank disclosure* both reflect an evaluator's obligation to serve not only her client or sponsor but also the broader public(s) who supposedly benefit from both the program and its accurate evaluation. In addition, the evaluator has loyalties to the profession of evaluation and the ethical canons on which it depends. That these canons are not crystal clear and the ethical dilemmas not all resolved is apparent from questions raised by Fetterman (1983):

How should evaluators respond when they obtain confidential knowledge of illegal or unethical practices? Should all potentially damaging information about the evaluation object be included in the report? With whom does the evaluator have a moral responsibility to share the findings of her research? That these questions are not yet fully answered by the published sets of standards suggests that we need continually to refine and expand our understanding of ethical standards in such areas.

Rights of human subjects are broadly understood to include such things as obtaining informed consent, maintaining rights to privacy, and assuring confidentiality. But human rights extend also into the standard of *human interactions* in three basic principles outlined by the National Commission for the Protection of Human Subjects of Biomedical and Behavioral Research, namely, beneficence, respect, and justice.

> Beneficence means avoidance of unnecessary harm and the maximization of good outcomes. . . .
>
> . . . respect refers to respect for the autonomy or freedom of persons and for the well-being of nonautonomous persons (children, the mentally incompetent, prisoners). . . .
>
> Justice refers to equitable treatment and equitable representation of subgroups within society. (Sieber, 1980, p. 54)

Evaluation also carries nontrivial costs to personnel involved in that which is evaluated, including time and effort in providing, collecting, or facilitating the collection of information requested by the evaluator, and the time and energy expended in explaining the evaluation to various constituencies.

Ethics Are Not the Sole Responsibility of the Evaluator

Our emphasis on the evaluator's responsibility to carry out her activities in an ethical fashion may seem to suggest that ethics is the sole province of the evaluator. Obviously, such is not the case. Anderson and Ball (1978) stress that ethical responsibilities are shared by evaluation sponsors, participants, and audiences. Much of the work of the Joint Committee (1981) is also predicated on this understanding.

Many ethical issues pertain directly to the programs or products being evaluated—the extent to which they are fulfilling their objectives and the impact they have—for better or worse—on the lives of those they serve.

> Much of the work in evaluation ethics (i.e., the moral behavior of an individual as a professional evaluator) which has been done to date has focused on *evaluation* moral issues such as confidentiality of data, protection of human subjects, proper professional behavior, and so on. Little has been done on *program* moral issues, such as: Is this mental hospital placing the community at risk by its early release of patients? Is this nursing home meeting residents' physical needs but at the cost of their human rights of privacy, freedom of movement, and individual expression? Is this educational program for talented students enchancing cognitive skills but reinforcing their emotional dependency on special recognition and privileges? (N. L. Smith, 1983a, p. 11)

Ethics Beyond a Code of Ethics

The evaluation standards described earlier are, in our judgment, singularly useful in improving the practice of evaluation in education and related fields. We urge anyone aspiring to do high-quality evaluation to become intimately familiar with those standards and to apply them diligently. At the same time, we caution that mere adherence to ethical standards—however sound—does not assure ethical behavior. It is impossible to draft standards that anticipate all potential ethical problems or dilemmas.

Perhaps Sieber stated it best:

> A code of ethics specifically for program evaluators... would be a minimum standard; it would only state what the profession expects of every evaluator in the way of honesty, competence, and decency in relation to those ethical problems that are clearly defined at present.
>
> In contrast, being ethical is a broad, evolving personal process that both resembles and is related to the process involved in becoming a competent social scientist. Ethical problems in program evaluation are problems having to do with unanticipated conflicts of obligation and interest and with unintended harmful side effects of evaluation. To be ethical is to evolve an ability to anticipate and circumvent such problems. It is an acquired ability.... As one undertakes new and different kinds of evaluation and as society changes, one's ability to be ethical must grow to meet new challenges. Thus, being ethical in program evaluation is a process of growth in understanding, perception, and creative problem-solving ability that respects the interests of individuals and of society. (Sieber, 1980, p. 53)

COPING WITH POLITICAL PRESSURES AND PROBLEMS IN EVALUATION

Cronbach and his colleagues (1980) present the view that evaluation is essentially a political activity. They describe evaluation as a "novel political institution" that is part of the governance of social programs. They assert that evaluators and their patrons often mount unrealistic "truth" or "right" decisions, rather than the more pertinent task of simply enlightening all participants so as to facilitate a democratic, pluralist decision-making process. Although some may reject this view as overstated, it underscores the fact that evaluation of publicly supported enterprises is inextricably intertwined with public policy formulation and all the political forces involved in that process. Evaluators who fail to understand this basic fact squander human and financial resources by conducting evaluations that are largely irrelevant because of their "political naivete," however impeccably they are designed and conducted.

In this section, therefore, we discuss the political nature of evaluation and ways of coping with unwarranted political influences that can otherwise subvert evaluation efforts.

Evaluation as a Political Activity

The term *politics* has been applied so broadly to so many different phenomena that it has all but lost its meaning. It has come to stand for everything from power plays and machination within a university department to political campaigns or relations among governmental agencies. Whatever its obscure connotations, "politics" is viewed by many evaluators as merely an eight-letter dirty word. The belief that evaluation should shun the realm of politics altogether stems from a failure to perceive the highly political nature of the beast. Our view that evaluation is a largely political activity should by now be apparent to the reader. Effective evaluators must recognize and cope with political influences as they occur. To ignore them or assume "politics can be removed from this study" is both naive and erroneous. This perception is shared by many thoughtful evaluators:

> Whether evaluators recognize the political nature of evaluation or not, internal and external politics impinging on evaluation studies have persistently exerted both constraints and influence on evaluations. (Talmage, 1982, p. 601)
>
> Decision-making. . .is a euphemism for the allocation of resources—money, position, authority. . . . Thus, to the extent that information is an instrument, basis, or excuse for changing power relationships within or among institutions, evaluation is a political activity. (Cohen, 1970, p. 214)

Expanding on Cohen's position, Weiss (1975) describes evaluation as a rational enterprise occurring within a political context. According to Weiss, political factors "intrude" upon evaluations in three ways: (1) the policies and programs with which evaluation deals are themselves the creatures of political decisions; (2) because evaluation feeds decision making, its reports enter the political arena; and (3) evaluation, by its very nature, makes implicit political statements (such as those challenging the legitimacy of certain program goals or implementation strategies).

According to Tumin (1975) the "politics of evaluation" refers to partisan activities meant to influence the conduct of evaluation in ways that favor one group or another. Given this view, political considerations enter into almost every evaluation at almost every stage. Cronbach and his colleagues recognize this fact in stressing the importance of the evaluator's representing *all* stakeholders:

> If the evaluator does not try to see the program through the eyes of diverse partisans, the posing of the questions may itself—myopically or intentionally—favor the interests of one agency, one sector of society, or the ideology of the evaluator himself.
>
> For our part, we advise the evaluator to be multipartisan, to make the best case he can for each side in turn. (Cronbach and others, 1980, pp. 208, 210)

The Joint Committee (1981) also recognizes the importance of the evaluator's sensitivity to the various partisan views of stakeholder groups; the committee proposes the following standard:

> *Political Viability.* The evaluation should be planned and conducted with anticipation of the different positions of various interest groups, so that their cooperation may be obtained, and so that possible attempts by any of these groups to curtail evaluation

operations or to bias or misapply the results can be averted or counteracted. (Joint Committee on Standards for Educational Evaluation, 1981, p. 56)

Coping with Political Pressures on Evaluation Studies

Political pressures are inevitably part of evaluation. And the professional evaluator who prefers to eschew "politics" and deal only with technical considerations has made a strange career choice.

Some political pressures, however, can interfere with evaluation in ways that are patently unethical. We are not concerned here with legitimate political processes or problems that naturally arise whenever an evaluation is conducted, but rather with those emanating from the *unethical* use of political influence.

Brickell (1978) describes several situations in which evaluators have experienced unethical political influence. We present them here, along with our suggestions for coping with the pressures involved in each case:

1. *The client makes it clear from the start what the evaluator should report at the end of the evaluation. Anything different will be unacceptable.* The evaluator could explain how a professional evaluator works and describe the standards (see Chapter 21) of the profession that apply in this situation. If the client persists in prescribing the outcomes expected, the evaluator should abort the evaluation and consider reporting the incident to a higher authority.

2. *The client rewrites the evaluation report, changing the evaluator's findings and interpretations.* Obviously the evaluator should protest and request that such self-interested editing be deleted. If that request is ignored, assuming the evaluator stipulated in the evaluation agreement that she had control of final reports (editing and distribution), she could offer to correct the client's error by distributing the original report, could sue the client for violation of the contract, or could expose the client for unethical practices, perhaps through the public media.

3. *The client makes the possibility of obtaining future evaluation contracts contingent on positive findings in the current evaluation. If the evaluator turns in a negative report, her future work is jeopardized.* If unethical evaluation practice were to result from the evaluator's bowing to this conflict of interest, she would be better foregoing future work than gaining notoriety through a breach of ethics. The evaluator and client could agree to allow other, independent evaluators to conduct or review the evaluation. The evaluator could, as Cronbach and others (1980) propose, appeal to a profession-wide group to support her in seeking both employment security and independence. She should also avoid tying her well-being to one client or project.

4. *The client introduces new requests that throw both schedule and budget off, then complains when things are not done on time.* Once the evaluation agreement is signed, all new requests should be accompanied by renegotiation of the agreement (including time frames and budget). The evaluator needs to be careful not to overpromise because of political pressure or desire to be "nice."

It is the evaluator's responsibility to see that political forces such as these are not allowed to subvert an otherwise good evaluation study. Of course, it is easier to propose coping strategies from an armchair than from one of the hot spots just described. In reality, the difficulty of dealing with unethical political pressures is often acute. For this reason, it is often advisable for evaluators to work in teams, rather than alone. There *is* safety—to say nothing of commiseration—in numbers.

After offering several "tongue-in-cheek" rules for escaping the influence of external political factors (Do not work for anyone who has anything to do with the project you are evaluating... Be independently wealthy...), Brickell makes the following serious suggestions for dealing with political influences in evaluation:

1. Try to understand how the client thinks. Find out what he has to gain or lose from the evaluation....
2. Reassure the client at the outset that you can interpret the findings so as to give helpful suggestions for program improvement—no matter what the findings of the study are.
3. Find out what the powerful decision-makers—the client and those who surround him—will actually use as criteria for judging the success of the project. Gather and present evidence addressed to those criteria. You may, if you wish, also gather data on the official objectives of the project or even on objectives that happen to interest you. But never try to substitute those for data addressed to criteria the decision-makers will use.
4. Try to get a supervisory mechanism set up for the evaluation contract that contains a cross section of all the powerful decision-makers. Try to get it designed so that the members have to resolve the conflicts among themselves before giving you marching orders for the study or deciding whether to accept your final report.
5. Write the report carefully, especially when describing shortcomings and placing blame, and do mention any extenuating circumstances.... Review the draft final report before submitting it to the client for his review, making sure in advance that you can defend any claim you make.

Following those rules will not help you escape political influences. The most they can do is help you cope with them. (Brickell, 1978, p. 98)

Fortunately, the Joint Committee on Standards for Educational Evaluation (1981) provides the evaluator with professional standards that emphasize the importance of formal evaluation agreements and the judicious use of an outside consultant to help mediate conflicts. In addition, avoiding conflict of interest and insisting upon open, fair, and complete disclosure of findings are two of the most important principles an evaluator can remember when it comes to coping with unethical political pressures.

CASE STUDY APPLICATION

January 8. I'm a tad frustrated tonight, and it's my own fault, I guess. Called Mrs. Janson yesterday to get her approval of the individuals I'd selected to be on the site-visit team. She asked me to get the OK of the Radnor humanities faculty, saying she had no objection if they didn't. I explained that I had asked her faculty earlier this week to nominate humanities experts they thought could do a good, fair review of their curriculum, and that I had selected one of the two they proposed. But she still thought they might feel better if they reviewed the list of everyone who would be on the team, and after reflecting for a minute, I agreed. So I asked if she might run the list past them this second time and let me know their reaction (there's more than one way to stretch a pitifully small telephone budget!).

Anyway, she called this morning and said that the faculty felt rather strongly that they wanted *both* of their nominees on the team, suggesting I drop someone else if necessary (not caring who, since they had no objection to any particular team member). I told Mrs. Janson I had only asked the faculty to *nominate* humanities experts, that I had honored that by choosing one of their nominees, and that I felt it was my prerogative to make the final selection of team members. Besides, I told her that I know the second humanities expert that I did list on the team, and she is excellent—not only sharp, but unbiased, plus experienced in doing curriculum reviews.

She said OK, but later today she called back and said she'd been talking with one of her faculty who was *insistent* that I use *both* nominees on the team. Mrs. Janson said she was uneasy, and wondered whether I might compromise a bit on this, rather than creating a furor in the faculty before we even got the evaluation started. She said she had reviewed my evaluation plan and couldn't find anything that said I would choose the team or that their district couldn't, so she felt on shaky ground being too hard-nosed about telling her staff that I had the sole right to make final decisions about team composition.

Well, that really got to me, and I had to bite my tongue to keep from telling her that we didn't have a legalistic contract, for goodness' sake, and that she also couldn't find anywhere in our agreed–upon plan that said I *couldn't* pick the team either. But I resisted. Maybe I should have drafted a more formal evaluation contract, at least laying out who makes key decisions pertaining to key aspects of the evaluation. But I hadn't. So I had to reveal something to her that I had hoped might be left unsaid, and that is the reason why I didn't include the faculty's one nominee I had dropped. So I told her that when I called both proposed consultants to see if they might have the time and interest to be involved, one chap nearly panted after the opportunity, saying he would "love to get back to Radnor again." *Again,* I asked? Turns out he was one of the people who helped set up the Radnor humanities program in the first place. So I drew a line through his name. Having him evaluate that curriculum would be a bit like having a mother evaluate her own baby.

When I explained, Mrs. Janson thanked me, suggested she talk to the faculty again. A bit later she got back to me and said everyone was satisfied with the team I'd selected. She apologized for her staff, saying they hadn't thought very deeply about the fact that prior involvement as a consultant might tend to color one's judgment. So she gave me the green light to proceed.

It still annoys me a bit that I hadn't been more precise with the evaluation agreement, but even then I may not have thought to include anything about who made the final choice of team members. Seems there are so many political or personal issues that crop up in every evaluation that I don't know how anyone would anticipate them all. Of course, that's no excuse for failing to get agreements on those you *can* anticipate, I guess.

Author Comments. None. Does that surprise you? Well, sometimes an evaluator's journal entry says it all.

APPLICATION EXERCISE

1. Refer to the evaluation plan you developed in the prior chapters. Identify three people who might conduct the evaluation, one who is closely associated with whatever you have selected to evaluate, one who works within the same

agency but is not closely associated, and one who is external to the agency. Determine how much you believe the financial, organizational, and interpersonal relationship of each of these three individuals (with the evaluation object) would bias the evaluation.

2. In the above situation, analyze the extent to which the evaluation will be both a political and technical activity.

SUGGESTED READINGS

ANDERSON, S. B., & BALL, S. (1978). *The profession and practice of program evaluation.* San Francisco: Jossey-Bass.

BRICKELL, H. M. (1978). The influence of external political factors on the role and methodology of evaluation. In T. D. COOK and others (Eds.), *Evaluation studies review annual* (Vol. 3). Beverly Hills, CA: Sage.

CRONBACH, L. J., AMBRON, S. R., DORNBUSCH, S. M., HESS, R. D., HORNIK, R. C., PHILLIPS, D. C., WALKER, D. F., & WEINER, S. S. (1980). *Toward reform of program evaluation.* San Francisco: Jossey-Bass.

HOUSE, E. R. (Ed.). (1973). *School evaluation: The politics and process.* Berkeley, CA: McCutchan.

Joint Committee on Standards for Educational Evaluation. (1981). *Standards for evaluations of educational programs, projects, and materials.* New York: McGraw-Hill.

Chapter 18
Collecting Evaluation Information

Orienting Questions

1. What techniques and procedures are useful for collecting important evaluation information?
2. Assuming that Murphy's Law holds for educational evaluation (as it seems to for most human endeavors), what can go wrong in data collection, storage, and retrieval?
3. What criteria would you use to separate "good" information from "bad," no matter how that information was collected?
4. What is *unobtrusive measurement* and how might it be useful in educational evaluation?
5. What investigative journalism methods and principles seem particularly useful to educational evaluators?

The government is very keen on amassing statistics. They collect them, add them, raise them to the *n*th power, take the cube root and prepare wonderful diagrams. But you must never forget that every one of these figures comes in the first instance from the village watchman, who just puts down what he pleases. [Sir Josiah Stamp, as quoted by Light & Smith (1970)]

The collection of information is fundamental to evaluation. Although educators sometimes joke about "data-free" or "fact-free" evaluations, no reputable evaluator would presume to make evaluative judgments without first assembling a solid base of evidence.

Still, information is situational and changes with every evaluation. Similarly, the methods evaluators must use to collect information must also change. Sometimes alternative data-collection methods are available, and the evaluator must make a choice, considering cost, precision (reliability), stability, relevance, validity of measurements, feasibility, political advisability, and acceptability to various audiences. The evaluator must be ready to use whichever method or methods appear most appropriate. And "being prepared" usually means having prior experience. We advise evaluators to gain experience with any methods that may be new to them—and that means actually using the methods, not just reading about them.

Entire books have been written on a single data-collection technique, instrument, or procedure.[98] We could not hope to cover in comparable detail the many data-collection methods that educational evaluators have come to use and value. Instead, we will briefly discuss those most commonly used and suggest references for those wanting additional information.

Before discussing specific methods and techniques, we need to comment briefly on dealing with protocol and other potential problems in collecting evaluation data, as well as the importance of establishing procedures for information control, organization, storage, and retrieval.

PROTOCOL AND POTENTIAL PROBLEMS IN COLLECTING EVALUATION INFORMATION

Whatever the evaluator's data-collection methods, they must be sanctioned by the proper authorities. In schools, approval of the school superintendent—and possibly the school board—is often required. Approval is usually also obtained from the school building principal, involved teachers, and parents of involved children. Most school districts have policies governing data collection in their schools; however, such policies do not always cover all the steps a thoughtful evaluator would include in order to establish and maintain good rapport.

Obtaining permission and cooperation requires clear communication, in non-technical language, about the reasons and proposed methods for data collection, requirements of participants, and potential benefits of participation. It is often appropriate to promise participants a chance to see the results that their cooperation helped to generate.

Potential problems that evaluators may encounter in collecting evaluation information fall into two categories: (1) problems of cooperation or access to data; and (2) technical problems in data collection.

Problems of Cooperation or Access to Data

There are many ways to keep an evaluator from collecting essential information. Authorities may refuse to open files or may be unavailable for interviews. To avoid such problems, the evaluator can counter by negotiating a clause covering access to data. He could also review the entire evaluation procedure with participants in positions of authority (such as the school district superintendent, the school principal, and the teachers' union) prior to signing an agreement, obtaining their support and sanction in writing if necessary.

Participants' motivations can affect the quality of data collected. Informants may give misleading or false information, for example, if they believe it is in their best interest. Others simply may not take the data collection seriously. Explaining the importance of their cooperation can prevent many potential problems. Sometimes participants raise fewer objections if confidentiality or anonymity can be guaranteed. Rewards—such as released time or feedback from the study—may also encourage full cooperation. Adherence to ethical practices that protect participants' rights is also essential to assure access to data sources.

Technical Problems in Data Collection

The evaluator's version of Murphy's Law goes something like this: "If anything can go wrong in collecting information, it will." A comprehensive list of potential problems would fill this chapter. But here are a few of the major ones:

- *Respondents misunderstanding directions and consequently responding inappropriately* (Always pilot-test your methods.)
- *Inexperienced data collectors reducing the quality of the information being collected* (Always include extensive training and trial runs. Eliminate potential problem staff before they hit the field. Monitor and document data-collection procedures.)
- *Partial or complete loss of information* (Duplicate records; keep records and raw data under lock and key at all times.)
- *Information being recorded incorrectly* (Always check data collection in progress. Cross-checks of recorded information are frequently necessary.)
- *Outright fraud* (Always have more than one person supplying data. Compare information, looking for the "hard to believe.")
- *Procedural breakdowns* (Keep logistics simple. Use supervisors. Minimize control for responsible evaluation staff. Avoid mailing critical information. Keep copies of irreplaceable instruments, raw data, records, and the like.)
- *Instruments thought appropriate for collecting information prove to be insensitive or off target, or give inconsistent readings* (Pilot-test all instruments before using them, whenever possible.)
- *Information that is thought to be factual proves to be inaccurate* (Include confirmations, cross-checks, triangulation steps in data collection whenever the accuracy of information is important and open to question.)[99]

INFORMATION CONTROL, ORGANIZATION, AND RETRIEVAL

An aspect of information collection that proves troublesome in many evaluations is the handling of data. Let us consider five steps involved in managing information: organization, control, checks, storage, and retrieval.

Information organization requires a filing system. Potentially important information is often lost if it is not placed in the proper location. In naturalistic studies, field notes are often organized on the spot for future reference. Tests and questionnaires should be categorized by grade level or early and late return, as appropriate for evaluation. The important thing to remember in collecting information is that everything fits somewhere. When information does not fit readily into place, it is time to rethink or perhaps rework the way data are organized.

Information control requires assurance that nothing is lost, overlooked, released prematurely, or used inappropriately in violation of evaluation policy or human rights. As information manager, the evaluator has a responsibility to see that collected information is safeguarded. The evaluation staff member who takes data home and then misplaces the data is a threat to the evaluation. In addition, the evaluator must honor commitments to participants to keep information confidential. Few things can damage an evaluation more than premature or inappropriate use of privileged information. As noted earlier, freedom of information—the legal right for anyone to access existing information—can be threatening to the evaluator when information is subpoenaed for purposes other than those for which it has been collected. The conscientious evaluator will consider first whether information should be recorded, and then how the procedures for recording can protect the information source or others from unwarranted disclosure. Using fictitious names or numerical labels, for example, is one way to control inappropriate uses of information, while still serving evaluation purposes.

Information checks provide assurance that both quantitative and qualitative information is recorded accurately. With quantitative information, this means that data collectors should check, while data are being gathered, to see that respondents have filled out forms correctly. Coding of responses should be checked while coding is being done (supervisors often sample and check coded forms for this purpose). The reading and storage of coded forms should also be checked for accuracy. With qualitative information, confirmation, cross-checks, and triangulation all reduce misunderstanding or misinterpretation.

Information storage is handled in two ways. In one, coded information, field note analyses, and the like are put into the computer or written records for future analysis. Information stored in this form should be verified for accuracy. In the other approach, raw data or raw field notes and artifacts are filed in case they are needed for future reference or reanalysis. It is good practice to arrange for a locked data storage room where raw evaluation data can be filed and kept safely. Once the evaluation is completed, plan to store raw data in boxes for at least three years before destroying it.[100] Follow-up studies, reanalyses, and questions about the evaluation can all require the use of the raw data.

Uncomplicated *retrieval of stored information* is vital to later analysis, yet it should be controlled so that unauthorized users cannot gain access to the data. When storing information, the evaluator needs to plan and discuss with data-processing staff the ways in which the information is to be analyzed. Storage, retrieval, and analysis of information must work together.

METHODS FOR COLLECTING EVALUATION INFORMATION

There are many potentially useful methods of information collection an evaluator needs to know. The most commonly used methods for collecting evaluation information are discussed in this section, along with references to more detailed treatments of each. The methods that follow might be considered an inventory of tools that the professional evaluator should be able to employ. None is to be used indiscriminately in every evaluation. Each should be used only after careful thought has been given to the information that is required to conduct a thorough evaluation, and to the potential contributions of particular techniques or procedures.

Testing

Volumes have been written on testing, and we neither hope nor wish to re-cover that ground here. We do believe, however, that some confusion has appeared in achievement testing in recent years; we will attempt to sort out some basic distinctions and comment on their relative utility in educational evaluation.[101] Such a discussion is important because achievement testing often represents a major part of the educational evaluator's work.

A *test* is a collection of items developed to measure some human educational or psychological attribute. An *item* on a test includes a set of instructions that (1) presents a situation (the stimulus), (2) records the examinee's response, and (3) provides for some way of scoring the response.

In achievement testing, recent advances have greatly extended the testing options available to the evaluator. Four approaches to achievement testing have dominated recent discussions:

- Norm-referenced testing (NRT)
- Criterion-referenced testing (CRT)
- Objectives-referenced testing (ORT)
- Domain-referenced testing (DRT)

These four strategies have many elements in common, but depending on which strategy is chosen, the procedures for test development and interpretation can be quite different.

An abundance of information could be provided on any one of the four strategies. The most salient points are summarized in Table 18.1, under the following categories (Sanders and Murray, 1976):

1. *Definition.* A brief description of the nature of the testing process and the basis for interpretation.
2. *Key emphasis.* The major distinguishing characteristics of the testing approach.
3. *Development procedure.* The key steps used in preparing tests for each approach.
4. *Item selection.* How test items or exercises are selected or generated for each approach.
5. *Necessary input for test development.* The primary information required to initiate the test-development process.
6. *Types of scores reported.* Examples of characteristic reporting formats.
7. *Examples of test interpretations.* The kind of information a relevant item yields, and sample interpretations for each testing approach.
8. *Recommended uses.* A brief description of the uses to which each testing approach may be put.
9. *Inappropriate uses and limitations.* A brief description of inappropriate uses.

The descriptions of alternative approaches to achievement testing contained in Table 18.1 provide a glimpse of current knowledge. We need to learn a great deal about the best way to design an achievement-testing program, but there is also a good deal we already know. The best achievement-testing system is probably a combination, or variation, of the approaches. Analyzing each separately simply allows us to see where relative strengths lie so that we can achieve the best combination to meet the needs of a particular testing program.

Norm-referenced and criterion-referenced tests both yield evaluative results in the sense that both provide standards for judging students' performance. Objectives-referenced and domain-referenced tests yield descriptive data about student performance, with no judgments attached.

Naturally, there are many types of tests used in education besides achievement tests. Most testing textbooks list intelligence, scholastic aptitude, special aptitude, personality, and other tests as important tools of the school psychologist or counselor. Achievement testing is an important tool of the evaluator.

Criteria that may be used to evaluate tests should include the following:

1. Administrative concerns such as cost, time needed to administer and score, and special facility or equipment requirements
2. Adequacy of the test manual in providing directions for administration and correct interpretation of results
3. Qualifications required of the examiner
4. Time elapsed since test revision
5. Evidence of validity for each intended use
6. Evidence that scores are sufficiently reliable (dependable)
7. Appropriate use of sampling procedures to gain validity and reliability evidence
8. Sufficient detail in directions for test administration, scoring, and interpretation
9. Availability of alternative forms
10. Availability and adequacy of norms for intended cases
11. Appropriate use of scoring scales.

The evaluator is referred to Thorndike and Hagen (1969), Cronbach (1979), Hopkins and Stanley (1981), or Worthen, Borg, and White (in press) for more detailed discussions of alternative testing methods and test development. The series of *Mental Measurements Yearbooks* and *Tests in Print* (developed originally by O. K. Buros and currently managed by the Buros Institute at the University of Nebraska) are invaluable reference works when selecting a test for data collection. We have also found the text by Mehrens and Lehmann (1969) to be a valuable reference on standardized testing.

Attitude Measurement

Scales developed to measure attitudes toward individuals, groups, institutions, programs, and other entities are time-consuming to construct. Often the investment cannot be justified when resources are limited.

Fortunately, excellent collections of well-developed attitude scales are available.

TABLE 18.1

A Comparative Analysis of Basic Achievement Test Approaches

Characteristic	Norm	Criterion	Objectives	Domain
1. Definition/Interpretation	Test performance as compared against others taking the same test.	Test performance as compared against absolute standards.	Test performance on behaviorally stated objectives.	Test performance as an estimate of performance on a universe of similar items.
2. Key Emphasis	Maximize individual differences. Survey of generally accepted skills and knowledge. Items logically sampled, then sorted, from generally defined content area. Evaluative results.	Explicit standards used for interpreting test performance. Items taken directly from specific curriculum. All items for unit used—no sampling. Evaluative results.	Use of behaviorally stated objectives to describe types of desired behaviors. Test items prepared for priority areas of concern. Items judgmentally sampled from all possibilities. Descriptive results.	Explicitly defining content area of test. Creation of item pools or item forms. Developing estimates of performance over a large number of similar items. Items randomly sampled from domain. Descriptive results.
3. Development Procedure	1. State content area. 2. Test items developed to discriminate. 3. Norms developed. 4. Appropriate validity and reliability estimates documented.	1. Curriculum or content analysis. 2. Test items written to match analysis in form and content. 3. Standards established. 4. Appropriate validity and real reliability estimates documented.	1. Objectives stated and selected. 2. Test items written to match objectives. 3. Appropriate validity and reliability estimates documented.	1. Content limits provided. 2. Item forms established. 3. Sample items written. 4. Sample of items drawn from domain. 5. Appropriate validity and reliability estimates documented.
4. Item Selection	Sample on a logical basis from theoretically defined content. Select items that discriminate.	Use items that replicate behaviors called for in specific instructions.	Use items that are indicators of achievement of objectives of interest.	Develop item forms for specified domains. Draw a representative sample of all items that could be generated using an item form.
5. Necessary input for the Test Development Process	Knowledge of a curriculum content area or a construct on which students can be expected to differ.	Performance objectives that include an acceptable level (standard) of performance.	A statement of objectives in terms of student behavior.	A content domain either explicit in a curriculum or explicitly stated in the form of objectives.

6. Types of Scores Reported	1. A percentile rank. 2. A standard score. 3. A stanine score (a special case of standard score). 4. A grade equivalent score.	1. A statement of whether or not a student has achieved a predetermined percentage or number correct. 2. A statement of whether or not a group of students has (on the average) achieved a predetermined level of performance. 3. The time taken to perform a given task and an indication of whether or not the task was completed in the allotted time.	1. Number of correct items for a student. 2. Percent correct for a student. 3. The percentage of students in a program who pass each item.	1. The percentage of correct items for a student and an estimate of the percentage of items that a student could get correct in a universe of items.
7. Example of Test Interpretation	"You performed better on this test than approximately 79 percent of the children in the group against which you are being compared."	"You have answered 80 percent of the items for this unit correctly so you may move on to the next unit."	"You have gotten 3 out of the 4 items written for this objective correct."	"You have answered 90 percent of the items correctly so we estimate that you will answer about 9 out of 10 similar items correctly."
8. Recommended Uses	1. Selection. 2. Classification.	1. Progress in specific curriculum.	1. Gathering information about priority area.	1. Instruction or education.
9. Inappropriate Uses and Limitations	1. Not best-suited for program or curriculum evaluation. 2. Not for frequent use in instruction.	1. Not for cross-curriculum testing. 2. Not for discrimination (selection, classification).	1. Not for comprehensive coverage of instruction. 2. Not for discrimination (selection, classification).	1. Not for low-cost budgets (can be expensive to set up). 2. Not for discrimination (selection, classification).

Source: Sanders & Murray, 1976.

Shaw and Wright (1967) have compiled scales that may be used or adapted for measuring attitudes toward virtually any social object. Each scale is accompanied by reliability and validity information that enables the evaluator to make informed decisions.

Likewise, Robinson, Athanasiou, and Head (1969) and Robinson and Shaver (1973a, 1973b) have compiled instruments for measuring social-psychological, occupational, and political attitudes. They also provide technical information about the instruments in their collections.

Buros's *Mental Measurements Yearbooks* also describe and reference numerous attitude scales. We highly recommend adapting available attitude scales whenever possible. When the evaluator must develop new attitude instruments, the following hints offered by Edwards (1957) may prove useful:

- Avoid statements that refer to the past rather than to the present.
- Avoid statements that are factual or capable of being interpreted as factual.
- Avoid statements that may be interpreted in more than one way.
- Avoid statements that are irrelevant to the object under consideration.
- Avoid statements that are believed to cover the entire range of the affective scale of interest.
- Avoid statements that are likely to be endorsed by almost everyone or by almost no one.
- Keep the language of the statements simple, clear, and direct.
- Keep statements short, rarely exceeding 20 words.
- Express only one complete thought per statement.
- Avoid statements containing universals such as *all, always, none,* and *never.*
- Use words such as *only, just, merely,* and others of a similar nature with care and moderation.
- Whenever possible, use simple rather than compound or complex sentences.
- Avoid words that may not be understood by users.
- Avoid double negatives.

Survey Questionnaires and Survey Methods

The development of questionnaires is the most critical and possibly the most underemphasized part of a survey. Educational evaluators often have a disturbing predisposition to list questions quickly, put them on a form, and call the result a questionnaire. In reality, unless it has undergone careful, critical appraisal before being sent to potential respondents, a questionnaire will yield little usable information.

The early stages of survey design center on decision making about the aims of the study and identification of hypotheses to be tested or questions to be answered. By talking to experts and reviewing relevant literature, the evaluator should be able to identify the most appropriate questions. Once questions are selected, it is important to consider how the responses will be analyzed and whether the results will adequately answer the questions. At that point, the evaluator should decide how the questionnaire items will be posed and whether answers will be quantified, categorized, or submitted to content analysis. Careful development of the questionnaire draft, instructions, and cover letter (if distributed by mail) then follow.

A first draft of the questionnaire should meet these criteria:

1. *Question sequence*
   a. Are later responses biased by early questions?
   b. Is the questionnaire attractive and interesting? Does it start off with easy, unthreatening questions?
   c. Are leading questions asked? Is there a logical, efficient sequencing of questions (for example, from general to specific questions; use of filter questions when appropriate)?
   d. Are closed/open-ended questions appropriate? If closed, are the categories exhaustive, mutually exclusive? (Could ordinal or nominal data be collected as interval data?)
   e. Are the major issues covered thoroughly while minor issues are passed over quickly?
   f. Are questions with similar content grouped logically?
2. *Question wording*
   a. Are questions stated precisely? (Who, what, when, where, why, how?)
   b. Does the questionnaire assume too much knowledge on the part of the respondent?
   c. Does each item ask only one question?
   d. Is the respondent in a position to answer the question, or must he make guesses?
   e. Are definitions clear?
   f. Are emotionally tinged words used?
   g. Are technical terms, jargon, slang, words with double meanings avoided?
   h. Are the methods for responding consistent?
   i. Are the questions impersonal?
   j. Are the questions appropriately brief and uncomplicated?
3. *Establishing and keeping rapport and eliciting cooperation*
   a. Is the questionnaire easy to answer?
   b. Is the time required to respond reasonable?
   c. Does the questionnaire look attractive? (that is, layout, quality of paper, etc.)
   d. Is there a "respondent orientation"?
   e. Is the questionnaire introduced with an explanation of purpose, sponsorship, method of respondent selection, anonymity?
   f. Is appropriate incentive provided for the respondent's cooperation?
4. *Instructions*
   a. Is the respondent clearly told how to record his responses?
   b. Are instructions for return due date and procedures included?
5. *Technical quality*
   a. Validity
      (1) Are second information sources used as cross-checks (for example, interviewer ratings, other findings)?
      (2) Are responses of like respondents (for example, husband/wife) checked?

    (3) Have content experts read pilot versions of the questionnaire?
  b. Reliability
    (1) Are factual questions repeated?
    (2) Are phony or dummy items used?
    (3) Are respondents reinterviewed?
    (4) Have responses been checked for logical consistency?
  c. External validity
    (1) Are nonresponse bias checks planned?

An excellent annotated bibliography on the design, construction, and use of questionnaires for inquiry is provided by Potter, Sharpe, Hendee, and Clark (1972). Texts by Berdie and Anderson (1974) and Oppenheim (1966) provide readable and detailed discussions of questionnaire development. Covert's (1977) paper on constructing questionnaires is helpful, and Kornhauser and Sheatsley's (1959) instructions for constructing questionnaires are still a standard. Payne's (1951) book on asking questions is indispensable.

Demaline and Quinn (1979) provide an excellent step-by-step guide and a 365-item bibliography on conducting mail surveys. They cover (1) preparation of instruments and cover letters; (2) delivery of the questionnaire; (3) analyzing responses and nonresponses; (4) follow-ups; (5) coding; and (6) checking for coding errors.

Interviews

A major difference between using questionnaires and collecting data via personal or telephone interviews is that interviews allow clarification and probing. Personal contact by field agents (interviewers), however, can also be a detriment. Extensive training with practice sessions and "scripts" for answering common questions is essential.

Following are some helpful hints in planning and conducting interviews:

1. Keep the language pitched to the level of the respondent. Questions posed to specialists can rely on the terminology with which they are familiar. But questions posed to the general public must use language more commonly understood.

2. Try to choose words that have the same meaning for everyone. If two groups lack a common language (or dialect), they should be given separate questionnaires.

3. Avoid long questions. They often become ambiguous and confusing.

4. Do not assume that your respondent possesses factual or firsthand information. A mother may be able to report what books her child reads, but only the child can tell you accurately how much he enjoys reading.

5. Establish the frame of reference you have in mind. For example, if interested in reader preferences in magazines, don't ask, "*How many* magazines do you read?" Ask, "*Which* magazines do you read?"

6. Either suggest all possible answers to a question or don't suggest any. Don't ask, "Do you think the husband should help with dressing and feeding the small children when he's home?" Ask, "Do you think the husband should help with dressing and feeding the small children when he's home, or do you think it's the wife's job in any case?"

7. Protect your respondent's ego. Don't ask, "Do you know the name of the Chief Justice of the Supreme Court?" Ask, "Do you happen to know the name of the Chief Justice of the Supreme Court?"

8. If you are after unpleasant orientations, give your respondent a chance to express his positive feelings first, so that he is not put in an unfavorable light. First ask, "What do you like about X?" Then ask, "What don't you like about X?"

9. Decide whether you need a direct question, an indirect question, or a combination. An example of a direct question is, "Do you ever steal on the job?" An indirect question might be, "Do you know of anyone ever stealing on the job?" A combination might be, "Do you know of anyone ever stealing on the job? Have you ever taken anything while on the job?"

An interviewer manual developed by the University of Michigan Institute for Social Research (1971) provides excellent coverage of interviewer training. Gordon's (1975) text is a thorough and readable treatment of interviewing methods. In addition, Guba and Lincoln (1981) provide an excellent discussion of interviews and guidelines for interviewers in naturalistic evaluations that has broad applicability to most educational uses. McDonald and Sanger (1982) provide a helpful analysis of notetaking versus tape recording in recording interview data. These sources are highly recommended for evaluators who plan on using interviews to collect information.

Observation Methods

Observation methods for collecting evaluation information may be quantitative or qualitative, structured or unstructured, depending on the approach that best suits the evaluation.

Structured and quantitative observation methods involve using checklists or forms for recording observations—often called *observation schedules*. Simon and Boyer (1974) have collected observation instruments that may be used to study educational processes. As with attitude measurement, the procedures required for developing good observation checklists and schedules are complex and costly. Whenever quantitative observation data are needed, we advise going to the Simon and Boyer collection and adapting an instrument that already exists.

Qualitative observation depends less on available instruments and more on the evaluator or observer. Checklists may be used, but typically they are informal. Denzin (1978) has distinguished among the following arrangements for qualitative observation: the complete participant, the participant as observer, the observer as participant, and the complete observer. The most appropriate arrangement depends on the observer's role in the processes being observed.

Guba and Lincoln (1981) provide an excellent discussion of the evaluator as observer by describing various concerns and listing several methods of qualitative observation, including the following:

1. *Running notes*—a pad may be used to jot down observations as they occur.

2. *Field experience log or diary*—detailed notes on a particular concern, such as how a school principal organizes for a faculty meeting.

3. *Notes on themes*—detailed notes on a particular theme, such as how the building principal typically organizes for a faculty meeting.

4. *Chronologs*—a step-by-step running account over a unit of time (for example, a day).

5. *Context maps*—a diagram of the contextual layout in which observations take place.

6. *Taxonomies or category systems*—predetermined categories for which instances are sought in open-ended fashion.

7. *Schedules*—specified place, times, duration of observation, and method of notation for the observation.

8. *Sociometrics*—relational diagrams indicating social intercourse.

9. *Panels*—periodic observations of the same persons over time.

10. *Debriefing questionnaires*—completed by the observers, not the subjects of the observation.

11. *Unobtrusive methods*—use of concealed devices or indirect measures.

The stages of qualitative observation often include (1) thorough preparation through reading or "chatting" with informants; (2) thinking out a point of view and establishing expectations before entering the setting; (3) looking *at* (not *for*) what occurs; (4) listening; (5) asking questions; (6) assimilating and synthesizing information; (7) checking working hypotheses; and (8) triangulating, confirming, and cross-checking.

On-site Evaluation Methods

The utility of site visits has made them a frequent requirement of funding for regulatory agencies. Though most frequently used for summative evaluation, or for educational or financial audits, on-site visits can also be very useful for formative evaluation (Worthen, 1983). Some of the advantages and deficits of site visits in evaluation are mentioned in the following observation by Stake:

> ...the *site visit* is a widely used evaluation method. When a large-scale program is under way at some distant place, the most common way to evaluate it is to appoint a small number of respected persons to go there and inspect it. This method receives a proper share of criticism. It is evident that the program staff works hard to make the operation atypically handsome during the visit and the visitors grasp at the slimmest shred of evidence for something to report. Despite these defects, the method of site visits deserves its eminence because it is designed for the most sensitive instruments available: experienced and insightful men. Furthermore, it is capable of quick adaptation to local circumstances. Its failings could be remedied by heeding Helen Peak's advice: train (even briefly) the visitors and provide a set of standardized scales for directing visitor attention for describing what is seen. (Stake, 1970, pp. 192–193)

An on-site visit is often only one facet of an overall evaluation design, and exclusive reliance on site-visit data is usually unwise. Site visits can be profitably combined with mailed questionnaire surveys, student testing, attitude measurement, and other methods described in this chapter. When site visits are preceded by other data-collection methods, they will often provide clues to possible problems or issues that can be probed during the on-site visit by use of interviews or observations.

Site visits range from brief, informal observations by one professional to extended, rigorous probing by a team of professionals. The comprehensiveness and thoroughness of a site-visit evaluation depends mainly on the time and personnel available to conduct the visit.

Inadequate preparation limits the usefulness of many site visits. Completing the following activities will greatly enhance the success of the visit itself.

1. *Identifying specific information needed*
2. *Developing evaluation questions* to be posed during on-site interviews
3. *Developing on-site instruments* (for example, interview forms, checklists, or rating scales)
4. *Selection of on-site visitor(s)*
5. *Previsit communications and arrangements*
6. *Conducting the on-site evaluation visit,* considering
   a. Amount of time to be spent on site
   b. An initial on-site team meeting, prior to meeting with on-site administrators or staff, to reemphasize the purpose, procedures, and expected products of the visit
   c. An initial briefing by site administrator(s) and/or staff to orient the team to specific nuances or idiosyncratic information not readily available in previsit materials
   d. Efficient interviewing and observation by splitting the team up to cover more activities or interviewees, having the entire team together only for key events or interviews with key personnel
   e. Interspersed team meetings to debrief and share impressions, and a final team formulation of their overall evaluation
   f. Exit interview with the site administrator(s) and, if appropriate, site staff
7. *Writing, disseminating, and using the final report of the on-site evaluation.*

For a comprehensive, detailed discussion of on-site evaluation guidelines and procedures, evaluators are referred to Worthen and White (1986). That text includes examples of on-site evaluation interview forms, rating scales, previsit information forms, team-training materials, and sample exit and final reports.

Unobtrusive Measurements

An unfortunate side effect of many information-collection methods is that subjects alter their behavior when they know information is being collected about or from them.

Webb and others (1966) suggest many ways to get around this reaction, including reliance on the following data sources:

1. *Physical traces*—physical evidence left from some past behavior. Such evidence would include natural erosion (worn carpeting in front of a particular painting in

an art museum), natural accretion (deposits of information such as creative work done by past civilizations), controlled erosion measures (such as pre- and post-measures of shoe wear on children), and controlled accretion measures (such as lightly sealing with glue the pages of a book to detect how many and which pages are read).

2. *Archival records*—the ongoing, continuing records of society, including actuarial records, political and judicial records, government records, and mass media files.

3. *Private records*—those not ordinarily left open to the public, including sales records, institutional records, and written documents such as diaries.

4. *Contrived observation*—the use of hardware devices for observation (video-tapes, audiotapes). When hardware devices are used, they should be a familiar part of the environment, or hidden, if reactivity is to be minimized.

Metfessel and Michael (1967) also inventoried alternative ways of unobtrusively collecting information about educational outcomes. Their list of unobtrusive indicators includes attendance records, anecdotal records, appointments, news items, assignments, awards, program changes, citations, disciplinary actions, dropouts, grades, groupings, leisure activities, library cards, PTA participation, and even telephone calls from parents or other interested parties.

Guba and Lincoln (1981) have extended earlier discussions of unobtrusive measurement to applications in naturalistic evaluations.

One word of caution: Unobtrusive measures tend to be unreliable. Never base a conclusion on just one measurement. Always triangulate, confirm, and cross-check.

Delphi Technique

A variant of survey procedures for collecting group consensus and judgmental data is the *Delphi technique*, in which a panel of experts responds independently to a mailed set of questions. A follow-up report to the panel summarizes responses, using the median and interquartile range as descriptive statistics for the responses to each original question. Each panel member also receives a reminder of how he responded to each of the original questions. He is asked to compare his first response to the panel summary and revise any response if he desires. If his second response is outside the interquartile range, he is asked to justify his deviation from the panel's majority judgment. Then, in a third-round questionnaire, the second-round responses are summarized together with a summary of the reasons listed by deviants for their positions. Each panel member is asked to reconsider his second-round responses, given the results and reasons yielded from that round.

A respondent who desires to remain outside the interquartile range on the third round is asked to present his reasons. This iterative procedure can continue for several more rounds, but the payoff usually begins to diminish quickly after the third round. On the final round, panel members are asked to revise their responses one last time, given the results and arguments yielded by the previous round.

This procedure has been used by management to attain consensus from a panel of experts. A variation of the procedure has used committee meetings to obtain convergence after the first round. This is also a procedure that the evaluator may find useful in the early stages of program development when commitments on selected developmental goals must be made. References for further information about the Delphi technique include Helmer (1967) and Hencley and Yates (1974).

Q-sort

A technique for evaluating needs and objectives, frequently mentioned in recent papers on formative evaluation, is the *Q-sort*. Methods for collecting appraisal or judgmental data from relevant groups on simply and tersely stated needs or objectives is used in evaluation to determine group judgments. The procedures developed by Stephenson (1953), labeled *Q methodology*, are appropriate for this purpose.

Briefly, a Q-sort uses lists of need statements or goal (objective) statements that have been assigned numerals, placed on cards, and ranked according to some predetermined rules. The ordinal data that result from the sorts may be analyzed to yield a number of useful statistics, including the following:

1. Consistency or homogeneity of ranking within a group (indicating what degree people agree in their perceptions about needs or objectives).

2. Overall (and subgrouped) rankings (or sets of priorities) on the list of needs or objectives (and also the variance for each need or objective statement).

3. Differences in ranking profiles among groups of persons (for example, a summary of differences among a school board, the school teachers, the school administrators, and parents on the priorities or values assigned to a list of needs of objectives).

4. Clusters of needs or objectives as ranked by a given group.

5. Clusters of persons as they rank needs or objectives (for example, do Republicans and Democrats cluster differently on their priorities?).

6. Similarity of the distribution of rankings by a group of persons to an ideal or criterion distribution (for example, are teachers normally distributed in their rankings of objectives for school improvement?).

There are two basic types of Q-sort—structured and unstructured—and each has a particular use. A *structured Q-sort* includes a set of rules whereby a certain number of cards (needs or objectives) must be placed in each of a certain number of piles (for instance, left-hand piles for most valuable and right-hand piles for least valuable needs or objectives). Sorting is forced into a predetermined distribution, according to some theory.

In an *unstructured Q-sort*, there is no underlying theory, and a person is asked merely to place the cards into a predetermined number of piles according to his own perceptions. This approach, in essence, "lets the cards fall where they may."

Collecting Q-sort data generally includes the following steps:

1. Place unambiguous statements of needs or objectives on cards, one to a card. Theoretically, at least 75 but no more than 140 items should be sorted.

2. Shuffle or randomly order the cards and give them to someone to sort. The same random order should be given to each person.

3. Sort the cards into some predetermined distribution. Usually 7 to 13 piles of cards are used, but this can be modified, depending on the needs of the investigator. For example, if 80 items were to be sorted into a somewhat normal distribution, the instruction might be to sort the cards into 9 piles, with the left-most pile representing most valuable needs or objectives and the right-most pile representing least valuable needs or objectives, and the number in each pile set as follows:

4   6   10   12   16   12   10   6   4

4. Collect the cards as sorted by the person and assign ranks to the cards in each pile (for example, a value of "1" to cards in the left-most pile and "10" to cards in the right-most pile).

5. Calculate desired statistics on resultant data.

Content Analysis

In reviewing documents, content analysis procedures have much to offer. Informal content analysis provides qualitative summaries of documents. Formal content analysis seeks to quantify content objectively, according to explicitly formulated rules and mutually exclusive and exhaustive categories. The content analyst actually counts *coding units* (for example, words, themes, paragraphs) and places them within the categories. A sample set of categories (Sanders & Cunningham, 1974) reflecting themes in newspaper articles on sex education is shown in Figure 18.1.

Content analysis has many uses in evaluation. Thematic analyses of board meetings or editorials in professional journals or word counts on federal policy statements can help identify and clarify values in an objective way no other source can match. Detailed discussions of content analysis may be found in Budd, Thop, and Donohew (1967), Holsti (1969), Grobman (1972), Krippendorff (1980), and Guba and Lincoln (1981).

Sampling

Sampling is drawing a portion of a target population for observation. If we were to test only a portion of the children in a state, we would be sampling. We could then use data from the sample to make inferences about the characteristics of the entire target population (in this case, all the children in the state).

A *sampling unit* is an element or collection of elements in the target population. Within a given state, sampling units could be pupils, classrooms, schools, school districts, or regions. Care must be taken to select a sampling unit that is consistent with the element about which one would like to make inferences. That is, if we want to draw conclusions about individual schools, we should use schools as the sampling unit.

A *sample design* is the plan by which a sample is to be drawn. This is to be distinguished from *sample selection*, which is the actual drawing and listing of specific sampling units to be observed.

A *sampling frame* is the list, map, directory, or other source in which sampling units are defined and from which a set of units are selected. If the target population were all small elementary schools (fewer than 200 children) in Iowa, our sampling frame would be a list or directory of those schools.

It is vital to select the best approach for any given situation, so that bias can be controlled and accurate inferences made. The most common sampling approaches in educational evaluation are these three:

1. *Haphazard sampling.* In haphazard sampling, elements are drawn on the basis of accessibility, with little concern for the composition of the sample as a whole. If

Newspaper:	Date:	Story Source:

− (Negative)	+ (Positive)
Expressions of opposition to sex education	Expressions favoring sex education
Actions in opposition to sex education	Actions in support of sex education
Statements attacking proponents of sex education	Statements supporting proponents of sex education
Statements listing opponents of sex education	Statements listing proponents of sex education
Provisions of alternate plans	Statements opposing alternate plans
Some other plan satisfactory	Authorities insist on current objectives
Miscellaneous−	Miscellaneous+

0 (Neutral)	Other themes
School board to discuss issue	
School board vote to be close	
Possible areas of compromise	
Miscellaneous	

Content totals	Headline	Headline Content
+ _____	Head size _____	(+1, −1, or 0)
− _____	Location on page _____	
0 _____	Length _____	
	Total score and direction _____	

FIGURE 18.1 Sample Set of Content Analysis Categories

Source: Sanders & Cunningham, 1974.

we were to select the first four people coming into a classroom for our sample, regardless of who they were, we would be drawing a haphazard sample. Conclusions about a whole population based on haphazard sample are very likely to be erroneous.

2. *Judgment sampling.* In this approach, a sample is drawn based on expert judgment or "best guesses" about which units may best reflect the characteristics of a population. If we were to choose three rural schools that, in our estimation, were like the typical rural schools in the state of Florida, we would be drawing a judgment sample. Making inferential leaps from judgment samples is risky business that rarely lands one on solid footing.

3. *Probability sampling.* In this approach, the sample is drawn based on selection probabilities assigned to every unit in the sampling frame. These probabilities need not be equal, but the most common type of probability sampling (random sampling) does use the assignment of equal probabilities. Most large assessment projects (for example, the United States' National Assessment of Education Progress) use probability sampling.

References to comprehensive discussions of sampling include Cochran (1963), Kish (1965), and Jaeger (1984). We also recommend that the evaluator study the well-designed sampling procedures used by large-scale assessment projects, such as the National Assessment of Educational Progress (NAEP) or survey studies such as those conducted by the Institute for Social Research at the University of Michigan. Many existing sampling designs can be adopted or adapted by the evaluator. As a further aid, a guide to estimating sample size for common surveys has been developed by Krejcie and Morgan (1970).

Experimental and Quasi-Experimental Design Methods

Misuses of experimental designs have been legitimately criticized (Guba & Stufflebeam, 1968; Guba, 1969); yet we disagree with those who contend that the experimental paradigm is inapplicable in educational evaluations. Comparative experimental and quasi-experimental designs have legitimate and valuable uses in educational evaluation when effects of well-defined treatments need to be estimated.

Comparative studies can provide extremely useful evidence regarding the value of an intervention. Random or true comparative experiments assign subjects from a qualified pool for a study to one of several possible controlled treatments using a table of random numbers or some other random process. Pretests may be given to each group if the tests are nonreactive, but posttests are essential. Comparisons of posttest results across the groups can provide convincing evidence of intervention effects, as Boruch and Riecken (1975) have shown.

In response to those who argue that comparative experiments are not feasible in field studies, Cook and Campbell (1979) list several situations when randomized experiments or quasi-experiments are entirely appropriate and possible:

- When lotteries or other chance drawings are expected
- When demand outstrips supply

- When an innovation cannot be delivered in all units at once
- When experimental units can be temporarily isolated
- When experimental units are spatially separated or interunit communication is low
- When change is mandated and solutions are unknown
- When a tie can be broken
- When some persons express no preference among alternatives.

In comparative studies, two or more programs, products, or methods are compared on common criteria. For example, assume a public school system is planning to establish an elementary language program in Spanish. All but two sets of curriculum materials have been excluded on the basis of such considerations as cost or guaranteed availability of replacement materials. In addition to the two sets of printed materials still being considered, some teachers have expressed enthusiasm for a new conversational approach that uses no written materials whatever. A comparative study might be designed involving a random sample of six elementary schools in the district, with one of the three curriculum approaches randomly assigned to each school as the exclusive treatment there. The outcomes of the three Spanish curriculum approaches could be compared on such criteria as students' ability to converse in or read Spanish, and a judgment made as to which approach produces the best results. Obviously, this example is oversimplified because it ignores other possibly useful measures and criteria, treatment-aptitude interactions, weighting of criteria, and the like, but it should serve to illustrate the point.

Noncomparative or single-program evaluations obviously lack any comparison group. The focus of such evaluations is often internal and goal-directed, although neither of these is a requisite condition. Single-program evaluations are the most common type of evaluation conducted in education today. In the previous example, the school system would make a decision on some relevant basis (for example, reputation of publisher or cost) to try a particular approach to teaching Spanish. Objectives for the program might be carefully noted, the program implemented, and, after it had run its course, measures applied to see if it had attained its objectives. The program's success would not be judged according to how it compared with any other program, but simply according to how well it fulfilled its promise in meeting important objectives.

Both comparative and single-program paradigms are well entrenched in education, and each has its advocates and opponents. Cronbach takes the following stance:

> *The aim to compare one course with another should not dominate plans for evaluation.* To be sure, decision makers have to choose between courses, and any evaluation report will be interpreted in part comparatively. But formally designed experiments pitting one course against another are rarely definitive enough to justify their cost. . . .
>
> Ours is a problem like that of the engineer examining a new automobile. He can set himself the task of defining its performance characteristics and its dependability. It would merely be distracting to put his question in the form: "Is this car better or worse than the competing brand?" (Cronbach, 1973, pp. 48–49)

In a response to Cronbach, Scriven champions comparative evaluation, arguing that no automobile engineer ever has had or will have the pure interest Cronbach describes, adding:

> Objectives do not come "important" except in a context of practical choice.... The very measures of the performance and dependability of an automobile and our interest in them spring *entirely* from knowledge of what has and has not so far proved possible, or possible within a certain price-class, or possible with certain interior space, or with a certain overall weight, etc....
>
> The same applies in the field of curriculum development. We already have curricula aimed at almost every subject known to man, and there isn't any real interest in producing curricula for curricula's sake; to the extent that there is, there isn't any interest in evaluating them. We are interested in curricula because they may prove to be better than what we now have, in some important way. We may assign someone the task of rating a curriculum on certain variables, without asking them simultaneously to look up the performance of other curricula on these variables. But when we come to *evaluate* the curriculum, as opposed to merely describing its performance, then we inevitably confront the question of its superiority or inferiority to the competition. (Scriven, 1973, pp. 84–85)

Scriven (undated) also proposes the concept of "critical competitors" for educational evaluations, noting that the most important of all comparisons in evaluation is that between alternatives that use similar fiscal and human resources. Using *Consumer Reports* evaluations as an analog, Scriven describes the difficulty of selecting the most crucial comparisons, recounting the following:

> One of their most brilliant choices occurred when testing proprietary carpet cleaners; instead of just testing these against each other, they tossed a dilute solution of Tide into the race. It won in a canter, at less than one-tenth the price. Teachers have to be tested against texts (in their cognitive role); texts against television (when Children's Television Workshop efforts are irrelevant); live lectures against closed circuit television; CAI against programmed texts, etc. And more imaginative comparisons are important, against created competitors.
>
> ... I have frequently found that a push for what I've called a "cheapie version" of some very expensive product provides by far the best critical competitor to the original product. It also proves extremely unpalatable for the producers to work up such versions. But trimming off the gingerbread often cuts the price in half and rarely has much effect on teaching effectiveness.... There's no doubt that pushing for these things encourages the evaluator's reputation as a bean counter, nitpicker, or cost accountant-type. But then the value of an evaluator is not to be found in his image but in the educational gains he can facilitate. (Scriven, undated, pp. 29, 33)

We could extend the productive and provocative dialogue among Cronbach, Scriven, and others on this point. But the appropriateness of comparative, experimental paradigms depends on—among other things—the questions to be answered and the resources available. Obviously, comparative studies are sometimes impractical or irrelevant to the questions posed (for example, in some internal formative evaluations). Unfortunately, many appropriate opportunities to conduct comparative evaluations are lost because educators view "comparative experiments" as useless or even harmful.[102] The experimental paradigm has a place in educational evaluation *if* used properly. Negative perceptions typically stem from instances where comparisons have been unintelligently conducted by those who misunderstood the methodology. As evaluators learn to structure alternatives in more useful ways, the reputation of experimental evaluation should improve among decision-makers.

The best references for detailed discussion of experimental and quasi-experimental design methods and the analysis of information that they yield may be found in Campbell and Stanley (1966), Boruch (1976), and Cook and Campbell (1979).

AN OVERVIEW OF TWO ADDITIONAL METHODS FOR COLLECTING EVALUATION INFORMATION

In this section we will look at two less commonly used methods that have received relatively little attention but are nonetheless useful. They are *investigative journalism* and *goal-free evaluation*.

Investigative Journalism Methods

Guba (1981a, 1981b) notes that investigative reporting, which can focus on both *events* and *processes*, requires disclosure of information that may be secret, inaccessible, not easily observed, or hard to discover. Investigative journalism is ostensibly done in the public interest and requires great personal effort on the part of the reporter. It is evident there are a few parallels between educational evaluation and investigative reporting.

What can the educational evaluator learn from investigative journalism? Guba (1981a) suggests that evaluators pay heed to these journalistic methods and principles:

1. *Pursuing a variety of sources of information.* Many evaluation studies depend on information from one or a handful of traditional sources. Yet, it is clear to the investigative reporter that the most critical information often comes from nontraditional sources. Investigative journalists depend not only on routine information sources but also on tips, repetitive questioning of sources, leg work (getting out and seeing people), insights gained from other investigations, their own observations and experiences, conversations with contradictory sources, and the like. "Truth," for the journalist, evolves through multiple, not limited, sources.

2. *Decision points.* Several times during most inquiry activities, the investigator asks, "Should I continue?" One must be willing to abort a study if it becomes evident that the payoff will not justify the cost of continuing.

3. *The "fast study."* Investigative journalists immerse themselves quickly in the context of their inquiry. Evaluators too must learn to assimilate background information rapidly—to "get smart" and learn the territory early.

4. *Key interviews.* Interviews with key actors in the study should be characterized by (1) preparation—full background briefing, logical, organized questions, and preparation with at least one other interviewer (be sure to define roles and responsibilities); (2) control—ensuring that the interviewer remains in control throughout; and (3) information collection—not only checking existing information but also ferreting out new and elusive details.

5. *Reporting.* Selecting themes, checking accuracy, and arranging follow-up are important tasks for the reporter and evaluator. Like the reporter, the evaluator should ask

- What is this story about?
- Who cares?
- Why will my primary audience care?

6. *Skepticism.* It is often realistic to suspect that people may be selectively providing or even withholding information. The reporter uses this skepticism to advantage as a motivator for checking additional sources, probing, questioning, and verifying all facts. The evaluator, too, can make his skepticism work to his advantage.

7. *Use of records.* Contrary to popular belief, not all public records are legally open to the public. Not all evaluators know how to locate or access records, though like reporters they need this skill. The concept of tracking and using records does have a parallel in Scriven's (1974a) modus operandi method.

8. *Confrontation.* Sometimes it is necessary to take the offensive if information is being withheld. Some techniques used by reporters include

- Increasing the specificity of questions.
- Showing documentation that supports allegations.
- Demonstrating contradictions as they occur.
- Registering indignation if an interviewer is lying or continues to do so.
- Shifting gears if the confrontation becomes too heated (changing topics or switching to another interviewer).

9. *Dealing with constraints.* Investigators need to recognize and work within certain constraints. Some common constraints in investigative reporting include

- Resources (time, staff, budget, lost opportunities).
- Law (libel, slander, censorship, access to data).
- Attitudes among management (the boss may want to avoid controversy or negative public response).
- Attitudes among reporters (unwillingness to offend, personal pressures, peer pressure, lack of stamina).
- Skills (lack of training, experience, ability).
- Hazards (physical, psychological, legal harassment).
- Provincialism (lack of trust in work done by others).

10. *Circling, shuffling, and filling.* In order to extend and check information, the investigator may (1) run information obtained from one source past cooperative informants for refutation or confirmation (circling); (2) run information obtained from one source past others who are assumed to be uncooperative, pressing for details, asking what *really* did happen, and then passing new information by other informants (shuffling); or (3) build boundaries around a subject area and then fill in the gaps (filling).

For a comprehensive treatment of the use of investigative journalism in educational evaluation, the reader is referred to Guba (1981a) and Nelson (1982).

Goal-Free Evaluation Methods

As noted briefly in Chapter 5, goal-free evaluation (GFE) is the evaluation of interim and ultimate *outcomes*, regardless of whether they were intended. Scriven (1978) states that goal-free evaluation involves conducting an evaluation of outcomes without the evaluator being exposed to, or contaminated by, awareness of the purposes or goals.

Interest in studying side effects in evaluation did not originate with Scriven's proposal of GFE. He and other specialists in evaluation had noted earlier a need to attend to side effects (Scriven, 1967; Glass, 1969) or unintended outcomes (Cronbach, 1963; Stake, 1967) as well as to the objectives of educational programs. It was Scriven, however, who coined the term *goal-free evaluation* and articulated and popularized the concept.

Scriven did not propose that GFE be the only strategy used to evaluate a program's worth; other evaluative data (including objectives-referenced data) should also be used. His point was that goal-free information would be less subject than goal-based information to contamination by the evaluator's prior knowledge of program goals, and that it should *supplement* rather than replace other goal-based evaluation methods.

Scriven's approach to GFE *forces the evaluator into serious needs assessment*. The evaluator does not look to see if the performance matches the project director's goals. Instead, criteria against which the project is compared reflect the needs of the target population.

Thus, GFE begins when the evaluator and client first meet. Assuming interest, the first consideration is the feasibility of using GFE. The evaluator should avoid any questions that would lead the client to disclose the goals or objectives of the project. Instead, the evaluator must determine the context and scope of the project being evaluated by asking questions like these:

1. *Where is the project being implemented?* If the project is being implemented in inaccessible sites or over a wide geographical area, then the goal-free approach may not be feasible.

2. *How long has the project been running? How long will it run?* If the project has been running a long time, or is almost over, the goal-free approach may not be appropriate.

3. *What is the total number of participants in the project?* The number of participants gives the evaluator some indication of the relative size of the project and corresponding budget and personnel requirements.

4. *What are the evaluation's cost constraints?* Determining cost constraints early is essential in assessing feasibility. For instance, the GFE may require site visitations that prove prohibitively costly given available resources.

5. *Can written permission and site-access be obtained?* If not, the goal-free approach may not be feasible.

6. *What other evaluation work is planned?* In most cases, the GFE approach should be used in conjunction with other evaluation strategies.

If GFE seems feasible, staffing and designing the study are the next steps. Besides the evaluator, GFE calls for a project manager and, depending on the size of the project, several observers. Hiring staff with a variety of relevant experiences is advisable because it adds credibility and validity to the evaluation report. In particular, observers need experience related to the object of evaluation. For example, evaluation of a project for children in grades K–6 requires observers who are knowledgeable and experienced in elementary education. Training sessions should be used before actual field work to develop observation skills and calibrate observers.

Data–collection procedures should be standardized so that observers are directed to gather comparable data (for example, file data on school curricula and student characteristics; teacher responses to a structured interview about students' attitudes, special problems that affect students' physical, social, or mental development). Observational procedures should ensure comparable and comprehensive data across settings. Observer bias can be controlled in part by insisting that all observations be documented and confirmed by a second observer.

The first consideration in actual field work is collecting baseline and/or comparison group data. All observers should participate. By comparing preimplementation data with data collected during project implementation, and by comparing comparison group data with those collected for the treatment group, the goal-free evaluators can begin to formulate hypotheses about any changes the project has brought about. As new data are gathered, these hypotheses can be modified or dismissed. It is important to record each hypothesis and to trace the reasons for either supporting or dismissing it. Treatment findings and effects may then be contrasted with the intents or goals of the product during the analysis phase of the GFE.

When field–data collection begins, copies of all documents pertaining to the project (including statements of agreement, press releases, minutes of meetings, and so on) should be requested and "filtered" by the project manager to the goal-free evaluator, with both explicit and implicit goal statements expunged.

Following the baseline observations, the goal-free evaluator should arrange multiple observations/ratings by different staff members for each project document or site. These should be done not only by different observers at the same time but also across time (for example, same classrooms before, during, and after treatment). Multiple observations help the goal-free evaluator estimate interobserver reliability and increase the validity of the final report by allowing cross-checks and triangulations. Observers would be well-advised to make observations for a period of time (say, 20 to 30 minutes) before and after treatment, whenever possible.

Observers who work in pairs should *not* be allowed to discuss their observations until that day's written reports have been completed. Even then, discussions should be limited to the GFE design and should not reveal the substance of the observations. This assures independent perspectives. Likewise, if staff members rate various products, they should not discuss those products until after reports have been turned in.

As reports are turned in, it is the project manager's duty to review and organize them for writing a preliminary report. They should be reviewed by the project manager as soon as they are submitted to see if the instrument design can be improved. The manager should also look for patterns that might be verified by field observers—hiring extra consultants if necessary. Translating noticeable patterns into working hypotheses is a critical step. Once all observations or ratings are completed, all staff members should help synthesize and draft the preliminary report. Only after that report has been completed should information on program goals be disclosed to GFE staff.

The last step in GFE is the *reversal* phase; here GFE staff inspect various background materials, guidelines, products, aims, and objectives of the project and contrast them with the goal-free report as a means of comparing what actually happened with what was originally intended. The idea is that one can obtain most of the advantages of a goal-based evaluation *after* completing a goal-free initial phase. The initial report is not revised on the basis of this review; rather, the goal-free evaluator uses any additional information in completing the final GFE report.

Noted in the report will be a list of working hypotheses developed during the GFE, along with the reasons for their support or dismissal. Contrasts between the supported hypotheses and the stated intended outcomes of the project should be noted. Objectives of the project for which few results were observed should also be noted. Finally, possible contaminations of the goal-free process should be noted, along with any limitations of the study. The final reporting step should include a discussion with all individuals involved in the GFE, with opportunity for them to examine openly GFE findings and conclusions and to revise the report or append further information as warranted by the discussion and review.

For more complete discussions of GFE, the reader is referred to Scriven (1972, 1974a, 1978).

CASE STUDY APPLICATION

January 15. I'm beat tonight, having spent all day working on instruments and procedures for collecting the data we agreed to collect for the Radnor evaluation. Thinking is tiring work.

But the day was productive. I was able to get several instruments developed, in first draft form at least. Did review Buros's *Mental Measurement Yearbook* and the social psychology handbook of tests and found some possibly useful tests for humanities knowledge, and ordered specimen sets of those. Picked up a possible instrument for testing critical thinking also. But for the most part, it looks like a do-it-yourself instrument development effort. So far I have completed a first draft of the following:

• interview schedules for students, teachers, parents, and board members, using the questions I know so far to be important; I'll probably add others suggested by the site-visit team of experts, once they're selected.

- a classroom observation instrument (this one is hurting; I am comfortable with the parts dealing with general classroom stuff like attention, time-on-task, etc., but am still fuzzy about what to look for relating to humanities, per se. Guess it's time to call good old Dewey Pitcher again. Maybe he'll help me once more if I promise to quit teasing him about the unfortunate ways some of his faculty keep abbreviating his title).

- both a Likert scale and a semantic differential to get at some of the attitudinal stuff—thought I'd try both out with the Radnor staff before I decide on one.

- a very rough draft of some criterion-referenced tests, mostly useful, I suspect, as a starting place to work with the Radnor humanities faculty—even though I pulled the concepts from their materials, I'm not certain my items reflect the concepts they view as important.

- variations of a questionnaire that I hope will get at a lot of opinions and factual information that might otherwise fall through the cracks. People who dash off casual questions surely fall under the "ignorance is bliss" rubric. By the time I'd torn up my third draft today, I was almost wishing I had never minored in sociology.

Didn't get around to worrying about just how I will go about using existing records or unobtrusive measures, but I will before we fire off our salvo of data-collection techniques. Right now I'm more concerned with getting the draft instruments off for the Radnor folks to review.

Author Comments. Were I actually to conduct this evaluation, I would turn quickly to Buros's *Mental Measurements Yearbooks* or other collections that may contain well-developed instruments relevant to some of the data-collection needs. Even though I am never too optimistic about finding just the right instrument, I suspect useful instruments on variables such as critical thinking, writing and language arts, and attitudes toward different cultural groups and ethnicity could be located in these sources.

Even if one did not find usable instruments, there is a high probability of finding useful strategies and formats for asking questions that will make instrument design an easier task.

Where no instruments exist—and I suspect that would be the case for most of the specific content of the humanities curriculum—homemade (do not misread that as *carelessly* made) cognitive measures would need to be fashioned. How to construct those with an eye to validity and other technical considerations is another day's tale. Suffice it to say here that I would work closely with the humanities faculty and members of the humanities study committee in designing those instruments. That not only assures relevance, but it also is an excellent way to build rapport and trust with those whose program is being evaluated. I would also pilot drafts of the resulting criterion-referenced instruments with small samples of students. The strategy for designing affective measures would be similar.

Although student measures are often viewed as the most difficult to construct, the most poorly designed instruments in most educational evaluations are usually questionnaires or interview schedules. If one traces the professional genealogy of most educational evaluators, their parentage is frequently found to consist of educational and psychological methodologists. Small wonder that our evaluators seem to have inherited an ancestral sneer toward mailed questionnaire surveys or interview studies. Most educational and psychological methodologists have long misunderstood (or worse, never studied) the data-collection methods and strategies of the sociometrician and are more likely to mistake Kornhauser and Sheatsley for a law firm rather than recognizing them as authors of a very useful set of guidelines for designing good mailed questionnaires. Rather than expanding on a pet peeve here, let me simply indicate that the design of good questionnaires and interview schedules is a task that demands every bit as much time and creativity as the design of more traditional cognitive and affective measures.

April 20. Sorry, journal, for the neglect, but these past few months have been "the pits," as my son would say. My heaviest teaching load always comes during winter and spring, so, with the addition of the Radnor contract I took on, this year my cup "runneth over," so to speak. But so did the river—with a flood unlike anything ever seen in this country. The mountain snowfall this winter was over 200 percent of normal, and when the Spring thaw hit, half our valley was under water, or so it seemed. As chairman of our community's Emergency Preparedness Committee, I lost a good part of several weeks coordinating sand-bag efforts, etc. Governor M. is right when he says this is surely a poor way to run a desert! Who would have thought that I'd welcome the shuttle flights back and forth to Pennsylvania just so I could get away from here long enough to get my feet dry?

Anyway, things are nearly back to normal; the river is back in its banks, and I'm catching up. The Radnor evaluation is almost on schedule, and the data-collection effort is nearly completed. The site visit is the only major evaluation activity still ahead, and it appears my idea of having the humanities experts on that team also to do the expert review of the humanities curriculum materials will work out well. No hitches in the testing or attitude measurement, and the second follow-up on the mailed survey of parents and community leaders has boosted the response rate over 70 percent, and still climbing. Guess there is some genuine interest in this program to get that good a response rate (or perhaps we've just been good nags). I'd rather work to get a good response rate than have to fall back on checking nonresponse bias any day.

Anyway, as soon as we get the last data in, we'll be able to start thinking about analysis and reporting. Of course, we're getting a pretty good picture already about opinion data, etc., from the interviews, and we'll soon know what the experts think. But I'll try to keep an open (don't read that as empty) mind until all the data are in and analyzed.

Author Comments. Most of the information-collection activities I might actually have conducted in an evaluation of this type can be readily inferred from the evaluation plan outline in Chapter 15, but three comments may be helpful.

First, it is important to capitalize on what is known about survey methods if one intends to obtain an adequate response rate to a mailed questionnaire. There exists a body of literature on how to increase response rates (see Worthen & Valcarce, 1985, for information and references in this area). In addition, it would be important to know and use appropriate techniques for assessing whether respondents and nonrespondents differ significantly on relevant variables that might bias the results.

Second, little has been said about observation within classrooms; yet I would see that as a pivotal part of the study. Here I would want the humanities specialist(s) to accompany me, or perhaps take the lead. The evaluator should be able to get a fairly good feel for the classroom climate, the effectiveness of the instruction, whether the curriculum objectives were being translated into learning activities for students, and how students react to those activities. The humanities expert is needed, however, to get at the more subtle nuances to judge whether what students are learning in the classroom is really the essence of what is important for them to know about the humanities.

Finally, although I may nowhere label it as such, a data-collection effort such as that outlined here is obviously an instance of multiple-method, multiple-source evaluation.

APPLICATION EXERCISE

1. Recheck your worksheets from Chapter 15. Are there plans that you would like to change, using what you just learned in this chapter? Would you want to add procedures? Approach things a little differently?
2. Develop a chart, listing each of the methods covered in this chapter, and then for each describe some types of information that might be collected with its use.

SUGGESTED READINGS

BERDIE, D., & ANDERSON, J. (1974). *Questionnaires*. Metuchen, NJ: Scarecrow Press.

BORG, W. R., & GALL, M. D. (1983). *Educational research: An introduction* (4th ed.). New York: Longman.

DEMALINE, R., & QUINN, W. (1979). *Hints for planning and conducting a survey and a bibliography of survey methods*. Kalamazoo, MI: Western Michigan University Evaluation Center.

GORDON, R. L. (1975). *Interviewing strategy, techniques, and factors*. Homewood, IL: Dorsey Press.

GUBA, E. G. (1981b). Investigative reporting. In N. L. SMITH (Ed.), *Metaphors for evaluation: Sources of new methods* (pp. 67–87). Beverly Hills, CA: Sage.

GUBA, E. G., & LINCOLN, Y. S. (1981). *Effective evaluation*. San Francisco: Jossey-Bass.

HENCLEY, S. P., & YATES, J. R. (Eds.). (1974). *Futurism in education*. Berkeley, CA: McCutchan.

HOPKINS, K. D., & STANLEY, J. C. (1981). *Educational and psychological measurement and evaluation*. Englewood Cliffs, NJ: Prentice-Hall.

ISAAC, S., & MICHAEL, W. B. (1981). *Handbook in research and evaluation*. San Diego, CA: Edits.

JAEGER, R. M. (1983). *Statistics: A spectator sport*. Beverly Hills, CA: Sage.

JAEGER, R. M. (1984). *Sampling in education and the social sciences*. New York: Longman.

MEHRENS, W. A., & LEHMANN, I. J. (1969). *Standardized tests in education*. New York: Holt, Rinehart, & Winston.

NELSON, D. E. (1982). Investigative journalism methods in educational evaluation. In N. L. SMITH (Ed.), *Field assessments of innovative evaluation methods*. New Directions in Program Evaluation, No. 13. San Francisco: Jossey-Bass.

SCRIVEN, M. (1974a). Evaluation perspectives and procedures. In W. J. POPHAM (Ed.), *Evaluation in education* (pp. 1–93). Berkeley, CA: McCutchan.

WEBB, E. J., CAMPBELL, D. T., SCHWARTZ, R. D., & SECHREST, L. (1966). *Unobtrusive measures: Nonreactive research in the social sciences.* Chicago: Rand McNally.

WORTHEN, B. R., & WHITE, K. R. (1986). *Evaluating educational and social programs: Guidelines for proposal reviews, onsite evaluation, evaluation contracts, and technical assistance.* Boston: Kluwer–Nijhoff.

Chapter 19

Analyzing and Interpreting Evaluation Information

Orienting Questions

1. How can you look for patterns and draw defensible conclusions from all the information an evaluation study generates?
2. What must you consider when deciding how to analyze evaluation data?
3. How can evaluation findings be interpreted so that the most relevant perspectives have been used?
4. How do you analyze program costs?

Evaluations involve processing mountains of information that—if not organized in a form that permits meaningful interpretation—is often worthless, or worse yet, misleading.

The aim of *data analysis* is to reduce and synthesize information—to "make sense" out of it—and to allow inferences about populations. The aim of *interpretation* is to combine the results of data analysis with value statements, criteria, and standards in order to produce conclusions, judgments, and recommendations. Both data analysis and interpretation rely on empirical and logical methods. Values, too, obviously play a major role in both.

We are concerned with analyzing and interpreting two general types of data: *qualitative* and *quantitative*. These terms are used to distinguish between the use of natural language (qualitative) and the use of numerical values (quantitative) to record observations. Each data type requires systematic analysis and interpretation.

In this chapter we discuss briefly how to analyze and interpret both qualitative and quantitative data, along with a special category, *cost data*. Most of the methods for extracting meaning from quantitative and qualitative data are adequately covered in books on data analysis and sources of information on cost analysis, to which we will direct the reader's attention. Our goal here is simply to map the terrain.

CONSIDERATIONS IN ANALYZING AND INTERPRETING EVALUATION INFORMATION

Methods for data analysis and interpretation should be selected at the time decisions are being made about how information will be collected and which questions or issues will guide the evaluation. All these evaluation activities work together. No one aspect of evaluation should be planned without thought to the others. And all parts should relate to the overall purpose of the evaluation.

When considering alternative methods for data analysis or interpretation, the evaluator should ask herself these questions:

1. What methods of data analysis and interpretation are appropriate for the *questions* I am trying to answer, the *information* that I plan to collect, and the *method* I will use to collect information?

2. What methods of data analysis and interpretation are most likely to be *understood* and to be *credible* to the audiences who will receive reports?

3. For quantitative data, what *measurement scale* should be used when observations are quantified, and which analysis methods are appropriate for such scales?

4. For qualitative data, how should observations be recorded?

5. Who should be involved in interpreting the results of data analysis?

The answers will help the evaluator select appropriate data analysis and interpretation methods. At this early stage of planning, the evaluator should also involve technical consultants, such as statisticians, if she feels they are needed.

METHODS USED FOR QUALITATIVE DATA ANALYSIS

Wilcox (1982) has noted that the analysis of qualitative data depends on the nature of the data and the conceptual framework employed in the analysis. Methods for qualitative data analysis range from narrative description to quantitative analyses of narrative components (for example, words, phrases, sentences, paragraphs, themes).

Analysis methods for qualitative data usually involve some form of analytic induction. Discussions of specific techniques such as the "key incident" approach (Wilcox, 1982), analysis in the field (Bogdan & Biklen, 1982), and searching for patterns and categories (Guba, 1978a; Guba & Lincoln, 1981; Patton, 1980; Bogdan & Biklen, 1982) have given evaluators direction in processing qualitative information.

The "key incident" approach described by Wilcox involves analyzing qualitative descriptions of educational incidents or events that the evaluator identifies as key incidents or concrete examples of an abstract principle. Erickson describes this approach as follows:

> This involves pulling out from field notes a key incident, linking it to other incidents, phenomena, and theoretical constructs, and writing it up so others can see the generic in

the particular, the universal in the concrete, the relation between part and whole. (Erickson, 1977, p. 16)

Wilcox notes that

the key incident approach may involve massive leaps of inference over many different kinds of data from different sources, including field notes, documents, elicited texts, demographic information, unstructured interviews, and so on. (Wilcox, 1982, p. 462)

The process of "analysis in the field," as described by Bogdan and Biklen (1982), directs the evaluator to spend time each day (some have estimated that one hour of data analysis for each hour of observation is realistic) reviewing field notes, reflecting on what has been learned and what merits further study, writing "observer's comments" into the field notes while experiences are still fresh, and writing short summaries about what is being learned. This continuous data analysis encourages the evaluator to draw tentative conclusions that can then be checked. Evidence supporting conclusions or validating facts can be gathered for use when reports are written.

Searching for patterns and categories is part of the analytic induction that undergirds all qualitative analysis. This search "builds levels of confidence" in the evaluation's ultimate conclusions through these steps:

1. *Exploring and forming impressions*, recorded in field notes.

2. *Identifying themes*, recorded in memos or short concept statements.

3. *Focusing and concentrating*, using "working hypotheses" as focal points for further observation and documentation. As these "working hypotheses" are "tested," those that are supported receive further attention, whereas those that are not supported are noted, along with the evidence used to reject them. Meanwhile, the exploring and forming of impressions (step 1 above) continues.

4. *Verification.* "Working hypotheses" are given the status of tentative conclusions; scenarios and thick, detailed descriptions are developed to make them come alive. These tentative conclusions are then tested for authenticity by the subjects in the study. Confirmation checks and triangulation are used to increase the certainty that these conclusions are accurate.

5. *Assimilation.* Conclusions are placed in the broader context of what else is known about the object of the evaluation.

Whereas much qualitative data analysis is conducted while the study is in progress, some analyses are delayed until after the evaluator leaves the field. Patton (1980) outlines several steps for processing the voluminous amount of qualitative data most evaluations will generate, including the following:

1. Make sure it is all there.

2. Make copies for safe storage, for writing on, and for cutting and pasting.

3. Organize the data into topics and files. (Bogdan & Biklen, 1982, suggest an excellent set of coding categories for this purpose. Guba, 1978a, Patton, 1980, and Guba & Lincoln, 1981, also discuss category systems for organizing qualitative data.)

4. Look for causes, consequences, and relationships. (Bodgan & Biklen, 1982, suggested using a cut-up-and-put-in-folders approach, or a card system.)
5. Validate the findings of the analysis, using
    a. examinations of rival explanations;
    b. reviews of negative cases (exceptions);
    c. triangulation; reconciling qualitative and quantitative data; comparing multiple qualitative data sources, and multiple perspectives from multiple observers;
    d. design checks (examining distortions due to design decisions);
    e. evaluator effects (reviewing distortions due to the evaluator's perspectives or behavior);
    f. quality of the data;
    g. reactions to reported data and analyses by stakeholders and subjects; and
    h. intellectual rigor (justification of conclusions).

For detailed discussions of qualitative data-analysis methods, the reader is referred to Miles and Huberman's (1984) text detailing methods for qualitative data analysis; Williams's (1986a) monograph on qualitative methods; entries concerning "making sense of qualitative data" in Filstead's (1981) bibliography; Bogdan and Taylor's (1975) introduction to qualitative research; and relevant articles by Becker (1958), Fienberg (1977), and Kennedy (1984).

METHODS USED FOR QUANTITATIVE DATA ANALYSIS

Once more we defer to the excellent textbooks available on data-analysis methods.

Easily read texts on quantitative data-analysis methods have been prepared by Hinkle, Wiersma, and Jurs (1979), Hopkins and Glass (1978), and Jaeger (1983). In addition, Hoaglin, Light, McPeek, Mosteller, and Stoto (1982) have published readable summaries of data-analysis methods useful in many recent large-scale studies.

Brinkerhoff and others (1983) have provided a succinct summary of data-analysis techniques that are frequently employed in evaluation.

METHODS USED FOR INTERPRETING EVALUATION INFORMATION

Data analysis focuses on organizing and reducing information and making statistical inferences; interpretation, on the other hand, attaches meaning to organized information and draws conclusions. Analysis may be thought of as organizing and verifying facts; interpretation as applying values, perspective, and conceptual ability to formulate supportable conclusions.

Interpretation should be characterized by careful, fair, open methods of inquiry. Anyone who claims that the "numbers speak for themselves" is either naive or a shyster.

Components of Interpreting Data Analyses

Interpretation means judging the object of the evaluation and considering the implications of those judgments. Recall that Stake's countenance model (discussed in Chapter 10) includes in the "judgment matrix" both *standards* and *judgments*. These are part of interpretation, but there is more.

The evaluator's perspective also influences her interpretation of the data. Perspective is a result of experience, of unique views and orientations developed over idiosyncratic life histories, and of a tendency to attend to certain details. Thus all interpretations, to some extent, are personal and idiosyncratic. Consequently, not only interpretations but the *reasons* behind them should be made explicit.

Conceptual ability can also affect interpretation. Each evaluator looks at the evaluation information, twists it around, discovers nuances, and generates insights—things that others may never have seen without the evaluator's help—in an individual way that affects the outcomes of the evaluation. If evaluation is to serve an educational function, as Cronbach and his associates (1980) claim, results must be interpreted so that audiences know how best to use or consider them.

Guidelines for Interpreting Data Analyses

Evaluators are just beginning to develop systematic methods of interpretation, and new methods will likely be generated in the future. Among those interpretation methods that have served well in the recent past are the following:[103]

1. Determining whether objectives have been achieved;
2. Determining whether laws, democratic ideals, regulations, or ethical principles have been violated;
3. Determining whether assessed needs have been reduced;
4. Determining the value of accomplishments;
5. Asking critical reference groups to review the data and to provide their judgments of successes and failures, strengths and weaknesses;
6. Comparing results with those reported by similar entities or endeavors;
7. Comparing assessed performance levels on critical variables to expectations of performance;
8. Interpreting results in light of evaluation procedures that generated them.

Interpretation of data analyses is not the sole province of the evaluator. No one is omniscient. Most evaluators have learned that interpreting and summarizing results in isolation is generally an unsound practice. The evaluator brings only one of many pertinent perspectives to bear and, in fact, is sometimes less well prepared to offer insightful interpretations than others who can look at the data through fresh eyes.

One method for bringing multiple perspectives to the interpretation task is to use *stakeholder meetings*. Small groups of five to eight people meet for several hours to discuss their interpretations of printouts, tables, charts, and other information collected and analyzed during the evaluation. Stakeholders can be supplied in advance with the results, along with other pertinent information such as the evaluation plan and the list of criteria, questions and issues that guided the evaluation; that way, meeting time can be devoted to discussion rather than presentation. At the meeting, findings are systematically reviewed in their entirety, with each participant interpreting each finding: for example, What does this mean? Is it good, bad, neutral? Consequential or inconsequential? What are the implications? What, if anything, should be done?

Besides contributing her own interpretations, the evaluator serves as transcriber so that all interpretations and the reasons for them can be recorded and included in the evaluation reports. These interpretative sessions not only capture diverse perspectives and original thinking but they also frequently disclose values previously undetected. All this contributes to the utility of the evaluation while assuring that those who should be involved are.

Other methods of interpretation suggested by the Joint Committee on Standards for Educational Evaluation (1981) include

- Having different teams write advocacy reports representing the various perspectives
- Conducting a jury trial or administrative hearing to review evidence concerning the object of the evaluation
- Seeking convergence of opinion about interpretation of results through use of a Delphi study.

Some additional useful guidelines suggested by Brinkerhoff and others (1983) for interpreting the results of analysis include the following:

1. Seeking confirmation and consistency with other sources of information;
2. Dealing with contradictory and conflicting evidence; not forcing consensus when none exists;
3. Not confusing statistical significance with practical significance (a point we shall discuss in detail shortly);
4. Considering and citing limitations of the analysis.

Some Common Misinterpretations of Evaluation Findings. Data-analysis results can be misinterpreted in myriad ways. One of the most common is to impute causation, based only on correlational data. In most areas of life, common sense limits impulsiveness. For example, when a medical study reports a significant *inverse relationship* between church attendance and serious coronary incidents, few people dash out to "get religion." They recognize that freedom from heart disease is more likely attributable to some other causal culprit (for example, life style, or abstinence from alcohol or drugs) than to religion per se. Yet, as Anderson and Ball point out, evaluators do not always seek out the underlying cause:

> some hard-pressed program evaluators have been tempted to draw causal inferences about programs from simple correlational status studies. . . . For example, when they obtain negative correlations between number of full-time aides in the classroom and pupil achievement, they conclude that aides are not worthwhile, without stopping to think that aides are likely to be assigned to classrooms where pupil achievement has already been determined to be low. Or they have looked at correlations between frequency of public

service TV "spots" and reductions in traffic accidents and conclude that the program was effective, without taking into account the gasoline shortage that occurred during the same period. (Anderson & Ball, 1978, p. 50)

Another common error is to confuse statistical significance with practical significance. For example, finding that a particular educational program produces statistically significant gains in students' achievement test scores only means that the finding is not likely to be a fluke. That is, the relationship between the program and the achievement scores is real. The gains may or may not be *educationally* significant; maybe they are great enough to warrant continuation of the program, maybe not.

Statistical significance is influenced by many factors, not the least of which is the sample size. The more observations or measurements included in the analysis, the more likely it is that observed differences will be found. The more critical question is whether these differences have any educational significance.

The evaluator can seldom judge educational significance alone; the client and other stakeholders who know what they want from the program are often in a better position to determine practical significance of the findings. For this reason, it is important that the evaluator provide an opportunity for various evaluation audiences to review and react to the findings and their educational impact.

For those who wish to pursue further the issue of statistical versus practical significance of research and evaluation results, Shaver (1985a, 1985b) has provided an excellent discussion. Porter, Schmidt, Floden, and Freemen (1978) have also provided a useful discussion of how to determine practical significance in program evaluations.

COST ANALYSIS

Educators are not econometricians and should not be expected to be skilled in identifying all the financial, human, or time costs associated with programs they operate. That leniency cannot extend to the evaluator, however, for it is her job to bring precise information on costs to the attention of developers, teachers, and administrators who are responsible for their products or programs. Educators are often faulted for choosing the more expensive of two equally effective programs— just because the expensive one is packaged more attractively or advertised more widely. The real fault lies with the program evaluations, which failed to consider cost along with the other variables. As any insightful administrator knows, sound decision making depends on knowing how much Program X will accomplish *at what cost*. Decision-makers should be fully aware not only of what they are gaining but also of what they are giving up.

Extensive discussions of cost analysis of education may be found in Levin (1981, 1983), Scriven (1974a, 1984), and Thompson (1980).[104] Wortman (1984), Smith and Smith (1985), Pezzino (1984), and St. John (1985) have provided useful reviews or analyses, and good illustrations of the application of various cost-analysis procedures can be seen in the work of Quinn, Van Mondfrans, and

Worthen (1984), Weinrott, Jones, and Howard (1982), and Franklin and Sparkman (1978). Despite the abundance of such information, cost analysis receives light treatment in most widely used texts on data analysis and evaluation in education. For this reason, we give separate treatment to it here.

The complexity of analyzing educational costs and benefits leads us to the conclusion that only well-defined, limited-scope cost analyses are possible in educational evaluation, given our current state-of-the-art methodology. We have found Levin's (1983) discussions of cost-benefit, cost-effectiveness, cost-utility, and cost-feasibility analyses to be a useful guide to what is possible.

Cost-benefit analysis is defined as the analysis of well-defined alternatives by comparing their costs and benefits when each is measured in monetary terms. Each alternative is examined to see if benefits exceed costs. The alternative with the highest benefit-to-cost ratio is then selected. Educational benefits are often translated into projected gains in earnings, or into the amount of money one would have to pay for educational services if they were not provided.

The disadvantage in cost-benefit analysis is that even measureable benefits are not always translatable into monetary terms. Only under certain circumstances (when it makes sense to talk about gains in earnings, for example) is cost-benefit analysis appropriate.

Cost-effectiveness analysis involves assessing the costs and effects of alternatives according to common outcomes. When selecting among alternatives for attaining a particular objective, this method would be the correct choice. It is among the most useful decision-making approaches in education. Under cost-effectiveness analysis, the alternative to be selected would be the one with the lowest cost per student gain in test score, per prevented dropout, or per some other appropriate criterion. Only alternatives with common goals and common measure of effectiveness can be compared using this method. Examples of effectiveness measures that may be analyzed using this method are listed by Levin (1983) as program completions, dropout reduction, employment placements, student learning, physical performance, and college placements.

Cost-utility analysis is used to analyze alternatives by comparing their costs and estimated utility. Estimated utility is a subjective estimate of the probability of a unit gain (for example, one grade-equivalent level) and of the value of the outcome (scored, for example, on a 0 to 10 scale). Expected utility can be calculated by multiplying the subjective probability by the estimated utility for each outcome associated with each alternative, then adding the products for each outcome for each alternative. The sum of the products for each alternative is then compared. The subjectivity of this method makes it hard to replicate and defend the results. It is a method that a planner might use, however, when time and data are minimal.

Cost-feasibility analysis is used to determine whether the costs of an alternative prohibit its consideration. The evaluator simply looks at the costs of each alternative and compares those costs to the available budget. Cost-feasibility studies should be conducted before too much has been invested in program development.

Levin (1983) provides the following set of questions that should help the evaluator judge the utility of cost-analysis reports in education:

1. What is the decision framework? What criteria will be used to guide the decision?
2. Which alternatives are considered?
3. How are costs estimated?
4. Are the costs analyzed according to who pays them? Are costs categorized by constituents?
5. Are costs presented in an appropriate mode?
6. Is the criterion of effectiveness appropriate?
7. Are there different effects across subpopulations?
8. Does the estimate of effects meet technical standards (for example, design, measurement, data-analysis standards?)
9. Are the cost comparisons appropriate?
10. How generalizable are the results to other settings?

We hope this brief discussion of cost analysis provides a sufficient overview to help the reader understand basic approaches and necessary steps. The sources cited in this section offer additional helpful information.

CASE STUDY APPLICATION

May 4. For once I believe I did something right. Remember all the time I spent last year planning for the analysis of all of the data that I would collect on the Radnor evaluation? Well it's paying off now. There is nothing more frustrating than to get to the end of a long and expensive data-collection effort only to find that certain controls or certain question formats should have been used to allow me to use the analysis techniques that I wanted to use. It's usually too late to go back and do it again by the time data analysis is begun. But this time things worked out well.

I've collected both quantitative and qualitative data in this evaluation, and thus used a variety of procedures for data analysis. Mrs. Janson asked how I would be analyzing the data, so I summarized that briefly and sent it off to her today.

Artifact No. 7

Data	Quantitative or Qualitative?	Techniques Used for Analysis
1. Interviews with students, teachers, parents, and board members	1. Qualitative and quantitative	1. Description statistics (means, standard deviations, frequency distributions) were used for the structured, standard questions. A content analysis and summary of response types with their frequencies were done for the qualitative, probing, and follow-up questions that were added to each interview.

Artifact No. 7 continued \

Data	Quantitative or Qualitative?	Techniques Used for Analysis
2. Classroom observations	2. Quantitative and qualitative	2. Descriptive statistics (again, means, standard deviations, and frequencies) were used to analyze data collected in each classroom on each dimension in my observation schedule. In addition, I had asked observers to write short, descriptive narratives about what went on in each classroom so that we could get a sense of what it was like to be there. I had two independent readers read these accounts and then list what they thought were important events or transactions. They then compared their analyses and resolved any differences between them. Both the full descriptions and the readers' analyses will be used in our reports.
3. Likert scale and semantic differential data on attitudes toward values and concepts taught in the curriculum.	3. Quantitative	3. There is some debate over whether data collected with such scales should be considered interval or ordinal. Being conservative, I treated these data as ordinal scale measurements and used medians and semi-interquartile ranges, plus frequency distributions to summarize item-by-item (scale-by-scale) responses. My factor analysis of the instruments revealed that several possible dimensions were present. It was tempting to report summary, summated ratings for each resulting dimension, but without further research on the instruments I was uncertain enough about stability of these dimensions so I avoided using them in the analysis.
4. Criterion-referenced test results	4. Quantitative	4. I had spent a lot of time pilot-testing the CRT items and was relatively confident that every item correlated highly with total test scores. My internal consistency (KR_{20}) for the test was high. I used the test to collect pre- and posttest data on participating classrooms

Artifact No. 7 (continued)

Data	Quantitative or Qualitative?	Techniques Used for Analysis
		and matched nonparticipating classrooms. An analysis of covariance was done to look for statistical significance. I also ran a *t*-test for dependent samples on the gain scores for participating and for nonparticipating students. Finally, I asked teachers to rate the practical significance of gains reflected in the descriptive statistics (means and standard deviations for participating students).
5. Survey questionnaires	5. Quantitative	5. All questions on my questionnaires were structured and standard for all respondents. I used frequencies and percentages to report responses on each individual question. I also looked at cross-tabulations, using chi-square tests for certain demographic variables crossed with the responses for certain questions.
6. Faculty analyses of curriculum; expert reviews of lesson plans and materials (from site visit)	6. Quantitative and qualitative	6. I used a standard analysis form for these analyses and then allowed reviewers to provide open-ended comments as well. Responses to the structured questions were summarized with frequency distributions and with the appropriate measure of central tendency and dispersion for each question (for example, mode/ median/mean, semi-interquartile range/standard deviation). There were so few on-site reviewers that I reported their open-ended comments verbatim in the report of my analyses.

Author Comments.   Several precautions are in order as the raw data from the instruments are prepared for data analysis. With the advent of desk-top micro-computers, it is possible to do most of the analyses right in the office. No need exists to remove the raw data from the office, and a strict policy of keeping the data secure is in place. Before any data can be entered into the computer, a coding handbook should be developed and checked by a colleague. After each form has been coded and entered, a printout of the entered data should be prepared and checked for accuracy. Format statements in the statistical software program should always be checked by a colleague to make sure the data are being read as intended. Finally, the numbers on the printouts should be checked to make sure they are reasonable and within the range of possibilities.

There is nothing (well, almost nothing) more embarrassing than to discover that some particular point I am stressing heavily in the report is wrong, attributable to human error in the analysis. My credibility is also at stake, and no evaluator can afford to lose that.

Confidentiality is also a concern at this point, and I need to make sure that the raw data are stored in a secure area. I promised my respondents that their names would never be associated with their responses. Their trust and my professional integrity are at stake here, so I must be careful. The data entered into the computer only had ID numbers associated with the responses—I am safe there. But the raw data are going to be locked in a data-storage cabinet, never to be opened (unless a reanalysis is in order) for several years to come. My rule of thumb is to not discard any raw data from projects for at least three years.

May 10. The numbers have been cranked out of the computer and the last qualitative data summary has just been received from my faithful typist. Enough copies have been made of each for me to distribute them to my steering committee (made up of trusted representatives of each stakeholder group) for their review and interpretation. These aren't reports—just data summaries. And, of course, the site-visit information is missing, because that occurs later this week.

A half-day meeting has been scheduled at the high school for us to go through the results, instrument by instrument, question by question, and to share our reading and interpretation of the preliminary findings. What do they mean to us? What conclusions can we draw? I am doing my homework now and I am sure each of the stakeholders will also. This step is important to all of us, because it ensures a place for our values to be reflected in the report. So much the better if we all agree on an interpretation. But if we don't, there is a place for multiple interpretations of the same results. This is part of the educational process—where people learn about differing perspectives and expectations. I am really looking forward to this meeting.

APPLICATION EXERCISE

1. Revisit your data-collection plans that you developed as an application exercise in previous chapters. For each set of data that you would collect, indicate how the resulting information should be analyzed.

2. Once you get computer printouts for a quantitative data analysis, or draft field notes for a qualitative data analysis, indicate how you would handle the interpretation stage of data analysis. Propose specific steps that you would take.

3. Work out the details for conducting one type of cost analysis for a program of your choice.

SUGGESTED READINGS

Bogdan, R. C., & Biklen, S. K. (1982). *Qualitative research for education*. Boston: Allyn & Bacon.

Guba, E. G., & Lincoln, Y. S. (1981). *Effective evaluation*. San Francisco: Jossey-Bass.

Hoaglin, D. C., Light, R. J., McPeek, B., Mosteller, F., & Stoto, M. A. (1982). *Data for decisions*. Cambridge, MA: Abt.

Hopkins, K. D., & Glass, G. V. (1978). *Basic statistics for the behavioral sciences*. Englewood Cliffs, NJ: Prentice-Hall.

Jaeger, R. M. (1983). *Statistics: A spectator sport*. Beverly Hills, CA: Sage.

Levin, H. M. (1983). *Cost-effectiveness: A primer*. Beverly Hills, CA: Sage.

Patton, M. Q. (1980). *Qualitative evaluation methods*. Beverly Hills, CA: Sage.

Spindler, G. (Ed.). (1982). *Doing the ethnography of schooling*. New York: Holt, Rinehart, & Winston.

Chapter 20
Reporting and Using Evaluation Information

Orienting Questions

1. What considerations are important in tailoring an evaluation report to audience needs?
2. What components should be included in an evaluation report? Why is each of them important?
3. If someone asked you how to make an evaluation report effective, what suggestions would you give?
4. How can you present an oral evaluation report so that it will have substantial impact on your audiences?
5. What factors have been found to influence the use of evaluation information?

In the prior two chapters we have discussed the collection, analysis, and interpretation of evaluation information. Obviously, these activities are not ends in themselves, but terribly important means to making evaluation information useful. It seems obvious that such information is not likely to be used effectively unless it has been communicated effectively. Yet reporting is too often the step to which many evaluators give the least thought.

In this chapter we address the following topics: clarifying reporting purposes; timing reports for maximum effectiveness; tailoring reports to meet the needs of various audiences; shaping content; presenting information effectively; protecting clients' and participants' rights and sensitivities; avoiding common reporting failures; and understanding factors that influence the use of evaluation reports.

PURPOSES OF EVALUATION REPORTS

We noted in Chapter 1 that evaluation (and evaluators) can play many different roles, and the information produced can be put to very different uses. We noted, for example, that formative-evaluation information is typically used by those wanting to improve a program they are developing or operating, whereas summative-evaluation information is typically used by funders and potential consumers, as well as program staff, to certify a program's utility.

The purpose of an evaluation report is directly linked to the role the evaluation was intended to play. If the evaluation is formative, its overall purpose is to improve the program, and the report should inform program staff early about how the program is functioning and what changes must be made to improve it. If the role of the evaluation is summative, the report should provide information and judgments about the mature program's utility to those who: (1) may wish to adopt it; or (2) will determine resource allocation for its continuation; or (3) who have a right to know about the program for other reasons.

Given that the purpose of an evaluation report follows naturally from the role evaluation plays, it is apparent that evaluation reports can serve many purposes. Both Patton (1978) and Alkin and others (1979) have discussed the range of ways evaluation findings can be used. As should be apparent from our discussion in Chapter 17, evaluation reports may often serve political or public relations purposes. Brinkerhoff and others (1983) also underscored this point, listing—in addition to decision making—nine other possible purposes served by evaluation reports:

- To demonstrate accountability
- To convince
- To educate
- To explore and investigate
- To document
- To involve
- To gain support
- To promote understanding
- To promote public relations.

Indeed, evaluation reports serve many purposes. Central to all of them, however, is that of "delivering the message"—informing the appropriate audience(s) about the findings and conclusions resulting from the collection, analysis, and interpretation of evaluation information.

IDENTIFYING AUDIENCES FOR EVALUATION REPORTS

In Chapter 13 we discussed the importance of identifying the multiple audiences for an evaluation and suggested procedures for how to do so. An evaluation report obviously cannot be well targeted without clear definition of its audience(s) and the types of questions those audiences are likely to raise about findings. Writing an evaluation report before defining the audience is like firing a gun blind, then hurrying to draw the bull's-eye in the path of the speeding bullet. As Lee and Holley (1978) note, "Identify your audience" may be an obvious, overworked platitude, but unfortunately it is often an overlooked step. They cite some common mistakes that have particular relevance for evaluation reports:

Most evaluations have many audiences. Not identifying all of them is a common mistake. An ignored audience can on occasion get pretty testy and introduce a lot of undesired commotion into the situation. More typically, an audience who needs certain information but never gets it, will make its decisions in ignorance of some perhaps vital information. . . .

Another mistake you can make in identifying your audience is to identify too broad or too narrow an audience. An example of this would be for an evaluator to think a parent committee is the evaluation audience, when the actual audience is the committee chairperson. (She is the respected opinion leader of the group and always determines the action the committee will take on any issue.) Therefore, the majority of the evaluator's dissemination efforts toward the committee should be directed at informing and persuading the chairperson of the validity and implications of the evaluation information. (Lee & Holley, 1978, p. 2)

TAILORING EVALUATION REPORTS TO THEIR AUDIENCE(S)

Multiple audiences have different informational needs. Knowledge of the values held by those who receive information from the evaluator can help him to shape communications effectively. We suggest that an *audience analysis* should be completed for all pertinent stakeholders for the evaluation. Such an audience analysis would involve determining what information that particular audience should be receiving or is interested in receiving and the best channels and procedures to transmit such information.[105]

For example, when an evaluator completes an evaluation, his methodologically oriented colleagues will be interested in a complete, detailed report of the data-collection procedures, analysis techniques, and the like. Not so the school board, or the PTA, or the chairman of the local taxpayer group. These audiences do not share the evaluator's grasp of technical details, his interest in test reliability and validity, or his concern over the appropriate choice of an error term in a randomized blocks design. The evaluator will have to tailor reports for these groups so that they depend on nontechnical language and avoid overuse of tabular data presentation. A typical evaluation might end up with one omnibus technical evaluation report that self-consciously includes all the details and one or more nontechnical evaluation report aimed at important audience(s).

In preparing an evaluation report, the evaluator should consider what type of evidence his audiences will find most compelling, as well as the particular medium, format, and style they are likely to appreciate.

Tailoring Report Content to the Evaluation's Audience(s)

Because of their diverse backgrounds, interests, preferences, and motivations, those who receive and use evaluation reports look for different things. The evaluator who neglects to identify his audiences' needs and preferences will generally find that audiences respond by neglecting his evaluation reports. Lee and Holley say it succinctly:

> An audience of teachers who are primed to find out what teaching strategies are most effective with low income students are not going to be fascinated with your report on teacher attitudes. (Lee & Holley, 1978, p. 3)

In addition to including the specific content important to each audience, the evaluator must also account for differences in the ways audiences interpret and accept evaluation reports. One group may find inferences drawn from certain information credible and useful, whereas another group may scoff at the same conclusions (no matter how "scientifically" defensible). Testimonials of students and teachers may be the most persuasive information possible for some audiences, whereas others would insist on statistical summaries of student test performance. The evaluator must also take into account the criteria various audiences will use to make judgments and what standards they will employ to determine the success or failure of that which is evaluated. Evaluation reports must present results in a believable way.

Evaluators can learn from the research of Weiss and Bucuvalas (1980), who state that evaluation reports are most likely to be heard and used by policymakers if they meet two criteria—those of *truth value* and *utility value* for the recipient. Truth value refers to the technical quality of the study, and to whether the findings correspond to policymakers' previous understanding and experience with how the world works (expectations). Utility value refers to the extent to which the study provides explicit and practical direction on matters the policymakers can do something about and challenges the status quo (with new formulations and approaches).

Tailoring Report Format and Style to the Evaluation Audience(s)

Evaluation reports are often thought of as written documents. But slide-tape presentations, oral reports, or a variety of other forms can also be effective. Good evaluations seldom depend solely on the printed word. An important challenge for the evaluator is to present the report in the medium and format that will both appeal to and convince the evaluation's audience(s).

Whatever the form of the report, it is also important to tailor the level of sophistication so that evaluation findings can be clearly understood. The evaluator must decide whether the report should be general or specific, technical or nontechnical.

In tailoring the presentation of findings to audience needs, the evaluator might choose from many different media and modes of display:[106]
- Written reports
- Photo essays
- Audiotape reports
- Slide-tape presentations
- Film or videotape reports

- Multimedia presentations
- Dialogues/testimonies
- Hearings or mock trials
- Product displays
- Simulations
- Scenarios
- Portrayals
- Case studies
- Graphs and charts
- Test score summaries
- Questions/answers.

Audiences Can Help Tailor Reports to Fit Their Needs

Patton (1978) points out that evaluation data are used more if the evaluator discusses and negotiates the format, style, and organization of evaluation reports with primary users. Brinkerhoff and his colleagues (1983) suggest some ways audiences might be involved in influencing the evaluation reports: (1) suggesting dates on which they need information; (2) stating in advance what information would be of interest; (3) requesting specific kinds of recommendations; and (4) suggesting displays and graphs they would find useful.

It is beyond the scope of this book to discuss specifics of all the alternative reporting schedules, types, and formats the evaluator might use, but we will deal in the following sections with the issue of timing of reports and the two most common types of reports: written and oral.

TIMING OF EVALUATION REPORTS

As purposes and audiences for evaluation reports vary, so obviously will the timing of those reports. Formative-evaluation reports designed to inform program administrators of needed improvements in a developing, pilot program obviously cannot be delivered after the project has been completed (although that might be appropriate for a summative-evaluation report to the program's sponsors or regulatory agency). An evaluation report that is limited in scope and perhaps even in rough draft form, but presented prior to relevant decisions, is preferable to a polished, comprehensive report that is delivered after those decisions have been made. Even informal verbal briefings that serve an early warning function are preferable to formal but tardy reports. Timeliness is critical in evaluation.

The scheduling of evaluation findings must be guided in a general way by the role of the study. It is obvious, for example, that early reporting will be more customary in a formative evaluation than in a summative study. But it would be an error to conclude that summative reporting is restricted to formal, written reports. Indeed, too much formality may well lessen the likelihood that evaluation findings will be used, for an evaluation's primary audience often will not take the time to study a report. Higher-level administrators and policymakers often hear evaluation findings only from underlings or others who have read the report and distilled from it the particular message they prefer. This has led some analysts (for example, Sproull & Larkey, 1979) to suggest that the evaluator who wishes his message to be heard by managers has to rely largely on interim reports, using "nonprint" strategies such as:

- Being around and available to provide information that managers request
- Talking to those people on whom the manager trusts and relies
- Using examples, stories, and anecdotes to make succinct, memorable points
- Talking often, but briefly.

To these four suggestions, we would add a fifth, suggested by Guba and Lincoln (1981):

- Communicating in the audience's language.

Scheduled Interim Reports. Throughout the development, operation, and adoption of the entity that is evaluated, it is often appropriate to schedule a report of whatever evaluation information is available at that time. For example, we spoke in Chapter 16 of evaluation "milestones"; an interim evaluation report may well coincide with (or represent) each of these milestones (for example, completion or acceptance of the evaluation plan and/or data-collection instruments; a report of results obtained at the conclusion of each exploratory report; pilot-test, or field-test of an instructional innovation; or the end-of-year report). Interim reports may also coincide with natural milestones in whatever is being evaluated (for example, completion of each successive draft of a set of curriculum materials; student performance at the end of each semester in a particular university program). In addition, interim reports may be scheduled at regular time intervals (monthly, semiannually, annually) or to precede or coincide with major events for which the evaluation information is particularly relevant (for instance, scheduled funding decisions about the evaluation object; scheduled meetings of review committees, governing boards or regulatory bodies; or scheduled legislative sessions).

Unscheduled Interim Reports. The need for interim evaluation reports cannot always be seen in advance. No matter how carefully interim reports have been scheduled, there will be additional times when available evaluation information should be shared. In a formative evaluation, for example, the evaluator may discover a major problem or impediment, such as the fact that video monitors used in an experimental program designed to teach algebra are too small for students beyond the third row to see the numerical symbols clearly. It would be a gross disservice to withhold that information until the next *scheduled* interim report, which might be weeks away, and then deliver the not-too-surprising message that a majority of students did not seem to be learning much algebra from the experimental program. Helpful evaluators will deliver many unscheduled interim reports, as the information is needed, whenever unexpected events or results pop up. For this reason, we propose that the formative evaluator maintain some form of "hotline" to key managers and policymakers so that even informal evaluation results can be transmitted as soon as the evaluator is sufficiently certain of his data. Of course, unscheduled sharing of evaluation information is not limited to formative evaluation; as was noted earlier, the summative evaluator who wishes to see his results used by managers learns to "be around" to share the emerging results of the evaluation informally and frequently.

Final Reports. Final reports are so familiar as to require no further comment here except to note that they may be incremental (that is, a preliminary final report released for review and reaction by stakeholders, followed by a later *final* report).

IMPORTANT INGREDIENTS IN A GOOD WRITTEN EVALUATION REPORT

No one best outline or suggested table of contents fits all written evaluation reports. Evaluation roles, objects, and contexts are simply too diverse to permit that. Each evaluation contains idiosyncracies peculiar to itself, and reports must be tailored to reflect such uniqueness.

Yet there are some important items that should be included in almost every written evaluation (at least every formal, final evaluation report, and interim reports as appropriate). These items are the core of most good written evaluation reports.

We agree with Stake (1969a) that one must worry much more about the form of formal reports intended for external audiences. We see the following outline as applicable in other situations as well, however, and offer it as a heuristic checklist evaluators might consider as they prepare any written evaluation report.

In our judgment, a written, comprehensive, technical evaluation report will typically contain the sections listed in the following "generic" table of contents.

   I. Executive Summary
  II. Introduction to the Report
      A. Purpose of the evaluation
      B. Audiences for the evaluation report
      C. Limitations of the evaluation and explanation of disclaimers (if any)
      D. Overview of report contents
 III. Focus of the Evaluation
      A. Description of the evaluation object
      B. Evaluative questions or objectives used to focus the study
      C. Information needed to complete the evaluation
  IV. Evaluation Plan and Procedures
      A. Information collection plan; design of the study
      B. Overview of evaluation instruments
      C. Overview of data analysis and interpretation
   V. Presentation of Evaluation Results
      A. Summary of evaluation findings
      B. Interpretation of evaluation findings
  VI. Conclusions and Recommendations
      A. Criteria and standards used to judge evaluation object
      B. Judgments about evaluation object (strengths and weaknesses)
      C. Recommendations

VII. Minority Reports or Rejoinders (if any)
VIII. Appendices
    A. Detailed tabulations or analyses of data
    B. Instruments and/or detailed procedures used
    C. Other information.

A brief discussion of each of these major sections and their contents follows.

Executive Summary

One feature of many evaluation reports that makes them so formidable is their organization, which often requires that the busy reader ferret out from a compulsively detailed report why and how the study was conducted and what important information it yielded. Sometimes a brief summary of essential information is wedged somewhere between the presentation of the findings and the appendices, but often readers are left to sift out the most valuable nuggets of information for themselves.

Most evaluation audiences do not have (or will not take) the time or energy necessary to read a thick report laden with tabular information or narrative details. It makes good sense, therefore, to provide a brief executive summary in one of the following forms:

Executive Summary within a Report. For most evaluation studies, an executive summary might best be included within the report itself, preferably right up front where it is the first thing the busy administrator sees when the report is opened. We also propose that the executive summary be printed on a different color paper to draw attention to it. This summary should usually be somewhere between 3 and 15 pages in length, depending on the scope and complexity of the evaluation. In addition to a very brief description of the study's purpose, questions, and procedures, the summary should contain the most important findings, judgments, and recommendations, perhaps organized in a simple question-answer format. The summary should also contain references directing the reader to further information on salient points. If the evaluation report is large and interest in it broad, then it is sometimes more economical to distribute a *separately bound executive summary* similar in all other respects to that described previously.

Executive Abstract. With a large evaluation audience, it may be necessary to condense the executive summary to a one- or two-page abstract that contains only the major findings and recommendations without any supporting documentation. Such abstracts are often useful in communicating evaluation results to parents, board members, or community leaders.

In one statewide evaluation of a controversial school program with which we are familiar, three interrelated written evaluation reports were prepared: (1) a large, detailed technical report containing most of the information called for in the earlier outline; (2) a medium-sized summary of major interpretations and judgments drawn from the data; (3) a brief executive summary of the study procedures, findings, and conclusions. Availability of these three reports was broadly announced in the newspapers and on television. Readership was estimated by the number of people who requested a copy or checked one out in the several repositories in which they were made available. Nearly 400 individuals read the executive summary, 40 read the mid-sized interpretive report, and only one person ever even requested the complete report (and he was an expert methodologist hired by opponents of the evaluation to see if he could find fault with it).

Introduction to the Report

Despite its prominent placement in the report, the executive summary is only a brief abstract, not an introduction. An adequate introduction will set the stage for the remainder of the report by outlining the basic purpose(s) of the evaluation and the audiences the report is intended to serve. For example, is the evaluation intended to provide information to legislative budget analysts who will determine future funding of a statewide vocational education program, or is it to document the performance of a new instructional product in a true field test? Is the evaluation audience the state legislature, the administrators and staff operating the state-supported vocational education programs, or both?

One good way to ensure that a report will be relevant is to describe thoroughly the rationale for the evaluation. The rationale should address such questions as: Why was the evaluation conducted? What is the evaluation intended to accomplish? What questions was it intended to answer? Why was the evaluation conducted the way it was? Once this information is provided, audiences can determine whether the report is relevant by asking how well each question is answered.

The introduction is also one logical place to caution the reader about limitations that affect the collection, analysis, or interpretation of information. Such limitations should be openly disclosed here (or in a later section dealing with evaluation procedures). Similarly, disclaimers are sometimes placed at the beginning of a report (for example, in the preface or on the title page) to clarify what the evaluation is and is not, thus protecting both clients and evaluators from criticisms based on misunderstandings.

It is also useful to provide in the introduction a brief "reader's guide" to the report. The table of contents only lists major topics. The reader's guide explains what each topic comprises.

Focus of the Evaluation

This section provides a focus to the evaluation, summarizing those evaluation activities we described in Chapters 12 through 14. We stressed in Chapter 13, for example, the importance of describing the evaluation object accurately, so everyone could agree on precisely what was (and was not) being evaluated. It is not only essential to agree on such a description at the beginning of an evaluation but also to share that description prominently in an early section of the report. Descriptions of evaluation objects obviously should not be limited to physical characteristics but should also include (1) rationale, goals, and objectives;[107] (2) students or other recipients/participants to be benefited; (3) substantive or subject matter focus; (4) strategies and procedures used for implementation; (5) operating context; and (6) human and other resource requirements needed.

It is also important to list in an early section the evaluative questions, objectives, or other organizers used to focus the evaluation. If differential priorities were assigned to the questions or objectives, that process should be explained.

Finally, it is useful to include a subsection outlining the needed information the evaluation was intended to collect, analyze, and report. Such a list helps make the rationale for the next section much more apparent.

Evaluation Plan and Procedures

Any complete evaluation report must include a detailed presentation of the evaluation plan, the data-collection instruments, and the methods and techniques used to analyze and interpret data. Not all details must be included in this section, however; a careful and complete summary will suffice if detailed procedures (and possibly even the instruments themselves) are contained in supporting appendices. This is the place to present any information needed to help the reader understand such things as what (if any) sampling procedures were used, how the information was collected to ensure its accuracy, what specific statistical analysis procedure was used, and why. In short, this is where the evaluator provides the methodological and technical information needed not only by primary audiences but also by fellow evaluators who will decide whether the conduct of the study was adequate to make its results believable. Evaluation reports must be usable by administrators and staffs who are not steeped in methodology or techniques; at the same time, the evaluator cannot forget that fellow evaluators keenly interested in methodological and technical adequacy will also be perusing those reports. It is wise to remember Campbell's insistence on "having available (along with the data available for reanalysis) a full academic analysis for cross-examination by our applied social science colleagues" (Campbell, 1984, p. 41).

Presentation of Evaluation Results

This section of the report contains the results of the evaluation and represents the source of subsequent conclusions and recommendations, preferably in the form of a complete summary, using tables and displays as appropriate, and referencing more detailed data summaries in supporting appendices.

The interpretation of the results is as important as their presentation. Evaluation depends, after all, on the evaluator's ability to perceive and interpret. Interpreting data should not be an informal or casual activity. Rather, it should be a careful process, made as public as possible by the evaluator's careful listing of all content and steps followed to reach the particular judgments and recommendations presented.

One of the most disconce ting deficits of many evaluation reports is the lack of any organization to assist the reader in relating findings to the major evaluative questions posed. Without organization or categorization, findings often blur, becoming less understandable. We urge evaluators to relate their findings to the most logical set of organizers. We prefer to organize the findings around the evaluative questions posed for the study, in a question-and-answer format. Other organizers might include the goals or objectives (if that is the evaluation's focus), or even the instruments used to collect data. Whatever the organizer, some structure must be given to all but the most simplistic, single-variable, single-question evaluations.

Conclusions and Recommendations

In this section of the report we would propose that the evaluator list the standards and criteria used, provide his best judgments about the quality of what has been evaluated, and provide whatever recommendations he feels follow from those judgments.

Standards and criteria should be listed explicitly. The data do not speak for themselves. The evaluator who knows those data well is in the best position to apply the standards to the data to reach a judgment of whether the evaluation object is effective or ineffective, valuable or worthless. Making judgments is an essential part of the evaluator's job. An evaluation without clear criteria is as much an indictment of its author's lack of sophistication as one where judgments are not based on the data.

We strongly prefer organizing evaluative judgments under the headings *strengths* (presented first) and *limitations* (or the parallel and more familiar *strengths* and *weaknesses*, if client and evaluator are less squeamish). Several advantages accrue to this dichotomous presentation:

- Attention is focused on both positive and negative judgments
- Audiences can conveniently locate the evaluator's positive or negative judgments
- Presenting strengths first generally helps those responsible for the evaluation object to accept the weaknesses listed thereafter.

The discussion of strengths and limitations must be sufficiently complete to allow the audience(s) to see the rationale and judgments on which later recommendations are based.

Although we strongly prefer the inclusion of recommendations, there are times when they might be appropriately omitted. In an adversary evaluation hearing, for instance, it may be best to use all the evaluation's resources to present the best cases possible, but leaving the "jury" to draw the final conclusions and make recommendations. Even here, however, each team could add recommendations they viewed as logical, allowing the jury to sift out the pros and cons. But for most evaluations, recommendations are a key responsibility of the evaluator.

This does not necessarily mean, however, that the evaluator's recommendations should automatically be adopted. As Nowakowski (1985) cautions, evaluators may be better at identifying how well things are working than they are at recommending how necessary corrections should be made. She proposes that evaluator and client work together to design corrective action. The client and other audiences may have more confidence in co-authored recommendations.

Minority Reports or Rejoinders

Sometimes, under circumstances discussed in a later section, it may be important to include a section in which those who disagree with the evaluator's judgments, conclusions, or recommendations are provided space to share their distaff views. Or, if one member of an evaluation team disagrees with the majority view, it seems sensible to insert any rebuttals or "minority reports" as a last section.

Appendices

Supporting appendices (bound within the report or as a separate volume) might include detailed descriptions of evaluation procedures, detailed data tabulations or analyses, complete transcripts of important interviews, and other information that is relevant but too detailed to present in the body of the report. Appendices might also include the actual data-collection instruments and any other information (for example, boundary maps of sampling units in a community survey) deemed of interest and importance to the audiences, but inappropriately detailed and/or extensive for inclusion in the body of the report. Appropriate use of appendices will make the report itself much more streamlined and eminently more readable.

SUGGESTIONS FOR PRESENTING INFORMATION IN WRITTEN EVALUATION REPORTS

Written evaluation reports are nearly as varied as those who write them. But the great majority share a common characteristic: They make tedious and tiresome reading. Indeed, their variety seems limited only by the number of ways that can be found to make written information boring. Many deserve Mark Twain's waggish opprobrium: "chloroform in print." One sometimes wonders whether such dreadful dullness reflects a purposeful design to discourage readers.

Not that all evaluation reports are awful. Now and then one appears that is both interesting and informative, both enlightening and entertaining, both comprehensive and captivating. But these, like other gems, are rare. In this and the following section we suggest several considerations to help make the evaluator's written presentation effective, interesting, and fair.

Accuracy, Balance, and Fairness

It goes without saying that evaluation reports should not be unfair, imbalanced, or inaccurate. Yet truth is elusive, and even the most scrupulous evaluator must struggle to see that carefully collected and analyzed information is not later distorted, intentionally or unintentionally, in its presentation. As the Joint Committee states: "Oral and written evaluation reports should be open, direct, and honest in their disclosure of pertinent findings" (Joint Committee on Standards for Educational Evaluation, 1981, p. 74).

Similarly, the evaluator must make certain that nothing is allowed to color the presentation of information. Suppose the personality traits of a program director offend the evaluator. It is important to prevent that fact from negatively tainting the judgments and language in the evaluation report (unless, of course, the program director also offends others in ways that have a negative effect on the program). Fairness in reporting is the hallmark of a professional evaluator.

Finally, there are two or more sides to every story. It is essential that legitimate positions be reported in a balanced way. No evaluator will ever be completely free of bias, but every effort must be made to control bias in reporting.[108] The Joint Committee, evidencing its concern in this area, articulated the following as one standard of propriety:

> *Balanced Reporting.* The evaluation should be complete and fair in its presentation of strengths and weaknesses of the object under investigation, so that strengths can be built upon and problem areas addressed. (Joint Committee on Standards for Educational Evaluation, 1981, p. 90)

Communication and Persuasion

Communication plays an important role in all stages of evaluation. Good communication is essential if the evaluator is to understand the origins and context for an evaluation, elicit the evaluative questions and criteria from stakeholders, reach agreements with clients concerning the evaluation plan, deal with political and interpersonal aspects of evaluation studies, maintain rapport and protocol during data collection, and so on. But nowhere is clarity of communication more central than during reporting. The quality of that communication will determine whether the evaluator's message comes through clear or garbled.

Construed broadly, communication may be thought of as all the procedures one person uses to inform another. Presenting information in a way that it is not understood is simply poor communication (no matter how *correct* the information). Presenting statistical summaries to lay audiences who do not understand statistics is poor communication (or noncommunication), regardless of how well a more statistically oriented audience might receive the same information. It is essential that the evaluator tailor every presentation to make it understandable to its audience(s).

This requires care and creativity. To present statistical evaluation results to audiences who are not schooled in statistics, Brager and Mazza (1979) suggest using (1) analogies, (2) graphs or pictorial displays, (3) well-explained summaries to highlight selected findings, (4) a television newscast format to underscore concise, important findings, and (5) a minimal number of judiciously inserted statistics. Lee and Holley (1978) suggest relating evaluation information to an action that must be taken (for example, a pending decision or a plan).

No matter how dispassionate the presentation, if the communication seeks to bring the reader to the same conclusions the evaluator has reached, then its intent is not only to inform but also to persuade. House (1980) analyzed in one study the contrast between impersonal, neutral presentation of evaluation procedures and the dramatic use of imagery in presenting the implications for action. But, as House notes, both are used to persuade. Describing the discussion of methodology in the study as being "conducted with painstaking neutrality," he observes that

> The resulting "scientific" style is clinical, detached, impersonal, and lacks imagery. The author presents the external world and allows it to persuade the reader. The style suggests that the observer is governed by method and by the rules of scientific integrity. (House, 1980, p. 99)

In speaking of the study's implications for action, House notes that facts are converted to imagery, and comments,

> Imagery, dramatic structure, and mode of presentation are central considerations for the import of an evaluation. These elements, often thought of as merely cosmetic, can affect what people believe and do. (House, 1980, p. 100)

House also relates both styles of presentation to the coherence he believes is essential, a coherence he says can be attained through "storytelling":

> Every evaluation must have a minimum degree of coherence. The minimum coherence is that the evaluation tell a story. . . .
>
> There are at least two conventional ways of telling the story. One way is to present the evaluator as a neutral, scientific observer. In this case, the story line is implied. It runs something like, "I am a detached, neutral observer who has made measurements according to the canons of science and have found certain things to be so. The program was conducted as I have described it, and I have found the following outcomes. . . ." Usually the story line concludes that "the program was implemented, and such and such were the results." Actual description is often sparse. . . . The usual presentation is to describe the project or the goals of the project, the treatment, the results or effects, and the conclusions.
>
> The second major way of telling the story is for the evaluator to stand closer to the program, as reflected in the narrator's "voice," and to tell the story by describing the events in detail. To this end the evaluator may use emotionally charged language and a narrative presentation. The story may look like a newspaper report. (House, 1980, pp. 102–103)

Wachtman (1978) and Denny (1980) have also expounded on the importance of telling a story through the evaluation, whether that be through careful narrative description or usual displays. Whatever tactic is used, it is imperative that the evaluator take pains to communicate his message clearly and persuasively.

Level of Detail

The notion that all evaluators suffer from compulsive-obsessive personality disorders may be an unfounded rumor, but it is probably rooted in some real-world evaluation reports. We have all seen (if not produced) such reports, two inches or more in thickness, crammed full of all conceivable (and some inconceivable) details about the evaluation study and everything associated with it. Some evaluators confuse the call for comprehensiveness with the compulsion to collect. Cronbach and his colleagues (1980) made this wry observation:

> ...comprehensive examination of a program does not necessarily justify an exhaustive report....
>
> Many evaluations are reported with self-defeating thoroughness.... A normal human being will try to assimilate only so many numbers, and not much more prose. When an avalanche of words and tables descends, everyone in its path dodges. (Cronbach and others, 1980, p. 186)

How much detail should be included in an evaluation report? Owens has suggested the following guidelines:

> The question of how detailed or specific to make a report also relates back to an understanding of the audience. If the report is to be given about individual classrooms, teachers are usually interested in specifics. If the report contains data for an entire district, it may be best to simply summarize it and place the details in an appendix. The same data may be reported to various audiences at various levels of specificity. For example, a complete evaluation report may be a summary description of the instruments used to measure a particular objective, the student population or sample, procedures used to analyze the data, the statistical findings and a discussion of the findings related to that objective. Project staff may be primarily interested in a discussion of how recommendations could be used to improve the program. Parents or community persons may simply be interested in a single sentence summarizing how students performed on a particular objective.
>
> A written evaluation report should be organized so that various audiences can quickly assess the information of particular interest to them. If a program evaluation report is intended for the funding agency, don't forget to see what forms or report format they might require or suggest. A moderately detailed table of contents can be very helpful to the reader. (Owens, 1977, p. 57)

Technical Writing Style

Earlier we spoke about communication and persuasion in a broader sense. There we were concerned mostly with communicating clearly, avoiding unnecessary ambiguity, and making certain the evaluation story was clearly understood. In a written report, the use of language, as well as pictures, graphs, and tabular displays, will determine whether or not the communication is effective.

Nothing is as tiresome as reading tedious, unnecessarily convoluted, imprecise and sometimes inconvenient and awkward expression (see what we mean?) Wouldn't it have been better if we had said simply, "Nothing is as tiresome as reading complicated writing"?

We offer these few rules for improving writing style in evaluation reports:

- *Avoid jargon*[109] (if you don't know what it is, you're probably using it).
- *Use simple, direct language* (make certain the level of language is appropriate for the audience; don't ramble).

- *Use examples, anecdotes, illustrations* (don't forget a picture is worth a thousand words—and don't be flippant by asking why we forgot to illustrate this text).
- *Use correct grammar and punctuation* (and spelling should also be appropriate for the country in which the report is to be used).
- *Avoid cluttering narrative with reference notes* (yes, we know we have done just that, but then this is a text and reference book, not an evaluation report, and you are not the typical evaluation audience).
- *Use language that is interesting, not dull.*

Lee and Holley (1978) also give these helpful tips, several of which deal directly with writing style:

1. Start with the most important information (not only within the report, but within each section).
2. Highlight the important points.
3. Keep the readability level low.
   a. Use a shorter, more familiar word if it will work as well.
   b. If you must use a technical term, define it clearly.
   c. Use active verbs.
   d. Cut out the deadwood.
   e. Shorten your sentences.
   f. Shorten your paragraphs.
   g. Personalize your text (by using personal pronouns, contractions, and "shirtsleeves" language).

Appearance of the Report

It would be interesting to do a bit of "free-response research" to determine what is the first word that pops into people's minds when they hear "evaluation report." We cannot predict the most common responses, but we would be amazed if they included "attractive," "handsome," or "visually appealing." Concern with aesthetics has historically been as common among evaluators as compassion has been among tax collectors. Most evaluators have been preoccupied with what the report said, not with how attractively the message came packaged.

Appearance counts, however, because it will often influence how (or whether) a document will be read. Market analysts and advertising specialists know much that would be useful to evaluators who want their products used (like how long it takes the average administrator to transmit most items from the "incoming" mailbox to the "outgoing" wastebasket).

Of course, few evaluators will adopt the slick and glossy visual tricks of advertising. But much can be modified and tastefully applied to make evaluation reports more visually appealing and readable. Five suggestions follow:

1. *Print quality.* If you have ever tried to read a faded, purple copy of a report reproduced on the school's nearly worn out "ditto machine" (spirit duplicator), you know that only a rare report will be judged worth the effort. Sharp, dark printing in standard size or larger is essential.

2. *Graphics.* Evaluators (and their secretaries) are not necessarily competent

in drafting or in art. Yet visual displays should be used in evaluation reports wherever they would be helpful in telling (or better yet, *showing*) the story. The fee paid to someone to produce clear, attractive graphs may be as wise an investment of evaluation resources as any.

3. *Page appearance.* Most technical reports are overwhelmed with a sense of "grayness"—page after page of long, uninterrupted paragraphs with nothing to relieve the monotony (small wonder the eye sometimes responds by closing). Good copy editors have long since learned the advantage of "breaking up the page," using strategies such as

- White space (to separate and relieve printed sections)
- Varied headings (regular and boldface)
- Underlining or italics (not only to give emphasis but also to add interest)
- Use of numbered or "bulleted" lists (such as this one)
- Insertion of visuals (graphs, pictures, or even cartoons)
- Boxes (or other visual displays of selected materials).

4. *Color.* Careful use of color can make an evaluation report more attractive, as well as more functional. When the executive summary appears as the first section in an evaluation report, we prefer to print it on colored paper. This not only gives some visual appeal but also draws attention to the summary and makes it easy for the reader to locate later. Consider printing appendices on yet another color. It will be easy to turn to, and the combination of colors with the predominantly white body of the report enhances the visual appeal of the whole.

5. *Cover.* Obviously not all written evaluation reports warrant preparing and printing a cover. A typed and stapled cover page will serve well in many formative evaluation studies, and possibly some summative evaluation studies as well. But a more attractive report cover may entice readers and suggest that the evaluator thought the information contained in the report was worthy of a professional presentation. Of course, no cover will compensate for an inadequate evaluation report.

HUMAN AND HUMANE CONSIDERATIONS IN REPORTING EVALUATION FINDINGS

Many evaluators become so preoccupied with preparing and presenting their messages that they forget the impact that those messages will have. If an evaluation report labels a new math curriculum as ill-conceived and its implementation as inadequate, the personal egos (and perhaps the professional reputations) of the curriculum designer and the staff implementing the program will not go unscathed. This doesn't mean that truth should be diluted to protect feelings, but only that it be communicated as carefully, sensitively, and professionally as possible. Beyond obvious idealistic reasons for protecting the rights and sensitivities of those on whom the evaluation might reflect, there are also some obvious (if you think about it for a moment) pragmatic reasons. For example, in many evaluations, results are reported directly to those responsible for planning or running the program. Evaluators far too wise to tell any mother that her baby is ugly may tactlessly tell an administrator and staff that the program to which they have devoted three years of their lives is a disaster. Not surprisingly, the program practitioners may exercise the limits of their ingenuity in seeking ways to discount both the evaluation and the evaluator. The opportunity for the message to be of use has been irretrievably lost.

The evaluator must take appropriate steps to protect the rights and sensitivities of all those involved in the evaluation. In this section we offer our suggestions for (1) delivering negative messages and (2) providing those affected with the opportunity to review a draft report (and suggest modifications) prior to its final release.

Delivering Negative Messages

In olden days, the messenger who delivered news to the king lived a life fraught with risk. If the news was bad, the messenger might lose his tongue—or even his head. Nowadays, the bearers of bad evaluation tidings may still find themselves savaged (though in a somewhat more polite manner).

Sometimes evaluation clients (or others involved with the evaluation) are so sensitive to any criticism, any hint of imperfection, that it would not matter much how negative findings were reported—the reaction would still be defensive. But more often we have observed that defensive reactions are exacerbated by the manner in which the negative results are conveyed.

Earlier we proposed one simple solution: to present the strengths of the program first. (To those who say they cannot *find* any strengths to report, we suggest they are not very thorough or insightful; in even the most awful program, one can usually comment sincerely on the efforts, dedication, and hard work of the staff.) We also reiterate the following suggestions of Van Mondfrans for helping those involved in evaluation to "swallow bitter pills":

1. In an oral debriefing where the major events of the evaluation are reviewed and where the major findings are previewed, the negative information is stated in as positive a context as possible. It seems easier for clients to accept negative information in an oral form in a relatively friendly encounter.

2. A preliminary written report is presented in which the negative information is described in a straightforward factual manner but in as positive a perspective as possible. Often a personal visit needs to follow in which the preliminary report is discussed and the client allowed to propose changes if the information is viewed as unfair. No changes ought to occur in the preliminary report which would hide negative information or which would allow the misinterpretation of negative information; however, it may be that in discussing the negative information, the client will bring up other factors which were not known to the evaluator at the time the preliminary report was written. These other factors may be included in the final report in juxtaposition with the negative information thus allowing better interpretation.

3. A final written report is prepared in which the negative information is accurately and fully presented. Having undergone previous steps, the client is better prepared to deal with the negative information, having had a chance to review it several times, to think

other factors which are relevant, and present those to the evaluator. The evaluator had the opportunity to review other factors and include them in the report if they aid the interpretation of the negative information. (Van Mondfrans, 1985, pp. 3–4)

Earlier in this chapter we mentioned that disclaimers could be inserted early in an evaluation report to protect both client and evaluator. Such disclaimers are intended to prevent misinterpretation and to put any negative messages in proper perspective. An example of such a disclaimer follows:[110]

This report describes the procedures and results of a formative/summative evaluation of (name of product/project). The client, (name of client), reserves all rights to this information. The purpose of this evaluation was to (state purpose). Any other use of this report may be subject to serious errors since the information was collected with the above purpose as the focus. Information relevant to other purposes was either not collected or not reported.

It is often useful to expand on such cryptic disclaimers. Errors and misunderstandings can arise if evaluation results are used for purposes other than those intended.

Providing an Opportunity for Review of the Report

Only the most arrogant evaluator would assume that his work and the report that presents it are completely accurate and fair in all regards. Small factual errors can lead to nontrivial errors in judgment and conclusions. Interpretations can overlook contextual factors that the evaluator failed to understand, and thus be spurious. And the evaluator's bias can creep into evaluation narratives unnoticed, especially by the evaluator.

For all of these reasons, we strongly urge that the evaluator circulate a draft of his evaluation report to the client and other key stakeholders for comments, asking that they point out (and correct where appropriate) all

- Minor errors (for example, misspellings)
- Factual errors (wrong names or titles, errors in numbers of students participating etc.)
- Interpretive errors.

Reviewers should be asked not only to challenge anything that they perceive to be an error but also to provide substantiation for the alternative facts or interpretations that they propose as correct. Reviewers should be informed that the evaluator is under no obligation to accept their suggestions (the intent is not to allow clients to rewrite the report any way they wish), but only to give those suggestions serious consideration. The evaluator reserves the right to ignore suggestions and to make only those changes that are warranted.

Circulating a preliminary draft report can increase the number of individuals who read the report carefully; shared responsibility for the report's accuracy is a good motivator. Some (see Parlett & Dearden, 1977) worry that use of drafts may lessen interest in the final report. That concerns us less than the very real possibility that many key persons who are not asked to review a draft may never read the report at all.

What if the evaluator refuses to accept a proposed change in the report, but the reviewer who suggested it continues to contend that the report is inaccurate, misleading, or unfair? Simple. Invite the reviewer to share that view, in writing, and include it in a concluding section of the report, as we proposed earlier. We see no problem with permitting reviewers to include their rebuttals, rejoinders, or contrary comments. If the evaluator's data analysis, interpretation, judgments, and conclusions are on solid ground, they should not be harmed by such detraction. If they are shaky and cannot withstand such challenge, then they deserve to be taken to task.

SUGGESTIONS FOR EFFECTIVE ORAL REPORTING

Written evaluation reports, although most common, are not necessarily the most effective medium for evaluation reporting. Oral reports, supported by appropriate visual aids, are often very effective.

Many of the earlier suggestions for improving written reports are pertinent for oral reports as well. Audiences who listen to oral reports need an introduction that explains the purpose of the evaluation, what was evaluated, the questions addressed, and the evaluation procedures used. Presenting positive conclusions followed by negative conclusions and recommendations is still appropriate. And the evaluator should still be as concerned about such items as the following:

- Accuracy, balance, and fairness
- Communication and persuasion
- Level of detail
- Use of simple, direct, correct, and interesting language
- Avoidance of jargon and unnecessary technical language
- Use of examples, anecdotes, and illustrations
- Sensitivity to the rights and feelings of those involved

Oral reports also require particular attention to audiovisual presentation of information. Obviously the suggestions commonly offered in speech and communications courses and texts are relevant here. But some suggestions have particular relevance for oral presentation of evaluation reports. Lee and Holley (1978) offer the following tips on making effective oral evaluation reports:

1. Make the presentation format interesting and varied.
   a. Do not use the format the audience expects; do something different.
   b. Put variety in the format, using multiple media, multiple presenters, or other variations.
2. Develop a presentation that feels natural and comfortable to you, then practice until you are at ease delivering it.
3. Make all visuals large and simple, using only a few words on each.
4. Involve the audience in the presentation through questions and answers, show of hands or other interaction, providing written issues they would like you to address, and the like.

Developing and adhering to an agenda, with appropriate breaks, is also helpful. Protracted oral reports will have people slumping in their seats (or worse, out of their seats).

A CHECKLIST FOR GOOD EVALUATION REPORTS

Ingredients of a good evaluation report can readily be inferred from our earlier suggestions, but here, for convenience, is a checklist of things that would typify most good evaluation reports.

Check each that applies
- _____ Interim and final reports provided in time to be most useful
- _____ Report content tailored to the audience(s)
- _____ Report format and style tailored to the audience(s)
- _____ Involvement of audiences in determining the format and style of the report
- _____ An executive summary
- _____ An adequate introduction to "set the stage"
- _____ Mention of limitations of the study
- _____ Adequate presentation of evaluation plan and procedures
- _____ Effective organization in the presentation of results
- _____ All necessary technical information provided (preferably in appendices)
- _____ Evaluative judgments
- _____ Specification of standards and criteria for evaluative judgments
- _____ Lists of *both* identified strengths and weaknesses
- _____ Recommendations for action
- _____ Protection of clients' and stakeholders' interests
- _____ Sensitivity to those affected by the evaluation findings
- _____ Provision for minority reports or rejoinders
- _____ Accurate and unbiased presentation
- _____ Effective communication and persuasion through "telling the story"
- _____ Appropriate level of detail
- _____ Lack of technical jargon
- _____ Use of correct, uncomplicated and interesting language
- _____ Use of examples and illustrations
- _____ Attention to visual appearance and eye appeal

THE USE OF EVALUATION REPORTS

The utility of any evaluation is a prime criterion for judging its worth (Joint Committee on Standards for Educational Evaluation, 1981). If an evaluation is not used, it must be judged harshly regardless of its technical, practical, and ethical merits.

Cost-effectiveness is an important argument for using evaluation in education. As Scriven (1974a, 1984) and Cronbach and others (1980) have argued so well, evaluation is justified only to the extent that it saves the client resources or adds substantially to the community's well-being.

For the above reasons, we believe it is important to examine (1) research on the ways in which evaluation has been used, and (2) research on factors found to influence its use.

Research on Use of Evaluation

It has been reported (Lyon, Doscher, McGranahan, & Williams, 1978) that about 90 percent of the metropolitan (45,000-plus students) school districts in the United States have testing or evaluation offices, whereas about 60 percent of the school districts serving 25,000 to 45,000 students have such offices, and 33 percent of the school districts serving 10,000 to 25,000 students have them. Little is known about the extent to which school districts serving fewer than 10,000 students have evaluation or testing offices. But the existence of evaluation offices tells little about how much of the information generated by those offices is actually used.

Compilations of research focused directly on the use of evaluation have been published by Braskamp and Brown (1980), Davis and Salasin (1975), King, Thompson, and Pechman (1981), Patton (1978), Weiss (1977), Smith (1980), Leviton and Hughes (1981), and Cousins and Leithwood (1985).

This research has been extended by Alkin and others (1979), Dickey (1980), Florio, Behrmann, and Goltz (1979), King and others (1982), Patton and others (1975), King and Pechman (1982, 1984), Brown and Newmann (1979), Kennedy and others (1980), and Kennedy (1984).

Until recently, the Center for the Study of Evaluation at UCLA published a newsletter titled *Using School Evaluations*. It is evident that evaluation use has been receiving the attention that it deserves.

What has been found from all of this research and conceptual activity? We have learned that evaluation is used in many different ways, some of which are difficult to document (Alkin and others, 1979; Patton, 1978). King and others (1982) defined three categories of evaluation use that may be used to guide our thinking about the utility of evaluation in education:

1. *Instrumental or allocative uses*—direct use of evaluation to make decisions or changes in education. Only infrequently does a single evaluation study or a particular piece of information resulting from an evaluation get used immediately for decision making.

2. *Conceptual uses*—indirect and cumulative uses of evaluation to shape the thinking of the policy-shaping community. Cronbach and his colleagues (1980) saw this use as the typical and most effective use of evaluation. By drawing attention to critical variables or issues, evaluation affects discussions that eventually lead to changes or new initiatives.

3. *Symbolic uses*—evaluation used for other than that for which it may have been intended. Examples of such use include pro forma submission of a mandated evaluation report just to fulfill funding requirements; uses of evaluation information to support or attack a point of view that may or may not have been

associated with the evaluation; drawing from evaluation findings as needed to prepare a new proposal or program design; using evaluation findings to legitimate decisions; and showing the public that evaluation indeed is being done. These are not discrete, nonoverlapping categories. In fact, evaluation may be used for any or all of these uses by the same or different users.

We have also learned from research on evaluation use that the needs for evaluation differ at different levels of the school organization. At the local level, Kennedy and colleagues (1980) reported these different uses:

1. *Classroom or guidance level*
   - students' instructional needs
   - students' social and emotional needs
   - referrals of students to special programs
2. *Building level*
   - implementing district policies
   - building management
   - program improvement
3. *Program level*
   - responsibility and authority
   - compliance
   - funding
4. *Districtwide level*
   - federal influences
   - student behavior
   - testing

We have also learned that evaluation use differs somewhat depending on school size. Stufflebeam (1980) reported the following evaluation functions to be found in large urban school systems that he studied: (1) administrative support services, (2) planning and development, (3) funded project evaluations, (4) instructional studies, (5) testing and test development, (6) needs assessment, and (7) special ad hoc studies. Conversely, forms of evaluation that Sanders (1983a) found occurring naturally in small rural schools included the following:

1. Classroom teachers solving problems of instruction and classroom management
2. Periodic curriculum and curriculum materials (for example, textbook) reviews
3. Standardized testing, and using the test results to check teacher perceptions of student development
4. Discussion and use of new ideas for school programs
5. Accumulation of tacit knowledge about students by classroom teachers
6. Allocation of resources for the school year by the principal (for instance, in-service days, committee assignments, conference attendance)
7. Indirect reformulation of curriculum (such as through benign neglect).

Awareness of the advantages of having evaluation information available has escaped many educators and policymakers. As one school superintendent said some years after becoming convinced of the utility of evaluation, "I don't really know how many potential problems our evaluative feedback has helped detect and how many crises have been avoided as a result, but I do know that I wouldn't want to go back to the old ways and find out" (Taylor, 1974, p. 19).

Research on Factors Found to Influence Evaluation Use

As was mentioned earlier in this chapter, evaluators can learn from the research of Weiss and Bucuvalas (1980) the importance of producing reports that are viewed by audiences as truthful and useful. Other researchers have investigated additional variables. For example, Kennedy and others (1980) reported that different influences existed on the use of information found at the different levels of the school districts they studied. For example, at the district-wide level, use was influenced by a predisposition to deal with situations that require a response. Use at this level was also influenced by the availability of information and the nature of the decision-making process used in the school district. At the program level, influences were found to be the problems that program directors were faced with, the amount of personal knowledge that they already had about the program, and the availability of formative evaluation. Influences at the building level included the availability of information, existence of informal personal information, and awareness of goals. Finally, influences at the classroom or guidance level (called the *clinical level* by Kennedy and others) included overlap of test coverage with what the teacher covers, teacher opinions about tests, preference for personal knowledge, and recognized need for information.

In studying the use of Title I evaluation in school districts, Alkin, Stecher, and Geiger (1982) concluded that six factors were most responsible for the use of evaluation information:

- the reputation of the evaluator
- the evaluator's commitment to evaluation use
- the interest of decision-makers and the community in the evaluation
- the extent to which the evaluation focused on local needs
- the degree to which evaluation was presented in graphic, nontechnical form
- the development of procedures that assisted decision-makers to use the information.

Leviton and Hughes (1981) found five clusters of factors that affect evaluation use: (1) relevance of evaluation to decision-maker's needs, (2) credibility of the evaluation and the evaluator, (3) communication of evaluation results, (4) translation of evaluation results into specific implications, and (5) evaluation user involvement and advocacy.

Kennedy and colleagues (1980) found several methods that school district evaluation units were using to promote evaluation use. These included "staff development through workshops and inservice programs, participation on committees, discussions with parent groups, and encouraging school boards to develop policies regarding information use" (Kennedy and others, 1980, p. 113). They also found evaluators promoting evaluation use by negotiating with potential users during the design stage of the evaluation (for example, by requiring program managers to respond in writing) and by demonstrating to the school board how evaluation studies can save money.

Patton and colleagues (1975) have been widely cited for reporting evidence that a *personal factor* (an individual takes personal responsibility for getting the information to the right people) is a critical determiner of evaluation use. Later, Patton (1978) reported that the impact of evaluation was most frequently seen as providing additional pieces of information, permitting some reduction in uncertainty for program decision-makers. This conclusion was based on the analysis of 20 national health program evaluations. He added:

> Our findings, then, suggest that the predominant image of non-utilization that characterizes much of the commentary on evaluation research can be attributed in substantial degree to a definition of utilization that is too narrow in its emphasis on seeing immediate, direct, and concrete impact on program decisions. Such a narrow definition fails to take into account the nature of most actual program development processes. (Patton, 1978, p. 33)

Because use of evaluation information is context specific, we agree with others (see Van de Vall & Bolas, 1982; Tash & Stahler, 1982; Sproull & Zubrow, 1981) who believe that evaluators need to adapt to the demands of the client and organization they serve. Those who cannot adapt will find their usefulness limited.

Support from those in positions of power over the school or system in question is essential, for school staff often look to those individuals for sanction, and their commitment is necessary to allow evaluation to run unimpeded. Stufflebeam (1980) has made the point that the support of the school superintendent is a necessary ingredient for a school evaluation system to function (see also Van de Vall & Bolas, 1982, and Rich, 1979, in this regard).

Most reviews of research on factors affecting the use of evaluation also show that involving potential users throughout the evaluation is a critical ingredient to evaluation use. They need to be involved at the beginning so that their expectations for the evaluation are understood. They need to feel ownership in the evaluation design and its methods of operation. They need to be kept informed while the evaluation is in progress. They need to understand the evaluation's findings and its implications for action. They need to be involved in evaluation decisions. Failure in any of these forms of involvement and communication are likely to reduce the potential for the use of the information yielded by the evaluation.

Finally, Cousins and Leithwood (1985) have confirmed that the quality of the evaluation itself is the factor that seems to be most strongly associated with evaluation use.

Based on the foregoing discussion of research on evaluation use, we have a sense that an empirical basis for making decisions about evaluation is beginning to emerge. As this research literature matures, we expect to see increasing sophistication in the practice of evaluation.

CASE STUDY APPLICATION

May 11. Today I had the first of the usual flurry of requests for preliminary information that come on nearly every evaluation. But we've not even held our steering committee meeting to review the preliminary data analyses yet, and anything we said at this point would be too subjective for my taste. I usually don't mind giving a few impressions, if people will remember that's all they are, but my sense is that this humanities program is controversial enough that it's likely some people might extract only the message they want to hear from whatever we say. I know we can't guard against that completely, even with the most polished final report, but if I do the best I can to present data I'm confident of, in as careful and balanced fashion as possible, then I can sleep easier at night if someone misuses it than I can if I contribute to the misuse through casual or careless communication.

Of course, key folk on the committee are now aware of *some* of the preliminary analyses, but that's not in very "disseminable" form, even if we had finished interpreting it, which we haven't. So, there is a need for some interim information; I don't think it necessary to keep everyone waiting with bated breath right up to the final written report. Methinks I'll let the site-visit exit interview later this week be the first interim report— probably the only one, really, with the final report coming on fairly soon.

Author Comments.   Few evaluation reports hold such general interest that they are media events. In contexts like the Radnor humanities curriculum, however, several individuals and groups will generally press to get a preview of the findings at the earliest possible moment. The more visible the evaluation, the more curious the local folk get about the outcomes. When outside experts begin roaming through, requests for evaluation findings often spring up in their wake.

In the Radnor case, I would probably restrict early release of information to the previously mentioned exit interview at the conclusion of the on-site evaluation visit. This is a natural and expected time to share at least general impressions of the evaluation team. The audiences for the report (probably the humanities staff, the principal, and representatives of the humanities committee and the board) should be reminded that this is only one facet of the evaluation, and that the results of the on-site evaluation will have to be integrated with those from the other evaluation activities (being reviewed by the steering committee) into a more comprehensive report before they will have the full picture that the evaluation will provide.

May 25. Some day I hope to learn not to procrastinate (does anyone ever learn that, really?) With spring clean-up along our creek and spraying the aspen groves for black-spot disease (whoever said "natural" landscaping needed little care never saw natural groves of naturally sickly and naturally dead aspens, I've decided), the last few evenings have gotten away from me, and the final report on the Radnor program is due soon. Time to put pen to paper. Lots of the basic stuff is already there in our data summaries, on-site visit reports, etc., but it needs to be pulled together into a cohesive, coherent report, complete with executive summary and all the trimmings. I promised Mrs. Janson a draft copy for review by her and the other audiences by the end of next week, so I'd best let the aspens care for themselves for a week or two. Maybe I can get the draft off to her before the county agent tells us its time to spray the birch trees to keep down damage by leaf miners and bronze-headed borers. Oh the joys of a residence in the country!

Author Comments. In preparing the final report, I would produce a complete first draft including at least the following:

1. An introduction describing the humanities curriculum, purposes and audiences for the evaluation, and an overview of the rest of the report.

2. A list of evaluative questions used to guide the study.

3. Overview of the evaluation plan and procedures, with a supporting appendix to provide detail. (The matrix described earlier is often a helpful inclusion in the overview section of the plan.)

4. Discussion of findings, probably organized around the evaluative questions. (Again, detailed presentations of findings generated by each instrument could be provided in an appendix.)

5. Judgments, in the form of strengths and weaknesses, along with recommendations, with sufficient rationale and linkage to findings to demonstrate that the recommendations are warranted.

Once it is completed, I would submit the draft copy of the final report to the principal and ask that she review it and also have it reviewed by the head of the humanities faculty, other selected members of the humanities study committee, and the board president. The intent of this review would be twofold: first, to identify any factual inaccuracies; second, to challenge any inferences, conclusions, or recommendations these partisan reviewers think are inappropriate, unwarranted, or unfair. It is important, in asking for these reviews, to communicate that you will take them very seriously and will consider carefully each suggested revision, whether it be minor editing or deletion of a major recommendation. It is equally important to make very clear that the ultimate decision for what goes into the final report draft belongs to the evaluator and that there is no guarantee that all of their suggestions will be incorporated. Failure to get these ground rules clear at the outset can lead to all manner of problems.[111]

Having the client review a draft of the report and vouchsafe its factual accuracy is good insurance against the evaluator committing serious blunders. Helpful clients have saved me embarrassment by correcting nontrivial errors I failed to spot in draft reports (like the "typo" that turned a K–3 program into K–8, or the instance when I described a project director as single-minded, but the typewriter rendered it "simple-minded").

Even small factual errors, uncorrected, give comfort to the critic bent on discrediting the report. Consider, for instance, the PTA president who had opposed a new curriculum designed to teach reading through a study of local cultures, only to find that our evaluation showed clearly that the curriculum was having a very positive effect on student learning. "How," he thundered at a collective PTA and school board meeting, "can you believe anything else is accurate if the evaluator can't even spell the name of the school or its principal right!" (Now before you judge too harshly, you should try to evaluate the curriculum at Tchesinkut School, where Mr. Nakinilerak presides.) It was there in the Alaskan bush that I first learned the value of asking clients to review and share responsibility for accuracy of the final report.

Several references have been made previously to an executive summary. This might take the form of a parsimonious introductory chapter to the evaluation report, including a synopsis of the findings and references to other sections of the report of interest to particular audiences. Or, the executive summary might be a separate, self-contained document of 5 to 10 pages for use with interested parties who need results but are not concerned with details. In larger evaluations, where more people need to be informed, a brief evaluation abstract of one or two pages might be useful.

One ethical consideration that should not be neglected in report writing is preserving desired confidentiality and anonymity. Evaluators generally promise that individual responses or test scores will not be divulged (except with the individuals' express approval). Unfortunately, that promise is sometimes forgotten at the report-writing stage.

APPLICATION EXERCISE

1. Apply the "good evaluation report" checklist from this chapter to an evaluation study of your choosing. Do the strengths and weaknesses of the reporting process you reviewed suggest procedures that you will want to adopt in the future?

2. List questions that you think future research on evaluation reporting and use should answer. What questions do you have for which there are no good answers?

SUGGESTED READINGS

ALKIN, M. C., DAILLAK, R., & WHITE, P. (1979). *Using evaluation: Does evaluation make a difference?* Beverly Hills, CA: Sage.

BRASKAMP, L., & BROWN, R. D. (Eds.). (1980). *Utilization of evaluative information.* New Directions for Program Evaluation, No. 5. San Francisco: Jossey-Bass.

PATTON, M. Q. (1978). *Utilization-focused evaluation.* Beverly Hills, CA: Sage.

SMITH, N. L. (Ed.). (1982a). *Communication strategies in evaluation.* Beverly Hills, CA: Sage.

Chapter 21
Evaluating Evaluations

Orienting Questions

1. Why should evaluations be evaluated? When would you want to commission a meta-evaluation?
2. What are the attributes of good evaluation?
3. What guidelines and steps would you use in carrying out a meta-evaluation?
4. What are the major contributions of the Joint Committee on Standards for Educational Evaluation? Of other sets of meta-evaluation criteria?

Any evaluation study is biased to some extent. Decisions that an evaluator makes about what to examine, what methods and instruments to use, who to talk to and who to listen to—all influence the outcome of the evaluation. Even the evaluator's personal background, biases, professional training, and experience all affect the way the study is conducted.

Both evaluator and client must be concerned about evaluation bias: the evaluator because her personal standards and professional reputation are at stake; the client because he doesn't want to invest (either politically or financially) in findings that are off target. Both have a lot to lose if an evaluation is shown to be deficient in some critical aspect.

This is why *meta-evaluation*—the evaluation of an evaluation—is important. Formative meta-evaluation can improve an evaluation study before it is irretrievably too late. Summative meta-evaluations can add credibility to final results.

In this chapter we discuss the concept of meta-evaluation, standards and criteria for evaluating evaluations, and meta-evaluation procedures that can be used to enhance the quality of evaluations done in education.

THE CONCEPT AND EVOLUTION
OF META-EVALUATION

Not even the most enthusiastic advocate would assert that all evaluation activities are intrinsically valuable, or even well-intentioned. Thoughtful observers have even asked, from time to time, whether evaluation results warrant their cost in human and other resources. As Nilsson and Hogben (1983) correctly point out, meta-evaluation refers not only to the evaluation of particular studies but also to evaluation of the very function and practice of evaluation itself.

This broader definition of meta-evaluation, however, goes beyond the scope of both this chapter and book. By now our bias must be clear to the reader: We are thoroughly convinced of evaluation's importance in educational improvement. *Properly practiced*, evaluation has led to direct and incontestable improvements in educational systems, programs, and practices—improvements that would have occurred in no other way. Given the number and frequency of evaluation failures, however, we understand why some question the basic concept. When evaluation goes wrong, the fault lies, we believe, not with the concept but with the way in which the evaluation is conducted. The purpose of meta-evaluation is to help evaluation live up to its potential. For this chapter, then, we restrict our discussion to evaluation of individual evaluation designs, studies, and reports.

The Evolution of Meta-Evaluation

In an informal sense, meta-evaluation has been around as long as evaluation, for someone has had an opinion about the quality of every evaluation study ever conducted. During the 1960s, however, evaluators began to discuss formal meta-evaluation procedures and criteria, writers began to suggest what constituted good and bad evaluations (for example, Scriven, 1967; Stake, 1967, 1970; Stufflebeam, 1968), and unpublished checklists of evaluation standards began to be exchanged informally among educational evaluators. In addition, several evaluators published their proposed guidelines, or "meta-evaluation" criteria, for use in judging evaluation plans or reports (Guba & Stufflebeam, 1968; Stake, 1969a; Stufflebeam and others, 1971; Stufflebeam, 1974b; Scriven, 1974b; Worthen, 1974a; Sanders & Nafziger, 1975).

In general, evaluators welcomed these lists of proposed meta-evaluation criteria. In addition, several authors of the criteria attempted to make them useful to evaluation consumers, thinking that perhaps if evaluation clients were more skillful in judging an evaluation's adequacy, the number of unhelpful and wasteful evaluations might diminish. Clients can demand high quality only if they can recognize what it is that makes one evaluation better or worse than another. For this to occur, evaluators and those they serve must reach shared agreements about what constitutes a good evaluation, in terms both can understand.

Although some of the published and fugitive meta-evaluation documents were purported to be for school administrators, they still depended largely on specialized terminology or technical knowledge that school personnel would not normally be expected to possess. Consequently, useful as they were, their primary users continued to be evaluators.

Also, the many different sets of proposed criteria proved disconcerting to evaluators and consumers alike. Was one set better than another? Which was best? Which was most acceptable?

No one could answer such questions well, for none of the proposed sets of criteria offered by educational evaluators carried any profession-wide endorsement. Consequently, an ambitious effort was launched in the late 1970s to develop a comprehensive set of standards explicitly tailored for use in educational evaluations and containing generally agreed-upon standards for quality evaluation. Development of these standards began in 1975, under the direction of Daniel Stufflebeam, at Western Michigan University's Evaluation Center. Guidance and authorization were provided by a profession-wide Joint Committee on Standards for Educational Evaluation (hereafter referred to as the Joint Committee) (Ridings & Stufflebeam, 1981).[112]

The result of the Joint Committee's work was the *Standards for Evaluations of Educational Programs, Projects, and Materials* (Joint Committee, 1981), which has received widespread attention in education. In the introduction to the *Standards,* as we shall call them, the Joint Committee stated that development of sound standards could provide the following benefits:

> a common language to facilitate communication and collaboration in evaluation; a set of general rules for dealing with a variety of specific evaluation problems; a conceptual framework by which to study the often-confusing world of evaluation; a set of working definitions to guide research and development on the evaluation process; a public statement of the state of the art in educational evaluation; a basis for self-regulation and accountability by professional evaluators; and an aid to developing public credibility for the educational evaluation field. (Joint Committee, 1981, p. 5)

Other efforts to set standards for evaluation and for certain professions (Ridings, 1982; Rossi, 1982b) will not be discussed in this chapter, except to note the following. The Evaluation Research Society (ERS), established to serve the needs of program evaluators in a wide spectrum of applied social science disciplines and health, law enforcement, and public policy fields, developed a set of standards for program evaluation, borrowing and incorporating ideas from the Joint Committee's *Standards* (as well as from guidelines of the United States General Accounting Office and the Office of the Auditor General of Canada). We do not provide comparable detail about the ERS standards because (1) there is a heavy overlap in the coverage of the two sets; (2) the ERS standards are restricted solely to program evaluation, whereas the Joint Committee *Standards* include evaluation of projects and materials as well; (3) the Joint Committee *Standards* deal directly with evaluation of *educational* entities, the focus of this book; and (4) we accept the Joint Committee *Standards* as the canon of practice for educational evaluation.

THE JOINT COMMITTEE STANDARDS FOR EDUCATIONAL EVALUATION

The Joint Committee *Standards* are a set of 30 standards, each with an overview that provides definitions and a rationale for the standard, a list of guidelines, potential pitfalls and caveats, an illustrative case describing an evaluation practice that could have been guided by that particular standard, and an analysis of that case. The result is a work so comprehensive that it fills a book (Joint Committee, 1981).

One of the most important insights that the Joint Committee provides with the *Standards* is the concept that the quality of an evaluation study can be determined by looking at its (1) utility, (2) feasibility, (3) propriety, and (4) accuracy. The 30 standards are grouped according to their potential contribution to each of these four attributes. Utility is purposely listed first, for the Joint Committee recognized that without utility, an evaluation will be judged harshly, no matter how well it focuses on feasibility, propriety, and accuracy.

Following are the 30 Joint Committee *Standards*, with a brief explanation of each.

A   *Utility Standards*

The Utility Standards are intended to ensure that an evaluation will serve the practical information needs of given audiences. These standards are:

A1 *Audience Identification*

Audiences involved in or affected by the evaluation should be identified, so that their needs can be addressed.

A2 *Evaluator Credibility*

The persons conducting the evaluation should be both trustworthy and competent to perform the evaluation, so that their findings achieve maximum credibility and acceptance.

A3 *Information Scope and Selection*

Information collected should be of such scope and selected in such ways as to address pertinent questions about the object of the evaluation and be responsive to the needs and interests of specified audiences.

A4 *Valuational Interpretation*

The perspectives, procedures, and rationale used to interpret the findings should be carefully described, so that the bases for value judgments are clear.

A5 *Report Clarity*

The evaluation report should describe the object being evaluated and its context, and the purposes, procedures, and findings of the evaluation, so that the audiences will readily understand what was done, why it was done, what information was obtained, what conclusions were drawn, and what recommendations were made.

A6 *Report Dissemination*

Evaluation findings should be disseminated to clients and other right-to-know audiences, so that they can assess and use the findings.

A7 *Report Timeliness*

Release of reports should be timely, so that audiences can best use the reported information.

A8 *Evaluation Impact*

Evaluations should be planned and conducted in ways that encourage follow-through by members of the audiences.

B *Feasibility Standards*

The feasibility standards are intended to ensure that an evaluation will be realistic, prudent, diplomatic, and frugal. They are:

B1 *Practical Procedures*

The evaluation procedures should be practical, so that disruption is kept to a minimum, and that needed information can be obtained.

B2 *Political Viability*

The evaluation should be planned and conducted with anticipation of different positions of various interest groups, so that their cooperation may be obtained, and so that possible attempts by any of these groups to curtail evaluation operations or to bias or misapply the results can be averted or counteracted.

B3 *Cost-Effectiveness*

The evaluation should produce information of sufficient value to justify the resources extended.

C *Propriety Standards*

The propriety standards are intended to ensure that an evaluation will be conducted legally, ethically, and with due regard for the welfare of those involved in the evaluation as well as those affected by its results. These standards are:

C1 *Formal Obligation*

Obligations of the formal parties to an evaluation (what is to be done, how, by whom, when) should be agreed to in writing, so that these parties are obligated to adhere to all conditions of the agreement or formally to renegotiate it.

C2 *Conflict of Interest*

Conflict of interest, frequently unavoidable, should be dealt with openly and honestly, so that it does not compromise the evaluation processes and results.

C3 *Full and Frank Disclosure*

Oral and written evaluation reports should be open, direct, and honest in their disclosure of pertinent findings, including the limitations of the evaluation.

C4 *Public's Right to Know*

The formal parties to an evaluation should respect and assure the public's right to know, within the limits of other related principles and statutes, such as those dealing with public safety and the right to privacy.

C5 *Rights of Human Subjects*

Evaluations should be designed and conducted, so that the rights and welfare of the human subjects are respected and protected.

C6 *Human Interactions*

Evaluators should respect human dignity and worth in their interactions with other persons associated with an evaluation.

C7 *Balanced Reporting*

The evaluation should be complete and fair in its presentation of strengths and weaknesses of the object under investigation, so that strengths can be built upon and problem areas addressed.

C8 *Fiscal Responsibility*

The evaluator's allocation and expenditure of resources should reflect sound accountability procedures and otherwise be prudent and ethically responsible.

D *Accuracy Standards*

The Accuracy Standards are intended to ensure that an evaluation will reveal and convey technically adequate information about the features of the object being studied that determine its worth or merit. These standards are:

D1 *Object Identification*

The object of the evaluation (program, project, material) should be sufficiently examined, so that the form(s) of the object being considered in the evaluation can be clearly identified.

D2 *Context Analysis*

The context in which the program, project, or material exists should be examined in enough detail, so that its likely influences on the object can be identified.

D3 *Described Purposes and Procedures*

The purposes and procedures of the evaluation should be monitored and described in enough detail, so that they can be identified and assessed.

D4 *Defensible Information Sources*

The sources of information should be described in enough detail so that the adequacy of the information can be assessed.

D5 *Valid Measurement*

The information-gathering instruments and procedures should be chosen or developed and then implemented in ways that will assure that the interpretation arrived at is valid for the given use.

D6 *Reliable Measurement*

The information-gathering instruments and procedures should be chosen or developed and then implemented in ways that will assure that the information obtained is sufficiently reliable for the intended use.

D7 *Systematic Data Control*

The data collected, processed, and reported in an evaluation should be reviewed and corrected, so that the results of the evaluation will not be flawed.

D8 *Analysis of Quantitative Information*

Quantitative information in an evaluation should be appropriately and systematically analyzed to ensure supportable interpretations.

D9 *Analysis of Qualitative Information*

Qualitative information in an evaluation should be appropriately and systematically analyzed to ensure supportable interpretations.

D10 *Justified Conclusions*

The conclusions reached in an evaluation should be explicitly justified, so that the audience can assess them.

D11 Objective Reporting

The evaluation procedures should provide safeguards to protect the evaluation findings and reports against distortion by the personal feelings and biases of any party to the evaluation.

Utility of the Standards

School evaluators and other educators may use the *Standards* in planning or reviewing evaluations, organizing preservice and in-service education in evaluation, and monitoring or auditing formally commissioned evaluations. Ridings and Stufflebeam (1981) provide an excellent analysis of the relative importance of the *Standards* to various evaluation tasks, as shown in Figure 21.1.

A useful byproduct of the *Standards* is an annotated bibliography of references addressing each of the 30 standards. The bibliography was compiled by Wildemuth (1981) at the ERIC Clearinghouse on Tests, Measurements, and Evaluation and is available through the ERIC system.

In our judgment, the Joint Committee *Standards* continue as the ultimate benchmark against which both evaluations and other sets of meta-evaluation criteria and standards should be judged.

Application of the Standards

The *Standards* are not a cookbook list of steps to follow. Rather, they are a compilation of commonly agreed upon characteristics of good evaluation practice. In the final analysis, choices and trade-offs relating to each standard are the province of the evaluator.

A checklist (based on the *Standards*) for judging the adequacy of evaluation designs and reports could be developed easily using a format somewhat like that shown in the following sample.

Title of Evlauation Document: _____

Name of Reviewer: _____

	Criterion Met?	*Elaboration*

Standard: AUDIENCE IDENTIFICATION
Specific Criteria:

a. Are the audiences for the evaluation identified?	Yes No ? NA	
b. Have the needs of the audiences been identified?	Yes No ? NA	
c. Are the objectives of the evaluation consistent with the needs of the audiences?	Yes No ? NA	
d. Does the information to be provided allow necessary decisions about the program or product to be made?	Yes No ? NA	

Standard: RELIABLE MEASUREMENT
Specific Criteria:

a. Are data-collection procedures described well?	Yes	No	?	NA
b. Will care be taken to assure minimal error?	Yes	No	?	NA
c. Are scoring or coding procedures objective?	Yes	No	?	NA
d. Are the evaluation instruments reliable (that is, is reliability information included)?	Yes	No	?	NA

Standard: PRACTICAL PROCEDURES
Specific Criteria:

a. Are the evaluation resources (time, money, and personnel) adequate to carry out the projected activities?	Yes	No	?	NA
b. Are management plans specified for conducting the evaluation?	Yes	No	?	NA
c. Has adequate planning been done to support the feasibility of conducting complex activities?	Yes	No	?	NA

PROFESSIONAL STANDARDS AND EQUITY

We should not leave this discussion without commenting on the importance of making standards sensitive to equity concerns. We live in an era when regulatory agencies and litigation both play a role in ensuring that the civil and constitutional rights of women and ethnic, racial, and other minorities are not abridged. Yet as Tittle so appropriately reminds us, "While there has not been litigation to make evaluation standards responsive to equity concerns, natural rights and laws create an ethical imperative for evaluation standards as well" (Tittle, 1984, p. 21). Her analysis of several sets of standards (including the ERS standards and the Joint Committee *Standards*) suggests that no extant set of evaluation standards is yet as responsive as it should be to equity concerns.

We urge those who use any meta-evaluation standards or criteria to consider in reviewing any evaluation design or report whether the effort has in any way hindered the goal of equity, which is a hallmark of civilized societies.

THE ROLE OF META-EVALUATOR

As we implied earlier, nearly everyone does informal meta-evaluation. But *formal* evaluation is something else entirely. Ostensibly, a meta-evaluator must possess at least as much evaluation acumen as whoever conducted the original study. As Brinkerhoff and others (1983) state, "Not only should they [meta-evaluators] be competent enough to *do* the original evaluation, but they also have to be able to tell if it was a good or bad one and be able to convince others that they know the difference" (Brinkerhoff and others, 1983, p. 208).

Accurate as this observation is, it does create a dilemma: It calls for development of a "super-evaluator" with sufficient competence to evaluate almost any evaluation that is done. But who then will be competent to evaluate the super-evaluator's work? Other super-evaluators? Or will it be necessary to develop *super*-super-evaluators who are even more competent than the super-evaluators whose work they judge?

Evaluation Function Standards (Descriptors)	1. Deciding Whether to do a Study	2. Clarifying and Assessing Purpose	3. Ensure Political Viability	4. Contract	5. Staff the Study	6. Manage the Study	7. Collect Data	8. Analyze Data	9. Report Findings	10. Apply Results
A1 Audience Identification	×	×	×	×		×			×	×
A2 Evaluator Credibility	×		×	×	×	×	×			
A3 Information Scope and Selection			×				×		×	
A4 Valuational Interpretation	×	×					×	×	×	×
A5 Timely Reporting				×		×			×	
A6 Report Dissemination			×	×		×			×	×
A7 Clear Reporting									×	
A8 Evaluation Impact	×	×	×						×	×
B1 Practical Procedures			×				×	×		
B2 Political Viability	×		×	×	×	×	×			×
B3 Cost Effectiveness	×	×				×				
C1 Formal Obligation	×		×	×		×	×			×
C2 Conflict of Interest	×	×	×	×	×	×				×
C3 Full & Frank Disclosure									×	
C4 Public's Right to Know			×	×					×	×
C5 Rights of Human Subjects			×	×		×	×			×
C6 Human Interactions			×			×	×			
C7 Balanced Reporting							×		×	×
C8 Fiscal Responsibility			×	×		×				
D1 Object Identification	×	×		×			×	×	×	
D2 Context Analysis	×	×					×	×	×	×
D3 Described Purposes and Procedures	×	×	×	×		×	×		×	×
D4 Defensible Information Sources		×					×		×	
D5 Valid Measurement							×			
D6 Reliable Measurement							×			
D7 Systematic Data Control						×	×			
D8 Quantitative Analysis								×		
D9 Qualitative Analysis										
D10 Justified Conclusions		×						×	×	×
D11 Objective Reporting			×		×				×	

FIGURE 21.1 Analysis of the Relative Importance of Thirty Standards in Performing Ten Tasks in an Evaluation

Source: Ridings and Stufflebeam, 1981.

377

Of course, the answer to such circular concerns is that in meta-evaluation, as in many other efforts, we simply do the best we can. Much as we would prefer to have every meta-evaluation conducted by a second superbly skilled evaluator, that is often not feasible. Time or resource constraints sometimes force the evaluator who wishes to determine the adequacy of her own work to be her own meta-evaluator. Similarly, administrators who receive evaluation proposals or reports often lack the time or resources to permit a meta-evaluation by a second evaluator. It is largely for that reason that we include in this chapter samples of less-detailed sets of meta-evaluation criteria that administrators and other evaluation consumers might find useful.

We see all of the following persons as being appropriate individuals to conduct meta-evaluations, at the same time recognizing that the sophistication, certainty, and objectivity of their judgments are likely to vary according to their competence and conflict of interest:

1. *Meta-Evaluation conducted by the original evaluator.* We discussed earlier the possible biases that can accrue from evaluating one's own work. The evaluator is not immune to personal biases, and it is always advisable to have another evaluator review one's work—even if it is only a critique by a friendly but frank colleague down the hall. Should that not be possible, however, we think it better for an evaluator to measure her own evaluation work against one of the sets of meta-evaluation criteria provided earlier than to allow it to go unmeasured simply because there is a risk of bias.

2. *Meta-Evaluation conducted by evaluation consumers.* Often the evaluation sponsor, client, or other stakeholders are left to judge the adequacy of an evaluation plan or report without assistance from a professional evaluator. The success of this approach depends heavily on the technical competence of the consumer to judge how well the evaluation meets such standards as "valid measurement" or "analysis of quantitative information." Many of the criteria and standards listed in this chapter do not, however, require specialized technical training. It may be quite feasible for a client to apply most of the criteria effectively, calling on a technical expert to clarify anything that seems complex or unclear. Of course, if the evaluation is judged to be irrelevant, unintelligible, biased, or untimely, its technical adequacy may be of little concern.

3. *Meta-Evaluation conducted by competent evaluators.* This would seem to be the best arrangement, all else being equal. Still, there are important choices to be made. As Brinkerhoff and others (1983) remind us, (1) external meta-evaluators are generally more credible than internal meta-evaluators; and (2) a team may bring a greater range of skills to a meta-evaluation than can an individual evaluator.

SOME GENERAL GUIDELINES FOR CONDUCTING META-EVALUATIONS

Evaluators are well-advised to plan both internal and external reviews of evaluation at critical points: once after an evaluation plan or design has been finalized, at periodic intervals during the evaluation to check progress and identify problems, and at the end of the evaluation to review findings and reports, and audit the evaluation procedures and conclusions. Many evaluators use internal and external reviews to guide their work.

The *internal review* can be conducted by an evaluation committee or advisory group. While the evaluation is in progress, the evaluator could enlist a group of stakeholders and evaluation staff, asking for their reactions to the evaluation plan, its implementation, the relative timeliness and costs of various evaluation tasks, and the need for any revisions. The minutes of such meetings provide useful progress reports for the client.

The *external review* is best conducted by a disinterested outside party with successful experience in similar evaluations. If called in early enough, the outside evaluator can review the evaluation design and offer recommendations for strengthening it. An external reviewer can also provide technical assistance during the evaluation and at the end of the project, can review evaluation procedures, findings, and reports. The external reviewer may need to schedule a site visit at each review stage to gain full access to evaluation files, instruments, data, reports, and audiences. Such an arrangement takes both planning and knowledge of how and where to access pertinent evaluation information. The evaluator should be able to show how the evaluation has been adjusted in response to recommendations by the external reviewer.

Brinkerhoff and colleagues (1983) provide a helpful list of procedural options (Fig. 21.2) from which one might choose in focusing a meta-evaluation:

As noted above, one can evaluate evaluation plans, designs, activities, reports, or even the financing and management of an evaluation. We choose to emphasize in the remainder of our discussion the evaluation of the evaluation design.

	Focus of the Meta-Evaluation		
	Formative Uses		*Summative Uses*
	Evaluating Evaluation Plans	*Evaluating Evaluation in Progress*	*Evaluating Evaluation After Its Completion*
Procedures for Doing the Meta-Evaluation	hire consultant, e.g., evaluator, measurement specialist, or content specialist	independent observers, e.g., meta-evaluator, evaluation team, review panel	review of final reports, e.g., send reports to evaluator, consultant, advisory group
	review panel, e.g, advisory group	review of progress reports, e.g., logs, interim reports, budget update, management plan, collection schedule	meta-evaluator, e.g., sponsors or funding agent, advisory panel, professional evaluator(s)
	review of evaluation plans, e.g., design, contract management plan		

FIGURE 21.2   Procedural Options for Doing the Meta-evaluation

Source: Brinkeroff and others, 1983, p. 221.

In evaluation, design is critical. Poor designs do not lead to satisfactory evaluations. Yet meta-evaluation has to cover more than evaluation design. It is equally important to monitor the evaluation in progress and to review reports to ensure that the promises outlined in evaluation plans have been kept. It would be foolish to wait until the report is filed to assess the adequacy of the evaluation and thus find it too late to correct many deficiencies that might otherwise be identified. In short, a complete meta-evaluation includes:

- Reviewing the proposed design to ensure it is feasible and sound
- Monitoring the design to see that tasks are completed as planned and within budget
- Checking the quality of instruments, procedures, and products (such as data and reports)
- Reviewing the design for possible midstream revisions (especially in light of the utility the evaluation has shown so far for important audiences or of problems the evaluation was running into)
- Checking the effects of meta-evaluation on the evaluation.

Because of limited space, we limit this discussion and our remaining examples to evaluating the design. Readers should easily be able to extrapolate criteria from this discussion for meta-evaluations of other aspects of an evaluation.

Steps to Take in Evaluating an Evaluation Design

The following steps are proposed for conducting a meta-evaluation of an evaluation design:

1. *Obtain a copy of the design in a form ready for review.* Formative evaluation of a meta-evaluation is obviously desirable once the design is sufficiently formulated to make such a review productive. There is little utility in telling an evaluator that her unfinished design is incomplete.

2. *Identify who will do the meta-evaluation.* Check our comments in the previous section on "The Role of Meta-Evaluator" for help in this decision.

3. *Assure that authorization exists to evaluate the design.* If you are a sponsor or client and you receive a design submitted by an evaluator who proposes to contract with you to do an evaluation, you are obviously free to evaluate it, and normally there would be no professional or legal restraint on your arranging for another competent "meta-evaluator" to assist you in doing so. Conversely, suppose the chair of a "Concerned Citizens Against Year-Round Education" committee asks you to find flaws in an internal evaluation design the school proposes to use in evaluating its year-round program. You should question the appropriateness of that role, especially if you find the design is in rough draft form, circulated only for internal reactions, and surreptitiously spirited from the school to the committee by a disgruntled school custodian. Meta-evaluators (like evaluators) can find themselves used as "hired guns," and it is important before buckling on the holster to be certain that the meta-evaluation desired by your paymaster will not violate ethical or legal principles.

4. *Choose the meta-evaluation criteria or standards to apply.* If the sponsor or client is to do the meta-evaluation, this choice may be theirs alone. If an evaluation specialist is selected to do the meta-evaluation, then the criteria or standards should be agreed upon by the evaluator and the sponsor/client. Any of the lists referenced in this chapter would seem appropriate. Tailoring criteria to the particular situation is another option, although given the careful thought that lies behind already developed standards, the value in expending resources to invent new standards seems highly questionable.

5. *Apply the criteria or standards to the evaluation design.* Some of the meta-evaluation criteria and standards we have referenced include their own aids to application. For example, the Joint Committee encourages use of the *Standards* by appending a checklist to its publication. The Sanders and Nafziger (1975) criteria we presented also have a response scale appended, as well as a format for summarizing reactions to the evaluation design on several criterion categories. If one prefers to apply a set of criteria that is not accompanied by any such checklist or response scale, it is advisable to create at least a simple scale for recording how well the design meets each criterion, even if that scale is as simple as "high-medium-low," or "acceptable-unacceptable."

6. *Judge the adequacy of the evaluation design.* No evaluation design is perfect. The question is whether, on balance, after summarizing judgments across scales, the evaluation seems to achieve its purposes at an acceptable level of quality. Some authors of meta-evaluation criteria provide no suggestions for making this decision, whereas others suggest priorities among their standards or criteria (for example, the Joint Committee suggests that an evaluation that lacks "utility" will not be acceptable, regardless of its other redeeming features).

A SIMPLE EXAMPLE OF META-EVALUATION

As we stated earlier, the ultimate meta-evaluation yardstick, in our opinion, is the Joint Committee's *Standards*; yet other sets of criteria or standards are useful and appropriate in given circumstances.[113] For example, sometimes the comprehensiveness of a set of criteria can mitigate against their use (at least in their entirety), in circumstances where time is short or the inclusiveness of the criteria makes them intimidating to users. In such cases, even simple (but defensible) lists of meta-evaluation criteria are better than nothing.

For the sake of simplicity, we will present here a very simple example of meta-evaluation, based on Worthen's (1974a) 11 criteria, one of the more general and brief lists we referenced earlier. Our choice of simplicity is purposeful and may help make another point.

Like most professionals, evaluators (intentionally or not) have allowed their use of specialized techniques and terminology to hinder communication with laypersons and colleagues in other areas. The tendency of many practitioners to accord evaluation plans or reports a certain mystique (perhaps because of their statistical symbols) further compounds the problem. As a result, a typical practitioner's critique of an evaluation study may go something like this: "Why can't those people quit using jargon and write in simple English?" or "Surely the evaluator must know that the board of education isn't going to read a lot of tables!''

Sound familiar? It should, for such statements are all too representative of many teachers' and administrators' reactions to well-intentioned and perhaps well-conducted evaluation studies. The tragedy is that such blanket reactions may spotlight basic deficiencies common to many evaluation designs and reports, but they fail completely to deal with deeper issues: Is the design technically sound? Is the information in the study believable? Is it unbiased? Does it reflect the full range of information necessary to judge the program's worth? The frequent failure to deal with evaluation studies on this more meaningful level is less the fault of the school practitioner than of the evaluator. Ironically, many evaluators, whose very profession requires them to articulate criteria for judging quality, are casual about informing clients of the existence of simple, uncomplicated sets of criteria for use in judging the quality of evaluation studies. Only if evaluators begin to communicate more effectively and simply will clients learn to differentiate between a good evaluation and a poor one.

The section that follows is meant to show evaluation consumers how even a simple list of 11 general criteria might be used in judging an evaluation study. A fictional example is used to illustrate how one might tell whether a proposed evaluation study possesses each characteristic deemed critical.

Before launching into this example, we must briefly summarize the 11 general criteria that we will use.

The 11 Touchstones of Good Evaluations

The following 11 characteristics of good evaluations are proposed for use in judging the quality of evaluation studies:

1. *Conceptual clarity* (the extent to which the evaluation is well focused and the purpose, role, and general approach are clearly stated).

2. *Characterization of the object of the evaluation* (the extent to which the evaluation contains a thorough, detailed description of that which is evaluated).

3. *Recognition and representation of legitimate audiences* (the extent to which all legitimate evaluation audiences have a voice in focusing the study and an opportunity to review results).

4. *Sensitivity to political problems in evaluation* (the extent to which the evaluation has been sensitive to and coped satisfactorily with potentially disruptive political, interpersonal, and ethical issues).

5. *Specification of information needs and sources* (the extent to which the evaluation specifies needed information and sources of that information).

6. *Comprehensiveness/inclusiveness* (the extent to which the evaluation has collected data on all important variables and issues, without getting bogged down in inconsequential data).

7. *Technical adequacy* (the extent to which the evaluation design and procedures yielded information that meets scientific criteria of validity, reliability, and objectivity).

8. *Consideration of costs* (the extent to which the evaluation considered cost factors along with other variables).

9. *Explicit standards/criteria* (the extent to which the evaluation contained an explicit listing and/or discussion of the criteria and standards used to make judgments about the evaluation object).

10. *Judgments and/or recommendations* (the extent to which the evaluation goes beyond reporting findings to offer judgments and recommendations suggested by the data).

11. *Reports tailored to audiences* (the extent to which the evaluation reports are provided at appropriate times and in appropriate formats to the identified audiences for the evaluation information).

Now to apply these criteria to our fictional example.

Enter the Actors...

The scenario is as follows. The Board of Education of a large city school district has called for an evaluation of the district's primary-grade team-teaching program. The associate superintendent for instruction, Frank Overly, has asked each of the district's two full-time evaluators, Lotta Smart and Les Wise,[114] to prepare independent plans detailing how they would propose to conduct the evaluation. The plans have been prepared and reviewed by Frank Overly. He has asked for a discussion with each evaluator before deciding which plan he will recommend to the board. Portions of the two dialogues that ensue appear throughout the balance of this text under each of 11 general characteristics proposed for use in judging the quality of an evaluation study.

Conceptual Clarity: Interview with Les Wise

FRANK: I've finished reading your evaluation plan, Les, and want to make sure I understand it completely before I make my recommendation to the Board of Education tonight. They're eager to take a close look at the team-teaching program, so I want to make sure our plan will provide them with all the information they need. I need to ask a few questions about your plan, if that's OK with you.

LES: Go ahead, although I believe most of it is pretty straightforward. But if there's something you don't understand, we probably should get it clarified.

FRANK: As I read through your plan, I'm not entirely clear about whether you see the data being produced primarily for the staff to use in improving the program or for the board to use in deciding whether or not to continue it.

LES: I don't really think it matters very much because the information can be used by both. Data are data, and they don't much care what you use them for.

You said the board needed to decide whether to continue the program, so I see that as the main purpose of the evaluation. But the staff is welcome to the data too, as far as I'm concerned.

FRANK: Shouldn't we really collect different kinds of data for the board to use for their decision than for the staff to use for formative purposes?

LES: Not in my view. The data I propose to collect for the board are no different than what we've collected for the staff for two years now. As I said before, data are data, and they don't much care. . . .

FRANK: Yes, I understand your point. But that brings up another concern. You have been working on our district's internal evaluation of this program for two years. Can you really be impartial enough to judge whether the program should be continued or not?

LES: I don't see why not. Look, Frank, I'm an evaluator. I'm trained to be impartial, right? That means that I don't let my personal feelings, if I have any, get in the way of my work. When I look at what the data say, there isn't any way I am going to let my ideas get into the mix—I'll just tell it like it is. Besides, numbers don't lie. If the program kids score low on the test, that's just the way it is, and that's the way it will be written up.

FRANK: I'm not suggesting you wouldn't be honest, but I can't help wondering if all of us aren't sometimes influenced, even subconsciously, by our biases. Aren't there ways that your bias can creep in unaware, even to yourself? What about the kind of instruments you choose, or the emphasis you place on certain outcomes in writing your report? I see nothing in your plan to guard against such possibilities.

LES: Like I said before, that's not a problem with me, because I'm trained to be objective. Who in the district is any more objective than I? I didn't help plan the program, so I'm about the only one who doesn't really have any reason to care about how the evaluation comes out. Just because some of my friends are in it doesn't change that fact. So when I analyze the data and tell you what the board should do with the program, that's the most objective decision you'll be able to get.

FRANK: Perhaps part of my unease about objectivity is that I'm not really very clear about just what type of evaluation you're proposing or what the guiding framework is for your study. I've reread it once or twice, but I don't have a real sense of whether you will be making comparisons and, if so, with what, how—or whether—you intend to decide whether objectives are attained, and so on. But maybe that will come clear to me if we talk about some of the specifics of your document.

Conceptual Clarity: Interview with Lotta Smart

FRANK: I've finished reading your evaluation plan, Lotta, and want to make sure I understand it completely before I make my recommendation to the Board of Education tonight. They're eager to take a close look at the team-teaching program, so I want to make sure our plan will provide them with all the information they need. I need to ask a few questions about your plan, if that's OK with you.

LOTTA: By all means—that might help me see if I have covered everything adequately in the plan.

FRANK: As I understand it, you're proposing that the evaluation be summative, that the data will help the board decide whether or not to continue the program.

LOTTA: Yes, that's true. The program has run for two full years and all the staff seem to agree the bugs are all out and it's working as well as it can. It seems fair to give it a full-blown evaluation now to see if it's really worth the resources we're putting into it.

FRANK: I keep wondering if the information will still not really be more useful as formative evaluation for the staff. Isn't it really a formative evaluation?

LOTTA: Only if the program continues, Frank. We've been giving the staff formative data for two years so they could use it to improve the program. Now we're talking about collecting some pretty hard data for the board to use to decide whether to keep funding the program. That really means we're summing it up, not forming or shaping it—that's why I see this as primarily a summative evaluation. Of course, if the program is continued, the staff can still use this evaluation in a formative sense to correct any additional problems that show up.

FRANK: Can you really be impartial enough to judge whether the program should be continued or not? After all, you have been one of the formative evaluators for two years, and I know you've gotten to know many of the staff quite well.

LOTTA: You have good reason to question whether I can really be objective after getting fairly close to some people in the program. But keep in mind three things. First, although my preference would be to have the evaluation contracted to someone else, you know the superintendent has already said there is simply no money for extensive consultant help or outside contracts. And the board *is* going to make a decision about the program this year. It may not be ideal, but if I don't conduct the evaluation, they will be making it on the basis of no evaluation data at all. Second, I'm not going to decide whether or not the program should continue. That decision is up to you administrators and the board. My role is to get you the information and present it so you can analyze it on the criteria you intend to use in making the decision. I may add standards I think you should use, and I surely will make some overall judgments and recommendations, but I am not the only judge. The final judgment is yours and the board's. And that brings up the third point. We may all of us, collectively, be too close to the program to be able to judge it objectively. That's why I've built-in limited use of an external evaluator to review my work at key points where my bias could enter in. For example, he has already reviewed this plan and agrees to review the data-collection instruments, audit my scoring and analysis of data, and review all reports. If he finds any bias I have slipped in, we will correct it. In that way, I can get a somewhat "external" flavor into what is mostly an internal evaluation. It isn't ideal or as pure as I would like, but I believe it will assure acceptable objectivity.

FRANK: Yes, I saw the use of the external evaluator in your plan and liked it. What you say impresses me even more with the idea. I don't believe I have any other questions about the overview or introduction to your design. I understand why you propose a comparative evaluation, and the way you laid out and discussed the use of objectives and evaluation questions is very clear.

Characteristics of the Evaluation Object:
Interview with Les Wise (continued)

FRANK: One thing I need to correct. Your plan calls for you to collect data on the district's "K–6 team-teaching program." The program is still only a K–3 program.

LES: That's right, I should have remembered that from the formative evaluation. That will make it easier, since I'll only have to test all the K–3 classrooms in the district and....

FRANK: Excuse me for interrupting, Les, but keep in mind that the program hasn't been implemented in *all* the classrooms, just the half selected two years ago when we decided to try the idea.

LES: Oh, that's right. Well, anyway, I'll need data from pupils, plus I want to observe the two teachers in each classroom sometime during the evaluation.

FRANK: Umm...observations could probably be arranged, but you do remember that you won't see two teachers in the modified team classrooms, don't you?

LES: Modified?

FRANK: Yes, those are the schools where the principals wanted to try one teacher and two aides in two classrooms, remember? Les, this conversation makes me wonder if you wouldn't be wise to add a phase to your plan in which you prepare a careful description of the program. That would probably reassure the board that you were evaluating the same components of the program they want to look at.

Characterization of the Evaluation Object:
Interview with Lotta Smart (continued)

FRANK: I notice that one of the first activities called for in your plan is a "description of the program." I don't have any particular objection to it, but why would you need to do that? We have a pretty good description in our original proposal, which led the board to approve the program two years ago.

LOTTA: That description was probably accurate then, but I'm not sure it still is two years later. I know there have been some changes in the program because of information from the formative evaluation, and I would be willing to bet there are lots of other changes I don't know about. My belief is that I can't really do a fair and complete evaluation of a program unless I have a thorough understanding of all aspects of the program. In this case, I need to understand all of the objectives and activities of the program. If I were doing a "goal-free" evaluation—which is a good idea in a lot of cases, but not very feasible here—I would still need to be able to describe the operation of the program accurately before I could evaluate it fairly. I also find it useful to have staff review my program description to correct any misimpressions which are revealed when I change their terminology into mine. Reaching agreement with staff has another fringe benefit. When the results are in and reported, staff are much less likely to reject the findings on the basis that they merely reflect the evaluator's misunderstanding of their program.

Recognition and Representation of Legitimate Audiences: Interview with Les Wise (continued)

FRANK: I note that your plan calls for you to meet with each board member to find out what information they want from the evaluation. I like that, but don't you intend to talk to anyone else, maybe the staff or some of the parents—maybe to find out what they think you should look for in the evaluation?

LES: What for? The Board of Education has called for the evaluation and they're going to make the decision, so I don't see what I'd gain by talking to the bystanders. Like I said before, they're welcome to see the data.

FRANK: Well, it just seems like there are a lot of people more involved in the program than the board, so maybe they have some ideas about what important features of the program we need to look at. It seems that something like teacher morale or job satisfaction might be....

LES: Frank, the purpose of evaluation isn't to make everybody feel good, but to find out whether the program works. That means just one thing—did the kids learn more or better because of the program? The rest is just window dressing, and that's what you're likely to get if you trot around asking for ideas from all the self-interest groups.

Recognition and Representation of Legitimate Audiences: Interview with Lotta Smart (continued)

FRANK: I was intrigued by your listing several audiences for your evaluation, Lotta. Sometimes I have seen evaluators focus exclusively on what the board or district administrators want to know and forget that other people have legitimate questions and concerns that should also be considered. My only worry is that you don't spend so much time on touching base with all the interested parties that you short-shrift the evaluation itself.

LOTTA: That's a good caution, although it seems to me that the base-touching is one of the most important parts of the evaluation. Everyone knows the evaluation is being conducted for the board and administration, but a lot of other people have legitimate concerns about what is emphasized in the evaluation. The principals and teachers hope the board will not overlook some of the fringe benefits of the program, and the PTA has already asked whether they will have a chance to give their opinion about what the important outcomes of the program are.

FRANK: Do you expect that talking with all these different groups will really result in a different evaluation than if you just went after the information you know the board wants?

LOTTA: Yes, let me give you an example. The board is interested in whether kids are learning more in the team-teaching classes, and I guess that is pretty much what I had in mind, too. But yesterday the PTA president mentioned that a lot of parents think one of the best features of the program is the fact that there are two teachers for the child to relate to, which means fewer children will get stuck with a teacher they can't stand. There may be something worth looking at in that area too, and while I might have thought to include it, I could just as easily have missed it.

Sensitivity to Political Problems in Evaluation:
Interview with Les Wise (continued)

FRANK: I notice your plan calls for you to look at program costs. Are you aware of the fact that the teachers' union may take a strong stand against the whole program just because of the use of teacher aides to replace teachers on the modified teams? They see that as a sneaky way for the board to save money and avoid hiring more union teachers.

LES: I heard some rumbling to that effect. So?

FRANK: It just seems to me that you're dealing with a sensitive issue that could cloud your whole evaluation, especially since a lot of teachers will probably have to cooperate in any classroom data collection.

LES: I'm not going to worry about things like that, Frank. You could spend all your time worrying about personalities and politics if you let yourself, and I just don't intend to spend my time that way. My job is to get you guys the data, and if someone won't cooperate, you can bet I'll let you know. No need worrying now about something that may not occur.

Sensitivity to Political Problems in Evaluation:
Interview with Lotta Smart (continued)

LOTTA: I would like to test my perception on another point, Frank. You'll notice that my plan has a blank space under the heading "Implications for Personnel Costs and Policy." I really am not sure how to tackle that area. I know the teachers' union is really up in arms about the possibility of the district's using one teacher's salary to hire two teacher aides. That issue has gotten so hot that I suspect the business manager may stall on giving me access to salary information I need to calculate costs. You will have to check to make sure I can get that data before I promise more than we can deliver. Also, we may need to make sure the union will agree to let us into classrooms for observation before we place too much dependency on that as a way of getting data.

FRANK: I'm glad you're aware of those issues. I'll be happy to help you check whatever you need to know so you can flesh out those parts of your plan.

Specification of Information Needs and Sources: Interview with Les Wise (continued)

FRANK: I've scanned your design again while we've been talking, Les, and I'm still having trouble getting clear on just what information you intend to collect. You mention student-achievement data, but I'm not too sure of just what you are after in that area. Maybe my problem is that your plan launches right into a discussion of the CTBS test you intend to use without ever talking about why you're using it. If I know the board members, some of them will ask whether you intend to collect only that information listed in your plan.

LES: I've never conducted an evaluation where I've been able to predict in advance just exactly what data I would want to gather. When you actually get further into it, other leads turn up and you can rest assured I'll pursue them.

FRANK: I don't doubt that and I like the idea of flexibility, but I would still be more comfortable if you had given a little more thought at the outset to some of the places you might look for information you need.

Specification of Information Needs and Sources: Interview with Lotta Smart (continued)

FRANK: You know what part of your plan I liked best? The chart where you laid out every objective of the program and the information you plan to collect to tell whether the program met those goals. Laying it out in those columns, "information needed, source of information, instrument," and so forth, is really a help. That's the first evaluation plan where I could actually see, for every objective, just what data were going to be collected, from whom, with what type of instrument, when and by whom, etc. That kind of presentation makes a lot more sense to me than a lot of the more complicated evaluation plans I have seen.

LOTTA: Well, I always prefer a simple-minded approach so I can understand it! But seriously, if I don't do something like this to organize my thinking, I'm likely to run off in various directions and still never cover all the bases. I think identifying the information needs and sources is probably the most important part of planning an evaluation. Which reminds me, I need to add a note to indicate that this chart is still incomplete and tentative because I haven't had time to get around to all of the audiences we talked about earlier to see what information they think is important. When I get their ideas in, it will probably result in a refined or expanded chart that I will bring back to you for final approval.

Comprehensiveness/Inclusiveness:
Interview with Les Wise (continued)

FRANK: In reviewing your plan, I still have the feeling you may be overlooking something important. I don't mean to harp on the point, but just how do you propose to identify all of the things you should be looking at? Do you just pick your pet variables—the ones that appeal to you—and assume the rest don't matter?

LES: Of course not. I also ask whoever is paying for the evaluation. If what I propose to measure isn't complete, I'm sure the board will tell me what else they want me to include.

FRANK: What about unforeseen benefits or problems caused by the program? Do you have any plans for trying to pick up information on such—what do you evaluators call them—side effects?

LES: Like I said before, I'll be flexible and look at anything important that turns up. But it seems to me that if it doesn't relate to student achievement, you're going to be hard-pressed to convince me that it's important enough to spend much time on. Especially if it gets as far afield as the teacher morale stuff you were talking about earlier. Obviously, I'll measure whatever you tell me, since you're the boss, but I sure hope you remember what this evaluation is about, and that's whether kids learn more!

Comprehensive/Inclusiveness: Interview
with Lotta Smart (continued)

LOTTA: Do you see any important outcomes of the program that I've neglected to put in the design? I don't want to waste time on trivia or be too compulsive, but I would hate to overlook an area of real importance.

FRANK: Won't you get that kind of check from talking to the parents and staff and so on?

LOTTA: I should—that's one of the major reasons for talking to them, but that will take some time. In the meantime, I would like your reaction, if for no other reason than to keep the board from thinking they have employed an evaluator with tunnel vision. What do you think? Does anything occur to you as a serious omission?

FRANK: Well, there is one area. I think we really need to know whether there are any cost savings in the team program because principals choose not to hire substitutes when a teacher is absent. You can bet the money-minded members of the board will be raising that question.

LOTTA: That's a good idea. I'll add it. That brings a related area to mind, and that is teacher absenteeism. Would there be any interest in seeing whether teachers in the team program were absent more or less than those in regular classes? You could argue that the program. . . .

Technical Adequacy: Interview with Les Wise (continued)

FRANK: I'm frankly confused by some aspects of your plan. You have a section on statistical analysis of data, but you only mention two things. First, you talk about using multivariate analysis of the CTBS test results. Now I don't pretend to know much about statistics, but I understand that technique is useful when you want to look simultaneously at the effects of several variables. But I don't see any variables besides student achievement that you intend to look at. Are you looking at subtest scores on the CTBS or what? Maybe I'm way off base, but it seems you've proposed a technique for analyzing data before you have really thought-through what it is you want to learn.

LES: I don't think it would be helpful to put on paper all the reasons for using the techniques I do in carrying out an evaluation study. After all, Frank, you pay me to know my stuff—I hope I don't have to justify everything I do to people who may not understand it if I did.

FRANK: That's a cop-out, Les. If you don't, how can you expect me to defend your plan to the board? It surely isn't convincing to me. Here's another place, where you talk about the teacher observations. You say, "Appropriate statistical analyses will be employed." OK, even if I grant that you will choose an appropriate technique, I still have other serious questions. For example, do you have any check on bias in the observations? Do you intend to use an instrument? You never mention one. If you do, are you going to develop it from scratch and, if so, are you really up on classroom–climate research to make sure that your approach is as good as it might be? And what about sampling, do you intend to use samples or....

LES: Hold on, I almost feel like you're questioning my competence. When you do your job, no one asks you to write down a detailed management plan defending everything you are going to do in the future. If you really trust my judgment, why do you need everything spelled out in advance?

FRANK: For the simple reason that your role is to produce information that we need to make important decisions. If we aren't really sure of how your information has been produced, or whether it's completely believable, then it isn't of much use to us. I don't pretend to be a statistician or measurement expert, but I do know that there are some basic concerns, like validity, and generalizability, and so on. I don't think it insulting or unreasonable to expect an evaluator to present a plan in a way that the reasons for choosing certain techniques are clear, even to a layman. If a plan doesn't do that, it isn't very reassuring.

Technical Adequacy: Interview with Lotta Smart (continued)

FRANK: Lotta, I'm no technician, but I really appreciate the section on "evaluation procedures" you put in your plan. It is straightforward and I believe it will help prepare the board for your report. I thought the description of procedures for sampling and for selecting and developing instruments was especially helpful. Board members should surely be impressed with your review of relevant classroom-climate instruments. Another thing I liked was your plan to use the outside expert to check your technical plan and suggest improvements.

LOTTA: What about the sections on design and analysis of data? I tried to avoid getting too technical, but I did want the board to understand the rationale for the statistical tests I plan to run on the achievement-test data.

FRANK: No, I think they will understand it; in fact, I believe that is the first time I have really understood why you can't use pre- and posttest gains without some comparison. Putting it in simple terms is really helpful. I did have one concern, though. Do you really need to use that "matrix sampling" approach for testing students? I know you're concerned about testing time, but I wonder if the cost of printing different instruments with different items, not to mention the logistical problems, is really worth the 45 minutes testing time you save?

Consideration of Costs: Interview with Les Wise (continued)

FRANK: Another question. You've mentioned that you intend to collect cost data, but I'm not quite sure what type of costs you mean.

LES: Actual dollar costs. Isn't that what the Board of Education is concerned about?

FRANK: Yes, but they are also likely to be interested in things like personnel and time costs, which I don't see covered in your plan.

LES: Isn't that really the same thing? Personnel costs translate into salaries, and that's dollars.

FRANK: Yes, but that is only part of it. What about time costs and things like "opportunity costs," where doing one thing costs you the opportunity of doing something else? For example, what are we giving up when we ask teachers to spend time planning for team teaching, working out their schedules, etc.? Would the same time spent in reviewing subject matter for "solo" teaching yield greater payoff? I know that's a tough evaluation question, but isn't that what evaluation is all about, giving us a notion of the relative costs and benefits from a program?

LES: Uh, that's a good idea. Could we switch topics for a moment and talk about the final report?

Consideration of Costs: Interview with Lotta Smart (continued)

LOTTA: Could you help me a bit with my efforts to get at cost data? You can see that I intend to look at several cost factors, like personnel costs, time costs, any costs for in-service workshops on team teaching, and so on. When we get into the evaluation, the interviews will help me find costs I may have over-looked in these categories. But what I am worried about is that I might miss a whole category of hidden costs if I fail to probe carefully enough. Would you help by racking your brain for any categories I may have missed?

FRANK: I already have one I intended to suggest to you—administrative costs here in our central office. Although I'm not sure why, it turns out that we spend more time assisting principals in the team-teaching schools than in the regular schools. Perhaps you would have picked that up under your category of "time costs."

LOTTA: I doubt it. I was zeroing in on teachers' and aides' contact hours with students, planning time, and the like. That's a helpful suggestion, and I'll pursue it to see if others share your perception.

Explicit Standards/Criteria: Interview with Les Wise (continued)

FRANK: Before we talk about the report, Les, I want to ask about the criteria or standards you propose to use to judge whether objectives have been met. Just what do you have in mind?

LES: That's up to you and the board. I'll report the results, and you can decide if the objectives have been met.

FRANK: Yes, but using whose criteria? Each of us with our own different set? Of course the board could set the criteria as a group, but should they do so without first considering criteria suggested by other groups? These are some of the things your evaluation plan doesn't seem to explain.

LES: Still sounds unnecessary to me, but I'll write something up if you want. Now can we talk about the report?

Explicit Standards/Criteria: Interview with Lotta Smart (continued)

FRANK: I couldn't help chuckling when I got to the section of your plan on "Criteria for judging attainment of objectives" and found it completely blank. Couldn't you think of any criteria or did you simply run out of gas?

LOTTA: Neither. I would be quite happy to list *my* preferred criteria for deciding when an objective has been attained, but I doubt you really want that. The board has to make the decision, so they will also have to decide what criteria they want to use. Before they decide, I want them to consider the standards suggested by the other audiences we spoke of earlier. Since talking to those groups is still in the future, well, that's why the section is blank.

FRANK: Why not write a description of the process you will use for setting criteria and insert that in your blank section? Then the actual criteria can be developed as part of the evaluation process.

Judgments and/or Recommendations:
Interview with Les Wise (continued)

FRANK: Since you want to talk about reports, let me ask if you intend to provide recommendations to the board or just summaries of data analyses. I can't really tell from your plan.

LES: The latter. My thought was to give the board the results of the evaluation— the findings. They're the ones to judge or make decisions.

FRANK: I'm not suggesting you should make the decision. But as a person who has been close to the data, probably closer than anyone else, shouldn't you try to put it together with the criteria we talked about a moment ago? My goodness, Les, if all I wanted was the results of summarizing the data, I could get a research assistant from the university to provide that—at half the cost of what we pay you.

Judgments and/or Recommendations:
Interview with Lotta Smart (continued)

FRANK: One area of your plan about which I had no question at all was your discussion of the type of judgments and recommendations you will give us. As I understand it, you propose to take the evaluation results, apply the criteria to the data to determine if the objective has been met, and so on for each objective. Then, based on the overall performance on the objectives and the standards we've set, you will make a recommendation or set of recommendations about whether we should continue, modify, or terminate the program. Then, using your evaluation report and recommendation, along with anything else we feel is relevant, we—really the Board of Education —make the decision. Is that right?

LOTTA: One hundred percent.

Reports Tailored to Audiences:
Interview with Les Wise (continued)

LES: Can we talk about the final report now? How do you like the outline? Pretty complete, isn't it?

FRANK: It sure looks like all the technical stuff will be there, "procedures, instruments, analysis plan, summary of analyses, limitations of the study," and so forth. I assume you would be able and willing to add other things I've mentioned?

LES: Yes, if you're sure you really want me to.

FRANK: I would request that you do before I would recommend your plan. Now, what about shorter reports for the people who don't want or need all that technical detail? What did you have in mind?

LES: I didn't plan on any other reports. If I produce one really complete final report, it seems to me everyone can find the section they need, without having to have separate reports.

FRANK: Some people don't want to have to dig through big reports.

LES: I don't have much patience with some people who want to be spoon-fed all the time. You'd think they didn't know how to use a table of contents!

FRANK: Let me be a little more blunt, Les. I am still getting complaints from some board members about the CAI evaluation report you delivered to them last year. The table of contents wasn't much help when all it did was refer the reader to other tables. Really now, don't you think that 85 pages of analysis of variance tables was a bit much to expect the board to wade through, especially since the only place they could find the results was buried between the tables? I think Mrs. Dithers is still suffering "symbol shock" from that one.

LES: Well, I'm not sure what kind of report would be any better and still be complete enough.

FRANK: Les, I'm afraid that our talk hasn't really solved some of the problems I've tried to communicate to you. I just don't think your plan is very good or at all complete. I can't tell from it whether it would give us a good evaluation or not. Frankly, I'm pessimistic enough that I can't recommend it to the board. I'm sorry.... By the way, switching topics, did you see the announcement of the new position that is opening up in the computer center? You know, they could sure use someone with your technical skills.

Reports Tailored to Audiences:
Interview with Lotta Smart (continued)

FRANK: Lotta, I really like your idea of multiple reports, if you think you can pull it off without burning up our year's printing budget.

LOTTA: Actually it will probably cost you less because you won't need to produce many copies of the big report.

FRANK: OK, but let's see if I have it right. First, you will prepare a complete technical report, with all the tables and a description of the procedures and instruments, and so on. That will be run off in a small number of copies for use by anyone who really wants to dig into the study. If you expect so few readers, do you really need it at all?

LOTTA: Yes. It is the proof that the evaluation was done correctly and has all the necessary information for anyone who wants to challenge it—or defend it, for that matter.

FRANK: All right. Your second report would be a brief, written executive summary, almost an abstract, of the major findings and recommendations, along with a very brief description of the study. This will be for the staff, parents, or anyone else who wants to know about the evaluation. Then your last report consists of a series of overhead transparencies you'll prepare for your report to the Board of Education, right? What if the board wants more information?

LOTTA: They will also have the copies of the executive summary and complete technical report. There's another report I didn't want to put in the plan until we talked about it—a press release. I know the press will print something, and I would like it to be accurate. Even the executive summary is likely to be too long. Any chance of getting the district public relations officer to help draft a press release with a brief summary of major findings?

FRANK: By all means, Lotta. I am really pleased with your ideas and your whole evaluation plan. I will give it my full support and I have little doubt that the board will approve it. It should really be a good study!

A NEED FOR MORE META-EVALUATION

With any luck we have convinced the reader that the concept of meta-evaluation is useful and that there are many appropriate tools that can be used for that purpose. Despite the wide publicity, acceptance, and availability of even such tools as the Joint Committee's *Standards*, however, few educational evaluations are being subjected to any closer scrutiny now than before their publication. Even casual inspection reveals that only a small proportion of evaluation studies are ever evaluated, even in the most perfunctory fashion. Of the few meta-evaluations that do occur, most are internal evaluations done by the evaluator who produced the evaluation in the first place. It is rare indeed to see an evaluator call in an outside expert to evaluate her evaluation efforts. Perhaps the reasons are many and complex why this is so, but one seems particularly compelling—evaluators are human and are no more ecstatic about having their work evaluated than are professionals in other areas of endeavor.[115] It can be a profoundly unnerving experience to swallow one's own prescriptions. Although the infrequency of good meta-evaluation might be understandable, it is not easily forgivable, for it enables shoddy evaluation practices to go undetected and, worse, to be repeated again and again, to the detriment of the profession.

CASE STUDY APPLICATION

June 4. My final report went to Mrs. Janson today, so this evaluation is completed at last! Or is it? I did suggest to the folks at Radnor that it would be in their best interest to have the completed evaluation reviewed by an outside evaluator. Masochistic as this may seem, I strongly believe that there is more to be learned by involving other eyes and ears, perspectives, experience, and, of course, expertise, in any evaluation. To the extent that we become aware of limitations and strong points in the evaluation, I and my Radnor friends can weigh how much confidence to place in the results. We can also learn something that can help us when we undertake evaluation in the future. The learning process in evaluation never stops. That's one reason why I keep at it, I guess. Of course Brad's orthodontics bill is another.

June 16. Just received a package from Radnor. Mrs. Janson got a professor who teaches evaluation courses in Philadelphia to agree to review the evaluation as a volunteer service to the school district. She used the Joint Committee *Standards* as the basis for her review. Mrs. Janson kindly sent me a copy of the review. Brief, but helpful.

Artifact No. 8

Mrs. Janson, my reaction to the external evaluation you had conducted for your district is summarized below, using only the category headings for the Joint Committee's *Standards* we discussed. Sorry time did not permit me to provide more detail.

1. *Utility of the Evaluation.* It appears that the groundwork has been laid for producing an evaluation report that has impact. It remains to be seen, however, whether the utility of the evaluation will be worth its cost. You should follow up with the recommendations that resulted from the evaluation and should monitor changes in the program. Because the evaluator has become so knowledgeable about the program, he is a resource that might be tapped in the future for advice on follow-up reviews. My advice to you is not to look at this evaluation as a one-shot study; build on it, continue your reviews and use further internal evaluation for planning and development. Strong points of this study related to utility were stakeholder involvement throughout the evaluation, the credibility that the evaluator established for himself and the evaluation, the scope of the evaluation, the integration of multiple value orientations into the study, and clarity and timing of the report.

A possible limitation may be the question of commitment of top administrators to the program itself, as well as to using the evaluation. Although they have said they are committed, actions speak louder than words.

2. *Feasibility of the Evaluation.* The evaluation was tailored to meet budget and time constraints of the client. The logistics of all phases of the evaluation were kept manageable and enabled the study to be completed on time and within budget. The evaluator did a nice job of not overpromising. He delivered what he said he would. Political viability was built by involving everyone who wanted to be involved or who had something to say about the program.

An unknown yet is the cost-effectiveness of the evaluation, and this is something you can affect. The way in which the evaluation is used should justify its cost. A lot of money and energy that might have been better spent on other work will have been wasted if this evaluation has no demonstrable impact. On the other hand, considerable cost savings could occur if the evaluation prevents investments in future unproductive program activities. This remains to be seen.

3. *Propriety of the Evaluation.* This aspect of the evaluation looks fairly good. A brief agreement clarified most expectations for the evaluation, and everything that was promised was delivered in a quality manner. (But the agreement was a bit too brief and I suspect you and the evaluator must have developed a fair bit of mutual trust to get through the study without major misunderstandings.) There were no conflicts of interest evident in the evaluation. It was wise to hire an impartial and independent evaluation methodologist for the study. Reports were full, frank, and fair, and the rights of participants and informants were respected and protected. Strengths and weaknesses of the program were both addressed. Interactions during the evaluation appeared to be very professional and respectful.

4. *Accuracy of the Evaluation.* The evaluator compensated well for his lack of expertise in humanities education. The use of outside experts and humanities

instructors from Radnor rounded out the team of evaluators that, in my judgment, was needed to do a good job of evaluating this program. The evaluator was at somewhat of a disadvantage in that instruments for data collection were not readily available, so that several had to be developed ad hoc. This is a fairly common circumstance in evaluation, but instrument development is expensive and time-consuming. The evaluator did a good job of balancing resource allocations to instrument development with his constraints, maybe even an outstanding job, given the limitations placed on him. By using multiple methods and sources, he was able to triangulate in gathering information that is not misleading. It was evident that if he had used just one source and one method (interviews), he might have been led to far different findings that would have been off target. His methods of data control, data analysis, and interpretation addressed the standards of systematic data control, analysis of quantitative and qualitative information, justified conclusions, and objective reporting.

The one limitation that I saw in the reports was the lack of thoroughness of object identification and context analysis. Although the informed reader is well-informed about the program and its context, the uninformed reader of the evaluation reports is left wondering about pertinent characteristics of the school district and participating faculty and students. History and philosophy of the program received too little attention, as did implications of the evaluation for other educators who might be considering a similar undertaking. Perhaps a separate report for other educators is in order, so that they can be better informed about its transportability, processes, content, and impact.

Author Comments.   Just as I thought. Well done, but not perfect. There was something to be learned from having the evaluation evaluated by an impartial expert in evaluation. There always is.

October 10. Had a telephone call from Pennsylvania today, requesting some extra copies of the evaluation report I wrote last spring. I was interested to learn that the Radnor folk *did* use that evaluation to make some very sensible decisions about their humanities program. That's the good news. But the bad news is that they've just launched a new districtwide, computer-assisted math curriculum, with absolutely no plans to evaluate it to see how well it works. Mrs. Janson said she argued vigorously that an evaluation should be built-in from the outset, but she lost out.

It beats me why evaluation isn't a regular part of every school's planning, budgeting, program development, textbook and test selection, performance reviews and staff development, educational reform, school board deliberations, mileage requests, and the like.

I suspect the problem is that few leadership figures in education, in politics, and in the community have much real understanding about evaluation. There are few who are aware of the potential or who have seen the impact that evaluation can have. There are few who have seen *good* evaluation, in fact. And, there are probably many who have seen or experienced poorly done evaluations. We have come a long way during the past 20 years in our understanding of the role and proper conduct of evaluation. We are still learning, but I shouldn't forget that we now know a lot more than we did then.

Seems to me evaluators should be working with school districts, school boards, politicians, and community groups to share what they know and to work out plans for using evaluation effectively. Wouldn't it be something if educational leaders figured out how to recognize and reward exemplary evaluation efforts, or maybe even some sensible way to penalize those who spend large chunks of public funds without any effort to evaluate the quality or usefulness of those expenditures? With that kind of leadership, and real effort from the evaluation community, we should be able to make evaluation more useful so it will be used more often and more intelligently.

My word—I just reread this entry, and I wonder where I left my drums and bugle. If I'm not careful, I'll be marching forth, flags flying, to increase the "espirit de evaluation!" Best put a leash on my enthusiasm, I guess. I'd rather hate having my colleagues discount me as some wild-eyed fanatic who gets high by ranting about how evaluation can vanquish the evils of education. That would surely be a totally exaggerated caricature. Well, at least a somewhat exaggerated caricature.

Author Comments. And so we come to the end of our fictional evaluation. Yet I have only scratched the surface of what actually happens in carrying out any real evaluation. Most evaluation studies are complex and comprehensive enterprises. Beneath the complexity, however, lie many simple, straightforward steps on which the evaluator and client can work as partners. I hope my imaginary case study has been instructive on some of those practical guidelines. Also, I hope it has shown that evaluation studies are strongest when tailored specifically to meet the client's needs, drawing as necessary on multiple perspectives rather than following the prescriptions of any one evaluation model or method. It would be disappointing if my contrived evaluation failed to make that point.

I must confess that writing this fictional Radnor evaluation has been therapeutic. It is the only evaluation I have ever conducted from the comfort of my armchair, and it is the only evaluation where no one has raised questions about my design or my motives, or even my ancestry. Yes indeed, doing these make-believe evaluations could prove addictive.

CONCLUSION

We have reached the end of the book, except for the appendices. But we have only begun to share what is known about educational evaluation. Even the abundance of references we have made to other writings we consider especially important reflect only a fraction of the existing literature in this growing field. In choosing to focus attention on (1) alternative approaches to educational evaluation, and (2) practical guidelines for planning, conducting, reporting, and using evaluation studies, we have tried to emphasize what we believe is most important to include in any single volume that aspires to give a broad overview of such a complex and multifaceted field. We hope we have selected well. But we encourage students and evaluation practitioners to go beyond this text to explore the richness and depth of other evaluation literature.

We leave the reader with two final thoughts.

First, all that experience and research can teach convinces us that evaluation—properly conducted—has great potential for improving the practice and products of education. Evaluators have become self-consciously aware that evaluation studies are often misused or ignored, with the result that some individuals have argued for decreased emphasis on the evaluative process. But that seems no more sensible than abandoning medical diagnosis because science has not yet sucessfully eliminated all disease. Knowledge about evaluation has grown impressively in the dozen-plus years since our last book was published, but its conclusion still rings true:

> Educational systems have most of the earmarks of classical bureaucracies and, historically, have been reasonably successful in resisting change in practices and policies. Recently, strong social forces have coalesced to push many educational systems out from behind their barriers; change in education has become a much more frequent reality. However, without a tradition of planned change or systematic inquiry into the effectiveness of potential new programs, the changes which are occurring in education can be often little more than random adoption of faddish innovations. Perhaps the most important deficiency which fosters such a situation is the lack of dependable information in the performance of educational products, practices, and programs. Without such information, educators cannot readily correct deficiencies or malfunctions in present practices or intelligently select new products or practices for adoption.
>
> Evaluation, as described in this volume, holds great promise in providing educators with badly needed information which can be used to improve the process of education. While obviously not a panacea, evaluation can have a profound impact on the field of education. (Worthen & Sanders, 1973, pp. 348–349)

The second thought we wish to leave with readers is this: Despite great strides, it is increasingly apparent how little we really do know about evaluation, compared to what we need to know. N. L. Smith said it well when he likened the progress of educational evaluation to a raft trip. Evaluation, he argued, has barely rounded the first bend in the river:

> We can expect major shifts in emphasis, expanding horizons, and radical alternatives to emerge as educational evaluation continues in its current period of expansive growth. Like shooting the rapids, living through such turmoil will result in greater security in the knowledge gained upon reaching the other side.
>
> We have only just started our evaluation trip. The current is swift, and we have only made the first few turns in the river, so our vision is limited. Perhaps considering visions of what is possible ahead will help us deal with the future of educational evaluation as it unfolds before us. (N. L. Smith, 1983b, pp. 383, 391)

Much of the river on which evaluation will travel remains uncharted. We hope this book has helped to pique your spirit of adventure and that the hard-won knowledge we've gained from experience has left us better prepared for whatever awaits around the next bend.

APPLICATION EXERCISE

1. Use the Joint Committee *Standards* to evaluate a completed evaluation study of your choice. For what aspects of the study do you lack information? What can you learn from the strengths and weaknesses of the work of other evaluators?

2. Select a class of evaluation studies (for example, project evaluations in one large urban school district completed from 1980 until the present). Use the Joint Committee *Standards* to evaluate each study. From these data, can you draw any inferences about project evaluation in the school district? Are there any patterns that emerge? You could repeat this exercise with other classes of evaluations, looking for patterns and drawing conclusions.

SUGGESTED READINGS

Joint Committee on Standards for Educational Evaluation (1981). *Standards for evaluations of educational programs, projects, and materials.* New York: McGraw–Hill.

STUFFLEBEAM, D. L. (1974b). *Metaevaluation.* (Occasional Paper No. 3). Kalamazoo, MI: Western Michigan University Evaluation Center.

Appendix 1
Some General Areas of Competence Important in Educational Evaluation

The following (drawn from Sanders, 1979) describes 11 general areas of competence important for evaluators to conduct high-quality educational evaluations. We do not propose the list as all-inclusive of all the areas of competence necessary in the broad range of evaluation approaches that might be applied in education. No doubt some abilities important to conduct certain educational evaluations have been omitted, but we believe these 11 areas are representative areas of competence that cut across almost all educational evaluations.

We believe, then, that the competent evaluator must be able to:

1. *Describe the object of an evaluation*—that is, be able to communicate to others what is being evaluated, what its limits are, and what its important characteristics are. This is necessary, regardless of the object being evaluated (a program, a project, an idea, human performance, materials, etc.). Objects change over time, with different staff, in new settings, from plans to actual operations. Labels are not enough to communicate what has been evaluated.

2. *Describe the context of an evaluation*—that is, be able to communicate to others what factors in the environment have affected the object of an evaluation, as well as the evaluation itself. The results of most educational evaluations are specific to a particular setting, time, and set of human actors. The findings are often idiosyncratic because factors in the environment affect the object and its performance in a way that cannot be replicated. Taking knowledge about these factors into account can greatly help us to understand evaluation findings.

3. *Conceptualize appropriate purposes and frameworks for evaluation*—that is, be able to use existing information to make decisions about the most appropriate framework for planning the evaluation. Does the situation call for a formative or summative design? Should the study be objectives-oriented or expertise-oriented? Should the unit being studied be an individual, a classroom, a curriculum, a school system, a region or state?[116]

4. *Identify and select appropriate evaluation questions, information needs, and sources of information*—that is, be able to determine what we need to know about an object before judgments can be made and where we might learn about those charac-

402

teristics. Determining what we need to know is dependent on the criteria that will be used to determine value. Standard criteria can be found in books and articles dealing with entities similar to the object of the evaluation, and these criteria are linked to substantive theory and earlier research. There are also expectations of important evaluation stakeholders that help establish criteria. Finally, proposed evaluation approaches and evaluation textbooks suggest additional criteria. Evaluators must be able to set priorities and justify them for collecting information when lists of information needs become unwieldy. Evaluators must also be able to sort out which of the alternative sources of information (for example, students, parents, administrators, teachers, files, etc.) will provide the best information (objective, reliable, valid, representative, relevant) within our constraints (time, cost, personnel, logistics).

5. *Identify, select, and apply appropriate techniques and procedures for information collection, processing, and analysis*—that is, be able to develop and select various types of information-gathering instruments (tests, scales, questionnaires, interview schedules, observation checklists, or other forms) and procedures (experimental design, survey methods, or the like), being able to record and process various types of information (qualitative and quantitative measurement, coding and computer storage and retrieval), and being able to analyze the information (data reduction and summarization, statistical analysis, assimilation of qualitative data). These technical skills involve identifying and selecting the best approach and then being able to do it. Evaluators need to be skilled technical generalists. Fortunately, graduate course work and textbooks in many relevant skill areas are available to build this competence, but it does take time and opportunity to apply newly gained knowledge.

6. *Determine value of the object of an evaluation*—that is, be able to apply criteria to descriptive information about an object in order to arrive at defensible value statements. There are several routes to determining value, and no one basis for value can be claimed as the correct one. Nevertheless, the competent evaluator must be able to proceed in a systematic and justifiable way to the point of preparing judgments or value statements.

7. *Communicate evaluation plans and results effectively*—that is, be able to understand the information needs of important audiences, prepare appropriate messages, and deliver each message in a way that it will be heard. Written documents and long technical reports are usually expected from evaluators, but they are not necessarily the best way to communicate plans or results. They might best serve as necessary supporting documents that are available for anyone wanting to pursue a particular point. The evaluator must know the audience for evaluative information, select the most appropriate way to bring that information to the attention of the audience, and then do so in an understandable and timely way. Follow-up communication with an audience is often an important part of the overall communication process.

8. *Manage evaluations*—that is, be able to plan evaluation activities, allocate human and fiscal resources to carry out evaluation tasks, and provide leadership throughout the study, supporting, monitoring, and supervising as necessary other personnel to complete a high-quality evaluation. The competent evaluator must be able to use available resources to produce on schedule a quality evaluation that delivers on all the promises made when the study was commissioned. This requires task orientation, expertise in working with people, planning skills, and good decision-making skills.

9. *Maintain ethical standards*—that is, be able to demonstrate professional behavior during all aspects of an evaluation. Knowing laws regarding protection of human subjects and freedom of information is certainly one part of this competency. In addition, evaluators frequently deal with confidential information, produce value judgments, affect the work and well-being of others, give people "bitter pills" to swallow, and address moral issues. Knowing and maintaining ethical principles as an evaluator is part of professional behavior.

10. *Adjust for external factors that affect an evaluation*—that is, be able to remain flexible during an evaluation. The competent evaluator must be able to assimilate new information into the procedures of the evaluation as such information becomes known. Constraints that may affect even the most well-conceived plan include those that are legal, logistical, political, administrative, human, and methodological. The competent evaluator cannot be dogmatic in implementation of the evaluation plan.

11. *Evaluate the evaluation (meta-evaluate)*—that is, be able to critique, revise, and learn from evaluation experiences. Evaluation is a young profession and there is much to be learned. Furthermore, no evaluation can be bias-free. The competent evaluator will include procedures to review plans, techniques, and procedures, and apply appropriate criteria (see criteria for use in evaluating evaluations discussed in Chapter 21) to improve the quality of an evaluation.

Although perhaps hinted at in items 9 and 10 above, professional, ethical, and interpersonal sensitivities are essential for any educational evaluator. As Sechrest concluded:

> In many ways, attitudes or outlook may be as important as specific skills. Certainly the evaluation researcher must have an ability to work closely with others in a sensitive way. The field is no place for loners nor for those inclined to be oblivious to the attitudes, feelings, and problems of others. Attitudes and outlook are difficult to impart by direct instruction, but must be carefully nurtured in students who were selected because they seemed hospitable to the learning. (Sechrest, 1980, p. 90)

Certainly one would hope to select an evaluator who possesses not only these sensitivities but also those reflected in the 11 general areas of competence outlined above.

Appendix 2
Task-Oriented Teacher Education Programme (TOTE)

A. *Programme Description*
   1. *Short Title Used in This Report*: TOTE
   2. *Date Started*: 1974
   3. *Needs*: A need exists for a competency-based teacher education programme that is perceived by students as relevant, integrated and coherent. The TOTE Programme should appear relevant because the learning activities are directly related to teaching tasks. The fact that everyone making inputs to the programme will be working from a common conceptualization of teaching tasks should allow students to perceive the programme as integrated and coherent. In addition, there is a need for students to have an opportunity to apply the learned abilities in instructional planning and in the classroom.
   4. *Programme Goals*: The general objectives of the programme are: (1) to equip beginning social studies teachers with the abilities needed to carry out successfully the tasks of teaching and (2) to equip them with the understanding necessary for critically analyzing and reconstructing their teaching practices in the light of subsequent teaching experience.
   5. *Types of Students for Whom the Programme Is Designed*: This programme is designed for regular Faculty of Education students who decide to do their professional year in their fourth year and also for graduate transfers planning to be Social Studies teachers in secondary schools.
   6. *Student Outcomes Expected from the Programme*: Students will develop competence in performing the following kinds of teaching functions or tasks: (1) establishing and clarifying objectives, (2) selecting and organizing the content of instruction, (3) devising and employing appropriate teaching techniques, (4) managing the learning environment humanely, and (5) evaluating pupil growth. The students will learn to perform the teaching functions to achieve objectives in three areas:
   (a) Develop the critical thinking of their pupils by (1) effective questioning, (2) teaching concepts and generalizations, (3) teaching inquiry skills and, (4) teaching pupils to assess the quality of inductive and deductive arguments. Student teachers will become competent at using historical documents, maps, photos, charts and graphs as means to develop the

critical thinking abilities of pupils. In addition, student teachers will become competent in assessing pupil need for structure and in using standardized tests of critical thinking.

(b) Develop pupil ability to make rational value judgments by: (1) teaching pupils tests of principle: the new cases, role exchange, universal consequences and subsumption tests; (2) teaching pupils to construct valid normative arguments, assess empirical and conceptual claims and to assess authorities; (3) assessing the level of moral maturity of pupils and conducting discussions aimed at raising levels of moral maturity.

Sociodrama, role-playing and simulations are some of the means by which the ability to make rational value judgments will be developed.

(c) Competencies in the area of human development include: (1) the application of models of adolescent growth and development such as Piaget and Erikson; (2) the application of models to enhance self-concept; (3) assessing individual differences by observation and measures of personality, attitudes, intelligence, and achievement; (4) the application of models for effective interpersonal communication.

7. *Basic Structure and Scheduling Characteristics*: Three features distinguish the TOTE Programme. First, it is competency-based. The programme analyzes the various tasks a teacher must be able to perform and it develops student competency in performing each of these tasks. Second, TOTE provides students with extensive school experience early in the programme so that they can reflect on these experiences in subsequent work. Third, TOTE involves sponsor teachers in a two week seminar with UBC faculty in order to acquaint them with the programme in some detail.

The programme focuses upon the following teaching strategies and learning activities: (1) reading and discussion to gain prerequisite understanding, (2) demonstration or modeling of the desired performances, (3) simulation of the desired performance, (4) actual practice of the desired performance with guided self analysis of the record of the performance. In addition the programme is individualized through the use of self instructional modules on some specific competencies.

The instructional timetable for TOTE is outlined as follows:

Week 1 and 2: Preparation for First School Experience
> A survival kit approach includes topics such as basic lesson planning, classroom management and discussion techniques.

Week 3 to 8: First School Experience
> Student teachers gradually assume full-time teaching responsibilities in the classroom, working from lesson plans approved by the sponsor teacher. Daily conferences are held between sponsor and student to plan lessons and discuss strengths and weaknesses of the student's performance. UBC faculty attend at least one of these conferences per week.

Week 9 to 26: Instruction and Practice
> Student teachers work individually and attend sessions on campus to

prepare competencies for actual practice in the classroom. The competencies may be done individually or in blocks. As a result, the student teacher may be back in the school for an hour one day or continuously for a week or more. An estimate of the anticipated proportion of time spent on campus would be three to four days per week and in the schools one to two days per week.

After students have demonstrated competence in individual functions they are assigned to a second major school experience lasting four weeks. An effort is made to assign the student teacher to a classroom where the supervising teacher will allow the student teacher considerable freedom in selecting objectives, and selecting and organizing the content for instruction. Members of the TOTE faculty team will evaluate the student teacher's ability to integrate the full range of teaching activities.

Weeks 27 and 28: (end of April) Follow-up Workshop

Follow-up workshops and teaching practice on designated competencies as required by individual students are held. Final evaluation of student growth on all competencies and evaluation of the TOTE Programme occurs.

8. *Content*: Course equivalents for the on-campus instructional periods are 3 units each of Philosophy of Education, Social Studies Methods, Educational Media; 1.5 units of Educational Psychology and of Education Evaluation; plus a teaching practicum.

9. *Administrative and Managerial Procedures*: The programme has the cooperation of eleven classroom teachers in three schools. Two student teachers are assigned to each supervising teacher.

UBC faculty responsibilities include: (1) conducting the initial intensive preparation for the first school experience; (2) supervising students in cooperation with classroom teachers during first school experience; (3) guiding students through steps in achieving competencies; (4) evaluating success of the competency; (5) supervising and evaluating success of student teacher in integrating competencies in the final four week teaching experience.

A paid graduate student is assigned responsibilities as an office manager. His responsibilities include: (1) keeping records, (2) signing out competencies and equipment, (3) making arrangements with schools on behalf of student teachers.

10. *Number and Types of Instructional Personnel*:

4 UBC Faculty (1.3 FTE)

11 Sponsor Teachers

11. *Approximate Number of Students Enrolled*: 20

(Worthen and others, 1975, pp. 174–176)

Notes

CHAPTER 1. THE ROLE OF EVALUATION IN IMPROVING EDUCATION

[1]"Formative" and "summative" evaluation will be discussed in greater detail in Chapter 3.

[2]Only rarely, in our experience, can this purpose be achieved in a program evaluation without compromising more basic evaluation purposes.

[3]For further reading about evaluation objects, you may wish to refer to Sanders (1978), Martin (1981), or Nowakowski and others (1985) for reviews of attempts to identify objects for educational evaluation.

[4]An illustration of just how limited an evaluation can be, compared to the expectations held for it, may be found in House's (1980) fascinating account of the 1967–1977 evaluation of the federal government's Follow-Through Program.

CHAPTER 2. THE HISTORY OF EVALUATION IN EDUCATION

[5]However, Travers (1983) did note that prior to 1840, McGuffey had engaged in the earliest recorded form of curriculum materials evaluations—at least in the United States. McGuffey read selections of material to children of various ages at his home. Observing differential age-group responses to the materials, he sorted out content that would eventually be incorporated into the *McGuffey Readers*. His evaluation efforts, although informal, must have paid off, for more than 90 million copies of the *Readers* were sold.

[6]This is a lesson that school superintendents are rediscovering constantly, especially those who wish to innovate. Accurate information outweighs opinion and polemics in any debate over policy or issues. Moreover, superintendents after Washburne have continued to find that their credibility is greatly enhanced when they can cite objective, accurate information in public presentations or written reports.

[7]These associations included The American Association of School Administrators, American Educational Research Association, American Federation of Teachers, American Personnel and Guidance Association, American Psychological Association, Association for Supervision and Curriculum Development, Council for American Private Education, Education Commission of the States, National Association of Elementary School Principals, National Council on Measurement in Education, National Education Association, and National School Boards Association.

CHAPTER 3. THE CONCEPT OF EVALUATION: AN OVERVIEW

[8]Portions of this section and of some later sections in this chapter follow in part earlier writings by Glass and Worthen (1972) and Worthen and Sanders (1973).

[9]We shall say more later about the fact that determination of value is tied closely to specific purposes for doing so, such as making decisions.

[10]Apologies to mathematics, history, philosophy, and so forth, for the obvious empirical social science bias in our definition and thinking.

[11]Guba and Clark (n.d.) argued that the basic-applied distinction is dysfunctional and that the two kinds of activity do not rightfully belong on the same continuum. The authors admit to problems with this, as with any, classification scheme. However, attempts to replace such accepted distinctions with yet another classification system seem destined to have the same success one would have in discarding the descriptors "Democrat" and "Republican" because of recognition of wide variance within the political parties thus identified.

[12]The practitioner who is already convinced that research and evaluation are different may wish to skip to the next major section, recognizing it is possible to return to read this section should that conviction waiver in the future.

[13]It is not our position that, for any one study, the characteristics must be all evaluation attributes to be an evaluation study, or all research characteristics to be a research study. Inquiry assumes many forms and few studies have all evaluation or all research characteristics. However, it does seem useful to make distinctions as sharp as possible to help the would-be evaluator recognize differences between research and evaluation.

[14]That evaluators must "presume" that certain conditions are worthwhile and to be sought after leads to what Scriven called the "point-of-entry problem in evaluation" (personal communication). Every act of evaluation must enter a chain of justification of valued states at some point short of the philosopher's rationalization of such elusive concepts as "the good life." Educational evaluation cannot solve the problems of philosophy. Perhaps the best advice for the evaluator is to enter at one stage above her client, seeking justification for the client's definition of "worth" but not for her own.

[15]The discussion has taken on a utopian tone. In reality, much evaluation is becoming as stereotyped as most research. Evaluators often take part in asking the questions they will ultimately answer, and they are all too prone to generate questions out of a particular "evaluation model" (for example, the UCLA model, discrepancy evaluation) rather than out of a "discipline." We have even witnessed the specter of a governmental agency imposing a particular evaluation approach on all who would choose to conduct evaluation studies for that agency. Stereotyping of method threatens evaluation as it threatens research (Glass, 1969).

[16]Not that everyone agrees as to their importance or utility, but rather about what they are and how they can be differentiated.

[17]The discussion in the remainder of this book is intended to apply equally to evaluation of educational programs, projects, products, and processes—indeed, any object of an educational evaluation. However, to avoid tedious redundancy, only one term ("program" or "curriculum") will generally be used hereafter in each example or concept presented. The other possible objects of educational evaluation can be assumed to be included by implication.

[18]There are some exceptions to this statement. For example, Harlan (1975) suggests that her evaluation of Science 5/13 in the United Kingdom shows that the classical objectives-based evaluation approach (see Chapter 5) is less useful in formative evaluation than some alternatives. We shall attempt to note these exceptions as they are discussed in later chapters.

[19]We are indebted to our colleague Adrian Van Mondfrans for most of the content of this figure, although we have adapted his ideas somewhat here.

CHAPTER 4. ALTERNATIVE VIEWS OF EVALUATION

[20]More will be said about such multiple methods in later chapters of this book.

[21]We are indebted to these colleagues for their contribution to our thinking and for permission to quote liberally from their work in this section.

[22]Kaplan (1964) described this fallacy by noting that if you give a small boy a hammer, suddenly

everything he encounters needs hammering. The same tendency is true, he asserts, for scientists who gain familiarity and comfort in using a particular method or technique; suddenly all problems will be wrested into a form where they may be addressed in that fashion, whether or not that is appropriate.

[23]Some promising starts have been made at broadening our methodological base in evaluation during recent years. Colleagues have begun to adapt aspects of the judicial model, ethnography, aesthetic criticism, investigative journalism, and the like into evaluative terms, as noted in Chapters 8 through 10 of this text. But for the most part, the methods and techniques from other disciplines remain relatively unknown terrain to educational evaluators, and our attempt in later chapters to portray our embryonic efforts to understand and apply these efforts to educational evaluation does not negate our point or the methodological predominance we note here.

[24]A metaphor is a figure of speech, an implied comparison in which the meaning of a term or phrase is transferred from the object it ordinarily designates to another object so as to provide new insight or perspective on the latter. In a broader sense, metaphor may also designate a process whereby the meanings and relationships of one theory or model may be used to suggest meanings and relationships in another arena for which no theory or model currently exists. For example, a researcher interested in how rumors spread might use epidemiology, the theory of how diseases spread, as a metaphor. This theory would suggest that the researcher look for carriers of rumor, that rumors spread from epicenters in regional clusters, and so on.

CHAPTER 5. OBJECTIVES-ORIENTED EVALUATION APPROACHES

[25]This approach to evaluation has also been called the "EPIC" Evaluation Model because it was developed and used by an evaluation center at the University of Arizona (Project EPIC) during the time Hammond was employed there.

[26]Although "standards" and "objectives" are not synonymous, they were used by Provus interchangeably. Stake (1970) also stated that, "Standards are another form of objective: those seen by outside authority-figures who know little or nothing about the specific program being evaluated but whose advice is relevant to programs in many places" (p. 185). Provus's use of the term is generally consistent with such accepted usage.

[27]Provus earlier used "Pittsburgh Evaluation Model" to label his approach.

CHAPTER 7. CONSUMER-ORIENTED EVALUATION APPROACHES

[28]A list of reports is available from the EPIE Institute, 475 Riverside Drive, New York, NY 10027.

[29]These categories are drawn from the CMAS outline, which is not reproduced here in its entirety. We take full responsibility for any distortion of intent or content that may have resulted from our selective presentation.

[30]We have slightly modified this checklist (for example, by inserting category headings) and take full responsibility for any distortions of intent or content that may have resulted from such alterations.

CHAPTER 8. EXPERTISE-ORIENTED EVALUATION APPROACHES

[31]A comprehensive and detailed discussion of guidelines and procedures for site visits and proposal reviews may be found in Worthen and White (1986).

[32]Floden (1983) has noted that jurisdictional disputes *within* professions exist, as with the long-standing tension over who should control accreditation of teacher education programs, elementary and secondary school teachers or faculties of teacher education institutions. Though beyond the scope of

this chapter, issues of who should participate in and who should control accreditation processes are obviously important.

[33]For example, the American Psychological Association omits any self-study by professional psychology programs under its accreditation review.

[34]More information on the Utah review system can be obtained by writing to the Office of the Commissioner of Higher Education, Utah State Board of Regents, Utah System of Higher Education, 3 Triad Center, Suite 550, 355 West North Temple, Salt Lake City, UT 84180–1205.

[35]For an example of such a system, see Worthen (1983).

[36]In peer evaluation, a "peer" might be thought of as anyone who is an expert in the substantive and procedural areas in which the individual or group's competence or contribution is being judged—an "expert" being anyone having recognized expertise in such substance or procedures.

[37]"Field readers" who respond individually from afar may collectively make up a panel if they or their opinions are later brought together to arrive at a group judgment concerning that which is evaluated.

[38]This is an important point lost on some who employ Eisner's notions as the *sole* evaluation of an educational entity, overlooking the fact that Eisner never proposed his approach as sufficient in and of itself.

[39]We add that Eisner doubtlessly had *quality* of experience in mind as much or more than *quantity*. The connoisseur of wine and the lush are worlds apart.

[40]Obviously, in single-purpose institutions, such as a dental school with no other programs, this distinction is meaningless.

[41]One of the present authors resides in an academic department that received four external professional reviews by national professional associations and state regulatory bodies in one three-year period. The costs borne by the department for these reviews so depleted the budget that supplies (for example, mimeo paper) were exhausted midway through each academic year.

CHAPTER 9. ADVERSARY-ORIENTED EVALUATION APPROACHES

[42]As will be shown later, we would also consider as adversary-oriented those evaluations where more than two opposing views exist. We use the term to include all cases where opposing advocates or positions, no matter how many, are represented in an evaluation, just so those multiple views are clearly in opposition to one another and the evaluation is structured and conducted to highlight the opposition among the views. For now, however, we prefer to use the more simple, two-view "pro and con" case to make our points more clearly.

[43]Many writers today use the term *advocate-adversary evaluation* to refer to what we call adversary-oriented evaluation in this chapter. Although the advocate-adversary label is not incorrect, because generally one evaluator serves as an advocate and the other an adversary, we prefer to reserve that term to describe cases where opposite views are given but the evaluation is not structured to take full advantage of one of the paradigms underlying truly adversarial evaluation. Also, we prefer the single term *adversary* not only because the program's advocate and adversary are adversaries to one another's views, but also to encompass situations where multiple positions exist, varying in their advocacy or opposition to the program but clearly at odds with one another.

[44]We agree that all adversary models should be concerned with judicious evaluation, but we wonder whether it is realistic to expect that winning will not continue to be such a part of human nature as to suggest this hope may be overly optimistic, as we shall discuss later. In the meantime, we do not accept that the judicial evaluation model is not a perfect example of adversary-oriented evaluation, as defined in this chapter.

[45]Portions of this section draw on an earlier article by Worthen and Rogers (1980).

[46]Madaus (1982) disagrees with us, cautioning that the judicial evaluation approach may be inappropriate for controversial issues such as busing to create ethnic ratios in schools, because of their potential

of touching off "protests from groups on the left and right of the issue. Cooperation and data sharing would be difficult. I would anticipate bitter fights over the admissibility of evidence and witness testimony." Perhaps he is correct, at least on the deepest schisms society faces.

[47]Estes and Demaline (1982) found in an evaluation of one adversary evaluation that participants suggested that cross-examination may increase interest more than it enhances understanding. They suggested that direct examination without cross-examination may be just as effective.

[48]Braithwaite and Thompson (1981) disagree with us on this point.

[49]Although we would not disagree, we might point out that the same deficit extends to other evaluation approaches, which also lack a mechanism for appealing improper conclusions. Perhaps the visibility associated with the "findings" in an adversary evaluation makes this a more serious concern here, however.

CHAPTER 10. NATURALISTIC AND PARTICIPANT-ORIENTED EVALUATION APPROACHES

[50]Obviously "naturalistic" and "participant-oriented" are not synonymous; a naturalistic evaluation could focus on description and portrayal, while ignoring participants' views, just as an evaluation might be built around issues selected by participants without using naturalistic methods. The tendency for the two somewhat different approaches to overlap heavily in practice—most evaluations which are examples of one are also examples of the other—is our justification for treating them as one general evaluation approach.

[51]"Stakeholders" are various persons and publics who may be affected by a program or who hold a stake in determining the direction of an educational endeavor, identifying concerns and issues to be addressed in evaluating a program, and selecting the criteria and variables that will be used in judging its value.

[52]Stake's assertion is confirmed by personal experience. After being skeptical for several years about the usefulness of responsive evaluation, one of the authors of this text was asked to describe in print how he would evaluate a particular curriculum (Worthen, 1981). This expedition into "logic-in-use" (see Kaplan, 1964) was revealing because it forced recognition that Stake's description of responsive evaluation had indeed captured those activities and procedures so long used by many experienced evaluators as to become second nature. Stake has served well by articulating and bringing to a level of public discourse and analysis procedures that have previously existed largely at the subconscious level of practicing evaluators.

[53]"Preordinate" evaluation refers to evaluation studies that rely on prespecification, where inquiry tends to follow a prescribed plan and does not go beyond the predetermined issues and predefined problems.

[54]We are indebted to our colleague Adrian Van Mondfrans for informal communication in which he has suggested these ways in which the informant is central to naturalistic inquiry.

[55]It should be noted that recent advances in the methodology of naturalistic and participant-oriented approaches (see Guba, 1978a; Stake, 1980; Guba & Lincoln, 1981; Spindler, 1982) have largely neutralized these latter concerns, however.

CHAPTER 11. ALTERNATIVE EVALUATION APPROACHES: A SUMMARY AND COMPARATIVE ANALYSIS

[56]The work by Stufflebeam and others (1971) may come closest here in its attention to knowledge about decision theory.

[57]Readers are reminded of Kaplan's "law of the instrument" analogy to show the fallacy of such thinking (see Chapter 4).

[58]We view this, not lack of interest or effort, as the most likely reason that no synthesis has been

forthcoming since the profession-wide discussion of that issue in 1977. We should also note that this does not negate the possibility of eclectically combining compatible portions of different approaches, as discussed later in this chapter.

[59]Notable exceptions do exist: for example, the National Institute of Education research sponsored at Northwest Regional Educational Laboratory and the UCLA Center for the Study of Evaluation. These research efforts did not focus on the type of research called for here, however useful they have been in other ways.

[60]Guba and Lincoln (1981) give examples of some incompatible assumptions in the scientific and naturalistic paradigms in asking, "Can one assume both singular reality and multiple realities at the same time? How can one believe in insularity between the investigator and the object of his investigation while also allowing for their mutual interaction? How can one work simultaneously toward the development of nomothetic and idiographic science" (Guba & Lincoln, 1981, p. 77). Despite this pessimism, these authors maintain that "complementarity [between these two paradigms] is not only possible but desirable" (p. 77).

CHAPTER 12. CLARIFYING THE EVALUATION REQUEST AND RESPONSIBILITIES

[61]Brickell (1978) has provided an example of a situation in which hiring of minorities as teacher aides in a large city school system carried such potent political appeal that even had the evaluation findings been negative, they would almost certainly have been ignored by the school administrators.

[62]An argument for external formative evaluation has been made previously (Worthen, 1974a) and we accept the contention that this is an important activity. However, relatively few educational agencies have yet sought external formative evaluations of their programs. It therefore seems appropriate to focus attention in this chapter on the more typical external summative evaluation. Were an agency to decide to seek an external formative evaluation, discussions in later sections of this chapter on how to select an external evaluator would also apply.

[63]Individual consultants and external contracting agencies are not treated separately in the remainder of this discussion because procedures for obtaining assistance would be similar in both cases.

[64]Of course, external evaluators are not without bias, and they can be co-opted by their interest in follow-up consulting contracts, references for work with other potential clients, and the like. Yet it would seem that conflict of interest for the external evaluator is usually very slight, compared to that for the internal evaluator—especially if the evaluation serves a summative role.

[65]This statement and many others made in this section are obviously applicable to the internal evaluator as well; those statements peculiarly applicable to the external evaluator will be apparent.

[66]Selection of an external evaluation agency as opposed to an individual is not treated separately here because the quality of work done by an agency depends primarily on the individuals who do the work.

[67]For example, because of frequent forays into their state by unqualified but persuasive "evaluators," the Alaska Department of Education commissioned development of a system (Wright & Worthen, 1975) that included standards and procedures for selecting individuals qualified to do high-quality evaluation work.

[68]These approaches have been drawn primarily from Wright and Worthen (1975) but we also have been influenced by the thoughts of Brophy and others (1974) and Lai (1978) on this topic.

[69]This and subsequent criteria stated as applicable to an individual evaluator should also be construed to apply to the personnel of evaluation agencies under consideration as potential contractors, especially persons who would play a major role in the evaluation.

[70]Obviously the criteria must be combined and trade-offs made. It would seem preferable, for example, to contract with a novice who was trained thoroughly in evaluation rather than a person who has no formal training in evaluation but has served for a year or two in a minor evaluation capacity.

[71]Each item in this checklist is written to apply to an individual. If the potential evaluator is an agency, the question should be recast accordingly.

[72]This section and parallel sections that follow at the end of chapters are taken from Worthen (1981), with adaptations and expansions as necessary for our purposes here. The Radnor humanities curriculum, which is evaluated in this "imaginary" evaluation, is described in Part Three of the present volume, beginning on p. 162.

[73]Any resemblance to persons living or dead is purely coincidental.

CHAPTER 13. SETTING BOUNDARIES AND ANALYZING THE EVALUATION CONTEXT

[74]Although our checklist bears only superficial resemblance to and is substantially different from Owen's checklist, we owe the idea and format to his earlier efforts.

[75]For the sake of readability, we refer to the entity being evaluated as a *program*, recognizing that in some cases it will be a project, strategy, or the like.

[76]The actual description of the program, reprinted from the original evaluation report, appears in Appendix 2.

[77]This is not to say there is no cost for such personnel services, but only that it may be possible to obtain some assistance with evaluation tasks from on-site personnel within existing operating budgets.

[78]An evaluation in which, if the results come out right, will be used to support a preconceived position, but if results come out wrong, will be suppressed or ignored.

CHAPTER 14. IDENTIFYING AND SELECTING THE EVALUATIVE QUESTIONS, CRITERIA, AND ISSUES

[79]Advantages and disadvantages of having the evaluator serve in the dual capacity of expert in both the substantive content and evaluation methods are discussed in Worthen and Sanders (1984).

[80]Obviously the criteria guiding selection of evaluation questions differ from those governing research, where interest alone may justify inquiry.

CHAPTER 15. PLANNING THE INFORMATION COLLECTION, ANALYSIS, AND INTERPRETATION

[81]We have stated previously that although evaluative objectives, issues, or other organizers might be used, we find questions preferable. For simplicity, in later chapters, we will refer only to evaluative questions as organizers for an evaluation. The points we make would be as pertinent in most instances to other organizers as well.

[82]For simplicity of presentation, this list assumes that an educational *program* is being evaluated.

[83]This set of categories draws on Furst (1958) and Worthen, Borg, and White (unpublished manuscript).

[84]Even these samples are only partial, providing the first four columns of a matrix. Subsequent columns that would need to be completed for each evaluative question (but omitted here to conserve space) include *at least* the following: arrangement for collecting information (by whom, when, under what conditions), analysis of information, and reporting of information (to whom, when, how).

CHAPTER 16. DEVELOPING A MANAGEMENT PLAN FOR THE EVALUATION

[85]Another management approach, Critical Path Management (CPM), is not discussed here because it is quite similar to PERT. For further information on that technique, see Stires and Murphy (1962).

[86]We know of one three-month project, for example, where seven weeks were consumed laying out

a compulsively complete and detailed PERT network for the entire project, with the predictable result that the project was nearly two months tardy, and the evaluation report delivered after the decisions had all been made.

[87]Case (1969) has made an excellent case (no pun intended) for the utility of PERT in large-scale research and evaluation studies.

[88]Where doing one thing "costs" the system the opportunity of doing something that could have been accomplished with the same amount of time, energy, and resources.

[89]This list was originally published as part of an earlier discussion (Sanders, 1983b) of the direct dollar costs of evaluation.

[90]As judged by the American Educational Research Association in its annual competition for "best evaluation study."

[91]We leave that exercise to the reader as an application to check your skills in developing Gantt charts.

[92]See Worthen (1974a); a more complete discussion of criteria for evaluating evaluations appears in Chapter 21 of the present text.

[93]Joint Committee on Standards for Educational Evaluation (1981).

CHAPTER 17. DEALING WITH POLITICAL, ETHICAL, AND INTERPERSONAL ASPECTS OF EVALUATION

[94]See, for example, Smith's (1982a) volume on communication strategies in evaluation or Cronbach and his associates' (1980) discussion of evaluators' communications. We shall say more about communication in discussing evaluation reports in Chapter 20.

[95]We are grateful to Vincent Greaney of the Educational Research Centre at St. Patrick's College in Dublin, Ireland, for participating in discussions that led us to formulate these recommendations.

[96]The remainder of this section draws not only on our own prior work (see Worthen, 1980) but is also influenced by Scriven's (1976a) discussion of evaluator relationships and bias and Anderson and Ball's (1978) excellent discussion of internal and external relationships in evaluation.

[97]The names, organizations, and titles in this summary and the following letter have been changed to provide anonymity and "protect the innocent," so to speak. But the essential content has not been altered and is reproduced here *verbatim*.

CHAPTER 18. COLLECTING EVALUATION INFORMATION

[98]For examples, see Osgood, Suci, and Tannenbaum's (1957) book on the semantic differential as an instrument for assessing attitudes, Stephenson (1953) on Q-sorts, or Helmer's (1967) book on how to conduct Delphi studies.

[99]Further discussions of problems to look for in data handling may be found in Brinkerhoff and others (1983), pp. 119–126, and Levine (1985).

[100]Storage may be considerably longer if the data represent an important data base that is comprehensive, expensive to collect, and/or useful for follow-up analyses.

[101]An earlier version of the discussion in this section appeared in Sanders and Murray (1976).

[102]Although this discussion centers on the appropriateness of the experimental paradigm, it should be noted that comparative evaluation is not synonymous with comparative experimentation, in the methodological sense. There are numerous comparisons that do not depend on the methodology of experimental design.

CHAPTER 19. ANALYZING AND INTERPRETING EVALUATION INFORMATION

[103]These guidelines draw on suggestions of the Joint Committee on Standards for Educational Evaluation (1981).

[104]Discussions of the cost of evaluation are provided in Alkin and Solmon (1983), but we limit our discussion here to analysis methods for costs in education, not costs of evaluation.

CHAPTER 20. REPORTING AND USING EVALUATION INFORMATION

[105]King, Thompson, and Pechman (1982) and N. L. Smith (1982a) have completed thorough reviews of literature on communication strategies and their effect on the use of evaluation in education. Space does not permit us to give adequate coverage to those works here; readers interested in pursuing this subject in greater depth are referred to the original sources.

[106]Some of the alternatives listed in this section are drawn from Brophy and others, (1974).

[107]Unless, of course, this is a goal-free evaluation study.

[108]Of course, in an adversary–oriented evaluation, balance exists not *within* one set of evaluation findings, as is the goal of most evaluation approaches, but in the balance *between* the two alternative viewpoints built into the evaluation.

[109]See Brown, Braskamp, and Newmann (1978) for an interesting study of the impact of professional jargon on the credibility of an evaluation report. Also see Stalford's (1985) reflection about the importance of using everyday language rather than technical terminology in reporting to school practitioners and policymakers, even if some precision is lost.

[110]We are indebted for this example to our colleague, Adrian Van Mondfrans, who notes no legal status should be assumed for it, because it was not drafted by an attorney. If legal status is desired for any disclaimer, an attorney should be consulted.

[111]Brickell (1978) has described in his delightful paper a number of these problems (including the client who insists on final editing of the evaluator's report).

CHAPTER 21. EVALUATING EVALUATIONS

[112]The following professional organizations in the United States appointed members to the Joint Committee: American Association of School Administrators, American Educational Research Association, American Federation of Teachers, American Personnel and Guidance Association, American Psychological Association, Association for Supervision and Curriculum Development, Council for American Private Education, Education Commission of the States, National Association of Elementary School Principals, National Council on Measurement in Education, National Education Association, and National School Boards Association. In addition, numerous professional evaluators assisted in the development of standards, testing them, and drafting instructional materials to help others apply them.

[113]Portions of this example are drawn from an earlier article (Worthen, 1977a).

[114]We trust the reader will permit the mnemonic puns in these names to go unpunished and will agree that the names are descriptive.

[115]Scriven (1984) has attributed this at least in part to "valuephobia, a pervasive fear of being evaluated," which is a part of the general human condition that afflicts not only evaluators but also others in every walk of life.

APPENDIX 1. SOME GENERAL AREAS OF COMPETENCE IMPORTANT IN EDUCATIONAL EVALUATION

[116]The analysis of different evaluation frameworks provided in Chapters 4 through 12 should prove useful in sorting out and choosing among various frameworks for evaluation, but there are many more details to be determined than any textbook can teach. This competency is somewhat subjective, an art that requires wisdom that only experience can provide.

References

ALEXANDER, R. R. (1977). *Educational criticism of three art history classes*. Unpublished doctoral dissertation, Stanford University. (University Microfilms No. 78–2125)

ALKIN, M. C. (1969). Evaluation theory development. *Evaluation Comment, 2*, 2–7.

ALKIN, M. C., DAILLAK, R., & WHITE, P. (1979). *Using evaluation: Does evaluation make a difference?* Beverly Hills, CA: Sage.

ALKIN, M. C., & SOLMON, L. C. (Eds.). (1983). *The costs of evaluation*. Beverly Hills, CA: Sage.

ALKIN, M. C., STECHER, B. M., & GEIGER, F. L. (1982). *Title I evaluation: Utility and factors influencing use*. Northridge, CA: Educational Evaluation Associates.

ANDERSON, R. C. (1983). Reflections on the role of peer review in competitions for federal research. *Educational Researcher, 12*, 3–5.

ANDERSON, R. D., SOPTICK, J. M., ROGERS, W. T., & WORTHEN, B. R. (1971). *An analysis and interpretation of tasks and competencies required of personnel conducting exemplary research and research-related activities in education* (Tech. Paper No. 52). Washington, DC: AERA Task Force on Research Training.

ANDERSON, S. B., & BALL, S. (1978). *The profession and practice of program evaluation*. San Francisco: Jossey-Bass.

ANTONOPLOS, D. P. (1977, April). Evaluation reconsidered: Pied pipers of pedagogy. Paper presented at the annual meeting of the American Educational Research Association, New York City.

ARNSTEIN, G. (1975). Trial by jury: A new evaluation method. II. The outcome. *Phi Delta Kappan, 57*(3), 188–190.

ATKIN, J. M. (1968). Behavioral objectives in curriculum design: A cautionary note. *The Science Teacher, 35*, 27–30.

AUERBACH, C., GARRISON, L. K., HURST, W., & MERMIN, S. (1961). The adversary system. In C. AUERBACH & S. MERMIN (Eds.), *The Legal Process*. San Francisco: Chandler.

BAKER, E. L. (1978). Evaluation dimensions for program development and improvement. In S. B. ANDERSON & C. D. COLES (Eds.), *Exploring purposes and dimensions*. New Directions for Program Evaluation, No. 1. San Francisco: Jossey-Bass.

BECKER, H. S. (1958). Problems of influence and proof in participant observation. *American Sociological Review, 23*(6), 652–660.

BERDIE, D., & Anderson, J. (1974). *Questionnaires*. Metuchen, NJ: Scarecrow Press.

BERNHARDT, V. L. (1984, April). *Evaluation processes of regional and national education accrediting agencies: Implications for redesigning an evaluation process in California*. Paper presented at the annual meeting of the American Educational Research Association, New Orleans.

BLANPIED, W. A., & BORG, A. F. (1979). Peer review of science education proposals at the National Science Foundation. *Science Education, 63*(3), 417–421.

BLOOM, B. S., ENGELHART, M. D., FURST, E. J., HILL, W. H., & KRATHWOHL, D. R. (1956).

Taxonomy of educational objectives: Handbook I: Cognitive domain. New York: David McKay.

BLOOM, B. S., HASTINGS, J. T., & MADAUS, G. F. (1971). *Handbook on formative and summative evaluation of student learning.* New York: McGraw-Hill.

BOGDAN, R. C., & BIKLEN, S. K. (1982). *Qualitative research for education.* Boston: Allyn & Bacon.

BOGDAN, R. C., & TAYLOR, S. J. (1975). *Introduction to qualitative research methods: A phenomenological approach to the social sciences.* New York: Wiley.

BORG, W. R., & GALL, M. D. (1983). *Educational research: An introduction* (4th ed.). New York: Longman.

BORUCH, R. F. (1976). On common contentions about randomized field experiments. In G. V. GLASS (Ed.), *Evaluation studies review annual* (Vol. 1). Beverly Hills, CA: Sage.

BORUCH, R. F., & CORDRAY, D. S. (Eds.). (1980). *An appraisal of educational program evaluations: Federal, state, and local agencies.* Washington, DC: U.S. Department of Education.

BORUCH, R. F., & RIECKEN, H. W. (Eds.). (1975). *Experimental testing of public policy.* Boulder, CO: Westview Press.

BRACHT, G. H. (1974, May). *Planning evaluation studies.* Paper presented at the Minnesota Round Table in Early Childhood Education II, Spring Hill, MN.

BRACHT, G. H., & GLASS, G. V. (1968). The external validity of experiments. *American Educational Research Journal*, 5(4), 437–474.

BRAGER, G. L., & MAZZA, P. (1979). The level of analysis and the level of presentation are not the same. *Educational Evaluation and Policy Analysis*, 1(3), 105–106.

BRAITHWAITE, R. L., & THOMPSON, R. L. (1981). Application of the judicial evaluation model within an employment and training program. *Center on Evaluation, Development, and Research (CEDR) Quarterly*, 14(2), 13–16.

BRANDT, R. S. (Ed.). (1981). *Applied strategies for curriculum evaluation.* Alexandria, VA: Association for Supervision and Curriculum Development.

BRASKAMP, L., & BROWN, R. D. (Eds.). (1980). *Utilization of evaluative information.* New Directions for Program Evaluation, No. 5. San Francisco: Jossey-Bass.

BRAYBROOKE, D., & LINDBLOM, C. E. (1963). *A strategy of decision.* New York: The Free Press.

BRICKELL, H. M. (1978). The influence of external political factors on the role and methodology of evaluation. In T. D. COOK, M. L. DEL ROSARIO, K. M. HENNIGAN, M. M. MARK, & W. M. K. TROCHIM (Eds.), *Evaluation studies review annual* (Vol. 3). Beverly Hills, CA: Sage.

BRINKERHOFF, R. O., BRETHOWER, D. M., HLUCHYJ, T., & NOWAKOWSKI, J. R. (1983). *Program evaluation: A practitioner's guide for trainers and educators.* Boston: Kluwer-Nijhoff.

BROPHY, K., GROTELUESCHEN, A., & GOOLER, D. (1974). *A blueprint for program evaluation* (Occasional Paper No. 1). Urbana-Champaign: University of Illinois, College of Education, Office for Professional Services.

BROWDER, L. H., ATKINS, W. A., & KAYA, E. (1973). *Developing an educationally accountable program.* Berkeley, CA: McCutchan.

BROWN, R. D., BRASKAMP, L. A., & NEWMANN, D. L. (1978). Evaluator credibility as a function of report style: Do jargon and data make a difference? *Evaluation Quarterly*, 2(2), 331–341.

BROWN, R. D., & NEWMANN, D. L. (1979). *A schematic approach to studying evaluation utilization.* Paper presented at the annual meeting of the American Educational Research Association, Minneapolis, MN.

BRYK, A. S. (Ed.). (1983). *Stakeholder-based evaluation.* New Directions for Program Evaluation, No. 17. San Francisco: Jossey-Bass.

BUDD, R. W., THOP, R. K., & DONOHEW, L. (1967). *Content analysis of communication.* New York: Macmillan.

BULLOCK, C. C. (1982). Interactionist evaluators look for "what is" not "what should be." *Parks and Recreation, 17,* 37–39.

BUNDA, M. A., & SANDERS, J. R. (Eds.). (1979). *Practices and problems in competency-based measurement.* Washington, DC: National Council on Measurement in Education.

CAMPBELL, D. T. (1984). Can we be scientific in applied social science? In R. F. CONNER, D. G. ALTMAN, & C. JACKSON (Eds.), *Evaluation studies review annual* (Vol. 9). Beverly Hills, CA: Sage.

CAMPBELL, D. T., & STANLEY, J. C. (1963). Experimental and quasi-experimental designs for research of teaching. In N. L. GAGE (Ed.), *Handbook of research on teaching.* Chicago: Rand McNally.

CAMPBELL, D. T., & STANLEY, J. C. (1966). *Experimental and quasi-experimental designs for research.* Chicago: Rand McNally.

CARO, F. G. (1971). *Readings in evaluation research.* New York: Russell Sage Foundation.

CARTER, L. R. (1982). The standards for program evaluation and the large for-profit social science research and evaluation companies. In P. H. ROSSI (Ed.), *Standards for evaluation practice.* New Directions for Program Evaluation, No. 15. San Francisco: Jossey-Bass.

CASE, C. M. (1969). The application of PERT to large-scale educational research and evaluation studies. *Educational Technology, 9,* 79–83.

CLARK, N. (1952). *The Gantt chart.* London: Pitman and Sons.

CLEARINGHOUSE FOR APPLIED PERFORMANCE TESTING. (1974). *Bibliographies on applied performance testing.* Portland, OR: Northwest Regional Educational Laboratory.

CLIFFORD, G. J. (1973). A history of the impact of research on teaching. In R. M. W. TRAVERS (Ed.), *Second handbook of research on teaching.* Chicago: Rand McNally.

CLYNE, S. F. (1982). *The judicial evaluation model: A case study.* Unpublished doctoral dissertation, Boston College.

COCHRAN, W. R. (1963). *Sampling techniques.* New York: Wiley.

COHEN, D. K. (1970). Politics and research: Evaluation of social action programs in education. *Review of Educational Research, 40,* 213–238.

COHEN, S. (1978). Science and the tabloid press. *APA Monitor, 9*(3), 1.

CONNER, R. F., ALTMAN, D. G., & JACKSON C. (Eds.). (1984). *Evaluation studies review annual* (Vol. 9). Beverly Hills, CA: Sage.

COOK, D. L. (1966). *Program evaluation and review techniques: Applications in education* (Monograph No. 17). Washington, DC: U.S. Office of Education Cooperative Research.

COOK, T. D., & CAMPBELL, D. T. (1979). *Quasi-experimentation: Design and analysis issues for field settings.* Chicago: Rand McNally.

COOK, T. D., & REICHARDT, C. S. (Eds.). (1979). *Qualitative and quantitative methods in evaluation research.* Beverly Hills, CA: Sage.

COUSINS, J. B., & LEITHWOOD, K. A. (1985). *The state of the art of empirical research on evaluation utilization.* Toronto: The Ontario Institute for Studies in Education.

COVERT, R. W. (1977). *Guidelines and criteria for constructing questionnaires.* Unpublished manuscript, University of Virginia, Evaluation Research Center.

CRITTENDEN, B. (1978). Product or process in curriculum evaluation? *Australian Educational Researcher, 5*(1), 29–52.

CRONBACH, L. J. (1963). Course improvement through evaluation. *Teachers College Record, 64,* 672–683.

CRONBACH, L. J. (1973). Course improvement through evaluation. In B. R. WORTHEN & J. R. SANDERS, *Educational evaluation: Theory and practice.* Belmont, CA: Wadsworth.

CRONBACH, L. J. (1977). Remarks to the new society. *Evaluation Research Society Newsletter,* *1*(1), 1–3.

CRONBACH, L. J. (1979). *Essentials of psychological testing.* New York: Harper & Row.

CRONBACH, L. J. (1982). *Designing evaluations of educational and social programs.* San Francisco: Jossey-Bass.

CRONBACH. L. J., AMBRON, S. R., DORNBUSCH, S. M., HESS, R. D., HORNIK, R. C., PHILLIPS, D. C., WALKER, D. F., & WEINER, S. S. (1980). *Toward reform of program evaluation.* San Francisco: Jossey-Bass.

CRONBACH, L. J., & SUPPES, P. (1969). *Research for tomorrow's schools: Disciplined inquiry for education.* New York: Macmillan.

CURRICULUM DEVELOPMENT CENTRE. (1977). *Curriculum evaluation.* Canberra, Australia: Author.

DAVIS, H. R., & SALASIN, S. E. (1975). The utilization of evaluation. In E. L. STRUENING & M. GUTTENTAG (Eds.), *Handbook of evaluation research* (Vol. 1). Beverly Hills, CA: Sage.

DEMALINE, R., & QUINN, W. (1979). *Hints for planning and conducting a survey and a bibliography of survey methods.* Kalamazoo, MI: Western Michigan University Evaluation Center.

DENNY, T. (1980). *Storytelling and educational understanding* (Occasional Paper No. 12). Kalamazoo, MI: Western Michigan University Evaluation Center.

DENZIN, N. K. (1978). *The research act.* Chicago: Aldine.

DICKEY, B. (1980). Utilization of evaluations of small-scale innovative educational projects. *Educational Evaluation and Policy Analysis, 2,* 65–77.

DICKEY, F. G., & MILLER, J. W. (1972). *A current perspective on accreditation.* Washington, DC: American Association for Higher Education.

DONMOYER, R. (Undated). *Evaluation as deliberation: Theoretical and empirical explorations* (Grant No. G 810083). National Institute of Education, Ohio State University.

DOUGLAS, J. D. (1976). *Investigative social research.* Beverly Hills, CA: Sage.

EASH, M. J. (1970). *Developing an instrument for the assessment of instructional materials.* Paper presented at the annual meeting of the American Educational Research Association, Minneapolis, MN.

EDWARDS, A. L. (1957). *Techniques of attitude scale construction.* New York: Appleton-Century-Crofts.

EDWARDS, W., GUTTENTAG, M., & SNAPPER, K. (1975). A decision-theoretic approach to evaluation research. In E. L. STRUENING & M. GUTTENTAG (Eds.), *Handbook of evaluation research* (Vol. 1). Beverly Hills, CA: Sage.

EISNER, E. W. (1975, March). *The perceptive eye: Toward the reformation of educational evaluation.* Invited address at the American Educational Research Association, Washington, DC.

EISNER, E. W. (1976). Educational connoisseurship and criticism: Their form and function in educational evaluation. *Journal of Aesthetic Education, 10,* 135–150.

EISNER, E. W. (1979a). *The educational imagination: On the design and evaluation of school programs.* New York: Macmillan.

EISNER, E. W. (1979b). The use of qualitative forms of evaluation for improving educational practice. *Educational Evaluation and Policy Analysis, 1*(6), 11–19.

ERICKSON, F. (1977). Some approaches to inquiry in school community ethnography. *Anthropology and Education Quarterly, 8,* 58–69.

ESTES, G. D., & DEMALINE, R. E. (1982). Outcomes of the MCT clarification process. In

E. R. House, S. Mathison, J. A. Pearsol, & H. Preskill (Eds.), *Evaluation studies review annual* (Vol. 7). Beverly Hills, CA: Sage.

Evaluation Research Society Standards Committee (1982). Evaluation Research Society standards for program evaluation. In R. F. Conner, D. G. Altman, & C. Jackson (Eds.), *Standards for evaluation practice.* New Directions for Program Evaluation, No. 15. San Francisco: Jossey-Bass.

Fetterman, D. M. (1983). Guilty knowledge, dirty hands, and other ethical dilemmas: The hazards of contract research. *Human Organization, 42*(3), 214–224.

Fetterman, D. M. (1984). *Ethnography in educational evaluation.* Beverly Hills, CA: Sage.

Fienberg, S. E. (1977). The collection and analysis of ethnographic data in educational research. *Anthropology and Education Quarterly, 8*(2), 50–57.

Filstead, W. J. (1981). Using qualitative methods in evaluation research: An illustrative bibliography. *Evaluation Review, 5*(2), 259–268.

Flexner, A. (1910). *Medical education in the United States and Canada* (Bulletin No. 4). New York: Carnegie Foundation for the Advancement of Teaching.

Flexner, A. (1960). *Abraham Flexner: An autobiography.* New York: Simon & Schuster.

Floden, R. E. (1983). Flexner, accreditation, and evaluation. In G. F. Madaus, M. Scriven, & D. L. Stufflebeam (Eds.), *Evaluation models: Viewpoints on educational and human services evaluation.* Boston: Kluwer-Nijhoff.

Florida Department of Education. (1980). *Guidelines for the review and selection of instructional materials for competency-based education* (Project No. 9–1C12). Tallahassee: Florida Department of Education, Division of Vocational Education.

Florio, D. H., Behrmann, M. M., & Goltz, D. L. (1979). What do policy makers think of educational research and evaluation? Or do they? *Educational Evaluation and Policy Analysis, 1*, 61–87.

Frank, J. N. (1949). *Courts on trial.* Princeton, NJ: Princeton University Press.

Franklin, G. S., & Sparkman, W. E. (1978). The cost effectiveness of two program delivery systems for exceptional children. *Journal of Education Finance, 3*(3), 305–314.

Franks, M. E., & Fortune, J. C. (1984, April). *A study of the impact of Chapter 2 of the Education Consolidation and Improvement Act on local education agencies.* Paper presented at the annual meeting of the American Educational Research Association, New Orleans.

Furst, E. J. (1958). *Constructing evaluation instruction.* New York: David McKay.

Gagné, R. M. (1975). Qualifications of professionals in educational R. & D. *Educational Researcher, 4*(2), 7–11.

Gephart, W. J. (1977). *Toward a synthesis of evaluation models.* Paper presented at the annual meeting of the American Educational Research Association, New York City.

Gephart, W. J. (1978). *The facets of the evaluation process: A starter set.* Unpublished manuscript, Bloomington, IN: Phi Delta Kappa.

Gideonse, H. D. (1969). Behavioral objectives: Continuing the dialogue. *The Science Teacher, 36*, 51–54.

Glass, G. V (1969). *The growth of evaluation methodology.* Boulder, CO: University of Colorado, Laboratory of Educational Research.

Glass, G. V (1975). A paradox about the excellence of schools and the people in them. *Educational Researcher, 4*, 9–13.

Glass, G. V, & Worthen, B. R. (1970). *Essential knowledge and skills for educational research and evaluation* (Tech. Paper No. 5). Washington, DC: AERA Task Force on Research Training.

Glass, G. V, & Worthen, B. R. (1972). Educational inquiry and the practice of education.

In H. D. Schalock (Ed.), *Conceptual frameworks for viewing educational research, development, diffusion, and evaluation.* Monmouth, OR: State System of Higher Education.

Goetz, J. P., & LeCompte, M. D. (1981). Ethnographic research and the problem of data reduction. *Anthropology and Education Quarterly, 12,* 51–70.

Goodlad, J. (1979). *What schools are for.* Bloomington, IN: Phi Delta Kappa Educational Foundation.

Goodlad, J. (1984). *A place called school.* New York: McGraw-Hill.

Gordon, R. L. (1975). *Interviewing strategy, techniques, and factors.* Homewood, IL: Dorsey Press.

Grobman, H. (1972). *Content analysis as a tool in formative and summative evaluation.* Paper presented at the annual meeting of the American Educational Research Association, Chicago.

Guba, E. G. (1965). *Evaluation in field studies.* Address at evaluation conference sponsored by the Ohio State Department of Education, Columbus.

Guba, E. G. (1967). Evaluation and the process of change. In *Notes and working papers concerning the administration of programs: Title III ESEA.* Washington, DC: U.S. Senate Committee on Labor and Public Welfare, Subcommittee on Education.

Guba, E. G. (1969). The failure of educational evaluation. *Educational Technology, 9,* 29–38.

Guba, E. G. (1975). Problems in utilizing the results of evaluation. *Journal of Research and Development in Education, 8,* 42–54.

Guba, E. G. (1978a). *Toward a methodology of naturalistic inquiry in educational evaluation* (Monograph Series No. 8). Los Angeles: University of California, Center for the Study of Evaluation.

Guba, E. G. (1978b). *The use of metaphors in constructing theory* (Paper and Report Series, No. 3). Portland, OR: Northwest Regional Educational Laboratory, Research on Evaluation Program.

Guba, E. G. (1981a). Investigative journalism. In N. L. Smith (Ed.), *New techniques for evaluation.* Beverly Hills, CA: Sage.

Guba, E. G. (1981b). Investigative reporting. In N. L. Smith (Ed.), *Metaphors for evaluation: Sources of new methods.* Beverly Hills, CA: Sage.

Guba, E. G., & Clark, D. L. (undated mimeo). *Types of educational research.* Columbus: Ohio State University.

Guba, E. G., & Clark, D. L. (1976). *Contemporary scenarios of knowledge production and utilization in schools, colleges, and departments of education.* Bloomington, IN: Research on Institutions of Teacher Education. (ERIC Document Reproduction Service No. ED 139 809)

Guba, E. G., & Lincoln, Y. S. (1981). *Effective evaluation.* San Francisco: Jossey-Bass.

Guba, E. G., & Stufflebeam, D. L. (1968). *Evaluation: The process of stimulating, aiding, and abetting insightful action.* Paper presented at the 2nd Phi Delta Kappa National Symposium for Professors of Educational Research, Boulder, CO.

Gustafson, T. (1975). The controversy over peer review. *Science, 190*(4219), 1060–1066.

Halpern, E. S. (1983, April). *Auditing naturalistic inquiries: Some preliminary applications. Part 1: Development of the process. Part 2: Case study application.* Paper presented at the annual meeting of the American Educational Research Association, Montreal, Quebec, Canada.

Hamilton, D. (1976). *Curriculum evaluation.* London: Open Books.

Hamilton, D. (1977). Making sense of curriculum evaluation: Continuities and discontinuities in an educational idea. In L. Shulman (Ed.), *Review of research in education* (Vol. 5). Itasca, IL: Peacock.

HAMILTON, D., JENKINS, D., KING, C., MACDONALD, B., & PARLETT, M. (Eds.). (1977). *Beyond the numbers game: A reader in educational evaluation.* Berkeley, CA: McCutchan.

HAMMOND, R. L. (1973). Evaluation at the local level. In B. R. WORTHEN & J. R. SANDERS, *Educational evaluation: Theory and practice.* Belmont, CA: Wadsworth.

HARLAN, W. (1975). A critical look at the classical strategy applied to formative curriculum evaluation. *Studies in Evaluation, 1,* 37–53.

HÉBERT, Y. M. (1986). Naturalistic evaluation in practice: A case study. In D. D. WILLIAMS (Ed.), *Naturalistic evaluation.* New Directions for Program Evaluation, No. 30. San Francisco: Jossey-Bass.

HELMER, O. (1967). *Analysis of the future: The delphi method.* Santa Monica, CA: Rand Corporation.

HENCLEY, S. P., & YATES, J. R. (Eds.). (1974). *Futurism in education.* Berkeley, CA: McCutchan.

HERNDON, E. B. (1980). *NIE's study of minimum competency testing: A process for the clarification of issues.* Washington, DC: National Institute of Education.

HINKLE, D., WIERSMA, W., & JURS, S. (1979). *Applied statistics for the behavioral sciences.* Chicago: Rand McNally.

HISCOX, M. D., & OWENS, T. R. (1975). *Attempts at implementing an educational adversary model.* Paper presented at the third annual Pacific Northwest Educational Research and Evaluation Conference, Seattle, WA.

HIVELY, W., MAXWELL, G., RABEHL, G., SENSION, D., & LUNDIN, S. (1973). *Domain-referenced curriculum evaluation: A technical handbook and a case study from the Minnemast project* (CSE Monograph Series in Evaluation No. 1). Los Angeles: University of California, Center for the Study of Evaluation.

HOAGLIN, D. C., LIGHT, R. J., McPEEK, B., MOSTELLER, F., & STOTO, M. A. (1982). *Data for decisions.* Cambridge, MA: Abt.

HODGKINSON, H. (1957). Action research: A critique. *Journal of Educational Sociology, 31*(4), 137–153.

HODGKINSON, H., HURST, J., & LEVINE, H. (1975). *Improving and assessing performance: Evaluation in higher education.* Berkeley, CA: University of California Center for Research and Development in Higher Education.

HOLSTI, O. (1969). *Content analysis for the social sciences and humanities.* Reading, MA: Addison-Wesley.

HOPKINS, K. D., & GLASS, G. V (1978). *Basic statistics for the behavioral sciences.* Englewood Cliffs, NJ: Prentice-Hall.

HOPKINS, K. D., & STANLEY, J. C. (1981). *Educational and psychological measurement and evaluation.* Englewood Cliffs, NJ: Prentice-Hall.

HOUSE, E. R. (Ed.). (1973). *School evaluation: The politics and process.* Berkeley, CA: McCutchan.

HOUSE, E. R. (1976). Justice in evaluation. In G. V. GLASS (Ed.), *Evaluation studies review annual* (Vol. 1). Beverly Hills, CA: Sage.

HOUSE, E. R. (1980). *Evaluating with validity.* Beverly Hills, CA: Sage.

HOUSE, E. R. (1983a). Assumptions underlying evaluation models. In G. F. MADAUS, M. SCRIVEN, & D. L. STUFFLEBEAM (Eds.), *Evaluation models: Viewpoints on educational and human services evaluation.* Boston: Kluwer-Nijhoff.

HOUSE, E. R. (Ed.). (1983b). *Philosophy of evaluation.* New Directions for Program Evaluation, No. 19. San Francisco: Jossey-Bass.

HOUSE, E. R., MATHISON, S., PEARSOL, J. A., & PRESKILL, H. (Eds.). (1982). *Evaluation studies review annual* (Vol. 7). Beverly Hills, CA: Sage.

HOUSE, E. R., THURSTON, P., & HAND, J. (1984). The adversary hearing as a public forum. *Studies in Educational Evaluation, 10,* 111–123.

HOWE, K. R. (1985). Two dogmas of educational research. *Educational Researcher, 14*(8), 10–18.

HUXLEY, E. (1982). *The flame trees of Thika: Memories of an African childhood.* London: Chatto and Windus.

ILLINOIS STATE BOARD OF EDUCATION. (1982). *Handbook for evaluation of special education effectiveness.* Springfield, IL: Author.

INSTRUCTIONAL OBJECTIVES EXCHANGE. (1969). *Objectives and test item collections.* Los Angeles, CA: Instructional Objectives Exchange, Box 24095.

ISAAC, S., & MICHAEL, W. B. (1981). *Handbook in research and evaluation.* San Diego, CA: Edits.

JAEGER, R. M. (1983). *Statistics: A spectator sport.* Beverly Hills, CA: Sage.

JAEGER, R. M. (1984). *Sampling in education and the social sciences.* New York: Longman.

JAEGER, R. M., & TITTLE, C. K. (Eds.). (1980). *Minimum competency achievement testing.* Berkeley, CA: McCutchan.

JOINT COMMITTEE ON STANDARDS FOR EDUCATIONAL EVALUATION. (1981). *Standards for evaluations of educational programs, projects, and materials.* New York: McGraw-Hill.

JUNG, S. M., & SCHUBERT, J. G. (1983). Evaluability assessment: A two-year retrospective. *Educational Evaluation and Policy Analysis, 5*(4), 435–444.

JUSTIZ, M. J., & MOORMAN, H. N. (1985). New NIE peer review procedures. *Educational Researcher, 14*(1), 5–11.

KAPLAN, A. (1964). *The conduct of inquiry.* San Francisco: Chandler.

KELLS, H. R., & ROBERTSON, M. P. (1980). Post-secondary accreditation: A current bibliography. *North Central Association Quarterly, 54,* 411–426.

KELLY, E. F. (1975). Curriculum evaluation and literary criticism. Comments on the anthology. *Curriculum Theory Network, 5,* 87–106.

KELLY, E. F. (1978). Curriculum criticism and literary criticism: Comments on the anthology. In G. WILLIS (Ed.), *Qualitative evaluation.* Berkeley, CA: McCutchan.

KEMMIS, S. (1977). Telling it like it is: The problem of making a portrayal of an educational program. In L. RUBIN (Ed.), *Curriculum handbook: Administration and theory.* Boston: Allyn & Bacon.

KENNEDY, M. (1984). How evidence alters understanding and decisions. *Educational Evaluation and Policy Analysis, 6,* 207–226.

KENNEDY, M., APLING, R., & NEUMANN, W. (1980). *The role of evaluation and test information in public schools.* Cambridge, MA: The Huron Institute.

KERLINGER, F. N. (1975). *Foundations of behavioral research: Educational, psychological, and sociological inquiry* (2nd ed.). New York: Holt, Rinehart, & Winston.

KING, J. A., & PECHMAN, E. M. (1982). *The process of evaluation use in local school settings* (Final report of NIE Grant No. 81–0900). New Orleans: New Orleans Public Schools.

KING, J. A., & PECHMAN, E. M. (1984). Pinning the wave to the shore: Conceptualizing evaluation use in school systems. *Educational Evaluation and Policy Analysis, 6,* 241–253.

KING, J. A., THOMPSON, B., & PECHMAN, E. M. (1981). *Evaluation utilization: A bibliography.* New Orleans: New Orleans Public Schools.

KING, J. A., THOMPSON, B., & PECHMAN, E. M. (1982). *Improving evaluation use in local schools* (Final report for NIE Grant NIE–G–80–0082). New Orleans: New Orleans Public Schools.

KIRKWOOD, R. (1982). Accreditation. In H. E. MITZEL (Ed.), *Encyclopedia of educational research* (Vol. 1, 5th ed.). New York: Macmillan and The Free Press.

KISH, L. (1965). *Survey sampling*. New York: Wiley.

KORNHAUSER, A., & SHEATSLEY, P. (1959). Questionnaire construction and interview procedure. In C. SELLTIZ, L. WRIGHTSMAN, & S. COOK (Eds.), *Research methods in social relations*. New York: Holt, Rinehart, & Winston.

KOURILSKY, M. (1973). An adversary model for educational evaluation. *Evaluation Comment*, 4(2), 3–6.

KOURILSKY, M., & BAKER, E. (1976). An experimental comparison of interaction, advocacy, and adversary evaluation. *Center on Evaluation, Development, and Research (CEDR) Quarterly*, 9(2), 4–8.

KRATHWOHL, D. R., BLOOM, B. S., & MASIA, B. B. (1964). *Taxonomy of educational objectives: Handbook II: Affective domain*. New York: David McKay.

KREJCIE, R. V., & MORGAN, D. W. (1970). Determining sample size for research activities. *Educational and Psychological Measurement*, 30, 607–610.

KRIPPENDORFF, K. (1980). *Content analysis: An introduction to its methodology*. Beverly Hills, CA: Sage.

LAI, M. K. (1978, March). *Consumer's guide to educational evaluation*. Paper presented at the annual meeting of the American Educational Research Association, Toronto, Ontario, Canada.

LANG, K., & LANG, G. (1953). The unique perspective of television and its effects: A pilot study. *American Sociological Review*, 18, 3–12.

LEE, A. M., & HOLLEY, F. R. (1978, March). *Communicating evaluation information: Some practical tips that work*. Paper presented at the annual meeting of the American Educational Research Association, Toronto, Ontario, Canada.

LESSINGER, L. M. (1970). Engineering accountability for results in public education. *Phi Delta Kappan*, 52, 217–225.

LESSINGER, L. M., & TYLER, R. W. (Eds.). (1971). *Accountability in education*. Worthington, OH: Charles A. Jones.

LEVIN, H. M. (1981). Cost analysis. In N. L. SMITH (Ed.), *New techniques for evaluation*. Beverly Hills, CA: Sage.

LEVIN, H. M. (1983). *Cost-effectiveness: A primer*. Beverly Hills, CA: Sage.

LEVINE, M. (1974). Scientific method and the adversary model. Some preliminary thoughts. *American Psychologist*, 29, 661–677.

LEVINE, M. (1976). *Experiences in adapting the jury trial to the problem of educational program evaluation*. Unpublished manuscript, State University of New York at Buffalo.

LEVINE, M. (1982). Adversary hearings. In N. L. SMITH (Ed.), *Communication strategies in evaluation*. Beverly Hills, CA: Sage.

LEVINE, M. (1985). Principles of data storage and retrieval for use in qualitative evaluations. *Educational Evaluation and Policy Analysis*, 7(2), 169–186.

LEVINE, M., BROWN, E., FITZGERALD, C., GOPLERUD, E., GORDON, M. E., JAYNE-LAZARUS, C., ROSENBERG, N., & SLATER, J. (1978). Adapting the jury trial for program evaluation: A report of an experience. *Evaluation and Program Planning*, 1, 177–186.

LEVINE, M., & ROSENBERG, N. (1979). An adversary model of fact finding and decision making for program evaluation: Theoretical considerations. In H. C. SCHULBERG & F. BAKER (Eds.), *Program evaluation in the health field* (Vol. 2). New York: Behavioral Publications.

LEVITON, L. C., & HUGHES, E. F. X. (1981). Research on the utilization of evaluations: A review and synthesis. *Evaluation Review*, 5, 524–548.

LEWY, A. (1977). Responsive evaluation: An interpretation. *Studies in Educational Evaluation*, 3(2), 143–148.

LIGHT, R. J., & SMITH, P. V. (1970). Choosing a future: Strategies for designing and evaluating new programs. *Harvard Educational Review*, *40*(1), 1–28.

LINCOLN, Y. S., & GUBA, E. G. (1985). *Naturalistic inquiry*. Beverly Hills, CA: Sage.

LINDVALL, C. M. (Ed.). (1964). *Defining educational objectives*. Pittsburgh: University of Pittsburgh Press.

LYON, C., DOSCHER, L., McGRANAHAN, P., & WILLIAMS, R. (1978). *Evaluation and school districts*. Los Angeles: UCLA Center for the Study of Evaluation.

MacDONALD, B., & WALKER, R. (1977). Case study and the social philosophy of educational research. In D. HAMILTON and others (Eds.), *Beyond the Numbers Game*. Berkeley, CA: McCutchan.

MacDONALD, J. B. (1974). An evaluation of evaluation. *Urban Review*, *7*(1), 3–14.

MacDONALD, J. B. (1976). Evaluation and the control of education. In D. TAWNEY (Ed.), *Curriculum evaluation today: Trends and implications*. Schools Council Research Studies, London: Macmillan.

MADAUS, G. F. (1981). NIE clarification hearing: The negative team's case. *Phi Delta Kappan*, *63*(2), 92–94.

MADAUS, G. F. (1982). The clarification hearing: A personal view of the process. *Educational Researcher*, *11*(1), 4, 6–11.

MADAUS, G. F. (Ed.). (1983). *The courts, validity, and minimum competency testing*. Boston: Kluwer-Nijhoff.

MADAUS, G. F., AIRASIAN, P., & KELLAGHAN, T. (1980). *School effectiveness*. New York: McGraw-Hill.

MADAUS, G. F., SCRIVEN, M., & STUFFLEBEAM, D. L. (1983). *Evaluation models: Viewpoints on educational and human services evaluation*. Boston: Kluwer-Nijhoff.

MADAUS, G. F., STUFFLEBEAM, D. L., & SCRIVEN, M. (1983). Program evaluation: A historical overview. In G. F. MADAUS, M. SCRIVEN, & D. L. STUFFLEBEAM (Eds.), *Evaluation models: Viewpoints on educational and human services evaluation*. Boston: Kluwer-Nijhoff.

MADEY, D. L. (1982). Some benefits of integrating qualitative and quantitative methods in program evaluation, with illustrations. *Educational Evaluation and Policy Analysis*, *4*(2), 223–236.

MAGER, R. F. (1962). *Preparing instructional objectives*. Palo Alto, CA: Fearon Press.

MALCOLM, C., & WELCH, W. (1981). *Case study evaluations: A case in point. An illustrative report and methodological analysis of case study evaluations*. Minneapolis: University of Minnesota, Minnesota Research and Evaluation Center.

MARTIN, M. A. (1981). *A framework for identifying information needs for evaluation planning* (Instructional Aids Series No. 4). Kalamazoo, MI: Western Michigan University, Evaluation Center.

MAXWELL, G. S. (1984). A rating scale for assessing the quality of responsive/illuminative evaluations. *Educational Evaluation and Policy Analysis*, *6*, 131–138.

McCUTCHEON, G. (1978). Of solar systems, responsibility and basics: An educational criticism of Mr. Clement's fourth grade. In G. WILLIS (Ed.), *Qualitative evaluation*. Berkeley, CA: McCutchan.

McDONALD, B., & SANGER, J. (1982). Just for the record? Notes toward a theory of interviewing in evaluation. In E. R. HOUSE, S. MATHISON, J. A. PEARSOL, & H. PRESKILL (Eds.), *Evaluation studies review annual* (Vol. 7.). Beverly Hills, CA: Sage.

McLAUGHLIN, M. W. (1980). Evaluation and alchemy. In J. PINCUS (Ed.), *Educational evaluation in public policy setting*. Santa Monica, CA: Rand Corporation.

MEHRENS, W. A., & LEHMANN, I. J. (1969). *Standardized tests in education*. New York: Holt, Rinehart, & Winston.

METFESSEL, N. S., & MICHAEL, W. B. (1967). A paradigm involving multiple criterion measures for the evaluation of the effectiveness of school programs. *Educational and Psychological Measurement, 27,* 931–943.

MILES, M. B., & HUBERMAN, A. M. (1984). *Qualitative data analysis: A sourcebook of new methods.* Beverly Hills, CA: Sage.

MILLMAN, J. (1975). *Selecting educational researchers and evaluators* (TM Report 48). Princeton, NJ: ERIC Clearinghouse on tests, measurement, and evaluation. (ERIC Document Reproduction Service No. ED 117 191)

MITCHELL, J. V. (Ed.). (1985). *The ninth mental measurement yearbook.* Lincoln, NB: University of Nebraska Press. (See also the 1938 and 1940 Mental Measurement Yearbooks and the third through eighth Mental Measurement Yearbooks edited by O. K. BUROS; also BUROS, O. K., *Tests in print.* Highland Park, NJ: The Gryphon Press.)

MITROFF, I. (1974). *The subjective side of science.* New York: American Elsevier.

MORRIS, L. L., & FITZGIBBON, C. T. (1978). *How to deal with goals and objectives.* Beverly Hills, CA: Sage.

MORRISETT, I., & STEVENS, W. W. (1967). *Steps in curriculum analysis outline.* Boulder, CO: University of Colorado, Social Science Education Consortium.

NAFZIGER, D. H., WORTHEN, B. R., & BENSON, J. (1977). *3 on 2 evaluation report: Volume I, technical report.* Portland, OR: Northwest Regional Educational Laboratory.

NATIONAL COMMISSION ON EXCELLENCE IN EDUCATION (1983). *A nation at risk: The imperative for educational reform.* Washington, DC: U.S. Government Printing Office.

NATIONAL COMMITTEE FOR CITIZENS IN EDUCATION. (1982). *Your school: How well is it working?* Columbia, MD: Author.

NATIONAL INSTITUTE OF EDUCATION. (1981, July). *Minimum competency testing clarification hearing, transcript* (Vol. 1–3). Washington, DC: Author.

NATIONAL SCHOOL PUBLIC RELATIONS ASSOCIATION. (1981). *Good schools: What makes them work?* Arlington, VA: Author.

NATIONAL SCIENCE FOUNDATION. (1960). *Reviews of data on research and development* (No. 17, NSF–60–10). Washington, DC: Author.

NATIONAL STUDY OF SCHOOL EVALUATION. (1978). *Evaluative criteria.* Arlington, VA: Author.

NATIONAL STUDY OF SECONDARY SCHOOL EVALUATION. (1973). *Evaluative Criteria 1973 edition.* Washington, DC: Author.

NELSON, D. E. (1982). Investigative journalism methods in educational evaluation. In N. L. SMITH (Ed.), *Field assessments of innovative evaluation methods.* New Directions in Program Evaluation, No. 13. San Francisco: Jossey-Bass.

NEURATH, O., CARNAP, R., & MORRIS, C. (Eds.). (1955). *Fundamentals of the unity of science: Toward an international encyclopedia of unified science.* Foundations of the Unity of Science Series (Vol. 1 and 2). University of Chicago Press.

NILSSON, N., & HOGBEN, D. (1983). Metaevaluation. In E. R. HOUSE (Ed.), *Philosophy of evaluation.* New Directions for Program Evaluation, No. 19. San Francisco: Jossey-Bass.

NOWAKOWSKI, J. (1985). Evaluation for strategy setting. *Evaluation News, 6*(4), 57–67.

NOWAKOWSKI, J., BUNDA, M. A., WORKING, R., BERNACKI, G., & HARRINGTON, P. (1985). *A handbook of educational variables.* Boston: Kluwer-Nijhoff.

OPPENHEIM, A. (1966). *Questionnaire design and attitude measurement.* New York: Basic Books.

ORLANS, H. (1971). The political uses of social research. *American Academy of Political and Social Science Annals, 394,* 28–35.

ORLANS, H. (1975). *Private accreditation and public eligibility.* Lexington, MA: D.C. Heath.

OSGOOD, C. E., SUCI, G. J., & TANNENBAUM, P. H. (1957). *The measurement of meaning.* Urbana: University of Illinois.

OWENBY, E. M., & THOMAS, H. B. (1978, March). *Research and evaluation competencies needed by vocational educators.* Paper presented at the annual meeting of the American Educational Research Association, Toronto, Ontario, Canada.

OWENS, T. R. (1968). *The roles of evaluation specialists in Title I and Title III Elementary and Secondary Education Act projects.* Unpublished doctoral dissertation, the Ohio State University Evaluation Center.

OWENS, T. R. (1971). *Application of adversary proceedings for educational evaluation and decision making.* Paper presented at the annual meeting of the American Educational Research Association, New York City.

OWENS, T. R. (1973). Educational evaluation by adversary proceeding. In E. R. HOUSE (Ed.), *School evaluation: The politics and process.* Berkeley, CA: McCutchan.

OWENS, T. R. (1977). *Program evaluation skills for busy administrators.* Portland, OR: Northwest Regional Educational Laboratory.

OWENS, T. R., HAENN, J. F., & FEHRENBACHER, H. L. (1976). *The use of multiple strategies in evaluating an experienced based career education program* (Paper and Report Series No. 9). Portland, OR: Northwest Regional Educational Laboratory, Research on Evaluation Program.

OWENS, T. R., & HISCOX, M. D. (1977). *Alternative models for adversary evaluation: Variations on a theme.* Paper presented at the annual meeting of the American Educational Research Association, New York City.

OWENS, T. R., & OWEN, T. R. (1981). Law. In N. L. SMITH (Ed.), *Metaphors for evaluation: Sources of new methods.* Beverly Hills, CA: Sage.

PAGE, E. B., & STAKE, R. E. (1979). Should educational evaluation be more objective or more subjective? *Educational Evaluation and Policy Analysis, 1*(1), 45–47.

PALUMBO, D. J., & NACHMIAS, D. (1984). The preconditions for successful evaluation: Is there an ideal paradigm? In R. F. CONNOR, D. G. ALTMAN, & C. JACKSON (Eds.), *Evaluation studies review annual* (Vol. 9). Beverly Hills, CA: Sage.

PARLETT, M., & DEARDEN, G. (Eds.). (1977). *Introduction to illumination evaluation: Studies in higher education.* Cardiff-by-the-Sea, CA: Pacific Soundings Press.

PARLETT, M., & HAMILTON, D. (1976). Evaluation as illumination: A new approach to the study of innovatory programs. In G. V. GLASS (Ed.), *Evaluation studies review annual* (Vol. 1). Beverly Hills, CA: Sage.

PATTERSON, M. (undated). *Instructional materials review form.* Tallahassee: Florida State University, Center for Studies in Vocational Education, Vocational Instructional Materials Acquisition System.

PATTON, M. Q. (1975). *Alternative evaluation research paradigm.* Grand Forks, ND: North Dakota Study Group on Evaluation.

PATTON, M. Q. (Ed.). (1978). *Utilization-focused evaluation.* Beverly Hills, CA: Sage.

PATTON, M. Q. (1980). *Qualitative evaluation methods.* Beverly Hills, CA: Sage.

PATTON, M. Q., GRIMES, P. S., GUTHRIE, K. M., BRENNAN, N. J., FRENCH, B. D., & BLYTH, D. A. (1975). *In search of impact: An analysis of the utilization of federal health evaluation research* (Unpublished manuscript). Minneapolis: University of Minnesota, Center for Sociological Research.

PATTON, M. Q., GRIMES, P. S., GUTHRIE, K. M., BRENNAN, N. J., FRENCH, B. D., & BLYTH, D. A. (1978). In search of impact: An analysis of the utilization of federal health evaluation research. In T. D. COOK and others (Eds.), *Evaluation studies review annual* (Vol. 3). Beverly Hills, CA: Sage.

PAULSON, S. F. (1964, November). The effects of the prestige of the speaker and acknowledgment of opposing arguments on audience retention and shift of opinion. *Speech Monographs,* 267–271.

PAYNE, D. A. (Ed.). (1974). *Curriculum evaluation: Commentaries on purposes, process, product.* Lexington, MA: D.C. Heath.

PAYNE, S. L. (1951). *The art of asking questions.* Princeton, NJ: Princeton University Press.

PERLOFF, R. M., PADGETT, V. R., & BROCK, T. C. (1980). Sociocognitive biases in the evaluation process. In R. PERLOFF & E. PERLOFF (Eds.), *Values, ethics, and standards in evaluation.* New Directions for Program Evaluation, No. 7. San Francisco: Jossey-Bass.

PEZZINO, J. (1984, March). *Cost-effectiveness methods in human services management.* Paper presented at the meeting of the National Association of Developmental Disabilities Managers, Las Vegas, NV.

POPHAM, W. J. (1973a). *Evaluating instruction.* Englewood Cliffs, NJ: Prentice-Hall.

POPHAM, W. J. (1973b). Objectives and instruction. In B. R. WORTHEN & J. R. SANDERS (Eds.), *Educational evaluation: Theory and practice.* Belmont, CA: Wadsworth.

POPHAM, W. J. (1975). *Educational evaluation.* Englewood Cliffs, NJ: Prentice-Hall.

POPHAM, W. J. (1981). The case for minimum competency testing. *Phi Delta Kappan, 63*(2), 89–91.

POPHAM, W. J., & CARLSON D. (1977). Deep dark deficits of the adversary evaluation model. *Educational Researcher, 6*(6), 3–6.

POPHAM, W. J., EISNER, E. W., SULLIVAN, H. J., & TYLER, L. L. (1969). *Instructional objectives.* American Educational Research Association Monograph Series on Curriculum Evaluation, 3. Chicago: Rand McNally.

PORTER, A. C., SCHMIDT, W. H., FLODEN, R. E., & FREEMEN, D. J. (1978). Practical significance in program evaluation. *American Educational Research Journal, 15*(4), 529–539.

POTTER, D., SHARPE, K., HENDEE, J., & CLARK, R. (1972). *Questionnaires for research: An annotated bibliography on design, construction, and use.* Portland, OR: Pacific Northwest Forest and Range Experiment Station.

PROVUS, M. M. (1969). Evaluation of ongoing programs in the public school system. In R. W. TYLER (Ed.), *Educational evaluation: New roles, new means.* The 68th yearbook of the National Society for the Study of Education, Part II. Chicago: University of Chicago Press.

PROVUS, M. M. (1971). *Discrepancy evaluation.* Berkeley, CA: McCutchan.

PROVUS, M. M. (1973). Evaluation of ongoing programs in the public school system. In B. R. WORTHEN & J. R. SANDERS, *Educational evaluation: Theory and practice.* Belmont, CA: Wadsworth.

QUINN, D. W., VAN MONDFRANS, A. L., & WORTHEN, B. R. (1984). Cost-effectiveness of two math programs as moderated by pupil SES. *Educational Evaluation and Policy Analysis, 6*(1), 39–52.

RAIZEN, S. A., & ROSSI, P. H. (1981). *Program evaluation in education: When? How? To what ends?* Washington, DC: National Academy Press.

RAIZEN, S. A., & ROSSI, P. H. (1982). Summary of program evaluation in education: When? How? To what ends? In E. R. HOUSE, S. MATHISON, J. A. PEARSOL, & H. PRESKILL (Eds.), *Evaluation studies review annual* (Vol. 7). Beverly Hills, CA: Sage.

REINHARD, D. (1972). *Methodology for input evaluation utilizing advocate and design teams.* Unpublished doctoral dissertation, The Ohio State University.

RICE, J. M. (1915). *The people's government: Efficient, bossless, graftless.* Philadelphia: John C. Winston.

RICH, R. F. (1979). Problem solving and evaluation research. Unemployment insurance policy. In R. F. RICH (Ed.), *Translating evaluation into policy.* Beverly Hills, CA: Sage.

RICKS, F. A. (1976). Training program evaluators. *Professional Psychology, 7,* 339–343.

RIDINGS, J. M. (1982). *Standard setting: The crucial issues.* Kalamazoo, MI: Western Michigan University, Evaluation Center.

RIDINGS, J. M., & STUFFLEBEAM, D. L. (1981). Evaluation reflections: The project to develop standards for educational evaluation: Its past and future. *Studies in Educational Evaluation,* 7, 3–16.

RIPPEY, R. M. (Ed.). (1973). *Studies in transactional evaluation.* Berkeley, CA: McCutchan.

RIST, R. (1980). Blitzkrieg ethnography: On the transformation of a method into a movement. *Educational Researcher, 9*(2), 8–10.

RIVLIN, A. M. (1971). *Systematic thinking for social action.* Washington, DC: The Brookings Institution.

ROBINSON, J. P., ATHANASIOU, R., & HEAD, K. B. (1969). *Measures of occupational attributes and occupational characteristics.* Ann Arbor, MI: Institute for Social Research.

ROBINSON, J. P., & SHAVER, P. R. (1973a). *Measures of social psychological attitudes.* Ann Arbor, MI: Institute for Social Research.

ROBINSON, J. P., & SHAVER, P. R. (1973b). *Measures of political attitudes.* Ann Arbor, MI: Institute for Social Research.

ROSS, L., & CRONBACH, L. J. (Eds.). (1976). Handbook of evaluation research: Essay review by a task force of the Stanford Evaluation Consortium. *Educational Researcher, 5,* 9–19.

ROSSI, P. H. (1982a). Some dissenting comments on Stake's review. In E. R. HOUSE, S. MATHISON, J. A. PEARSOL, & H. PRESKILL (Eds.), *Evaluation studies review annual* (Vol. 7). Beverly Hills, CA: Sage.

ROSSI, P. H. (Ed.). (1982b). *Standards for evaluation practice.* New Directions for Program Evaluation, No. 15. San Francisco: Jossey-Bass.

ROSSI, P. H., FREEMAN, H. E., & WRIGHT, S. R. (1979). *Evaluation: A systematic approach.* Beverly Hills, CA: Sage.

SADLER, D. R. (1981). Intuitive data processing as a potential source of bias in naturalistic evaluations. *Educational Evaluation and Policy Analysis, 3*(4), 25–31.

SANDERS, J. R. (1974). *Criteria for the validation of products for dissemination.* Paper presented at the Western Regional Planning Conference, Honolulu, HI.

SANDERS, J. R. (1978). School professionals and the evaluation function. *Journal of School Psychology, 16,* 301–311.

SANDERS, J. R. (1979). The technology and art of evaluation. A review of seven evaluation primers. *Evaluation News, 12,* 2–7.

SANDERS, J. R. (1982). *A design for improving level 2 and low achieving student performance in the Shaker Heights City School District.* Kalamazoo, MI: Western Michigan University, Evaluation Center.

SANDERS, J. R. (1983a). *A strategy for evaluation in the small rural elementary school.* Kalamazoo, MI: Western Michigan University Evaluation Center. (ERIC Document Reproduction Service No. ED 251 275)

SANDERS, J. R. (1983b). Cost implications of the standards. In M. C. ALKIN & L. C. SOLMAN (Eds.), *The cost of evaluation.* Beverly Hills, CA: Sage.

SANDERS, J. R., & CUNNINGHAM, D. J. (1973). A structure for formative evaluation in product development. *Review of Educational Research, 43,* 217–236.

SANDERS, J. R., & CUNNINGHAM, D. J. (1974). Techniques and procedures for formative evaluation. In G. BORICH (Ed.), *Evaluating educational programs and products.* Englewood Cliffs, NJ: Educational Technology Publications.

SANDERS, J. R., & MURRAY, S. L. (1976). Alternatives for achievement testing. *Educational Technology, 16,* 17–23.

SANDERS, J. R., & NAFZIGER, D. H. (1975). *A basis for determining the adequacy of evaluation designs.* Portland, OR: Northwest Regional Educational Laboratory.

SANDERS, J. R., & SACHSE, T. P. (1977). Applied performance testing in the classroom. *Journal of Research and Development in Education, 10,* 92–104.

SANDERS, J. R., & SONNAD, S. R. (1982). *Research on the impact of ThinkAbout* (Vol. I–V). Bloomington, IN: Agency for Instructional Television.

SAX, G. (1980). *Principles of educational and psychological measurement and evaluation.* Belmont, CA: Wadsworth.

SCHALOCK, H. D., & SELL, G. R. (1972). *The Oregon studies in educational research, development, diffusion, and evaluation: Vol. 1, Summary report (with appendices)* (USOE Grant OEG–0–70–4977, Project No. 0–0701). Monmouth, OR: Oregon State System of Higher Education, Teaching Research Division.

SCHOFIELD, J. W., & ANDERSON, K. M. (1984, January). *Combining quantitative and qualitative methods in research on ethnic identity and intergroup relations.* Paper presented at the Society for Research on Child Development Study Group on Ethnic Socialization, Los Angeles.

SCRIVEN, M. (undated mimeo). *The evaluation of educational goals, instructional procedures and outcomes or the iceman cometh.* Unpublished manuscript, University of California, Berkeley.

SCRIVEN, M. (1967). The methodology of evaluation. In R. E. STAKE (Ed.), *Curriculum evaluation.* American Educational Research Association Monograph Series on Evaluation, No. 1. Chicago: Rand McNally.

SCRIVEN, M. (1972). Pros and cons about goal-free evaluation. *Evaluation Comment, 3*(4), 1–7.

SCRIVEN, M. (1973). The methodology of evaluation. In B. R. WORTHEN & J. R. SANDERS, *Educational evaluation: Theory and practice.* Belmont, CA: Wadsworth.

SCRIVEN, M. (1974a). Evaluation perspectives and procedures. In W. J. POPHAM (Ed.), *Evaluation in education.* Berkeley, CA: McCutchan.

SCRIVEN, M. (1974b). Standards for the evaluation of educational programs and products. In G. D. BORICH (Ed.), *Evaluating educational programs and products.* Englewood Cliffs, NJ: Educational Technology Publications.

SCRIVEN, M. (1976a). Evaluation bias and its control. In G. V. GLASS (Ed.), *Evaluation studies review annual* (Vol. 1). Beverly Hills, CA: Sage.

SCRIVEN, M. (1976b, May). *The intellectual dimensions of evaluation research.* Paper presented at the fourth annual Pacific Northwest Research and Evaluation Conference, Seattle, WA.

SCRIVEN, M. (1978). *Goal-free evaluation in practice.* Paper presented at the annual meeting of the American Educational Research Association, Toronto, Ontario, Canada.

SCRIVEN, M. (1981). *Evaluation thesaurus* (3rd ed.). Pt. Reyes, CA: Edgepress.

SCRIVEN, M. (1984). Evaluation ideologies. In R. F. CONNOR, D. G. ALTMAN, & C. JACKSON (Eds.), *Evaluation studies review annual* (Vol. 9). Beverly Hills, CA: Sage.

SECHREST, L. (Ed.). (1980). *Training program evaluators.* New Directions for Program Evaluation, No. 8. San Francisco: Jossey-Bass.

SHAVER, J. P. (1985a). Chance and nonsense: A conversation about interpreting tests of statistical significance, Part 1. *Phi Delta Kappan, 67*(1), 57–60.

SHAVER, J. P. (1985b). Chance and nonsense: A conversation about interpreting tests of statistical significance, Part 2. *Phi Delta Kappan, 67*(2), 138–141.

SHAW, M. R., & WRIGHT, J. M. (1967). *Scales for the measurement of attitudes.* New York: McGraw-Hill.

SHULMAN, L. S. (1985). Peer reviews: The many sides of virtue. *Educational Researcher, 14*(1), 12–13.

SIEBER, J. E. (1980). Being ethical: Professional and personal decisions in program evaluation. In R. PERLOFF & E. PERLOFF (Eds.), *Values, ethics, and standards in evaluation.* New Directions for Program Evaluation, No. 7. San Francisco: Jossey-Bass.

SIMON, A., & BOYER, E. G. (1974). *Mirrors for behavior III: An anthology of observation instruments.* Philadelphia: Research for Better Schools.

SIMONS, H. (1984). Against the rules: Procedural problems in institutional self-evaluation. Unpublished manuscript.

SMITH, E. R., & TYLER, R. W. (1942). *Appraising and recording student progress.* New York: Harper & Row.

SMITH, J. K. (1983). Quantitative versus interpretive: The problem of conducting social inquiry. In E. R. HOUSE (Ed.), *Philosophy of education.* New Directions for Program Evaluation, No. 19. San Francisco: Jossey-Bass.

SMITH, J. K., & SMITH, N. L. (1985). *An investigation of program evaluation budgets* (Paper and Report Series No. 108). Portland, OR: Northwest Regional Educational Laboratory, Research on Evaluation Program.

SMITH, N. L. (1980). *Bibliography on evaluation utilization.* Portland, OR: Northwest Regional Educational Laboratory.

SMITH, N. L. (1981a). *Evaluation contracting checklist.* Portland, OR: Northwest Regional Educational Laboratory, Research on Evaluation Program.

SMITH, N. L. (1981b). *Metaphors for evaluation: Sources of new methods: New perspectives in evaluation* (Vol. 1). Beverly Hills, CA: Sage.

SMITH, N. L. (1981c). *New techniques for evaluation: New perspectives in evaluation* (Vol. 2). Beverly Hills, CA: Sage.

SMITH, N. L. (Ed.). (1982a). *Communication strategies in evaluation: New Perspectives in Evaluation* (Vol. 3). Beverly Hills, CA: Sage.

SMITH, N. L. (1982b). *Public data resources for educational policy analysis and evaluation* (Paper and Report Series No. 75). Portland, OR: Northwest Regional Educational Laboratory, Research on Evaluation Program.

SMITH, N. L. (Ed.). (1983a). *Dimensions of moral and ethical problems in evaluation* (Paper and Report Series No. 92). Portland, OR: Northwest Regional Educational Laboratory, Research on Evaluation Program.

SMITH, N. L. (1983b). The progress of educational evaluation: Rounding the first bends in the river. In G. F. MADAUS, M. S. SCRIVEN, & D. L. STUFFLEBEAM (Eds.), *Evaluation models: Viewpoints on educational and human services evaluation.* Boston: Kluwer-Nijhoff.

SMITH, N. L. (1985). *Adversary and committee hearings as evaluation methods* (Paper and Report Series No. 110). Portland, OR: Northwest Regional Educational Laboratory, Research on Evaluation Program.

SMITH, R. (1984). *The new aesthetic curriculum theorists and their astonishing ideas: Some critical observations* (The Monograph Series). Vancouver, Canada: University of British Columbia, Center for the Study of Curriculum and Instruction.

Southern Association Cooperative Study in Elementary Education. (1951). *Evaluating the elementary school.* Atlanta, GA: Author.

SPENCER, R. L. (1964). Do it yourself evaluation. *The National Elementary Principal, 44,* 51–52.

SPINDLER, G. (Ed.). (1982). *Doing the ethnography of schooling.* New York: Holt, Rinehart, & Winston.

SPROULL, L., & LARKEY, P. (1979). Managerial behavior and evaluator effectiveness. In *The evaluator and management.* Beverly Hills, CA: Sage.

SPROULL, L., & ZUBROW, D. (1981). Standardized testing from the administrative perspective. *Phi Delta Kappan, 62,* 628–631.

STAKE, R. E. (1967). The countenance of educational evaluation. *Teachers College Record, 68,* 523–540.

STAKE, R. E. (1969a). Evaluation design, instrumentation, data collection, and analysis of data. In J. L. DAVIS (Ed.), *Educational evaluation.* Columbus, OH: State Superintendent of Public Instruction.

STAKE, R. E. (1969b). Generalizability of program evaluation: The need for limits. *Educational Product Report, 2*(5), 39–40.

STAKE, R. E. (1970). Objectives, priorities, and other judgment data. *Review of Educational Research, 40*(2), 181–212.

STAKE, R. E. (1972). *Responsive evaluation.* Unpublished manuscript.

STAKE, R. E. (1975a). *Evaluating the arts in education: A responsive approach.* Columbus, OH: Charles E. Merrill.

STAKE, R. E. (1975b). *Program evaluation, particularly responsive evaluation* (Occasional Paper, No. 5). Kalamazoo, MI: Western Michigan University Evaluation Center.

STAKE, R. E. (1976). *Evaluating educational programmes: The need and response.* Urbana-Champaign, IL: Center for Educational Research and Innovation.

STAKE, R. E. (1978). The case study method in social inquiry. *Educational Researcher, 7,* 5–8.

STAKE, R. E. (1980). *Recommendations for those considering the support of naturalistic case-study research.* Champaign, IL: University of Illinois, Center for Instructional Research and Curriculum Evaluation.

STAKE, R. E. (1982). A peer response: A review of program evaluation in education: When? How? To What ends? In E. R. HOUSE, S. MATHISON, J. A. PEARSOL, & H. PRESKILL (Eds.), *Evaluation studies review annual* (Vol. 7). Beverly Hills, CA: Sage.

STAKE, R. E., & DENNY, T. (1969). Needed concepts and techniques for utilizing more fully the potential of evaluation. In R. W. TYLER (Ed.), *Educational evaluation: New roles, new means.* The 68th Yearbook of the National Society for the Study of Education, Part II. Chicago: National Society for the Study of Education.

STAKE, R. E., & EASELY, J. A., Jr. (Eds.). (1978). *Case studies in science education.* Champaign, IL: University of Illinois, Center for Instructional Research and Curriculum Evaluation.

STAKE, R. E., & GJERDE, C. (1974). An evaluation of T-CITY, The Twin City Institute for Talented Youth. In R. H. P. KRAFT, L. M. SMITH, R. A. POHLAND, C. J. BRAUNER, & C. GJERDE (Eds.), *Four evaluation examples: Anthropological, economic, narrative and portrayal.* AERA Monograph Series on Curriculum Evaluation, No. 7. Chicago: Rand McNally.

STALFORD, C. B. (1985). Reflections on writing a clear evaluation summary. *Evaluation News, 6*(4), 10–16.

STENHOUSE, L. (1975). *An introduction to curriculum research and development.* London: Heinemann.

STENZEL, N. (1975). *Adversary processes and their potential use in evaluation for the Illinois Office of Education.* Springfield, IL: Illinois Department of Education.

STENZEL, N. (1976). *Meta-evaluation of the IPS adversary hearing evaluation: Variations on a theme.* Springfield, IL: Illinois Department of Education.

STENZEL, N. (1982). Committee hearings as an evaluation format. In N. L. SMITH (Ed.), *Field assessments of innovative evaluation methods.* New Directions for Program Evaluation, No. 13. San Francisco: Jossey-Bass.

STEPHENSON, W. (1953). *The study of behavior: Q-technique and its methodology.* Chicago: University of Chicago Press.

STIRES, D. M., & MURPHY, M. M. (1962). *Modern management methods—PERT and CPM.* Boston: Materials Management Institute.

ST. JOHN, M. (Undated). Committee hearings: Their use in evaluation (Contract No. 400–80–0105). *Evaluation Guides, 8,* 2–12. Portland, OR: Northwest Regional Educational Laboratory.

ST. JOHN, M. (1985). Toward streamlining methods of cost analysis. *Research on evaluation program* (Paper and Report Series No. 112). Portland, OR: Northwest Regional Educational Laboratory, Research on Evaluation Program.

ST. PIERRE, R. G. (Ed.). (1983). *Management and organization of program evaluation.* New Directions for Program Evaluation, No. 18. San Francisco: Jossey-Bass.

STONE, L. (1984). *Results from a global curriculum project evaluation: Practical problems—theoretical questions.* Paper presented at the annual meeting of the American Educational Research Association, New Orleans.

STRATON, R. G. (1977). *Research of the evaluation process: Current status and future directions.* Paper presented at the annual conference of the Australian Association for Research in Education, Canberra, Australia.

STUDY COMMISSION ON UNDERGRADUATE EDUCATION AND THE EDUCATION OF TEACHERS. (1976). *Teacher education in the United States: The responsibility gap.* Lincoln, NB: University of Nebraska Press.

STUFFLEBEAM, D. L. (1968). *Evaluation as enlightenment for decision making.* Columbus, OH: Ohio State University, Evaluation Center.

STUFFLEBEAM, D. L. (1969). Evaluation as enlightenment for decision making. In W. H. BEATTY & A. B. WALCOTT (Eds.), *Improving educational assessment and an inventory of measures of affective behavior.* Washington, DC: Association for Supervision and Curriculum Development.

STUFFLEBEAM, D. L. (1971). The relevance of The CIPP Evaluation Model for Educational Accountability. *Journal of Research and Development in Education, 5*(1), 19–25.

STUFFLEBEAM, D. L. (1973a). An introduction to the PDK book: Educational evaluation and decision-making. In B. R. WORTHEN & J. R. SANDERS, *Educational evaluation: Theory and practice.* Belmont, CA: Wadsworth.

STUFFLEBEAM, D. L. (1973b). Excerpts from "Evaluation as enlightenment for decision making." In B. R. WORTHEN & J. R. SANDERS, *Educational evaluation: Theory and practice.* Belmont, CA: Wadsworth.

STUFFLEBEAM, D. L. (1974a). *A response to the Michigan Education Department's defense of their accountability system* (Occasional Paper No. 1). Kalamazoo, MI: Western Michigan University, School of Education.

STUFFLEBEAM, D. L. (1974b). *Metaevaluation.* (Occasional Paper No. 3). Kalamazoo, MI: Western Michigan University Evaluation Center.

STUFFLEBEAM, D. L. (1977). *Working paper on needs assessment in evaluation.* Paper presented at the American Educational Research Association Evaluation Conference, San Francisco.

STUFFLEBEAM, D. L. (1980). Evaluation in large urban school systems. In F. S. CHASE (Ed.), *Educational quandaries and opportunities.* Dallas, TX: Urban Education Studies.

STUFFLEBEAM, D. L. (1981, November). *A review of progress in educational evaluation.* Paper presented at the annual meeting of the Evaluation Network, Austin, TX.

STUFFLEBEAM, D. L. (1982). *Daniel Stufflebeam's improvement oriented evaluation.* Kalamazoo, MI: Western Michigan University, Evaluation Center.

STUFFLEBEAM, D. L. (1983). The CIPP model for program evaluation. In G. F. MADAUS, M. SCRIVEN, & D. L. STUFFLEBEAM (Eds.), *Evaluation models: Viewpoints on educational and human services evaluation.* Boston: Kluwer-Nijhoff.

STUFFLEBEAM, D. L. (1984). Has the profession of educational evaluation changed with changing times? *Evaluation Comment, 7*(1), 9–11.

STUFFLEBEAM, D. L., FOLEY, W. J., GEPHART, W. J., GUBA, E. G., HAMMOND, R. L., MERRIMAN, H. O., & PROVUS, M. M. (1971). *Educational evaluation and decision making.* Itasca, IL: F. E. Peacock.

STUFFLEBEAM, D. L., & SHINKFIELD, A. J. (1985). *Systematic evaluation.* Boston: Kluwer-Nijhoff.

STUFFLEBEAM, D. L., & WEBSTER, W. J. (1980). An analysis of alternative approaches to evaluation. *Educational Evaluation and Policy Analysis, 2*(3), 5–19.

SUAREZ, T. M. (1981). *A planning guide for the evaluation of educational programs.* Unpublished manuscript. Chapel Hill, NC: University of North Carolina.

TABA, H. (1962). *Curriculum development.* New York: Harcourt, Brace, and World.

TALLMADGE, G. K. (1977). *Ideabook: JDRP* (ERIC DL 48329). Washington, DC: U.S. Government Printing Office.

TALLMADGE, G. K., & WOOD, C. T. (1976). *Users guide. ESEA Title I evaluation and reporting system.* Mountain View, CA: RMC Research Corporation.

TALMAGE, H. (1982). Evaluation of programs. In H. E. MITZEL (Ed.), *Encyclopedia of educational research* (5th ed.). New York: The Free Press.

TASH, W., & STAHLER, G. (1982). Enhancing the utilization of evaluation findings. *Community Mental Health Journal, 18,* 180–189.

TAYLOR, J. (1974). *An administrator's perspective of evaluation* (Occasional Paper, No. 2). Kalamazoo, MI: Western Michigan University, Evaluation Center.

THOMPSON, M. S. (1980). *Benefit-cost analysis for program evaluation.* Beverly Hills, CA: Sage.

THORNDIKE, R. L., & HAGEN, E. (1969). *Measurement and evaluation in psychology and education.* New York: Wiley.

TITTLE, C. K. (1984). *Professional standards and equity: The role of evaluators and researchers.* Paper presented at the annual meeting of the American Educational Research Association, New Orleans.

TRAVERS, R. M. W. (1983). *How research has changed American schools.* Kalamazoo, MI: Mythos Press.

TUMIN, M. M. (1975). Politics of evaluation. In S. B. ANDERSON and others (Eds.), *Encyclopedia of education evaluation: Concepts and techniques for evaluating education and training programs.* San Francisco: Jossey-Bass.

TYLER, L. L., & KLEIN, F. (1967). *Recommendations for curriculum and instructional materials.* Unpublished manuscript, University of California, Los Angeles.

TYLER, R. W. (1942). General statement on evaluation. *Journal of Educational Research, 35,* 492–501.

TYLER, R. W. (1950). *Basic principles of curriculum and instruction.* Chicago: University of Chicago Press.

UNIVERSITY OF MICHIGAN INSTITUTE FOR SOCIAL RESEARCH. (1971). *Interviewer's Manual.* Ann Arbor: Author.

VALLANCE, E. (1978). Scanning horizons and looking at weeks: A critical description of "The Great Plains Experience." In G. WILLIS (Ed.), *Qualitative evaluation.* Berkeley, CA: McCutchan.

VAN DE VALL, M., & BOLAS, C. (1982). Using social policy research for reducing social problems: An empirical analysis of structure and functions. *Journal of Applied Behavioral Science, 18,* 49–67.

VAN MONDFRANS, A. (1985). *Guidelines for reporting evaluation findings.* Unpublished manuscript. Provo, UT: Brigham Young University, College of Education.

WACHTMAN, E. L. (1978). *Evaluation as a story: The narrative quality of educational evaluation.* Paper presented at the annual meeting of the American Educational Research Association, Toronto, Ontario, Canada.

WAKS, L. J. (1975). Educational objectives and existential heros. In R. A. SMITH (Ed.), *Regaining educational leadership.* New York: Wiley.

WALKER, R. (1974). The conduct of educational case study: Ethics, theory and procedures. In Safari-Project (Ed.), *SAFARI-Innovation, evaluation, research and the problem of control: Some interim papers.* Norwich, UK: University of East Anglia, Centre for Applied Research in Education.

WAPLES, D., & TYLER, R. W. (1930). *Research methods and teacher problems*. New York: Macmillan.

WEBB, E. J., CAMPBELL, D. T., SCHWARTZ, R. D., & SECHREST, L. (1966). *Unobtrusive measures: Nonreactive research in the social sciences*. Chicago: Rand McNally.

WEBSTER'S NEW WORLD DICTIONARY (1960). Concise edition. New York: World.

WEBSTER, W. J. (1977, September). *Sensible school district evaluation*. Paper presented at the American Educational Research Association Evaluation Conference, San Francisco.

WEINROTT, M. R., JONES, R. R., & HOWARD, J. R. (1982). Cost effectiveness of teaching family programs for delinquents: Results of a national evaluation. *Evaluation Review*, 6(2), 173–201.

WEISS, C. H. (1975). Evaluation research in the political context. In E. L. STRUENING & M. GUTTENTAG (Eds.), *Handbook of evaluation research* (Vol. 1). Beverly Hills, CA: Sage.

WEISS, C. H. (Ed.). (1977). *Using social research in public policy making*. Lexington, MA: Lexington Books.

WEISS, C. H. (1984). Toward the future of stakeholder approaches in evaluation. In R. F. CONNOR, D. G. ALTMAN, & C. JACKSON (Eds.), *Evaluation studies review annual* (Vol. 9). Beverly Hills, CA: Sage.

WEISS, C. H., & BUCUVALAS, M. J. (1980). Truth tests and utility tests: Decision-makers' frames of reference for social science research. *American Sociological Review*, 45, 302–313.

WELCH, W. W. (Ed.). (1981). *Case study methodology in educational evaluation*. Minneapolis, MN: Minnesota Research and Evaluation Center.

WELCH, W. W., & WALBERG, H. J. (1968). A design for curriculum evaluation. *Science Education*, 52, 10–16.

WHOLEY, J. S. (1979). *Evaluation: Promise and performance*. Washington, DC: The Urban Institute.

WILCOX, K. (1982). Ethnography as a methodology and its application to the study of schooling. In G. SPINDLER (Ed.), *Doing the ethnography of schooling*. New York: Holt, Rinehart, & Winston.

WILDEMUTH, B. M. (1981). A bibliography to accompany the Joint Committee's standards on educational evaluation (ERIC/TM Report 81). Princeton, NJ: ERIC Clearinghouse on Tests, Measurement, and Evaluation, Educational Testing Service.

WILLIAMS, D. D. (Ed.). (1986a). *Naturalistic evaluation*. New Directions for Program Evaluation, No. 30. San Francisco: Jossey-Bass.

WILLIAMS, D. D. (1986b). Naturalistic evaluation: Potential conflicts between evaluation standards and criteria for conducting naturalistic inquiry. *Educational Evaluation and Policy Analysis*, 8(1), 87–99.

WOLCOTT, H. (1976). Criteria for an ethnographic approach to research in schools. In J. T. ROBERTS & S. K. AKINSANGA (Eds.), *Schooling in the cultural context*. New York: David McKay.

WOLF, R. L. (1973). *The application of select legal concepts to educational evaluation*. Unpublished doctoral dissertation, University of Illinois, Urbana-Champaign.

WOLF, R. L. (1975). Trial by jury: A new evaluation method. *Phi Delta Kappan*, 57(3), 185–187.

WOLF, R. L. (1978). *Studying school governance through judicial evaluation procedures*. Bloomington, IN: Indiana Center for Evaluation.

WOLF, R. L. (1979). The use of judicial evaluation methods in the formulation of educational policy. *Educational Evaluation and Policy Analysis*, 1(3), 19–28.

WOLF, R. L., & TYMITZ, B. (1977). Toward more natural inquiry in education. *Center on Evaluation, Development, and Research (CEDR) Quarterly*, 10, 7–9.

WORTHEN, B. R. (1972a, April). *Certification for educational evaluators: Problem and potential.* Paper presented at the annual meeting of the American Educational Research Association, Chicago.

WORTHEN, B. R. (1972b, April). *Impediments to the practice of educational evaluation.* Paper presented at the annual meeting of the American Educational Research Association, Chicago.

WORTHEN, B. R. (1974a). *A look at the mosaic of educational evaluation and accountability* (Research, Evaluation and Development Paper No. 3). Portland, OR: Northwest Regional Educational Laboratory. Also reprinted in the *Educational Reports* series of the University of Colorado Bureau of Educational Field Services, 1974.

WORTHEN, B. R. (1974b, April). *Content specialization and educational evaluation: A necessary marriage?* Paper presented at the annual meeting of the American Educational Research Association, Chicago.

WORTHEN, B. R. (1975a). Competencies for educational research and evaluation. *Educational Researcher, 4*(1), 13–16.

WORTHEN, B. R. (1975b). *Evaluation in education.* Paper presented at the Evaluation Network Conference, Snowmass, CO, August 12–14.

WORTHEN, B. R. (1977a). Characteristics of good evaluation studies. *Journal of Research and Development in Education, 10*(3), 3–20.

WORTHEN, B. R. (1977b, April). *Eclecticism and evaluation models: Snapshots of an elephant's anatomy?* Paper presented at the annual meeting of the American Educational Research Association, New York City.

WORTHEN, B. R. (1978, March). *Metaphors and methodologies for evaluation.* Paper presented at the annual meeting of the American Educational Research Association, Toronto, Ontario, Canada.

WORTHEN, B. R. (1980). *Curriculum evaluation: An instructional manual.* Alexandria, VA: Association for Supervision and Curriculum Development.

WORTHEN, B. R. (1981). Journal entries of an eclectic evaluator. In R. S. BRANDT (Ed.), *Applied strategies for curriculum evaluation.* Alexandria, VA: Association for Supervision and Curriculum Development.

WORTHEN, B. R. (1982). *Proposal review guidelines and instruments: A manual for external review panels.* Salt Lake City: Utah State Office of Education.

WORTHEN, B. R. (1983). *Onsite evaluation guidelines and procedures: A manual for onsite evaluators.* Salt Lake City: Utah State Office of Education.

WORTHEN, B. R. (1984). Program evaluation. In *International encyclopedia of education: Research and studies.* Oxford, England: Pergamon Press, Ltd.

WORTHEN, B. R., BORG, W. R., & WHITE, K. *Measurement and evaluation in the schools.* Unpublished manuscript.

WORTHEN, B. R., & GAGNÉ, R. M. (1969). *The development of a classification system for functions and skills required of research and research-related personnel in education* (Technical Paper No. 1). Washington, DC: AERA Task Force on Research Training.

WORTHEN, B. R., OWENS, T. R., & ANDERSON, B. (1975). *Evaluation of the alternative teacher education programs of the University of British Columbia faculty of education.* A Report to the Policy Council of the University of British Columbia Faculty of Education and Supervisors of the Alternative Teacher Education Programs, Northwest Regional Educational Laboratory.

WORTHEN, B. R., & OWENS, T. R. (1978). Adversary evaluation and the school psychologist. *Journal of School Psychology, 16*(4), 334–345.

WORTHEN, B. R., & ROADEN, A. L. (1975). *The research assistantship: Recommendations for colleges and universities.* Bloomington, IN: Phi Delta Kappa International.

WORTHEN, B. R., & ROGERS, W. T. (1977, April). *Uses and abuses of adversary evaluation: A consumer's guide.* Paper presented at the annual meeting of the American Educational Research Association, New York City.

WORTHEN, B. R., & ROGERS, W. T. (1980). Pitfalls and potential of adversary evaluation. *Educational Leadership, 37*(7), 536–543.

WORTHEN, B. R., & SANDERS, J. R. (1973). *Educational evaluation: Theory and practice.* Belmont, CA: Wadsworth.

WORTHEN, B. R., & SANDERS, J. R. (1984). *Content specialization and educational evaluation: A necessary marriage?* (Occasional Paper No. 14). Kalamazoo: Western Michigan University, Evaluation Center. (Update and expansion of the senior author's paper by this title read at the AERA 1974 annual meeting.)

WORTHEN, B. R., & VALCARCE, R. W. (1985). Relative effectiveness of personalized and form covering letters in initial and follow-up mail surveys. *Psychological Reports, 57,* 735–744.

WORTHEN, B. R., & WHITE, K. R. (1986). *Evaluating educational and social programs: Guidelines for proposal review, onsite evaluation, evaluation contracts and technical assistance.* Boston: Kluwer-Nijhoff.

WORTMAN, P. M. (1984). Cost effectiveness: A review. In R. F. CONNOR, D. G. ALTMAN, & C. JACKSON (Eds.), *Evaluation studies review annual* (Vol. 9). Beverly Hills, CA: Sage.

WRIGHT, W. J., & SACHSE, T. (1977). *Payoffs of adversary evaluation.* Paper presented at the annual meeting of the American Educational Research Association, New York City.

WRIGHT, W. J., & WORTHEN, B. R. (1975). *Standards and procedures for evaluation contracting.* Portland, OR: Northwest Regional Educational Laboratory.

YAVORSKY, D. K. (1976). *Discrepancy evaluation: A practitioner's guide.* Charlottesville, VA: University of Virginia Evaluation Research Center.

Name Index

Subject Index

AROUND THE WORLD
IN EIGHTY DAYS

A Jules Verne's Classic Novel With 55 Original Illustrations
(100th Anniversary Collection Edition, #1)

AROUND THE WORLD IN EIGHTY DAYS

A Jules Verne's Classic Novel With 55 Original Illustrations
(100th Anniversary Collection Edition, #1)

JULES VERNE

PHILEAS FOGG

CONTENTS

CHAPTER XXXVI

CHAPTER XXXVII

ILLUSTRATIONS

They had forced the doors, and were fighting hand to hand with

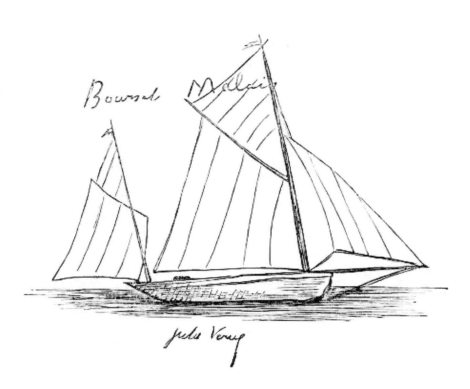

THE "SAINT MICHEAL"

INTRODUCTION.

JULES VERNE.

The autographic sketch on the opposite page represents the " St. Michael," a little decked bark belonging to the author of "Around the World in Eighty Days."

The sketch, which Verne executed in the twinkling of an eye, on our own desk, without suspecting that it would receive the honours of publicity, is accompanied by the inscription, "Bourset Malais," which two words indicate the type of craft of which the " St. Michael " is an example. It is on this frail skiff that Jules Verne goes upon long voyages, and has already explored the English coast and ascended as far as Scotland.

Verne recently took a trip in her to Jersey, in the English Channel, accompanied by his factotum, Antonie Delon, a veritable sea-wolf, who loves danger because he has always overcome it.

These daring peregrinations gave the author of " Twenty Thousand Leagues under the Sea " the ideas and subjects of his remarkable works, which have been translated into many languages, and have found readers in two worlds.

Verne passes half of his existence on board the "St. Michael ; " dividing the remainder of his time between Amiens, where his family resides, and Paris, where he attends the sessions of the Geographical Society, of which

he is the most honoured member, and where he collects, in its museums and library, the numerous materials necessary to the scientific perfection of his works.

Verne receives letters, in which his correspondents give him their impressions and ideas, and sometimes foolish observations, from all parts of the world. Those who have read " Around the World in Eighty Days " recall, no doubt, that Phileas Fogg, its hero, undertook his journey after reading an article in the Daily Telegraph at the Reform Club. The other day Verne received a letter from a member of that famous club, in which he said, somewhat bluntly, that the political tone of the Daily Telegraph excluded that sheet from the Reform.

" It is as if you should say that M. de Belcastel sub- scribed for the Republique Frangaise!" added this pert correspondent.

Verne laughed heartily at the illustration, and, as he is amiability itself, apprised the member of the club that in the next edition of the book he would substitute for the obnoxious sheet one admitted into the club to which the famous Phileas Fogg belonged ; and, as the editions are rapidly succeeding each other, the discon- tented gentleman will doubtless ere long be fully satisfied.

The author of our little sketch leads the laborious, regular, and sober life of a student. Wherever he may be, he works from five in the morning till one in the afternoon, passes the day visiting shops and factories, where he carefully studies the machinery, and goes to bed at seven o'clock. Extended on his bed, he devours all the scientific publications till midnight, and when they fail him he looks over books of travel and tourist adventures. He has no need, however, of borrowing ideas of travel or geography from others, for he has himself travelled much, and is quite familiar with Scotland, Ireland, Denmark, Norway, and Sweden.

He had an adventure in Sweden, with which I must enliven this brief biography.

Verne was stopping at a hotel in Stockholm. As he was on the point of ascending the coast to the northern part of that picturesque country, he wished to pay his bill, and began searching in his pocket-book for the draft at sight, which he had procured of the Rothschilds before leaving Paris. But he searched for it in vain. There was no doubt about it — he had been robbed !

He found himself, as the Bohemians say, flat on his back. The landlord stared at him, and he thought he heard him mutter, " Adventurer ! " Verne took his " Swedish Guide," which he was learning by heart, under his arm, and wandered about the city, calling on all the bankers to apprise them of his misfortune, and warn them lest the robber should forge his name.

After three days of going backwards and forwards, our unhappy author climbed up to the last banker's,, with his guide-book, as usual, under his arm. He placed the book on the desk, and began to tell the clerk of his misfortune. The latter, indifferent to the tale, took up Verne's book and began carelessly turning over its leaves. As he was doing this, a slip of paper, which served as a mark in the middle of a chapter, fell out on the floor.

The clerk took it up, and unfolding it, cried : "Why here's your draft, after all ! "

I leave you to imagine Verne's triumphant entrance into his hotel.

Verne studied law, and became a barrister. Then, under the auspices of Captain Darpentigny, a well-known chiro- mancer, he became intimate with the Dumases, father and son, wrote pieces in conjunction with them, and afterwards worked alone, producing several libretti which had some success at the Theatre Lyrique, under the direction of the Sevestes and Rety. Among them were "Les Pailles Rompus," "L'Auberge des Ardennes," "Le Colin Mail- lard," " Onze Jours de Siege," and some operettas, the titles

of which escape me. He makes verses with extreme ease ; and if ever there was a person who could be called marvellously gifted, it is Jules Verne.

He was a broker in the firm of Eggley, in which he had, and still has, a pecuniary interest, when the success of " Five Weeks in a Balloon " induced him to turn his whole atten- tion to scientific romance.

He brings to his so justly popular works an ardour and faith which greatly contribute to their success. He shrinks from no pains to procure information, and he is careful to fully establish beforehand the facts which he asserts.

He went to America, and returned with the plan of the " Floating City." He accomplished his voyage in ninety- six days, on the "Great Eastern." On reaching New York, hedid not saunter about Broadway, looking in shop- windows, but took the railway and went six hundred leagues to see Niagara Falls, of which he cannot yet speak without emotion.

Verne is overwhelmed with requests from dramatists to be permitted to dramatize his works. He is not disinclined to yield to their wishes, and has shown me some very original ideas in regard to scenery, which seem likely to enrich the managers, who may choose to put some hundreds of thousands of francs at the service of his labours, by millions. He has nearly finished, with Cadol, the " Around the World," and proposes to substitute for the ordinary drop-curtain a planisphere, on which a luminous trail shall mark between each act the road gone over by the heroes in their tour across the four quarters of the globe. He is also preparing "The Marvels of Science," a great piece of mechanism, which will borrow its effect, not only from painting, velvet, and the ballet, but from the dynamic agents of physics, chemistry, and mechanics. But I must stop. I might write a volume about this eloquent, witty, affable, and sympathetic man, whose biography may, however, be included in these words : " A Breton, a Catholic, and a sailor."

Adrien Marx.

CHAPTER I

IN WHICH PHILEAS FOGG AND PASSEPARTOUT ACCEPT EACH OTHER, THE ONE AS MASTER, THE OTHER AS MAN

Mr. Phileas Fogg lived, in 1872, at No. 7, Saville Row, Burlington Gardens, the house in which Sheridan died in 1814. He was one of the most noticeable members of the Reform Club, though he seemed always to avoid attracting attention; an enigmatical personage, about whom little was known, except that he was a polished man of the world. People said that he resembled Byron—at least that his head was Byronic; but he was a bearded, tranquil Byron, who might live on a thousand years without growing old.

Certainly an Englishman, it was more doubtful whether Phileas Fogg was a Londoner. He was never seen on 'Change, nor at the Bank, nor in the counting-rooms of the "City"; no ships ever came into London docks of which he was the owner; he had no public employment; he had never been entered at any of the Inns of Court, either at the Temple, or Lincoln's Inn, or Gray's Inn; nor had his voice ever resounded in the Court of Chancery, or in the Exchequer, or the Queen's Bench, or the Ecclesiastical Courts. He certainly was not a manufacturer; nor was he a merchant or a gentleman farmer. His name was strange to the scientific and learned societies, and he never was known to take part in the sage deliberations of the Royal Institution or the London Institution, the Artisan's Association, or the Institution of Arts and Sciences. He belonged, in fact, to none of the numerous societies which swarm in the English capital, from the Harmonic to that of the Entomologists, founded mainly for the purpose of abolishing pernicious insects.

Phileas Fogg was a member of the Reform, and that was all.

The way in which he got admission to this exclusive club was simple enough.

He was recommended by the Barings, with whom he had an open credit. His cheques were regularly paid at sight from his account current, which was always flush.

Was Phileas Fogg rich? Undoubtedly. But those who knew him best could not imagine how he had made his fortune, and Mr. Fogg was the last person to whom to apply for the information. He was not lavish, nor, on the contrary, avaricious; for, whenever he knew that money was needed for a noble, useful, or benevolent purpose, he supplied it quietly and sometimes anonymously. He was, in short, the least communicative of men. He talked very little, and seemed all the more mysterious for his taciturn manner. His daily habits were quite open to observation; but whatever he did was so exactly the same thing that he had always done before, that the wits of the curious were fairly puzzled.

Had he travelled? It was likely, for no one seemed to know the world more familiarly; there was no spot so secluded that he did not appear to have an intimate acquaintance with it. He often corrected, with a few clear words, the thousand conjectures advanced by members of the club as to lost and unheard-of travellers, pointing out the true probabilities, and seeming as if gifted with a sort of second sight, so often did events justify his predictions. He must have travelled everywhere, at least in the spirit.

It was at least certain that Phileas Fogg had not absented himself from London for many years. Those who were honoured by a better acquaintance with him than the rest, declared that nobody could pretend to have ever seen him anywhere else. His sole pastimes were reading the papers and playing whist. He often won at this game, which, as a silent one, harmonised with his nature; but his winnings never went into his purse, being reserved as a fund for his charities. Mr. Fogg played, not to win, but for the sake of playing. The game was in his eyes a contest, a struggle with a difficulty, yet a motionless, unwearying struggle, congenial to his tastes.

Phileas Fogg was not known to have either wife or children, which may happen to the most honest people; either relatives or near friends, which is certainly more unusual. He lived alone in his house in Saville Row, whither none penetrated. A single domestic sufficed to serve him. He breakfasted and dined at the club, at hours mathematically fixed, in the same room, at the same table, never taking his meals with other members, much less bringing a guest with him; and went home at exactly midnight, only to retire at once to bed. He never used the cosy chambers which the Reform provides for its favoured members. He passed ten hours out of the twenty-four in Saville Row, either in sleeping or making his toilet. When he chose to take a walk it was with a regular step in the entrance hall with its mosaic flooring, or in the circular gallery with its dome supported by twenty red porphyry Ionic columns, and illuminated by blue painted windows. When he breakfasted or dined all the resources of the club—its kitchens and pantries, its buttery and dairy—aided to crowd his table with their most succulent stores; he was served by the gravest waiters, in dress coats, and shoes with swan-skin soles, who proffered the viands in special porcelain, and on the finest linen; club decanters, of a lost mould, contained his sherry, his port, and his cinnamon-spiced claret; while his beverages were refreshingly cooled with ice, brought at great cost from the American lakes.

If to live in this style is to be eccentric, it must be confessed that there is something good in eccentricity.

The mansion in Saville Row, though not sumptuous, was exceedingly comfortable. The habits of its occupant were such as to demand but little from the sole domestic, but Phileas Fogg required him to be almost superhumanly prompt and regular. On this very 2nd of October he had dismissed James Forster, because that luckless youth had brought him shaving-water at eighty-four degrees Fahrenheit instead of eighty-six; and he was awaiting his successor, who was due at the house between eleven and half-past.

Phileas Fogg was seated squarely in his armchair, his feet close together like those of a grenadier on parade, his hands resting on his knees, his body straight, his head erect; he was steadily watching a complicated clock which indicated the hours, the minutes, the seconds, the days, the months, and the years. At exactly half-past eleven Mr. Fogg would, according to his daily habit, quit Saville Row, and repair to the Reform.

A rap at this moment sounded on the door of the cosy apartment where Phileas Fogg was seated, and James Forster, the dismissed servant, appeared.

"The new servant," said he.

A young man of thirty advanced and bowed.

"You are a Frenchman, I believe," asked Phileas Fogg, "and your name is John?"

JEAN PASSEPARTOUT

"Jean, if monsieur pleases," replied the newcomer, "Jean Passepartout, a surname which has clung to me because I have a natural aptness for going out of one business into another. I believe I'm honest, monsieur, but, to be outspoken, I've had several trades. I've been an itinerant singer, a circus-rider, when I used to vault like Leotard, and dance on a rope like Blondin. Then I got to be a professor of gymnastics, so as to make better use of my talents; and then I was a sergeant fireman at Paris, and assisted at many a big fire. But I quitted France five years ago, and, wishing to taste the sweets of domestic life, took service as a valet here in England. Finding myself out of place, and hearing that Monsieur Phileas Fogg was the most exact and settled gentleman in the United Kingdom, I have come to monsieur in the hope of living with him a tranquil life, and forgetting even the name of Passepartout."

"Passepartout suits me," responded Mr. Fogg. "You are well recommended to me; I hear a good report of you. You know my conditions?"

"Yes, monsieur."

"Good! What time is it?"

"Twenty-two minutes after eleven," returned Passepartout, drawing an enormous silver watch from the depths of his pocket.

"You are too slow," said Mr. Fogg.

"Pardon me, monsieur, it is impossible—"

"You are four minutes too slow. No matter; it's enough to mention the error. Now from this moment, twenty-nine minutes after eleven, a.m., this Wednesday, 2nd October, you are in my service."

Phileas Fogg got up, took his hat in his left hand, put it on his head with an automatic motion, and went off without a word.

Passepartout heard the street door shut once; it was his new master going out. He heard it shut again; it was his predecessor, James Forster, departing in his turn. Passepartout remained alone in the house in Saville Row.

CHAPTER II

IN WHICH PASSEPARTOUT IS CONVINCED THAT HE HAS AT LAST FOUND HIS IDEAL

"Faith," muttered Passepartout, somewhat flurried, "I've seen people at Madame Tussaud's as lively as my new master!"

Madame Tussaud's "people," let it be said, are of wax, and are much visited in London; speech is all that is wanting to make them human.

During his brief interview with Mr. Fogg, Passepartout had been carefully observing him. He appeared to be a man about forty years of age, with fine, handsome features, and a tall, well-shaped figure; his hair and whiskers were light, his forehead compact and unwrinkled, his face rather pale, his teeth magnificent. His countenance possessed in the highest degree what physiognomists call "repose in action," a quality of those who act rather than talk. Calm and phlegmatic, with a clear eye, Mr. Fogg seemed a perfect type of that English composure which Angelica Kauffmann has so skilfully represented on canvas. Seen in the various phases of his daily life, he gave the idea of being perfectly well-balanced, as exactly regulated as a Leroy chronometer. Phileas Fogg was, indeed, exactitude personified, and this was betrayed even in the expression of his very hands and feet; for in men, as well as in animals, the limbs themselves are expressive of the passions.

He was so exact that he was never in a hurry, was always ready, and was economical alike of his steps and his motions. He never took one step too many, and always went to his destination by the shortest cut; he made no superfluous gestures, and was never seen to be moved or agitated. He was the most deliberate person in the world, yet always reached his destination at the exact moment.

He lived alone, and, so to speak, outside of every social relation; and as he knew that in this world account must be taken of friction, and that friction retards, he never rubbed against anybody.

As for Passepartout, he was a true Parisian of Paris. Since he had abandoned his own country for England, taking service as a valet, he had in vain searched for a master after his own heart. Passepartout was by no means one of those pert dunces depicted by Moliere with a bold gaze and a nose held high in the air; he was an honest fellow, with a pleasant face, lips a trifle protruding, soft-mannered and serviceable, with a good round head, such as one likes to see on the shoulders of a friend. His eyes were blue, his complexion rubicund, his figure almost portly and well-built, his body muscular, and his physical powers fully developed by the exercises of his younger days. His brown hair was somewhat tumbled; for, while the ancient sculptors are said to have known eighteen methods of arranging Minerva's tresses, Passepartout was familiar with but one of dressing his own: three strokes of a large-tooth comb completed his toilet.

It would be rash to predict how Passepartout's lively nature would agree with Mr. Fogg. It was impossible to tell whether the new servant would turn out as absolutely methodical as his master required; experience alone could solve the question. Passepartout had been a sort of vagrant in his early years, and now yearned for repose; but so far he had failed to find it, though he had already served in ten English houses. But he could not take root in any of these; with chagrin, he found his masters invariably whimsical and irregular, constantly running about the country, or on the look-out for adventure. His last master, young Lord Longferry, Member of Parliament, after passing his nights in the Haymarket taverns, was too often brought home in the morning on policemen's shoulders. Passepartout, desirous of respecting the gentleman whom he served, ventured a mild remonstrance on such conduct; which, being ill-received, he took his leave. Hearing that Mr. Phileas Fogg was looking for a servant, and that his life was one of unbroken regularity, that he neither travelled nor stayed from home overnight, he felt sure that this would be the place he was after. He presented himself, and was accepted, as has been seen.

At half-past eleven, then, Passepartout found himself alone in the house in Saville Row. He began its inspection without delay, scouring it from cellar to garret. So clean, well-arranged, solemn a mansion pleased him; it seemed to him like a snail's shell, lighted and warmed by gas, which sufficed for both these purposes. When Passepartout reached the second story he recognised at once the room which he was to inhabit, and he was well satisfied with it. Electric bells and speaking-tubes afforded communication with the lower stories; while on the mantel stood an electric clock, precisely like that in Mr. Fogg's bedchamber, both beating the same second at the same instant. "That's good, that'll do," said Passepartout to himself.

He suddenly observed, hung over the clock, a card which, upon inspection, proved to be a programme of the daily routine of the house. It comprised all that was required of the servant, from eight in the morning, exactly at which hour Phileas Fogg rose, till half-past eleven, when he left the house for the Reform Club—all the details of service, the tea and toast at twenty-three minutes past eight, the shaving-water at thirty-seven minutes past nine, and the toilet at twenty minutes before ten. Everything was regulated and foreseen that was to be done from half-past eleven a.m. till midnight, the hour at which the methodical gentleman retired.

Mr. Fogg's wardrobe was amply supplied and in the best taste. Each pair of trousers, coat, and vest bore a number, indicating the time of year and season at which they were in turn to be laid out for wearing; and the same system was applied to the master's shoes. In short, the house in Saville Row, which must have been a very temple of disorder and unrest under the illustrious but dissipated Sheridan, was cosiness, comfort, and method idealised. There was no study, nor were there books, which would have been quite useless to Mr. Fogg; for at the Reform two libraries, one of general literature and the other of law and politics, were at his service. A moderate-sized safe stood in his bedroom, constructed so as to defy fire as well as burglars; but Passepartout found neither arms nor hunting weapons anywhere; everything betrayed the most tranquil and peaceable habits.

Having scrutinised the house from top to bottom, he rubbed his hands, a broad smile overspread his features, and he said joyfully, "This is just what I wanted! Ah, we shall get on together, Mr. Fogg and I! What a domestic and regular gentleman! A real machine; well, I don't mind serving a machine."

CHAPTER III

IN WHICH A CONVERSATION TAKES PLACE WHICH SEEMS LIKELY TO COST PHILEAS FOGG DEAR

Phileas Fogg, having shut the door of his house at half-past eleven, and having put his right foot before his left five hundred and seventy-five times, and his left foot before his right five hundred and seventy-six times, reached the Reform Club, an imposing edifice in Pall Mall, which could not have cost less than three millions. He repaired at once to the dining-room, the nine windows of which open upon a tasteful garden, where the trees were already gilded with an autumn colouring; and took his place at the habitual table, the cover of which had already been laid for him. His breakfast consisted of a side-dish, a broiled fish with Reading sauce, a scarlet slice of roast beef garnished with mushrooms, a rhubarb and gooseberry tart, and a morsel of Cheshire cheese, the whole being washed down with several cups of tea, for which the Reform is famous. He rose at thirteen minutes to one, and directed his steps towards the large hall, a sumptuous apartment adorned with lavishly-framed paintings. A flunkey handed him an uncut Times, which he proceeded to cut with a skill which betrayed familiarity with this delicate operation. The perusal of this paper absorbed Phileas Fogg until a quarter before four, whilst the Standard, his next task, occupied him till the dinner hour. Dinner passed as breakfast had done, and Mr. Fogg re-appeared in the reading-room and sat down to the Pall Mall at twenty minutes before six. Half an hour later several members of the Reform came in and drew up to the fireplace, where a coal fire was steadily burning. They were Mr. Fogg's usual partners at whist: Andrew Stuart, an engineer; John Sullivan and Samuel Fallentin, bankers; Thomas Flanagan, a brewer; and Gauthier Ralph, one of the Directors of the Bank of England—all rich and highly respectable personages, even in a club which comprises the princes of English trade and finance.

"Well, Ralph," said Thomas Flanagan, "what about that robbery?"

"Oh," replied Stuart, "the Bank will lose the money."

"On the contrary," broke in Ralph, "I hope we may put our hands on the robber. Skilful detectives have been sent to all the principal ports of America and the Continent, and he'll be a clever fellow if he slips through their fingers."

"But have you got the robber's description?" asked Stuart.

"In the first place, he is no robber at all," returned Ralph, positively.

"What! a fellow who makes off with fifty-five thousand pounds, no robber?"

"No."

"Perhaps he's a manufacturer, then."

"The Daily Telegraph says that he is a gentleman."

It was Phileas Fogg, whose head now emerged from behind his newspapers, who made this remark. He bowed to his friends, and entered into the conversation. The affair which formed its subject, and which was town talk, had occurred three days before at the Bank of England. A package of banknotes, to the value of fifty-five thousand pounds, had been taken from the principal cashier's table, that functionary being at the moment engaged in registering the receipt of three shillings and sixpence. Of course, he could not have his eyes everywhere. Let it be observed that the Bank of England reposes a touching confidence in the honesty of the public. There are neither guards nor gratings to protect its treasures; gold, silver, banknotes are freely exposed, at the mercy of the first comer. A keen observer of English customs relates that, being in one of the rooms of the Bank one day, he had the curiosity to examine a gold ingot weighing some seven or eight pounds. He took it up, scrutinised it, passed it to his neighbour, he to the next man, and so on until the ingot, going from hand to hand, was transferred to the end of a dark entry; nor did it return to its place for half an hour. Meanwhile, the cashier had not so much as raised his head. But in the present instance things had not gone so smoothly. The package of notes not being found when five o'clock sounded from the ponderous clock in the "drawing office," the amount was passed to the account of profit and loss. As soon as the robbery was discovered, picked detectives hastened off to Liverpool, Glasgow, Havre, Suez, Brindisi, New York, and other ports, inspired by the proffered reward of two thousand pounds, and five per cent. on the sum that might be recovered. Detectives were also charged with narrowly watching those who arrived at or left London by rail, and a judicial examination was at once entered upon.

There were real grounds for supposing, as the Daily Telegraph said, that the thief did not belong to a professional band. On the day of the robbery a well-dressed gentleman of polished manners, and with a well-to-do air, had been observed going to and fro in the paying room where the crime was committed. A description of him was easily procured and sent to the detectives; and some hopeful spirits, of whom Ralph was one, did not despair of his apprehension. The papers and clubs were full of the affair, and everywhere people were discussing the probabilities of a successful pursuit; and the Reform Club was especially agitated, several of its members being Bank officials.

Ralph would not concede that the work of the detectives was likely to be in vain, for he thought that the prize offered would greatly stimulate their zeal and activity. But Stuart was far from sharing this confidence; and, as they placed themselves at the whist-table, they continued to argue the matter. Stuart and Flanagan played together, while Phileas Fogg had Fallentin for his partner. As the game proceeded the conversation ceased, excepting between the rubbers, when it revived again.

"I maintain," said Stuart, "that the chances are in favour of the thief, who must be a shrewd fellow."

"Well, but where can he fly to?" asked Ralph. "No country is safe for him."

"Pshaw!"

"Where could he go, then?"

"Oh, I don't know that. The world is big enough."

"It was once," said Phileas Fogg, in a low tone. "Cut, sir," he added, handing the cards to Thomas Flanagan.

The discussion fell during the rubber, after which Stuart took up its thread.

"What do you mean by `once'? Has the world grown smaller?"

"Certainly," returned Ralph. "I agree with Mr. Fogg. The world has grown smaller, since a man can now go round it ten times more quickly than a hundred years ago. And that is why the search for this thief will be more likely to succeed."

"And also why the thief can get away more easily."

"Be so good as to play, Mr. Stuart," said Phileas Fogg.

But the incredulous Stuart was not convinced, and when the hand was finished, said eagerly: "You have a strange way, Ralph, of proving that the world has grown smaller. So, because you can go round it in three months—"

"In eighty days," interrupted Phileas Fogg.

"That is true, gentlemen," added John Sullivan. "Only eighty days, now that the section between Rothal and Allahabad, on the Great Indian Peninsula Railway, has been opened. Here is the estimate made by the Daily Telegraph:

From London to Suez via Mont Cenis and
    Brindisi, by rail and steamboats................ 7 days
From Suez to Bombay, by steamer....................13 "
From Bombay to Calcutta, by rail .... 3"
From Calcutta to Hong Kong, by steamer .... 13"
From Hong Kong to Yokohama (Japan), by steamer.....6 "
From Yokohama to San Francisco, by steamer .... 22"
From San Francisco to New York, by rail .... 7"
From New York to London, by steamer and rail........ 9"

Total.. 80 days."

"Yes, in eighty days!" exclaimed Stuart, who in his excitement made a false deal. "But that doesn't take into account bad weather, contrary winds, shipwrecks, railway accidents, and so on."

"All included," returned Phileas Fogg, continuing to play despite the discussion.

"But suppose the Hindoos or Indians pull up the rails," replied Stuart; "suppose they stop the trains, pillage the luggage-vans, and scalp the passengers!"

"All included," calmly retorted Fogg; adding, as he threw down the cards, "Two trumps."

Stuart, whose turn it was to deal, gathered them up, and went on: "You are right, theoretically, Mr. Fogg, but practically—"

"Practically also, Mr. Stuart."

"I'd like to see you do it in eighty days."

"It depends on you. Shall we go?"

"Heaven preserve me! But I would wager four thousand pounds that such a journey, made under these conditions, is impossible."

"Quite possible, on the contrary," returned Mr. Fogg.

"Well, make it, then!"

A POOR MENDICANT

"The journey round the world in eighty days?"

"Yes."

"I should like nothing better."

"When?"

"At once. Only I warn you that I shall do it at your expense."

"It's absurd!" cried Stuart, who was beginning to be annoyed at the persistency of his friend. "Come, let's go on with the game."

"Deal over again, then," said Phileas Fogg. "There's a false deal."

Stuart took up the pack with a feverish hand; then suddenly put them down again.

"Well, Mr. Fogg," said he, "it shall be so: I will wager the four thousand on it."

"Calm yourself, my dear Stuart," said Fallentin. "It's only a joke."

"When I say I'll wager," returned Stuart, "I mean it."

"All right," said Mr. Fogg; and, turning to the others, he continued: "I have a deposit of twenty thousand at Baring's which I will willingly risk upon it."

"Twenty thousand pounds!" cried Sullivan. "Twenty thousand pounds, which you would lose by a single accidental delay!"

"The unforeseen does not exist," quietly replied Phileas Fogg.

"But, Mr. Fogg, eighty days are only the estimate of the least possible time in which the journey can be made."

"A well-used minimum suffices for everything."

"But, in order not to exceed it, you must jump mathematically from the trains upon the steamers, and from the steamers upon the trains again."

"I will jump—mathematically."

"You are joking."

"A true Englishman doesn't joke when he is talking about so serious a thing as a wager," replied Phileas Fogg, solemnly. "I will bet twenty thousand pounds against anyone who wishes that I will make the tour of the world in eighty days or less; in nineteen hundred and twenty hours, or a hundred and fifteen thousand two hundred minutes. Do you accept?"

"We accept," replied Messrs. Stuart, Fallentin, Sullivan, Flanagan, and Ralph, after consulting each other.

"Good," said Mr. Fogg. "The train leaves for Dover at a quarter before nine. I will take it."

"This very evening?" asked Stuart.

"WELL, MR. FOGG." SAID HE, "IT SHALL, BE SO : I WILL WA-
GER £4000 ON IT!

"This very evening," returned Phileas Fogg. He took out and consulted a pocket almanac, and added, "As today is Wednesday, the 2nd of October, I shall be due in London in this very room of the Reform Club, on Saturday, the 21st of December, at a quarter before nine p.m.; or else the twenty thousand pounds, now deposited in my name at Baring's, will belong to you, in fact and in right, gentlemen. Here is a cheque for the amount."

A memorandum of the wager was at once drawn up and signed by the six parties, during which Phileas Fogg preserved a stoical composure. He certainly did not bet to win, and had only staked the twenty thousand pounds, half of his fortune, because he foresaw that he might have to expend the other half to carry out this difficult, not to say unattainable, project. As for his antagonists, they seemed much agitated; not so much by the value of their stake, as because they had some scruples about betting under conditions so difficult to their friend.

The clock struck seven, and the party offered to suspend the game so that Mr. Fogg might make his preparations for departure.

"I am quite ready now," was his tranquil response. "Diamonds are trumps: be so good as to play, gentlemen."

CHAPTER IV

IN WHICH PHILEAS FOGG ASTOUNDS PASSEPARTOUT, HIS SERVANT

Having won twenty guineas at whist, and taken leave of his friends, Phileas Fogg, at twenty-five minutes past seven, left the Reform Club.

Passepartout, who had conscientiously studied the programme of his duties, was more than surprised to see his master guilty of the inexactness of appearing at this unaccustomed hour; for, according to rule, he was not due in Saville Row until precisely midnight.

Mr. Fogg repaired to his bedroom, and called out, "Passepartout!"

Passepartout did not reply. It could not be he who was called; it was not the right hour.

"Passepartout!" repeated Mr. Fogg, without raising his voice.

Passepartout made his appearance.

"I've called you twice," observed his master.

"But it is not midnight," responded the other, showing his watch.

"I know it; I don't blame you. We start for Dover and Calais in ten minutes."

A puzzled grin overspread Passepartout's round face; clearly he had not comprehended his master.

"Monsieur is going to leave home?"

"Yes," returned Phileas Fogg. "We are going round the world."

Passepartout opened wide his eyes, raised his eyebrows, held up his hands, and seemed about to collapse, so overcome was he with stupefied astonishment.

"Round the world!" he murmured.

"In eighty days," responded Mr. Fogg. "So we haven't a moment to lose."

"But the trunks?" gasped Passepartout, unconsciously swaying his head from right to left.

"We'll have no trunks; only a carpet-bag, with two shirts and three pairs of stockings for me, and the same for you. We'll buy our clothes on the way. Bring down my mackintosh and traveling-cloak, and some stout shoes, though we shall do little walking. Make haste!"

Passepartout tried to reply, but could not. He went out, mounted to his own room, fell into a chair, and muttered: "That's good, that is! And I, who wanted to remain quiet!"

He mechanically set about making the preparations for departure. Around the world in eighty days! Was his master a fool? No. Was this a joke, then? They were going to Dover; good! To Calais; good again! After all, Passepartout, who had been away from France five years, would not be sorry to set foot on his native soil again. Perhaps they would go as far as Paris, and it would do his eyes good to see Paris once more. But surely a gentleman so chary of his steps would stop there; no doubt—but, then, it was none the less true that he was going away, this so domestic person hitherto!

By eight o'clock Passepartout had packed the modest carpet-bag, containing the wardrobes of his master and himself; then, still troubled in mind, he carefully shut the door of his room, and descended to Mr. Fogg.

Mr. Fogg was quite ready. Under his arm might have been observed a red-bound copy of Bradshaw's Continental Railway Steam Transit and General Guide, with its timetables showing the arrival and departure of steamers and railways. He took the carpet-bag, opened it, and slipped into it a goodly roll of Bank of England notes, which would pass wherever he might go.

"You have forgotten nothing?" asked he.

"Nothing, monsieur."

"My mackintosh and cloak?"

"Here they are."

"Good! Take this carpet-bag," handing it to Passepartout. "Take good care of it, for there are twenty thousand pounds in it."

Passepartout nearly dropped the bag, as if the twenty thousand pounds were in gold, and weighed him down.

Master and man then descended, the street-door was double-locked, and at the end of Saville Row they took a cab and drove rapidly to Charing Cross. The cab stopped before the railway station at twenty minutes past eight. Passepartout jumped off the box and followed his master, who, after paying the cabman, was about to enter the station, when a poor beggar-woman, with a child in her arms, her naked feet smeared with mud, her head covered with a wretched bonnet, from which hung a tattered feather, and her shoulders shrouded in a ragged shawl, approached, and mournfully asked for alms.

Mr. Fogg took out the twenty guineas he had just won at whist, and handed them to the beggar, saying, "Here, my good woman. I'm glad that I met you;" and passed on.

Passepartout had a moist sensation about the eyes; his master's action touched his susceptible heart.

Two first-class tickets for Paris having been speedily purchased, Mr. Fogg was crossing the station to the train, when he perceived his five friends of the Reform.

"Well, gentlemen," said he, "I'm off, you see; and, if you will examine my passport when I get back, you will be able to judge whether I have accomplished the journey agreed upon."

"Oh, that would be quite unnecessary, Mr. Fogg," said Ralph politely. "We will trust your word, as a gentleman of honour."

"You do not forget when you are due in London again?" asked Stuart.

"In eighty days; on Saturday, the 21st of December, 1872, at a quarter before nine p.m. Good-bye, gentlemen."

Phileas Fogg and his servant seated themselves in a first-class carriage at twenty minutes before nine; five minutes later the whistle screamed, and the train slowly glided out of the station.

The night was dark, and a fine, steady rain was falling. Phileas Fogg, snugly ensconced in his corner, did not open his lips. Passepartout, not yet recovered from his stupefaction, clung mechanically to the carpet-bag, with its enormous treasure.

Just as the train was whirling through Sydenham, Passepartout suddenly uttered a cry of despair.

"What's the matter?" asked Mr. Fogg.

"Alas! In my hurry—I—I forgot—"

"What?"

"To turn off the gas in my room!"

"Very well, young man," returned Mr. Fogg, coolly; "it will burn—at your expense."

CHAPTER V

IN WHICH A NEW SPECIES OF FUNDS, UNKNOWN TO THE MONEYED MEN, APPEARS ON 'CHANGE

Phileas Fogg rightly suspected that his departure from London would create a lively sensation at the West End. The news of the bet spread through the Reform Club, and afforded an exciting topic of conversation to its members. From the club it soon got into the papers throughout England. The boasted "tour of the world" was talked about, disputed, argued with as much warmth as if the subject were another Alabama claim. Some took sides with Phileas Fogg, but the large majority shook their heads and declared against him; it was absurd, impossible, they declared, that the tour of the world could be made, except theoretically and on paper, in this minimum of time, and with the existing means of travelling. The Times, Standard, Morning Post, and Daily News, and twenty other highly respectable newspapers scouted Mr. Fogg's project as madness; the Daily Telegraph alone hesitatingly supported him. People in general thought him a lunatic, and blamed his Reform Club friends for having accepted a wager which betrayed the mental aberration of its proposer.

Articles no less passionate than logical appeared on the question, for geography is one of the pet subjects of the English; and the columns devoted to Phileas Fogg's venture were eagerly devoured by all classes of readers. At first some rash individuals, principally of the gentler sex, espoused his cause, which became still more popular when the Illustrated London News came out with his portrait, copied from a photograph in the Reform Club. A few readers of the Daily Telegraph even dared to say, "Why not, after all? Stranger things have come to pass."

At last a long article appeared, on the 7th of October, in the bulletin of the Royal Geographical Society, which treated the question from every point of view, and demonstrated the utter folly of the enterprise.

Everything, it said, was against the travellers, every obstacle imposed alike by man and by nature. A miraculous agreement of the times of departure and arrival, which was impossible, was absolutely necessary to his success. He might, perhaps, reckon on the arrival of trains at the designated hours, in Europe, where the distances were relatively moderate; but when he calculated upon crossing India in three days, and the United States in seven, could he rely beyond misgiving upon accomplishing his task? There were accidents to machinery, the liability of trains to run off the line, collisions, bad weather, the blocking up by snow—were not all these against Phileas Fogg? Would he not find himself, when travelling by steamer in winter, at the mercy of the winds and fogs? Is it uncommon for the best ocean steamers to be two or three days behind time? But a single delay would suffice to fatally break the chain of communication; should Phileas Fogg once miss, even by an hour; a steamer, he would have to wait for the next, and that would irrevocably render his attempt vain.

This article made a great deal of noise, and, being copied into all the papers, seriously depressed the advocates of the rash tourist.

Everybody knows that England is the world of betting men, who are of a higher class than mere gamblers; to bet is in the English temperament. Not only the members of the Reform, but the general public, made heavy wagers for or against Phileas Fogg, who was set down in the betting books as if he were a race-horse. Bonds were issued, and made their appearance on 'Change; "Phileas Fogg bonds" were offered at par or at a premium, and a great business was done in them. But five days after the article in the bulletin of the Geographical Society appeared, the demand began to subside: "Phileas Fogg" declined. They were offered by packages, at first of five, then of ten, until at last nobody would take less than twenty, fifty, a hundred!

Lord Albemarle, an elderly paralytic gentleman, was now the only advocate of Phileas Fogg left. This noble lord, who was fastened to his chair, would have given his fortune to be able to make the tour of the world, if it took ten years; and he bet five thousand pounds on Phileas Fogg. When the folly as well as the uselessness of the adventure was pointed out to him, he contented himself with replying, "If the thing is feasible, the first to do it ought to be an Englishman."

The Fogg party dwindled more and more, everybody was going against him, and the bets stood a hundred and fifty and two hundred to one; and a week after his departure an incident occurred which deprived him of

READERS OF ALL CLASSES DEVOURED THE NEWS RELATING
TO PHILEAS FOGG

backers at any price.

The commissioner of police was sitting in his office at nine o'clock one evening, when the following telegraphic dispatch was put into his hands:

Suez to London.

Rowan, Commissioner of Police, Scotland Yard:

I've found the bank robber, Phileas Fogg. Send with out delay warrant of arrest to Bombay.

Fix, Detective.

The effect of this dispatch was instantaneous. The polished gentleman disappeared to give place to the bank robber. His photograph, which was hung with those of the rest of the members at the Reform Club, was minutely examined, and it betrayed, feature by feature, the description of the robber which had been provided to the police. The mysterious habits of Phileas Fogg were recalled; his solitary ways, his sudden departure; and it seemed clear that, in undertaking a tour round the world on the pretext of a wager, he had had no other end in view than to elude the detectives, and throw them off his track.

CHAPTER VI

IN WHICH FIX, THE DETECTIVE, BETRAYS A VERY NATURAL IMPA-TIENCE

The circumstances under which this telegraphic dispatch about Phileas Fogg was sent were as follows:

The steamer Mongolia, belonging to the Peninsular and Oriental Company, built of iron, of two thousand eight hundred tons burden, and five hundred horse-power, was due at eleven o'clock a.m. on Wednesday, the 9th of October, at Suez. The Mongolia plied regularly between Brindisi and Bombay via the Suez Canal, and was one of the fastest steamers belonging to the company, always making more than ten knots an hour between Brindisi and Suez, and nine and a half between Suez and Bombay.

Two men were promenading up and down the wharves, among the crowd of natives and strangers who were sojourning at this once straggling village—now, thanks to the enterprise of M. Lesseps, a fast-growing town. One was the British consul at Suez, who, despite the prophecies of the English Government, and the unfavourable predictions of Stephenson, was in the habit of seeing, from his office window, English ships daily passing to and fro on the great canal, by which the old roundabout route from England to India by the Cape of Good Hope was abridged by at least a half. The other was a small, slight-built personage, with a nervous, intelligent face, and bright eyes peering out from under eyebrows which he was incessantly twitching. He was just now manifesting unmistakable signs of impatience, nervously pacing up and down, and unable to stand still for a moment. This was Fix, one of the detectives who had been dispatched from England in search of the bank robber; it was his task to narrowly watch every passenger who arrived at Suez, and to follow up all who seemed to be suspicious characters, or bore a resemblance to the description of the criminal, which he had received two days before from the police headquarters at London.

DETECTIVE FIX

The detective was evidently inspired by the hope of obtaining the splendid reward which would be the prize of success, and awaited with a feverish impatience, easy to understand, the arrival of the steamer Mongolia.

"So you say, consul," asked he for the twentieth time, "that this steamer is never behind time?"

"No, Mr. Fix," replied the consul. "She was bespoken yesterday at Port Said, and the rest of the way is of no account to such a craft. I repeat that the Mongolia has been in advance of the time required by the company's regulations, and gained the prize awarded for excess of speed."

"Does she come directly from Brindisi?"

"Directly from Brindisi; she takes on the Indian mails there, and she left there Saturday at five p.m. Have patience, Mr. Fix; she will not be late. But really, I don't see how, from the description you have, you will be able to recognise your man, even if he is on board the Mongolia."

"A man rather feels the presence of these fellows, consul, than recognises them. You must have a scent for them, and a scent is like a sixth sense which combines hearing, seeing, and smelling. I've arrested more than one of these gentlemen in my time, and, if my thief is on board, I'll answer for it; he'll not slip through my fingers."

"I hope so, Mr. Fix, for it was a heavy robbery."

"A magnificent robbery, consul; fifty-five thousand pounds! We don't often have such windfalls. Burglars are getting to be so contemptible nowadays! A fellow gets hung for a handful of shillings!"

"Mr. Fix," said the consul, "I like your way of talking, and hope you'll succeed; but I fear you will find it far from easy. Don't you see, the description which you have there has a singular resemblance to an honest man?"

"Consul," remarked the detective, dogmatically, "great robbers always resemble honest folks. Fellows who have rascally faces have only one course to take, and that is to remain honest; otherwise they would be arrested off-hand. The artistic thing is, to unmask honest countenances; it's no light task, I admit, but a real art."

Mr. Fix evidently was not wanting in a tinge of self-conceit.

Little by little the scene on the quay became more animated; sailors of various nations, merchants, ship-brokers, porters, fellahs, bustled to and fro as if the steamer were immediately expected. The weather was clear, and slightly chilly. The minarets of the town loomed above the houses in the pale rays of the sun. A jetty pier, some two thousand yards along, extended into the roadstead. A number of fishing-smacks and coasting boats, some retaining the fantastic fashion of ancient galleys, were discernible on the Red Sea.

As he passed among the busy crowd, Fix, according to habit, scrutinised the passers-by with a keen, rapid glance.

It was now half-past ten.

"The steamer doesn't come!" he exclaimed, as the port clock struck.

"She can't be far off now," returned his companion.

"How long will she stop at Suez?"

"Four hours; long enough to get in her coal. It is thirteen hundred and ten miles from Suez to Aden, at the other end of the Red Sea, and she has to take in a fresh coal supply."

"And does she go from Suez directly to Bombay?"

"Without putting in anywhere."

"Good!" said Fix. "If the robber is on board he will no doubt get off at Suez, so as to reach the Dutch or French colonies in Asia by some other route. He ought to know that he would not be safe an hour in India, which is English soil."

"Unless," objected the consul, "he is exceptionally shrewd. An English criminal, you know, is always better concealed in London than anywhere else."

This observation furnished the detective food for thought, and meanwhile the consul went away to his office. Fix, left alone, was more impatient than ever, having a presentiment that the robber was on board the Mongolia. If he had indeed left London intending to reach the New World, he would naturally take the route via India, which was less watched and more difficult to watch than that of the Atlantic. But Fix's reflections were soon interrupted by a succession of sharp whistles, which announced the arrival of the Mongolia. The porters and fellahs rushed down the quay, and a dozen boats pushed off from the shore to go and meet the steamer. Soon her gigantic hull appeared passing along between the banks, and eleven o'clock struck as she anchored in the road. She brought an unusual number of passengers, some of whom remained on deck to scan the picturesque panorama of the town, while the greater part disembarked in the boats, and landed on the quay.

Fix took up a position, and carefully examined each face and figure which made its appearance. Presently one of the passengers, after vigorously pushing his way through the importunate crowd of porters, came up to him and politely asked if he could point out the English consulate, at the same

AFTER VIGOROUSLY REPULSING THE FELLAHS WHO OF-
FERED THEIR ASSISTANCE

time showing a passport which he wished to have visaed. Fix instinctively took the passport, and with a rapid glance read the description of its bearer. An involuntary motion of surprise nearly escaped him, for the description in the passport was identical with that of the bank robber which he had received from Scotland Yard.

"Is this your passport?" asked he.

"No, it's my master's."

"And your master is—"

"He stayed on board."

"But he must go to the consul's in person, so as to establish his identity."

"Oh, is that necessary?"

"Quite indispensable."

"And where is the consulate?"

"There, on the corner of the square," said Fix, pointing to a house two hundred steps off.

"I'll go and fetch my master, who won't be much pleased, however, to be disturbed."

The passenger bowed to Fix, and returned to the steamer.

CHAPTER VII

WHICH ONCE MORE DEMONSTRATES THE USELESSNESS OF PASSPORTS AS AIDS TO DETECTIVES

The detective passed down the quay, and rapidly made his way to the consul's office, where he was at once admitted to the presence of that official.

"Consul," said he, without preamble, "I have strong reasons for believing that my man is a passenger on the Mongolia." And he narrated what had just passed concerning the passport.

"Well, Mr. Fix," replied the consul, "I shall not be sorry to see the rascal's face; but perhaps he won't come here—that is, if he is the person you suppose him to be. A robber doesn't quite like to leave traces of his flight behind him; and, besides, he is not obliged to have his passport countersigned."

"If he is as shrewd as I think he is, consul, he will come."

"To have his passport visaed?"

"Yes. Passports are only good for annoying honest folks, and aiding in the flight of rogues. I assure you it will be quite the thing for him to do; but I hope you will not visa the passport."

"Why not? If the passport is genuine I have no right to refuse."

"Still, I must keep this man here until I can get a warrant to arrest him from London."

"Ah, that's your look-out. But I cannot—"

The consul did not finish his sentence, for as he spoke a knock was heard at the door, and two strangers entered, one of whom was the servant whom Fix had met on the quay. The other, who was his master, held out his passport with the request that the consul would do him the favour to visa it. The consul took the document and carefully read it, whilst Fix observed, or rather devoured, the stranger with his eyes from a corner of the room.

"You are Mr. Phileas Fogg?" said the consul, after reading the passport.

"I am."

"And this man is your servant?"

"He is: a Frenchman, named Passepartout."

"You are from London?"

"Yes."

"And you are going—"

"To Bombay."

"Very good, sir. You know that a visa is useless, and that no passport is required?"

"I know it, sir," replied Phileas Fogg; "but I wish to prove, by your visa, that I came by Suez."

"Very well, sir."

The consul proceeded to sign and date the passport, after which he added his official seal. Mr. Fogg paid the customary fee, coldly bowed, and went out, followed by his servant.

"Well?" queried the detective.

"Well, he looks and acts like a perfectly honest man," replied the consul.

"Possibly; but that is not the question. Do you think, consul, that this phlegmatic gentleman resembles, feature by feature, the robber whose description I have received?"

'I concede that; but then, you know, all descriptions—"

"I'll make certain of it," interrupted Fix. "The servant seems to me less mysterious than the master; besides, he's a Frenchman, and can't help talking. Excuse me for a little while, consul."

Fix started off in search of Passepartout.

Meanwhile Mr. Fogg, after leaving the consulate, repaired to the quay, gave some orders to Passepartout, went off to the Mongolia in a boat, and descended to his cabin. He took up his note-book, which contained the following memoranda:

"Left London, Wednesday, October 2nd, at 8.45 p.m. "Reached Paris, Thursday, October 3rd, at 7.20 a.m. "Left Paris, Thursday, at 8.40 a.m. "Reached Turin by Mont Cenis, Friday, October 4th, at 6.35 a.m. "Left Turin, Friday, at 7.20 a.m. "Arrived at Brindisi, Saturday, October 5th, at 4 p.m. "Sailed on the Mongolia, Saturday, at 5 p.m. "Reached Suez, Wednesday, October 9th, at 11 a.m. "Total of hours spent, 158+; or, in days, six days and a half."

These dates were inscribed in an itinerary divided into columns, indicating the month, the day of the month, and the day for the stipulated and actual arrivals at each principal point Paris, Brindisi, Suez, Bombay, Calcutta, Singapore, Hong Kong, Yokohama, San Francisco, New York, and London—from the 2nd of October to the 21st of December; and giving a space for setting down the gain made or the loss suffered on arrival at each locality. This methodical record thus contained an account of everything needed, and Mr. Fogg always knew whether he was behind-hand or in advance of his time. On this Friday, October 9th, he noted his arrival at Suez, and observed that he had as yet neither gained nor lost. He sat down quietly to breakfast in his cabin, never once thinking of inspecting the town, being one of those Englishmen who are wont to see foreign countries through the eyes of their domestics.

CHAPTER VIII

IN WHICH PASSEPARTOUT TALKS RATHER MORE, PERHAPS, THAN IS PRUDENT

Fix soon rejoined Passepartout, who was lounging and looking about on the quay, as if he did not feel that he, at least, was obliged not to see anything.

"Well, my friend," said the detective, coming up with him, "is your passport visaed?"

"Ah, it's you, is it, monsieur?" responded Passepartout. "Thanks, yes, the passport is all right."

"And you are looking about you?"

"Yes; but we travel so fast that I seem to be journeying in a dream. So this is Suez?"

"Yes."

"In Egypt?"

"Certainly, in Egypt."

"And in Africa?"

"In Africa."

"In Africa!" repeated Passepartout. "Just think, monsieur, I had no idea that we should go farther than Paris; and all that I saw of Paris was between twenty minutes past seven and twenty minutes before nine in the morning, between the Northern and the Lyons stations, through the windows of a car, and in a driving rain! How I regret not having seen once more Pere la Chaise and the circus in the Champs Elysees!"

"You are in a great hurry, then?"

"I am not, but my master is. By the way, I must buy some shoes and shirts. We came away without trunks, only with a carpet-bag."

"I will show you an excellent shop for getting what you want."

"Really, monsieur, you are very kind."

And they walked off together, Passepartout chatting volubly as they went along.

"Above all," said he; "don't let me lose the steamer."

"You have plenty of time; it's only twelve o'clock."

Passepartout pulled out his big watch. "Twelve!" he exclaimed; "why, it's only eight minutes before ten."

"Your watch is slow."

"My watch? A family watch, monsieur, which has come down from my great-grandfather! It doesn't vary five minutes in the year. It's a perfect chronometer, look you."

"I see how it is," said Fix. "You have kept London time, which is two hours behind that of Suez. You ought to regulate your watch at noon in each country."

"I regulate my watch? Never!"

"Well, then, it will not agree with the sun."

"So much the worse for the sun, monsieur. The sun will be wrong, then!"

And the worthy fellow returned the watch to its fob with a defiant gesture. After a few minutes silence, Fix resumed: "You left London hastily, then?"

"I rather think so! Last Friday at eight o'clock in the evening, Monsieur Fogg came home from his club, and three-quarters of an hour afterwards we were off."

"But where is your master going?"

"Always straight ahead. He is going round the world."

"Round the world?" cried Fix.

"Yes, and in eighty days! He says it is on a wager; but, between us, I don't believe a word of it. That wouldn't be common sense. There's something else in the wind."

"Ah! Mr. Fogg is a character, is he?"

"I should say he was."

"Is he rich?"

"No doubt, for he is carrying an enormous sum in brand new banknotes with him. And he doesn't spare the money on the way, either: he has offered a large reward to the engineer of the Mongolia if he gets us to Bombay well in advance of time."

"MY WATCH? A FAMILY WATCH!"

"And you have known your master a long time?"

"Why, no; I entered his service the very day we left London."

The effect of these replies upon the already suspicious and excited detective may be imagined. The hasty departure from London soon after the robbery; the large sum carried by Mr. Fogg; his eagerness to reach distant countries; the pretext of an eccentric and foolhardy bet—all confirmed Fix in his theory. He continued to pump poor Passepartout, and learned that he really knew little or nothing of his master, who lived a solitary existence in London, was said to be rich, though no one knew whence came his riches, and was mysterious and impenetrable in his affairs and habits. Fix felt sure that Phileas Fogg would not land at Suez, but was really going on to Bombay.

"Is Bombay far from here?" asked Passepartout.

"Pretty far. It is a ten days' voyage by sea."

"And in what country is Bombay?"

"India."

"In Asia?"

"Certainly."

"The deuce! I was going to tell you there's one thing that worries me— my burner!"

"What burner?"

"My gas-burner, which I forgot to turn off, and which is at this moment burning at my expense. I have calculated, monsieur, that I lose two shillings every four and twenty hours, exactly sixpence more than I earn; and you will understand that the longer our journey—"

Did Fix pay any attention to Passepartout's trouble about the gas? It is not probable. He was not listening, but was cogitating a project. Passepartout and he had now reached the shop, where Fix left his companion to make his purchases, after recommending him not to miss the steamer, and hurried back to the consulate. Now that he was fully convinced, Fix had quite recovered his equanimity.

"Consul," said he, "I have no longer any doubt. I have spotted my man. He passes himself off as an odd stick who is going round the world in eighty days."

"Then he's a sharp fellow," returned the consul, "and counts on returning to London after putting the police of the two countries off his track."

"We'll see about that," replied Fix.

"But are you not mistaken?"

"I am not mistaken."

"Why was this robber so anxious to prove, by the visa, that he had passed through Suez?"

"Why? I have no idea; but listen to me."

He reported in a few words the most important parts of his conversation with Passepartout.

"In short," said the consul, "appearances are wholly against this man. And what are you going to do?"

"Send a dispatch to London for a warrant of arrest to be dispatched instantly to Bombay, take passage on board the Mongolia, follow my rogue to India, and there, on English ground, arrest him politely, with my warrant in my hand, and my hand on his shoulder."

Having uttered these words with a cool, careless air, the detective took leave of the consul, and repaired to the telegraph office, whence he sent the dispatch which we have seen to the London police office. A quarter of an hour later found Fix, with a small bag in his hand, proceeding on board the Mongolia; and, ere many moments longer, the noble steamer rode out at full steam upon the waters of the Red Sea.

CHAPTER IX

IN WHICH THE RED SEA AND THE INDIAN OCEAN PROVE PROPITIOUS TO THE DESIGNS OF PHILEAS FOGG

The distance between Suez and Aden is precisely thirteen hundred and ten miles, and the regulations of the company allow the steamers one hundred and thirty-eight hours in which to traverse it. The Mongolia, thanks to the vigorous exertions of the engineer, seemed likely, so rapid was her speed, to reach her destination considerably within that time. The greater part of the passengers from Brindisi were bound for India some for Bombay, others for Calcutta by way of Bombay, the nearest route thither, now that a railway crosses the Indian peninsula. Among the passengers was a number of officials and military officers of various grades, the latter being either attached to the regular British forces or commanding the Sepoy troops, and receiving high salaries ever since the central government has assumed the powers of the East India Company: for the sub-lieutenants get 280 pounds, brigadiers, 2,400 pounds, and generals of divisions, 4,000 pounds. What with the military men, a number of rich young Englishmen on their travels, and the hospitable efforts of the purser, the time passed quickly on the Mongolia. The best of fare was spread upon the cabin tables at breakfast, lunch, dinner, and the eight o'clock supper, and the ladies scrupulously changed their toilets twice a day; and the hours were whirled away, when the sea was tranquil, with music, dancing, and games.

But the Red Sea is full of caprice, and often boisterous, like most long and narrow gulfs. When the wind came from the African or Asian coast the Mongolia, with her long hull, rolled fearfully. Then the ladies speedily disappeared below; the pianos were silent; singing and dancing suddenly ceased. Yet the good ship ploughed straight on, unretarded by wind or wave, towards the straits of Bab-el-Mandeb. What was Phileas Fogg doing all this time? It might be thought that, in his anxiety, he would be constantly

watching the changes of the wind, the disorderly raging of the billows—
every chance, in short, which might force the Mongolia to slacken her speed,
and thus interrupt his journey. But, if he thought of these possibilities, he
did not betray the fact by any outward sign.

Always the same impassible member of the Reform Club, whom
no incident could surprise, as unvarying as the ship's chronometers, and
seldom having the curiosity even to go upon the deck, he passed through
the memorable scenes of the Red Sea with cold indifference; did not
care to recognise the historic towns and villages which, along its borders,
raised their picturesque outlines against the sky; and betrayed no fear of
the dangers of the Arabic Gulf, which the old historians always spoke of
with horror, and upon which the ancient navigators never ventured without
propitiating the gods by ample sacrifices. How did this eccentric personage
pass his time on the Mongolia? He made his four hearty meals every day,
regardless of the most persistent rolling and pitching on the part of the
steamer; and he played whist indefatigably, for he had found partners as
enthusiastic in the game as himself. A tax-collector, on the way to his post
at Goa; the Rev. Decimus Smith, returning to his parish at Bombay; and a
brigadier-general of the English army, who was about to rejoin his brigade
at Benares, made up the party, and, with Mr. Fogg, played whist by the hour
together in absorbing silence.

As for Passepartout, he, too, had escaped sea-sickness, and took his
meals conscientiously in the forward cabin. He rather enjoyed the voyage,
for he was well fed and well lodged, took a great interest in the scenes
through which they were passing, and consoled himself with the delusion
that his master's whim would end at Bombay. He was pleased, on the day
after leaving Suez, to find on deck the obliging person with whom he had
walked and chatted on the quays.

"If I am not mistaken," said he, approaching this person, with his most
amiable smile, "you are the gentleman who so kindly volunteered to guide
me at Suez?"

"Ah! I quite recognise you. You are the servant of the strange
Englishman—"

"Just so, monsieur—"

"Fix."

"Monsieur Fix," resumed Passepartout, "I'm charmed to find you on
board. Where are you bound?"

"Like you, to Bombay."

MR. FIX ON THE WATCH

"That's capital! Have you made this trip before?"

"Several times. I am one of the agents of the Peninsular Company."

"Then you know India?"

"Why yes," replied Fix, who spoke cautiously.

"A curious place, this India?"

"Oh, very curious. Mosques, minarets, temples, fakirs, pagodas, tigers, snakes, elephants! I hope you will have ample time to see the sights."

"I hope so, Monsieur Fix. You see, a man of sound sense ought not to spend his life jumping from a steamer upon a railway train, and from a railway train upon a steamer again, pretending to make the tour of the world in eighty days! No; all these gymnastics, you may be sure, will cease at Bombay."

"And Mr. Fogg is getting on well?" asked Fix, in the most natural tone in the world.

"Quite well, and I too. I eat like a famished ogre; it's the sea air."

"But I never see your master on deck."

"Never; he hasn't the least curiosity."

"Do you know, Mr. Passepartout, that this pretended tour in eighty days may conceal some secret errand—perhaps a diplomatic mission?"

"Faith, Monsieur Fix, I assure you I know nothing about it, nor would I give half a crown to find out."

After this meeting, Passepartout and Fix got into the habit of chatting together, the latter making it a point to gain the worthy man's confidence. He frequently offered him a glass of whiskey or pale ale in the steamer bar-room, which Passepartout never failed to accept with graceful alacrity, mentally pronouncing Fix the best of good fellows.

Meanwhile the Mongolia was pushing forward rapidly; on the 13th, Mocha, surrounded by its ruined walls whereon date-trees were growing, was sighted, and on the mountains beyond were espied vast coffee-fields. Passepartout was ravished to behold this celebrated place, and thought that, with its circular walls and dismantled fort, it looked like an immense coffee-cup and saucer. The following night they passed through the Strait of Bab-el-Mandeb, which means in Arabic The Bridge of Tears, and the next day they put in at Steamer Point, north-west of Aden harbour, to take in coal. This matter of fuelling steamers is a serious one at such distances from the coal-mines; it costs the Peninsular Company some eight hundred thousand pounds a year. In these distant seas, coal is worth three or four pounds

THEY PUT IN AT STEAMER POINT

sterling a ton.

The Mongolia had still sixteen hundred and fifty miles to traverse before reaching Bombay, and was obliged to remain four hours at Steamer Point to coal up. But this delay, as it was foreseen, did not affect Phileas Fogg's programme; besides, the Mongolia, instead of reaching Aden on the morning of the 15th, when she was due, arrived there on the evening of the 14th, a gain of fifteen hours.

Mr. Fogg and his servant went ashore at Aden to have the passport again visaed; Fix, unobserved, followed them. The visa procured, Mr. Fogg returned on board to resume his former habits; while Passepartout, according to custom, sauntered about among the mixed population of Somalis, Banyans, Parsees, Jews, Arabs, and Europeans who comprise the twenty-five thousand inhabitants of Aden. He gazed with wonder upon the fortifications which make this place the Gibraltar of the Indian Ocean, and the vast cisterns where the English engineers were still at work, two thousand years after the engineers of Solomon.

"Very curious, very curious," said Passepartout to himself, on returning to the steamer. "I see that it is by no means useless to travel, if a man wants to see something new." At six p.m. the Mongolia slowly moved out of the roadstead, and was soon once more on the Indian Ocean. She had a hundred and sixty-eight hours in which to reach Bombay, and the sea was favourable, the wind being in the north-west, and all sails aiding the engine. The steamer rolled but little, the ladies, in fresh toilets, reappeared on deck, and the singing and dancing were resumed. The trip was being accomplished most successfully, and Passepartout was enchanted with the congenial companion which chance had secured him in the person of the delightful Fix. On Sunday, October 20th, towards noon, they came in sight of the Indian coast: two hours later the pilot came on board. A range of hills lay against the sky in the horizon, and soon the rows of palms which adorn Bombay came distinctly into view. The steamer entered the road formed by the islands in the bay, and at half-past four she hauled up at the quays of Bombay.

Phileas Fogg was in the act of finishing the thirty-third rubber of the voyage, and his partner and himself having, by a bold stroke, captured all thirteen of the tricks, concluded this fine campaign with a brilliant victory.

The Mongolia was due at Bombay on the 22nd; she arrived on the 20th. This was a gain to Phileas Fogg of two days since his departure from London, and he calmly entered the fact in the itinerary, in the column of gains.

CHAPTER X

IN WHICH PASSEPARTOUT IS ONLY TOO GLAD TO GET OFF WITH THE LOSS OF HIS SHOES

Everybody knows that the great reversed triangle of land, with its base in the north and its apex in the south, which is called India, embraces fourteen hundred thousand square miles, upon which is spread unequally a population of one hundred and eighty millions of souls. The British Crown exercises a real and despotic dominion over the larger portion of this vast country, and has a governor-general stationed at Calcutta, governors at Madras, Bombay, and in Bengal, and a lieutenant-governor at Agra.

But British India, properly so called, only embraces seven hundred thousand square miles, and a population of from one hundred to one hundred and ten millions of inhabitants. A considerable portion of India is still free from British authority; and there are certain ferocious rajahs in the interior who are absolutely independent. The celebrated East India Company was all-powerful from 1756, when the English first gained a foothold on the spot where now stands the city of Madras, down to the time of the great Sepoy insurrection. It gradually annexed province after province, purchasing them of the native chiefs, whom it seldom paid, and appointed the governor-general and his subordinates, civil and military. But the East India Company has now passed away, leaving the British possessions in India directly under the control of the Crown. The aspect of the country, as well as the manners and distinctions of race, is daily changing.

Formerly one was obliged to travel in India by the old cumbrous methods of going on foot or on horseback, in palanquins or unwieldy coaches; now fast steamboats ply on the Indus and the Ganges, and a great railway, with branch lines joining the main line at many points on its route, traverses the peninsula from Bombay to Calcutta in three days. This railway does not run in a direct line across India. The distance between Bombay and Calcutta, as

PASSEPARTOUT, FOLLOWING HIS USUAL CUSTOM, TAKES A
STROLL

the bird flies, is only from one thousand to eleven hundred miles; but the deflections of the road increase this distance by more than a third.

The general route of the Great Indian Peninsula Railway is as follows: Leaving Bombay, it passes through Salcette, crossing to the continent opposite Tannah, goes over the chain of the Western Ghauts, runs thence north-east as far as Burhampoor, skirts the nearly independent territory of Bundelcund, ascends to Allahabad, turns thence eastwardly, meeting the Ganges at Benares, then departs from the river a little, and, descending south-eastward by Burdivan and the French town of Chandernagor, has its terminus at Calcutta.

The passengers of the Mongolia went ashore at half-past four p.m.; at exactly eight the train would start for Calcutta.

Mr. Fogg, after bidding good-bye to his whist partners, left the steamer, gave his servant several errands to do, urged it upon him to be at the station promptly at eight, and, with his regular step, which beat to the second, like an astronomical clock, directed his steps to the passport office. As for the wonders of Bombay—its famous city hall, its splendid library, its forts and docks, its bazaars, mosques, synagogues, its Armenian churches, and the noble pagoda on Malabar Hill, with its two polygonal towers—he cared not a straw to see them. He would not deign to examine even the masterpieces of Elephanta, or the mysterious hypogea, concealed south-east from the docks, or those fine remains of Buddhist architecture, the Kanherian grottoes of the island of Salcette.

Having transacted his business at the passport office, Phileas Fogg repaired quietly to the railway station, where he ordered dinner. Among the dishes served up to him, the landlord especially recommended a certain giblet of "native rabbit," on which he prided himself.

Mr. Fogg accordingly tasted the dish, but, despite its spiced sauce, found it far from palatable. He rang for the landlord, and, on his appearance, said, fixing his clear eyes upon him, "Is this rabbit, sir?"

"Yes, my lord," the rogue boldly replied, "rabbit from the jungles."

"And this rabbit did not mew when he was killed?"

"Mew, my lord! What, a rabbit mew! I swear to you—"

"Be so good, landlord, as not to swear, but remember this: cats were formerly considered, in India, as sacred animals. That was a good time."

"For the cats, my lord?"

"Perhaps for the travellers as well!"

After which Mr. Fogg quietly continued his dinner. Fix had gone on shore shortly after Mr. Fogg, and his first destination was the headquarters of the Bombay police. He made himself known as a London detective, told his business at Bombay, and the position of affairs relative to the supposed robber, and nervously asked if a warrant had arrived from London. It had not reached the office; indeed, there had not yet been time for it to arrive. Fix was sorely disappointed, and tried to obtain an order of arrest from the director of the Bombay police. This the director refused, as the matter concerned the London office, which alone could legally deliver the warrant. Fix did not insist, and was fain to resign himself to await the arrival of the important document; but he was determined not to lose sight of the mysterious rogue as long as he stayed in Bombay. He did not doubt for a moment, any more than Passepartout, that Phileas Fogg would remain there, at least until it was time for the warrant to arrive.

Passepartout, however, had no sooner heard his master's orders on leaving the Mongolia than he saw at once that they were to leave Bombay as they had done Suez and Paris, and that the journey would be extended at least as far as Calcutta, and perhaps beyond that place. He began to ask himself if this bet that Mr. Fogg talked about was not really in good earnest, and whether his fate was not in truth forcing him, despite his love of repose, around the world in eighty days!

Having purchased the usual quota of shirts and shoes, he took a leisurely promenade about the streets, where crowds of people of many nationalities—Europeans, Persians with pointed caps, Banyas with round turbans, Sindes with square bonnets, Parsees with black mitres, and long-robed Armenians—were collected. It happened to be the day of a Parsee festival. These descendants of the sect of Zoroaster—the most thrifty, civilised, intelligent, and austere of the East Indians, among whom are counted the richest native merchants of Bombay—were celebrating a sort of religious carnival, with processions and shows, in the midst of which Indian dancing-girls, clothed in rose-coloured gauze, looped up with gold and silver, danced airily, but with perfect modesty, to the sound of viols and the clanging of tambourines. It is needless to say that Passepartout watched these curious ceremonies with staring eyes and gaping mouth, and that his countenance was that of the greenest booby imaginable.

Unhappily for his master, as well as himself, his curiosity drew him unconsciously farther off than he intended to go. At last, having seen the Parsee carnival wind away in the distance, he was turning his steps towards the station, when he happened to espy the splendid pagoda on Malabar Hill, and was seized with an irresistible desire to see its interior. He was quite ignorant that it is forbidden to Christians to enter certain Indian temples, and that even the faithful must not go in without first leaving their shoes outside the door. It may be said here that the wise policy of the British Government severely punishes a disregard of the practices of the native religions.

Passepartout, however, thinking no harm, went in like a simple tourist, and was soon lost in admiration of the splendid Brahmin ornamentation which everywhere met his eyes, when of a sudden he found himself sprawling on the sacred flagging. He looked up to behold three enraged priests, who forthwith fell upon him; tore off his shoes, and began to beat him with loud, savage exclamations. The agile Frenchman was soon upon his feet again, and lost no time in knocking down two of his long-gowned adversaries with his fists and a vigorous application of his toes; then, rushing out of the pagoda as fast as his legs could carry him, he soon escaped the third priest by mingling with the crowd in the streets.

At five minutes before eight, Passepartout, hatless, shoeless, and having in the squabble lost his package of shirts and shoes, rushed breathlessly into the station.

Fix, who had followed Mr. Fogg to the station, and saw that he was really going to leave Bombay, was there, upon the platform. He had resolved to follow the supposed robber to Calcutta, and farther, if necessary. Passepartout did not observe the detective, who stood in an obscure corner; but Fix heard him relate his adventures in a few words to Mr. Fogg.

"I hope that this will not happen again," said Phileas Fogg coldly, as he got into the train. Poor Passepartout, quite crestfallen, followed his master without a word. Fix was on the point of entering another carriage, when an idea struck him which induced him to alter his plan.

"No, I'll stay," muttered he. "An offence has been committed on Indian soil. I've got my man."

Just then the locomotive gave a sharp screech, and the train passed out into the darkness of the night.

HE KNOCKED DOWN TWO OF HIS ADVERSARIES

CHAPTER XI

IN WHICH PHILEAS FOGG SECURES A CURIOUS MEANS OF CONVEYANCE AT A FABULOUS PRICE

The train had started punctually. Among the passengers were a number of officers, Government officials, and opium and indigo merchants, whose business called them to the eastern coast. Passepartout rode in the same carriage with his master, and a third passenger occupied a seat opposite to them. This was Sir Francis Cromarty, one of Mr. Fogg's whist partners on the Mongolia, now on his way to join his corps at Benares. Sir Francis was a tall, fair man of fifty, who had greatly distinguished himself in the last Sepoy revolt. He made India his home, only paying brief visits to England at rare intervals; and was almost as familiar as a native with the customs, history, and character of India and its people. But Phileas Fogg, who was not travelling, but only describing a circumference, took no pains to inquire into these subjects; he was a solid body, traversing an orbit around the terrestrial globe, according to the laws of rational mechanics. He was at this moment calculating in his mind the number of hours spent since his departure from London, and, had it been in his nature to make a useless demonstration, would have rubbed his hands for satisfaction. Sir Francis Cromarty had observed the oddity of his travelling companion—although the only opportunity he had for studying him had been while he was dealing the cards, and between two rubbers—and questioned himself whether a human heart really beat beneath this cold exterior, and whether Phileas Fogg had any sense of the beauties of nature. The brigadier-general was free to mentally confess that, of all the eccentric persons he had ever met, none was comparable to this product of the exact sciences.

Phileas Fogg had not concealed from Sir Francis his design of going round the world, nor the circumstances under which he set out; and the general only saw in the wager a useless eccentricity and a lack of sound common sense. In the way this strange gentleman was going on, he would leave the world without having done any good to himself or anybody else.

An hour after leaving Bombay the train had passed the viaducts and the Island of Salcette, and had got into the open country. At Callyan they reached the junction of the branch line which descends towards south-eastern India by Kandallah and Pounah; and, passing Pauwell, they entered the defiles of the mountains, with their basalt bases, and their summits crowned with thick and verdant forests. Phileas Fogg and Sir Francis Cromarty exchanged a few words from time to time, and now Sir Francis, reviving the conversation, observed, "Some years ago, Mr. Fogg, you would have met with a delay at this point which would probably have lost you your wager."

"How so, Sir Francis?"

"Because the railway stopped at the base of these mountains, which the passengers were obliged to cross in palanquins or on ponies to Kandallah, on the other side."

"Such a delay would not have deranged my plans in the least," said Mr. Fogg. "I have constantly foreseen the likelihood of certain obstacles."

"But, Mr. Fogg," pursued Sir Francis, "you run the risk of having some difficulty about this worthy fellow's adventure at the pagoda." Passepartout, his feet comfortably wrapped in his travelling-blanket, was sound asleep and did not dream that anybody was talking about him. "The Government is very severe upon that kind of offence. It takes particular care that the religious customs of the Indians should be respected, and if your servant were caught—"

"Very well, Sir Francis," replied Mr. Fogg; "if he had been caught he would have been condemned and punished, and then would have quietly returned to Europe. I don't see how this affair could have delayed his master."

The conversation fell again. During the night the train left the mountains behind, and passed Nassik, and the next day proceeded over the flat, well-cultivated country of the Khandeish, with its straggling villages, above which rose the minarets of the pagodas. This fertile territory is watered by numerous small rivers and limpid streams, mostly tributaries of the Godavery.

Passepartout, on waking and looking out, could not realise that he was actually crossing India in a railway train. The locomotive, guided by an English engineer and fed with English coal, threw out its smoke upon cotton, coffee, nutmeg, clove, and pepper plantations, while the steam curled in spirals around groups of palm-trees, in the midst of which were seen picturesque bungalows, viharis (sort of abandoned monasteries), and marvellous temples enriched by the exhaustless ornamentation of Indian architecture. Then they came upon vast tracts extending to the horizon, with jungles inhabited by snakes and tigers, which fled at the noise of the train; succeeded by forests penetrated by the railway, and still haunted by elephants which, with pensive eyes, gazed at the train as it passed. The travellers crossed, beyond Milligaum, the fatal country so often stained with blood by the sectaries of the goddess Kali. Not far off rose Ellora, with its graceful pagodas, and the famous Aurungabad, capital of the ferocious Aureng-Zeb, now the chief town of one of the detached provinces of the kingdom of the Nizam. It was thereabouts that Feringhea, the Thuggee chief, king of the stranglers, held his sway. These ruffians, united by a secret bond, strangled victims of every age in honour of the goddess Death, without ever shedding blood; there was a period when this part of the country could scarcely be travelled over without corpses being found in every direction. The English Government has succeeded in greatly diminishing these murders, though the Thuggees still exist, and pursue the exercise of their horrible rites.

At half-past twelve the train stopped at Burhampoor where Passepartout was able to purchase some Indian slippers, ornamented with false pearls, in which, with evident vanity, he proceeded to encase his feet. The travellers made a hasty breakfast and started off for Assurghur, after skirting for a little the banks of the small river Tapty, which empties into the Gulf of Cambray, near Surat.

Passepartout was now plunged into absorbing reverie. Up to his arrival at Bombay, he had entertained hopes that their journey would end there; but, now that they were plainly whirling across India at full speed, a sudden change had come over the spirit of his dreams. His old vagabond nature returned to him; the fantastic ideas of his youth once more took possession of him. He came to regard his master's project as intended in good earnest, believed in the reality of the bet, and therefore in the tour of the world and the necessity of making it without fail within the designated period. Already he began to worry about possible delays, and accidents which might happen on the way. He recognised himself as being personally interested in the wager, and trembled at the thought that he might have been the means of losing it by his unpardonable folly of the night before. Being much less cool-headed than Mr. Fogg, he was much more restless, counting

THE SMOKE FORMED INTO SPIRAL COLUMNS

and recounting the days passed over, uttering maledictions when the train stopped, and accusing it of sluggishness, and mentally blaming Mr. Fogg for not having bribed the engineer. The worthy fellow was ignorant that, while it was possible by such means to hasten the rate of a steamer, it could not be done on the railway.

The train entered the defiles of the Sutpour Mountains, which separate the Khandeish from Bundelcund, towards evening. The next day Sir Francis Cromarty asked Passepartout what time it was; to which, on consulting his watch, he replied that it was three in the morning. This famous timepiece, always regulated on the Greenwich meridian, which was now some seventy-seven degrees westward, was at least four hours slow. Sir Francis corrected Passepartout's time, whereupon the latter made the same remark that he had done to Fix; and upon the general insisting that the watch should be regulated in each new meridian, since he was constantly going eastward, that is in the face of the sun, and therefore the days were shorter by four minutes for each degree gone over, Passepartout obstinately refused to alter his watch, which he kept at London time. It was an innocent delusion which could harm no one.

The train stopped, at eight o'clock, in the midst of a glade some fifteen miles beyond Rothal, where there were several bungalows, and workmen's cabins. The conductor, passing along the carriages, shouted, "Passengers will get out here!"

Phileas Fogg looked at Sir Francis Cromarty for an explanation; but the general could not tell what meant a halt in the midst of this forest of dates and acacias.

Passepartout, not less surprised, rushed out and speedily returned, crying: "Monsieur, no more railway!"

"What do you mean?" asked Sir Francis.

"I mean to say that the train isn't going on."

The general at once stepped out, while Phileas Fogg calmly followed him, and they proceeded together to the conductor.

"Where are we?" asked Sir Francis.

"At the hamlet of Kholby."

"Do we stop here?"

"Certainly. The railway isn't finished."

"What! not finished?"

"No. There's still a matter of fifty miles to be laid from here to Allahabad, where the line begins again."

"But the papers announced the opening of the railway throughout."

"What would you have, officer? The papers were mistaken."

"Yet you sell tickets from Bombay to Calcutta," retorted Sir Francis, who was growing warm.

"No doubt," replied the conductor; "but the passengers know that they must provide means of transportation for themselves from Kholby to Allahabad."

Sir Francis was furious. Passepartout would willingly have knocked the conductor down, and did not dare to look at his master.

"Sir Francis," said Mr. Fogg quietly, "we will, if you please, look about for some means of conveyance to Allahabad."

"Mr. Fogg, this is a delay greatly to your disadvantage."

"No, Sir Francis; it was foreseen."

"What! You knew that the way—"

"Not at all; but I knew that some obstacle or other would sooner or later arise on my route. Nothing, therefore, is lost. I have two days, which I have already gained, to sacrifice. A steamer leaves Calcutta for Hong Kong at noon, on the 25th. This is the 22nd, and we shall reach Calcutta in time."

There was nothing to say to so confident a response.

It was but too true that the railway came to a termination at this point. The papers were like some watches, which have a way of getting too fast, and had been premature in their announcement of the completion of the line. The greater part of the travellers were aware of this interruption, and, leaving the train, they began to engage such vehicles as the village could provide four-wheeled palkigharis, waggons drawn by zebus, carriages that looked like perambulating pagodas, palanquins, ponies, and what not.

Mr. Fogg and Sir Francis Cromarty, after searching the village from end to end, came back without having found anything.

"I shall go afoot," said Phileas Fogg.

Passepartout, who had now rejoined his master, made a wry grimace, as he thought of his magnificent, but too frail Indian shoes. Happily he too had been looking about him, and, after a moment's hesitation, said, "Monsieur, I think I have found a means of conveyance."

"What?"

"An elephant! An elephant that belongs to an Indian who lives but a hundred steps from here."

"Let's go and see the elephant," replied Mr. Fogg.

THERE THEY FOUND THEMSELVES IN THE PRESENCE OF AN
ADMIRAL

They soon reached a small hut, near which, enclosed within some high palings, was the animal in question. An Indian came out of the hut, and, at their request, conducted them within the enclosure. The elephant, which its owner had reared, not for a beast of burden, but for warlike purposes, was half domesticated. The Indian had begun already, by often irritating him, and feeding him every three months on sugar and butter, to impart to him a ferocity not in his nature, this method being often employed by those who train the Indian elephants for battle. Happily, however, for Mr. Fogg, the animal's instruction in this direction had not gone far, and the elephant still preserved his natural gentleness. Kiouni—this was the name of the beast—could doubtless travel rapidly for a long time, and, in default of any other means of conveyance, Mr. Fogg resolved to hire him. But elephants are far from cheap in India, where they are becoming scarce, the males, which alone are suitable for circus shows, are much sought, especially as but few of them are domesticated. When therefore Mr. Fogg proposed to the Indian to hire Kiouni, he refused point-blank. Mr. Fogg persisted, offering the excessive sum of ten pounds an hour for the loan of the beast to Allahabad. Refused. Twenty pounds? Refused also. Forty pounds? Still refused. Passepartout jumped at each advance; but the Indian declined to be tempted. Yet the offer was an alluring one, for, supposing it took the elephant fifteen hours to reach Allahabad, his owner would receive no less than six hundred pounds sterling.

Phileas Fogg, without getting in the least flurried, then proposed to purchase the animal outright, and at first offered a thousand pounds for him. The Indian, perhaps thinking he was going to make a great bargain, still refused.

Sir Francis Cromarty took Mr. Fogg aside, and begged him to reflect before he went any further; to which that gentleman replied that he was not in the habit of acting rashly, that a bet of twenty thousand pounds was at stake, that the elephant was absolutely necessary to him, and that he would secure him if he had to pay twenty times his value. Returning to the Indian, whose small, sharp eyes, glistening with avarice, betrayed that with him it was only a question of how great a price he could obtain. Mr. Fogg offered first twelve hundred, then fifteen hundred, eighteen hundred, two thousand pounds. Passepartout, usually so rubicund, was fairly white with suspense.

At two thousand pounds the Indian yielded.

"What a price, good heavens!" cried Passepartout, "for an elephant."

It only remained now to find a guide, which was comparatively easy.

A young Parsee, with an intelligent face, offered his services, which Mr. Fogg accepted, promising so generous a reward as to materially stimulate his zeal. The elephant was led out and equipped. The Parsee, who was an accomplished elephant driver, covered his back with a sort of saddle-cloth, and attached to each of his flanks some curiously uncomfortable howdahs. Phileas Fogg paid the Indian with some banknotes which he extracted from the famous carpet-bag, a proceeding that seemed to deprive poor Passepartout of his vitals. Then he offered to carry Sir Francis to Allahabad, which the brigadier gratefully accepted, as one traveller the more would not be likely to fatigue the gigantic beast. Provisions were purchased at Kholby, and, while Sir Francis and Mr. Fogg took the howdahs on either side, Passepartout got astride the saddle-cloth between them. The Parsee perched himself on the elephant's neck, and at nine o'clock they set out from the village, the animal marching off through the dense forest of palms by the shortest cut.

CHAPTER XII

IN WHICH PHILEAS FOGG AND HIS COMPANIONS VENTURE ACROSS THE INDIAN FORESTS, AND WHAT ENSUED

In order to shorten the journey, the guide passed to the left of the line where the railway was still in process of being built. This line, owing to the capricious turnings of the Vindhia Mountains, did not pursue a straight course. The Parsee, who was quite familiar with the roads and paths in the district, declared that they would gain twenty miles by striking directly through the forest.

Phileas Fogg and Sir Francis Cromarty, plunged to the neck in the peculiar howdahs provided for them, were horribly jostled by the swift trotting of the elephant, spurred on as he was by the skilful Parsee; but they endured the discomfort with true British phlegm, talking little, and scarcely able to catch a glimpse of each other. As for Passepartout, who was mounted on the beast's back, and received the direct force of each concussion as he trod along, he was very careful, in accordance with his master's advice, to keep his tongue from between his teeth, as it would otherwise have been bitten off short. The worthy fellow bounced from the elephant's neck to his rump, and vaulted like a clown on a spring-board; yet he laughed in the midst of his bouncing, and from time to time took a piece of sugar out of his pocket, and inserted it in Kiouni's trunk, who received it without in the least slackening his regular trot.

After two hours the guide stopped the elephant, and gave him an hour for rest, during which Kiouni, after quenching his thirst at a neighbouring spring, set to devouring the branches and shrubs round about him. Neither Sir Francis nor Mr. Fogg regretted the delay, and both descended with a feeling of relief. "Why, he's made of iron!" exclaimed the general, gazing admiringly on Kiouni.

PASSEPARTOUT'S UNEASY RIDE ON THE BACK OF THE ELE-
PHANT.

"Of forged iron," replied Passepartout, as he set about preparing a hasty breakfast.

At noon the Parsee gave the signal of departure. The country soon presented a very savage aspect. Copses of dates and dwarf-palms succeeded the dense forests; then vast, dry plains, dotted with scanty shrubs, and sown with great blocks of syenite. All this portion of Bundelcund, which is little frequented by travellers, is inhabited by a fanatical population, hardened in the most horrible practices of the Hindoo faith. The English have not been able to secure complete dominion over this territory, which is subjected to the influence of rajahs, whom it is almost impossible to reach in their inaccessible mountain fastnesses. The travellers several times saw bands of ferocious Indians, who, when they perceived the elephant striding across-country, made angry and threatening motions. The Parsee avoided them as much as possible. Few animals were observed on the route; even the monkeys hurried from their path with contortions and grimaces which convulsed Passepartout with laughter.

In the midst of his gaiety, however, one thought troubled the worthy servant. What would Mr. Fogg do with the elephant when he got to Allahabad? Would he carry him on with him? Impossible! The cost of transporting him would make him ruinously expensive. Would he sell him, or set him free? The estimable beast certainly deserved some consideration. Should Mr. Fogg choose to make him, Passepartout, a present of Kiouni, he would be very much embarrassed; and these thoughts did not cease worrying him for a long time.

The principal chain of the Vindhias was crossed by eight in the evening, and another halt was made on the northern slope, in a ruined bungalow. They had gone nearly twenty-five miles that day, and an equal distance still separated them from the station of Allahabad.

The night was cold. The Parsee lit a fire in the bungalow with a few dry branches, and the warmth was very grateful, provisions purchased at Kholby sufficed for supper, and the travellers ate ravenously. The conversation, beginning with a few disconnected phrases, soon gave place to loud and steady snores. The guide watched Kiouni, who slept standing, bolstering himself against the trunk of a large tree. Nothing occurred during the night to disturb the slumberers, although occasional growls from panthers and chatterings of monkeys broke the silence; the more formidable beasts made no cries or hostile demonstration against the occupants of the bungalow. Sir Francis slept heavily, like an honest soldier overcome with fatigue.

Passepartout was wrapped in uneasy dreams of the bouncing of the day before. As for Mr. Fogg, he slumbered as peacefully as if he had been in his serene mansion in Saville Row.

The journey was resumed at six in the morning; the guide hoped to reach Allahabad by evening. In that case, Mr. Fogg would only lose a part of the forty-eight hours saved since the beginning of the tour. Kiouni, resuming his rapid gait, soon descended the lower spurs of the Vindhias, and towards noon they passed by the village of Kallenger, on the Cani, one of the branches of the Ganges. The guide avoided inhabited places, thinking it safer to keep the open country, which lies along the first depressions of the basin of the great river. Allahabad was now only twelve miles to the north-east. They stopped under a clump of bananas, the fruit of which, as healthy as bread and as succulent as cream, was amply partaken of and appreciated.

At two o'clock the guide entered a thick forest which extended several miles; he preferred to travel under cover of the woods. They had not as yet had any unpleasant encounters, and the journey seemed on the point of being successfully accomplished, when the elephant, becoming restless, suddenly stopped.

It was then four o'clock.

"What's the matter?" asked Sir Francis, putting out his head.

"I don't know, officer," replied the Parsee, listening attentively to a confused murmur which came through the thick branches.

The murmur soon became more distinct; it now seemed like a distant concert of human voices accompanied by brass instruments. Passepartout was all eyes and ears. Mr. Fogg patiently waited without a word. The Parsee jumped to the ground, fastened the elephant to a tree, and plunged into the thicket. He soon returned, saying:

"A procession of Brahmins is coming this way. We must prevent their seeing us, if possible."

The guide unloosed the elephant and led him into a thicket, at the same time asking the travellers not to stir. He held himself ready to bestride the animal at a moment's notice, should flight become necessary; but he evidently thought that the procession of the faithful would pass without perceiving them amid the thick foliage, in which they were wholly concealed.

The discordant tones of the voices and instruments drew nearer, and now droning songs mingled with the sound of the tambourines and cymbals. The head of the procession soon appeared beneath the trees, a hundred paces away; and the strange figures who performed the religious

BANDS OF HINDOOS OF BOTH SEXES

ceremony were easily distinguished through the branches. First came the priests, with mitres on their heads, and clothed in long lace robes. They were surrounded by men, women, and children, who sang a kind of lugubrious psalm, interrupted at regular intervals by the tambourines and cymbals; while behind them was drawn a car with large wheels, the spokes of which represented serpents entwined with each other. Upon the car, which was drawn by four richly caparisoned zebus, stood a hideous statue with four arms, the body coloured a dull red, with haggard eyes, dishevelled hair, protruding tongue, and lips tinted with betel. It stood upright upon the figure of a prostrate and headless giant.

Sir Francis, recognising the statue, whispered, "The goddess Kali; the goddess of love and death."

"Of death, perhaps," muttered back Passepartout, "but of love—that ugly old hag? Never!"

The Parsee made a motion to keep silence.

A group of old fakirs were capering and making a wild ado round the statue; these were striped with ochre, and covered with cuts whence their blood issued drop by drop—stupid fanatics, who, in the great Indian ceremonies, still throw themselves under the wheels of Juggernaut. Some Brahmins, clad in all the sumptuousness of Oriental apparel, and leading a woman who faltered at every step, followed. This woman was young, and as fair as a European. Her head and neck, shoulders, ears, arms, hands, and toes were loaded down with jewels and gems with bracelets, earrings, and rings; while a tunic bordered with gold, and covered with a light muslin robe, betrayed the outline of her form.

The guards who followed the young woman presented a violent contrast to her, armed as they were with naked sabres hung at their waists, and long damascened pistols, and bearing a corpse on a palanquin. It was the body of an old man, gorgeously arrayed in the habiliments of a rajah, wearing, as in life, a turban embroidered with pearls, a robe of tissue of silk and gold, a scarf of cashmere sewed with diamonds, and the magnificent weapons of a Hindoo prince. Next came the musicians and a rearguard of capering fakirs, whose cries sometimes drowned the noise of the instruments; these closed the procession.

Sir Francis watched the procession with a sad countenance, and, turning to the guide, said, "A suttee."

The Parsee nodded, and put his finger to his lips. The procession slowly wound under the trees, and soon its last ranks disappeared in the depths of the wood. The songs gradually died away; occasionally cries were heard in the distance, until at last all was silence again.

Phileas Fogg had heard what Sir Francis said, and, as soon as the procession had disappeared, asked: "What is a suttee?"

"A suttee," returned the general, "is a human sacrifice, but a voluntary one. The woman you have just seen will be burned to-morrow at the dawn of day."

"Oh, the scoundrels!" cried Passepartout, who could not repress his indignation.

"And the corpse?" asked Mr. Fogg.

"Is that of the prince, her husband," said the guide; "an independent rajah of Bundelcund."

"Is it possible," resumed Phileas Fogg, his voice betraying not the least emotion, "that these barbarous customs still exist in India, and that the English have been unable to put a stop to them?"

"These sacrifices do not occur in the larger portion of India," replied Sir Francis; "but we have no power over these savage territories, and especially here in Bundelcund. The whole district north of the Vindhias is the theatre of incessant murders and pillage."

"The poor wretch!" exclaimed Passepartout, "to be burned alive!"

"Yes," returned Sir Francis, "burned alive. And, if she were not, you cannot conceive what treatment she would be obliged to submit to from her relatives. They would shave off her hair, feed her on a scanty allowance of rice, treat her with contempt; she would be looked upon as an unclean creature, and would die in some corner, like a scurvy dog. The prospect of so frightful an existence drives these poor creatures to the sacrifice much more than love or religious fanaticism. Sometimes, however, the sacrifice is really voluntary, and it requires the active interference of the Government to prevent it. Several years ago, when I was living at Bombay, a young widow asked permission of the governor to be burned along with her husband's body; but, as you may imagine, he refused. The woman left the town, took refuge with an independent rajah, and there carried out her self-devoted purpose."

While Sir Francis was speaking, the guide shook his head several times, and now said: "The sacrifice which will take place to-morrow at dawn is not a voluntary one."

"How do you know?"

"Everybody knows about this affair in Bundelcund."

IT WAS A YOUNG WOMAN

"But the wretched creature did not seem to be making any resistance," observed Sir Francis.

"That was because they had intoxicated her with fumes of hemp and opium."

"But where are they taking her?"

"To the pagoda of Pillaji, two miles from here; she will pass the night there."

"And the sacrifice will take place—"

"To-morrow, at the first light of dawn."

The guide now led the elephant out of the thicket, and leaped upon his neck. Just at the moment that he was about to urge Kiouni forward with a peculiar whistle, Mr. Fogg stopped him, and, turning to Sir Francis Cromarty, said, "Suppose we save this woman."

"Save the woman, Mr. Fogg!"

"I have yet twelve hours to spare; I can devote them to that."

"Why, you are a man of heart!"

"Sometimes," replied Phileas Fogg, quietly; "when I have the time."

CHAPTER XIII

IN WHICH PASSEPARTOUT RECEIVES A NEW PROOF THAT FORTUNE FAVORS THE BRAVE

The project was a bold one, full of difficulty, perhaps impracticable. Mr. Fogg was going to risk life, or at least liberty, and therefore the success of his tour. But he did not hesitate, and he found in Sir Francis Cromarty an enthusiastic ally.

As for Passepartout, he was ready for anything that might be proposed. His master's idea charmed him; he perceived a heart, a soul, under that icy exterior. He began to love Phileas Fogg.

There remained the guide: what course would he adopt? Would he not take part with the Indians? In default of his assistance, it was necessary to be assured of his neutrality.

Sir Francis frankly put the question to him.

"Officers," replied the guide, "I am a Parsee, and this woman is a Parsee. Command me as you will."

"Excellent!" said Mr. Fogg.

"However," resumed the guide, "it is certain, not only that we shall risk our lives, but horrible tortures, if we are taken."

"That is foreseen," replied Mr. Fogg. "I think we must wait till night before acting."

"I think so," said the guide.

The worthy Indian then gave some account of the victim, who, he said, was a celebrated beauty of the Parsee race, and the daughter of a wealthy Bombay merchant. She had received a thoroughly English education in that city, and, from her manners and intelligence, would be thought an European. Her name was Aouda. Left an orphan, she was married against her will to the old rajah of Bundelcund; and, knowing the fate that awaited her, she escaped, was retaken, and devoted by the rajah's relatives, who had an interest in her death, to the sacrifice from which it seemed she could not escape.

The Parsee's narrative only confirmed Mr. Fogg and his companions in their generous design. It was decided that the guide should direct the elephant towards the pagoda of Pillaji, which he accordingly approached as quickly as possible. They halted, half an hour afterwards, in a copse, some five hundred feet from the pagoda, where they were well concealed; but they could hear the groans and cries of the fakirs distinctly.

They then discussed the means of getting at the victim. The guide was familiar with the pagoda of Pillaji, in which, as he declared, the young woman was imprisoned. Could they enter any of its doors while the whole party of Indians was plunged in a drunken sleep, or was it safer to attempt to make a hole in the walls? This could only be determined at the moment and the place themselves; but it was certain that the abduction must be made that night, and not when, at break of day, the victim was led to her funeral pyre. Then no human intervention could save her.

As soon as night fell, about six o'clock, they decided to make a reconnaissance around the pagoda. The cries of the fakirs were just ceasing; the Indians were in the act of plunging themselves into the drunkenness caused by liquid opium mingled with hemp, and it might be possible to slip between them to the temple itself.

The Parsee, leading the others, noiselessly crept through the wood, and in ten minutes they found themselves on the banks of a small stream, whence, by the light of the rosin torches, they perceived a pyre of wood, on the top of which lay the embalmed body of the rajah, which was to be burned with his wife. The pagoda, whose minarets loomed above the trees in the deepening dusk, stood a hundred steps away.

"Come!" whispered the guide.

He slipped more cautiously than ever through the brush, followed by his companions; the silence around was only broken by the low murmuring of the wind among the branches.

Soon the Parsee stopped on the borders of the glade, which was lit up by the torches. The ground was covered by groups of the Indians, motionless in their drunken sleep; it seemed a battlefield strewn with the dead. Men, women, and children lay together.

In the background, among the trees, the pagoda of Pillaji loomed distinctly. Much to the guide's disappointment, the guards of the rajah, lighted by torches, were watching at the doors and marching to and fro with

THE RAJAH'S GUARDS

naked sabres; probably the priests, too, were watching within.

The Parsee, now convinced that it was impossible to force an entrance to the temple, advanced no farther, but led his companions back again. Phileas Fogg and Sir Francis Cromarty also saw that nothing could be attempted in that direction. They stopped, and engaged in a whispered colloquy.

"It is only eight now," said the brigadier, "and these guards may also go to sleep."

"It is not impossible," returned the Parsee.

They lay down at the foot of a tree, and waited.

The time seemed long; the guide ever and anon left them to take an observation on the edge of the wood, but the guards watched steadily by the glare of the torches, and a dim light crept through the windows of the pagoda.

They waited till midnight; but no change took place among the guards, and it became apparent that their yielding to sleep could not be counted on. The other plan must be carried out; an opening in the walls of the pagoda must be made. It remained to ascertain whether the priests were watching by the side of their victim as assiduously as were the soldiers at the door.

After a last consultation, the guide announced that he was ready for the attempt, and advanced, followed by the others. They took a roundabout way, so as to get at the pagoda on the rear. They reached the walls about half-past twelve, without having met anyone; here there was no guard, nor were there either windows or doors.

The night was dark. The moon, on the wane, scarcely left the horizon, and was covered with heavy clouds; the height of the trees deepened the darkness.

It was not enough to reach the walls; an opening in them must be accomplished, and to attain this purpose the party only had their pocket-knives. Happily the temple walls were built of brick and wood, which could be penetrated with little difficulty; after one brick had been taken out, the rest would yield easily.

They set noiselessly to work, and the Parsee on one side and Passepartout on the other began to loosen the bricks so as to make an aperture two feet wide. They were getting on rapidly, when suddenly a cry was heard in the interior of the temple, followed almost instantly by other cries replying from the outside. Passepartout and the guide stopped. Had they been heard? Was the alarm being given? Common prudence urged them to retire, and they did so, followed by Phileas Fogg and Sir Francis. They again hid themselves in the wood, and waited till the disturbance, whatever it might be, ceased, holding themselves ready to resume their attempt without delay. But, awkwardly enough, the guards now appeared at the rear of the temple, and there installed themselves, in readiness to prevent a surprise.

It would be difficult to describe the disappointment of the party, thus interrupted in their work. They could not now reach the victim; how, then, could they save her? Sir Francis shook his fists, Passepartout was beside himself, and the guide gnashed his teeth with rage. The tranquil Fogg waited, without betraying any emotion.

"We have nothing to do but to go away," whispered Sir Francis.

"Nothing but to go away," echoed the guide.

"Stop," said Fogg. "I am only due at Allahabad tomorrow before noon."

"But what can you hope to do?" asked Sir Francis. "In a few hours it will be daylight, and—"

"The chance which now seems lost may present itself at the last moment."

Sir Francis would have liked to read Phileas Fogg's eyes. What was this cool Englishman thinking of? Was he planning to make a rush for the young woman at the very moment of the sacrifice, and boldly snatch her from her executioners?

This would be utter folly, and it was hard to admit that Fogg was such a fool. Sir Francis consented, however, to remain to the end of this terrible drama. The guide led them to the rear of the glade, where they were able to observe the sleeping groups.

Meanwhile Passepartout, who had perched himself on the lower branches of a tree, was resolving an idea which had at first struck him like a flash, and which was now firmly lodged in his brain.

He had commenced by saying to himself, "What folly!" and then he repeated, "Why not, after all? It's a chance,—perhaps the only one; and with such sots!" Thinking thus, he slipped, with the suppleness of a serpent, to the lowest branches, the ends of which bent almost to the ground.

The hours passed, and the lighter shades now announced the approach of day, though it was not yet light. This was the moment. The slumbering multitude became animated, the tambourines sounded, songs and cries arose; the hour of the sacrifice had come. The doors of the pagoda swung open, and a bright light escaped from its interior, in the midst of which Mr. Fogg and Sir Francis espied the victim. She seemed, having shaken off the stupor of intoxication, to be striving to escape from her executioner. Sir

THERE WAS A CRY OF TERROR

Francis's heart throbbed; and, convulsively seizing Mr. Fogg's hand, found in it an open knife. Just at this moment the crowd began to move. The young woman had again fallen into a stupor caused by the fumes of hemp, and passed among the fakirs, who escorted her with their wild, religious cries.

Phileas Fogg and his companions, mingling in the rear ranks of the crowd, followed; and in two minutes they reached the banks of the stream, and stopped fifty paces from the pyre, upon which still lay the rajah's corpse. In the semi-obscurity they saw the victim, quite senseless, stretched out beside her husband's body. Then a torch was brought, and the wood, heavily soaked with oil, instantly took fire.

At this moment Sir Francis and the guide seized Phileas Fogg, who, in an instant of mad generosity, was about to rush upon the pyre. But he had quickly pushed them aside, when the whole scene suddenly changed. A cry of terror arose. The whole multitude prostrated themselves, terror-stricken, on the ground.

The old rajah was not dead, then, since he rose of a sudden, like a spectre, took up his wife in his arms, and descended from the pyre in the midst of the clouds of smoke, which only heightened his ghostly appearance.

Fakirs and soldiers and priests, seized with instant terror, lay there, with their faces on the ground, not daring to lift their eyes and behold such a prodigy.

The inanimate victim was borne along by the vigorous arms which supported her, and which she did not seem in the least to burden. Mr. Fogg and Sir Francis stood erect, the Parsee bowed his head, and Passepartout was, no doubt, scarcely less stupefied.

The resuscitated rajah approached Sir Francis and Mr. Fogg, and, in an abrupt tone, said, "Let us be off!"

It was Passepartout himself, who had slipped upon the pyre in the midst of the smoke and, profiting by the still overhanging darkness, had delivered the young woman from death! It was Passepartout who, playing his part with a happy audacity, had passed through the crowd amid the general terror.

A moment after all four of the party had disappeared in the woods, and the elephant was bearing them away at a rapid pace. But the cries and noise, and a ball which whizzed through Phileas Fogg's hat, apprised them that the trick had been discovered.

The old rajah's body, indeed, now appeared upon the burning pyre; and the priests, recovered from their terror, perceived that an abduction had taken place. They hastened into the forest, followed by the soldiers, who fired a volley after the fugitives; but the latter rapidly increased the distance between them, and ere long found themselves beyond the reach of the bullets and arrows.

CHAPTER XIV

IN WHICH PHILEAS FOGG DESCENDS THE WHOLE LENGTH OF THE BEAUTIFUL VALLEY OF THE GANGES WITHOUT EVER THINKING OF SEEING IT

The rash exploit had been accomplished; and for an hour Passepartout laughed gaily at his success. Sir Francis pressed the worthy fellow's hand, and his master said, "Well done!" which, from him, was high commendation; to which Passepartout replied that all the credit of the affair belonged to Mr. Fogg. As for him, he had only been struck with a "queer" idea; and he laughed to think that for a few moments he, Passepartout, the ex-gymnast, ex-sergeant fireman, had been the spouse of a charming woman, a venerable, embalmed rajah! As for the young Indian woman, she had been unconscious throughout of what was passing, and now, wrapped up in a travelling-blanket, was reposing in one of the howdahs.

The elephant, thanks to the skilful guidance of the Parsee, was advancing rapidly through the still darksome forest, and, an hour after leaving the pagoda, had crossed a vast plain. They made a halt at seven o'clock, the young woman being still in a state of complete prostration. The guide made her drink a little brandy and water, but the drowsiness which stupefied her could not yet be shaken off. Sir Francis, who was familiar with the effects of the intoxication produced by the fumes of hemp, reassured his companions on her account. But he was more disturbed at the prospect of her future fate. He told Phileas Fogg that, should Aouda remain in India, she would inevitably fall again into the hands of her executioners. These fanatics were scattered throughout the county, and would, despite the English police, recover their victim at Madras, Bombay, or Calcutta. She would only be safe by quitting India for ever.

Phileas Fogg replied that he would reflect upon the matter.

The station at Allahabad was reached about ten o'clock, and, the interrupted line of railway being resumed, would enable them to reach Calcutta in less than twenty-four hours. Phileas Fogg would thus be able to arrive in time to take the steamer which left Calcutta the next day, October 25th, at noon, for Hong Kong.

The young woman was placed in one of the waiting-rooms of the station, whilst Passepartout was charged with purchasing for her various articles of toilet, a dress, shawl, and some furs; for which his master gave him unlimited credit. Passepartout started off forthwith, and found himself in the streets of Allahabad, that is, the City of God, one of the most venerated in India, being built at the junction of the two sacred rivers, Ganges and Jumna, the waters of which attract pilgrims from every part of the peninsula. The Ganges, according to the legends of the Ramayana, rises in heaven, whence, owing to Brahma's agency, it descends to the earth.

Passepartout made it a point, as he made his purchases, to take a good look at the city. It was formerly defended by a noble fort, which has since become a state prison; its commerce has dwindled away, and Passepartout in vain looked about him for such a bazaar as he used to frequent in Regent Street. At last he came upon an elderly, crusty Jew, who sold second-hand articles, and from whom he purchased a dress of Scotch stuff, a large mantle, and a fine otter-skin pelisse, for which he did not hesitate to pay seventy-five pounds. He then returned triumphantly to the station.

The influence to which the priests of Pillaji had subjected Aouda began gradually to yield, and she became more herself, so that her fine eyes resumed all their soft Indian expression.

When the poet-king, Ucaf Uddaul, celebrates the charms of the queen of Ahmehnagara, he speaks thus:

"Her shining tresses, divided in two parts, encircle the harmonious contour of her white and delicate cheeks, brilliant in their glow and freshness. Her ebony brows have the form and charm of the bow of Kama, the god of love, and beneath her long silken lashes the purest reflections and a celestial light swim, as in the sacred lakes of Himalaya, in the black pupils of her great clear eyes. Her teeth, fine, equal, and white, glitter between her smiling lips like dewdrops in a passion-flower's half-enveloped breast. Her delicately formed ears, her vermilion hands, her little feet, curved and tender as the lotus-bud, glitter with the brilliancy of the loveliest pearls of Ceylon, the most dazzling diamonds of Golconda. Her narrow and supple waist, which a hand may clasp around, sets forth the outline of her rounded

PASSEPARTOUT NOT AT ALL FRIGHTENED

figure and the beauty of her bosom, where youth in its flower displays the wealth of its treasures; and beneath the silken folds of her tunic she seems to have been modelled in pure silver by the godlike hand of Vicvarcarma, the immortal sculptor."

It is enough to say, without applying this poetical rhapsody to Aouda, that she was a charming woman, in all the European acceptation of the phrase. She spoke English with great purity, and the guide had not exaggerated in saying that the young Parsee had been transformed by her bringing up.

The train was about to start from Allahabad, and Mr. Fogg proceeded to pay the guide the price agreed upon for his service, and not a farthing more; which astonished Passepartout, who remembered all that his master owed to the guide's devotion. He had, indeed, risked his life in the adventure at Pillaji, and, if he should be caught afterwards by the Indians, he would with difficulty escape their vengeance. Kiouni, also, must be disposed of. What should be done with the elephant, which had been so dearly purchased? Phileas Fogg had already determined this question.

"Parsee," said he to the guide, "you have been serviceable and devoted. I have paid for your service, but not for your devotion. Would you like to have this elephant? He is yours."

The guide's eyes glistened.

"Your honour is giving me a fortune!" cried he.

"Take him, guide," returned Mr. Fogg, "and I shall still be your debtor."

"Good!" exclaimed Passepartout. "Take him, friend. Kiouni is a brave and faithful beast." And, going up to the elephant, he gave him several lumps of sugar, saying, "Here, Kiouni, here, here."

The elephant grunted out his satisfaction, and, clasping Passepartout around the waist with his trunk, lifted him as high as his head. Passepartout, not in the least alarmed, caressed the animal, which replaced him gently on the ground.

Soon after, Phileas Fogg, Sir Francis Cromarty, and Passepartout, installed in a carriage with Aouda, who had the best seat, were whirling at full speed towards Benares. It was a run of eighty miles, and was accomplished in two hours. During the journey, the young woman fully recovered her senses. What was her astonishment to find herself in this carriage, on the railway, dressed in European habiliments, and with travellers who were quite strangers to her! Her companions first set about fully reviving her with a little liquor, and then Sir Francis narrated to her what had passed, dwelling upon the courage with which Phileas Fogg had not hesitated to risk his life to save her, and recounting the happy sequel of the venture, the result of Passepartout's rash idea. Mr. Fogg said nothing; while Passepartout, abashed, kept repeating that "it wasn't worth telling."

Aouda pathetically thanked her deliverers, rather with tears than words; her fine eyes interpreted her gratitude better than her lips. Then, as her thoughts strayed back to the scene of the sacrifice, and recalled the dangers which still menaced her, she shuddered with terror.

Phileas Fogg understood what was passing in Aouda's mind, and offered, in order to reassure her, to escort her to Hong Kong, where she might remain safely until the affair was hushed up—an offer which she eagerly and gratefully accepted. She had, it seems, a Parsee relation, who was one of the principal merchants of Hong Kong, which is wholly an English city, though on an island on the Chinese coast.

At half-past twelve the train stopped at Benares. The Brahmin legends assert that this city is built on the site of the ancient Casi, which, like Mahomet's tomb, was once suspended between heaven and earth; though the Benares of to-day, which the Orientalists call the Athens of India, stands quite unpoetically on the solid earth, Passepartout caught glimpses of its brick houses and clay huts, giving an aspect of desolation to the place, as the train entered it.

Benares was Sir Francis Cromarty's destination, the troops he was rejoining being encamped some miles northward of the city. He bade adieu to Phileas Fogg, wishing him all success, and expressing the hope that he would come that way again in a less original but more profitable fashion. Mr. Fogg lightly pressed him by the hand. The parting of Aouda, who did not forget what she owed to Sir Francis, betrayed more warmth; and, as for Passepartout, he received a hearty shake of the hand from the gallant general.

The railway, on leaving Benares, passed for a while along the valley of the Ganges. Through the windows of their carriage the travellers had glimpses of the diversified landscape of Behar, with its mountains clothed in verdure, its fields of barley, wheat, and corn, its jungles peopled with green alligators, its neat villages, and its still thickly-leaved forests. Elephants were bathing in the waters of the sacred river, and groups of Indians, despite the advanced season and chilly air, were performing solemnly their pious ablutions. These were fervent Brahmins, the bitterest foes of Buddhism, their deities being Vishnu, the solar god, Shiva, the divine impersonation of natural forces, and Brahma, the supreme ruler of priests and legislators. What would these divinities think of India, anglicised as it is to-day, with steamers whistling and scudding along the Ganges, frightening the gulls which float upon its surface, the turtles swarming along its banks, and the faithful dwelling upon its borders?

The panorama passed before their eyes like a flash, save when the steam concealed it fitfully from the view; the travellers could scarcely discern the fort of Chupenie, twenty miles south-westward from Benares, the ancient stronghold of the rajahs of Behar; or Ghazipur and its famous rose-water factories; or the tomb of Lord Cornwallis, rising on the left bank of the Ganges; the fortified town of Buxar, or Patna, a large manufacturing and trading-place, where is held the principal opium market of India; or Monghir, a more than European town, for it is as English as Manchester or Birmingham, with its iron foundries, edgetool factories, and high chimneys puffing clouds of black smoke heavenward.

Night came on; the train passed on at full speed, in the midst of the roaring of the tigers, bears, and wolves which fled before the locomotive; and the marvels of Bengal, Golconda ruined Gour, Murshedabad, the ancient capital, Burdwan, Hugly, and the French town of Chandernagor, where Passepartout would have been proud to see his country's flag flying, were hidden from their view in the darkness.

Calcutta was reached at seven in the morning, and the packet left for Hong Kong at noon; so that Phileas Fogg had five hours before him.

According to his journal, he was due at Calcutta on the 25th of October, and that was the exact date of his actual arrival. He was therefore neither behind-hand nor ahead of time. The two days gained between London and Bombay had been lost, as has been seen, in the journey across India. But it is not to be supposed that Phileas Fogg regretted them.

CHAPTER XV

IN WHICH THE BAG OF BANKNOTES DISGORGES SOME THOUSANDS OF POUNDS MORE

The train entered the station, and Passepartout jumping out first, was followed by Mr. Fogg, who assisted his fair companion to descend. Phileas Fogg intended to proceed at once to the Hong Kong steamer, in order to get Aouda comfortably settled for the voyage. He was unwilling to leave her while they were still on dangerous ground.

Just as he was leaving the station a policeman came up to him, and said, "Mr. Phileas Fogg?"

"I am he."

"Is this man your servant?" added the policeman, pointing to Passepartout.

"Yes."

"Be so good, both of you, as to follow me."

Mr. Fogg betrayed no surprise whatever. The policeman was a representative of the law, and law is sacred to an Englishman. Passepartout tried to reason about the matter, but the policeman tapped him with his stick, and Mr. Fogg made him a signal to obey.

"May this young lady go with us?" asked he.

"She may," replied the policeman.

Mr. Fogg, Aouda, and Passepartout were conducted to a palkigahri, a sort of four-wheeled carriage, drawn by two horses, in which they took their places and were driven away. No one spoke during the twenty minutes which elapsed before they reached their destination. They first passed through the "black town," with its narrow streets, its miserable, dirty huts, and squalid population; then through the "European town," which presented a relief in its bright brick mansions, shaded by coconut-trees and bristling with masts, where, although it was early morning, elegantly dressed horsemen and handsome equipages were passing back and forth.

The carriage stopped before a modest-looking house, which, however, did not have the appearance of a private mansion. The policeman having requested his prisoners—for so, truly, they might be called—to descend, conducted them into a room with barred windows, and said: "You will appear before Judge Obadiah at half-past eight."

He then retired, and closed the door.

"Why, we are prisoners!" exclaimed Passepartout, falling into a chair.

Aouda, with an emotion she tried to conceal, said to Mr. Fogg: "Sir, you must leave me to my fate! It is on my account that you receive this treatment, it is for having saved me!"

Phileas Fogg contented himself with saying that it was impossible. It was quite unlikely that he should be arrested for preventing a suttee. The complainants would not dare present themselves with such a charge. There was some mistake. Moreover, he would not, in any event, abandon Aouda, but would escort her to Hong Kong.

"But the steamer leaves at noon!" observed Passepartout, nervously.

"We shall be on board by noon," replied his master, placidly.

It was said so positively that Passepartout could not help muttering to himself, "Parbleu that's certain! Before noon we shall be on board." But he was by no means reassured.

At half-past eight the door opened, the policeman appeared, and, requesting them to follow him, led the way to an adjoining hall. It was evidently a court-room, and a crowd of Europeans and natives already occupied the rear of the apartment.

Mr. Fogg and his two companions took their places on a bench opposite the desks of the magistrate and his clerk. Immediately after, Judge Obadiah, a fat, round man, followed by the clerk, entered. He proceeded to take down a wig which was hanging on a nail, and put it hurriedly on his head.

"The first case," said he. Then, putting his hand to his head, he exclaimed, "Heh! This is not my wig!"

"No, your worship," returned the clerk, "it is mine."

"My dear Mr. Oysterpuff, how can a judge give a wise sentence in a clerk's wig?"

The wigs were exchanged.

Passepartout was getting nervous, for the hands on the face of the big clock over the judge seemed to go around with terrible rapidity.

"The first case," repeated Judge Obadiah.

"Phileas Fogg?" demanded Oysterpuff.

"I am here," replied Mr. Fogg.

"Passepartout?"

"Present," responded Passepartout.

"Good," said the judge. "You have been looked for, prisoners, for two days on the trains from Bombay."

"But of what are we accused?" asked Passepartout, impatiently.

"You are about to be informed."

"I am an English subject, sir," said Mr. Fogg, "and I have the right—"

"Have you been ill-treated?"

"Not at all."

"Very well; let the complainants come in."

A door was swung open by order of the judge, and three Indian priests entered.

"That's it," muttered Passepartout; "these are the rogues who were going to burn our young lady."

The priests took their places in front of the judge, and the clerk proceeded to read in a loud voice a complaint of sacrilege against Phileas Fogg and his servant, who were accused of having violated a place held consecrated by the Brahmin religion.

"You hear the charge?" asked the judge.

"Yes, sir," replied Mr. Fogg, consulting his watch, "and I admit it."

"You admit it?"

"I admit it, and I wish to hear these priests admit, in their turn, what they were going to do at the pagoda of Pillaji."

The priests looked at each other; they did not seem to understand what was said.

"Yes," cried Passepartout, warmly; "at the pagoda of Pillaji, where they were on the point of burning their victim."

The judge stared with astonishment, and the priests were stupefied.

"What victim?" said Judge Obadiah. "Burn whom? In Bombay itself?"

"Bombay?" cried Passepartout.

"Certainly. We are not talking of the pagoda of Pillaji, but of the pagoda of Malabar Hill, at Bombay."

"And as a proof," added the clerk, "here are the desecrator's very shoes, which he left behind him."

Whereupon he placed a pair of shoes on his desk.

"My shoes!" cried Passepartout, in his surprise permitting this imprudent

" MY SHOES ! " CRIED PASSEPARTOUT

exclamation to escape him.

The confusion of master and man, who had quite forgotten the affair at Bombay, for which they were now detained at Calcutta, may be imagined.

Fix the detective, had foreseen the advantage which Passepartout's escapade gave him, and, delaying his departure for twelve hours, had consulted the priests of Malabar Hill. Knowing that the English authorities dealt very severely with this kind of misdemeanour, he promised them a goodly sum in damages, and sent them forward to Calcutta by the next train. Owing to the delay caused by the rescue of the young widow, Fix and the priests reached the Indian capital before Mr. Fogg and his servant, the magistrates having been already warned by a dispatch to arrest them should they arrive. Fix's disappointment when he learned that Phileas Fogg had not made his appearance in Calcutta may be imagined. He made up his mind that the robber had stopped somewhere on the route and taken refuge in the southern provinces. For twenty-four hours Fix watched the station with feverish anxiety; at last he was rewarded by seeing Mr. Fogg and Passepartout arrive, accompanied by a young woman, whose presence he was wholly at a loss to explain. He hastened for a policeman; and this was how the party came to be arrested and brought before Judge Obadiah.

Had Passepartout been a little less preoccupied, he would have espied the detective ensconced in a corner of the court-room, watching the proceedings with an interest easily understood; for the warrant had failed to reach him at Calcutta, as it had done at Bombay and Suez.

Judge Obadiah had unfortunately caught Passepartout's rash exclamation, which the poor fellow would have given the world to recall.

"The facts are admitted?" asked the judge.

"Admitted," replied Mr. Fogg, coldly.

"Inasmuch," resumed the judge, "as the English law protects equally and sternly the religions of the Indian people, and as the man Passepartout has admitted that he violated the sacred pagoda of Malabar Hill, at Bombay, on the 20th of October, I condemn the said Passepartout to imprisonment for fifteen days and a fine of three hundred pounds."

"Three hundred pounds!" cried Passepartout, startled at the largeness of the sum.

"Silence!" shouted the constable.

"And inasmuch," continued the judge, "as it is not proved that the act was not done by the connivance of the master with the servant, and as the master in any case must be held responsible for the acts of his paid servant, I condemn Phileas Fogg to a week's imprisonment and a fine of one hundred and fifty pounds."

Fix rubbed his hands softly with satisfaction; if Phileas Fogg could be detained in Calcutta a week, it would be more than time for the warrant to arrive. Passepartout was stupefied. This sentence ruined his master. A wager of twenty thousand pounds lost, because he, like a precious fool, had gone into that abominable pagoda!

Phileas Fogg, as self-composed as if the judgment did not in the least concern him, did not even lift his eyebrows while it was being pronounced. Just as the clerk was calling the next case, he rose, and said, "I offer bail."

"You have that right," returned the judge.

Fix's blood ran cold, but he resumed his composure when he heard the judge announce that the bail required for each prisoner would be one thousand pounds.

"I will pay it at once," said Mr. Fogg, taking a roll of bank-bills from the carpet-bag, which Passepartout had by him, and placing them on the clerk's desk.

"This sum will be restored to you upon your release from prison," said the judge. "Meanwhile, you are liberated on bail."

"Come!" said Phileas Fogg to his servant.

"But let them at least give me back my shoes!" cried Passepartout angrily.

"Ah, these are pretty dear shoes!" he muttered, as they were handed to him. "More than a thousand pounds apiece; besides, they pinch my feet."

Mr. Fogg, offering his arm to Aouda, then departed, followed by the crestfallen Passepartout. Fix still nourished hopes that the robber would not, after all, leave the two thousand pounds behind him, but would decide to serve out his week in jail, and issued forth on Mr. Fogg's traces. That gentleman took a carriage, and the party were soon landed on one of the quays.

The Rangoon was moored half a mile off in the harbour, its signal of departure hoisted at the mast-head. Eleven o'clock was striking; Mr. Fogg was an hour in advance of time. Fix saw them leave the carriage and push off in a boat for the steamer, and stamped his feet with disappointment.

"The rascal is off, after all!" he exclaimed. "Two thousand pounds sacrificed! He's as prodigal as a thief! I'll follow him to the end of the world if necessary; but, at the rate he is going on, the stolen money will soon be exhausted."

The detective was not far wrong in making this conjecture. Since leaving

London, what with travelling expenses, bribes, the purchase of the elephant, bails, and fines, Mr. Fogg had already spent more than five thousand pounds on the way, and the percentage of the sum recovered from the bank robber promised to the detectives, was rapidly diminishing.

CHAPTER XVI

IN WHICH FIX DOES NOT SEEM TO UNDERSTAND IN THE LEAST WHAT IS SAID TO HIM

The Rangoon—one of the Peninsular and Oriental Company's boats plying in the Chinese and Japanese seas—was a screw steamer, built of iron, weighing about seventeen hundred and seventy tons, and with engines of four hundred horse-power. She was as fast, but not as well fitted up, as the Mongolia, and Aouda was not as comfortably provided for on board of her as Phileas Fogg could have wished. However, the trip from Calcutta to Hong Kong only comprised some three thousand five hundred miles, occupying from ten to twelve days, and the young woman was not difficult to please.

During the first days of the journey Aouda became better acquainted with her protector, and constantly gave evidence of her deep gratitude for what he had done. The phlegmatic gentleman listened to her, apparently at least, with coldness, neither his voice nor his manner betraying the slightest emotion; but he seemed to be always on the watch that nothing should be wanting to Aouda's comfort. He visited her regularly each day at certain hours, not so much to talk himself, as to sit and hear her talk. He treated her with the strictest politeness, but with the precision of an automaton, the movements of which had been arranged for this purpose. Aouda did not quite know what to make of him, though Passepartout had given her some hints of his master's eccentricity, and made her smile by telling her of the wager which was sending him round the world. After all, she owed Phileas Fogg her life, and she always regarded him through the exalting medium of her gratitude.

Aouda confirmed the Parsee guide's narrative of her touching history. She did, indeed, belong to the highest of the native races of India. Many of the Parsee merchants have made great fortunes there by dealing in cotton;

110

SHE SHOWED HIM THE MOST LIVELY GRATITUDE

and one of them, Sir Jametsee Jeejeebhoy, was made a baronet by the English government. Aouda was a relative of this great man, and it was his cousin, Jeejeeh, whom she hoped to join at Hong Kong. Whether she would find a protector in him she could not tell; but Mr. Fogg essayed to calm her anxieties, and to assure her that everything would be mathematically—he used the very word—arranged. Aouda fastened her great eyes, "clear as the sacred lakes of the Himalaya," upon him; but the intractable Fogg, as reserved as ever, did not seem at all inclined to throw himself into this lake.

The first few days of the voyage passed prosperously, amid favourable weather and propitious winds, and they soon came in sight of the great Andaman, the principal of the islands in the Bay of Bengal, with its picturesque Saddle Peak, two thousand four hundred feet high, looming above the waters. The steamer passed along near the shores, but the savage Papuans, who are in the lowest scale of humanity, but are not, as has been asserted, cannibals, did not make their appearance.

The panorama of the islands, as they steamed by them, was superb. Vast forests of palms, arecs, bamboo, teakwood, of the gigantic mimosa, and tree-like ferns covered the foreground, while behind, the graceful outlines of the mountains were traced against the sky; and along the coasts swarmed by thousands the precious swallows whose nests furnish a luxurious dish to the tables of the Celestial Empire. The varied landscape afforded by the Andaman Islands was soon passed, however, and the Rangoon rapidly approached the Straits of Malacca, which gave access to the China seas.

What was detective Fix, so unluckily drawn on from country to country, doing all this while? He had managed to embark on the Rangoon at Calcutta without being seen by Passepartout, after leaving orders that, if the warrant should arrive, it should be forwarded to him at Hong Kong; and he hoped to conceal his presence to the end of the voyage. It would have been difficult to explain why he was on board without awakening Passepartout's suspicions, who thought him still at Bombay. But necessity impelled him, nevertheless, to renew his acquaintance with the worthy servant, as will be seen.

All the detective's hopes and wishes were now centred on Hong Kong; for the steamer's stay at Singapore would be too brief to enable him to take any steps there. The arrest must be made at Hong Kong, or the robber would probably escape him for ever. Hong Kong was the last English ground on which he would set foot; beyond, China, Japan, America offered to Fogg an almost certain refuge. If the warrant should at last make its appearance at Hong Kong, Fix could arrest him and give him into the hands of the local police, and there would be no further trouble. But beyond Hong Kong, a simple warrant would be of no avail; an extradition warrant would be necessary, and that would result in delays and obstacles, of which the rascal would take advantage to elude justice.

Fix thought over these probabilities during the long hours which he spent in his cabin, and kept repeating to himself, "Now, either the warrant will be at Hong Kong, in which case I shall arrest my man, or it will not be there; and this time it is absolutely necessary that I should delay his departure. I have failed at Bombay, and I have failed at Calcutta; if I fail at Hong Kong, my reputation is lost: Cost what it may, I must succeed! But how shall I prevent his departure, if that should turn out to be my last resource?"

Fix made up his mind that, if worst came to worst, he would make a confidant of Passepartout, and tell him what kind of a fellow his master really was. That Passepartout was not Fogg's accomplice, he was very certain. The servant, enlightened by his disclosure, and afraid of being himself implicated in the crime, would doubtless become an ally of the detective. But this method was a dangerous one, only to be employed when everything else had failed. A word from Passepartout to his master would ruin all. The detective was therefore in a sore strait. But suddenly a new idea struck him. The presence of Aouda on the Rangoon, in company with Phileas Fogg, gave him new material for reflection.

Who was this woman? What combination of events had made her Fogg's travelling companion? They had evidently met somewhere between Bombay and Calcutta; but where? Had they met accidentally, or had Fogg gone into the interior purposely in quest of this charming damsel? Fix was fairly puzzled. He asked himself whether there had not been a wicked elopement; and this idea so impressed itself upon his mind that he determined to make use of the supposed intrigue. Whether the young woman were married or not, he would be able to create such difficulties for Mr. Fogg at Hong Kong that he could not escape by paying any amount of money.

But could he even wait till they reached Hong Kong? Fogg had an abominable way of jumping from one boat to another, and, before anything could be effected, might get full under way again for Yokohama.

Fix decided that he must warn the English authorities, and signal the Rangoon before her arrival. This was easy to do, since the steamer stopped at Singapore, whence there is a telegraphic wire to Hong Kong. He finally resolved, moreover, before acting more positively, to question Passepartout.

It would not be difficult to make him talk; and, as there was no time to lose, Fix prepared to make himself known.

It was now the 30th of October, and on the following day the Rangoon was due at Singapore.

Fix emerged from his cabin and went on deck. Passepartout was promenading up and down in the forward part of the steamer. The detective rushed forward with every appearance of extreme surprise, and exclaimed, "You here, on the Rangoon?"

"What, Monsieur Fix, are you on board?" returned the really astonished Passepartout, recognising his crony of the Mongolia. "Why, I left you at Bombay, and here you are, on the way to Hong Kong! Are you going round the world too?"

"No, no," replied Fix; "I shall stop at Hong Kong—at least for some days."

"Hum!" said Passepartout, who seemed for an instant perplexed. "But how is it I have not seen you on board since we left Calcutta?"

"Oh, a trifle of sea-sickness—I've been staying in my berth. The Gulf of Bengal does not agree with me as well as the Indian Ocean. And how is Mr. Fogg?"

"As well and as punctual as ever, not a day behind time! But, Monsieur Fix, you don't know that we have a young lady with us."

"A young lady?" replied the detective, not seeming to comprehend what was said.

Passepartout thereupon recounted Aouda's history, the affair at the Bombay pagoda, the purchase of the elephant for two thousand pounds, the rescue, the arrest, and sentence of the Calcutta court, and the restoration of Mr. Fogg and himself to liberty on bail. Fix, who was familiar with the last events, seemed to be equally ignorant of all that Passepartout related; and the later was charmed to find so interested a listener.

"But does your master propose to carry this young woman to Europe?"

"Not at all. We are simply going to place her under the protection of one of her relatives, a rich merchant at Hong Kong."

"Nothing to be done there," said Fix to himself, concealing his disappointment. "A glass of gin, Mr. Passepartout?"

"Willingly, Monsieur Fix. We must at least have a friendly glass on board the Rangoon."

CHAPTER XVII

SHOWING WHAT HAPPENED ON THE VOYAGE FROM SINGAPORE TO HONG KONG

The detective and Passepartout met often on deck after this interview, though Fix was reserved, and did not attempt to induce his companion to divulge any more facts concerning Mr. Fogg. He caught a glimpse of that mysterious gentleman once or twice; but Mr. Fogg usually confined himself to the cabin, where he kept Aouda company, or, according to his inveterate habit, took a hand at whist.

Passepartout began very seriously to conjecture what strange chance kept Fix still on the route that his master was pursuing. It was really worth considering why this certainly very amiable and complacent person, whom he had first met at Suez, had then encountered on board the Mongolia, who disembarked at Bombay, which he announced as his destination, and now turned up so unexpectedly on the Rangoon, was following Mr. Fogg's tracks step by step. What was Fix's object? Passepartout was ready to wager his Indian shoes—which he religiously preserved—that Fix would also leave Hong Kong at the same time with them, and probably on the same steamer.

Passepartout might have cudgelled his brain for a century without hitting upon the real object which the detective had in view. He never could have imagined that Phileas Fogg was being tracked as a robber around the globe. But, as it is in human nature to attempt the solution of every mystery, Passepartout suddenly discovered an explanation of Fix's movements, which was in truth far from unreasonable. Fix, he thought, could only be an agent of Mr. Fogg's friends at the Reform Club, sent to follow him up, and to ascertain that he really went round the world as had been agreed upon.

"It's clear!" repeated the worthy servant to himself, proud of his shrewdness. "He's a spy sent to keep us in view! That isn't quite the thing, either, to be spying Mr. Fogg, who is so honourable a man! Ah, gentlemen of the Reform, this shall cost you dear!"

Passepartout, enchanted with his discovery, resolved to say nothing to his master, lest he should be justly offended at this mistrust on the part of his adversaries. But he determined to chaff Fix, when he had the chance, with mysterious allusions, which, however, need not betray his real suspicions.

During the afternoon of Wednesday, 30th October, the Rangoon entered the Strait of Malacca, which separates the peninsula of that name from Sumatra. The mountainous and craggy islets intercepted the beauties of this noble island from the view of the travellers. The Rangoon weighed anchor at Singapore the next day at four a.m., to receive coal, having gained half a day on the prescribed time of her arrival. Phileas Fogg noted this gain in his journal, and then, accompanied by Aouda, who betrayed a desire for a walk on shore, disembarked.

Fix, who suspected Mr. Fogg's every movement, followed them cautiously, without being himself perceived; while Passepartout, laughing in his sleeve at Fix's manoeuvres, went about his usual errands.

The island of Singapore is not imposing in aspect, for there are no mountains; yet its appearance is not without attractions. It is a park checkered by pleasant highways and avenues. A handsome carriage, drawn by a sleek pair of New Holland horses, carried Phileas Fogg and Aouda into the midst of rows of palms with brilliant foliage, and of clove-trees, whereof the cloves form the heart of a half-open flower. Pepper plants replaced the prickly hedges of European fields; sago-bushes, large ferns with gorgeous branches, varied the aspect of this tropical clime; while nutmeg-trees in full foliage filled the air with a penetrating perfume. Agile and grinning bands of monkeys skipped about in the trees, nor were tigers wanting in the jungles.

After a drive of two hours through the country, Aouda and Mr. Fogg returned to the town, which is a vast collection of heavy-looking, irregular houses, surrounded by charming gardens rich in tropical fruits and plants; and at ten o'clock they re-embarked, closely followed by the detective, who had kept them constantly in sight.

Passepartout, who had been purchasing several dozen mangoes—a fruit as large as good-sized apples, of a dark-brown colour outside and a bright red within, and whose white pulp, melting in the mouth, affords gourmands a delicious sensation—was waiting for them on deck. He was only too glad to offer some mangoes to Aouda, who thanked him very gracefully for them.

IN A FINE EQUIPAGE, DRAWN BY SPLENDID HORSES, AOUDA
AND PHILEAS FOGG DROVE THROUGH THE RICH FOREST

SCENERY

At eleven o'clock the Rangoon rode out of Singapore harbour, and in a few hours the high mountains of Malacca, with their forests, inhabited by the most beautifully-furred tigers in the world, were lost to view. Singapore is distant some thirteen hundred miles from the island of Hong Kong, which is a little English colony near the Chinese coast. Phileas Fogg hoped to accomplish the journey in six days, so as to be in time for the steamer which would leave on the 6th of November for Yokohama, the principal Japanese port.

The Rangoon had a large quota of passengers, many of whom disembarked at Singapore, among them a number of Indians, Ceylonese, Chinamen, Malays, and Portuguese, mostly second-class travellers.

The weather, which had hitherto been fine, changed with the last quarter of the moon. The sea rolled heavily, and the wind at intervals rose almost to a storm, but happily blew from the south-west, and thus aided the steamer's progress. The captain as often as possible put up his sails, and under the double action of steam and sail the vessel made rapid progress along the coasts of Anam and Cochin China. Owing to the defective construction of the Rangoon, however, unusual precautions became necessary in unfavourable weather; but the loss of time which resulted from this cause, while it nearly drove Passepartout out of his senses, did not seem to affect his master in the least. Passepartout blamed the captain, the engineer, and the crew, and consigned all who were connected with the ship to the land where the pepper grows. Perhaps the thought of the gas, which was remorselessly burning at his expense in Saville Row, had something to do with his hot impatience.

"You are in a great hurry, then," said Fix to him one day, "to reach Hong Kong?"

"A very great hurry!"

"Mr. Fogg, I suppose, is anxious to catch the steamer for Yokohama?"

"Terribly anxious."

"You believe in this journey around the world, then?"

"Absolutely. Don't you, Mr. Fix?"

"I? I don't believe a word of it."

"You're a sly dog!" said Passepartout, winking at him.

This expression rather disturbed Fix, without his knowing why. Had the Frenchman guessed his real purpose? He knew not what to think. But how could Passepartout have discovered that he was a detective? Yet, in speaking as he did, the man evidently meant more than he expressed.

Passepartout went still further the next day; he could not hold his tongue.

"Mr. Fix," said he, in a bantering tone, "shall we be so unfortunate as to lose you when we get to Hong Kong?"

"Why," responded Fix, a little embarrassed, "I don't know; perhaps—"

"Ah, if you would only go on with us! An agent of the Peninsular Company, you know, can't stop on the way! You were only going to Bombay, and here you are in China. America is not far off, and from America to Europe is only a step."

Fix looked intently at his companion, whose countenance was as serene as possible, and laughed with him. But Passepartout persisted in chaffing him by asking him if he made much by his present occupation.

"Yes, and no," returned Fix; "there is good and bad luck in such things. But you must understand that I don't travel at my own expense."

"Oh, I am quite sure of that!" cried Passepartout, laughing heartily.

Fix, fairly puzzled, descended to his cabin and gave himself up to his reflections. He was evidently suspected; somehow or other the Frenchman had found out that he was a detective. But had he told his master? What part was he playing in all this: was he an accomplice or not? Was the game, then, up? Fix spent several hours turning these things over in his mind, sometimes thinking that all was lost, then persuading himself that Fogg was ignorant of his presence, and then undecided what course it was best to take.

Nevertheless, he preserved his coolness of mind, and at last resolved to deal plainly with Passepartout. If he did not find it practicable to arrest Fogg at Hong Kong, and if Fogg made preparations to leave that last foothold of English territory, he, Fix, would tell Passepartout all. Either the servant was the accomplice of his master, and in this case the master knew of his operations, and he should fail; or else the servant knew nothing about the robbery, and then his interest would be to abandon the robber.

Such was the situation between Fix and Passepartout. Meanwhile Phileas Fogg moved about above them in the most majestic and unconscious indifference. He was passing methodically in his orbit around the world, regardless of the lesser stars which gravitated around him. Yet there was near by what the astronomers would call a disturbing star, which might have produced an agitation in this gentleman's heart. But no! the charms of

Aouda failed to act, to Passepartout's great surprise; and the disturbances, if they existed, would have been more difficult to calculate than those of Uranus which led to the discovery of Neptune.

It was every day an increasing wonder to Passepartout, who read in Aouda's eyes the depths of her gratitude to his master. Phileas Fogg, though brave and gallant, must be, he thought, quite heartless. As to the sentiment which this journey might have awakened in him, there was clearly no trace of such a thing; while poor Passepartout existed in perpetual reveries.

One day he was leaning on the railing of the engine-room, and was observing the engine, when a sudden pitch of the steamer threw the screw out of the water. The steam came hissing out of the valves; and this made Passepartout indignant.

"The valves are not sufficiently charged!" he exclaimed. "We are not going. Oh, these English! If this was an American craft, we should blow up, perhaps, but we should at all events go faster!"

HE TOOK A HAND AT EVERYTHING AND ASTONISHED THE
CREW

CHAPTER XVIII

IN WHICH PHILEAS FOGG, PASSEPARTOUT, AND FIX GO EACH ABOUT HIS BUSINESS

The weather was bad during the latter days of the voyage. The wind, obstinately remaining in the north-west, blew a gale, and retarded the steamer. The Rangoon rolled heavily and the passengers became impatient of the long, monstrous waves which the wind raised before their path. A sort of tempest arose on the 3rd of November, the squall knocking the vessel about with fury, and the waves running high. The Rangoon reefed all her sails, and even the rigging proved too much, whistling and shaking amid the squall. The steamer was forced to proceed slowly, and the captain estimated that she would reach Hong Kong twenty hours behind time, and more if the storm lasted.

Phileas Fogg gazed at the tempestuous sea, which seemed to be struggling especially to delay him, with his habitual tranquillity. He never changed countenance for an instant, though a delay of twenty hours, by making him too late for the Yokohama boat, would almost inevitably cause the loss of the wager. But this man of nerve manifested neither impatience nor annoyance; it seemed as if the storm were a part of his programme, and had been foreseen. Aouda was amazed to find him as calm as he had been from the first time she saw him.

Fix did not look at the state of things in the same light. The storm greatly pleased him. His satisfaction would have been complete had the Rangoon been forced to retreat before the violence of wind and waves. Each delay filled him with hope, for it became more and more probable that Fogg would be obliged to remain some days at Hong Kong; and now the heavens themselves became his allies, with the gusts and squalls. It mattered not that they made him sea-sick—he made no account of this inconvenience; and, whilst his body was writhing under their effects, his spirit bounded with hopeful exultation.

Passepartout was enraged beyond expression by the unpropitious weather. Everything had gone so well till now! Earth and sea had seemed to be at his master's service; steamers and railways obeyed him; wind and steam united to speed his journey. Had the hour of adversity come? Passepartout was as much excited as if the twenty thousand pounds were to come from his own pocket. The storm exasperated him, the gale made him furious, and he longed to lash the obstinate sea into obedience. Poor fellow! Fix carefully concealed from him his own satisfaction, for, had he betrayed it, Passepartout could scarcely have restrained himself from personal violence.

Passepartout remained on deck as long as the tempest lasted, being unable to remain quiet below, and taking it into his head to aid the progress of the ship by lending a hand with the crew. He overwhelmed the captain, officers, and sailors, who could not help laughing at his impatience, with all sorts of questions. He wanted to know exactly how long the storm was going to last; whereupon he was referred to the barometer, which seemed to have no intention of rising. Passepartout shook it, but with no perceptible effect; for neither shaking nor maledictions could prevail upon it to change its mind.

On the 4th, however, the sea became more calm, and the storm lessened its violence; the wind veered southward, and was once more favourable. Passepartout cleared up with the weather. Some of the sails were unfurled, and the Rangoon resumed its most rapid speed. The time lost could not, however, be regained. Land was not signalled until five o'clock on the morning of the 6th; the steamer was due on the 5th. Phileas Fogg was twenty-four hours behind-hand, and the Yokohama steamer would, of course, be missed.

The pilot went on board at six, and took his place on the bridge, to guide the Rangoon through the channels to the port of Hong Kong. Passepartout longed to ask him if the steamer had left for Yokohama; but he dared not, for he wished to preserve the spark of hope, which still remained till the last moment. He had confided his anxiety to Fix who—the sly rascal!—tried to console him by saying that Mr. Fogg would be in time if he took the next boat; but this only put Passepartout in a passion.

Mr. Fogg, bolder than his servant, did not hesitate to approach the pilot, and tranquilly ask him if he knew when a steamer would leave Hong Kong for Yokohama.

"At high tide to-morrow morning," answered the pilot.

"Ah!" said Mr. Fogg, without betraying any astonishment.

Passepartout, who heard what passed, would willingly have embraced the pilot, while Fix would have been glad to twist his neck.

"What is the steamer's name?" asked Mr. Fogg.

"The Carnatic."

"Ought she not to have gone yesterday?"

"Yes, sir; but they had to repair one of her boilers, and so her departure was postponed till to-morrow."

"Thank you," returned Mr. Fogg, descending mathematically to the saloon.

Passepartout clasped the pilot's hand and shook it heartily in his delight, exclaiming, "Pilot, you are the best of good fellows!"

The pilot probably does not know to this day why his responses won him this enthusiastic greeting. He remounted the bridge, and guided the steamer through the flotilla of junks, tankas, and fishing boats which crowd the harbour of Hong Kong.

At one o'clock the Rangoon was at the quay, and the passengers were going ashore.

Chance had strangely favoured Phileas Fogg, for had not the Carnatic been forced to lie over for repairing her boilers, she would have left on the 6th of November, and the passengers for Japan would have been obliged to await for a week the sailing of the next steamer. Mr. Fogg was, it is true, twenty-four hours behind his time; but this could not seriously imperil the remainder of his tour.

The steamer which crossed the Pacific from Yokohama to San Francisco made a direct connection with that from Hong Kong, and it could not sail until the latter reached Yokohama; and if Mr. Fogg was twenty-four hours late on reaching Yokohama, this time would no doubt be easily regained in the voyage of twenty-two days across the Pacific. He found himself, then, about twenty-four hours behind-hand, thirty-five days after leaving London.

The Carnatic was announced to leave Hong Kong at five the next morning. Mr. Fogg had sixteen hours in which to attend to his business there, which was to deposit Aouda safely with her wealthy relative.

On landing, he conducted her to a palanquin, in which they repaired to the Club Hotel. A room was engaged for the young woman, and Mr. Fogg, after seeing that she wanted for nothing, set out in search of her cousin Jeejeeh. He instructed Passepartout to remain at the hotel until his return, that Aouda might not be left entirely alone.

Mr. Fogg repaired to the Exchange, where, he did not doubt, every one would know so wealthy and considerable a personage as the Parsee merchant. Meeting a broker, he made the inquiry, to learn that Jeejeeh had left China two years before, and, retiring from business with an immense fortune, had taken up his residence in Europe—in Holland the broker thought, with the merchants of which country he had principally traded. Phileas Fogg returned to the hotel, begged a moment's conversation with Aouda, and without more ado, apprised her that Jeejeeh was no longer at Hong Kong, but probably in Holland.

Aouda at first said nothing. She passed her hand across her forehead, and reflected a few moments. Then, in her sweet, soft voice, she said: "What ought I to do, Mr. Fogg?"

"It is very simple," responded the gentleman. "Go on to Europe."

"But I cannot intrude—"

"You do not intrude, nor do you in the least embarrass my project. Passepartout!"

"Monsieur."

"Go to the Carnatic, and engage three cabins."

Passepartout, delighted that the young woman, who was very gracious to him, was going to continue the journey with them, went off at a brisk gait to obey his master's order.

CHAPTER XIX

IN WHICH PASSEPARTOUT TAKES A TOO GREAT INTEREST IN HIS MASTER, AND WHAT COMES OF IT

Hong Kong is an island which came into the possession of the English by the Treaty of Nankin, after the war of 1842; and the colonising genius of the English has created upon it an important city and an excellent port. The island is situated at the mouth of the Canton River, and is separated by about sixty miles from the Portuguese town of Macao, on the opposite coast. Hong Kong has beaten Macao in the struggle for the Chinese trade, and now the greater part of the transportation of Chinese goods finds its depot at the former place. Docks, hospitals, wharves, a Gothic cathedral, a government house, macadamised streets, give to Hong Kong the appearance of a town in Kent or Surrey transferred by some strange magic to the antipodes.

Passepartout wandered, with his hands in his pockets, towards the Victoria port, gazing as he went at the curious palanquins and other modes of conveyance, and the groups of Chinese, Japanese, and Europeans who passed to and fro in the streets. Hong Kong seemed to him not unlike Bombay, Calcutta, and Singapore, since, like them, it betrayed everywhere the evidence of English supremacy. At the Victoria port he found a confused mass of ships of all nations: English, French, American, and Dutch, men-of-war and trading vessels, Japanese and Chinese junks, sempas, tankas, and flower-boats, which formed so many floating parterres. Passepartout noticed in the crowd a number of the natives who seemed very old and were dressed in yellow. On going into a barber's to get shaved he learned that these ancient men were all at least eighty years old, at which age they are permitted to wear yellow, which is the Imperial colour. Passepartout, without exactly knowing why, thought this very funny.

On reaching the quay where they were to embark on the Carnatic, he was not astonished to find Fix walking up and down. The detective seemed very much disturbed and disappointed.

"This is bad," muttered Passepartout, "for the gentlemen of the Reform Club!" He accosted Fix with a merry smile, as if he had not perceived that gentleman's chagrin. The detective had, indeed, good reasons to inveigh against the bad luck which pursued him. The warrant had not come! It was certainly on the way, but as certainly it could not now reach Hong Kong for several days; and, this being the last English territory on Mr. Fogg's route, the robber would escape, unless he could manage to detain him.

"Well, Monsieur Fix," said Passepartout, "have you decided to go with us so far as America?"

"Yes," returned Fix, through his set teeth.

"Good!" exclaimed Passepartout, laughing heartily. "I knew you could not persuade yourself to separate from us. Come and engage your berth."

They entered the steamer office and secured cabins for four persons. The clerk, as he gave them the tickets, informed them that, the repairs on the Carnatic having been completed, the steamer would leave that very evening, and not next morning, as had been announced.

"That will suit my master all the better," said Passepartout. "I will go and let him know."

Fix now decided to make a bold move; he resolved to tell Passepartout all. It seemed to be the only possible means of keeping Phileas Fogg several days longer at Hong Kong. He accordingly invited his companion into a tavern which caught his eye on the quay. On entering, they found themselves in a large room handsomely decorated, at the end of which was a large camp-bed furnished with cushions. Several persons lay upon this bed in a deep sleep. At the small tables which were arranged about the room some thirty customers were drinking English beer, porter, gin, and brandy; smoking, the while, long red clay pipes stuffed with little balls of opium mingled with essence of rose. From time to time one of the smokers, overcome with the narcotic, would slip under the table, whereupon the waiters, taking him by the head and feet, carried and laid him upon the bed. The bed already supported twenty of these stupefied sots.

Fix and Passepartout saw that they were in a smoking-house haunted by those wretched, cadaverous, idiotic creatures to whom the English merchants sell every year the miserable drug called opium, to the amount of one million four hundred thousand pounds—thousands devoted to one of the most despicable vices which afflict humanity! The Chinese

IN HIS STROLL PASSEPARTOUT CAME ACROSS A NUMBER OF
OLD NATIVES

government has in vain attempted to deal with the evil by stringent laws. It passed gradually from the rich, to whom it was at first exclusively reserved, to the lower classes, and then its ravages could not be arrested. Opium is smoked everywhere, at all times, by men and women, in the Celestial Empire; and, once accustomed to it, the victims cannot dispense with it, except by suffering horrible bodily contortions and agonies. A great smoker can smoke as many as eight pipes a day; but he dies in five years. It was in one of these dens that Fix and Passepartout, in search of a friendly glass, found themselves. Passepartout had no money, but willingly accepted Fix's invitation in the hope of returning the obligation at some future time.

They ordered two bottles of port, to which the Frenchman did ample justice, whilst Fix observed him with close attention. They chatted about the journey, and Passepartout was especially merry at the idea that Fix was going to continue it with them. When the bottles were empty, however, he rose to go and tell his master of the change in the time of the sailing of the Carnatic.

Fix caught him by the arm, and said, "Wait a moment."

"What for, Mr. Fix?"

"I want to have a serious talk with you."

"A serious talk!" cried Passepartout, drinking up the little wine that was left in the bottom of his glass. "Well, we'll talk about it to-morrow; I haven't time now."

"Stay! What I have to say concerns your master."

Passepartout, at this, looked attentively at his companion. Fix's face seemed to have a singular expression. He resumed his seat.

"What is it that you have to say?"

Fix placed his hand upon Passepartout's arm, and, lowering his voice, said, "You have guessed who I am?"

"Parbleu!" said Passepartout, smiling.

"Then I'm going to tell you everything—"

"Now that I know everything, my friend! Ah! that's very good. But go on, go on. First, though, let me tell you that those gentlemen have put themselves to a useless expense."

"Useless!" said Fix. "You speak confidently. It's clear that you don't know how large the sum is."

"Of course I do," returned Passepartout. "Twenty thousand pounds."

"Fifty-five thousand!" answered Fix, pressing his companion's hand.

"What!" cried the Frenchman. "Has Monsieur Fogg dared—fifty-five thousand pounds! Well, there's all the more reason for not losing an instant," he continued, getting up hastily.

Fix pushed Passepartout back in his chair, and resumed: "Fifty-five thousand pounds; and if I succeed, I get two thousand pounds. If you'll help me, I'll let you have five hundred of them."

"Help you?" cried Passepartout, whose eyes were standing wide open.

"Yes; help me keep Mr. Fogg here for two or three days."

"Why, what are you saying? Those gentlemen are not satisfied with following my master and suspecting his honour, but they must try to put obstacles in his way! I blush for them!"

"What do you mean?"

"I mean that it is a piece of shameful trickery. They might as well waylay Mr. Fogg and put his money in their pockets!"

"That's just what we count on doing."

"It's a conspiracy, then," cried Passepartout, who became more and more excited as the liquor mounted in his head, for he drank without perceiving it. "A real conspiracy! And gentlemen, too. Bah!"

Fix began to be puzzled.

"Members of the Reform Club!" continued Passepartout. "You must know, Monsieur Fix, that my master is an honest man, and that, when he makes a wager, he tries to win it fairly!"

"But who do you think I am?" asked Fix, looking at him intently.

"Parbleu! An agent of the members of the Reform Club, sent out here to interrupt my master's journey. But, though I found you out some time ago, I've taken good care to say nothing about it to Mr. Fogg."

"He knows nothing, then?"

"Nothing," replied Passepartout, again emptying his glass.

The detective passed his hand across his forehead, hesitating before he spoke again. What should he do? Passepartout's mistake seemed sincere, but it made his design more difficult. It was evident that the servant was not the master's accomplice, as Fix had been inclined to suspect.

"Well," said the detective to himself, "as he is not an accomplice, he will help me."

He had no time to lose: Fogg must be detained at Hong Kong, so he resolved to make a clean breast of it.

"Listen to me," said Fix abruptly. "I am not, as you think, an agent of the members of the Reform Club—"

"Bah!" retorted Passepartout, with an air of raillery.

"I am a police detective, sent out here by the London office."

"You, a detective?"

"I will prove it. Here is my commission."

Passepartout was speechless with astonishment when Fix displayed this document, the genuineness of which could not be doubted.

"Mr. Fogg's wager," resumed Fix, "is only a pretext, of which you and the gentlemen of the Reform are dupes. He had a motive for securing your innocent complicity."

"But why?"

"Listen. On the 28th of last September a robbery of fifty-five thousand pounds was committed at the Bank of England by a person whose description was fortunately secured. Here is his description; it answers exactly to that of Mr. Phileas Fogg."

"What nonsense!" cried Passepartout, striking the table with his fist. "My master is the most honourable of men!"

"How can you tell? You know scarcely anything about him. You went into his service the day he came away; and he came away on a foolish pretext, without trunks, and carrying a large amount in banknotes. And yet you are bold enough to assert that he is an honest man!"

"Yes, yes," repeated the poor fellow, mechanically.

"Would you like to be arrested as his accomplice?"

Passepartout, overcome by what he had heard, held his head between his hands, and did not dare to look at the detective. Phileas Fogg, the saviour of Aouda, that brave and generous man, a robber! And yet how many presumptions there were against him! Passepartout essayed to reject the suspicions which forced themselves upon his mind; he did not wish to believe that his master was guilty.

"Well, what do you want of me?" said he, at last, with an effort.

"See here," replied Fix; "I have tracked Mr. Fogg to this place, but as yet I have failed to receive the warrant of arrest for which I sent to London. You must help me to keep him here in Hong Kong—"

"I! But I—"

"I will share with you the two thousand pounds reward offered by the Bank of England."

"Never!" replied Passepartout, who tried to rise, but fell back, exhausted in mind and body.

"Mr. Fix," he stammered, "even should what you say be true—if my master is really the robber you are seeking for—which I deny—I have been,

"LISTEN," SAID FIX IN AN UNDER TONE

am, in his service; I have seen his generosity and goodness; and I will never betray him—not for all the gold in the world. I come from a village where they don't eat that kind of bread!"

"You refuse?"

"I refuse."

"Consider that I've said nothing," said Fix; "and let us drink."

"Yes; let us drink!"

Passepartout felt himself yielding more and more to the effects of the liquor. Fix, seeing that he must, at all hazards, be separated from his master, wished to entirely overcome him. Some pipes full of opium lay upon the table. Fix slipped one into Passepartout's hand. He took it, put it between his lips, lit it, drew several puffs, and his head, becoming heavy under the influence of the narcotic, fell upon the table.

"At last!" said Fix, seeing Passepartout unconscious. "Mr. Fogg will not be informed of the Carnatic's departure; and, if he is, he will have to go without this cursed Frenchman!"

And, after paying his bill, Fix left the tavern.

CHAPTER XX

IN WHICH FIX COMES FACE TO FACE WITH PHILEAS FOGG

While these events were passing at the opium-house, Mr. Fogg, unconscious of the danger he was in of losing the steamer, was quietly escorting Aouda about the streets of the English quarter, making the necessary purchases for the long voyage before them. It was all very well for an Englishman like Mr. Fogg to make the tour of the world with a carpet-bag; a lady could not be expected to travel comfortably under such conditions. He acquitted his task with characteristic serenity, and invariably replied to the remonstrances of his fair companion, who was confused by his patience and generosity:

"It is in the interest of my journey—a part of my programme."

The purchases made, they returned to the hotel, where they dined at a sumptuously served table-d'hote; after which Aouda, shaking hands with her protector after the English fashion, retired to her room for rest. Mr. Fogg absorbed himself throughout the evening in the perusal of The Times and Illustrated London News.

Had he been capable of being astonished at anything, it would have been not to see his servant return at bedtime. But, knowing that the steamer was not to leave for Yokohama until the next morning, he did not disturb himself about the matter. When Passepartout did not appear the next morning to answer his master's bell, Mr. Fogg, not betraying the least vexation, contented himself with taking his carpet-bag, calling Aouda, and sending for a palanquin.

It was then eight o'clock; at half-past nine, it being then high tide, the Carnatic would leave the harbour. Mr. Fogg and Aouda got into the palanquin, their luggage being brought after on a wheelbarrow, and half an hour later stepped upon the quay whence they were to embark. Mr. Fogg then learned that the Carnatic had sailed the evening before. He had expected to find not only the steamer, but his domestic, and was forced to give up both; but no sign of disappointment appeared on his face, and he merely remarked to Aouda, "It is an accident, madam; nothing more."

At this moment a man who had been observing him attentively approached. It was Fix, who, bowing, addressed Mr. Fogg: "Were you not, like me, sir, a passenger by the Rangoon, which arrived yesterday?"

"I was, sir," replied Mr. Fogg coldly. "But I have not the honour—"

"Pardon me; I thought I should find your servant here."

"Do you know where he is, sir?" asked Aouda anxiously.

"What!" responded Fix, feigning surprise. "Is he not with you?"

"No," said Aouda. "He has not made his appearance since yesterday. Could he have gone on board the Carnatic without us?"

"Without you, madam?" answered the detective. "Excuse me, did you intend to sail in the Carnatic?"

"Yes, sir."

"So did I, madam, and I am excessively disappointed. The Carnatic, its repairs being completed, left Hong Kong twelve hours before the stated time, without any notice being given; and we must now wait a week for another steamer."

As he said "a week" Fix felt his heart leap for joy. Fogg detained at Hong Kong for a week! There would be time for the warrant to arrive, and fortune at last favoured the representative of the law. His horror may be imagined when he heard Mr. Fogg say, in his placid voice, "But there are other vessels besides the Carnatic, it seems to me, in the harbour of Hong Kong."

And, offering his arm to Aouda, he directed his steps toward the docks in search of some craft about to start. Fix, stupefied, followed; it seemed as if he were attached to Mr. Fogg by an invisible thread. Chance, however, appeared really to have abandoned the man it had hitherto served so well. For three hours Phileas Fogg wandered about the docks, with the determination, if necessary, to charter a vessel to carry him to Yokohama; but he could only find vessels which were loading or unloading, and which could not therefore set sail. Fix began to hope again.

But Mr. Fogg, far from being discouraged, was continuing his search, resolved not to stop if he had to resort to Macao, when he was accosted by a sailor on one of the wharves.

"Is your honour looking for a boat?"

"Have you a boat ready to sail?"

" IS YOUR HONOUR LOOKING FOR A VESSEL ?"

"Yes, your honour; a pilot-boat—No. 43—the best in the harbour."

"Does she go fast?"

"Between eight and nine knots the hour. Will you look at her?"

"Yes."

"Your honour will be satisfied with her. Is it for a sea excursion?"

"No; for a voyage."

"A voyage?"

"Yes, will you agree to take me to Yokohama?"

The sailor leaned on the railing, opened his eyes wide, and said, "Is your honour joking?"

"No. I have missed the Carnatic, and I must get to Yokohama by the 14th at the latest, to take the boat for San Francisco."

"I am sorry," said the sailor; "but it is impossible."

"I offer you a hundred pounds per day, and an additional reward of two hundred pounds if I reach Yokohama in time."

"Are you in earnest?"

"Very much so."

The pilot walked away a little distance, and gazed out to sea, evidently struggling between the anxiety to gain a large sum and the fear of venturing so far. Fix was in mortal suspense.

Mr. Fogg turned to Aouda and asked her, "You would not be afraid, would you, madam?"

"Not with you, Mr. Fogg," was her answer.

The pilot now returned, shuffling his hat in his hands.

"Well, pilot?" said Mr. Fogg.

"Well, your honour," replied he, "I could not risk myself, my men, or my little boat of scarcely twenty tons on so long a voyage at this time of year. Besides, we could not reach Yokohama in time, for it is sixteen hundred and sixty miles from Hong Kong."

"Only sixteen hundred," said Mr. Fogg.

"It's the same thing."

Fix breathed more freely.

"But," added the pilot, "it might be arranged another way."

Fix ceased to breathe at all.

"How?" asked Mr. Fogg.

"By going to Nagasaki, at the extreme south of Japan, or even to Shanghai, which is only eight hundred miles from here. In going to Shanghai we should not be forced to sail wide of the Chinese coast, which would be a great advantage, as the currents run northward, and would aid us."

"Pilot," said Mr. Fogg, "I must take the American steamer at Yokohama, and not at Shanghai or Nagasaki."

"Why not?" returned the pilot. "The San Francisco steamer does not start from Yokohama. It puts in at Yokohama and Nagasaki, but it starts from Shanghai."

"You are sure of that?"

"Perfectly."

"And when does the boat leave Shanghai?"

"On the 11th, at seven in the evening. We have, therefore, four days before us, that is ninety-six hours; and in that time, if we had good luck and a south-west wind, and the sea was calm, we could make those eight hundred miles to Shanghai."

"And you could go—"

"In an hour; as soon as provisions could be got aboard and the sails put up."

"It is a bargain. Are you the master of the boat?"

"Yes; John Bunsby, master of the Tankadere."

"Would you like some earnest-money?"

"If it would not put your honour out—"

"Here are two hundred pounds on account sir," added Phileas Fogg, turning to Fix, "if you would like to take advantage—"

"Thanks, sir; I was about to ask the favour."

"Very well. In half an hour we shall go on board."

"But poor Passepartout?" urged Aouda, who was much disturbed by the servant's disappearance.

"I shall do all I can to find him," replied Phileas Fogg.

While Fix, in a feverish, nervous state, repaired to the pilot-boat, the others directed their course to the police-station at Hong Kong. Phileas Fogg there gave Passepartout's description, and left a sum of money to be spent in the search for him. The same formalities having been gone through at the French consulate, and the palanquin having stopped at the hotel for the luggage, which had been sent back there, they returned to the wharf.

It was now three o'clock; and pilot-boat No. 43, with its crew on board, and its provisions stored away, was ready for departure.

The Tankadere was a neat little craft of twenty tons, as gracefully built as if she were a racing yacht. Her shining copper sheathing, her galvanised iron-work, her deck, white as ivory, betrayed the pride taken by John Bunsby

"I REGRET HAVING NOTHING BETTER TO OFFER YOU," SAID
MR. FOGG TO FIX

in making her presentable. Her two masts leaned a trifle backward; she carried brigantine, foresail, storm-jib, and standing-jib, and was well rigged for running before the wind; and she seemed capable of brisk speed, which, indeed, she had already proved by gaining several prizes in pilot-boat races. The crew of the Tankadere was composed of John Bunsby, the master, and four hardy mariners, who were familiar with the Chinese seas. John Bunsby, himself, a man of forty-five or thereabouts, vigorous, sunburnt, with a sprightly expression of the eye, and energetic and self-reliant countenance, would have inspired confidence in the most timid.

Phileas Fogg and Aouda went on board, where they found Fix already installed. Below deck was a square cabin, of which the walls bulged out in the form of cots, above a circular divan; in the centre was a table provided with a swinging lamp. The accommodation was confined, but neat.

"I am sorry to have nothing better to offer you," said Mr. Fogg to Fix, who bowed without responding.

The detective had a feeling akin to humiliation in profiting by the kindness of Mr. Fogg.

"It's certain," thought he, "though rascal as he is, he is a polite one!"

The sails and the English flag were hoisted at ten minutes past three. Mr. Fogg and Aouda, who were seated on deck, cast a last glance at the quay, in the hope of espying Passepartout. Fix was not without his fears lest chance should direct the steps of the unfortunate servant, whom he had so badly treated, in this direction; in which case an explanation the reverse of satisfactory to the detective must have ensued. But the Frenchman did not appear, and, without doubt, was still lying under the stupefying influence of the opium.

John Bunsby, master, at length gave the order to start, and the Tankadere, taking the wind under her brigantine, foresail, and standing-jib, bounded briskly forward over the waves.

CHAPTER XXI

IN WHICH THE MASTER OF THE "TANKADERE" RUNS GREAT RISK OF LOSING A REWARD OF TWO HUNDRED POUNDS

This voyage of eight hundred miles was a perilous venture on a craft of twenty tons, and at that season of the year. The Chinese seas are usually boisterous, subject to terrible gales of wind, and especially during the equinoxes; and it was now early November.

It would clearly have been to the master's advantage to carry his passengers to Yokohama, since he was paid a certain sum per day; but he would have been rash to attempt such a voyage, and it was imprudent even to attempt to reach Shanghai. But John Bunsby believed in the Tankadere, which rode on the waves like a seagull; and perhaps he was not wrong.

Late in the day they passed through the capricious channels of Hong Kong, and the Tankadere, impelled by favourable winds, conducted herself admirably.

"I do not need, pilot," said Phileas Fogg, when they got into the open sea, "to advise you to use all possible speed."

"Trust me, your honour. We are carrying all the sail the wind will let us. The poles would add nothing, and are only used when we are going into port."

"It's your trade, not mine, pilot, and I confide in you."

Phileas Fogg, with body erect and legs wide apart, standing like a sailor, gazed without staggering at the swelling waters. The young woman, who was seated aft, was profoundly affected as she looked out upon the ocean, darkening now with the twilight, on which she had ventured in so frail a vessel. Above her head rustled the white sails, which seemed like great white wings. The boat, carried forward by the wind, seemed to be flying in the air.

THE YOUNG WOMAN, SITTING IN THE STERN, WAS LOST IN
CONTEMPLATION

Night came. The moon was entering her first quarter, and her insufficient light would soon die out in the mist on the horizon. Clouds were rising from the east, and already overcast a part of the heavens.

The pilot had hung out his lights, which was very necessary in these seas crowded with vessels bound landward; for collisions are not uncommon occurrences, and, at the speed she was going, the least shock would shatter the gallant little craft.

Fix, seated in the bow, gave himself up to meditation. He kept apart from his fellow-travellers, knowing Mr. Fogg's taciturn tastes; besides, he did not quite like to talk to the man whose favours he had accepted. He was thinking, too, of the future. It seemed certain that Fogg would not stop at Yokohama, but would at once take the boat for San Francisco; and the vast extent of America would ensure him impunity and safety. Fogg's plan appeared to him the simplest in the world. Instead of sailing directly from England to the United States, like a common villain, he had traversed three quarters of the globe, so as to gain the American continent more surely; and there, after throwing the police off his track, he would quietly enjoy himself with the fortune stolen from the bank. But, once in the United States, what should he, Fix, do? Should he abandon this man? No, a hundred times no! Until he had secured his extradition, he would not lose sight of him for an hour. It was his duty, and he would fulfil it to the end. At all events, there was one thing to be thankful for; Passepartout was not with his master; and it was above all important, after the confidences Fix had imparted to him, that the servant should never have speech with his master.

Phileas Fogg was also thinking of Passepartout, who had so strangely disappeared. Looking at the matter from every point of view, it did not seem to him impossible that, by some mistake, the man might have embarked on the Carnatic at the last moment; and this was also Aouda's opinion, who regretted very much the loss of the worthy fellow to whom she owed so much. They might then find him at Yokohama; for, if the Carnatic was carrying him thither, it would be easy to ascertain if he had been on board.

A brisk breeze arose about ten o'clock; but, though it might have been prudent to take in a reef, the pilot, after carefully examining the heavens, let the craft remain rigged as before. The Tankadere bore sail admirably, as she drew a great deal of water, and everything was prepared for high speed in case of a gale.

Mr. Fogg and Aouda descended into the cabin at midnight, having been already preceded by Fix, who had lain down on one of the cots. The pilot and crew remained on deck all night.

At sunrise the next day, which was 8th November, the boat had made more than one hundred miles. The log indicated a mean speed of between eight and nine miles. The Tankadere still carried all sail, and was accomplishing her greatest capacity of speed. If the wind held as it was, the chances would be in her favour. During the day she kept along the coast, where the currents were favourable; the coast, irregular in profile, and visible sometimes across the clearings, was at most five miles distant. The sea was less boisterous, since the wind came off land—a fortunate circumstance for the boat, which would suffer, owing to its small tonnage, by a heavy surge on the sea.

The breeze subsided a little towards noon, and set in from the south-west. The pilot put up his poles, but took them down again within two hours, as the wind freshened up anew.

Mr. Fogg and Aouda, happily unaffected by the roughness of the sea, ate with a good appetite, Fix being invited to share their repast, which he accepted with secret chagrin. To travel at this man's expense and live upon his provisions was not palatable to him. Still, he was obliged to eat, and so he ate.

When the meal was over, he took Mr. Fogg apart, and said, "sir"—this "sir" scorched his lips, and he had to control himself to avoid collaring this "gentleman"—"sir, you have been very kind to give me a passage on this boat. But, though my means will not admit of my expending them as freely as you, I must ask to pay my share—"

"Let us not speak of that, sir," replied Mr. Fogg.

"But, if I insist—"

"No, sir," repeated Mr. Fogg, in a tone which did not admit of a reply. "This enters into my general expenses."

Fix, as he bowed, had a stifled feeling, and, going forward, where he ensconced himself, did not open his mouth for the rest of the day.

Meanwhile they were progressing famously, and John Bunsby was in high hope. He several times assured Mr. Fogg that they would reach Shanghai in time; to which that gentleman responded that he counted upon it. The crew set to work in good earnest, inspired by the reward to be gained. There was not a sheet which was not tightened, not a sail which was not vigorously hoisted; not a lurch could be charged to the man at the helm. They worked as desperately as if they were contesting in a Royal yacht regatta.

THE "TANKADERE" WAS TOSSED ABOUT LIKE A FEATHER

By evening, the log showed that two hundred and twenty miles had been accomplished from Hong Kong, and Mr. Fogg might hope that he would be able to reach Yokohama without recording any delay in his journal; in which case, the many misadventures which had overtaken him since he left London would not seriously affect his journey.

The Tankadere entered the Straits of Fo-Kien, which separate the island of Formosa from the Chinese coast, in the small hours of the night, and crossed the Tropic of Cancer. The sea was very rough in the straits, full of eddies formed by the counter-currents, and the chopping waves broke her course, whilst it became very difficult to stand on deck.

At daybreak the wind began to blow hard again, and the heavens seemed to predict a gale. The barometer announced a speedy change, the mercury rising and falling capriciously; the sea also, in the south-east, raised long surges which indicated a tempest. The sun had set the evening before in a red mist, in the midst of the phosphorescent scintillations of the ocean.

John Bunsby long examined the threatening aspect of the heavens, muttering indistinctly between his teeth. At last he said in a low voice to Mr. Fogg, "Shall I speak out to your honour?"

"Of course."

"Well, we are going to have a squall."

"Is the wind north or south?" asked Mr. Fogg quietly.

"South. Look! a typhoon is coming up."

"Glad it's a typhoon from the south, for it will carry us forward."

"Oh, if you take it that way," said John Bunsby, "I've nothing more to say." John Bunsby's suspicions were confirmed. At a less advanced season of the year the typhoon, according to a famous meteorologist, would have passed away like a luminous cascade of electric flame; but in the winter equinox it was to be feared that it would burst upon them with great violence.

The pilot took his precautions in advance. He reefed all sail, the pole-masts were dispensed with; all hands went forward to the bows. A single triangular sail, of strong canvas, was hoisted as a storm-jib, so as to hold the wind from behind. Then they waited.

John Bunsby had requested his passengers to go below; but this imprisonment in so narrow a space, with little air, and the boat bouncing in the gale, was far from pleasant. Neither Mr. Fogg, Fix, nor Aouda consented to leave the deck.

The storm of rain and wind descended upon them towards eight o'clock.

With but its bit of sail, the Tankadere was lifted like a feather by a wind, an idea of whose violence can scarcely be given. To compare her speed to four times that of a locomotive going on full steam would be below the truth.

The boat scudded thus northward during the whole day, borne on by monstrous waves, preserving always, fortunately, a speed equal to theirs. Twenty times she seemed almost to be submerged by these mountains of water which rose behind her; but the adroit management of the pilot saved her. The passengers were often bathed in spray, but they submitted to it philosophically. Fix cursed it, no doubt; but Aouda, with her eyes fastened upon her protector, whose coolness amazed her, showed herself worthy of him, and bravely weathered the storm. As for Phileas Fogg, it seemed just as if the typhoon were a part of his programme.

Up to this time the Tankadere had always held her course to the north; but towards evening the wind, veering three quarters, bore down from the north-west. The boat, now lying in the trough of the waves, shook and rolled terribly; the sea struck her with fearful violence. At night the tempest increased in violence. John Bunsby saw the approach of darkness and the rising of the storm with dark misgivings. He thought awhile, and then asked his crew if it was not time to slacken speed. After a consultation he approached Mr. Fogg, and said, "I think, your honour, that we should do well to make for one of the ports on the coast."

"I think so too."

"Ah!" said the pilot. "But which one?"

"I know of but one," returned Mr. Fogg tranquilly.

"And that is—"

"Shanghai."

The pilot, at first, did not seem to comprehend; he could scarcely realise so much determination and tenacity. Then he cried, "Well—yes! Your honour is right. To Shanghai!"

So the Tankadere kept steadily on her northward track.

The night was really terrible; it would be a miracle if the craft did not founder. Twice it could have been all over with her if the crew had not been constantly on the watch. Aouda was exhausted, but did not utter a complaint. More than once Mr. Fogg rushed to protect her from the violence of the waves.

Day reappeared. The tempest still raged with undiminished fury; but the wind now returned to the south-east. It was a favourable change, and the Tankadere again bounded forward on this mountainous sea, though the waves crossed each other, and imparted shocks and counter-shocks which would have crushed a craft less solidly built. From time to time the coast was visible through the broken mist, but no vessel was in sight. The Tankadere was alone upon the sea.

There were some signs of a calm at noon, and these became more distinct as the sun descended toward the horizon. The tempest had been as brief as terrific. The passengers, thoroughly exhausted, could now eat a little, and take some repose.

The night was comparatively quiet. Some of the sails were again hoisted, and the speed of the boat was very good. The next morning at dawn they espied the coast, and John Bunsby was able to assert that they were not one hundred miles from Shanghai. A hundred miles, and only one day to traverse them! That very evening Mr. Fogg was due at Shanghai, if he did not wish to miss the steamer to Yokohama. Had there been no storm, during which several hours were lost, they would be at this moment within thirty miles of their destination.

The wind grew decidedly calmer, and happily the sea fell with it. All sails were now hoisted, and at noon the Tankadere was within forty-five miles of Shanghai. There remained yet six hours in which to accomplish that distance. All on board feared that it could not be done, and every one—Phileas Fogg, no doubt, excepted—felt his heart beat with impatience. The boat must keep up an average of nine miles an hour, and the wind was becoming calmer every moment! It was a capricious breeze, coming from the coast, and after it passed the sea became smooth. Still, the Tankadere was so light, and her fine sails caught the fickle zephyrs so well, that, with the aid of the currents John Bunsby found himself at six o'clock not more than ten miles from the mouth of Shanghai River. Shanghai itself is situated at least twelve miles up the stream. At seven they were still three miles from Shanghai. The pilot swore an angry oath; the reward of two hundred pounds was evidently on the point of escaping him. He looked at Mr. Fogg. Mr. Fogg was perfectly tranquil; and yet his whole fortune was at this moment at stake.

At this moment, also, a long black funnel, crowned with wreaths of smoke, appeared on the edge of the waters. It was the American steamer, leaving for Yokohama at the appointed time.

"Confound her!" cried John Bunsby, pushing back the rudder with a desperate jerk.

"Signal her!" said Phileas Fogg quietly.

A small brass cannon stood on the forward deck of the Tankadere, for making signals in the fogs. It was loaded to the muzzle; but just as the pilot was about to apply a red-hot coal to the touchhole, Mr. Fogg said, "Hoist your flag!"

The flag was run up at half-mast, and, this being the signal of distress, it was hoped that the American steamer, perceiving it, would change her course a little, so as to succour the pilot-boat.

"Fire!" said Mr. Fogg. And the booming of the little cannon resounded in the air.

CHAPTER XXII

IN WHICH PASSEPARTOUT FINDS OUT THAT, EVEN AT THE ANTIPODES, IT IS CONVENIENT TO HAVE SOME MONEY IN ONE'S POCKET

The Carnatic, setting sail from Hong Kong at half-past six on the 7th of November, directed her course at full steam towards Japan. She carried a large cargo and a well-filled cabin of passengers. Two state-rooms in the rear were, however, unoccupied—those which had been engaged by Phileas Fogg.

The next day a passenger with a half-stupefied eye, staggering gait, and disordered hair, was seen to emerge from the second cabin, and to totter to a seat on deck.

It was Passepartout; and what had happened to him was as follows: Shortly after Fix left the opium den, two waiters had lifted the unconscious Passepartout, and had carried him to the bed reserved for the smokers. Three hours later, pursued even in his dreams by a fixed idea, the poor fellow awoke, and struggled against the stupefying influence of the narcotic. The thought of a duty unfulfilled shook off his torpor, and he hurried from the abode of drunkenness. Staggering and holding himself up by keeping against the walls, falling down and creeping up again, and irresistibly impelled by a kind of instinct, he kept crying out, "The Carnatic! the Carnatic!"

The steamer lay puffing alongside the quay, on the point of starting. Passepartout had but few steps to go; and, rushing upon the plank, he crossed it, and fell unconscious on the deck, just as the Carnatic was moving off. Several sailors, who were evidently accustomed to this sort of scene, carried the poor Frenchman down into the second cabin, and Passepartout did not wake until they were one hundred and fifty miles away from China. Thus he found himself the next morning on the deck of the Carnatic, and eagerly inhaling the exhilarating sea-breeze. The pure air sobered him. He began to collect his sense, which he found a difficult task; but at last he recalled the events of the evening before, Fix's revelation, and the opium-house.

"It is evident," said he to himself, "that I have been abominably drunk! What will Mr. Fogg say? At least I have not missed the steamer, which is the most important thing."

Then, as Fix occurred to him: "As for that rascal, I hope we are well rid of him, and that he has not dared, as he proposed, to follow us on board the Carnatic. A detective on the track of Mr. Fogg, accused of robbing the Bank of England! Pshaw! Mr. Fogg is no more a robber than I am a murderer."

Should he divulge Fix's real errand to his master? Would it do to tell the part the detective was playing? Would it not be better to wait until Mr. Fogg reached London again, and then impart to him that an agent of the metropolitan police had been following him round the world, and have a good laugh over it? No doubt; at least, it was worth considering. The first thing to do was to find Mr. Fogg, and apologise for his singular behaviour.

Passepartout got up and proceeded, as well as he could with the rolling of the steamer, to the after-deck. He saw no one who resembled either his master or Aouda. "Good!" muttered he; "Aouda has not got up yet, and Mr. Fogg has probably found some partners at whist."

He descended to the saloon. Mr. Fogg was not there. Passepartout had only, however, to ask the purser the number of his master's state-room. The purser replied that he did not know any passenger by the name of Fogg.

"I beg your pardon," said Passepartout persistently. "He is a tall gentleman, quiet, and not very talkative, and has with him a young lady—"

"There is no young lady on board," interrupted the purser. "Here is a list of the passengers; you may see for yourself."

Passepartout scanned the list, but his master's name was not upon it. All at once an idea struck him.

"Ah! am I on the Carnatic?"

"Yes."

"On the way to Yokohama?"

"Certainly."

Passepartout had for an instant feared that he was on the wrong boat; but, though he was really on the Carnatic, his master was not there.

He fell thunderstruck on a seat. He saw it all now. He remembered that the time of sailing had been changed, that he should have informed his master of that fact, and that he had not done so. It was his fault, then, that Mr. Fogg and Aouda had missed the steamer. Yes, but it was still more the fault of the traitor who, in order to separate him from his master, and detain the latter at Hong Kong, had inveigled him into getting drunk! He now saw the detective's trick; and at this moment Mr. Fogg was certainly ruined, his bet was lost, and he himself perhaps arrested and imprisoned! At this thought Passepartout tore his hair. Ah, if Fix ever came within his reach, what a settling of accounts there would be!

After his first depression, Passepartout became calmer, and began to study his situation. It was certainly not an enviable one. He found himself on the way to Japan, and what should he do when he got there? His pocket was empty; he had not a solitary shilling, not so much as a penny. His passage had fortunately been paid for in advance; and he had five or six days in which to decide upon his future course. He fell to at meals with an appetite, and ate for Mr. Fogg, Aouda, and himself. He helped himself as generously as if Japan were a desert, where nothing to eat was to be looked for.

At dawn on the 13th the Carnatic entered the port of Yokohama. This is an important port of call in the Pacific, where all the mail-steamers, and those carrying travellers between North America, China, Japan, and the Oriental islands put in. It is situated in the bay of Yeddo, and at but a short distance from that second capital of the Japanese Empire, and the residence of the Tycoon, the civil Emperor, before the Mikado, the spiritual Emperor, absorbed his office in his own. The Carnatic anchored at the quay near the custom-house, in the midst of a crowd of ships bearing the flags of all nations.

Passepartout went timidly ashore on this so curious territory of the Sons of the Sun. He had nothing better to do than, taking chance for his guide, to wander aimlessly through the streets of Yokohama. He found himself at first in a thoroughly European quarter, the houses having low fronts, and being adorned with verandas, beneath which he caught glimpses of neat peristyles. This quarter occupied, with its streets, squares, docks, and warehouses, all the space between the "promontory of the Treaty" and the river. Here, as at Hong Kong and Calcutta, were mixed crowds of all races, Americans and English, Chinamen and Dutchmen, mostly merchants ready to buy or sell anything. The Frenchman felt himself as much alone among them as if he had dropped down in the midst of Hottentots.

He had, at least, one resource,—to call on the French and English consuls at Yokohama for assistance. But he shrank from telling the story of his adventures, intimately connected as it was with that of his master; and, before doing so, he determined to exhaust all other means of aid. As chance did not favour him in the European quarter, he penetrated that inhabited by the native Japanese, determined, if necessary, to push on to Yeddo.

The Japanese quarter of Yokohama is called Benten, after the goddess of the sea, who is worshipped on the islands round about. There Passepartout beheld beautiful fir and cedar groves, sacred gates of a singular architecture, bridges half hid in the midst of bamboos and reeds, temples shaded by immense cedar-trees, holy retreats where were sheltered Buddhist priests and sectaries of Confucius, and interminable streets, where a perfect harvest of rose-tinted and red-cheeked children, who looked as if they had been cut out of Japanese screens, and who were playing in the midst of short-legged poodles and yellowish cats, might have been gathered.

The streets were crowded with people. Priests were passing in processions, beating their dreary tambourines; police and custom-house officers with pointed hats encrusted with lac and carrying two sabres hung to their waists; soldiers, clad in blue cotton with white stripes, and bearing guns; the Mikado's guards, enveloped in silken doubles, hauberks and coats of mail; and numbers of military folk of all ranks—for the military profession is as much respected in Japan as it is despised in China—went hither and thither in groups and pairs. Passepartout saw, too, begging friars, long-robed pilgrims, and simple civilians, with their warped and jet-black hair, big heads, long busts, slender legs, short stature, and complexions varying from copper-colour to a dead white, but never yellow, like the Chinese, from whom the Japanese widely differ. He did not fail to observe the curious equipages—carriages and palanquins, barrows supplied with sails, and litters made of bamboo; nor the women—whom he thought not especially handsome—who took little steps with their little feet, whereon they wore canvas shoes, straw sandals, and clogs of worked wood, and who displayed tight-looking eyes, flat chests, teeth fashionably blackened, and gowns crossed with silken scarfs, tied in an enormous knot behind an ornament which the modern Parisian ladies seem to have borrowed from the dames of Japan.

Passepartout wandered for several hours in the midst of this motley crowd, looking in at the windows of the rich and curious shops, the jewellery establishments glittering with quaint Japanese ornaments, the restaurants decked with streamers and banners, the tea-houses, where the odorous beverage was being drunk with saki, a liquor concocted from the fermentation of rice, and the comfortable smoking-houses, where they were puffing, not opium, which is almost unknown in Japan, but a very fine, stringy tobacco. He went on till he found himself in the fields, in the midst of vast rice plantations. There he saw dazzling camellias expanding themselves, with flowers which were giving forth their last colours and perfumes, not on bushes, but on trees, and within bamboo enclosures, cherry, plum, and apple trees, which the Japanese cultivate rather for their blossoms than their fruit, and which queerly-fashioned, grinning scarecrows protected from the sparrows, pigeons, ravens, and other voracious birds. On the branches of the cedars were perched large eagles; amid the foliage of the weeping willows were herons, solemnly standing on one leg; and on every hand were crows, ducks, hawks, wild birds, and a multitude of cranes, which the Japanese consider sacred, and which to their minds symbolise long life and prosperity.

As he was strolling along, Passepartout espied some violets among the shrubs.

"Good!" said he; "I'll have some supper."

But, on smelling them, he found that they were odourless.

"No chance there," thought he.

The worthy fellow had certainly taken good care to eat as hearty a breakfast as possible before leaving the Carnatic; but, as he had been walking about all day, the demands of hunger were becoming importunate. He observed that the butchers stalls contained neither mutton, goat, nor pork; and, knowing also that it is a sacrilege to kill cattle, which are preserved solely for farming, he made up his mind that meat was far from plentiful in Yokohama—nor was he mistaken; and, in default of butcher's meat, he could have wished for a quarter of wild boar or deer, a partridge, or some quails, some game or fish, which, with rice, the Japanese eat almost exclusively. But he found it necessary to keep up a stout heart, and to postpone the meal he craved till the following morning. Night came, and Passepartout re-entered the native quarter, where he wandered through the streets, lit by vari-coloured lanterns, looking on at the dancers, who were executing skilful steps and boundings, and the astrologers who stood in the open air with their telescopes. Then he came to the harbour, which was lit up by the resin torches of the fishermen, who were fishing from their boats.

NIGHT CAME ON, AND PASSEPARTOUT RETURNED TO THE TOWN

The streets at last became quiet, and the patrol, the officers of which, in their splendid costumes, and surrounded by their suites, Passepartout thought seemed like ambassadors, succeeded the bustling crowd. Each time a company passed, Passepartout chuckled, and said to himself: "Good! another Japanese embassy departing for Europe!"

CHAPTER XXIII

IN WHICH PASSEPARTOUT'S NOSE BECOMES OUTRAGEOUSLY LONG

The next morning poor, jaded, famished Passepartout said to himself that he must get something to eat at all hazards, and the sooner he did so the better. He might, indeed, sell his watch; but he would have starved first. Now or never he must use the strong, if not melodious voice which nature had bestowed upon him. He knew several French and English songs, and resolved to try them upon the Japanese, who must be lovers of music, since they were for ever pounding on their cymbals, tam-tams, and tambourines, and could not but appreciate European talent.

It was, perhaps, rather early in the morning to get up a concert, and the audience prematurely aroused from their slumbers, might not possibly pay their entertainer with coin bearing the Mikado's features. Passepartout therefore decided to wait several hours; and, as he was sauntering along, it occurred to him that he would seem rather too well dressed for a wandering artist. The idea struck him to change his garments for clothes more in harmony with his project; by which he might also get a little money to satisfy the immediate cravings of hunger. The resolution taken, it remained to carry it out.

It was only after a long search that Passepartout discovered a native dealer in old clothes, to whom he applied for an exchange. The man liked the European costume, and ere long Passepartout issued from his shop accoutred in an old Japanese coat, and a sort of one-sided turban, faded with long use. A few small pieces of silver, moreover, jingled in his pocket.

"Good!" thought he. "I will imagine I am at the Carnival!"

His first care, after being thus "Japanesed," was to enter a tea-house of modest appearance, and, upon half a bird and a little rice, to breakfast like a man for whom dinner was as yet a problem to be solved.

PASSEPARTOUT WENT OUT MUFFLED UP IN AN OLD JAPA-
NESE ROBE

"Now," thought he, when he had eaten heartily, "I mustn't lose my head. I can't sell this costume again for one still more Japanese. I must consider how to leave this country of the Sun, of which I shall not retain the most delightful of memories, as quickly as possible."

It occurred to him to visit the steamers which were about to leave for America. He would offer himself as a cook or servant, in payment of his passage and meals. Once at San Francisco, he would find some means of going on. The difficulty was, how to traverse the four thousand seven hundred miles of the Pacific which lay between Japan and the New World.

Passepartout was not the man to let an idea go begging, and directed his steps towards the docks. But, as he approached them, his project, which at first had seemed so simple, began to grow more and more formidable to his mind. What need would they have of a cook or servant on an American steamer, and what confidence would they put in him, dressed as he was? What references could he give?

As he was reflecting in this wise, his eyes fell upon an immense placard which a sort of clown was carrying through the streets. This placard, which was in English, read as follows:

ACROBATIC JAPANESE TROUPE,
HONOURABLE WILLIAM BATULCAR, PROPRIETOR,
LAST REPRESENTATIONS,
PRIOR TO THEIR DEPARTURE TO THE UNITED STATES, OF THE
LONG NOSES! LONG NOSES!
UNDER THE DIRECT PATRONAGE OF THE GOD TINGOU!
GREAT ATTRACTION!

"The United States!" said Passepartout; "that's just what I want!"

He followed the clown, and soon found himself once more in the Japanese quarter. A quarter of an hour later he stopped before a large cabin, adorned with several clusters of streamers, the exterior walls of which were designed to represent, in violent colours and without perspective, a company of jugglers.

This was the Honourable William Batulcar's establishment. That gentleman was a sort of Barnum, the director of a troupe of mountebanks, jugglers, clowns, acrobats, equilibrists, and gymnasts, who, according to the placard, was giving his last performances before leaving the Empire of the Sun for the States of the Union.

Passepartout entered and asked for Mr. Batulcar, who straightway appeared in person.

"What do you want?" said he to Passepartout, whom he at first took for a native.

"Would you like a servant, sir?" asked Passepartout.

"A servant!" cried Mr. Batulcar, caressing the thick grey beard which hung from his chin. "I already have two who are obedient and faithful, have never left me, and serve me for their nourishment and here they are," added he, holding out his two robust arms, furrowed with veins as large as the strings of a bass-viol.

"So I can be of no use to you?"

"None."

"The devil! I should so like to cross the Pacific with you!"

"Ah!" said the Honourable Mr. Batulcar. "You are no more a Japanese than I am a monkey! Who are you dressed up in that way?"

"A man dresses as he can."

"That's true. You are a Frenchman, aren't you?"

"Yes; a Parisian of Paris."

"Then you ought to know how to make grimaces?"

"Why," replied Passepartout, a little vexed that his nationality should cause this question, "we Frenchmen know how to make grimaces, it is true but not any better than the Americans do."

"True. Well, if I can't take you as a servant, I can as a clown. You see, my friend, in France they exhibit foreign clowns, and in foreign parts French clowns."

"Ah!"

"You are pretty strong, eh?"

"Especially after a good meal."

"And you can sing?"

"Yes," returned Passepartout, who had formerly been wont to sing in the streets.

"But can you sing standing on your head, with a top spinning on your left foot, and a sabre balanced on your right?"

"Humph! I think so," replied Passepartout, recalling the exercises of his younger ays.

"Well, that's enough," said the Honourable William Batulcar.

The engagement was concluded there and then.

Passepartout had at last found something to do. He was engaged to act in the celebrated Japanese troupe. It was not a very dignified position, but within a week he would be on his way to San Francisco.

The performance, so noisily announced by the Honourable Mr. Batulcar, was to commence at three o'clock, and soon the deafening instruments of a Japanese orchestra resounded at the door. Passepartout, though he had not been able to study or rehearse a part, was designated to lend the aid of his sturdy shoulders in the great exhibition of the "human pyramid," executed by the Long Noses of the god Tingou. This "great attraction" was to close the performance.

Before three o'clock the large shed was invaded by the spectators, comprising Europeans and natives, Chinese and Japanese, men, women and children, who precipitated themselves upon the narrow benches and into the boxes opposite the stage. The musicians took up a position inside, and were vigorously performing on their gongs, tam-tams, flutes, bones, tambourines, and immense drums.

The performance was much like all acrobatic displays; but it must be confessed that the Japanese are the first equilibrists in the world.

One, with a fan and some bits of paper, performed the graceful trick of the butterflies and the flowers; another traced in the air, with the odorous smoke of his pipe, a series of blue words, which composed a compliment to the audience; while a third juggled with some lighted candles, which he extinguished successively as they passed his lips, and relit again without interrupting for an instant his juggling. Another reproduced the most singular combinations with a spinning-top; in his hands the revolving tops seemed to be animated with a life of their own in their interminable whirling; they ran over pipe-stems, the edges of sabres, wires and even hairs stretched across the stage; they turned around on the edges of large glasses, crossed bamboo ladders, dispersed into all the corners, and produced strange musical effects by the combination of their various pitches of tone. The jugglers tossed them in the air, threw them like shuttlecocks with wooden battledores, and yet they kept on spinning; they put them into their pockets, and took them out still whirling as before.

It is useless to describe the astonishing performances of the acrobats and gymnasts. The turning on ladders, poles, balls, barrels, &c., was executed with wonderful precision.

But the principal attraction was the exhibition of the Long Noses, a show to which Europe is as yet a stranger.

The Long Noses form a peculiar company, under the direct patronage of the god Tingou. Attired after the fashion of the Middle Ages, they bore upon their shoulders a splendid pair of wings; but what especially distinguished them was the long noses which were fastened to their faces, and the uses which they made of them. These noses were made of bamboo, and were five, six, and even ten feet long, some straight, others curved, some ribboned, and some having imitation warts upon them. It was upon these appendages, fixed tightly on their real noses, that they performed their gymnastic exercises. A dozen of these sectaries of Tingou lay flat upon their backs, while others, dressed to represent lightning-rods, came and frolicked on their noses, jumping from one to another, and performing the most skilful leapings and somersaults.

As a last scene, a "human pyramid" had been announced, in which fifty Long Noses were to represent the Car of Juggernaut. But, instead of forming a pyramid by mounting each other's shoulders, the artists were to group themselves on top of the noses. It happened that the performer who had hitherto formed the base of the Car had quitted the troupe, and as, to fill this part, only strength and adroitness were necessary, Passepartout had been chosen to take his place.

The poor fellow really felt sad when—melancholy reminiscence of his youth!—he donned his costume, adorned with vari-coloured wings, and fastened to his natural feature a false nose six feet long. But he cheered up when he thought that this nose was winning him something to eat.

He went upon the stage, and took his place beside the rest who were to compose the base of the Car of Juggernaut. They all stretched themselves on the floor, their noses pointing to the ceiling. A second group of artists disposed themselves on these long appendages, then a third above these, then a fourth, until a human monument reaching to the very cornices of the theatre soon arose on top of the noses. This elicited loud applause, in the midst of which the orchestra was just striking up a deafening air, when the pyramid tottered, the balance was lost, one of the lower noses vanished from the pyramid, and the human monument was shattered like a castle built of cards!

It was Passepartout's fault. Abandoning his position, clearing the footlights without the aid of his wings, and, clambering up to the right-hand gallery, he fell at the feet of one of the spectators, crying, "Ah, my master! my master!"

"You here?"

"Myself."

"Very well; then let us go to the steamer, young man!"

162

THE MONUMENT COLLAPSED LIKE A CASTLE OF CARDS

Mr. Fogg, Aouda, and Passepartout passed through the lobby of the theatre to the outside, where they encountered the Honourable Mr. Batulcar, furious with rage. He demanded damages for the "breakage" of the pyramid; and Phileas Fogg appeased him by giving him a handful of banknotes.

At half-past six, the very hour of departure, Mr. Fogg and Aouda, followed by Passepartout, who in his hurry had retained his wings, and nose six feet long, stepped upon the American steamer.

CHAPTER XXIV

DURING WHICH MR. FOGG AND PARTY CROSS THE PACIFIC OCEAN

What happened when the pilot-boat came in sight of Shanghai will be easily guessed. The signals made by the Tankadere had been seen by the captain of the Yokohama steamer, who, espying the flag at half-mast, had directed his course towards the little craft. Phileas Fogg, after paying the stipulated price of his passage to John Busby, and rewarding that worthy with the additional sum of five hundred and fifty pounds, ascended the steamer with Aouda and Fix; and they started at once for Nagasaki and Yokohama.

They reached their destination on the morning of the 14th of November. Phileas Fogg lost no time in going on board the Carnatic, where he learned, to Aouda's great delight—and perhaps to his own, though he betrayed no emotion—that Passepartout, a Frenchman, had really arrived on her the day before.

The San Francisco steamer was announced to leave that very evening, and it became necessary to find Passepartout, if possible, without delay. Mr. Fogg applied in vain to the French and English consuls, and, after wandering through the streets a long time, began to despair of finding his missing servant. Chance, or perhaps a kind of presentiment, at last led him into the Honourable Mr. Batulcar's theatre. He certainly would not have recognised Passepartout in the eccentric mountebank's costume; but the latter, lying on his back, perceived his master in the gallery. He could not help starting, which so changed the position of his nose as to bring the "pyramid" pell-mell upon the stage.

All this Passepartout learned from Aouda, who recounted to him what had taken place on the voyage from Hong Kong to Shanghai on the Tankadere, in company with one Mr. Fix.

FOLLOWED BY PASSEPARTOUT WITH THE WINGS ON HIS
BACK

Passepartout did not change countenance on hearing this name. He thought that the time had not yet arrived to divulge to his master what had taken place between the detective and himself; and, in the account he gave of his absence, he simply excused himself for having been overtaken by drunkenness, in smoking opium at a tavern in Hong Kong.

Mr. Fogg heard this narrative coldly, without a word; and then furnished his man with funds necessary to obtain clothing more in harmony with his position. Within an hour the Frenchman had cut off his nose and parted with his wings, and retained nothing about him which recalled the sectary of the god Tingou.

The steamer which was about to depart from Yokohama to San Francisco belonged to the Pacific Mail Steamship Company, and was named the General Grant. She was a large paddle-wheel steamer of two thousand five hundred tons; well equipped and very fast. The massive walking-beam rose and fell above the deck; at one end a piston-rod worked up and down; and at the other was a connecting-rod which, in changing the rectilinear motion to a circular one, was directly connected with the shaft of the paddles. The General Grant was rigged with three masts, giving a large capacity for sails, and thus materially aiding the steam power. By making twelve miles an hour, she would cross the ocean in twenty-one days. Phileas Fogg was therefore justified in hoping that he would reach San Francisco by the 2nd of December, New York by the 11th, and London on the 20th— thus gaining several hours on the fatal date of the 21st of December.

There was a full complement of passengers on board, among them English, many Americans, a large number of coolies on their way to California, and several East Indian officers, who were spending their vacation in making the tour of the world. Nothing of moment happened on the voyage; the steamer, sustained on its large paddles, rolled but little, and the Pacific almost justified its name. Mr. Fogg was as calm and taciturn as ever. His young companion felt herself more and more attached to him by other ties than gratitude; his silent but generous nature impressed her more than she thought; and it was almost unconsciously that she yielded to emotions which did not seem to have the least effect upon her protector. Aouda took the keenest interest in his plans, and became impatient at any incident which seemed likely to retard his journey.

She often chatted with Passepartout, who did not fail to perceive the state of the lady's heart; and, being the most faithful of domestics, he never exhausted his eulogies of Phileas Fogg's honesty, generosity, and devotion.

He took pains to calm Aouda's doubts of a successful termination of the journey, telling her that the most difficult part of it had passed, that now they were beyond the fantastic countries of Japan and China, and were fairly on their way to civilised places again. A railway train from San Francisco to New York, and a transatlantic steamer from New York to Liverpool, would doubtless bring them to the end of this impossible journey round the world within the period agreed upon.

On the ninth day after leaving Yokohama, Phileas Fogg had traversed exactly one half of the terrestrial globe. The General Grant passed, on the 23rd of November, the one hundred and eightieth meridian, and was at the very antipodes of London. Mr. Fogg had, it is true, exhausted fifty-two of the eighty days in which he was to complete the tour, and there were only twenty-eight left. But, though he was only half-way by the difference of meridians, he had really gone over two-thirds of the whole journey; for he had been obliged to make long circuits from London to Aden, from Aden to Bombay, from Calcutta to Singapore, and from Singapore to Yokohama. Could he have followed without deviation the fiftieth parallel, which is that of London, the whole distance would only have been about twelve thousand miles; whereas he would be forced, by the irregular methods of locomotion, to traverse twenty-six thousand, of which he had, on the 23rd of November, accomplished seventeen thousand five hundred. And now the course was a straight one, and Fix was no longer there to put obstacles in their way!

It happened also, on the 23rd of November, that Passepartout made a joyful discovery. It will be remembered that the obstinate fellow had insisted on keeping his famous family watch at London time, and on regarding that of the countries he had passed through as quite false and unreliable. Now, on this day, though he had not changed the hands, he found that his watch exactly agreed with the ship's chronometers. His triumph was hilarious. He would have liked to know what Fix would say if he were aboard!

"The rogue told me a lot of stories," repeated Passepartout, "about the meridians, the sun, and the moon! Moon, indeed! moonshine more likely! If one listened to that sort of people, a pretty sort of time one would keep! I was sure that the sun would some day regulate itself by my watch!"

Passepartout was ignorant that, if the face of his watch had been divided into twenty-four hours, like the Italian clocks, he would have no reason for exultation; for the hands of his watch would then, instead of as now indicating nine o'clock in the morning, indicate nine o'clock in the evening, that is, the twenty-first hour after midnight precisely the difference between London time and that of the one hundred and eightieth meridian. But if Fix had been able to explain this purely physical effect, Passepartout would not have admitted, even if he had comprehended it. Moreover, if the detective had been on board at that moment, Passepartout would have joined issue with him on a quite different subject, and in an entirely different manner.

Where was Fix at that moment?

He was actually on board the General Grant.

On reaching Yokohama, the detective, leaving Mr. Fogg, whom he expected to meet again during the day, had repaired at once to the English consulate, where he at last found the warrant of arrest. It had followed him from Bombay, and had come by the Carnatic, on which steamer he himself was supposed to be. Fix's disappointment may be imagined when he reflected that the warrant was now useless. Mr. Fogg had left English ground, and it was now necessary to procure his extradition!

"Well," thought Fix, after a moment of anger, "my warrant is not good here, but it will be in England. The rogue evidently intends to return to his own country, thinking he has thrown the police off his track. Good! I will follow him across the Atlantic. As for the money, heaven grant there may be some left! But the fellow has already spent in travelling, rewards, trials, bail, elephants, and all sorts of charges, more than five thousand pounds. Yet, after all, the Bank is rich!"

His course decided on, he went on board the General Grant, and was there when Mr. Fogg and Aouda arrived. To his utter amazement, he recognised Passepartout, despite his theatrical disguise. He quickly concealed himself in his cabin, to avoid an awkward explanation, and hoped—thanks to the number of passengers—to remain unperceived by Mr. Fogg's servant.

On that very day, however, he met Passepartout face to face on the forward deck. The latter, without a word, made a rush for him, grasped him by the throat, and, much to the amusement of a group of Americans, who immediately began to bet on him, administered to the detective a perfect volley of blows, which proved the great superiority of French over English pugilistic skill.

When Passepartout had finished, he found himself relieved and comforted. Fix got up in a somewhat rumpled condition, and, looking at his adversary, coldly said, "Have you done?"

"For this time—yes."

"Then let me have a word with you."

"But I—"

"In your master's interests."

Passepartout seemed to be vanquished by Fix's coolness, for he quietly followed him, and they sat down aside from the rest of the passengers.

"You have given me a thrashing," said Fix. "Good, I expected it. Now, listen to me. Up to this time I have been Mr. Fogg's adversary. I am now in his game."

"Aha!" cried Passepartout; "you are convinced he is an honest man?"

"No," replied Fix coldly, "I think him a rascal. Sh! don't budge, and let me speak. As long as Mr. Fogg was on English ground, it was for my interest to detain him there until my warrant of arrest arrived. I did everything I could to keep him back. I sent the Bombay priests after him, I got you intoxicated at Hong Kong, I separated you from him, and I made him miss the Yokohama steamer."

Passepartout listened, with closed fists.

"Now," resumed Fix, "Mr. Fogg seems to be going back to England. Well, I will follow him there. But hereafter I will do as much to keep obstacles out of his way as I have done up to this time to put them in his path. I've changed my game, you see, and simply because it was for my interest to change it. Your interest is the same as mine; for it is only in England that you will ascertain whether you are in the service of a criminal or an honest man."

Passepartout listened very attentively to Fix, and was convinced that he spoke with entire good faith.

"Are we friends?" asked the detective.

"Friends?—no," replied Passepartout; "but allies, perhaps. At the least sign of treason, however, I'll twist your neck for you."

"Agreed," said the detective quietly.

Eleven days later, on the 3rd of December, the General Grant entered the bay of the Golden Gate, and reached San Francisco.

Mr. Fogg had neither gained nor lost a single day.

CHAPTER XXV

IN WHICH A SLIGHT GLIMPSE IS HAD OF SAN FRANCISCO

It was seven in the morning when Mr. Fogg, Aouda, and Passepartout set foot upon the American continent, if this name can be given to the floating quay upon which they disembarked. These quays, rising and falling with the tide, thus facilitate the loading and unloading of vessels. Alongside them were clippers of all sizes, steamers of all nationalities, and the steamboats, with several decks rising one above the other, which ply on the Sacramento and its tributaries. There were also heaped up the products of a commerce which extends to Mexico, Chili, Peru, Brazil, Europe, Asia, and all the Pacific islands.

Passepartout, in his joy on reaching at last the American continent, thought he would manifest it by executing a perilous vault in fine style; but, tumbling upon some worm-eaten planks, he fell through them. Put out of countenance by the manner in which he thus "set foot" upon the New World, he uttered a loud cry, which so frightened the innumerable cormorants and pelicans that are always perched upon these movable quays, that they flew noisily away.

Mr. Fogg, on reaching shore, proceeded to find out at what hour the first train left for New York, and learned that this was at six o'clock p.m.; he had, therefore, an entire day to spend in the Californian capital. Taking a carriage at a charge of three dollars, he and Aouda entered it, while Passepartout mounted the box beside the driver, and they set out for the International Hotel.

From his exalted position Passepartout observed with much curiosity the wide streets, the low, evenly ranged houses, the Anglo-Saxon Gothic churches, the great docks, the palatial wooden and brick warehouses, the numerous conveyances, omnibuses, horse-cars, and upon the side-walks, not only Americans and Europeans, but Chinese and Indians. Passepartout

THE PLANKS WERE ROTTEN

was surprised at all he saw. San Francisco was no longer the legendary city of 1849—a city of banditti, assassins, and incendiaries, who had flocked hither in crowds in pursuit of plunder; a paradise of outlaws, where they gambled with gold-dust, a revolver in one hand and a bowie-knife in the other: it was now a great commercial emporium.

The lofty tower of its City Hall overlooked the whole panorama of the streets and avenues, which cut each other at right-angles, and in the midst of which appeared pleasant, verdant squares, while beyond appeared the Chinese quarter, seemingly imported from the Celestial Empire in a toy-box. Sombreros and red shirts and plumed Indians were rarely to be seen; but there were silk hats and black coats everywhere worn by a multitude of nervously active, gentlemanly-looking men. Some of the streets—especially Montgomery Street, which is to San Francisco what Regent Street is to London, the Boulevard des Italiens to Paris, and Broadway to New York—were lined with splendid and spacious stores, which exposed in their windows the products of the entire world.

When Passepartout reached the International Hotel, it did not seem to him as if he had left England at all.

The ground floor of the hotel was occupied by a large bar, a sort of restaurant freely open to all passers-by, who might partake of dried beef, oyster soup, biscuits, and cheese, without taking out their purses. Payment was made only for the ale, porter, or sherry which was drunk. This seemed "very American" to Passepartout. The hotel refreshment-rooms were comfortable, and Mr. Fogg and Aouda, installing themselves at a table, were abundantly served on diminutive plates by negroes of darkest hue.

After breakfast, Mr. Fogg, accompanied by Aouda, started for the English consulate to have his passport visaed. As he was going out, he met Passepartout, who asked him if it would not be well, before taking the train, to purchase some dozens of Enfield rifles and Colt's revolvers. He had been listening to stories of attacks upon the trains by the Sioux and Pawnees. Mr. Fogg thought it a useless precaution, but told him to do as he thought best, and went on to the consulate.

He had not proceeded two hundred steps, however, when, "by the greatest chance in the world," he met Fix. The detective seemed wholly taken by surprise. What! Had Mr. Fogg and himself crossed the Pacific together, and not met on the steamer! At least Fix felt honoured to behold once more the gentleman to whom he owed so much, and, as his business recalled him to Europe, he should be delighted to continue the journey in such pleasant company.

Mr. Fogg replied that the honour would be his; and the detective—who was determined not to lose sight of him—begged permission to accompany them in their walk about San Francisco—a request which Mr. Fogg readily granted.

They soon found themselves in Montgomery Street, where a great crowd was collected; the side-walks, street, horsecar rails, the shop-doors, the windows of the houses, and even the roofs, were full of people. Men were going about carrying large posters, and flags and streamers were floating in the wind; while loud cries were heard on every hand.

"Hurrah for Camerfield!"

"Hurrah for Mandiboy!"

It was a political meeting; at least so Fix conjectured, who said to Mr. Fogg, "Perhaps we had better not mingle with the crowd. There may be danger in it."

"Yes," returned Mr. Fogg; "and blows, even if they are political are still blows."

Fix smiled at this remark; and, in order to be able to see without being jostled about, the party took up a position on the top of a flight of steps situated at the upper end of Montgomery Street. Opposite them, on the other side of the street, between a coal wharf and a petroleum warehouse, a large platform had been erected in the open air, towards which the current of the crowd seemed to be directed.

For what purpose was this meeting? What was the occasion of this excited assemblage? Phileas Fogg could not imagine. Was it to nominate some high official—a governor or member of Congress? It was not improbable, so agitated was the multitude before them.

Just at this moment there was an unusual stir in the human mass. All the hands were raised in the air. Some, tightly closed, seemed to disappear suddenly in the midst of the cries—an energetic way, no doubt, of casting a vote. The crowd swayed back, the banners and flags wavered, disappeared an instant, then reappeared in tatters. The undulations of the human surge reached the steps, while all the heads floundered on the surface like a sea agitated by a squall. Many of the black hats disappeared, and the greater part of the crowd seemed to have diminished in height.

"It is evidently a meeting," said Fix, "and its object must be an exciting one. I should not wonder if it were about the Alabama, despite the fact that that question is settled." "Perhaps," replied Mr. Fogg, simply.

IF FIX HAD NOT RECEIVED THE BLOW

175

"At least, there are two champions in presence of each other, the Honourable Mr. Camerfield and the Honourable Mr. Mandiboy."

Aouda, leaning upon Mr. Fogg's arm, observed the tumultuous scene with surprise, while Fix asked a man near him what the cause of it all was. Before the man could reply, a fresh agitation arose; hurrahs and excited shouts were heard; the staffs of the banners began to be used as offensive weapons; and fists flew about in every direction. Thumps were exchanged from the tops of the carriages and omnibuses which had been blocked up in the crowd. Boots and shoes went whirling through the air, and Mr. Fogg thought he even heard the crack of revolvers mingling in the din, the rout approached the stairway, and flowed over the lower step. One of the parties had evidently been repulsed; but the mere lookers-on could not tell whether Mandiboy or Camerfield had gained the upper hand.

"It would be prudent for us to retire," said Fix, who was anxious that Mr. Fogg should not receive any injury, at least until they got back to London. "If there is any question about England in all this, and we were recognised, I fear it would go hard with us."

"An English subject—" began Mr. Fogg.

He did not finish his sentence; for a terrific hubbub now arose on the terrace behind the flight of steps where they stood, and there were frantic shouts of, "Hurrah for Mandiboy! Hip, hip, hurrah!"

It was a band of voters coming to the rescue of their allies, and taking the Camerfield forces in flank. Mr. Fogg, Aouda, and Fix found themselves between two fires; it was too late to escape. The torrent of men, armed with loaded canes and sticks, was irresistible. Phileas Fogg and Fix were roughly hustled in their attempts to protect their fair companion; the former, as cool as ever, tried to defend himself with the weapons which nature has placed at the end of every Englishman's arm, but in vain. A big brawny fellow with a red beard, flushed face, and broad shoulders, who seemed to be the chief of the band, raised his clenched fist to strike Mr. Fogg, whom he would have given a crushing blow, had not Fix rushed in and received it in his stead. An enormous bruise immediately made its appearance under the detective's silk hat, which was completely smashed in.

"Yankee!" exclaimed Mr. Fogg, darting a contemptuous look at the ruffian.

"Englishman!" returned the other. "We will meet again!"

"When you please."

"What is your name?"

"Phileas Fogg. And yours?"

"Colonel Stamp Proctor."

The human tide now swept by, after overturning Fix, who speedily got upon his feet again, though with tattered clothes. Happily, he was not seriously hurt. His travelling overcoat was divided into two unequal parts, and his trousers resembled those of certain Indians, which fit less compactly than they are easy to put on. Aouda had escaped unharmed, and Fix alone bore marks of the fray in his black and blue bruise.

"Thanks," said Mr. Fogg to the detective, as soon as they were out of the crowd.

"No thanks are necessary," replied. Fix; "but let us go."

"Where?"

"To a tailor's."

Such a visit was, indeed, opportune. The clothing of both Mr. Fogg and Fix was in rags, as if they had themselves been actively engaged in the contest between Camerfield and Mandiboy. An hour after, they were once more suitably attired, and with Aouda returned to the International Hotel.

Passepartout was waiting for his master, armed with half a dozen six-barrelled revolvers. When he perceived Fix, he knit his brows; but Aouda having, in a few words, told him of their adventure, his countenance resumed its placid expression. Fix evidently was no longer an enemy, but an ally; he was faithfully keeping his word.

Dinner over, the coach which was to convey the passengers and their luggage to the station drew up to the door. As he was getting in, Mr. Fogg said to Fix, "You have not seen this Colonel Proctor again?"

"No."

"I will come back to America to find him," said Phileas Fogg calmly. "It would not be right for an Englishman to permit himself to be treated in that way, without retaliating."

The detective smiled, but did not reply. It was clear that Mr. Fogg was one of those Englishmen who, while they do not tolerate duelling at home, fight abroad when their honour is attacked.

At a quarter before six the travellers reached the station, and found the train ready to depart. As he was about to enter it, Mr. Fogg called a porter, and said to him: "My friend, was there not some trouble to-day in San Francisco?"

"It was a political meeting, sir," replied the porter.

"But I thought there was a great deal of disturbance in the streets."

"It was only a meeting assembled for an election."

"The election of a general-in-chief, no doubt?" asked Mr. Fogg.

"No, sir; of a justice of the peace."

Phileas Fogg got into the train, which started off at full speed.

CHAPTER XXVI

IN WHICH PHILEAS FOGG AND PARTY TRAVEL BY THE PACIFIC RAILROAD

"From ocean to ocean"—so say the Americans; and these four words compose the general designation of the "great trunk line" which crosses the entire width of the United States. The Pacific Railroad is, however, really divided into two distinct lines: the Central Pacific, between San Francisco and Ogden, and the Union Pacific, between Ogden and Omaha. Five main lines connect Omaha with New York.

New York and San Francisco are thus united by an uninterrupted metal ribbon, which measures no less than three thousand seven hundred and eighty-six miles. Between Omaha and the Pacific the railway crosses a territory which is still infested by Indians and wild beasts, and a large tract which the Mormons, after they were driven from Illinois in 1845, began to colonise.

The journey from New York to San Francisco consumed, formerly, under the most favourable conditions, at least six months. It is now accomplished in seven days.

It was in 1862 that, in spite of the Southern Members of Congress, who wished a more southerly route, it was decided to lay the road between the forty-first and forty-second parallels. President Lincoln himself fixed the end of the line at Omaha, in Nebraska. The work was at once commenced, and pursued with true American energy; nor did the rapidity with which it went on injuriously affect its good execution. The road grew, on the prairies, a mile and a half a day. A locomotive, running on the rails laid down the evening before, brought the rails to be laid on the morrow, and advanced upon them as fast as they were put in position.

The Pacific Railroad is joined by several branches in Iowa, Kansas, Colorado, and Oregon. On leaving Omaha, it passes along the left bank of the Platte River as far as the junction of its northern branch, follows its

THIS WAS A SLEEPING CAR

southern branch, crosses the Laramie territory and the Wahsatch Mountains, turns the Great Salt Lake, and reaches Salt Lake City, the Mormon capital, plunges into the Tuilla Valley, across the American Desert, Cedar and Humboldt Mountains, the Sierra Nevada, and descends, via Sacramento, to the Pacific—its grade, even on the Rocky Mountains, never exceeding one hundred and twelve feet to the mile.

Such was the road to be traversed in seven days, which would enable Phileas Fogg—at least, so he hoped—to take the Atlantic steamer at New York on the 11th for Liverpool.

The car which he occupied was a sort of long omnibus on eight wheels, and with no compartments in the interior. It was supplied with two rows of seats, perpendicular to the direction of the train on either side of an aisle which conducted to the front and rear platforms. These platforms were found throughout the train, and the passengers were able to pass from one end of the train to the other. It was supplied with saloon cars, balcony cars, restaurants, and smoking-cars; theatre cars alone were wanting, and they will have these some day.

Book and news dealers, sellers of edibles, drinkables, and cigars, who seemed to have plenty of customers, were continually circulating in the aisles.

The train left Oakland station at six o'clock. It was already night, cold and cheerless, the heavens being overcast with clouds which seemed to threaten snow. The train did not proceed rapidly; counting the stoppages, it did not run more than twenty miles an hour, which was a sufficient speed, however, to enable it to reach Omaha within its designated time.

There was but little conversation in the car, and soon many of the passengers were overcome with sleep. Passepartout found himself beside the detective; but he did not talk to him. After recent events, their relations with each other had grown somewhat cold; there could no longer be mutual sympathy or intimacy between them. Fix's manner had not changed; but Passepartout was very reserved, and ready to strangle his former friend on the slightest provocation.

Snow began to fall an hour after they started, a fine snow, however, which happily could not obstruct the train; nothing could be seen from the windows but a vast, white sheet, against which the smoke of the locomotive had a greyish aspect.

At eight o'clock a steward entered the car and announced that the time for going to bed had arrived; and in a few minutes the car was transformed into a dormitory. The backs of the seats were thrown back, bedsteads carefully packed were rolled out by an ingenious system, berths were suddenly improvised, and each traveller had soon at his disposition a comfortable bed, protected from curious eyes by thick curtains. The sheets were clean and the pillows soft. It only remained to go to bed and sleep which everybody did—while the train sped on across the State of California.

The country between San Francisco and Sacramento is not very hilly. The Central Pacific, taking Sacramento for its starting-point, extends eastward to meet the road from Omaha. The line from San Francisco to Sacramento runs in a north-easterly direction, along the American River, which empties into San Pablo Bay. The one hundred and twenty miles between these cities were accomplished in six hours, and towards midnight, while fast asleep, the travellers passed through Sacramento; so that they saw nothing of that important place, the seat of the State government, with its fine quays, its broad streets, its noble hotels, squares, and churches.

The train, on leaving Sacramento, and passing the junction, Roclin, Auburn, and Colfax, entered the range of the Sierra Nevada. 'Cisco was reached at seven in the morning; and an hour later the dormitory was transformed into an ordinary car, and the travellers could observe the picturesque beauties of the mountain region through which they were steaming. The railway track wound in and out among the passes, now approaching the mountain-sides, now suspended over precipices, avoiding abrupt angles by bold curves, plunging into narrow defiles, which seemed to have no outlet. The locomotive, its great funnel emitting a weird light, with its sharp bell, and its cow-catcher extended like a spur, mingled its shrieks and bellowings with the noise of torrents and cascades, and twined its smoke among the branches of the gigantic pines.

There were few or no bridges or tunnels on the route. The railway turned around the sides of the mountains, and did not attempt to violate nature by taking the shortest cut from one point to another.

The train entered the State of Nevada through the Carson Valley about nine o'clock, going always northeasterly; and at midday reached Reno, where there was a delay of twenty minutes for breakfast.

From this point the road, running along Humboldt River, passed northward for several miles by its banks; then it turned eastward, and kept by the river until it reached the Humboldt Range, nearly at the extreme eastern limit of Nevada.

Having breakfasted, Mr. Fogg and his companions resumed their places in the car, and observed the varied landscape which unfolded itself as they passed along the vast prairies, the mountains lining the horizon, and the creeks, with their frothy, foaming streams. Sometimes a great herd of buffaloes, massing together in the distance, seemed like a moveable dam. These innumerable multitudes of ruminating beasts often form an insurmountable obstacle to the passage of the trains; thousands of them have been seen passing over the track for hours together, in compact ranks. The locomotive is then forced to stop and wait till the road is once more clear.

This happened, indeed, to the train in which Mr. Fogg was travelling. About twelve o'clock a troop of ten or twelve thousand head of buffalo encumbered the track. The locomotive, slackening its speed, tried to clear the way with its cow-catcher; but the mass of animals was too great. The buffaloes marched along with a tranquil gait, uttering now and then deafening bellowings. There was no use of interrupting them, for, having taken a particular direction, nothing can moderate and change their course; it is a torrent of living flesh which no dam could contain.

The travellers gazed on this curious spectacle from the platforms; but Phileas Fogg, who had the most reason of all to be in a hurry, remained in his seat, and waited philosophically until it should please the buffaloes to get out of the way.

Passepartout was furious at the delay they occasioned, and longed to discharge his arsenal of revolvers upon them.

"What a country!" cried he. "Mere cattle stop the trains, and go by in a procession, just as if they were not impeding travel! Parbleu! I should like to know if Mr. Fogg foresaw this mishap in his programme! And here's an engineer who doesn't dare to run the locomotive into this herd of beasts!"

The engineer did not try to overcome the obstacle, and he was wise. He would have crushed the first buffaloes, no doubt, with the cow-catcher; but the locomotive, however powerful, would soon have been checked, the train would inevitably have been thrown off the track, and would then have been helpless.

The best course was to wait patiently, and regain the lost time by greater speed when the obstacle was removed. The procession of buffaloes lasted three full hours, and it was night before the track was clear. The last ranks of the herd were now passing over the rails, while the first had already disappeared below the southern horizon.

It was eight o'clock when the train passed through the defiles of the

Humboldt Range, and half-past nine when it penetrated Utah, the region of the Great Salt Lake, the singular colony of the Mormons.

A HERD OF TEN OR TWELVE THOUSAND' BUFFALO' BARRED
THE TRACK

CHAPTER XXVII

IN WHICH PASSEPARTOUT UNDER-GOES, AT A SPEED OF TWENTY MILES AN HOUR, A COURSE OF MORMON HISTORY

During the night of the 5th of December, the train ran south-easterly for about fifty miles; then rose an equal distance in a north-easterly direction, towards the Great Salt Lake.

Passepartout, about nine o'clock, went out upon the platform to take the air. The weather was cold, the heavens grey, but it was not snowing. The sun's disc, enlarged by the mist, seemed an enormous ring of gold, and Passepartout was amusing himself by calculating its value in pounds sterling, when he was diverted from this interesting study by a strange-looking personage who made his appearance on the platform.

This personage, who had taken the train at Elko, was tall and dark, with black moustache, black stockings, a black silk hat, a black waistcoat, black trousers, a white cravat, and dogskin gloves. He might have been taken for a clergyman. He went from one end of the train to the other, and affixed to the door of each car a notice written in manuscript.

Passepartout approached and read one of these notices, which stated that Elder William Hitch, Mormon missionary, taking advantage of his presence on train No. 48, would deliver a lecture on Mormonism in car No. 117, from eleven to twelve o'clock; and that he invited all who were desirous of being instructed concerning the mysteries of the religion of the "Latter Day Saints" to attend.

"I'll go," said Passepartout to himself. He knew nothing of Mormonism except the custom of polygamy, which is its foundation.

The news quickly spread through the train, which contained about one hundred passengers, thirty of whom, at most, attracted by the notice,

186

ensconced themselves in car No. 117. Passepartout took one of the front seats. Neither Mr. Fogg nor Fix cared to attend.

At the appointed hour Elder William Hitch rose, and, in an irritated voice, as if he had already been contradicted, said, "I tell you that Joe Smith is a martyr, that his brother Hiram is a martyr, and that the persecutions of the United States Government against the prophets will also make a martyr of Brigham Young. Who dares to say the contrary?"

No one ventured to gainsay the missionary, whose excited tone contrasted curiously with his naturally calm visage. No doubt his anger arose from the hardships to which the Mormons were actually subjected. The government had just succeeded, with some difficulty, in reducing these independent fanatics to its rule. It had made itself master of Utah, and subjected that territory to the laws of the Union, after imprisoning Brigham Young on a charge of rebellion and polygamy. The disciples of the prophet had since redoubled their efforts, and resisted, by words at least, the authority of Congress. Elder Hitch, as is seen, was trying to make proselytes on the very railway trains.

Then, emphasising his words with his loud voice and frequent gestures, he related the history of the Mormons from Biblical times: how that, in Israel, a Mormon prophet of the tribe of Joseph published the annals of the new religion, and bequeathed them to his son Mormon; how, many centuries later, a translation of this precious book, which was written in Egyptian, was made by Joseph Smith, junior, a Vermont farmer, who revealed himself as a mystical prophet in 1825; and how, in short, the celestial messenger appeared to him in an illuminated forest, and gave him the annals of the Lord.

Several of the audience, not being much interested in the missionary's narrative, here left the car; but Elder Hitch, continuing his lecture, related how Smith, junior, with his father, two brothers, and a few disciples, founded the church of the "Latter Day Saints," which, adopted not only in America, but in England, Norway and Sweden, and Germany, counts many artisans, as well as men engaged in the liberal professions, among its members; how a colony was established in Ohio, a temple erected there at a cost of two hundred thousand dollars, and a town built at Kirkland; how Smith became an enterprising banker, and received from a simple mummy showman a papyrus scroll written by Abraham and several famous Egyptians.

The Elder's story became somewhat wearisome, and his audience grew gradually less, until it was reduced to twenty passengers. But this did not

" AND YOU, MY FAITHFUL FRIEND

disconcert the enthusiast, who proceeded with the story of Joseph Smith's bankruptcy in 1837, and how his ruined creditors gave him a coat of tar and feathers; his reappearance some years afterwards, more honourable and honoured than ever, at Independence, Missouri, the chief of a flourishing colony of three thousand disciples, and his pursuit thence by outraged Gentiles, and retirement into the Far West.

Ten hearers only were now left, among them honest Passepartout, who was listening with all his ears. Thus he learned that, after long persecutions, Smith reappeared in Illinois, and in 1839 founded a community at Nauvoo, on the Mississippi, numbering twenty-five thousand souls, of which he became mayor, chief justice, and general-in-chief; that he announced himself, in 1843, as a candidate for the Presidency of the United States; and that finally, being drawn into ambuscade at Carthage, he was thrown into prison, and assassinated by a band of men disguised in masks.

Passepartout was now the only person left in the car, and the Elder, looking him full in the face, reminded him that, two years after the assassination of Joseph Smith, the inspired prophet, Brigham Young, his successor, left Nauvoo for the banks of the Great Salt Lake, where, in the midst of that fertile region, directly on the route of the emigrants who crossed Utah on their way to California, the new colony, thanks to the polygamy practised by the Mormons, had flourished beyond expectations.

"And this," added Elder William Hitch, "this is why the jealousy of Congress has been aroused against us! Why have the soldiers of the Union invaded the soil of Utah? Why has Brigham Young, our chief, been imprisoned, in contempt of all justice? Shall we yield to force? Never! Driven from Vermont, driven from Illinois, driven from Ohio, driven from Missouri, driven from Utah, we shall yet find some independent territory on which to plant our tents. And you, my brother," continued the Elder, fixing his angry eyes upon his single auditor, "will you not plant yours there, too, under the shadow of our flag?"

"No!" replied Passepartout courageously, in his turn retiring from the car, and leaving the Elder to preach to vacancy.

During the lecture the train had been making good progress, and towards half-past twelve it reached the northwest border of the Great Salt Lake. Thence the passengers could observe the vast extent of this interior sea, which is also called the Dead Sea, and into which flows an American Jordan. It is a picturesque expanse, framed in lofty crags in large strata, encrusted with white salt—a superb sheet of water, which was formerly of

THE GREAT SALT LAKE

190

larger extent than now, its shores having encroached with the lapse of time, and thus at once reduced its breadth and increased its depth.

The Salt Lake, seventy miles long and thirty-five wide, is situated three miles eight hundred feet above the sea. Quite different from Lake Asphaltite, whose depression is twelve hundred feet below the sea, it contains considerable salt, and one quarter of the weight of its water is solid matter, its specific weight being 1,170, and, after being distilled, 1,000. Fishes are, of course, unable to live in it, and those which descend through the Jordan, the Weber, and other streams soon perish.

The country around the lake was well cultivated, for the Mormons are mostly farmers; while ranches and pens for domesticated animals, fields of wheat, corn, and other cereals, luxuriant prairies, hedges of wild rose, clumps of acacias and milk-wort, would have been seen six months later. Now the ground was covered with a thin powdering of snow.

The train reached Ogden at two o'clock, where it rested for six hours, Mr. Fogg and his party had time to pay a visit to Salt Lake City, connected with Ogden by a branch road; and they spent two hours in this strikingly American town, built on the pattern of other cities of the Union, like a checker-board, "with the sombre sadness of right-angles," as Victor Hugo expresses it. The founder of the City of the Saints could not escape from the taste for symmetry which distinguishes the Anglo-Saxons. In this strange country, where the people are certainly not up to the level of their institutions, everything is done "squarely"—cities, houses, and follies.

The travellers, then, were promenading, at three o'clock, about the streets of the town built between the banks of the Jordan and the spurs of the Wahsatch Range. They saw few or no churches, but the prophet's mansion, the court-house, and the arsenal, blue-brick houses with verandas and porches, surrounded by gardens bordered with acacias, palms, and locusts. A clay and pebble wall, built in 1853, surrounded the town; and in the principal street were the market and several hotels adorned with pavilions. The place did not seem thickly populated. The streets were almost deserted, except in the vicinity of the temple, which they only reached after having traversed several quarters surrounded by palisades. There were many women, which was easily accounted for by the "peculiar institution" of the Mormons; but it must not be supposed that all the Mormons are polygamists. They are free to marry or not, as they please; but it is worth noting that it is mainly the female citizens of Utah who are anxious to marry, as, according to the Mormon religion, maiden ladies are not admitted to the possession of its highest joys. These poor creatures seemed to be neither well off nor happy. Some—the more well-to-do, no doubt—wore short, open, black silk dresses, under a hood or modest shawl; others were habited in Indian fashion.

Passepartout could not behold without a certain fright these women, charged, in groups, with conferring happiness on a single Mormon. His common sense pitied, above all, the husband. It seemed to him a terrible thing to have to guide so many wives at once across the vicissitudes of life, and to conduct them, as it were, in a body to the Mormon paradise with the prospect of seeing them in the company of the glorious Smith, who doubtless was the chief ornament of that delightful place, to all eternity. He felt decidedly repelled from such a vocation, and he imagined—perhaps he was mistaken—that the fair ones of Salt Lake City cast rather alarming glances on his person. Happily, his stay there was but brief. At four the party found themselves again at the station, took their places in the train, and the whistle sounded for starting. Just at the moment, however, that the locomotive wheels began to move, cries of "Stop! stop!" were heard.

Trains, like time and tide, stop for no one. The gentleman who uttered the cries was evidently a belated Mormon. He was breathless with running. Happily for him, the station had neither gates nor barriers. He rushed along the track, jumped on the rear platform of the train, and fell, exhausted, into one of the seats.

Passepartout, who had been anxiously watching this amateur gymnast, approached him with lively interest, and learned that he had taken flight after an unpleasant domestic scene.

When the Mormon had recovered his breath, Passepartout ventured to ask him politely how many wives he had; for, from the manner in which he had decamped, it might be thought that he had twenty at least.

"One, sir," replied the Mormon, raising his arms heavenward —"one, and that was enough!"

CHAPTER XXVIII

IN WHICH PASSEPARTOUT DOES NOT SUCCEED IN MAKING ANYBODY LISTEN TO REASON

The train, on leaving Great Salt Lake at Ogden, passed northward for an hour as far as Weber River, having completed nearly nine hundred miles from San Francisco. From this point it took an easterly direction towards the jagged Wahsatch Mountains. It was in the section included between this range and the Rocky Mountains that the American engineers found the most formidable difficulties in laying the road, and that the government granted a subsidy of forty-eight thousand dollars per mile, instead of sixteen thousand allowed for the work done on the plains. But the engineers, instead of violating nature, avoided its difficulties by winding around, instead of penetrating the rocks. One tunnel only, fourteen thousand feet in length, was pierced in order to arrive at the great basin.

The track up to this time had reached its highest elevation at the Great Salt Lake. From this point it described a long curve, descending towards Bitter Creek Valley, to rise again to the dividing ridge of the waters between the Atlantic and the Pacific. There were many creeks in this mountainous region, and it was necessary to cross Muddy Creek, Green Creek, and others, upon culverts.

Passepartout grew more and more impatient as they went on, while Fix longed to get out of this difficult region, and was more anxious than Phileas Fogg himself to be beyond the danger of delays and accidents, and set foot on English soil.

At ten o'clock at night the train stopped at Fort Bridger station, and twenty minutes later entered Wyoming Territory, following the valley of Bitter Creek throughout. The next day, 7th December, they stopped for a quarter of an hour at Green River station. Snow had fallen abundantly during the night, but, being mixed with rain, it had half melted, and did not interrupt their progress. The bad weather, however, annoyed Passepartout; for the accumulation of snow, by blocking the wheels of the cars, would certainly have been fatal to Mr. Fogg's tour.

"What an idea!" he said to himself. "Why did my master make this journey in winter? Couldn't he have waited for the good season to increase his chances?"

While the worthy Frenchman was absorbed in the state of the sky and the depression of the temperature, Aouda was experiencing fears from a totally different cause.

Several passengers had got off at Green River, and were walking up and down the platforms; and among these Aouda recognised Colonel Stamp Proctor, the same who had so grossly insulted Phileas Fogg at the San Francisco meeting. Not wishing to be recognised, the young woman drew back from the window, feeling much alarm at her discovery. She was attached to the man who, however coldly, gave her daily evidences of the most absolute devotion. She did not comprehend, perhaps, the depth of the sentiment with which her protector inspired her, which she called gratitude, but which, though she was unconscious of it, was really more than that. Her heart sank within her when she recognised the man whom Mr. Fogg desired, sooner or later, to call to account for his conduct. Chance alone, it was clear, had brought Colonel Proctor on this train; but there he was, and it was necessary, at all hazards, that Phileas Fogg should not perceive his adversary.

Aouda seized a moment when Mr. Fogg was asleep to tell Fix and Passepartout whom she had seen.

"That Proctor on this train!" cried Fix. "Well, reassure yourself, madam; before he settles with Mr. Fogg; he has got to deal with me! It seems to me that I was the more insulted of the two."

"And, besides," added Passepartout, "I'll take charge of him, colonel as he is."

"Mr. Fix," resumed Aouda, "Mr. Fogg will allow no one to avenge him. He said that he would come back to America to find this man. Should he perceive Colonel Proctor, we could not prevent a collision which might have terrible results. He must not see him."

"You are right, madam," replied Fix; "a meeting between them might ruin all. Whether he were victorious or beaten, Mr. Fogg would be delayed, and—"

"And," added Passepartout, "that would play the game of the gentlemen

194

of the Reform Club. In four days we shall be in New York. Well, if my master does not leave this car during those four days, we may hope that chance will not bring him face to face with this confounded American. We must, if possible, prevent his stirring out of it."

The conversation dropped. Mr. Fogg had just woke up, and was looking out of the window. Soon after Passepartout, without being heard by his master or Aouda, whispered to the detective, "Would you really fight for him?"

"I would do anything," replied Fix, in a tone which betrayed determined will, "to get him back living to Europe!"

Passepartout felt something like a shudder shoot through his frame, but his confidence in his master remained unbroken.

Was there any means of detaining Mr. Fogg in the car, to avoid a meeting between him and the colonel? It ought not to be a difficult task, since that gentleman was naturally sedentary and little curious. The detective, at least, seemed to have found a way; for, after a few moments, he said to Mr. Fogg, "These are long and slow hours, sir, that we are passing on the railway."

"Yes," replied Mr. Fogg; "but they pass."

"You were in the habit of playing whist," resumed Fix, "on the steamers."

"Yes; but it would be difficult to do so here. I have neither cards nor partners."

"Oh, but we can easily buy some cards, for they are sold on all the American trains. And as for partners, if madam plays—"

"Certainly, sir," Aouda quickly replied; "I understand whist. It is part of an English education."

"I myself have some pretensions to playing a good game. Well, here are three of us, and a dummy—"

"As you please, sir," replied Phileas Fogg, heartily glad to resume his favourite pastime even on the railway.

Passepartout was dispatched in search of the steward, and soon returned with two packs of cards, some pins, counters, and a shelf covered with cloth.

The game commenced. Aouda understood whist sufficiently well, and even received some compliments on her playing from Mr. Fogg. As for the detective, he was simply an adept, and worthy of being matched against his present opponent.

"Now," thought Passepartout, "we've got him. He won't budge."

At eleven in the morning the train had reached the dividing ridge of the waters at Bridger Pass, seven thousand five hundred and twenty-four feet above the level of the sea, one of the highest points attained by the track in crossing the Rocky Mountains. After going about two hundred miles, the travellers at last found themselves on one of those vast plains which extend to the Atlantic, and which nature has made so propitious for laying the iron road.

On the declivity of the Atlantic basin the first streams, branches of the North Platte River, already appeared. The whole northern and eastern horizon was bounded by the immense semi-circular curtain which is formed by the southern portion of the Rocky Mountains, the highest being Laramie Peak. Between this and the railway extended vast plains, plentifully irrigated. On the right rose the lower spurs of the mountainous mass which extends southward to the sources of the Arkansas River, one of the great tributaries of the Missouri.

At half-past twelve the travellers caught sight for an instant of Fort Halleck, which commands that section; and in a few more hours the Rocky Mountains were crossed. There was reason to hope, then, that no accident would mark the journey through this difficult country. The snow had ceased falling, and the air became crisp and cold. Large birds, frightened by the locomotive, rose and flew off in the distance. No wild beast appeared on the plain. It was a desert in its vast nakedness.

After a comfortable breakfast, served in the car, Mr. Fogg and his partners had just resumed whist, when a violent whistling was heard, and the train stopped. Passepartout put his head out of the door, but saw nothing to cause the delay; no station was in view.

Aouda and Fix feared that Mr. Fogg might take it into his head to get out; but that gentleman contented himself with saying to his servant, "See what is the matter."

Passepartout rushed out of the car. Thirty or forty passengers had already descended, amongst them Colonel Stamp Proctor.

The train had stopped before a red signal which blocked the way. The engineer and conductor were talking excitedly with a signal-man, whom the station-master at Medicine Bow, the next stopping place, had sent on before. The passengers drew around and took part in the discussion, in which Colonel Proctor, with his insolent manner, was conspicuous.

Passepartout, joining the group, heard the signal-man say, "No! you can't pass. The bridge at Medicine Bow is shaky, and would not bear the weight of the train."

This was a suspension-bridge thrown over some rapids, about a mile from the place where they now were. According to the signal-man, it was in a ruinous condition, several of the iron wires being broken; and it was impossible to risk the passage. He did not in any way exaggerate the condition of the bridge. It may be taken for granted that, rash as the Americans usually are, when they are prudent there is good reason for it.

Passepartout, not daring to apprise his master of what he heard, listened with set teeth, immovable as a statue.

"Hum!" cried Colonel Proctor; "but we are not going to stay here, I imagine, and take root in the snow?"

"Colonel," replied the conductor, "we have telegraphed to Omaha for a train, but it is not likely that it will reach Medicine Bow in less than six hours."

"Six hours!" cried Passepartout.

"Certainly," returned the conductor, "besides, it will take us as long as that to reach Medicine Bow on foot."

"But it is only a mile from here," said one of the passengers.

"Yes, but it's on the other side of the river."

"And can't we cross that in a boat?" asked the colonel.

"That's impossible. The creek is swelled by the rains. It is a rapid, and we shall have to make a circuit of ten miles to the north to find a ford."

The colonel launched a volley of oaths, denouncing the railway company and the conductor; and Passepartout, who was furious, was not disinclined to make common cause with him. Here was an obstacle, indeed, which all his master's banknotes could not remove.

There was a general disappointment among the passengers, who, without reckoning the delay, saw themselves compelled to trudge fifteen miles over a plain covered with snow. They grumbled and protested, and would certainly have thus attracted Phileas Fogg's attention if he had not been completely absorbed in his game.

Passepartout found that he could not avoid telling his master what had occurred, and, with hanging head, he was turning towards the car, when the engineer, a true Yankee, named Forster called out, "Gentlemen, perhaps there is a way, after all, to get over."

"On the bridge?" asked a passenger.

"On the bridge."

"With our train?"

"With our train."

Passepartout stopped short, and eagerly listened to the engineer.

"But the bridge is unsafe," urged the conductor.

"No matter," replied Forster; "I think that by putting on the very highest speed we might have a chance of getting over."

"The devil!" muttered Passepartout.

But a number of the passengers were at once attracted by the engineer's proposal, and Colonel Proctor was especially delighted, and found the plan a very feasible one. He told stories about engineers leaping their trains over rivers without bridges, by putting on full steam; and many of those present avowed themselves of the engineer's mind.

"We have fifty chances out of a hundred of getting over," said one.

"Eighty! ninety!"

Passepartout was astounded, and, though ready to attempt anything to get over Medicine Creek, thought the experiment proposed a little too American. "Besides," thought he, "there's a still more simple way, and it does not even occur to any of these people! Sir," said he aloud to one of the passengers, "the engineer's plan seems to me a little dangerous, but—"

"Eighty chances!" replied the passenger, turning his back on him.

"I know it," said Passepartout, turning to another passenger, "but a simple idea—"

"Ideas are no use," returned the American, shrugging his shoulders, "as the engineer assures us that we can pass."

"Doubtless," urged Passepartout, "we can pass, but perhaps it would be more prudent—"

"What! Prudent!" cried Colonel Proctor, whom this word seemed to excite prodigiously. "At full speed, don't you see, at full speed!"

"I know—I see," repeated Passepartout; "but it would be, if not more prudent, since that word displeases you, at least more natural—"

"Who! What! What's the matter with this fellow?" cried several.

The poor fellow did not know to whom to address himself.

"Are you afraid?" asked Colonel Proctor.

"I afraid? Very well; I will show these people that a Frenchman can be as American as they!"

"All aboard!" cried the conductor.

"Yes, all aboard!" repeated Passepartout, and immediately. "But they can't prevent me from thinking that it would be more natural for us to cross the bridge on foot, and let the train come after!"

But no one heard this sage reflection, nor would anyone have

THE BRIDGE, COMPLETELY RUINED, FELL WITH A CRASH

acknowledged its justice. The passengers resumed their places in the cars. Passepartout took his seat without telling what had passed. The whist-players were quite absorbed in their game.

The locomotive whistled vigorously; the engineer, reversing the steam, backed the train for nearly a mile—retiring, like a jumper, in order to take a longer leap. Then, with another whistle, he began to move forward; the train increased its speed, and soon its rapidity became frightful; a prolonged screech issued from the locomotive; the piston worked up and down twenty strokes to the second. They perceived that the whole train, rushing on at the rate of a hundred miles an hour, hardly bore upon the rails at all.

And they passed over! It was like a flash. No one saw the bridge. The train leaped, so to speak, from one bank to the other, and the engineer could not stop it until it had gone five miles beyond the station. But scarcely had the train passed the river, when the bridge, completely ruined, fell with a crash into the rapids of Medicine Bow.

CHAPTER XXIX

IN WHICH CERTAIN INCIDENTS ARE NARRATED WHICH ARE ONLY TO BE MET WITH ON AMERICAN RAILROADS

The train pursued its course, that evening, without interruption, passing Fort Saunders, crossing Cheyne Pass, and reaching Evans Pass. The road here attained the highest elevation of the journey, eight thousand and ninety-two feet above the level of the sea. The travellers had now only to descend to the Atlantic by limitless plains, levelled by nature. A branch of the "grand trunk" led off southward to Denver, the capital of Colorado. The country round about is rich in gold and silver, and more than fifty thousand inhabitants are already settled there.

Thirteen hundred and eighty-two miles had been passed over from San Francisco, in three days and three nights; four days and nights more would probably bring them to New York. Phileas Fogg was not as yet behindhand.

During the night Camp Walbach was passed on the left; Lodge Pole Creek ran parallel with the road, marking the boundary between the territories of Wyoming and Colorado. They entered Nebraska at eleven, passed near Sedgwick, and touched at Julesburg, on the southern branch of the Platte River.

It was here that the Union Pacific Railroad was inaugurated on the 23rd of October, 1867, by the chief engineer, General Dodge. Two powerful locomotives, carrying nine cars of invited guests, amongst whom was Thomas C. Durant, vice-president of the road, stopped at this point; cheers were given, the Sioux and Pawnees performed an imitation Indian battle, fireworks were let off, and the first number of the Railway Pioneer was printed by a press brought on the train. Thus was celebrated the inauguration of this great railroad, a mighty instrument of progress and civilisation, thrown across the desert, and destined to link together cities and towns which do not yet exist. The whistle of the locomotive, more powerful than Amphion's lyre, was about to bid them rise from American soil.

Fort McPherson was left behind at eight in the morning, and three hundred and fifty-seven miles had yet to be traversed before reaching Omaha. The road followed the capricious windings of the southern branch of the Platte River, on its left bank. At nine the train stopped at the important town of North Platte, built between the two arms of the river, which rejoin each other around it and form a single artery, a large tributary, whose waters empty into the Missouri a little above Omaha.

The one hundred and first meridian was passed.

Mr. Fogg and his partners had resumed their game; no one—not even the dummy—complained of the length of the trip. Fix had begun by winning several guineas, which he seemed likely to lose; but he showed himself a not less eager whist-player than Mr. Fogg. During the morning, chance distinctly favoured that gentleman. Trumps and honours were showered upon his hands.

Once, having resolved on a bold stroke, he was on the point of playing a spade, when a voice behind him said, "I should play a diamond."

Mr. Fogg, Aouda, and Fix raised their heads, and beheld Colonel Proctor.

Stamp Proctor and Phileas Fogg recognised each other at once.

"Ah! it's you, is it, Englishman?" cried the colonel; "it's you who are going to play a spade!"

"And who plays it," replied Phileas Fogg coolly, throwing down the ten of spades.

"Well, it pleases me to have it diamonds," replied Colonel Proctor, in an insolent tone.

He made a movement as if to seize the card which had just been played, adding, "You don't understand anything about whist."

"Perhaps I do, as well as another," said Phileas Fogg, rising.

"You have only to try, son of John Bull," replied the colonel.

Aouda turned pale, and her blood ran cold. She seized Mr. Fogg's arm and gently pulled him back. Passepartout was ready to pounce upon the American, who was staring insolently at his opponent. But Fix got up, and, going to Colonel Proctor said, "You forget that it is I with whom you have to deal, sir; for it was I whom you not only insulted, but struck!"

"Mr. Fix," said Mr. Fogg, "pardon me, but this affair is mine, and mine only. The colonel has again insulted me, by insisting that I should not play a

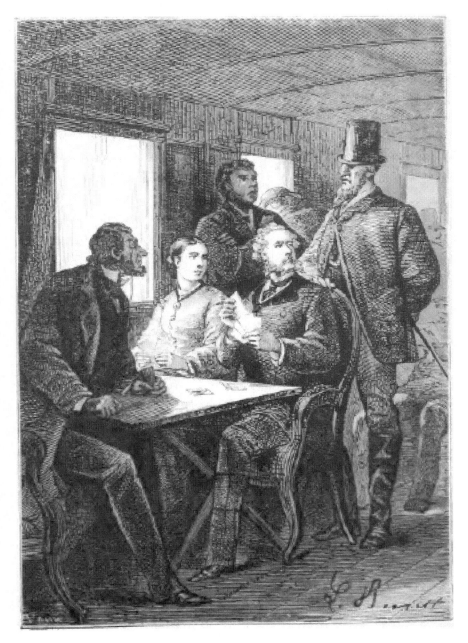

" I SHOULD PLAY A DIAMOND "

spade, and he shall give me satisfaction for it."

"When and where you will," replied the American, "and with whatever weapon you choose."

Aouda in vain attempted to retain Mr. Fogg; as vainly did the detective endeavour to make the quarrel his. Passepartout wished to throw the colonel out of the window, but a sign from his master checked him. Phileas Fogg left the car, and the American followed him upon the platform. "Sir," said Mr. Fogg to his adversary, "I am in a great hurry to get back to Europe, and any delay whatever will be greatly to my disadvantage."

"Well, what's that to me?" replied Colonel Proctor.

"Sir," said Mr. Fogg, very politely, "after our meeting at San Francisco, I determined to return to America and find you as soon as I had completed the business which called me to England."

"Really!"

"Will you appoint a meeting for six months hence?"

"Why not ten years hence?"

"I say six months," returned Phileas Fogg; "and I shall be at the place of meeting promptly."

"All this is an evasion," cried Stamp Proctor. "Now or never!"

"Very good. You are going to New York?"

"No."

"To Chicago?"

"No."

"To Omaha?"

"What difference is it to you? Do you know Plum Creek?"

"No," replied Mr. Fogg.

"It's the next station. The train will be there in an hour, and will stop there ten minutes. In ten minutes several revolver-shots could be exchanged."

"Very well," said Mr. Fogg. "I will stop at Plum Creek."

"And I guess you'll stay there too," added the American insolently.

"Who knows?" replied Mr. Fogg, returning to the car as coolly as usual. He began to reassure Aouda, telling her that blusterers were never to be feared, and begged Fix to be his second at the approaching duel, a request which the detective could not refuse. Mr. Fogg resumed the interrupted game with perfect calmness.

At eleven o'clock the locomotive's whistle announced that they were approaching Plum Creek station. Mr. Fogg rose, and, followed by Fix, went out upon the platform. Passepartout accompanied him, carrying a pair of revolvers. Aouda remained in the car, as pale as death.

The door of the next car opened, and Colonel Proctor appeared on the platform, attended by a Yankee of his own stamp as his second. But just as the combatants were about to step from the train, the conductor hurried up, and shouted, "You can't get off, gentlemen!"

"Why not?" asked the colonel.

"We are twenty minutes late, and we shall not stop."

"But I am going to fight a duel with this gentleman."

"I am sorry," said the conductor; "but we shall be off at once. There's the bell ringing now."

The train started.

"I'm really very sorry, gentlemen," said the conductor. "Under any other circumstances I should have been happy to oblige you. But, after all, as you have not had time to fight here, why not fight as we go along?"

"That wouldn't be convenient, perhaps, for this gentleman," said the colonel, in a jeering tone.

"It would be perfectly so," replied Phileas Fogg.

"Well, we are really in America," thought Passepartout, "and the conductor is a gentleman of the first order!"

So muttering, he followed his master.

The two combatants, their seconds, and the conductor passed through the cars to the rear of the train. The last car was only occupied by a dozen passengers, whom the conductor politely asked if they would not be so kind as to leave it vacant for a few moments, as two gentlemen had an affair of honour to settle. The passengers granted the request with alacrity, and straightway disappeared on the platform.

The car, which was some fifty feet long, was very convenient for their purpose. The adversaries might march on each other in the aisle, and fire at their ease. Never was duel more easily arranged. Mr. Fogg and Colonel Proctor, each provided with two six-barrelled revolvers, entered the car. The seconds, remaining outside, shut them in. They were to begin firing at the first whistle of the locomotive. After an interval of two minutes, what remained of the two gentlemen would be taken from the car.

Nothing could be more simple. Indeed, it was all so simple that Fix and Passepartout felt their hearts beating as if they would crack. They were listening for the whistle agreed upon, when suddenly savage cries resounded in the air, accompanied by reports which certainly did not issue from the car where the duellists were. The reports continued in front and the whole

THEY HAD FORCED THE DOORS, AND WERE FIGHTING
HAND TO HAND WITH THE TRAVELLERS

length of the train. Cries of terror proceeded from the interior of the cars.

Colonel Proctor and Mr. Fogg, revolvers in hand, hastily quitted their prison, and rushed forward where the noise was most clamorous. They then perceived that the train was attacked by a band of Sioux.

This was not the first attempt of these daring Indians, for more than once they had waylaid trains on the road. A hundred of them had, according to their habit, jumped upon the steps without stopping the train, with the ease of a clown mounting a horse at full gallop.

The Sioux were armed with guns, from which came the reports, to which the passengers, who were almost all armed, responded by revolver-shots.

The Indians had first mounted the engine, and half stunned the engineer and stoker with blows from their muskets. A Sioux chief, wishing to stop the train, but not knowing how to work the regulator, had opened wide instead of closing the steam-valve, and the locomotive was plunging forward with terrific velocity.

The Sioux had at the same time invaded the cars, skipping like enraged monkeys over the roofs, thrusting open the doors, and fighting hand to hand with the passengers. Penetrating the baggage-car, they pillaged it, throwing the trunks out of the train. The cries and shots were constant. The travellers defended themselves bravely; some of the cars were barricaded, and sustained a siege, like moving forts, carried along at a speed of a hundred miles an hour.

Aouda behaved courageously from the first. She defended herself like a true heroine with a revolver, which she shot through the broken windows whenever a savage made his appearance. Twenty Sioux had fallen mortally wounded to the ground, and the wheels crushed those who fell upon the rails as if they had been worms. Several passengers, shot or stunned, lay on the seats.

It was necessary to put an end to the struggle, which had lasted for ten minutes, and which would result in the triumph of the Sioux if the train was not stopped. Fort Kearney station, where there was a garrison, was only two miles distant; but, that once passed, the Sioux would be masters of the train between Fort Kearney and the station beyond.

The conductor was fighting beside Mr. Fogg, when he was shot and fell. At the same moment he cried, "Unless the train is stopped in five minutes, we are lost!"

"It shall be stopped," said Phileas Fogg, preparing to rush from the car.

"Stay, monsieur," cried Passepartout; "I will go."

Mr. Fogg had not time to stop the brave fellow, who, opening a door unperceived by the Indians, succeeded in slipping under the car; and while the struggle continued and the balls whizzed across each other over his head, he made use of his old acrobatic experience, and with amazing agility worked his way under the cars, holding on to the chains, aiding himself by the brakes and edges of the sashes, creeping from one car to another with marvellous skill, and thus gaining the forward end of the train.

There, suspended by one hand between the baggage-car and the tender, with the other he loosened the safety chains; but, owing to the traction, he would never have succeeded in unscrewing the yoking-bar, had not a violent concussion jolted this bar out. The train, now detached from the engine, remained a little behind, whilst the locomotive rushed forward with increased speed.

Carried on by the force already acquired, the train still moved for several minutes; but the brakes were worked and at last they stopped, less than a hundred feet from Kearney station.

The soldiers of the fort, attracted by the shots, hurried up; the Sioux had not expected them, and decamped in a body before the train entirely stopped.

But when the passengers counted each other on the station platform several were found missing; among others the courageous Frenchman, whose devotion had just saved them.

CHAPTER XXX

IN WHICH PHILEAS FOGG SIMPLY DOES HIS DUTY

Three passengers including Passepartout had disappeared. Had they been killed in the struggle? Were they taken prisoners by the Sioux? It was impossible to tell.

There were many wounded, but none mortally. Colonel Proctor was one of the most seriously hurt; he had fought bravely, and a ball had entered his groin. He was carried into the station with the other wounded passengers, to receive such attention as could be of avail.

Aouda was safe; and Phileas Fogg, who had been in the thickest of the fight, had not received a scratch. Fix was slightly wounded in the arm. But Passepartout was not to be found, and tears coursed down Aouda's cheeks.

All the passengers had got out of the train, the wheels of which were stained with blood. From the tyres and spokes hung ragged pieces of flesh. As far as the eye could reach on the white plain behind, red trails were visible. The last Sioux were disappearing in the south, along the banks of Republican River.

Mr. Fogg, with folded arms, remained motionless. He had a serious decision to make. Aouda, standing near him, looked at him without speaking, and he understood her look. If his servant was a prisoner, ought he not to risk everything to rescue him from the Indians? "I will find him, living or dead," said he quietly to Aouda.

"Ah, Mr.—Mr. Fogg!" cried she, clasping his hands and covering them with tears.

"Living," added Mr. Fogg, "if we do not lose a moment."

Phileas Fogg, by this resolution, inevitably sacrificed himself; he pronounced his own doom. The delay of a single day would make him lose the steamer at New York, and his bet would be certainly lost. But as he thought, "It is my duty," he did not hesitate.

HANGING BY ONE HAND BETWEEN THE TENDER AND THE
LUGGAGE VAN, HE

The commanding officer of Fort Kearney was there. A hundred of his soldiers had placed themselves in a position to defend the station, should the Sioux attack it.

"Sir," said Mr. Fogg to the captain, "three passengers have disappeared."

"Dead?" asked the captain.

"Dead or prisoners; that is the uncertainty which must be solved. Do you propose to pursue the Sioux?"

"That's a serious thing to do, sir," returned the captain. "These Indians may retreat beyond the Arkansas, and I cannot leave the fort unprotected."

"The lives of three men are in question, sir," said Phileas Fogg.

"Doubtless; but can I risk the lives of fifty men to save three?"

"I don't know whether you can, sir; but you ought to do so."

"Nobody here," returned the other, "has a right to teach me my duty."

"Very well," said Mr. Fogg, coldly. "I will go alone."

"You, sir!" cried Fix, coming up; "you go alone in pursuit of the Indians?"

"Would you have me leave this poor fellow to perish—him to whom every one present owes his life? I shall go."

"No, sir, you shall not go alone," cried the captain, touched in spite of himself. "No! you are a brave man. Thirty volunteers!" he added, turning to the soldiers.

The whole company started forward at once. The captain had only to pick his men. Thirty were chosen, and an old sergeant placed at their head.

"Thanks, captain," said Mr. Fogg.

"Will you let me go with you?" asked Fix.

"Do as you please, sir. But if you wish to do me a favour, you will remain with Aouda. In case anything should happen to me—"

A sudden pallor overspread the detective's face. Separate himself from the man whom he had so persistently followed step by step! Leave him to wander about in this desert! Fix gazed attentively at Mr. Fogg, and, despite his suspicions and of the struggle which was going on within him, he lowered his eyes before that calm and frank look.

"I will stay," said he.

A few moments after, Mr. Fogg pressed the young woman's hand, and, having confided to her his precious carpet-bag, went off with the sergeant and his little squad. But, before going, he had said to the soldiers, "My friends, I will divide five thousand dollars among you, if we save the prisoners."

211

It was then a little past noon.

Aouda retired to a waiting-room, and there she waited alone, thinking of the simple and noble generosity, the tranquil courage of Phileas Fogg. He had sacrificed his fortune, and was now risking his life, all without hesitation, from duty, in silence.

Fix did not have the same thoughts, and could scarcely conceal his agitation. He walked feverishly up and down the platform, but soon resumed his outward composure. He now saw the folly of which he had been guilty in letting Fogg go alone. What! This man, whom he had just followed around the world, was permitted now to separate himself from him! He began to accuse and abuse himself, and, as if he were director of police, administered to himself a sound lecture for his greenness.

"I have been an idiot!" he thought, "and this man will see it. He has gone, and won't come back! But how is it that I, Fix, who have in my pocket a warrant for his arrest, have been so fascinated by him? Decidedly, I am nothing but an ass!"

So reasoned the detective, while the hours crept by all too slowly. He did not know what to do. Sometimes he was tempted to tell Aouda all; but he could not doubt how the young woman would receive his confidences. What course should he take? He thought of pursuing Fogg across the vast white plains; it did not seem impossible that he might overtake him. Footsteps were easily printed on the snow! But soon, under a new sheet, every imprint would be effaced.

Fix became discouraged. He felt a sort of insurmountable longing to abandon the game altogether. He could now leave Fort Kearney station, and pursue his journey homeward in peace.

Towards two o'clock in the afternoon, while it was snowing hard, long whistles were heard approaching from the east. A great shadow, preceded by a wild light, slowly advanced, appearing still larger through the mist, which gave it a fantastic aspect. No train was expected from the east, neither had there been time for the succour asked for by telegraph to arrive; the train from Omaha to San Francisco was not due till the next day. The mystery was soon explained.

The locomotive, which was slowly approaching with deafening whistles, was that which, having been detached from the train, had continued its route with such terrific rapidity, carrying off the unconscious engineer and stoker. It had run several miles, when, the fire becoming low for want of fuel, the steam had slackened; and it had finally stopped an hour after, some

AN ENORMOUS SHADOW, PRECEDED BY A FLICKERING YEL-
LOW GLARE

twenty miles beyond Fort Kearney. Neither the engineer nor the stoker was dead, and, after remaining for some time in their swoon, had come to themselves. The train had then stopped. The engineer, when he found himself in the desert, and the locomotive without cars, understood what had happened. He could not imagine how the locomotive had become separated from the train; but he did not doubt that the train left behind was in distress.

He did not hesitate what to do. It would be prudent to continue on to Omaha, for it would be dangerous to return to the train, which the Indians might still be engaged in pillaging. Nevertheless, he began to rebuild the fire in the furnace; the pressure again mounted, and the locomotive returned, running backwards to Fort Kearney. This it was which was whistling in the mist.

The travellers were glad to see the locomotive resume its place at the head of the train. They could now continue the journey so terribly interrupted.

Aouda, on seeing the locomotive come up, hurried out of the station, and asked the conductor, "Are you going to start?"

"At once, madam."

"But the prisoners, our unfortunate fellow-travellers—"

"I cannot interrupt the trip," replied the conductor. "We are already three hours behind time."

"And when will another train pass here from San Francisco?"

"To-morrow evening, madam."

"To-morrow evening! But then it will be too late! We must wait—"

"It is impossible," responded the conductor. "If you wish to go, please get in."

"I will not go," said Aouda.

Fix had heard this conversation. A little while before, when there was no prospect of proceeding on the journey, he had made up his mind to leave Fort Kearney; but now that the train was there, ready to start, and he had only to take his seat in the car, an irresistible influence held him back. The station platform burned his feet, and he could not stir. The conflict in his mind again began; anger and failure stifled him. He wished to struggle on to the end.

Meanwhile the passengers and some of the wounded, among them Colonel Proctor, whose injuries were serious, had taken their places in the train. The buzzing of the over-heated boiler was heard, and the steam was escaping from the valves. The engineer whistled, the train started, and soon disappeared, mingling its white smoke with the eddies of the densely falling snow.

The detective had remained behind.

Several hours passed. The weather was dismal, and it was very cold. Fix sat motionless on a bench in the station; he might have been thought asleep. Aouda, despite the storm, kept coming out of the waiting-room, going to the end of the platform, and peering through the tempest of snow, as if to pierce the mist which narrowed the horizon around her, and to hear, if possible, some welcome sound. She heard and saw nothing. Then she would return, chilled through, to issue out again after the lapse of a few moments, but always in vain.

Evening came, and the little band had not returned. Where could they be? Had they found the Indians, and were they having a conflict with them, or were they still wandering amid the mist? The commander of the fort was anxious, though he tried to conceal his apprehensions. As night approached, the snow fell less plentifully, but it became intensely cold. Absolute silence rested on the plains. Neither flight of bird nor passing of beast troubled the perfect calm.

Throughout the night Aouda, full of sad forebodings, her heart stifled with anguish, wandered about on the verge of the plains. Her imagination carried her far off, and showed her innumerable dangers. What she suffered through the long hours it would be impossible to describe.

Fix remained stationary in the same place, but did not sleep. Once a man approached and spoke to him, and the detective merely replied by shaking his head.

Thus the night passed. At dawn, the half-extinguished disc of the sun rose above a misty horizon; but it was now possible to recognise objects two miles off. Phileas Fogg and the squad had gone southward; in the south all was still vacancy. It was then seven o'clock.

The captain, who was really alarmed, did not know what course to take. Should he send another detachment to the rescue of the first? Should he sacrifice more men, with so few chances of saving those already sacrificed? His hesitation did not last long, however. Calling one of his lieutenants, he was on the point of ordering a reconnaissance, when gunshots were heard. Was it a signal? The soldiers rushed out of the fort, and half a mile off they perceived a little band returning in good order.

Mr. Fogg was marching at their head, and just behind him were Passepartout and the other two travellers, rescued from the Sioux.

215

They had met and fought the Indians ten miles south of Fort Kearney. Shortly before the detachment arrived, Passepartout and his companions had begun to struggle with their captors, three of whom the Frenchman had felled with his fists, when his master and the soldiers hastened up to their relief.

All were welcomed with joyful cries. Phileas Fogg distributed the reward he had promised to the soldiers, while Passepartout, not without reason, muttered to himself, "It must certainly be confessed that I cost my master dear!"

Fix, without saying a word, looked at Mr. Fogg, and it would have been difficult to analyse the thoughts which struggled within him. As for Aouda, she took her protector's hand and pressed it in her own, too much moved to speak.

Meanwhile, Passepartout was looking about for the train; he thought he should find it there, ready to start for Omaha, and he hoped that the time lost might be regained.

"The train!the train!" cried he.

"Gone," replied Fix.

"And when does the next train pass here?" said Phileas Fogg.

"Not till this evening."

"Ah!" returned the impassible gentleman quietly.

THE FRENCHMAN HAD STUNNED THREE WITH HIS FISTS

CHAPTER XXXI

IN WHICH FIX, THE DETECTIVE, CONSIDERABLY FURTHERS THE INTERESTS OF PHILEAS FOGG

Phileas Fogg found himself twenty hours behind time. Passepartout, the involuntary cause of this delay, was desperate. He had ruined his master!

At this moment the detective approached Mr. Fogg, and, looking him intently in the face, said:

"Seriously, sir, are you in great haste?"

"Quite seriously."

"I have a purpose in asking," resumed Fix. "Is it absolutely necessary that you should be in New York on the 11th, before nine o'clock in the evening, the time that the steamer leaves for Liverpool?"

"It is absolutely necessary."

"And, if your journey had not been interrupted by these Indians, you would have reached New York on the morning of the 11th?"

"Yes; with eleven hours to spare before the steamer left."

"Good! you are therefore twenty hours behind. Twelve from twenty leaves eight. You must regain eight hours. Do you wish to try to do so?"

"On foot?" asked Mr. Fogg.

"No; on a sledge," replied Fix. "On a sledge with sails. A man has proposed such a method to me."

It was the man who had spoken to Fix during the night, and whose offer he had refused.

Phileas Fogg did not reply at once; but Fix, having pointed out the man, who was walking up and down in front of the station, Mr. Fogg went up to him. An instant after, Mr. Fogg and the American, whose name was Mudge, entered a hut built just below the fort.

There Mr. Fogg examined a curious vehicle, a kind of frame on two long beams, a little raised in front like the runners of a sledge, and upon which there was room for five or six persons. A high mast was fixed on the frame, held firmly by metallic lashings, to which was attached a large brigantine sail. This mast held an iron stay upon which to hoist a jib-sail. Behind, a sort of rudder served to guide the vehicle. It was, in short, a sledge rigged like a sloop. During the winter, when the trains are blocked up by the snow, these sledges make extremely rapid journeys across the frozen plains from one station to another. Provided with more sails than a cutter, and with the wind behind them, they slip over the surface of the prairies with a speed equal if not superior to that of the express trains.

Mr. Fogg readily made a bargain with the owner of this land-craft. The wind was favourable, being fresh, and blowing from the west. The snow had hardened, and Mudge was very confident of being able to transport Mr. Fogg in a few hours to Omaha. Thence the trains eastward run frequently to Chicago and New York. It was not impossible that the lost time might yet be recovered; and such an opportunity was not to be rejected.

Not wishing to expose Aouda to the discomforts of travelling in the open air, Mr. Fogg proposed to leave her with Passepartout at Fort Kearney, the servant taking upon himself to escort her to Europe by a better route and under more favourable conditions. But Aouda refused to separate from Mr. Fogg, and Passepartout was delighted with her decision; for nothing could induce him to leave his master while Fix was with him.

It would be difficult to guess the detective's thoughts. Was this conviction shaken by Phileas Fogg's return, or did he still regard him as an exceedingly shrewd rascal, who, his journey round the world completed, would think himself absolutely safe in England? Perhaps Fix's opinion of Phileas Fogg was somewhat modified; but he was nevertheless resolved to do his duty, and to hasten the return of the whole party to England as much as possible.

At eight o'clock the sledge was ready to start. The passengers took their places on it, and wrapped themselves up closely in their travelling-cloaks. The two great sails were hoisted, and under the pressure of the wind the sledge slid over the hardened snow with a velocity of forty miles an hour.

The distance between Fort Kearney and Omaha, as the birds fly, is at most two hundred miles. If the wind held good, the distance might be traversed in five hours; if no accident happened the sledge might reach Omaha by one o'clock.

What a journey! The travellers, huddled close together, could not speak for the cold, intensified by the rapidity at which they were going. The sledge sped on as lightly as a boat over the waves. When the breeze came skimming the earth the sledge seemed to be lifted off the ground by its sails. Mudge, who was at the rudder, kept in a straight line, and by a turn of his hand checked the lurches which the vehicle had a tendency to make. All the sails were up, and the jib was so arranged as not to screen the brigantine. A top-mast was hoisted, and another jib, held out to the wind, added its force to the other sails. Although the speed could not be exactly estimated, the sledge could not be going at less than forty miles an hour.

"If nothing breaks," said Mudge, "we shall get there!"

Mr. Fogg had made it for Mudge's interest to reach Omaha within the time agreed on, by the offer of a handsome reward.

The prairie, across which the sledge was moving in a straight line, was as flat as a sea. It seemed like a vast frozen lake. The railroad which ran through this section ascended from the south-west to the north-west by Great Island, Columbus, an important Nebraska town, Schuyler, and Fremont, to Omaha. It followed throughout the right bank of the Platte River. The sledge, shortening this route, took a chord of the arc described by the railway. Mudge was not afraid of being stopped by the Platte River, because it was frozen. The road, then, was quite clear of obstacles, and Phileas Fogg had but two things to fear—an accident to the sledge, and a change or calm in the wind.

But the breeze, far from lessening its force, blew as if to bend the mast, which, however, the metallic lashings held firmly. These lashings, like the chords of a stringed instrument, resounded as if vibrated by a violin bow. The sledge slid along in the midst of a plaintively intense melody.

"Those chords give the fifth and the octave," said Mr. Fogg.

These were the only words he uttered during the journey. Aouda, cosily packed in furs and cloaks, was sheltered as much as possible from the attacks of the freezing wind. As for Passepartout, his face was as red as the sun's disc when it sets in the mist, and he laboriously inhaled the biting air. With his natural buoyancy of spirits, he began to hope again. They would reach New York on the evening, if not on the morning, of the 11th, and there was still some chances that it would be before the steamer sailed for Liverpool.

Passepartout even felt a strong desire to grasp his ally, Fix, by the hand. He remembered that it was the detective who procured the sledge, the only means of reaching Omaha in time; but, checked by some presentiment, he kept his usual reserve. One thing, however, Passepartout would never forget, and that was the sacrifice which Mr. Fogg had made, without hesitation, to rescue him from the Sioux. Mr. Fogg had risked his fortune and his life. No!

THE COLD, INCREASED BY THE TREMENDOUS SPEED, DE-
PRIVED THEM OF THE POWER OF SPEECH

His servant would never forget that!

While each of the party was absorbed in reflections so different, the sledge flew past over the vast carpet of snow. The creeks it passed over were not perceived. Fields and streams disappeared under the uniform whiteness. The plain was absolutely deserted. Between the Union Pacific road and the branch which unites Kearney with Saint Joseph it formed a great uninhabited island. Neither village, station, nor fort appeared. From time to time they sped by some phantom-like tree, whose white skeleton twisted and rattled in the wind. Sometimes flocks of wild birds rose, or bands of gaunt, famished, ferocious prairie-wolves ran howling after the sledge. Passepartout, revolver in hand, held himself ready to fire on those which came too near. Had an accident then happened to the sledge, the travellers, attacked by these beasts, would have been in the most terrible danger; but it held on its even course, soon gained on the wolves, and ere long left the howling band at a safe distance behind.

About noon Mudge perceived by certain landmarks that he was crossing the Platte River. He said nothing, but he felt certain that he was now within twenty miles of Omaha. In less than an hour he left the rudder and furled his sails, whilst the sledge, carried forward by the great impetus the wind had given it, went on half a mile further with its sails unspread.

It stopped at last, and Mudge, pointing to a mass of roofs white with snow, said: "We have got there!"

Arrived! Arrived at the station which is in daily communication, by numerous trains, with the Atlantic seaboard!

Passepartout and Fix jumped off, stretched their stiffened limbs, and aided Mr. Fogg and the young woman to descend from the sledge. Phileas Fogg generously rewarded Mudge, whose hand Passepartout warmly grasped, and the party directed their steps to the Omaha railway station.

The Pacific Railroad proper finds its terminus at this important Nebraska town. Omaha is connected with Chicago by the Chicago and Rock Island Railroad, which runs directly east, and passes fifty stations.

A train was ready to start when Mr. Fogg and his party reached the station, and they only had time to get into the cars. They had seen nothing of Omaha; but Passepartout confessed to himself that this was not to be regretted, as they were not travelling to see the sights.

The train passed rapidly across the State of Iowa, by Council Bluffs, Des Moines, and Iowa City. During the night it crossed the Mississippi at Davenport, and by Rock Island entered Illinois. The next day, which was the

10th, at four o'clock in the evening, it reached Chicago, already risen from its ruins, and more proudly seated than ever on the borders of its beautiful Lake Michigan.

Nine hundred miles separated Chicago from New York; but trains are not wanting at Chicago. Mr. Fogg passed at once from one to the other, and the locomotive of the Pittsburgh, Fort Wayne, and Chicago Railway left at full speed, as if it fully comprehended that that gentleman had no time to lose. It traversed Indiana, Ohio, Pennsylvania, and New Jersey like a flash, rushing through towns with antique names, some of which had streets and car-tracks, but as yet no houses. At last the Hudson came into view; and, at a quarter-past eleven in the evening of the 11th, the train stopped in the station on the right bank of the river, before the very pier of the Cunard line.

The China, for Liverpool, had started three-quarters of an hour before!

CHAPTER XXXII

IN WHICH PHILEAS FOGG ENGAGES IN A DIRECT STRUGGLE WITH BAD FORTUNE

The China, in leaving, seemed to have carried off Phileas Fogg's last hope. None of the other steamers were able to serve his projects. The Pereire, of the French Transatlantic Company, whose admirable steamers are equal to any in speed and comfort, did not leave until the 14th; the Hamburg boats did not go directly to Liverpool or London, but to Havre; and the additional trip from Havre to Southampton would render Phileas Fogg's last efforts of no avail. The Inman steamer did not depart till the next day, and could not cross the Atlantic in time to save the wager.

Mr. Fogg learned all this in consulting his Bradshaw, which gave him the daily movements of the trans-Atlantic steamers.

Passepartout was crushed; it overwhelmed him to lose the boat by three-quarters of an hour. It was his fault, for, instead of helping his master, he had not ceased putting obstacles in his path! And when he recalled all the incidents of the tour, when he counted up the sums expended in pure loss and on his own account, when he thought that the immense stake, added to the heavy charges of this useless journey, would completely ruin Mr. Fogg, he overwhelmed himself with bitter self-accusations. Mr. Fogg, however, did not reproach him; and, on leaving the Cunard pier, only said: "We will consult about what is best to-morrow. Come."

The party crossed the Hudson in the Jersey City ferryboat, and drove in a carriage to the St. Nicholas Hotel, on Broadway. Rooms were engaged, and the night passed, briefly to Phileas Fogg, who slept profoundly, but very long to Aouda and the others, whose agitation did not permit them to rest.

The next day was the 12th of December. From seven in the morning of the 12th to a quarter before nine in the evening of the 21st there were nine days, thirteen hours, and forty-five minutes. If Phileas Fogg had left in the

AND SOMETIMES A PACK OF PRAIRIE WOLVES

China, one of the fastest steamers on the Atlantic, he would have reached Liverpool, and then London, within the period agreed upon.

Mr. Fogg left the hotel alone, after giving Passepartout instructions to await his return, and inform Aouda to be ready at an instant's notice. He proceeded to the banks of the Hudson, and looked about among the vessels moored or anchored in the river, for any that were about to depart. Several had departure signals, and were preparing to put to sea at morning tide; for in this immense and admirable port there is not one day in a hundred that vessels do not set out for every quarter of the globe. But they were mostly sailing vessels, of which, of course, Phileas Fogg could make no use.

He seemed about to give up all hope, when he espied, anchored at the Battery, a cable's length off at most, a trading vessel, with a screw, well-shaped, whose funnel, puffing a cloud of smoke, indicated that she was getting ready for departure.

Phileas Fogg hailed a boat, got into it, and soon found himself on board the Henrietta, iron-hulled, wood-built above. He ascended to the deck, and asked for the captain, who forthwith presented himself. He was a man of fifty, a sort of sea-wolf, with big eyes, a complexion of oxidised copper, red hair and thick neck, and a growling voice.

"The captain?" asked Mr. Fogg.

"I am the captain."

"I am Phileas Fogg, of London."

"And I am Andrew Speedy, of Cardiff."

"You are going to put to sea?"

"In an hour."

"You are bound for—"

"Bordeaux."

"And your cargo?"

"No freight. Going in ballast."

"Have you any passengers?"

"No passengers. Never have passengers. Too much in the way."

"Is your vessel a swift one?"

"Between eleven and twelve knots. The Henrietta, well known."

"Will you carry me and three other persons to Liverpool?"

"To Liverpool? Why not to China?"

"I said Liverpool."

"No!"

"No?"

"No. I am setting out for Bordeaux, and shall go to Bordeaux."

"Money is no object?"

"None."

The captain spoke in a tone which did not admit of a reply.

"But the owners of the Henrietta—" resumed Phileas Fogg.

"The owners are myself," replied the captain. "The vessel belongs to me."

"I will freight it for you."

"No."

"I will buy it of you."

"No."

Phileas Fogg did not betray the least disappointment; but the situation was a grave one. It was not at New York as at Hong Kong, nor with the captain of the Henrietta as with the captain of the Tankadere. Up to this time money had smoothed away every obstacle. Now money failed.

Still, some means must be found to cross the Atlantic on a boat, unless by balloon—which would have been venturesome, besides not being capable of being put in practice. It seemed that Phileas Fogg had an idea, for he said to the captain, "Well, will you carry me to Bordeaux?"

"No, not if you paid me two hundred dollars."

"I offer you two thousand."

"Apiece?"

"Apiece."

"And there are four of you?"

"Four."

Captain Speedy began to scratch his head. There were eight thousand dollars to gain, without changing his route; for which it was well worth conquering the repugnance he had for all kinds of passengers. Besides, passengers at two thousand dollars are no longer passengers, but valuable merchandise. "I start at nine o'clock," said Captain Speedy, simply. "Are you and your party ready?"

"We will be on board at nine o'clock," replied, no less simply, Mr. Fogg.

It was half-past eight. To disembark from the Henrietta, jump into a hack, hurry to the St. Nicholas, and return with Aouda, Passepartout, and even the inseparable Fix was the work of a brief time, and was performed by Mr. Fogg with the coolness which never abandoned him. They were on board when the Henrietta made ready to weigh anchor.

When Passepartout heard what this last voyage was going to cost, he uttered a prolonged "Oh!" which extended throughout his vocal gamut.

As for Fix, he said to himself that the Bank of England would certainly not come out of this affair well indemnified. When they reached England, even if Mr. Fogg did not throw some handfuls of bank-bills into the sea, more than seven thousand pounds would have been spent!

CHAPTER XXXIII

IN WHICH PHILEAS FOGG SHOWS HIMSELF EQUAL TO THE OCCASION

An hour after, the Henrietta passed the lighthouse which marks the entrance of the Hudson, turned the point of Sandy Hook, and put to sea. During the day she skirted Long Island, passed Fire Island, and directed her course rapidly eastward.

At noon the next day, a man mounted the bridge to ascertain the vessel's position. It might be thought that this was Captain Speedy. Not the least in the world. It was Phileas Fogg, Esquire. As for Captain Speedy, he was shut up in his cabin under lock and key, and was uttering loud cries, which signified an anger at once pardonable and excessive.

What had happened was very simple. Phileas Fogg wished to go to Liverpool, but the captain would not carry him there. Then Phileas Fogg had taken passage for Bordeaux, and, during the thirty hours he had been on board, had so shrewdly managed with his banknotes that the sailors and stokers, who were only an occasional crew, and were not on the best terms with the captain, went over to him in a body. This was why Phileas Fogg was in command instead of Captain Speedy; why the captain was a prisoner in his cabin; and why, in short, the Henrietta was directing her course towards Liverpool. It was very clear, to see Mr. Fogg manage the craft, that he had been a sailor.

How the adventure ended will be seen anon. Aouda was anxious, though she said nothing. As for Passepartout, he thought Mr. Fogg's manoeuvre simply glorious. The captain had said "between eleven and twelve knots," and the Henrietta confirmed his prediction.

If, then—for there were "ifs" still—the sea did not become too boisterous, if the wind did not veer round to the east, if no accident happened to the boat or its machinery, the Henrietta might cross the three thousand miles from New York to Liverpool in the nine days, between the

12th and the 21st of December. It is true that, once arrived, the affair on board the Henrietta, added to that of the Bank of England, might create more difficulties for Mr. Fogg than he imagined or could desire.

During the first days, they went along smoothly enough. The sea was not very unpropitious, the wind seemed stationary in the north-east, the sails were hoisted, and the Henrietta ploughed across the waves like a real trans-Atlantic steamer.

Passepartout was delighted. His master's last exploit, the consequences of which he ignored, enchanted him. Never had the crew seen so jolly and dexterous a fellow. He formed warm friendships with the sailors, and amazed them with his acrobatic feats. He thought they managed the vessel like gentlemen, and that the stokers fired up like heroes. His loquacious good-humour infected everyone. He had forgotten the past, its vexations and delays. He only thought of the end, so nearly accomplished; and sometimes he boiled over with impatience, as if heated by the furnaces of the Henrietta. Often, also, the worthy fellow revolved around Fix, looking at him with a keen, distrustful eye; but he did not speak to him, for their old intimacy no longer existed.

Fix, it must be confessed, understood nothing of what was going on. The conquest of the Henrietta, the bribery of the crew, Fogg managing the boat like a skilled seaman, amazed and confused him. He did not know what to think. For, after all, a man who began by stealing fifty-five thousand pounds might end by stealing a vessel; and Fix was not unnaturally inclined to conclude that the Henrietta under Fogg's command, was not going to Liverpool at all, but to some part of the world where the robber, turned into a pirate, would quietly put himself in safety. The conjecture was at least a plausible one, and the detective began to seriously regret that he had embarked on the affair.

As for Captain Speedy, he continued to howl and growl in his cabin; and Passepartout, whose duty it was to carry him his meals, courageous as he was, took the greatest precautions. Mr. Fogg did not seem even to know that there was a captain on board.

On the 13th they passed the edge of the Banks of Newfoundland, a dangerous locality; during the winter, especially, there are frequent fogs and heavy gales of wind. Ever since the evening before the barometer, suddenly falling, had indicated an approaching change in the atmosphere; and during the night the temperature varied, the cold became sharper, and the wind veered to the south-east.

This was a misfortune. Mr. Fogg, in order not to deviate from his course, furled his sails and increased the force of the steam; but the vessel's speed slackened, owing to the state of the sea, the long waves of which broke against the stern. She pitched violently, and this retarded her progress. The breeze little by little swelled into a tempest, and it was to be feared that the Henrietta might not be able to maintain herself upright on the waves.

Passepartout's visage darkened with the skies, and for two days the poor fellow experienced constant fright. But Phileas Fogg was a bold mariner, and knew how to maintain headway against the sea; and he kept on his course, without even decreasing his steam. The Henrietta, when she could not rise upon the waves, crossed them, swamping her deck, but passing safely. Sometimes the screw rose out of the water, beating its protruding end, when a mountain of water raised the stern above the waves; but the craft always kept straight ahead.

The wind, however, did not grow as boisterous as might have been feared; it was not one of those tempests which burst, and rush on with a speed of ninety miles an hour. It continued fresh, but, unhappily, it remained obstinately in the south-east, rendering the sails useless.

The 16th of December was the seventy-fifth day since Phileas Fogg's departure from London, and the Henrietta had not yet been seriously delayed. Half of the voyage was almost accomplished, and the worst localities had been passed. In summer, success would have been well-nigh certain. In winter, they were at the mercy of the bad season. Passepartout said nothing; but he cherished hope in secret, and comforted himself with the reflection that, if the wind failed them, they might still count on the steam.

On this day the engineer came on deck, went up to Mr. Fogg, and began to speak earnestly with him. Without knowing why it was a presentiment, perhaps Passepartout became vaguely uneasy. He would have given one of his ears to hear with the other what the engineer was saying. He finally managed to catch a few words, and was sure he heard his master say, "You are certain of what you tell me?"

"Certain, sir," replied the engineer. "You must remember that, since we started, we have kept up hot fires in all our furnaces, and, though we had coal enough to go on short steam from New York to Bordeaux, we haven't enough to go with all steam from New York to Liverpool." "I will consider," replied Mr. Fogg.

Passepartout understood it all; he was seized with mortal anxiety. The coal was giving out! "Ah, if my master can get over that," muttered he, "he'll be a famous man!" He could not help imparting to Fix what he had overheard.

"Then you believe that we really are going to Liverpool?"

"Of course."

"Ass!" replied the detective, shrugging his shoulders and turning on his heel.

Passepartout was on the point of vigorously resenting the epithet, the reason of which he could not for the life of him comprehend; but he reflected that the unfortunate Fix was probably very much disappointed and humiliated in his self-esteem, after having so awkwardly followed a false scent around the world, and refrained.

And now what course would Phileas Fogg adopt? It was difficult to imagine. Nevertheless he seemed to have decided upon one, for that evening he sent for the engineer, and said to him, "Feed all the fires until the coal is exhausted."

A few moments after, the funnel of the Henrietta vomited forth torrents of smoke. The vessel continued to proceed with all steam on; but on the 18th, the engineer, as he had predicted, announced that the coal would give out in the course of the day.

"Do not let the fires go down," replied Mr. Fogg. "Keep them up to the last. Let the valves be filled."

Towards noon Phileas Fogg, having ascertained their position, called Passepartout, and ordered him to go for Captain Speedy. It was as if the honest fellow had been commanded to unchain a tiger. He went to the poop, saying to himself, "He will be like a madman!"

In a few moments, with cries and oaths, a bomb appeared on the poop-deck. The bomb was Captain Speedy. It was clear that he was on the point of bursting. "Where are we?" were the first words his anger permitted him to utter. Had the poor man been an apoplectic, he could never have recovered from his paroxysm of wrath.

"Where are we?" he repeated, with purple face.

"Seven hundred and seven miles from Liverpool," replied Mr. Fogg, with imperturbable calmness.

"Pirate!" cried Captain Speedy.

"I have sent for you, sir—"

"Pickaroon!"

"—sir," continued Mr. Fogg, "to ask you to sell me your vessel."

" PIRATE !" CRIED ANDREW SPEEDY

"No! By all the devils, no!"

"But I shall be obliged to burn her."

"Burn the Henrietta!"

"Yes; at least the upper part of her. The coal has given out."

"Burn my vessel!" cried Captain Speedy, who could scarcely pronounce the words. "A vessel worth fifty thousand dollars!"

"Here are sixty thousand," replied Phileas Fogg, handing the captain a roll of bank-bills. This had a prodigious effect on Andrew Speedy. An American can scarcely remain unmoved at the sight of sixty thousand dollars. The captain forgot in an instant his anger, his imprisonment, and all his grudges against his passenger. The Henrietta was twenty years old; it was a great bargain. The bomb would not go off after all. Mr. Fogg had taken away the match.

"And I shall still have the iron hull," said the captain in a softer tone.

"The iron hull and the engine. Is it agreed?"

"Agreed."

And Andrew Speedy, seizing the banknotes, counted them and consigned them to his pocket.

During this colloquy, Passepartout was as white as a sheet, and Fix seemed on the point of having an apoplectic fit. Nearly twenty thousand pounds had been expended, and Fogg left the hull and engine to the captain, that is, near the whole value of the craft! It was true, however, that fifty-five thousand pounds had been stolen from the Bank.

When Andrew Speedy had pocketed the money, Mr. Fogg said to him, "Don't let this astonish you, sir. You must know that I shall lose twenty thousand pounds, unless I arrive in London by a quarter before nine on the evening of the 21st of December. I missed the steamer at New York, and as you refused to take me to Liverpool—"

"And I did well!" cried Andrew Speedy; "for I have gained at least forty thousand dollars by it!" He added, more sedately, "Do you know one thing, Captain—"

"Fogg."

"Captain Fogg, you've got something of the Yankee about you."

And, having paid his passenger what he considered a high compliment, he was going away, when Mr. Fogg said, "The vessel now belongs to me?"

"Certainly, from the keel to the truck of the masts—all the wood, that is."

"Very well. Have the interior seats, bunks, and frames pulled down, and burn them."

It was necessary to have dry wood to keep the steam up to the adequate pressure, and on that day the poop, cabins, bunks, and the spare deck were sacrificed. On the next day, the 19th of December, the masts, rafts, and spars were burned; the crew worked lustily, keeping up the fires. Passepartout hewed, cut, and sawed away with all his might. There was a perfect rage for demolition.

The railings, fittings, the greater part of the deck, and top sides disappeared on the 20th, and the Henrietta was now only a flat hulk. But on this day they sighted the Irish coast and Fastnet Light. By ten in the evening they were passing Queenstown. Phileas Fogg had only twenty-four hours more in which to get to London; that length of time was necessary to reach Liverpool, with all steam on. And the steam was about to give out altogether!

"Sir," said Captain Speedy, who was now deeply interested in Mr. Fogg's project, "I really commiserate you. Everything is against you. We are only opposite Queenstown."

"Ah," said Mr. Fogg, "is that place where we see the lights Queenstown?"

"Yes."

"Can we enter the harbour?"

"Not under three hours. Only at high tide."

"Stay," replied Mr. Fogg calmly, without betraying in his features that by a supreme inspiration he was about to attempt once more to conquer ill-fortune.

Queenstown is the Irish port at which the trans-Atlantic steamers stop to put off the mails. These mails are carried to Dublin by express trains always held in readiness to start; from Dublin they are sent on to Liverpool by the most rapid boats, and thus gain twelve hours on the Atlantic steamers.

Phileas Fogg counted on gaining twelve hours in the same way. Instead of arriving at Liverpool the next evening by the Henrietta, he would be there by noon, and would therefore have time to reach London before a quarter before nine in the evening.

The Henrietta entered Queenstown Harbour at one o'clock in the morning, it then being high tide; and Phileas Fogg, after being grasped heartily by the hand by Captain Speedy, left that gentleman on the levelled hulk of his craft, which was still worth half what he had sold it for.

THE CREW EVINCED AN INCREDIBLE ZEAL.

The party went on shore at once. Fix was greatly tempted to arrest Mr. Fogg on the spot; but he did not. Why? What struggle was going on within him? Had he changed his mind about "his man"? Did he understand that he had made a grave mistake? He did not, however, abandon Mr. Fogg. They all got upon the train, which was just ready to start, at half-past one; at dawn of day they were in Dublin; and they lost no time in embarking on a steamer which, disdaining to rise upon the waves, invariably cut through them.

Phileas Fogg at last disembarked on the Liverpool quay, at twenty minutes before twelve, 21st December. He was only six hours distant from London.

But at this moment Fix came up, put his hand upon Mr. Fogg's shoulder, and, showing his warrant, said, "You are really Phileas Fogg?"

"I am."

"I arrest you in the Queen's name!"

CHAPTER XXXIV

IN WHICH PHILEAS FOGG AT LAST REACHES LONDON

Phileas Fogg was in prison. He had been shut up in the Custom House, and he was to be transferred to London the next day.

Passepartout, when he saw his master arrested, would have fallen upon Fix had he not been held back by some policemen. Aouda was thunderstruck at the suddenness of an event which she could not understand. Passepartout explained to her how it was that the honest and courageous Fogg was arrested as a robber. The young woman's heart revolted against so heinous a charge, and when she saw that she could attempt to do nothing to save her protector, she wept bitterly.

As for Fix, he had arrested Mr. Fogg because it was his duty, whether Mr. Fogg were guilty or not.

The thought then struck Passepartout, that he was the cause of this new misfortune! Had he not concealed Fix's errand from his master? When Fix revealed his true character and purpose, why had he not told Mr. Fogg? If the latter had been warned, he would no doubt have given Fix proof of his innocence, and satisfied him of his mistake; at least, Fix would not have continued his journey at the expense and on the heels of his master, only to arrest him the moment he set foot on English soil. Passepartout wept till he was blind, and felt like blowing his brains out.

Aouda and he had remained, despite the cold, under the portico of the Custom House. Neither wished to leave the place; both were anxious to see Mr. Fogg again.

That gentleman was really ruined, and that at the moment when he was about to attain his end. This arrest was fatal. Having arrived at Liverpool at twenty minutes before twelve on the 21st of December, he had till a quarter before nine that evening to reach the Reform Club, that is, nine hours and a quarter; the journey from Liverpool to London was six hours.

I ARREST YOU IN THE NAME OF THE QUEEN

If anyone, at this moment, had entered the Custom House, he would have found Mr. Fogg seated, motionless, calm, and without apparent anger, upon a wooden bench. He was not, it is true, resigned; but this last blow failed to force him into an outward betrayal of any emotion. Was he being devoured by one of those secret rages, all the more terrible because contained, and which only burst forth, with an irresistible force, at the last moment? No one could tell. There he sat, calmly waiting—for what? Did he still cherish hope? Did he still believe, now that the door of this prison was closed upon him, that he would succeed?

However that may have been, Mr. Fogg carefully put his watch upon the table, and observed its advancing hands. Not a word escaped his lips, but his look was singularly set and stern. The situation, in any event, was a terrible one, and might be thus stated: if Phileas Fogg was honest he was ruined; if he was a knave, he was caught.

Did escape occur to him? Did he examine to see if there were any practicable outlet from his prison? Did he think of escaping from it? Possibly; for once he walked slowly around the room. But the door was locked, and the window heavily barred with iron rods. He sat down again, and drew his journal from his pocket. On the line where these words were written, "21st December, Saturday, Liverpool," he added, "80th day, 11.40 a.m.," and waited.

The Custom House clock struck one. Mr. Fogg observed that his watch was two hours too fast.

Two hours! Admitting that he was at this moment taking an express train, he could reach London and the Reform Club by a quarter before nine, p.m. His forehead slightly wrinkled.

At thirty-three minutes past two he heard a singular noise outside, then a hasty opening of doors. Passepartout's voice was audible, and immediately after that of Fix. Phileas Fogg's eyes brightened for an instant.

The door swung open, and he saw Passepartout, Aouda, and Fix, who hurried towards him.

Fix was out of breath, and his hair was in disorder. He could not speak. "Sir," he stammered, "sir—forgive me—most—unfortunate resemblance—robber arrested three days ago—you are free!"

Phileas Fogg was free! He walked to the detective, looked him steadily in the face, and with the only rapid motion he had ever made in his life, or which he ever would make, drew back his arms, and with the precision of a machine knocked Fix down.

"Well hit!" cried Passepartout, "Parbleu! that's what you might call a good application of English fists!"

Fix, who found himself on the floor, did not utter a word. He had only received his deserts. Mr. Fogg, Aouda, and Passepartout left the Custom House without delay, got into a cab, and in a few moments descended at the station.

Phileas Fogg asked if there was an express train about to leave for London. It was forty minutes past two. The express train had left thirty-five minutes before. Phileas Fogg then ordered a special train.

There were several rapid locomotives on hand; but the railway arrangements did not permit the special train to leave until three o'clock.

At that hour Phileas Fogg, having stimulated the engineer by the offer of a generous reward, at last set out towards London with Aouda and his faithful servant.

It was necessary to make the journey in five hours and a half; and this would have been easy on a clear road throughout. But there were forced delays, and when Mr. Fogg stepped from the train at the terminus, all the clocks in London were striking ten minutes before nine.

Having made the tour of the world, he was behind-hand five minutes. He had lost the wager!

HE HAD FOUND A BILL FROM THE GAS COMPANY

CHAPTER XXXV

IN WHICH PHILEAS FOGG DOES NOT HAVE TO REPEAT HIS ORDERS TO PASSEPARTOUT TWICE

The dwellers in Saville Row would have been surprised the next day, if they had been told that Phileas Fogg had returned home. His doors and windows were still closed, no appearance of change was visible.

After leaving the station, Mr. Fogg gave Passepartout instructions to purchase some provisions, and quietly went to his domicile.

He bore his misfortune with his habitual tranquillity. Ruined! And by the blundering of the detective! After having steadily traversed that long journey, overcome a hundred obstacles, braved many dangers, and still found time to do some good on his way, to fail near the goal by a sudden event which he could not have foreseen, and against which he was unarmed; it was terrible! But a few pounds were left of the large sum he had carried with him. There only remained of his fortune the twenty thousand pounds deposited at Barings, and this amount he owed to his friends of the Reform Club. So great had been the expense of his tour that, even had he won, it would not have enriched him; and it is probable that he had not sought to enrich himself, being a man who rather laid wagers for honour's sake than for the stake proposed. But this wager totally ruined him.

Mr. Fogg's course, however, was fully decided upon; he knew what remained for him to do.

A room in the house in Saville Row was set apart for Aouda, who was overwhelmed with grief at her protector's misfortune. From the words which Mr. Fogg dropped, she saw that he was meditating some serious project.

Knowing that Englishmen governed by a fixed idea sometimes resort to the desperate expedient of suicide, Passepartout kept a narrow watch upon his master, though he carefully concealed the appearance of so doing.

First of all, the worthy fellow had gone up to his room, and had extinguished the gas burner, which had been burning for eighty days. He had found in the letter-box a bill from the gas company, and he thought it more than time to put a stop to this expense, which he had been doomed to bear.

The night passed. Mr. Fogg went to bed, but did he sleep? Aouda did not once close her eyes. Passepartout watched all night, like a faithful dog, at his master's door.

Mr. Fogg called him in the morning, and told him to get Aouda's breakfast, and a cup of tea and a chop for himself. He desired Aouda to excuse him from breakfast and dinner, as his time would be absorbed all day in putting his affairs to rights. In the evening he would ask permission to have a few moment's conversation with the young lady.

PASSEPARTOUT PUTTING OUT THE GAS-LIGHT.

Passepartout, having received his orders, had nothing to do but obey them. He looked at his imperturbable master, and could scarcely bring his mind to leave him. His heart was full, and his conscience tortured by remorse; for he accused himself more bitterly than ever of being the cause of the irretrievable disaster. Yes! if he had warned Mr. Fogg, and had betrayed Fix's projects to him, his master would certainly not have given the detective passage to Liverpool, and then—

Passepartout could hold in no longer.

"My master! Mr. Fogg!" he cried, "why do you not curse me? It was my fault that—"

"I blame no one," returned Phileas Fogg, with perfect calmness. "Go!"

Passepartout left the room, and went to find Aouda, to whom he delivered his master's message.

"Madam," he added, "I can do nothing myself—nothing! I have no influence over my master; but you, perhaps—"

"What influence could I have?" replied Aouda. "Mr. Fogg is influenced by no one. Has he ever understood that my gratitude to him is overflowing? Has he ever read my heart? My friend, he must not be left alone an instant! You say he is going to speak with me this evening?"

"Yes, madam; probably to arrange for your protection and comfort in England."

"We shall see," replied Aouda, becoming suddenly pensive.

Throughout this day (Sunday) the house in Saville Row was as if uninhabited, and Phileas Fogg, for the first time since he had lived in that house, did not set out for his club when Westminster clock struck half-past eleven.

Why should he present himself at the Reform? His friends no longer expected him there. As Phileas Fogg had not appeared in the saloon on the evening before (Saturday, the 21st of December, at a quarter before nine), he had lost his wager. It was not even necessary that he should go to his bankers for the twenty thousand pounds; for his antagonists already had his cheque in their hands, and they had only to fill it out and send it to the Barings to have the amount transferred to their credit.

Mr. Fogg, therefore, had no reason for going out, and so he remained at home. He shut himself up in his room, and busied himself putting his affairs in order. Passepartout continually ascended and descended the stairs. The hours were long for him. He listened at his master's door, and looked through the keyhole, as if he had a perfect right so to do, and as if he feared that something terrible might happen at any moment. Sometimes he thought of Fix, but no longer in anger. Fix, like all the world, had been mistaken in Phileas Fogg, and had only done his duty in tracking and arresting him; while he, Passepartout. . . . This thought haunted him, and he never ceased cursing his miserable folly.

Finding himself too wretched to remain alone, he knocked at Aouda's door, went into her room, seated himself, without speaking, in a corner, and looked ruefully at the young woman. Aouda was still pensive.

About half-past seven in the evening Mr. Fogg sent to know if Aouda would receive him, and in a few moments he found himself alone with her.

Phileas Fogg took a chair, and sat down near the fireplace, opposite Aouda. No emotion was visible on his face. Fogg returned was exactly the Fogg who had gone away; there was the same calm, the same impassibility.

He sat several minutes without speaking; then, bending his eyes on Aouda, "Madam," said he, "will you pardon me for bringing you to England?"

"I, Mr. Fogg!" replied Aouda, checking the pulsations of her heart.

"Please let me finish," returned Mr. Fogg. "When I decided to bring you far away from the country which was so unsafe for you, I was rich, and counted on putting a portion of my fortune at your disposal; then your existence would have been free and happy. But now I am ruined."

"I know it, Mr. Fogg," replied Aouda; "and I ask you in my turn, will you forgive me for having followed you, and—who knows?—for having, perhaps, delayed you, and thus contributed to your ruin?"

"Madam, you could not remain in India, and your safety could only be assured by bringing you to such a distance that your persecutors could not take you."

"So, Mr. Fogg," resumed Aouda, "not content with rescuing me from a terrible death, you thought yourself bound to secure my comfort in a foreign land?"

"Yes, madam; but circumstances have been against me. Still, I beg to place the little I have left at your service."

"But what will become of you, Mr. Fogg?"

"As for me, madam," replied the gentleman, coldly, "I have need of nothing."

"But how do you look upon the fate, sir, which awaits you?"

"As I am in the habit of doing."

"At least," said Aouda, "want should not overtake a man like you. Your friends—"

"I have no friends, madam."

"Your relatives—"

"I have no longer any relatives."

246

"I pity you, then, Mr. Fogg, for solitude is a sad thing, with no heart to which to confide your griefs. They say, though, that misery itself, shared by two sympathetic souls, may be borne with patience."

"They say so, madam."

"Mr. Fogg," said Aouda, rising and seizing his hand, "do you wish at once a kinswoman and friend? Will you have me for your wife?"

Mr. Fogg, at this, rose in his turn. There was an unwonted light in his eyes, and a slight trembling of his lips. Aouda looked into his face. The sincerity, rectitude, firmness, and sweetness of this soft glance of a noble woman, who could dare all to save him to whom she owed all, at first astonished, then penetrated him. He shut his eyes for an instant, as if to avoid her look. When he opened them again, "I love you!" he said, simply. "Yes, by all that is holiest, I love you, and I am entirely yours!"

"Ah!" cried Aouda, pressing his hand to her heart.

Passepartout was summoned and appeared immediately. Mr. Fogg still held Aouda's hand in his own; Passepartout understood, and his big, round face became as radiant as the tropical sun at its zenith.

Mr. Fogg asked him if it was not too late to notify the Reverend Samuel Wilson, of Marylebone parish, that evening.

Passepartout smiled his most genial smile, and said, "Never too late."

It was five minutes past eight.

"Will it be for to-morrow, Monday?"

"For to-morrow, Monday," said Mr. Fogg, turning to Aouda.

"Yes; for to-morrow, Monday," she replied.

Passepartout hurried off as fast as his legs could carry him.

CHAPTER XXXVI

IN WHICH PHILEAS FOGG'S NAME IS ONCE MORE AT A PREMIUM ON 'CHANGE

It is time to relate what a change took place in English public opinion when it transpired that the real bankrobber, a certain James Strand, had been arrested, on the 17th day of December, at Edinburgh. Three days before, Phileas Fogg had been a criminal, who was being desperately followed up by the police; now he was an honourable gentleman, mathematically pursuing his eccentric journey round the world.

The papers resumed their discussion about the wager; all those who had laid bets, for or against him, revived their interest, as if by magic; the "Phileas Fogg bonds" again became negotiable, and many new wagers were made. Phileas Fogg's name was once more at a premium on 'Change.

His five friends of the Reform Club passed these three days in a state of feverish suspense. Would Phileas Fogg, whom they had forgotten, reappear before their eyes! Where was he at this moment? The 17th of December, the day of James Strand's arrest, was the seventy-sixth since Phileas Fogg's departure, and no news of him had been received. Was he dead? Had he abandoned the effort, or was he continuing his journey along the route agreed upon? And would he appear on Saturday, the 21st of December, at a quarter before nine in the evening, on the threshold of the Reform Club saloon?

The anxiety in which, for three days, London society existed, cannot be described. Telegrams were sent to America and Asia for news of Phileas Fogg. Messengers were dispatched to the house in Saville Row morning and evening. No news. The police were ignorant what had become of the detective, Fix, who had so unfortunately followed up a false scent. Bets increased, nevertheless, in number and value. Phileas Fogg, like a racehorse, was drawing near his last turning-point. The bonds were quoted, no longer at a hundred below par, but at twenty, at ten, and at five; and paralytic old Lord Albemarle bet even in his favour.

A great crowd was collected in Pall Mall and the neighbouring streets on Saturday evening; it seemed like a multitude of brokers permanently established around the Reform Club. Circulation was impeded, and everywhere disputes, discussions, and financial transactions were going on. The police had great difficulty in keeping back the crowd, and as the hour when Phileas Fogg was due approached, the excitement rose to its highest pitch.

The five antagonists of Phileas Fogg had met in the great saloon of the club. John Sullivan and Samuel Fallentin, the bankers, Andrew Stuart, the engineer, Gauthier Ralph, the director of the Bank of England, and Thomas Flanagan, the brewer, one and all waited anxiously.

When the clock indicated twenty minutes past eight, Andrew Stuart got up, saying, "Gentlemen, in twenty minutes the time agreed upon between Mr. Fogg and ourselves will have expired."

"What time did the last train arrive from Liverpool?" asked Thomas Flanagan.

"At twenty-three minutes past seven," replied Gauthier Ralph; "and the next does not arrive till ten minutes after twelve."

"Well, gentlemen," resumed Andrew Stuart, "if Phileas Fogg had come in the 7:23 train, he would have got here by this time. We can, therefore, regard the bet as won."

"Wait; don't let us be too hasty," replied Samuel Fallentin. "You know that Mr. Fogg is very eccentric. His punctuality is well known; he never arrives too soon, or too late; and I should not be surprised if he appeared before us at the last minute."

"Why," said Andrew Stuart nervously, "if I should see him, I should not believe it was he."

"The fact is," resumed Thomas Flanagan, "Mr. Fogg's project was absurdly foolish. Whatever his punctuality, he could not prevent the delays which were certain to occur; and a delay of only two or three days would be fatal to his tour."

"Observe, too," added John Sullivan, "that we have received no intelligence from him, though there are telegraphic lines all along his route."

"He has lost, gentleman," said Andrew Stuart, "he has a hundred times lost! You know, besides, that the China the only steamer he could have taken from New York to get here in time arrived yesterday. I have seen a list of the passengers, and the name of Phileas Fogg is not among them. Even if we admit that fortune has favoured him, he can scarcely have reached America. I think he will be at least twenty days behind-hand, and that Lord Albemarle will lose a cool five thousand."

"It is clear," replied Gauthier Ralph; "and we have nothing to do but to present Mr. Fogg's cheque at Barings to-morrow."

At this moment, the hands of the club clock pointed to twenty minutes to nine.

"Five minutes more," said Andrew Stuart.

The five gentlemen looked at each other. Their anxiety was becoming intense; but, not wishing to betray it, they readily assented to Mr. Fallentin's proposal of a rubber.

"I wouldn't give up my four thousand of the bet," said Andrew Stuart, as he took his seat, "for three thousand nine hundred and ninety-nine."

The clock indicated eighteen minutes to nine.

The players took up their cards, but could not keep their eyes off the clock. Certainly, however secure they felt, minutes had never seemed so long to them!

"Seventeen minutes to nine," said Thomas Flanagan, as he cut the cards which Ralph handed to him.

Then there was a moment of silence. The great saloon was perfectly quiet; but the murmurs of the crowd outside were heard, with now and then a shrill cry. The pendulum beat the seconds, which each player eagerly counted, as he listened, with mathematical regularity.

"Sixteen minutes to nine!" said John Sullivan, in a voice which betrayed his emotion.

One minute more, and the wager would be won. Andrew Stuart and his partners suspended their game. They left their cards, and counted the seconds.

At the fortieth second, nothing. At the fiftieth, still nothing.

At the fifty-fifth, a loud cry was heard in the street, followed by applause, hurrahs, and some fierce growls.

The players rose from their seats.

At the fifty-seventh second the door of the saloon opened; and the pendulum had not beat the sixtieth second when Phileas Fogg appeared, followed by an excited crowd who had forced their way through the club doors, and in his calm voice, said, "Here I am, gentlemen!"

" HERE I AM, GENTLEMEN," SAID HE

CHAPTER XXXVII

IN WHICH IT IS SHOWN THAT PHILEAS FOGG GAINED NOTHING BY HIS TOUR AROUND THE WORLD, UNLESS IT WERE HAPPINESS

Yes; Phileas Fogg in person.

The reader will remember that at five minutes past eight in the evening—about five and twenty hours after the arrival of the travellers in London—Passepartout had been sent by his master to engage the services of the Reverend Samuel Wilson in a certain marriage ceremony, which was to take place the next day.

Passepartout went on his errand enchanted. He soon reached the clergyman's house, but found him not at home. Passepartout waited a good twenty minutes, and when he left the reverend gentleman, it was thirty-five minutes past eight. But in what a state he was! With his hair in disorder, and without his hat, he ran along the street as never man was seen to run before, overturning passers-by, rushing over the sidewalk like a waterspout.

In three minutes he was in Saville Row again, and staggered back into Mr. Fogg's room.

He could not speak.

"What is the matter?" asked Mr. Fogg.

"My master!" gasped Passepartout—"marriage—impossible—"

"Impossible?"

"Impossible—for to-morrow."

"Why so?"

"Because to-morrow—is Sunday!"

"Monday," replied Mr. Fogg.

"No—to-day is Saturday."

"Saturday? Impossible!"

HIS HAIR ALL IN DISORDER, WITHOUT A HAT, KNOCKING
DOWN FOOT-PASSENGERS, ON HE RAN

"Yes, yes, yes, yes!" cried Passepartout. "You have made a mistake of one day! We arrived twenty-four hours ahead of time; but there are only ten minutes left!"

Passepartout had seized his master by the collar, and was dragging him along with irresistible force.

Phileas Fogg, thus kidnapped, without having time to think, left his house, jumped into a cab, promised a hundred pounds to the cabman, and, having run over two dogs and overturned five carriages, reached the Reform Club.

The clock indicated a quarter before nine when he appeared in the great saloon.

Phileas Fogg had accomplished the journey round the world in eighty days!

Phileas Fogg had won his wager of twenty thousand pounds!

How was it that a man so exact and fastidious could have made this error of a day? How came he to think that he had arrived in London on Saturday, the twenty-first day of December, when it was really Friday, the twentieth, the seventy-ninth day only from his departure?

The cause of the error is very simple.

Phileas Fogg had, without suspecting it, gained one day on his journey, and this merely because he had travelled constantly eastward; he would, on the contrary, have lost a day had he gone in the opposite direction, that is, westward.

In journeying eastward he had gone towards the sun, and the days therefore diminished for him as many times four minutes as he crossed degrees in this direction. There are three hundred and sixty degrees on the circumference of the earth; and these three hundred and sixty degrees, multiplied by four minutes, gives precisely twenty-four hours—that is, the day unconsciously gained. In other words, while Phileas Fogg, going eastward, saw the sun pass the meridian eighty times, his friends in London only saw it pass the meridian seventy-nine times. This is why they awaited him at the Reform Club on Saturday, and not Sunday, as Mr. Fogg thought.

And Passepartout's famous family watch, which had always kept London time, would have betrayed this fact, if it had marked the days as well as the hours and the minutes!

Phileas Fogg, then, had won the twenty thousand pounds; but, as he had spent nearly nineteen thousand on the way, the pecuniary gain was small. His object was, however, to be victorious, and not to win money. He divided the one thousand pounds that remained between Passepartout and the unfortunate Fix, against whom he cherished no grudge. He deducted, however, from Passepartout's share the cost of the gas which had burned in his room for nineteen hundred and twenty hours, for the sake of regularity.

That evening, Mr. Fogg, as tranquil and phlegmatic as ever, said to Aouda: "Is our marriage still agreeable to you?"

"Mr. Fogg," replied she, "it is for me to ask that question. You were ruined, but now you are rich again."

"Pardon me, madam; my fortune belongs to you. If you had not suggested our marriage, my servant would not have gone to the Reverend Samuel Wilson's, I should not have been apprised of my error, and—"

"Dear Mr. Fogg!" said the young woman.

"Dear Aouda!" replied Phileas Fogg.

It need not be said that the marriage took place forty-eight hours after, and that Passepartout, glowing and dazzling, gave the bride away. Had he not saved her, and was he not entitled to this honour?

The next day, as soon as it was light, Passepartout rapped vigorously at his master's door. Mr. Fogg opened it, and asked, "What's the matter, Passepartout?"

"What is it, sir? Why, I've just this instant found out—"

"What?"

"That we might have made the tour of the world in only seventy-eight days."

"No doubt," returned Mr. Fogg, "by not crossing India. But if I had not crossed India, I should not have saved Aouda; she would not have been my wife, and—"

Mr. Fogg quietly shut the door.

Phileas Fogg had won his wager, and had made his journey around the world in eighty days. To do this he had employed every means of conveyance—steamers, railways, carriages, yachts, trading-vessels, sledges, elephants. The eccentric gentleman had throughout displayed all his marvellous qualities of coolness and exactitude. But what then? What had he really gained by all this trouble? What had he brought back from this long and weary journey?

Nothing, say you? Perhaps so; nothing but a charming woman, who, strange as it may appear, made him the happiest of men!

Truly, would you not for less than that make the tour around the world?

THE END

Made in the USA
Coppell, TX
05 August 2022

80938503R10140